PARDON MY FRENCH!

POCKET FRENCH SLANG DICTIONARY

ENGLISH–FRENCH/FRENCH–EN

Ref

HARRAP

This second edition published
by Chambers Harrap Publishers Ltd 2003
7 Hopetoun Crescent
Edinburgh EH7 4AY
Great Britain

Previous edition published 1998

Reprinted 2004

ISBN 0245 50557 1 (France)
ISBN 0245 60720 X (UK)

Dépôt légal : février 2003

Designed and typeset by Chambers Harrap Publishers Ltd, Edinburgh
Printed in Great Britain by Clays Ltd, St Ives plc

Project Editors / Rédacteurs
Georges Pilard   Anna Stevenson

New Words Consultants / Consultants pour les néologismes
Dougal Campbell   Marie-Sandrine Cadudal

Publishing Manager / Direction éditoriale
Patrick White

Prepress / Prépresse
Marina Karapanovic

The editors would like to thank the students in Dougal Campbell's tutorial group at the University of Glasgow for their comments and suggestions, and Justine de Reyniès for her work on the thematic panels.

Les rédacteurs tiennent à remercier les étudiants de Dougal Campbell, de l'Université de Glasgow, pour leurs commentaires et leurs suggestions lors de la rédaction de cette nouvelle édition, ainsi que Justine de Reyniès pour son travail sur les encadrés thématiques français.

Contributors to the first edition/
Ont participé à la première édition

Project Editors / Rédacteurs
Georges Pilard   Anna Stevenson

with / avec
Laurence Larroche

American English Consultant / Spécialiste de l'anglais américain
Dr Jonathan E. Lighter

Publishing Manager / Direction éditoriale
Patrick White

Prepress / Prépresse
Sharon McTeir

Trademarks
Words considered to be trademarks have been designated in this dictionary by the symbol ®. However, no judgement is implied concerning the legal status of any trademark by virtue of the presence or absence of such a symbol.

Marques déposées
Les termes considérés comme des marques déposées sont signalés dans ce dictionnaire par le symbole ®. Cependant la présence ou l'absence de ce symbole ne constitue nullement une indication quant à la valeur juridique de ces termes.

Preface to the second edition

More than four years have passed since the first edition of *Pardon My French!* was published and since then both French and English slang have continued to evolve and expand at a steady rate. The time has now come for a new edition which reflects these changes.

The dictionary has been completely revised and updated and includes hundreds of new terms and expressions. We have included more regional varieties of French and English slang – the French side now contains many slang terms from Canada, Switzerland and Belgium, whilst Australian, Scottish and Irish English terms all now feature on the English side. Another new feature of this edition is the inclusion of thematic panels throughout the text devoted to some key themes in slang, such as sex, violence and drunkenness.

An insight into an often neglected aspect of the language, *Pardon My French!* is now, more than ever, an indispensable tool for all speakers and learners of French keen to uncover the mysteries of slang.

Preface to the first edition

Harrap has a long-standing reputation for giving excellent coverage of slang and colloquial language in all its dictionaries. Indeed, we are the only major dictionary publisher to publish a bilingual dictionary devoted entirely to this type of language. This book represents a continuation of that tradition, but takes a completely fresh look at the slang used as we move towards a new millennium. Since slang is a particularly productive and fast-growing area of language, we have had to be very selective in writing this dictionary. We do not claim to have compiled an exhaustive and comprehensive record of French and English slang. Rather, we have endeavoured to present a collection of the most common slang words and expressions heard in French- and English-speaking countries today. We have also included many humorous and colourful expressions, including popular catchphrases, which might usually be considered beyond the scope of such a small book. We encourage you to browse, to explore the more colourful side of the French language, and to revel in the rich exuberance of language at its most fun.

What is slang?

It should be easy for lexicographers to define the term "slang". A closer examination, however, shows that the word is used to refer to several different types of language. For example, "slang" is often used to refer to the sort of language used within particular social or professional groups, such as soldiers, criminals or even dentists. The function of this kind of slang is usually to reinforce group identity. These in-group terms, often called "jargon", have been deliberately excluded from these pages except when they have gained common currency. What is in this book represents our broader definition of slang, namely a wide range of non-standard language, from the colloquial to the vulgar – the language heard or used by us all every day in informal contexts.

Labelling

Despite the recent rise of political correctness, people are still using vulgar, racist, sexist and blasphemous language. Our extensive system of labelling those terms which are most likely to shock or offend should enable the reader to avoid making any embarrassing faux pas.

Although certain areas like sex, drugs, drunkenness, bodily functions and racism are particularly rich in slang expressions in both languages, there are nonetheless several areas where one language has generated more slang terms than the other. French, for example, seems to have a slang word for practically every mundane item from coffee (**kawa** or **caoua**) to dictionaries (**dico**), not forgetting old favourites like **boulot** (work/job). Where possible, a translation is given which matches the register (level of informality) of the source expression, but where there is no slang equivalent, as is the case for the above examples, a neutral translation has been given, followed by the symbol ᵔ.

The inclusion of a headword or expression in this slang dictionary implies that it is, by definition, familiar and should not be used in a formal context. There are, however, different degrees of informality, and these are clearly indicated. The symbol [!] denotes that the word or expression may cause offence and should be used with care. The symbol [!!] is reserved for vulgar and taboo words and phrases which will shock in most contexts. You should use these items with the greatest caution. We hope that these warning signs will help you to pick your way safely through the slang minefield.

Extra help

Sometimes translations are not enough on their own to render the full meaning of a word or expression. Therefore additional information is given at many entries in the form of usage notes. We hope you will find these enlightening and entertaining. They cover the following areas:

- Thematic panels giving explanations and examples of the different varieties of slang [**verlan**, **javanais**, **rhyming slang**, **Black American slang**]. There is also a panel explaining the typical patterns used in that most pure and visceral type of slang – insults [see the panel at **insultes** on the French side for examples of French insults];

- ▶ Fuller explanations of the subtleties of racist and homophobic terms [**Rital**, **Espingouin**, **Paki**, **queer**];

- ▶ Interesting etymologies [**bidochon**, **Château-Lapompe**, **cowabunga**, **not!**];

- ▶ Productive suffixes and prefixes [**-aille**, **archi-**, **-ard**, **-arama**, **-ville**, **mega-**];

- ▶ Explanations of set phrases that are hard to translate [**faire avancer le schmilblick**, **as the actress said to the bishop**, **beam me up Scotty!**];

- ▶ Cultural items that need fuller explanations [**BCBG**, **NAP**, **new lad**, **new man**, **Essex girl**, **trainspotter**].

Our friends across the pond

Although British slang is becoming increasingly Americanized through the influence of the media, many terms remain typically British or North American. These are clearly indicated with the geographical labels *Br* and *Am*, both at headword and at translation level. Our American consultant, Dr Jonathan E. Lighter of the University of Tennessee, has systematically verified all American material and has provided hundreds of new headwords. As author of the *Random House Historical Dictionary of American Slang*, Dr Lighter is a renowned specialist in North American slang, and we owe him a great debt of thanks for his invaluable contribution to this dictionary.

Préface de la deuxième édition

Il s'est écoulé plus de quatre ans depuis la publication de la première édition du *Harrap's Slang*, période pendant laquelle l'argot a continué à évoluer à un rythme soutenu tant en anglais qu'en français. Il était donc temps pour Harrap de proposer une nouvelle édition qui tienne compte de cette évolution et de ces changements. C'est aujourd'hui chose faite avec cette nouvelle mouture du *Harrap's Slang*.

L'ouvrage a fait l'objet d'une remise à jour complète et s'est enrichi de centaines de nouveaux termes et de nouvelles expressions de part et d'autre du dictionnaire. En outre, l'accent a été mis sur les variantes nationales des argots des mondes anglophone et francophone. Ainsi le côté anglais du dictionnaire voit l'arrivée de très nombreux termes australiens et d'un nombre conséquent de termes de l'anglais d'Écosse et d'Irlande, et le côté français s'enrichit de termes canadiens, belges et suisses. Cette nouvelle édition se distingue également par la présence d'encadrés thématiques qui font le point sur certains domaines-clés du vocabulaire argotique, tels que le sexe, la violence ou encore l'ivresse.

Fidèle reflet d'un aspect de la langue souvent négligé, le *Harrap's Slang* est plus que jamais l'outil indispensable de l'angliciste désireux de percer les mystères de l'argot.

Préface de la première édition

Les dictionnaires Harrap se sont toujours distingués par la place qu'ils accordent à l'argot et à la langue parlée en général. De toutes les grandes maisons d'édition, Harrap est la seule à publier un dictionnaire bilingue entièrement consacré à cet aspect de la langue. Le présent ouvrage privilégie particulièrement l'argot tel qu'on l'utilise en cette fin de millénaire. La partie français/anglais contient une part importante d'argot traditionnel ayant toujours cours aujourd'hui, ainsi que de nombreux termes de ce nouveau type d'argot que l'on appelle généralement argot des banlieues ou des cités.

La langue verte est une langue foisonnante, en constante évolution; de nouveaux termes, de nouvelles expressions apparaissent sans cesse et nous avons donc dû nous montrer sélectifs au moment d'établir notre nomenclature. Plutôt que de prétendre à l'exhaustivité, nous nous sommes efforcés de rassembler dans notre dictionnaire les mots et expressions argotiques les plus communément utilisés aujourd'hui dans les pays francophones et anglophones. Figurent également de nombreuses expressions humoristiques et pittoresques, ainsi qu'un grand nombre de formules popularisées par le cinéma et la télévision qui font partie intégrante de la langue parlée et qui posent souvent de gros problèmes de compréhension au locuteur étranger. Nous encourageons le lecteur à parcourir cet ouvrage pour le plaisir, pour découvrir une langue pleine de vitalité où l'humour règne en maître.

Qu'entend-on par argot?

Il n'est pas inutile de s'arrêter un instant sur la signification du mot "argot" car ce terme recouvre plusieurs réalités linguistiques bien différentes. Pour certains puristes l'argot désigne exclusivement la langue de la pègre (c'est "l'argot des vrais de vrais" d'Auguste Le Breton). Pour d'autres, l'argot est un jargon propre à un métier (le plus connu étant le *loucherbem* ou "argot des bouchers", aujourd'hui tombé en désuétude). Dans les deux cas, l'utilisation d'un jargon spécifique sert à renforcer la cohésion d'un groupe donné. Ce type d'argot ne nous intéresse que dans la mesure où il perd sa fonction purement cryptique pour être absorbé par la langue populaire. Notre ouvrage est donc un dictionnaire d'argot au sens le plus large du terme: un dictionnaire du français et de l'anglais non conventionnels, dont le registre s'étend du familier au très vulgaire.

Les indications d'usage

Malgré l'apparition du "politiquement correct", nombre de termes et expressions vulgaires, racistes et sexistes ont toujours cours. Des indicateurs d'usage éviteront au lecteur de se placer dans des situations embarrassantes en utilisant à son insu des mots qui ne manqueraient pas de choquer.

Les domaines les plus riches en termes argotiques sont peu ou prou les mêmes en anglais et en français: le sexe, le corps, la drogue, l'ivresse et le racisme sont particulièrement bien représentés dans les deux langues. Cela ne signifie pas que chaque terme dispose de son équivalent exact dans l'autre langue. L'argot et le slang ne coïncident pas en tous points. De nombreux termes de "rhyming slang", par exemple, n'ont pas d'équivalents argotiques en français; c'est le cas de **apples and pears** (escalier) et de **adam and eve** (croire). Il existe également des concepts qui ne peuvent pas être rendus de façon familière en français; c'est le cas de l'un des sens de l'adjectif **straight**, par exemple, que nous avons dû nous résoudre à traduire par "conventionnel".

Nous nous sommes efforcés, dans nos traductions, de respecter le niveau de langue des mots et expressions de la langue source. Cependant, lorsque ceci s'est avéré impossible, nous avons indiqué que la traduction donnée est neutre en lui accolant le symbole ᵡ.

Ceci étant un dictionnaire d'argot, le fait même qu'un terme (ou une expression) y soit traité est le signe qu'il appartient à la langue familière, et qu'il ne doit donc pas être utilisé dans un contexte neutre. Il existe cependant différents registres au sein de la langue familière, que nous avons choisi d'indiquer de la façon suivante: le symbole ⚠️ indique qu'un mot ou expression risque de choquer et doit être utilisé(e) avec circonspection; le symbole ‼️ est réservé aux termes et expressions vulgaires ou tabou. Les termes accompagnés de ce symbole doivent être utilisés avec la plus grande prudence. Nous espérons que ces indications vous aideront à éviter les principales embûches qui jalonnent la route de l'apprenti argotier.

Pour aider l'utilisateur

Il arrive qu'une simple traduction ne suffise pas à rendre fidèlement les subtilités ou parfois même le sens d'un mot ou d'une expression. C'est pourquoi de nombreuses entrées sont dotées de notes d'usage qui fournissent un complément d'information à l'utilisateur. Nous espérons que vous trouverez ces notes à la fois instructives et distrayantes. Elles comportent les éléments suivants:

▶ des encadrés sur les différentes variétés d'argot (**rhyming slang**, **Black American slang**, **verlan**, **javanais**). Vous trouverez également un tableau sur les différentes façons d'insulter son prochain dans la langue de Shakespeare (voir le tableau **insults** dans la partie anglais/français du dictionnaire);

▶ des compléments d'information expliquant les nuances d'usage de différents termes racistes, xénophobes ou insultants pour les homosexuels [**Paki**, **queer**, **Rital**, **Espingouin**];

▶ des explications sur certaines étymologies intéressantes [**cowabunga**, **not!**, **bidochon**, **Château-Lapompe**];

▶ des préfixes et des suffixes particulièrement générateurs [**mega-**, **-arama**, **-ville**, **archi-**, **-aille**, **-ard**];

▶ des explications sur des expressions et des formules toutes faites posant des problèmes de traduction particuliers [**as the actress said to the bishop**, **beam me up Scotty!**, **faire avancer le schmilblick**];

▶ des explications sur certains termes indissociables d'un contexte culturel ou social donné. (L'anglais britannique abonde en termes désignant des archétypes sociaux tels que **new lad**, **new man**, **Essex girl**, **trainspotter**).

L'argot américain

Bien que l'argot britannique subisse l'influence toujours croissante de l'anglais parlé aux États-Unis (principalement par le biais des médias), il existe de nombreux termes et expressions qui n'ont cours que d'un côté ou de l'autre de l'Atlantique. Ces termes sont précédés de la mention *Br* (britannique) et *Am* (américain); ces indications figurent aussi bien du côté anglais/français que dans les traductions de la partie français/anglais. Notre spécialiste en américanismes, le Professeur Jonathan E. Lighter, de l'Université du Tennessee, a vérifié tous les termes d'argot américain qui figurent dans cet ouvrage et a suggéré l'inclusion de centaines de nouvelles entrées et expressions. Le Professeur Lighter, auteur du *Random House Historical Dictionary of American Slang*, est l'un des grands spécialistes actuels de l'argot nord-américain.

Symboles Phonétiques de l'Anglais

Consonnes

[b]	bimbo ['bɪmbəʊ]
[d]	dishy ['dɪʃɪ]
[dʒ]	ginormous [dʒaɪ'nɔːməs]; jiffy ['dʒɪfɪ]
[f]	flunk [flʌŋk]
[g]	gaga ['gɑːgɑː]
[h]	hunky ['hʌŋkɪ]
[j]	yonks [jɒŋks]
[k]	conk [kɒŋk]
[l]	legless ['leglɪs]
[m]	manky ['mæŋkɪ]
[n]	naff [næf]
[ŋ]	banger ['bæŋə(r)]
[p]	prat [præt]
[r]	reefer ['riːfə(r)]
[(r)]	*(seulement prononcé en cas de liaison avec le mot suivant)* rotter ['rɒtə(r)]
[s]	scran [skræn]
[ʃ]	shooter ['ʃuːtə(r)]
[t]	tenner ['tenə(r)]
[tʃ]	chow [tʃaʊ]
[θ]	thicko ['θɪkəʊ]
[ð]	brother ['brʌðə(r)]
[v]	vibes [vaɪbz]
[w]	wacko ['wækəʊ]
[z]	zilch [zɪltʃ]
[ʒ]	casual ['kæʒʊəl]

Voyelles

[æ]	slammer ['slæmə(r)]
[ɑː]	barf [bɑːf]
[e]	preggers ['pregəz]
[ɜ]	hurl [hɜːl]
[ə]	gotcha ['gɒtʃə]
[iː]	geek [giːk]
[ɪ]	dippy ['dɪpɪ]
[ɒ]	pong [pɒŋ]
[ɔː]	awesome ['ɔːsəm]
[ʊ]	footie ['fʊtɪ]
[uː]	loony ['luːnɪ]
[ʌ]	junkie ['dʒʌŋkɪ]

Diphtongues

[aɪ]	wino ['waɪnəʊ]
[aʊ]	lousy ['laʊzɪ]
[eə]	yeah [jeə]
[eɪ]	flake [fleɪk]
[eʊ]	loaded ['leʊdɪd]
[ɪə]	weirdo ['wɪədəʊ]
[ɔɪ]	boyf [bɔɪf]

French Phonetic Symbols

Consonants

[b]   bagnole [baɲɔl]
[d]   draguer [drage]
[f]   frangin [frɑ̃ʒɛ̃]
[g]   greluche [grəlyʃ]
[ʒ]   gerber [ʒɛrbe]
[k]   costaud [kɔsto]
[l]   larguer [large]
[m]   mioche [mjɔʃ]
[n]   nul [nyl]
[ŋ]   feeling [filiŋ]
[ɲ]   guignol [giɲɔl]
[p]   pépé [pepe]
[r]   reum [rœm]
[s]   speeder [spide]
[ʃ]   chiper [ʃipe]
[t]   taré [tare]
[v]   vachement [vaʃmɑ̃]
[z]   zonard [zonar]

Vowels

[a]   aprème [aprɛm]
[ɑ]   pâlichon [pɑliʃɔ̃]
[e]   bourré [bure]
[ə]   peler [pəle]
[ø]   dégueu [degø]
[œ]   gueule [gœl]
[ɛ]   craignos [krɛɲos]
[i]   nippes [nip]
[ɔ]   hosto [ɔsto]
[o]   dope [dop]
[u]   roupiller [rupije]
[y]   nunuche [nynyʃ]
[ɑ̃]   lambin [lɑ̃bɛ̃]
[ɛ̃]   joint [ʒwɛ̃]
[ɔ̃]   défoncé [defɔ̃se]
[œ̃]   parfum [parfœ̃]

Semi-vowels

[w]   boîte [bwat]
[j]   flicaille [flikaj]
[ɥ]   puissant [pɥisɑ̃]

xiii

Labels
Indications d'Usage

English	Symbol	Français
gloss	=	glose
[introduces a brief explanation]		[introduit une explication]
cultural equivalent	≃	équivalent culturel
[introduces a translation which has a roughly equivalent status in the target language]		[introduit une traduction dont les connotations dans la langue cible sont comparables]
very familiar	!	très familier
vulgar	!!	vulgaire
neutral translation	▫	traduction neutre
abbreviation	*abbr, abrév*	abréviation
adjective	*adj*	adjectif
adverb	*adv*	adverbe
American English	*Am*	anglais d'Amérique du Nord
Australian English	*Aust*	anglais d'Australie
auxiliary	*aux*	auxiliaire
Belgian French	*Belg*	français de Belgique
British English	*Br*	anglais britannique
Canadian French	*Can*	canadianisme
exclamation	*exclam*	exclamation
feminine	*f*	féminin
humorous	*Hum*	humoristique
offensive	*Injurieux*	injurieux
[denotes a racist of homophobic term]		[signale un terme raciste ou homophobe]
invariable	*inv*	invariable
Irish English	*Ir*	anglais d'Irlande
ironic	*ironic, ironique*	ironique
masculine	*m*	masculin
modal auxiliary verb	*modal aux v*	auxiliaire modal
noun	*n*	nom
feminine noun	*nf*	nom féminin
feminine plural noun	*nfpl*	nom féminin pluriel
masculine noun	*nm*	nom masculin
masculine and feminine noun	*nmf*	nom masculin et féminin
(same form for both genders)		(formes identiques)
masculine and feminine noun	*nm,f*	nom masculin et féminin
(different form in the feminine)		(formes différentes)
masculine plural noun	*nmpl*	nom masculin pluriel
Black American English	*Noir Am*	anglais noir américain

plural noun	*npl*	nom pluriel
proper noun	*npr*	nom propre
offensive	*Offensive*	injurieux
[denotes a racist of homophobic term]		[signale un terme raciste ou homophobe]
pejorative	*Pej, Péj*	péjoratif
prefix	*prefix, préfixe*	préfixe
preposition	*prep, prép*	préposition
pronoun	*pron*	pronom
something	*qch*	quelque chose
somebody	*qn*	quelqu'un
registered trademark	®	marque déposée
somebody	*sb*	quelqu'un
Scottish English	*Scot*	anglais d'Écosse
something	*sth*	quelque chose
suffix	*suffix, suffixe*	suffixe
Swiss French	*Suisse*	helvétisme
verb	*v*	verbe
intransitive verb	*vi*	verbe intransitif
impersonal verb	*v imp*	verbe impersonnel
reflexive verb	*vpr*	verbe pronominal
transitive verb	*vt*	verbe transitif
inseparable transitive verb	*vt insép*	verbe transitif à particule inséparable
[phrasal verb where the verb and the adverb or preposition cannot be separated, e.g. **bunk off**; he **bunked off** school]		[par exemple: **bunk off** (sécher); he **bunked off** school (il a séché les cours)]
separable transitive verb	*vt sép*	verbe transitif à particule séparable
[phrasal verb where the verb and the adverb or preposition can be separated, e.g. **chuck in**; he **chucked** his job **in** or he **chucked in** his job]		[par exemple: **chuck in** (plaquer); he **chucked** his job **in** ou he **chucked in** his job (il a plaqué son travail)]

Thematic panels/Encadrés thématiques

English-French

Français-Anglais

English-French
Anglais-Français

A

Abo, abo ['æbəʊ] *n Austr Injurieux (abrév* **Aboriginal**) Aborigène □ *mf*

AC/DC [eɪsiː'diːsiː] *adj (bisexual)* à voile et à vapeur, bi

ace [eɪs] **1** *adj (excellent)* super, génial
2 *vt Am* **to ace an exam** réussir un examen les doigts dans le nez

aces ['eɪsəs] *adj Am (excellent)* super, génial

acid ['æsɪd] *n (LSD)* acide *m*; **to drop acid** prendre de l'acide; **acid house** *(music)* acid house *f*

acidhead ['æsɪdhed] *n* **to be an acidhead** consommer beaucoup de LSD □

act [ækt] *n* (**a**) **to get one's act together** se prendre en main □ (**b**) *Am* **to queer the act** tout faire foirer ▸ *voir aussi* **riot**

actress ['æktrɪs] *n Br Hum* **he's got a huge one… as the actress said to the bishop** il en a une énorme, si j'ose dire…

> "As the actress said to the bishop" est une formule humoristique prononcée lorsque l'on se rend compte que ce qui vient d'être dit peut être interprété de façon grivoise.

adam ['ædəm] *n (ecstasy)* ecstasy □ *f*, exta *f*

— *Pleins feux sur:* —

Alcohol

Il existe de multiples façons de désigner la boisson et l'ivresse dans les pays anglophones dont les habitants sont réputés pour aimer boire, notamment en Grande-Bretagne et en Australie. De quelqu'un qui sort avec l'intention explicite de s'enivrer, on utilisera entre autres les expressions **to go on a bender**, **to go on the piss** ou **on the bevvy**. À partir du mot **booze** (à la fois substantif = alcool, et verbe = picoler) de nombreux dérivés ont été créés : en anglais américain un **boozehound** signifie "poivrot" ; un **boozer** désigne un ivrogne et, en anglais britannique uniquement, un pub ; on emploiera **booze-up** pour une beuverie, et on dira d'une soirée qu'elle est **boozy** s'il y a beaucoup d'alcool à consommer. Parmi les autres termes désignant un ivrogne, citons **pisshead** et **piss-artist** (les deux étant d'un registre assez vulgaire), **lush** et, en anglais américain, **juicer**.

Il existe en anglais de très nombreux adjectifs argotiques pour dire d'une personne qu'elle est ivre. En anglais britannique les plus courants sont **legless**, **hammered**, **pissed** (ce dernier étant un peu plus vulgaire) et, plus récemment sont apparus les termes **bladdered** et **trousered**. En Écosse, on emploie aussi fréquemment l'adjectif **steaming**. L'expression **off one's face** s'utilise couramment, tout comme les expressions humoristiques (bien qu'un peu vulgaires) **pissed as a fart** et **pissed as a newt** ("bourré comme un triton"). Dans un registre encore plus vulgaire, on trouvera **shit-faced**. L'expression de l'argot rimé ("rhyming slang") **Brahms and Liszt** (= pissed) est pittoresque bien qu'en réalité rarement utilisée. **Blotto** s'employait souvent autrefois, mais ce terme est aujourd'hui vieilli.

The symbol □ indicates that a translation is neutral in register.

adam and eve ['ædəmən'iːv] *vt Br* (*rhyming slang* **believe**) croire $^□$; **would you adam and eve it!** tu te rends compte?

aggro ['ægrəʊ] *n Br* (*abrév* **aggravation**) (*violence*) castagne *f*; (*hassle*) problèmes $^□$ *mpl*; **my Mum's giving me so much aggro at the moment** ma mère est toujours sur mon dos en ce moment

aid [eɪd] *n* **what's that in aid of?** pourquoi t'as fait/dit ça, exactement?

air biscuit [eə'bɪskɪt] *n Br* (*fart*) perle *f*, prout *m*; **to float** or **launch an air biscuit** lâcher une perle, larguer une caisse

airhead ['eəhed] *n* = jolie nana pas très futée

alky ['ælkɪ] *n* (**a**) (*abrév* **alcoholic**) alcolo *mf*, poivrot(e) *m,f* (**b**) *Am* (*abrév* **alcohol**) gnôle *f*

all [ɔːl] *adv* (**a**) **the team was all over the place** l'équipe a joué n'importe comment $^□$; **at the interview he was all over the place** or **shop** il a complètement foiré son entretien; **he was pretending to be sober but he was all over the place** il était visiblement complètement bourré même s'il faisait tout son possible pour le dissimuler (**b**) **he's not all there** il n'a pas toute sa tête (**c**) **she was all over him at the party** elle l'a draguée tout le temps qu'a duré la soirée; *Hum* **he was all over her like a rash** or **a cheap suit** il l'a draguée de façon flagrante

all right [ɔːl'raɪt] **1** *adj* an **"I'm all right Jack" attitude** un comportement du style "moi d'abord, les autres ensuite"
2 *exclam* (**a**) (*as greeting*) salut, ça va? (**b**) (*in approval*) super!, cool! ▶ *voir aussi* **bit**

all that [ɔːl'ðæt] *adj* (*excellent*) super, génial; **she thinks she's all that** elle ne se prend pas pour n'importe qui

amber ['æmbə(r)] *n Br & Austr* **amber nectar** bière $^□$ *f*, mousse *f*

ambulance chaser ['æmbjʊlənst-ʃeɪsə(r)] *n Am Péj* = avocat qui ne s'occupe que d'affaires de demandes de dommages et intérêts pouvant rapporter gros

angel dust ['eɪndʒəldʌst] *n* PCP *f*, phéncyclidine $^□$ *f*

ankle-biter ['æŋkəlbaɪtə(r)] *n* gosse *mf*

anorak ['ænəræk] *n Br Péj* (*person*) ringard *m*

> Ce terme désigne un type de jeune homme généralement solitaire dont les activités vont à l'encontre de ce qui est considéré comme "cool". Un "anorak" ne s'intéresse pas à la mode (d'où le terme "anorak", symbole de l'absence de goût en matière vestimentaire) ni à l'actualité musicale ou sportive, et ne fréquente aucun endroit branché.

antsy ['æntsɪ] *adj Am* (*nervous*) agité $^□$, nerveux $^□$, sur des charbons ardents $^□$; (*irritable*) à cran

A-OK [eɪəʊ'keɪ] *Am* **1** *adj* super, génial; **everything's A-OK** tout baigne dans l'huile
2 *adv* **to go A-OK** se passer vachement bien

ape [eɪp] *adj* **to go ape (over)** (*lose one's temper*) piquer une crise, péter les plombs (à cause de); (*enthuse*) s'emballer (pour)

apeshit ⚠ ['eɪpʃɪt] *adj* **to go apeshit (over)** (*lose one's temper*) piquer une crise, péter les plombs (à cause de); (*enthuse*) s'emballer (pour)

apple ['æpəl] *n* (**a**) **the (Big) Apple** New York $^□$ (**b**) *Br* **apples and pears** (*rhyming slang* **stairs**) escaliers $^□$ *mpl* (**c**) *Austr* **she'll be apples!** tout baignera dans l'huile!

-arama [ə'rɑːmə] *suffixe Hum* **you should have seen how much we ate – it was pigarama!** t'aurais vu tout ce qu'on a mangé – une vraie orgie!; **try that new bar – it's babearama!** essaye ce nouveau bar – il y a toujours plein de canons

> Ce suffixe dénote l'abondance de ce qui le précède. On peut l'ajouter à presque n'importe quel nom, verbe ou adjectif pour introduire la notion de foisonnement.

The symbol $^□$ indicates that a translation is neutral in register.

argy-bargy ['ɑːdʒɪ'bɑːdʒɪ] n chamaille-
ries fpl; **there was a bit of argy-bargy
over who should do it** il y a eu des histoires pour savoir qui devait le faire

armpit ['ɑːmpɪt] n **the armpit of
the universe** (place) un coin paumé, un
trou

arse [!] [ɑːs] Br **1** n **(a)** (buttocks) cul m; **a
kick up the arse** un coup de pied au cul;
to make an arse of sth complètement
foirer qch; **to get one's arse in(to) gear**
se remuer le cul; **to work one's arse off**
bosser comme un nègre; **to talk out of
one's arse** dire des conneries; **his head's
completely up his arse** il se prend vraiment pas pour de la merde; **to be out on
one's arse** (get fired) se faire virer; **to go
arse over tit** or **tip** ramasser une gamelle; **my arse!** mon cul!; **aromather-
apy my arse!** aromathérapie mon cul!;
to kiss or **lick sb's arse** faire du lèche-
cul à qn; **kiss my arse!** va te faire foutre!;
get your arse over here! ramène ta
fraise!, amène-toi!; **move** or **shift your
arse!** pousse ton cul!; **come on, park
your arse, mate!** allez, pose ton cul,
vieux!; **stick** or **shove it up your arse!**
tu peux te le mettre au cul!; **a nice piece
of arse** une nénette bandante; **he's
been sitting on his arse all day** il a rien
foutu de la journée; **he doesn't know
his arse from his elbow** il est complètement nul; **she thinks the sun shines
out of his arse** elle le prend pour un dieu;
it's my arse that's on the line ça risque
de me retomber sur la gueule; **we had a
Ford Fiesta sitting on our arse the
whole way** une Ford Fiesta nous a collé
au cul pendant tout le trajet

(b) (person) crétin(e) m,f; **to make an
arse of oneself** se ridiculiser □

2 vt **why don't you come with us? – I
can't be arsed** tu viens avec nous? –
non, j'ai trop la flemme; **he can't be
arsed doing it himself** il a rien envie de
se faire chier à le faire lui-même ▶ voir
aussi **pain**

arse about [!], **arse around** [!] vi Br
(act foolishly) faire le con, déconner;
(waste time) glander, glandouiller

arse up [!] vt sép **to arse sth up** foirer
qch

arse-bandit [!] ['ɑːsbændɪt] n Br Injurieux pédale f, tapette f

arsehole [!] ['ɑːshəʊl] n Br **(a)** (anus) trou
m du cul; **the arsehole of nowhere** or
of the universe (place) un coin paumé,
un trou **(b)** (person) trou m du cul; **to
make an arsehole of oneself** se ridiculiser □

arseholed [!] ['ɑːshəʊld] adj Br (drunk)
bourré comme un coing, complètement
pété

arse-kisser [!] ['ɑːskɪsə(r)] n Br lèche-
cul mf

arse-kissing [!] ['ɑːskɪsɪŋ] Br **1** n lèche f
2 adj **he's nothing but an arse-
kissing bastard!** c'est qu'un lèche-cul!

arse-licker [!] ['ɑːslɪkə(r)] = **arse-
kisser**

arse-licking [!] ['ɑːslɪkɪŋ] = **arse-
kissing**

arsewipe [!] ['ɑːswaɪp] n Br (person) raclure f

arsey [!] ['ɑːsɪ] adj Br (stupid) débile; (not
trendy) ringard; **that was a bit of an arsey thing to say** c'est un peu débile de
dire un truc pareil

Arthur or Martha ['ɑːθərɔːmɑːθə]
adj Br & Austr Hum **he doesn't know if
he's Arthur or Martha** (is confused) il
est ou marche à côté de ses pompes; (is
unsure about his sexuality) il ne sait pas
trop lui-même s'il marche à voile ou à vapeur

arty-farty ['ɑːtɪ'fɑːtɪ], Am **artsy-
fartsy** ['ɑːtsɪ'fɑːtsɪ] adj (person) qui se
donne un genre artiste □; (film, activities)
qui se veut artistique □

arvo ['ɑːvəʊ] n Austr (afternoon) après-
midi mf, aprème mf

as if [æz'ɪf] exclam **am I a nag? – as if!**
est-ce que je suis une emmerdeuse? –
mais non! (dit ironiquement); **I'm going
on a diet tomorrow – as if!** je
commence un régime demain – c'est ça!
(dit ironiquement)

ass [!] [æs] n Am cul m; **a kick in the ass**

un coup de pied au cul; **to get one's ass in gear** se remuer le cul; **to work one's ass off** bosser comme un nègre; **to be on sb's ass** être sur le dos de qn; **to do sth ass backwards** faire qch à l'envers□; **to get one's ass in a sling** avoir des emmerdes; **to go ass over teakettle** ramasser une gamelle; **my (aching) ass!** mon cul!; **I don't want to put my ass on the line** je veux pas que ça me retombe sur la gueule; **to be out on one's ass** *(get fired)* se faire virer; **to haul** or **tear ass** se grouiller; **to kiss sb's ass** faire du lèche-cul à qn; **kiss my ass!** va te faire foutre!; **get your ass over here!** ramène ta fraise!, amène-toi!; **move your ass!** pousse ton cul!; **stick** or **shove it up your ass!** tu peux te le mettre au cul!; **a nice piece of ass** une nénette bandante; **he's been sitting on his ass all day** il n'a rien foutu de la journée; **he doesn't know his ass from his elbow** or **from a hole in the ground** il est complètement nul; **it's my ass that's on the line** ça risque de me retomber sur la gueule; **to kick sb's ass** *(defeat)* ratatiner qn; **to kick ass** assurer un max; **to break** or **bust one's ass** se casser le cul; **to be up to one's ass in work** crouler sous le travail; **up your ass!** va te faire mettre!; **you can**

bet your ass I will! un peu que je vais le faire!; **your ass is grass!** tu vas voir ce que tu vas prendre!; **they oughta fire his sorry ass!** ils devraient le virer! ▸ *voir aussi* **bite, pain, rat**

ass-bandit [!] ['æsbændɪt] *n Am Injurieux* pédale *f*, tapette *f*

asshole [!] ['æshəʊl] *n Am* **(a)** *(anus)* trou *m* du cul; **the asshole of the universe** or **world** *(place)* un coin paumé, un trou **(b)** *(person)* trou *m* du cul

ass-kisser [!] ['æskɪsə(r)] *n Am* lèche-cul *mf*

ass-kissing [!] ['æskɪsɪŋ] *Am* **1** *n* lèche *f* **2** *adj* **he's nothing but an ass-kissing bastard!** c'est qu'un lèche-cul!

ass-licker [!] ['æslɪkə(r)] *n Am* = **ass-kisser**

ass-licking [!] ['æslɪkɪŋ] *n Am* = **ass-kissing**

ass-wipe [!] ['æswaɪp] *n Am (person)* raclure *f*

at [æt] *prép* **that club is where it's at** c'est la boîte in; **that's not where I'm at** c'est pas mon truc

attitude ['ætɪtjuːd] *n (self-assurance, assertiveness)* assurance□ *f*; **to have attitude** avoir du caractère; **a car with attitude** une voiture qui a du caractère

Auntie ['ɑːntɪ] *n Br* **Auntie (Beeb)** la BBC

Australian slang

On désigne parfois l'argot australien par **strine** (un mot qui imite la façon dont les Australiens prononcent "Australian"). Étant donné les liens historiques étroits entre la Grande-Bretagne et l'Australie (appelée aussi familièrement **Oz**), il n'est pas surprenant qu'une grande partie de l'argot australien soit identique à l'argot britannique, notamment le "rhyming slang" ou argot rimé (voir encadré). Mais l'argot australien a aussi été influencé par l'anglais américain notamment lors de la ruée vers l'or en Australie. Il existe également un certain nombre d'inventions australiennes, bien que les deux mots les plus connus à l'étranger, **sheila** (fille) et **cobber** (ami), ne soient plus tellement employés aujourd'hui.

La création de mots par abréviation et ajout du suffixe **-o** est caractéristique de l'argot australien. On obtient par exemple **garbo** (diminutif de "garbage collector", éboueur) et **arvo** (diminutif de "afternoon", après-midi). Comme exemples typiques de l'argot d'Australie, on peut citer les mots **dag** (un ringard), **dunny** (des chiottes), **chook** (un poulet, et également "une femme") et la fameuse exclamation de surprise **strewth!**

The symbol □ indicates that a translation is neutral in register.

"Auntie" se traduit littéralement "tatie"; c'est le surnom affectueux donné à la BBC par les Britanniques, qui met en relief l'attitude quelque peu paternaliste de l'institution vis-à-vis du public, et un style qui manque parfois d'audace.

away [ə'weɪ] **1** *adj Br* **well away** *(drunk)* bourré, beurré, pété

  2 *adv* **to be away with the fairies** *(senile)* être complètement gaga; *(eccentric)* être farfelu; *(daydreaming)* être dans les nuages; *Br* **to play away** *(be unfaithful)* être infidèle ⁰

Le sens ci-dessus provient du vocabulaire sportif; en effet, "to play away" signifie "jouer à l'extérieur".

awesome ['ɔːsəm] *adj Am* super, génial

AWOL ['eɪwɒl] *adj Hum* **he goes AWOL whenever it's time to do the washing-up** il se débine à chaque fois qu'il s'agit de faire la vaisselle; **my keys have gone AWOL again** encore une fois, impossible de mettre la main sur mes clés

Il s'agit à l'origine d'un acronyme utilisé dans l'armée, dont la forme développée est "absent without leave" (absent sans permission).

awright [ɔː'raɪt] *exclam Br* (**a**) *(as greeting)* salut, ça va? (**b**) *(in approval)* super!, cool!

axe, *Am* **ax** [æks] *n (guitar)* gratte *f*, râpe *f*

Ayrton ['eətən] *n Br (rhyming slang* **Ayrton Senna** = **tenner**) = billet de dix livres

B

babe [beɪb] *n* (**a**) *(attractive woman)* canon *m*, bombe *f*; **his sister's friends are all absolute babes** les copines de sa sœur sont toutes des canons (**b**) *(term of address)* chéri(e) *m,f* (**c**) *Am (attractive man)* beau mec *m*; **my god, check out that total babe over there!** regarde un peu le beau mec là-bas! ▸ *voir aussi* **magnet**

backside [bæk'saɪd] *n* derrière *m*

bad [bæd] *adj* (**a**) *(not good)* **I'm having a bad hair day** *(my hair's a mess)* je n'arrive pas à me coiffer aujourd'hui □; *(I'm having a bad day)* aujourd'hui c'est un jour sans; **he's bad news** c'est quelqu'un de pas fréquentable □ (**b**) *(excellent)* super, génial; **this music's so bad** cette musique est vraiment super

badass [!] ['bædæs] *Am* **1** *n* *(person)* dur(e) *m,f* (à cuire)
2 *adj* (**a**) *(intimidating, tough)* **to be badass** être un(e) dur(e) à cuire; **her husband's some badass Mob guy** son mari est une espèce de dur à cuire qui bosse pour la Mafia (**b**) *(excellent)* super, génial; **her new sneakers are so badass** ils sont super, ses nouveaux tennis

badmouth ['bædmaʊθ] *vt* débiner

bag [bæg] *n* (**a**) *Péj (woman)* **old bag** vieille bique *f* (**b**) *(quantity of drugs)* dose *f* (en sachet ou dans un papier plié) (**c**) *(interest)* dada *m*; **he has a new bag** il a un nouveau dada; **it's not my bag** c'est pas mon truc (**d**) **it's in the bag** c'est dans la poche ▸ *voir aussi* **bum**

bag off *vi Br* **did you bag off last night?** t'as emballé hier soir?; **to bag off with sb** lever *ou* emballer qn

bahookie [bə'hʊkɪ] *n Scot (buttocks)* miches *fpl*, cul *m*

Baldwin ['bɔːldwɪn] *n Am (attractive male)* beau mec *m*

Il s'agit d'une référence à Alec Baldwin, acteur américain réputé pour son charme.

ball [!!] [bɔːl] *Am* **1** *vt (have sex with)* *(of man)* baiser, tringler, troncher; *(of woman)* baiser avec, s'envoyer
2 *vi (have sex)* baiser

ball up [!] *Am* = **balls up**

ball-breaker [!] ['bɔːlbreɪkə(r)], **ball-buster** [!] ['bɔːlbʌstə(r)] *n Am* (**a**) *(woman)* femme *f* de tête □ (**b**) *(problem, situation)* casse-tête *m*

ballistic [bə'lɪstɪk] *adv* **to go ballistic** piquer une crise, péter une durite

balls [!] [bɔːlz] *npl* (**a**) *(testicles)* couilles *fpl*; **to have blue balls** avoir les couilles pleines et douloureuses; **she's been breaking** *or* **busting my balls about it** elle arrête pas de me casser les couilles avec ça; **they've got us by the balls** ils nous tiennent à la gorge
(**b**) *(nonsense)* conneries *fpl*
(**c**) *(courage)* cran *m*; **to have the balls to do sth** avoir assez de cran pour faire qch; **his balls are bigger than his brains** il est pas bien, il est complètement malade

balls up [!] *vt sép* **to balls sth up** *(interview, exam)* foirer qch, se planter à qch; *(plan, arrangement)* faire foirer qch; **you've ballsed everything up** tu as tout fait foirer

balls-up [!] ['bɔːlzʌp] *n Br* merdier *m*; **to make a balls-up of sth** *(interview, exam)* foirer qch, se planter à qch; *(plan, arrangement)* faire foirer qch

ballsy ['bɔːlzɪ] *adj* qui en a; **his wife is one ballsy lady** elle a des couilles, sa femme

The symbol □ indicates that a translation is neutral in register.

ball-up ![] ['bɔːlʌp] *Am* = **balls-up**

baloney [bə'ləʊnɪ] **1** *n* (*nonsense*) foutaises *fpl*; **don't talk baloney!** arrête de raconter n'importe quoi!
2 *exclam* foutaises!

baltic ['bɔːltɪk] *adj Br* (*weather*) **it's baltic** il fait un froid de canard

bampot ['bæmpɒt] *n Scot* (*idiot*) andouille *f*

bananas [bə'nɑːnəz] *adj* (*mad*) dingue, cinglé, timbré; **to go bananas** devenir dingue *ou* cinglé *ou* timbré

bang [bæŋ] **1** *n* (**a**) (*sexual intercourse*) **to have a bang** ![!] baiser (**b**) *Am* **to get a bang out of sb/sth** s'éclater avec qn/en faisant qch
2 *adv Br* (**a**) (*exactly*) **bang on time** pile à l'heure; **bang up-to-date** hypermoderne; **bang in the middle** en plein milieu; **you were bang out of order calling him a fool in front of everybody!** tu n'avais pas à le traiter d'imbécile devant tout le monde!
(**b**) **bang on** (*guess, answer, calculation*) qui tombe pile; (*arrive, start*) pile à l'heure
(**c**) **bang goes that idea** c'est râpé; **bang goes my holiday** c'est foutu pour mes vacances
3 ![!] *vt* (*have sex with*) (*of man*) baiser, tringler, troncher; (*of woman*) baiser avec, s'envoyer
4 ![!] *vi* (*have sex*) baiser

bang on *vi Br* (*talk at length*) rabâcher; **he's forever banging on about Dido** il n'arrête pas de nous rebattre les oreilles avec Dido

bang up *vt sép Br* (*imprison*) boucler, coffrer

banger ['bæŋə(r)] *n* (**a**) (*car*) tas *m* de ferraille, vieille bagnole *f* (**b**) *Br* (*sausage*) saucisse ▯ *f*; **bangers and mash** saucisses-purée *f*

banging ['bæŋɪŋ] *adj Br* (*club, party*) hyper animé

bang-up ['bæŋʌp] *adj Br* (*excellent*) super, génial; **Russell Crowe has done a bang-up job of portraying the character** Russell Crowe est vraiment entré à fond dans la peau du personnage; **she did a bang-up job of throwing a good party** elle avait organisé une super soirée

banjax ['bændʒæks] *vt Scot & Ir* (*break*) bousiller

barbie ['bɑːbɪ] *n Austr & Br* (*barbecue*) barbecue ▯ *m*; **to have a barbie** faire un barbecue

bareback ['beəbæk] *adv Br Hum* **to ride bareback** (*have unprotected sex*) faire l'amour sans capote

barf [bɑːf] *vi* dégueuler, gerber

barfly ['bɑːflaɪ] *n Am* pilier *m* de bistrot

barhop ['bɑːhɒp] *vi Am* faire la tournée des bars ▯

barking ['bɑːkɪŋ] *adj Br* **barking (mad)** cinglé, toqué, taré

barmy ['bɑːmɪ] *adj Br* barjo

barnet *n Br* (*rhyming slang* **Barnet fair = hair**) tifs *mpl*

Barney ['bɑːnɪ] *n* (*ugly man*) mocheté *f*

> Barney Rubble est l'un des personnages de la bande dessinée américaine "les Flintstones".

barney ['bɑːnɪ] *n Br* (*argument*) prise *f* de bec

Barry White ![] [bærɪ'waɪt] *n Br* (*rhyming slang* **shite**) **to have a Barry White** couler un bronze

bar steward ['bɑːstjʊəd] *n Hum* salaud *m*, salopard *m*

> Il s'agit d'un jeu de mots sur "bastard".

bash [bæʃ] **1** *n* (**a**) (*party*) fiesta *f* (**b**) *Br* (*attempt*) **to have a bash (at sth/at doing sth)** essayer (qch/de faire qch) ▯; **I'll give it a bash** je vais essayer un coup
2 *vt* (*hit*) cogner; (*dent*) cabosser ▶ *voir aussi* **bishop**

basket case ['bɑːskɪtkeɪs] *n* cinglé(e) *m,f*, barjo *mf*

bastard ![] ['bɑːstəd] *n* (**a**) (*contemptible person*) salaud (salope) *m,f*; **some bastard traffic warden gave me a parking ticket** une salope de contractuelle m'a collé un papillon

---

The symbol ▯ indicates that a translation is neutral in register.

(b) *(any man)* **poor bastard!** le pauvre! ; **lucky bastard!** le veinard! ; **you sad bastard!** pauvre mec *ou* type, va! ; **he's a clever bastard** il en a dans le ciboulot; **her boyfriend's a big bastard** son copain est un sacré mastard; **all right, you old bastard?** *(as greeting)* ça va, vieux?

(c) *(thing)* truc *m* chiant; **a bastard of a job** un travail à la con; **this oven is a bastard to clean** ce four est vraiment chiant à nettoyer; **I can't get the bastard thing to start** j'arrive pas à faire démarrer cette saloperie

(d) it hurts like a bastard ça fait super *ou* vachement mal; **I raced round the shops like a bastard all day looking for a present** je me suis tapé tous les magasins au pas de course pendant toute la journée à la recherche d'un cadeau; **I've been working like a bastard while you've been lying in your pit all day** j'ai bossé comme un dingue alors que toi tu t'es prélassé dans ton pieu toute la journée

bat¹ [bæt] *n* **(a)** *Péj (woman)* old bat vieille bique *f* **(b)** *Am (drinking spree)* **to be on a bat** sortir prendre une cuite ▶ *voir aussi* **hell**

bat² *vi* **to bat for the other side** *or* **team** *(of gay man)* en être, être pédé; *(of lesbian)* être gouine; **to bat for both sides** *or* **teams** *(of bisexual)* marcher à voile et à vapeur

battered ['bætəd] *adj Br* bourré, beurré, pété

battleaxe, *Am* **battleax** ['bætəlæks] *n* *(woman)* dragon *m*, virago *f*

batty ['bætɪ] *adj* fêlé, timbré

bawl out [bɔːl] *vt sép* **to bawl sb out** enguirlander qn, passer un savon à qn

beak [biːk] *n (nose)* quart de brie *m*

beam [biːm] *vt Hum* **beam me up, Scotty!** que quelqu'un me sorte de là!

Il s'agit de l'expression utilisée par les membres d'équipage du vaisseau "Starship Enterprise" dans la série télévisée américaine culte *Star Trek* pour demander au technicien de l'équipe (nommé Scotty) de les ramener à bord du vaisseau grâce à un rayon spécial. Aujourd'hui, on utilise cette expression lorsque l'on se trouve dans une situation très désagréable, dont on voudrait bien être sorti comme par miracle.

bean [biːn], **beaner** ['biːnə(r)] *n Am Injurieux* métèque *mf (d'origine latino-américaine)*

bear [beə(r)] *n Hum* **does a bear shit in the woods?** ⚠ ça me paraît évident ▶ *voir aussi* **Pope**

beard [bɪəd] *n (woman going out with gay man)* = femme que fréquente un homosexuel de façon à dissimuler son homosexualité

beast [biːst] *n Am (ugly woman)* boudin *m*, cageot *m*

beat [biːt] *vt* **(a) to beat it**, *Am* **to beat feet** *(go away)* se tirer, se barrer **(b) to beat one's meat** ‼ *(masturbate)* se branler ▶ *voir aussi* **rap**

beat off ‼ *vi (masturbate)* se branler

beat-'em-up ['biːtəmʌp] *n* = film ou jeu vidéo comportant de nombreuses bagarres

beaut [bjuːt] **1** *n (beautiful thing)* splendeur *f*; **his new hi-fi's a beaut** sa nouvelle chaîne est géniale
2 *adj Austr* super, génial

beauty ['bjuːtɪ] **1** *n (beautiful thing)* splendeur *f*; **his new hi-fi's a beauty** sa nouvelle chaîne est géniale; **that black eye is a real beauty!** quel beau coquard!
2 *exclam Br* **(you) beauty!** super!

beaver ‼ ['biːvə(r)] *n (woman's genitals)* chatte *f*, cramouille *f*, chagatte *f*

bed [bed] *vt (have sex with)* coucher avec

beef [biːf] **1** *n (complaint)* **what's your beef?** c'est quoi, ton problème?; **my beef is with him** c'est avec lui que j'ai un problème
2 *vi (complain)* râler (**about** à propos de)

beefcake ['biːfkeɪk] *n (attractive men)* beaux mecs *mpl* musclés; *Br* **he's a real beefcake** il est vraiment bien foutu

The symbol ⁇ indicates that a translation is neutral in register.

beemer ['biːmə(r)] n (BMW) BM f

beer goggles ['bɪəɡɒɡəlz] npl **are you telling me you shagged her?! did you have your beer goggles on?** ⚠ quoi? tu l'as sautée? t'étais bourré ou quoi?

> "Beer goggles" signifie littéralement "lunettes de bière". Cette expression fait référence au fait qu'après avoir consommé quelques bières, un individu est susceptible de trouver du charme même aux personnes qui en sont presque totalement dépourvues.

bee stings ['biːstɪŋz] npl (small breasts) œufs mpl sur le plat (petite poitrine)

beezer ['biːzə(r)] n Am (nose) tarin m, blaire m

bell [bel] n Br (phone call) **to give sb a bell** passer un coup de fil à qn, bigophoner qn

bell-end ['bel'end] n (a) (head of penis) gland m (b) (contemptible man) gland m, trou du cul m

bellyache ['belɪeɪk] vi râler (**about** à propos de)

bellyful ['belɪfʊl] n **to have had a bellyful of sb/sth** en avoir ras le bol de qn/qch

belt [belt] **1** n (blow) gnon m, pain m; **to give sb a belt in the face** flanquer un gnon ou un pain dans la tronche à qn **2** vt (hit) (person) flanquer un gnon ou un pain à; (ball) flanquer un grand coup dans **3** vi (move quickly) **to belt along** aller à fond la caisse ou à toute blinde; **to belt down the stairs** descendre les escaliers à fond la caisse ou à toute blinde

belt up vi Br (be quiet) la fermer, la boucler; **belt up!** la ferme!, ta gueule!

belter ['beltə(r)] n Br **a belter of a film** un super film; **that last song was a belter** la dernière chanson était super

bend [bend] n **to be round the bend** être dingue ou cinglé; **to go round the bend** devenir dingue ou cinglé; **to drive sb round the bend** rendre qn dingue ou cinglé ▸ voir aussi **ear, elbow**

bender ['bendə(r)] n (a) (drinking session) beuverie f; **to go on a bender** aller se

cuiter (**b**) Injurieux (homosexual) pédale f, tantouze f

> Dans la catégorie (b), ce terme perd son caractère injurieux quand il est utilisé par des homosexuels.

bent [bent] adj (a) Br Injurieux (homosexual) pédé; **as bent as a nine bob note** or **as a three pound note** pédé comme un phoque (b) Br (corrupt, dishonest) pourri, ripou (c) Am **bent out of shape** (angry, upset) dans tous ses états (d) Am **get bent!** ⚠ va te faire voir!

> Dans la catégorie (a), ce terme perd son caractère injurieux quand il est utilisé par des homosexuels.

berk [bɜːk] n Br andouille f, débile mf

bet [bet] vi **you bet!** y a intérêt!, un peu!; **he says he's sorry – I bet!** il dit qu'il regrette – c'est ça! ou mon œil, oui!

Betty ['betɪ] n canon m, bombe f

> Il s'agit à l'origine d'un terme de l'argot des surfeurs. Betty est l'un des personnages féminins de la bande dessinée américaine "les Flintstones".

bevvied ['bevɪd] adj Br bourré, beurré; **to get bevvied** se cuiter, prendre une cuite

bevvy ['bevɪ] n Br (a) (alcohol) alcool ⁰ m, bibine f (b) (alcoholic drink) **to have a bevvy** boire un coup (c) (drinking session) beuverie f; **to go on the bevvy** aller se cuiter, aller prendre une cuite

bi [baɪ] adj (abrév **bisexual**) bi

Bible-basher ['baɪbəlbæʃə(r)], **Bible-thumper** ['baɪbəlθʌmpə(r)] n grenouille f de bénitier

biddy ['bɪdɪ] n **old biddy** vieille bique f

biff [bɪf] vt (person) foutre un pain ou un gnon à; (object) foutre un grand coup dans

biffer ['bɪfə(r)] n Br mocheté f

big [bɪɡ] adj (a) **to be into sb/sth big time** or **in a big way** être dingue de qn/qch; **he's been doing smack big time** or **in a big way** depuis quelque temps il arrête pas de prendre de l'héro; **he's**

messed up everything big time il a tout fait foirer dans les grandes largeurs; **did you have fun? – big time!** vous vous êtes bien amusés? – oui, vachement bien!

(b) **to make a big deal out of sth** faire tout un fromage de qch; **it's no big deal** c'est pas grave; *Ironique* **big deal!** la belle affaire!

(c) *Br* **big girl's blouse** *(wimp)* femme-lette *f*

(d) **to have big hair** = avoir une coiffure bouffante tenue par une grande quantité de laque

(e) *Am* **big house** *(prison)* taule *f*, placard *m*; **he's gone to the big house** on l'a mis à l'ombre ▶ *voir aussi* **cheese, E, enchilada, mama, shot, smoke, wheel**

big up *vt sép* faire du battage à propos de; **to big oneself up** se faire mousser; **all the radio stations are bigging up his new album** toutes les stations de radio font un sacré battage autour de son dernier album

biggie, biggy ['bɪgɪ] *n* **it's going to be a biggie** *or* **biggy!** *(new film, CD)* ça va faire un carton!; *(storm)* ça va faire mal!; *Am* **no biggie!** pas de problème!

bigwig ['bɪgwɪg] *n* huile *f*, grosse légume *f*, gros bonnet *m*

bike [baɪk] *n* (a) *Br* **on your bike!** *(go away)* casse-toi!, tire-toi!; *(don't talk nonsense)* n'importe quoi!; *(I don't believe you)* c'est ça!; (b) **she's the town bike** ⚠ *(promiscuous)* il n'y a que le train qui ne lui soit pas passé dessus

Bill [bɪl] *n Br* **the (Old) Bill** les flics *mpl*

Billy No Mates [bɪlɪ'nəʊmeɪts] *n Br Hum* = individu peu populaire; **nobody's called me for days, what a Billy No Mates...** ça fait des jours que personne m'a appelé; j'ai pas d'amis...

bimbo ['bɪmbəʊ] *n (woman)* jolie nana pas très futée

bin [bɪn] *n (psychiatric hospital)* maison *f* de fous

bint [bɪnt] *n Br* greluche *f*; **you stupid bint!** espèce d'andouille!

bird [bɜːd] *n* (a) *Br (woman, girlfriend)* nana *f*, gonzesse *f* (b) *Am (man)* mec *m* (c) *Am* **to give sb the bird** *(make fun of)* se foutre de la gueule de qn; *(gesture at)* faire un doigt d'honneur à qn; **to flip sb the bird** *(gesture at)* faire un doigt d'honneur à qn

birdbrain ['bɜːdbreɪn] *n* cervelle *f* d'oiseau

bishop ['bɪʃəp] *n* **to bang** *or Br* **bash the bishop** ⚠ *(masturbate)* se branler, se taper sur la colonne ▶ *voir aussi* **actress**

bit [bɪt] *n* (a) *Br* **a bit on the side** *(man)* amant ᵘ *m*; *(woman)* maîtresse ᵘ *f*; **she's a bit of all right!** elle est gironde! (b) *Am (term of imprisonment)* peine *f* de prison ᵘ; **he did a bit in Fort Worth** il a fait de la taule à Fort Worth ▶ *voir aussi* **stuff**

bitch [bɪtʃ] **1** *n* (a) *(nasty woman)* salope *f*, garce *f*; **she's a real bitch to her husband** c'est une vraie garce avec son mari

(b) *(any woman) Br* **the poor bitch** la pauvre; **the lucky bitch** la veinarde

(c) *(thing)* truc *m* chiant; **life's a bitch!** chienne de vie!; **I've had a bitch of a day** j'ai passé une sale journée; **her place is a bitch to find without a map** sa maison est vraiment chiante à trouver sans carte

2 *vi* (a) *Br (say nasty things)* déblatérer (**about** contre) (b) *(complain)* râler (**about** à propos de)

bitch up *vt sép* **to bitch sth up** saloper qch

bitchin ['bɪtʃɪn] *adj Am* super, génial

bitchy ['bɪtʃɪ] *adj (person)* salaud, dégueulasse; *(remark)* dégueulasse; **that was a bitchy thing to do** c'est vraiment salaud *ou* dégueulasse d'avoir fait ça

bite [baɪt] *Am* **1** *vt* **bite me!, bite my ass!** ⚠ va te faire voir!

2 *vi (be bad)* craindre; **this really bites!** ça craint vraiment!

biz [bɪz] *n Br (abrév* **business)** **it's the biz!** c'est impec'!

bizzies ['bɪzɪz] *npl Br* **the bizzies** *(the police)* les flics *mpl*

BJ ⚠ [biː'dʒeɪ] *n (abrév* **blow-job)** pipe *f*; **to give sb a BJ** faire une pipe à qn

The symbol ᵘ indicates that a translation is neutral in register.

blab [blæb] **1** vt (tell) raconter □
2 vi (**a**) (tell secret) vendre la mèche (**b**) (chatter) bavarder, jacasser

blabbermouth ['blæbəmaʊθ] n he's a **blabbermouth** il ne sait pas tenir sa langue

black [blæk] n (cannabis resin) hasch m, charas m, kif m

black man's wheels [blækmænz-'wiːlz] npl Br (BMW) BM f

Black Stump ['blæk'stʌmp] n Austr **beyond the Black Stump** en pleine cambrousse

bladdered ['blædəd] adj Br bourré, beurré, pété

blade [bleɪd] n (knife) lame f, surin m

blag [blæg] Br **1** n (robbery) braquage m
2 vt (**a**) (steal) piquer (**b**) (con) **to blag oneself sth** obtenir qch au culot; **to blag one's way in** resquiller

blah [blɑː] **1** n (**a**) (meaningless remarks, nonsense) blabla m, baratin m (**b**) blah, blah, blah (to avoid repetition) etc etc; **he went on for half an hour about how we all had to work harder, blah, blah, blah** il nous a rabâché pendant une demi-heure qu'il fallait qu'on fasse tous plus d'efforts, etc etc
2 adj (dull) sans intérêt □

blank [blæŋk] n **to shoot** or **fire blanks** (of man) être stérile □

blast [blɑːst] **1** n Am (good time) **it was a blast** c'était l'éclate; **we had a blast** on s'est éclatés
2 exclam Br **blast (it)!** crotte!, zut!

blasted ['blɑːstɪd] **1** adj (**a**) (drunk) bourré, beurré; (on drugs) défoncé (**b**) (for emphasis) **the blasted car** cette saleté de voiture; **the blasted child** ce sale môme; **it's a blasted nuisance** c'est sacrément embêtant
2 adv (for emphasis) **don't go so blasted fast!** ne va pas si vite, bon sang!

blazes ['bleɪzɪz] npl (**a**) **to run/work like blazes** courir/travailler comme un(e) fou (folle) (**b**) **what/who/why the blazes…?** que/qui/pourquoi diable…? (**c**) **go** or Br **get to blazes!** va au diable!

bleeder ['bliːdə(r)] n Br (person) salaud (salope) m,f; **the poor bleeder** le pauvre; **you lucky bleeder!** sacré veinard!

bleeding ['bliːdɪŋ] Br **1** adj (for emphasis) **you bleeding idiot!** espèce de con!; **what a bleeding nuisance!** quelle saloperie!
2 adv (for emphasis) foutrement; **you're bleeding (well) coming with me!** tu viens avec moi, un point c'est tout!; **that was bleeding stupid!** c'est vraiment

Black American slang

Il existe de nombreux termes d'argot Noir américain, qui, bien que désormais largement utilisés en Amérique du Nord et en Grande-Bretagne, retiennent néanmoins leur identité afro-américaine. Ces termes portent la mention Noir Am dans ce dictionnaire.

C'est dans le monde des musiciens, et particulièrement le monde des jazzmen des années trente, que tout un pan de l'argot Noir américain trouve ses origines. Le jargon des musiciens de jazz a par la suite été progressivement adopté par la jeunesse américaine. Depuis le début des années 80, c'est le rap qui est une source importante de termes d'argot. L'orthographe de ces termes est souvent modifiée de façon à en transcrire fidèlement la prononciation (par ex "ho", "nigga", "gangsta"). Le rap, en tant que forme d'expression d'une communauté défavorisée qui connaît un taux de criminalité très élevé, est une musique souvent violente, qui véhicule volontiers des clichés empreints de misogynie. Le rap continue d'exercer une très grande influence sur la façon dont s'expriment les jeunes.

The symbol □ indicates that a translation is neutral in register.

con, ce que tu as fait/dit!

blighter ['blaɪtə(r)] n (person) zigoto m; (thing) truc m, bidule m; **you cheeky blighter!** tu as un sacré culot toi!; **there's a wasp in the room and I'm terrified of the little blighters!** il y a une guêpe dans la pièce et j'ai horreur de ces bestioles!

blimey ['blaɪmɪ] exclam Br zut alors!, la vache!

blinder ['blaɪndə(r)] n Br (a) (drinking session) beuverie f; **to go on a blinder** aller se cuiter, aller prendre une cuite (b) (excellent performance) sacrée prestation f; **to play a blinder** faire un match/une partie d'enfer

blinding ['blaɪndɪŋ] adj Br (excellent) super, génial

bling bling ['blɪŋ'blɪŋ] **1** n (jewellery) bijoux □, quincaillerie f

2 adj (ostentatious) tape-à-l'œil; **that car is so bling bling!** cette voiture est vraiment tape-à-l'œil

3 vi (show off) frimer, taper la frime

> Il s'agit d'une onomatopée censée reproduire le bruit de bijoux que l'on agite. Il s'agit à l'origine d'un terme d'argot Noir américain mais on le rencontre également dans d'autres pays anglophones.

blink [blɪŋk] n **to be on the blink** (of TV, machine) déconner

blinking ['blɪŋkɪŋ] Br **1** adj (for emphasis) sacré; **the blinking thing won't work!** pas moyen de faire marcher cette saloperie!

2 adv (for emphasis) sacrément; **you're so blinking stubborn!** ce que tu peux être têtu!

blitzed [blɪtst] adj (drunk) bourré, beurré; (on drugs) défoncé

blob [blɒb] n Br **to be on the blob** avoir ses ragnagnas ou ses ours

bloke [bləʊk] n Br type m, mec m

blokeish ['bləʊkɪʃ] adj Br = typique d'un style de vie caractérisé par de fréquentes sorties entre copains, généralement copieusement arrosées, et un goût

prononcé pour le sport et les activités de groupe

bloody [!] ['blʌdɪ] Br **1** adj (for emphasis) **you bloody idiot!** espèce de con!; **bloody hell!** putain!; **where's my bloody pen?** où est ce putain de stylo?

2 adv (for emphasis) foutrement; **it's bloody hot!** il fait foutrement chaud!, il fait une chaleur à crever!; **it was bloody brilliant!** putain, c'était génial!; Ironique **that's just bloody marvellous!** il manquait plus que ça!; **I wish he'd bloody stop it!** quand est-ce qu'il va s'arrêter, merde!

blooming ['bluːmɪŋ] Br **1** adj (for emphasis) **I've lost my blooming keys** j'ai perdu ces saletés de clefs

2 adv (for emphasis) sacrément; **he's blooming useless!** il est vraiment nul!

blooter ['bluːtə(r)] vt Scot = donner un grand coup de pied dans

blootered ['bluːtəd] adj Scot (drunk) pété, bourré, beurré

blotto ['blɒtəʊ] adj complètement paf ou pété, bourré comme un coing

blow [bləʊ] **1** n Br (cannabis) shit m; Am (cocaine) coke f, neige f; (heroin) héro f, blanche f

2 vt (**a**) **to blow a gasket** or **a fuse** (of person) péter une durite, péter les plombs; **to blow one's top** or **one's stack** péter une durite, péter les plombs; **it blew my mind!** (of film, experience) ça m'a complètement emballé!

(**b**) (reveal) **to blow the gaff** vendre la mèche

(**c**) **to blow the whistle on sb** balancer qn; **to blow the whistle on sth** dénoncer qch □

(**d**) (waste) (chance) gâcher; **we should have won but we blew it** on aurait dû gagner mais on a tout fait foirer; **that's blown it!** ça a tout fait foirer!

(**e**) (money) claquer; **he blows all his salary on holidays/CDs** il claque tout son salaire en voyages/CD; **they blew £2,000 on an engagement ring** ils ont claqué 2.000 livres dans une bague de fiançailles

The symbol □ indicates that a translation is neutral in register.

(f) !! *(fellate)* tailler une pipe à **(g)** *Am* **to blow chunks** *(vomit)* gerber, dégobiller

blow away *vt sép* **(a)** *Am* **to blow sb away** *(shoot dead)* flinguer qn, descendre qn; *(defeat)* flanquer une raclée à qn **(b) to blow sb away** *(impress, bowl over)* complètement emballer qn; **the Grand Canyon just blew me away** le Grand Canyon m'a coupé le souffle

blower ['bləʊə(r)] *n Br (telephone)* bigophone *m*

blow-job !! ['bləʊdʒɒb] *n* pipe *f*; **to give sb a blow-job** tailler une pipe à qn

blub [blʌb], **blubber** ['blʌbə(r)] *vi* chialer comme un veau

bludge [blʌdʒ] *vi Austr* **(a)** *(shirk responsibilities)* se défiler **(b)** *(cadge)* quémander ᵒ **(c)** *(live off the State)* vivre en parasite de la société ᵒ

bludger ['blʌdʒə(r)] *n Austr* **(a)** *(shirker)* tire-au-flanc *m* **(b)** *(cadger)* pique-assiette *mf inv* **(c)** *(who lives off the State)* parasite ᵒ *m* de la société

blue-arsed fly ! ['bluːɑːst'flaɪ] *n Br* **to run about** *or* **around like a blue-arsed fly** courir dans tous les sens

blues [bluːz] *npl Am* **to sing the blues** *(complain)* geindre ᵒ, pleurnicher

BM [biː'em] *n Am (abrév* **bowel movement***)* **to have a BM** aller à la selle

boat [bəʊt] *n Br* **boat (race)** *(rhyming slang* **face***)* tronche *f*, trombine *f*

Bob [bɒb] *npr Br* **...and Bob's your uncle!** ...et le tour est joué!

bobby ['bɒbɪ] *n Br* flic *m*

bobo ['bəʊbəʊ] *n (abrév* **bohemian bourgeois***)* bobo *mf*

bod [bɒd] *n (abrév* **body***)* **(a)** *Br (person)* individu ᵒ *m*; **he's a strange bod** c'est un drôle de numéro ou de zèbre **(b)** *(physique)* corps ᵒ *m*; **she's got a great bod** elle est super bien roulée ou foutue

bodacious [bəʊ'deɪʃəs] *adj Am* incroyable

bog ! [bɒg] *n Br (toilet)* chiottes *fpl*; **bog roll** papier cul *m*, PQ *m*

bog off ! *vi Br* se barrer, se casser; **bog off!** *(go away)* barre-toi!, casse-toi!; *(expressing contempt, disagreement)* va te faire voir!

bogart ['bəʊgɑːt] *vt* **to bogart a joint** squatter un joint, bogarter

bogey ['bəʊgɪ] *n Br (nasal mucus)* crotte *f* de nez

boggin ['bɒgɪn] *adj Scot* dégueulasse; **that pizza was boggin!** cette pizza était vraiment dégueulasse!; **I don't know why you fancy him, he's boggin** je ne vois pas ce que tu lui trouves, c'est une vraie mocheté; **she was wearing these really boggin shoes** elle portait des chaussures hyper moches

bog-standard ['bɒgstændəd] *adj Br* tout ce qu'il y a d'ordinaire

bog-trotter ['bɒgtrɒtə(r)] *n* **(a)** *Injurieux (Irish person)* Irlandais(e) ᵒ *m,f* **(b)** *(country bumpkin)* plouc *m*, péquenaud *m*

bogus ['bəʊgəs] *adj Am (unpleasant)* chiant; *(unfashionable)* ringard

bohunk ['bəʊhʌŋk] *n Am* **(a)** *Injurieux (Eastern European immigrant)* = terme désignant un Américain originaire d'un pays d'Europe de l'Est ou ses descendants **(b)** *(country bumpkin)* bouseux(euse) *m,f*

boiler ['bɔɪlə(r)] *n Péj (old)* **boiler** vieille peau *f*

boink [bɔɪŋk] *Am* **1** *n* **to have a boink** faire une partie de jambes en l'air **2** *vt* s'envoyer en l'air avec **3** *vi* faire une partie de jambes en l'air

Bolivian marching powder [bə-'lɪvɪən'mɑːtʃɪŋpaʊdə(r)] *n Hum (cocaine)* coco *f*, coke *f*, reniflette *f*

bollock ! ['bɒlək] *Br* **1** *adv* **bollock naked** à poil, le cul à l'air **2** *vt* **to bollock sb** engueuler qn, passer un savon à qn

bollocking ! ['bɒləkɪŋ] *n Br* engueulade *f*, savon *m*; **to give sb a bollocking** engueuler qn, passer un savon à qn; **to get a bollocking** se faire engueuler, se faire passer un savon

bollocks ! ['bɒləks] *Br* **1** *npl* **(a)** *(testicles)* couilles *fpl* **(b)** *(nonsense)* conneries

---

fpl; **the film was a load of bollocks** c'était de la merde, ce film (**c**) **bollocks to him!** qu'il aille se faire foutre! **it's the bollocks** ou **the dog's bollocks** c'est super ou génial!

2 *exclam* des conneries, tout ça!

bollocks up ! *vt sép* **to bollocks sth up** *(interview, exam)* foirer qch, se planter à qch; *(plan, arrangement)* faire foirer qch

bolshie, bolshy ['bɒlʃɪ] *adj Br* râleur

bomb [bɒm] **1** *n* (**a**) *Br* **to go like a bomb** *(of fast car)* être un vrai bolide; *(of party)* se passer super bien; **he/the car was going like a bomb** il/la voiture roulait à fond la caisse (**b**) *Br (large sum of money)* **to cost a bomb** coûter bonbon ou la peau des fesses; **to make a bomb** se faire un fric fou (**c**) *Am (failure)* bide *m*

2 *vt Am (fail) (test)* se planter complètement à

3 *vi* (**a**) *(fail) (of film)* faire un four ou un bide; *Am (of student)* se planter complètement (**b**) **to bomb along** aller à fond la caisse ou à toute blinde

bomb out 1 *vt sép Br* **to bomb sb out** poser un lapin à qn

2 *vi (fail)* se faire sortir; **to bomb out of sth** se faire éjecter de qch

bombed [bɒmd] *adj (drunk)* bourré, beurré; *(on drugs)* défoncé

bomber ['bɒmə(r)] *n (cannabis cigarette)* cône *m*

bonce [bɒns] *n Br* caboche *f*, ciboulot *m*

bone !! [bəʊn] **1** *vt* baiser, troncher, tringler

2 *vi* baiser, s'envoyer en l'air

bone up on *vt insép* **to bone up on sth** potasser qch

bonehead ['bəʊnhed] *Am* **1** *n* débile *mf*, crétin(e) *m,f*

2 *adj* débile

boner ['bəʊnə(r)] *n* (**a**) *(erection)* **to have a boner** !! bander, avoir la trique (**b**) *Am (mistake)* bourde *f*, boulette *f*

bong [bɒŋ] *n* pipe *f* à eau □, bang *m*

bonk [bɒŋk] *Br* **1** *n* **to have a bonk** faire une partie de jambes en l'air

2 *vt* s'envoyer en l'air avec

3 *vi* faire une partie de jambes en l'air

bonkers ['bɒŋkəz] *adj* cinglé, fêlé, dingue, tapé

bonzer ['bɒnzə(r)] *Austr* **1** *adj* vachement bien, super, génial

2 *exclam* **bonzer!** super!, génial!

bonzo ['bɒnzəʊ] *adj Am* cinglé, fêlé, dingue, tapé

boob [bu:b] **1** *n* (**a**) *(breast)* nichon *m*; **to have a boob job** se faire refaire les nichons; **boob tube** *(garment)* bustier *m* extensible □ (**b**) *Br (mistake)* boulette *f*, bourde *f*; **to make a boob** faire une boulette (**c**) *Am (person)* abruti(e) *m,f*, andouille *f*, courge *f*; **boob tube** *(television)* téloche *f*

2 *vi Br (make mistake)* faire une bourde ou une boulette

boo-boo ['bu:bu:] *n Am* boulette *f*, bourde *f*; **to make a boo-boo** faire une boulette ou une bourde

booger ['bu:gə(r)] *n Am* (**a**) *(nasal mucus)* crotte *f* de nez (**b**) *(person)* garnement □ *m* (**c**) *(thing)* bidule *m*, machin *m*, truc *m*

boogie ['bu:gɪ] **1** *n (dance)* **to have a boogie** danser □, guincher

2 *vi* (**a**) *(dance)* danser □, guincher (**b**) *Am (leave)* mettre les bouts, se casser, s'arracher; **let's boogie on out of here** on met les bouts, on se casse

book [bʊk] *Am* **1** *vt* **to book it** *(leave)* mettre les bouts, se casser, s'arracher; **let's book it!** on se casse!, on s'arrache!

2 *vi* (**a**) *(leave)* mettre les bouts, se casser, s'arracher (**b**) *(move quickly)* foncer

boondocks ['bu:ndɒks], **boonies** ['bu:nɪz] *npl Am* **the boondocks, the boonies** la cambrousse; **in the boondocks, in the boonies** en pleine cambrousse

boost [bu:st] *Am* **1** *vt* (**a**) *(steal)* piquer, faucher (**b**) *(break into)* cambrioler □

2 *vi (steal)* voler □

boot [bu:t] **1** *n* (**a**) *(kick)* **to give sth a boot** donner un coup de latte dans qch; *Br* **he was trying to get up when they put the boot in** il essayait de se relever quand ils se sont mis à lui donner des coups de latte; Br **he'd already apologized, you didn't have to put the boot in like that** il s'était excusé, tu n'avais pas besoin d'insister à ce point $^\square$

  (**b**) **to give sb the boot** (fire) virer qn; **to get the boot** (get fired) se faire virer

  (**c**) Br Péj (ugly woman) **(old) boot** boudin m, cageot m

2 vt (kick) donner un coup de latte/des coups de latte à

3 vi (vomit) rendre, gerber

boot out vt sép **to boot sb out** foutre qn à la porte, vider qn

booty ['bu:tɪ] n (**a**) (buttocks) cul m, derche m (**b**) (sexual intercourse) **to get some booty** s'envoyer en l'air; **to make a booty call** = passer un coup de fil à son ami ou amie pour organiser une partie de jambes en l'air

booze [bu:z] 1 n (**a**) (alcohol) alcool $^\square$ m, bibine f; **to be on the booze** picoler; Austr **booze bus** = patrouille de police qui arrête les automobilistes au hasard pour leur faire passer l'alcootest

2 vi picoler

boozehound ['bu:zhaʊnd] n Am ivrogne mf, poivrot(e) m,f

boozer ['bu:zə(r)] n (**a**) Br (pub) pub $^\square$ m, troquet m (**b**) (person) ivrogne mf, poivrot(e) m,f

booze-up ['bu:zʌp] n beuverie f; **to have a booze-up** prendre une cuite

boozy ['bu:zɪ] adj (person) qui aime picoler; (occasion) où l'on picole beaucoup

bop¹ [bɒp] Br 1 n (dance) **to have a bop** danser $^\square$, guincher

2 vi (dance) danser $^\square$, guincher

bop² 1 n (punch) coup m de poing $^\square$, ramponneau m; **she gave him a bop on the head** elle lui a donné un coup de poing dans la tête

2 vt (hit) frapper $^\square$; **she bopped him on the head** elle lui a donné un coup de poing dans la tête

boracic [bə'ræsɪk] adj Br (rhyming slang **boracic lint = skint**) fauché, à sec, sans un

boss [bɒs] adj (excellent) super; **you're** **looking boss!** tu es superbe!

bottle ['bɒtəl] 1 n (**a**) Br (courage) courage $^\square$ m, cran m (**b**) (alcohol) **the bottle** l'alcool $^\square$ m; **to be on the bottle** picoler; **to hit the bottle** se mettre à picoler

2 vt Br **to bottle it** se dégonfler; **he was going to ask her out but he bottled it** il allait lui demander de sortir avec lui mais il s'est dégonflé

bottle out vi Br se dégonfler; **he bottled out of the fight** il s'est dégonflé au dernier moment et a refusé de se battre; **he bottled out of telling her the truth** finalement il a eu la trouille de lui dire la vérité

bottom feeder ['bɒtəmfi:də(r)] n (person) moins mf que rien

> Au sens littéral, ce terme désigne les poissons qui se nourrissent d'organismes se trouvant au fond des lacs, des rivières ou des océans.

botty ['bɒtɪ] n fesses $^\square$ fpl

bounce [baʊns] n Br **on the bounce** de suite; **they won three games on the bounce** ils ont gagné trois matchs de suite

bouncer ['baʊnsə(r)] n (doorman) videur m

Bourke [bɔːk] n Austr **in the back of Bourke** en pleine cambrousse

> Bourke est une petite ville au fin fond de la Nouvelle-Galles du Sud, en Australie.

bowfin' ['baʊfɪn] adj Scot dégueulasse; **that meal she cooked was bowfin'!** le repas qu'elle a préparé était vraiment dégueulasse!; **it's bowfin' in here!** (smelly) qu'est-ce que ça schlingue ici!

box [bɒks] n (**a**) Br **to be out of one's box** (drunk) être complètement pété, être plein comme une barrique (**b**) **the box** (television) la télé, la téloche (**c**) [!!] (vagina) chatte f, con m

boyf [bɔɪf] n Br (abrév **boyfriend**) **my/ her boyf** mon/son mec

boy racer [bɔɪ'reɪsə(r)] n Br jeune conducteur m imprudent $^\square$

Le "boy racer" est un jeune homme qui vient d'obtenir son permis de conduire et dont l'activité principale consiste à faire des tours en voiture avec ses copains, sans destination précise, pied au plancher, toutes vitres baissées tout en écoutant de la musique à plein volume.

boy toy ['bɔɪtɔɪ] *n Am Hum* jeune amant □ *m (d'une femme plus âgée)*

boys in blue ['bɔɪznblu] *nmpl Br* **the boys in blue** les flics *mpl*, les poulets *mpl*

bozo ['bəʊzəʊ] *n Am* crétin(e) *m,f*, andouille *f*, cruche *f*

bracelets ['breɪslɪts] *npl (handcuffs)* menottes □ *fpl*, bracelets *mpl*

Brahms and Liszt ['brɑːmɪən'lɪst] *adj Br (rhyming slang* **pissed**) bourré, pété, fait

brain [breɪn] **1** *n* (a) *to have brains* en avoir dans le ciboulot; *Br* **to have sth on the brain** faire une fixette sur qch (b) *(person)* tête *f*; **he's a real brain** c'est une vraie tête
2 *vt (hit)* donner un coup sur la cafetière à

brand new ['brænd'njuː] *adj Scot* super, génial, géant; **his new girlfriend's brand new** sa nouvelle copine est une perle

brass [brɑːs] *n Br* (a) *(money)* blé *m*, flouze *m* (b) **brass (neck)** *(cheek, nerve)* culot *m*, toupet *m*; **to have a brass neck** être culotté; **to have the brass (neck) to do sth** avoir le culot de faire qch (c) **it's brass monkeys** *or* **brass monkey weather** *(very cold)* il fait un froid de canard (d) *(prostitute)* pute *f*

brass off *vt sép* **to brass sb off** gonfler qn; **to be brassed off (with)** en avoir marre (de)

brassic ['bræsɪk] *Br* = **boracic**

bread [bred] *n* (a) *(money)* blé *m*, oseille *f* (b) *Br* **it's the best thing since sliced bread** c'est ce qu'on a fait de mieux depuis l'invention du fil à couper le beurre (c) *Br* **bread knife** *(rhyming slang* **wife**) bonne femme *f*, bourgeoise *f*, moitié *f*

break [breɪk] *n* **give me a break!** *(don't talk nonsense)* dis pas n'importe quoi!; *(stop nagging)* fiche-moi la paix! ▶ *voir aussi* **balls**

breeder ['briːdə(r)] *n Péj (heterosexual)* hétéro *m,f*

Il s'agit d'un terme dont la traduction littérale est "reproducteur". Ce mot n'est utilisé que par certains homosexuels par dérision envers les hétérosexuels.

breeze [briːz] *n* **it was a breeze** *(simple)* c'était du gâteau ▶ *voir aussi* **shoot**

brekky ['brekɪ] *n (abrév* **breakfast**) *Br* petit déj *m*

brew [bruː] *n Am (beer)* mousse *f*

brewer's droop ['bruːəz'druːp] *n Br Hum* = impuissance temporaire due à l'alcool; **he had brewer's droop** il bandait mou parce qu'il avait trop picolé

brewski ['bruːskɪ] *n Am* mousse *f*

brick [brɪk] **1** *n* **to be one brick short of a load** ne pas être net
2 *vt Br* **to brick it** les avoir à zéro; **they were absolutely bricking it when they saw the plod coming** ils les avaient vraiment à zéro quand ils ont vu le flic approcher

brill [brɪl] *adj Br (abrév* **brilliant**) super, génial

bring off ‼ [brɪŋ] *vt sép (masturbate)* **to bring sb off** branler qn; **to bring oneself off** se branler

bristols ['brɪstəlz] *npl Br (rhyming slang* **Bristols Cities** = **titties**) nichons *mpl*, roberts *mpl*

Bristol City est le nom d'une équipe de football de Bristol.

Brit [brɪt] **1** *n (abrév* **Britisher**) Angliche *mf*
2 *adj (abrév* **British**) angliche

Britney ['brɪtnɪ] *n Br (rhyming slang* **Britney Spears** = **beers**) mousse *f*, bière □ *f*

bro [brəʊ] *n (abrév* **brother**) (a) *(family member)* frangin *m*, frérot *m* (b) *Am (male friend)* pote *m*; **yo, bro!** salut mon pote! (c) *Am (black man)* = Noir américain; **go**

The symbol □ indicates that a translation is neutral in register.

ask that bro over there va demander au Noir, là-bas

broad [brɔːd] n Am (woman) gonzesse f, nana f

broke [brəʊk] adj (having no money) fauché, raide; **to go for broke** jouer le tout pour le tout

brolly ['brɒlɪ] n Br pébroc m, pépin m

brother ['brʌðə(r)] n Noir Am (black male) = Noir américain; **a brother got capped last night** un des nôtres s'est fait buter hier soir ► voir aussi **soul**

brown bread ['braʊn'bred] n Br (rhyming slang **dead**) clamsé, crevé

browned-off ['braʊnd'ɒf] adj Br **to be browned-off (with)** en avoir marre (de); **to be browned-off with doing sth** en avoir marre de faire qch

brown-nose ⚠ ['braʊnnəʊz] **1** n lèche-cul mf
2 vi faire de la lèche

Brum [brʌm] npr Br (abrév **Birmingham**) = surnom donné à la ville de Birmingham

Brummie ['brʌmɪ] n Br = natif de la ville de Birmingham

BS [biːˈes] n Am (abrév **bullshit**) conneries fpl

bubba ['bʌbə] n Am (a) (term of address) mec m, vieux m; **hey bubba, gimme a smoke!** hé, vieux! file-moi une clope! (b) Péj (redneck) plouc m (du sud des États-Unis)

bubbly ['bʌblɪ] n (champagne) champ' m

buck [bʌk] n Am (dollar) dollar ⁰ m; **got any bucks?** t'as du fric?

Buckley's ['bʌklɪz] n Austr **you don't have a Buckley's (chance)** tu n'as aucune chance

buddy ['bʌdɪ] n (a) (friend) pote m (b) (term of address) **thanks, buddy** (to friend) merci, vieux; (to stranger) merci, chef; **hey, buddy!** hé, toi!

buddy up vi **to buddy up to sb** faire de la lèche à qn

buddy-buddy ['bʌdɪbʌdɪ] adj Am Péj copain-copain; **they're very buddy-buddy** ils sont très copain-copain

buff [bʌf] n **in the buff** à poil

bug [bʌg] **1** vt (annoy, nag) enquiquiner, emmerder (**about** à cause de); (bother) turlupiner; **what's bugging him?** qu'est-ce qui le turlupine?
2 n Am **bug doctor** (psychiatrist) psychiatre ⁰ m

bug off vi Am (leave) se casser, s'arracher; **bug off!** casse-toi!

bug out vi Am (a) (leave) se casser, s'arracher (b) (go mad) déjanter

bugger ⚠ ['bʌgə(r)] Br **1** n (a) (person) salaud m; **the poor bugger** le pauvre; **the silly bugger** cet espèce d'imbécile; **to play silly buggers** faire le con
(b) (thing) truc m chiant; **a bugger of a job** un travail à la con; **her house is a bugger to find** sa maison est vachement dure à trouver
(c) **bugger all** (nothing) que dalle; **bugger all money/thanks** pas un sou/un merci; **that was bugger all help** ça n'a servi à rien
(d) **I don't give a bugger!** je m'en fous pas mal!
2 exclam **bugger (it)!** merde!, bordel!
3 vt (a) (exhaust) mettre sur les genoux, crever (b) (ruin, break) bousiller (c) (for emphasis) **bugger me!** putain!; **bugger the expense, let's buy it!** et puis merde, tant pis si c'est cher, achetons-le!

bugger about ⚠, **bugger around** ⚠ Br **1** vt sép **to bugger sb about** (treat badly) se foutre de la gueule de qn; (waste time of) faire perdre son temps à qn ⁰
2 vi (waste time) glander, glandouiller

bugger off ⚠ vi Br se barrer, se casser, s'arracher; **bugger off!** (go away) barre-toi!, casse-toi!; (expressing contempt, disagreement) va te faire foutre!

bugger up ⚠ vt sép **to bugger sth up** (ruin) foutre qch en l'air; (break) bousiller qch

buggeration [bʌgəˈreɪʃən] exclam Br bordel!, putain!, merde!

buggered ⚠ ['bʌgəd] adj Br (a) (exhausted) crevé, naze
(b) (broken) foutu, naze

The symbol ⁰ indicates that a translation is neutral in register.

(c) (amazed) **well, I'm buggered!** ben merde alors!

(d) (in trouble) foutu; **if we don't get the money soon, we're buggered** si on a pas l'argent rapidement, on est foutus

(e) (for emphasis) **I'll be buggered if I'm going to apologize!** plutôt crever que de m'excuser!; **I'm buggered if I know!** j'en sais foutre rien!

buggery [!] ['bʌgərɪ] n Br **like buggery!** ouais, mon cul!; **to run like buggery** courir comme un(e) dératé(e); **is he a good cook? – is he buggery!** il fait bien la cuisine? – tu veux rire!

builder's bum [bɪldəz'bʌm] n = phénomène censé se produire communément chez les ouvriers du bâtiment, dont le pantalon a tendance à tomber, exposant le haut de leur postérieur

bull [bʊl] **1** n (nonsense) conneries fpl; **he's talking bull** il raconte des conneries, il dit n'importe quoi

2 exclam n'importe quoi! ► voir aussi **shoot**

bulldyke ['bʊldaɪk] n Injurieux gouine f (d'apparence masculine)

bullshit [!] ['bʊlʃɪt] **1** n conneries fpl

2 exclam des conneries, tout ça!

3 vt **to bullshit sb** raconter des conneries à qn; **she bullshitted her way into the job** elle a eu le boulot au culot

4 vi raconter des conneries

bullshitter ['bʊlʃɪtə(r)] n (smooth talker) baratineur(euse) m,f; **he's a bullshitter** (he talks nonsense) il raconte des conneries

bum [bʌm] **1** n **(a)** (buttocks) fesses fpl, derrière m; **bum bag** banane f (sac); **bum fluff** (beard) barbe f très peu fournie □

(b) Am (tramp) **(stew) bum** clodo mf

(c) (enthusiast) **to be a beach/ski bum** passer son temps à la plage/sur les pistes □

(d) to give sb the bum's rush (dismiss) envoyer paître qn; (from work) virer qn; **to give sth the bum's rush** (idea, suggestion) rejeter qch □; **my idea got the bum's rush** mon idée est passée à la trappe

2 adj (worthless) merdique; **to get a bum deal** se faire avoir; **a bum rap** (false charge) une fausse accusation □

3 vt **(a)** (scrounge) **to bum sth (from** or **off sb)** taxer qch (à qn); **to bum a lift** or **a ride** se faire emmener en voiture □; **can I bum a lift** or **a ride to the station?** est-ce que tu peux me déposer à la gare?

(b) [!] (have anal sex with) enculer, entuber; **I walked in on him bumming his boyfriend** je suis entré et je suis tombé sur lui en train d'enculer son petit copain

bum about, bum around 1 vt insép (spend time in) **to bum about Australia/the country** parcourir l'Australie/le pays sac au dos □; **to bum about the house** rester chez soi à glander

2 vi (hang around) glander

bum-freezer ['bʌmfriːzə(r)] n Br Hum (jacket) veste f ultra-courte □; (skirt) jupe f ultra-courte □, jupe f ras la touffe

bummed [bʌmd] adj **to be bummed** l'avoir mauvaise

bummer ['bʌmə(r)] n (situation) **what a bummer!** la poisse!, c'est chiant!; **it was a real bummer being stuck at home all day** c'était vraiment la poisse ou chiant de devoir rester enfermé toute la journée

bump off [bʌmp] vt sép **to bump sb off** (murder) supprimer ou zigouiller ou buter qn

bumwad ['bʌmwɒd] n papier cul m, PQ m

bun [bʌn] n **(a) to have a bun in the oven** (be pregnant) être en cloque **(b)** Am **buns** (buttocks) fesses fpl, miches fpl

bundle ['bʌndəl] n **(a)** (large sum of money) **to cost a bundle** coûter bonbon ou la peau des fesses; **to make a bundle** se faire un fric fou □; Br **to go a bundle on sb** en pincer drôlement pour qn; **to go a bundle on sth** être fan de qch

bung [bʌŋ] Br **1** n (bribe) pot-de-vin □ m

2 vt (put) flanquer; (throw) balancer

bunk [bʌŋk] n Br **to do a bunk** (from home) fuguer, faire une fugue; (from prison) se faire la belle

The symbol □ indicates that a translation is neutral in register.

bunk off vt insép & vi Br sécher

bunny ['bʌnɪ] n (a) Am **ski** or **snow bunny** jeune minette f qui fait du ski (b) **bunny boiler** = femme obsessionnelle qui poursuit quelqu'un de ses assiduités ▶ voir aussi **jungle**

> C'est le film américain *Liaison fatale* qui est à l'origine de l'expression "bunny boiler". Dans une scène devenue célèbre, un personnage féminin assoiffé de vengeance (joué par l'actrice Glenn Close) fait cuire le lapin du fils de l'amant qui l'a délaissée (ce dernier étant incarné par Michael Douglas).

burbs [bɜːbz] npl Am (abrév **suburbs**) banlieue □ f; **they live in the burbs** ils habitent en banlieue

burl [bɜːl] n Austr (attempt) essai □ m; **give it a burl!** essaye!

burn [bɜːn] vt Am (a) (swindle) arnaquer (b) (anger) foutre en rogne

burn up vt sép Am (anger) foutre en rogne

bush [bʊʃ] n (a) ⚠ (woman's pubic hair) barbu m (b) (marijuana) herbe f

bushed [bʊʃt] adj crevé, lessivé, naze

business ['bɪznɪs] n **like nobody's business** (sing, tell jokes) vachement bien; (work) comme une bête; Br **it's the business** c'est impec'; **that new DVD player of his is the business** son nouveau lecteur de DVD est vraiment super; **did you do the business with her?** (have sex) est-ce que t'as couché avec elle? ▶ voir aussi **monkey**

bust [bʌst] **1** n (police raid) descente f; **drug bust** descente f des stups

     2 adj (a) (broken) foutu (b) (having no money) fauché; **to go bust** (of person, business) boire un bouillon

     3 vt (a) (arrest) agrafer (**for** pour) (b) (raid) faire une descente dans (c) Am

(demote) dégrader □; **he got busted to sergeant** il est repassé sergent ▶ voir aussi **balls**

buster ['bʌstə(r)] n Am (term of address) mec m; **who are you looking at, buster?** tu veux ma photo, Ducon?

bust-up ['bʌstʌp] n (a) (quarrel) engueulade f; **to have a bust-up** s'engueuler (b) (of relationship) rupture □ f

butch [bʊtʃ] **1** n (masculine lesbian) lesbienne f à l'allure masculine □

     2 adj (woman) hommasse; (man) macho

butcher's ['bʊtʃəz] n Br (rhyming slang **butcher's hook** = **look**) **to have a butcher's (at sb/sth)** mater (qn/qch)

butt [bʌt] n (buttocks) fesses fpl; **move your butt!** bouge-toi!

butt out vi s'occuper de ses fesses; **butt out!** occupe-toi de tes fesses!; **just butt out of my life!** laisse-moi vivre!

butthead ['bʌthed] n Am crétin(e) m,f, andouille f, cruche f

buttinski [bʌ'tɪnskɪ] n Am fouille-merde mf

button ['bʌtən] vt **to button it** (be quiet) la fermer; **button it!** ferme-la!

butty ['bʌtɪ] n Br sandwich □ m, casse-dalle m; **chip butty** sandwich m aux frites

buy [baɪ] vt Am **to buy the farm** (die) clamser, calancher, avaler son bulletin de naissance

buzz [bʌz] n (a) (phone call) **to give sb a buzz** passer un coup de fil à qn, bigophoner qn (b) (thrill) **to give sb a buzz** exciter qn □; **to get a buzz out of doing sth** prendre son pied à faire qch

buzz off vi dégager, mettre les bouts, se tirer; **buzz off!** dégage!, tire-toi!

buzzing ['bʌzɪŋ] adj (a) (party, nightclub) hyper animé (b) (hyper) speed, speedé

buzz-kill ['bʌzkɪl] n Am rabat-joie □ mf

The symbol □ indicates that a translation is neutral in register.

C

cabbage ['kæbɪdʒ] n (**a**) Br (brain-damaged person) légume m; (dull person) larve f (**b**) Am (money) fric m, blé m, oseille f

cabbaged ['kæbɪdʒd] adj Br pété, bourré

cable ['keɪbəl] n **to lay (a) cable** couler un bronze

cack [kæk] Br **1** n (**a**) (excrement) caca m (**b**) (nonsense) conneries fpl; **don't talk cack!** arrête de raconter n'importe quoi! (**c**) (worthless things) camelote f; **the film was a load of cack** le film était nul
2 adj (bad) nul; **her music is cack** sa musique est nulle
3 vt **he was cacking himself** (scared) il faisait dans son froc

cack-handed [kæk'hændɪd] adj Br maladroit ⁑, manche

cadge [kædʒ] **1** n Br (**a**) (person) pique-assiette mf, parasite ⁑ m (**b**) **to be on the cadge** jouer les parasites
2 vt (food, money) se procurer ⁑ (en quémandant); **he cadged a meal from** or **off his aunt** il s'est fait inviter à manger par sa tante; **she cadged £10 off me** elle m'a tapé de 10 livres; **they cadged a lift home** à force de quémander ils se sont fait ramener en voiture
3 vi quémander ⁑; **she's always cadging off her friends** elle est toujours en train de taper ses amis

cahoots [kə'huːts] n **to be in cahoots (with sb)** être de mèche (avec qn)

cakehole ['keɪkhəʊl] n Br bouche ⁑ f, clapet m; **shut your cakehole!** ferme-la!, ferme ton clapet!

calaboose ['kæləbuːs] n Am taule f, placard m; **in the calaboose** en taule, au placard, à l'ombre

camp [kæmp] adj efféminé; Hum **he's as camp as a row of tents** il fait très grande folle

can¹ [kæn] **1** n (**a**) Am (toilet) chiottes fpl (**b**) Am (prison) taule f, placard m; **in the can** en taule, au placard, à l'ombre (**c**) Am (buttocks) fesses fpl; **to kick sb in the can** botter les fesses à qn (**d**) Br **to carry the can** (take the blame) porter le chapeau
2 vt Am (**a**) (dismiss) virer, saquer (**b**) to can it (shut up) la fermer, la boucler; **can it!** ferme-la!, boucle-la!

can² modal aux v **no can do!** impossible!; Am **can do!** pas de problème!

cancer stick ['kænsəstɪk] n clope f

cane [keɪn] vt Br **to cane it** se bourrer ou se pinter la gueule

caned [keɪnd] adj Br bourré comme un coing

caner ['keɪnə(r)] n poivrot m, alcoolo m

canned [kænd] adj (drunk) beurré, bourré, pété

cap [kæp] Am **1** n (bullet) bastos f
2 vt (shoot) descendre

capper ['kæpə(r)] n Am **that was the capper!** c'est la goutte d'eau qui a fait déborder le vase!

cark [kɑːk] vt Br **to cark it** calancher, casser sa pipe, passer l'arme à gauche

carpet ['kɑːpɪt] **1** n (**a**) **to be on the carpet** (in trouble) être dans le caca; **to put sb on the carpet** (reprimand) enguirlander qn, passer un savon à qn (**b**) **to eat** or **munch carpet** [!!] pratiquer le cunnilingus ⁑
2 vt Br (reprimand) enguirlander, passer un savon à

carve up [kɑːv] vt sép **to carve sb up** (attack with knife) donner des coups de

---

The symbol ⁑ indicates that a translation is neutral in register.

couteau au visage à qn □; *(in car)* faire une queue de poisson à qn

case [keɪs] **1** *n* **he's always on my case** je l'ai tout le temps sur le dos; **get off my case!** lâche-moi les baskets!, oublie-moi!

2 *vt* **to case the joint** repérer les lieux *(avant un cambriolage)*

cash in [kæʃ] *Am* **1** *vt sép* **to cash in one's chips** *(die)* calancher, clamser, passer l'arme à gauche

2 *vi (die)* calancher, clamser, passer l'arme à gauche

casual ['kæʒʊəl] *n Br* jeune supporter *m* de foot

> Ce terme désigne un certain type de supporter de football. Le "casual" est un jeune homme, généralement issu d'un milieu modeste, qui dépense beaucoup d'argent en vêtements mais ne fait pas preuve d'un goût très sûr (ainsi les chaussures de sport et survêtements de marque côtoieront-ils les polos en laine vierge de coupe classique). Le "casual" se déplace le plus souvent en bande, consomme de la bière en grande quantité et est souvent l'auteur de violences lors des matchs.

cat [kæt] *n* **(a)** *Am (man)* mec *m*; *(woman)* nana *f*, gonzesse *f* **(b) to look like something the cat dragged in** ne ressembler à rien; **it's like herding cats** ce n'est vraiment pas une mince affaire ▸ *voir aussi* **fat**

cathouse ['kæthaʊs] *n* bordel *m*, claque *m*

cattle market ['kætəlmɑːkɪt] *n Br Péj (nightclub)* = boîte réputée pour être un lieu de drague

cha [tʃɑː] *n Br (tea)* thé □ *m*

chalfonts ['tʃælfɒnts] *npl Br (rhyming slang* **Chalfont St Giles = piles)** hémorroïdes □ *fpl*, émeraudes *fpl*

> Chalfont St Giles est une ville du Buckinghamshire.

champers ['ʃæmpəz] *n Br (abrév* **champagne)** champ' *m*

champion ['tʃæmpjən] **1** *adj* super, génial

2 *exclam* super!, génial!

chance [tʃɑːns] **1** *n* **no chance!** des clous!

2 *vt* **to chance one's arm** *(take a risk)* risquer le coup; *(push one's luck)* exagérer □, pousser

chancer ['tʃɑːnsə(r)] *n Br* opportuniste □ *mf*

chang [tʃæŋ] *n (cocaine)* coke *f*, neige *f*

char [tʃɑː(r)] = **cha**

charge [tʃɑːdʒ] *n Am (thrill)* **to get a charge out of sth/doing sth** s'éclater *ou* prendre son pied avec qch/en faisant qch

charlie ['tʃɑːlɪ] *n* **(a)** *(cocaine)* coke *f*, neige *f* **(b)** *Br (person)* andouille *f*, crétin(e) *m,f*; **to look/feel a right charlie** avoir l'air/se sentir con

chase [tʃeɪs] *vt* **to chase the dragon** chasser le dragon

chassis ['ʃæsɪ] *n (woman's body)* châssis *m*; *Hum* **she's got a classy chassis** elle est super bien foutue *ou* balancée *ou* carrossée

chat up [tʃæt] *vt sép Br* **to chat sb up** baratiner qn, draguer qn

chat-up line ['tʃætʌplaɪn] *n Br* = formule d'entrée en matière pour commencer à draguer quelqu'un; **do you come here often?! that's the worst chat-up line I've ever heard!** vous venez ici souvent?! on ne fait pas pire comme formule pour aborder quelqu'un!

cheapo ['tʃiːpəʊ] *adj* merdique; **he's bought some cheapo ghetto blaster** il a acheté une espèce de ghetto blaster merdique; **don't go to that cheapo supermarket, it's gross!** ne va pas dans ce supermarché au rabais, c'est vraiment nul

cheapskate ['tʃiːpskeɪt] *n* radin(e) *m,f*

check out [tʃek] **1** *vt sép (look at)* **to check sb/sth out** mater qn/qch; **there's a new pub we could check out** il y a un nouveau pub qu'on pourrait essayer; **check it/her out!** mate-moi ça!

2 vi Am (die) passer l'arme à gauche

cheers [tʃɪəz] exclam (**a**) Br (thank you) merci! ᵈ (**b**) Br (goodbye) salut!, ciao! (**c**) (as toast) santé!, à la tienne/vôtre!

cheese [tʃiːz] n (**a**) Br **hard cheese!** pas de pot ou veine! (**b**) **big cheese** (important person) huile f ▶ voir aussi **cut**

cheese off vt sép **to cheese sb off** gonfler qn; **to be cheesed off (with)** en avoir marre (de)

cheesecake ['tʃiːzkeɪk] n (attractive women) belles nanas fpl; Br **she's a real cheesecake** elle est vraiment bien foutue ou balancée ou carrossée

cheesy ['tʃiːzɪ] adj (**a**) (tasteless) ringard (**b**) **cheesy grin** large sourire ᵈ m

cheggers ['tʃegəz] adj Br en cloque

cherry ['tʃerɪ] **1** n (**a**) (virginity) berlingot m; **to lose one's cherry** perdre son berlingot; Am **to pop sb's cherry** dépuceler qn (**b**) (virgin) puceau (pucelle) m,f (**c**) Am (newcomer) bleu m
2 adj Am (in perfect condition) en parfait état ᵈ, impec!

Chevvy ['ʃevɪ] n Chevrolet® f

chew [tʃuː] vt **to chew the fat** or **the rag** tailler une bavette

chew out vt sép **to chew sb out** souffler dans les bronches à qn, passer un savon à qn; **to get chewed out** se faire souffler dans les bronches, se faire passer un savon

chib [tʃɪb] Scot **1** nm (knife) schlass m, lame f, surin m
2 vt suriner

chick [tʃɪk] n (woman) nana f, gonzesse f ▶ voir aussi **magnet**

chicken ['tʃɪkɪn] **1** n (**a**) (coward) dégonflé(e) m,f (**b**) (attractive young male) jeune mec m canon
2 adj (cowardly) dégonflé ▶ voir aussi **spring**

L'acception I (b) de ce terme appartient à l'argot homosexuel.

chicken out vi se dégonfler; **he chickened out of the fight** il s'est dégonflé au dernier moment et a refusé de se

battre; **he chickened out of telling her the truth** finalement il a eu la trouille de lui dire la vérité

chickenfeed ['tʃɪkɪnfiːd] n (small amount of money) cacahuètes fpl

chickenshit ! ['tʃɪkɪnʃɪt] adj Am dégonflé

chill (out) [tʃɪl] vi se détendre ᵈ; **I wish he'd chill out a bit** ça serait bien qu'il soit un peu plus cool; **he likes chilling out at home** il aime bien être chez lui, peinard; **what are you doing? – just chilling** qu'est-ce que tu fais? – rien, je me détends; **chill (out)!** relax!, calmos!

chilled [tʃɪld] adj relax

chillin ['tʃɪlɪn] adj Am super, génial, cool

chill pill ['tʃɪlpɪl] n Am **take a chill pill!** relax!, calmos!

china ['tʃaɪnə] n Br (rhyming slang **china plate** = **mate**) pote m; **alright, me old china?** ça va, mon pote?

Chink [tʃɪŋk] n Injurieux Chinetoc mf, Chinetoque mf

Chinky ['tʃɪŋkɪ] n Injurieux (**a**) (person) Chinetoc mf, Chinetoque mf (**b**) Br (meal) repas m chinois ᵈ; (restaurant) resto m chinois m; **to go for a Chinky** manger chinois

Lorsqu'il est question de nourriture, de cuisine, de restaurants, le terme "chinky" perd sa connotation raciste. Il est toutefois déconseillé de l'utiliser.

chinless wonder ['tʃɪnləs'wʌndə(r)] n Br = individu de bonne famille dépourvu de volonté et d'intelligence

Ce terme signifie littéralement "merveille au menton fuyant", ce trait physique étant censé être le signe d'un caractère faible et d'un patrimoine génétique peu enviable.

chintzy ['tʃɪntsɪ] adj Am (**a**) (cheap, of poor quality) toc et tape-à-l'œil (**b**) (miserly) radin

chinwag ['tʃɪnwæg] n Br converse f; **to have a chinwag (with sb)** tailler une bavette (avec qn)

chip in [tʃɪp] **1** vt sép (contribute) donner □; **everyone chipped in a fiver** tout le monde a donné cinq livres

2 vi (contribute money) participer □, donner □; **they all chipped in to buy her a present** ils se sont cotisés pour lui offrir un cadeau □

chippy ['tʃɪpi] n Br = boutique qui vend du poisson frit et des frites

chisel ['tʃɪzəl] vt (cheat) arnaquer; **to chisel sb out of sth** arnaquer qn de qch

chiseller ['tʃɪzələ(r)] n Ir gosse mf, môme mf

chocka ['tʃɒkə], **chock-a-block** [tʃɒkə'blɒk] adj Br plein à craquer

choke [tʃəʊk] vt Hum **to choke the chicken** !! (masturbate) se taper sur la colonne, se polir le chinois

chook [tʃʊk] n Austr (chicken) poulet □ m; (woman) nana f, gonzesse f

chop [tʃɒp] n **to get the chop** (of person) se faire virer; (of plan) passer à la trappe

chopper ['tʃɒpə(r)] n (a) (helicopter) hélico m (b) Br (penis) pine f, queue f

chops [tʃɒps] npl Br (mouth) gueule f; (face) gueule f, tronche f; **you're going to get a smack in the chops if you're not careful!** tu vas te prendre une baffe dans la gueule si tu fais pas gaffe!

chow [tʃaʊ] n (food) bouffe f

chow down vi Am attaquer

chowderhead ['tʃaʊdəhed] n Am crétin(e) m,f, imbécile mf

Christ [kraɪst] exclam **Christ (Almighty)!** nom de Dieu!; **for Christ's sake!** bon sang!

chrome dome ['krəʊmdəʊm] n Br **he's a chrome dome** il a une casquette en peau de fesse

chronic ['krɒnɪk] adj Br (very bad) nul

chuck [tʃʌk] **1** n Br **to give sb the chuck** plaquer qn

2 vt (a) (throw) balancer (b) (boyfriend, girlfriend) plaquer

chuck down vt sép **it's chucking it down** (raining) il tombe des cordes

chuck in vt sép **to chuck sth in** (job, studies) plaquer qch; (habit) se débarrasser de qch □

chuck out vt sép **to chuck sb out** flanquer qn à la porte; **to chuck sth out** balancer qch

chuck up vi Br (vomit) dégobiller, gerber, dégueuler

chucker-out [tʃʌkə'raʊt] n Br (doorman) videur m

chucking-out time ['tʃʌkɪŋ'aʊttaɪm] n Br (in pub) heure f de la fermeture □

chuff [tʃʌf] n Br (a) !! (vagina) craquette f, fente f; **to be as tight as a nun's chuff** (miserly) avoir des oursins dans le porte-monnaie, les lâcher avec des élastiques (b) !! (anus) trou m de balle (c) **for chuff's sake!** bordel de merde!

chuffed [tʃʌft] adj Br content □; **I was chuffed to bits** j'étais vachement content

chuffer ['tʃʌfə(r)] n Br trou m du cul, trouduc m

chuffing ['tʃʌfɪŋ] adj Br foutu, sacré; **that chuffing idiot** ce sombre crétin

chug [tʃʌg] **1** n Br **to have a chug** ! (masturbate) se branler

2 vt (drink quickly) descendre

3 ! vi Br (masturbate) se branler

chug down vt sép **to chug sth down** descendre qch

chump [tʃʌmp] n (a) Br **to be off one's chump** être cinglé ou timbré; **to go off one's chump** perdre la boule, disjoncter (b) Am **chump change** (small amount of money) cacahuètes fpl

chunder ['tʃʌndə(r)] vi Br & Austr dégobiller, gerber, dégueuler

cig [sɪg] n Am (abrév **cigarette**) clope f, tige f

cigar [sɪ'gɑː(r)] n **close, but no cigar!** c'est presque ça, mais pas tout à fait!

Il s'agit d'une expression humoristique utilisée lorsqu'une personne à qui l'on a posé une devinette donne une réponse inexacte mais très proche de la réponse juste, le cigare étant la récompense fictive à laquelle cette personne aurait eu droit si elle avait deviné juste. Cette expression a été popularisée par les animateurs de jeux télévisés.

ciggy ['sɪgɪ] n (abrév **cigarette**) clope f, tige f

cinch [sɪntʃ] n **it was a cinch** c'était du gâteau, c'était simple comme bonjour; **it's a cinch to use** c'est hyper facile à utiliser

cissy ['sɪsɪ] Br = **sissy**

city ['sɪtɪ] n Am **you should see the people at the gym – it's fat city!** si tu voyais les gens qui vont au club de gym – c'est tous des gros lards!; **try the park, it's dope city!** va voir au parc, c'est pas les dealers qui manquent! ▶ voir aussi **fat**

Ce mot dénote l'abondance de ce qui le précède. On peut l'ajouter à presque n'importe quel nom, verbe ou adjectif pour introduire la notion de foisonnement.

clam [klæm] n Am (dollar) dollar ᵁ m

clap [klæp] n **the clap** la chaude-pisse; **to have (a dose of) the clap** avoir la chaude-pisse

clapped-out [klæpt'aʊt] adj Br (person) crevé, lessivé, naze; (car, TV) fichu

clappers ['klæpəz] npl Br **to do sth like the clappers** faire qch comme un dingue

claret ['klærət] n (blood) raisiné m, sang ᵁ m

clart [klɑːt] n Scot (dirty person) = personne sale et négligée; **he's a pure clart!** ce qu'il peut être crade ou cradingue!

clarty ['klɑːtɪ] adj Scot (dirty) crade, cradingue, dégueulasse

class [klɑːs] adj (excellent) classe; **a class car/hi-fi** une voiture/chaîne classe

classic ['klæsɪk] **1** n **it was a classic!** ça payait!
2 adj **it was classic!** ça payait!

clean [kliːn] adj **to be clean** (not carrying drugs) ne pas avoir de drogue sur soi ᵁ; (not carrying weapons) ne pas être armé ᵁ; (no longer addicted to drugs) avoir décroché ▶ voir aussi **nose**

clean out vt sép **to clean sb out** (leave penniless) nettoyer qn

clean up vi (make large profit) gagner gros

clear off [klɪə(r)] vi Br dégager, se tirer; **clear off!** dégage!, tire-toi!

clear out vi dégager, se tirer; **clear out!** dégage!, tire-toi!

clever clogs ['klevəklɒgz], **clever dick** ['klevədɪk] n Br gros (grosse) malin(igne) m,f; **OK, clever clogs** or **dick, what do we do now?** alors, gros malin, qu'est-ce qu'on fait maintenant?

clink [klɪŋk] n (prison) taule f, placard m; **in the clink** en taule, à l'ombre, en cabane

clip [klɪp] **1** n (a) Br (blow) **to give sb a clip round the ear** flanquer une calotte à qn (b) **clip joint** = bar ou boîte de nuit où l'on se fait escroquer
2 vt Br **to clip sb round the ear** flanquer une calotte à qn

clipe [klaɪp] Scot **1** n (person) mouchard(e) m,f
2 vi moucharder, cafarder; **to clipe on sb** moucharder qn

clit [!!] [klɪt] n (abrév **clitoris**) clito m, clit m

clobber[1] ['klɒbə(r)] n Br (clothes) frusques fpl; (belongings) barda m

clobber[2] vt (a) (hit) (once) flanquer un pain ou gnon à; (repeatedly) flanquer une raclée à (b) (defeat) flanquer une raclée à (c) (penalize) écraser ᵁ, accabler ᵁ

clock [klɒk] **1** n Am **to clean sb's clock** (attack) rentrer dans qn; (defeat) écraser qn, battre qn à plates coutures
2 vt (a) (hit) flanquer un pain ou un gnon à (b) (notice) repérer

clogs [klɒgz] npl Br **to pop one's clogs** passer l'arme à gauche, calancher ▶ voir aussi **clever clogs**

closet ['klɒzɪt] **1** n **to come out of the closet** (of homosexual) faire son comeout
2 adj **closet communist/alcoholic** communiste mf/alcoolique mf honteux(euse); **closet queen** homo m honteux

clot [klɒt] n Br (person) nouille f, courge f, andouille f

The symbol ᵁ indicates that a translation is neutral in register.

cloud-cuckoo-land [ˈklaʊdˈkʊkuː
læ nd] n Br **to be living in cloud-cuckoo
-land** ne pas avoir les pieds sur terre

clout [klaʊt] **1** n (a) (influence) influence ᵁ
f; **to have a lot of clout** avoir le bras long
(b) (blow) calotte f; **to give sb a clout**
flanquer une calotte à qn; **to give sth a
clout** flanquer un coup dans qch
   2 vt (hit) (person) flanquer une calotte à;
(thing) flanquer un coup dans

clown [klaʊn] n Hum **to be one clown
short of a circus** ne pas être net

club [klʌb] n (a) Br **to be in the (pudding) club** (pregnant) être en cloque (b)
join the club! t'es pas le (la) seul(e)!

clueless [ˈkluːlɪs] adj nul

C-note [ˈsiːnəʊt] n Am billet m de cent
dollars ᵁ

cobber [ˈkɒbə(r)] n Austr copain m, pote
m

cobblers [!] [ˈkɒbləz] Br **1** npl (a) (testicles) balloches fpl, boules fpl (b) (nonsense) foutaises fpl
   2 exclam n'importe quoi!, des foutaises,
tout ça!

cock [kɒk] n (a) [!!] (penis) queue f, bite f
(b) Br (term of address) mon pote; **alright, me old cock!** salut, mon pote!

cock up vt sép **to cock sth up** (interview,
exam) foirer qch, se planter à qch; (plan,
arrangement) faire foirer qch

cocksucker [!!] [ˈkɒksʌkə(r)] n enculé m

cocktease [!!] [ˈkɒktiːz], **cockteaser**
[!!] [ˈkɒktiːzə(r)] n allumeuse f

cock-up [ˈkɒkʌp] n Br foirade f; **to make
a cock-up of sth** (interview, exam) foirer
qch, se planter à qch; (plan, arrangement)
faire foirer qch

coco [ˈkəʊkəʊ] vi Br **I should coco!** tu l'as
dit!

cod [kɒd] n Br (nonsense) foutaises fpl

codger [ˈkɒdʒə(r)] n **old codger** vieux
croulant m

codswallop [ˈkɒdzwɒləp] n Br foutaises
fpl; **it's a load of codswallop** tout ça,
c'est des foutaises

coffin [ˈkɒfɪn] n (a) Br Péj **coffin dodger**

(old person) croulant(e) m,f (b) **coffin nail**
(cigarette) clope f, tige f

coke [kəʊk] n (abrév **cocaine**) coke f

coked up [kəʊktˈʌp] adj défoncé à la
coke

cokehead [ˈkəʊkhed] n **to be a cokehead** marcher à la cocaïne

coldcock [ˈkəʊldkɒk] vt Am assommer ᵁ, estourbir

cold turkey [kəʊldˈtɜːkɪ] n **to be cold
turkey** être en manque; **to go cold turkey** décrocher d'un seul coup

comatose [ˈkəʊmətəʊs] adj (drunk) ivre
mort ᵁ

combi [ˈkɒmbɪ] n Austr **combi (van)**
camping-car ᵁ m

come [kʌm] **1** [!] n (semen) foutre m
   2 vi (a) [!] (reach orgasm) jouir (b) Br **to
come it** bluffer; **don't come it with me!**
arrête ton cinéma!

come off 1 vt insép **come off it!** arrête
ton char!
   2 [!] vi (reach orgasm) jouir

come on vi (a) **to come on to sb** faire du
rentre-dedans à qn (b) Br (start menstruating) avoir ses ragnagnas; **I came on
this morning** les Anglais ont débarqué
ce matin

come out vi (reveal homosexuality) faire
son comeout

come up vi Br (a) [!] (ejaculate) décharger
(b) (after taking drugs) décoller

come-on [ˈkʌmɒn] n **to give sb the
come-on** faire du rentre-dedans à qn

commando [kəˈmɑːndəʊ] n Hum **to go
commando** ne pas porter de slip/de culotte

commie [ˈkɒmɪ] n (abrév **communist**)
coco mf

con¹ [kɒn] **1** n (abrév **confidence trick**)
(swindle) arnaque f; **con man** arnaqueur
m
   2 vt arnaquer; **to con sth out of sb** arnaquer qn de qch; **to con sb into doing
sth** persuader qn de faire qch par la ruse ▸
voir aussi **merchant**

con² n (abrév **convict**) taulard(e) m, f

The symbol ᵁ indicates that a translation is neutral in register.

conk [kɒŋk] n Br (nose) tarin m, blaire m

conk out vi (a) (break down) tomber en rade (b) (fall asleep) s'endormir □, piquer du nez

connection [kə'nekʃən] n Am (drug dealer) dealer m

cook [kʊk] 1 vt to cook a shot préparer un shoot d'héroïne

2 vi what's cooking? (what's happening?) quoi de neuf?; now we're cooking with gas! maintenant tout marche comme sur des roulettes!

cook up 1 vt sép to cook up a shot préparer un shoot d'héroïne

2 vi (heat heroin) préparer un shoot d'héroïne

cookie ['kʊkɪ] n (a) (person) a tough cookie un(e) dur(e) m,f à cuire; a smart cookie une tête (b) that's the way the cookie crumbles c'est la vie (c) to toss or Am shoot one's cookies (vomit) gerber, dégueuler

cool [kuːl] 1 adj (a) (fashionable, sophisticated) branché; Glasgow's a really cool city Glasgow est une ville hyper-branchée; he still thinks it's cool to smoke il pense encore que ça fait bien de fumer

(b) (excellent) cool, super; we had a really cool weekend on a passé un super week-end; that's a cool jacket elle est cool ou super, cette veste

(c) (allowed, acceptable) is it cool to skin up in here? on peut se rouler un joint ici?; it's not cool to wear jeans in that restaurant on ne peut pas entrer dans ce restaurant si on porte un jean □

(d) (accepting, not upset) are you cool with that? ça te va?; they're not cool about me smoking at home ils n'aiment pas que je fume à la maison □; I thought she'd be angry, but she was really cool about it je pensais qu'elle se fâcherait, mais en fait elle a été très cool

2 exclam cool!, super!

3 vt to cool it se calmer □; cool it! du calme!, calmos! ▸ voir aussi **lose**

cooler ['kuːlə(r)] n (prison) taule f, cabane f; **in the cooler** en taule, en cabane, à l'ombre

coon [kuːn] n Injurieux (black person) nègre (négresse) m,f

cooties ['kuːtɪz] npl Am poux □ mpl; **don't sit beside her, she's got cooties!** ne t'assieds pas à côté d'elle, elle a des poux!

cooze [!!] [kuːz] n Am (female genitals) craquette f, fente f, cramouille f; (women) nanas fpl, cuisse f; **I'm gonna go out and get me some cooze tonight** j'ai bien l'intention de me mettre une nana sur le bout ce soir; **that new bar's oozing with cooze!** il y a de la cuisse dans ce nouveau bar!

cop [kɒp] 1 n (a) (police officer) flic m; **cop shop** (police station) poste m; **cop show** (on TV) série f télévisée policière

(b) Br Hum (arrest) **it's a fair cop!** je suis fait, y a rien à dire!

(c) Br **it's not much cop** (not very good) ce n'est pas terrible, ça ne casse pas trois pattes à un canard

2 vt (a) (catch) **to cop sb** pincer qn; **to get copped doing sth** se faire pincer en train de faire qch; **to cop hold of sth** choper qch; **cop (a load of) this!** (listen) écoute-moi ça!; (look) mate-moi ça!

(b) Br **to cop it** (be punished) prendre un savon; (die) clamser, calancher; **did he try to cop a feel?** il a essayé de te peloter?

(c) **to cop some** Br **zeds** or Am **zees** roupiller

cop off vi Br **did you cop off last night?** t'as réussi à lever quelqu'un hier soir?; **to cop off with sb** lever ou emballer qn

cop out vi (avoid responsibility) se défiler; (choose easy solution) choisir la solution de facilité □; **to cop out of doing sth** ne pas avoir le cran de faire qch

cop-out ['kɒpaʊt] n solution f de facilité □

copper ['kɒpə(r)] n (police officer) flic m

corker ['kɔːkə(r)] n Br (excellent thing) **their new CD is a corker** leur nouveau CD est vraiment super; **that was a corker of a party** c'était une super soirée

The symbol □ indicates that a translation is neutral in register.

corking ['kɔːkɪŋ] *adj Br* super, génial

cornball ['kɔːnbɔːl] *Am* **1** *n* personne *f* gnangnan
  2 *adj* cucul, gnangnan

cornhole ‼️ ['kɔːnhəʊl] *vt Am* enculer, enviander

cossie ['kɒzɪ] *n Br & Austr* maillot *m* de bain □

cottage ['kɒtɪdʒ] *n Br (public toilet)* tasse *f*, toilettes publiques □ *fpl (utilisées comme lieu de rencontre par certains homosexuels)*

cottaging ['kɒtɪdʒɪŋ] *n Br* = drague homosexuelle dans les toilettes publiques

couch potato ['kaʊtʃpə'teɪtəʊ] *n* flemmard(e) *m,f* qui passe sa vie devant la télé

cough up [kɒf] **1** *vt sép (money)* cracher, allonger
  2 *vi* cracher *ou* allonger le fric

coupon ['kuːpɒn] *n Scot (face)* tronche *f*, face *f*

cow [kaʊ] *n Br Péj (woman)* vache *f*, chameau *m*; **poor cow!** la pauvre!; **lucky cow!** la veinarde!; **you silly cow!** espèce de cloche! ▸ *voir aussi* **holy**

cowabunga [kaʊə'bʌŋgə] *exclam Am* = cri de joie ou de victoire

> Il s'agit d'un terme du monde des surfers, rendu célèbre par le dessin animé des Tortues Ninja.

cowboy ['kaʊbɔɪ] *n Br Péj (workman)* mauvais artisan □ *m*, fumiste *m*; **they're a cowboy outfit** ils sont vraiment pas sérieux dans cette entreprise

crab [kræb] *n (pubic louse)* morpion *m*; **to have crabs** avoir des morpions

crack [kræk] **1** *n* **(a)** **crack (cocaine)** crack *m* **(b)** ‼️ *(woman's genitals)* chatte *f*, con *m*, cramouille *f* **(c)** ‼️ *(anus)* troufignon *m*, trou *m* du cul **(d)** *(attempt)* **to have a crack at sth, to give sth a crack** essayer qch □
  2 *vi* **to get cracking** *(make a start)* se mettre au boulot; *(speed up)* se grouiller, se magner

crack up **1** *vt sép* **to crack sb up** *(cause to laugh hysterically)* faire éclater qn de rire
  2 *vi* **(a)** *Br (get angry)* péter les plombs

(b) *(have nervous breakdown)* craquer (nerveusement) **(c)** *(laugh hysterically)* éclater de rire

cracked [krækt] *adj (mad)* cinglé, toqué

cracker ['krækə(r)] *n* **(a)** *Br (excellent thing)* **to be a cracker** être génial; **it was a cracker of a goal** c'était un but magnifique; **she's a cracker** *(gorgeous)* elle est hyper canon **(b)** *Am (poor white person)* = pauvre originaire du sud des États-Unis

crackerjack ['krækədʒæk] *Am* **1** *n* **to be a crackerjack** *(person)* être un crack *ou* un as; *(thing)* être génial
  2 *adj (excellent)* génial, du tonnerre

crackers ['krækəz] *adj Br (mad)* cinglé, toqué

crackhead ['krækhed] *n* accro *mf* au crack

crackhouse ['krækhaʊs] *n* = lieu où l'on achète, vend et consomme du crack

cracking ['krækɪŋ] *adj Br (excellent)* super, génial

crackpot ['krækpɒt] **1** *n (person)* allumé(e) *m,f*
  2 *adj (scheme, idea)* loufoque

cradle-snatcher ['kreɪdəlsnætʃə(r)] *n* **he's a cradle-snatcher** il les prend au berceau

crank [kræŋk] *n* **(a)** *(eccentric)* allumé(e) *m,f* **(b)** *Am (grumpy person)* râleur(euse) *m,f*

crank up **1** *vt sép* **to crank sth up** *(music, volume)* monter qch
  2 *vi (inject drugs)* se piquer

cranky ['kræŋkɪ] *adj* **(a)** *Br (eccentric)* excentrique □, loufoque **(b)** *Am (grumpy)* grognon, grincheux

crap ❗ [kræp] **1** *n* **(a)** *(excrement)* merde *f*; **to have** *or* **take a crap** chier, couler un bronze; **he bores the crap out of me** je le trouve chiant comme la pluie
  (b) *(nonsense)* conneries *fpl*; **he's full of crap** il raconte n'importe quoi; **you're talking crap!** tu racontes n'importe quoi!; **cut the crap!** arrête tes conneries!, arrête de dire n'importe quoi!; **don't believe all that crap!** il faut pas écouter

toutes ces conneries!; **I can't be doing with all that New Age crap** je ne supporte pas toutes ces conneries New Age; **that's crap, I never said that!** c'est des conneries, j'ai jamais dit ça!; **what he's saying is a load of crap** il raconte n'importe quoi

(c) *(worthless things)* **the film/book was a load of crap** il était nul, ce film/bouquin

(d) *(useless things)* bazar *m*; **clear all your crap off the bed** enlève ton bazar du lit

(e) *(disgusting substance)* merde *f*, saloperie *f*; **he eats nothing but crap** il bouffe que de la merde

(f) *(unfair treatment)* **I'm not taking that crap from you!** si tu crois que je vais supporter tes conneries, tu te gourres!; **I don't need this crap!** je me passerais bien de ce genre de conneries!

(g) **to feel like crap** *(ill)* se sentir vraiment patraque

2 *adj (worthless)* merdique; *(nasty)* dégueulasse; **to feel crap** *(ill)* se sentir vraiment mal fichu; *(guilty)* se sentir coupable ᵈ; **her work is crap** elle fait de la merde; **he's a crap teacher** il est complètement nul comme prof

3 *vt* **to crap oneself** *(defecate, be scared)* faire dans son froc

4 *vi (defecate)* chier, couler un bronze

crap out ⚠ *vi* se dégonfler; **he crapped out of the fight** il s'est dégonflé au dernier moment et a refusé se battre; **he crapped out of telling her the truth** finalement il a eu la trouille de lui dire la vérité

crapper ⚠ ['kræpə(r)] *n (toilet)* chiottes *fpl*, gogues *mpl*

crappy ⚠ ['kræpɪ] *adj (worthless)* merdique; **to feel crappy** *(ill)* se sentir vraiment mal fichu; *(guilty)* se sentir coupable ᵈ; **he's a crappy teacher** il est complètement nul comme prof

crash [kræʃ] **1** *vt (party)* s'inviter à, taper l'incruste à

2 *vi (spend night, sleep)* pieuter; *(fall asleep)* s'endormir ᵈ; **can I crash at your place?** est-ce que je peux pieuter chez toi?

crash out *vi (spend night, sleep)* pieuter; *(fall asleep)* s'endormir ᵈ; **he was crashed out on the sofa** il roupillait dans le canapé

crate [kreɪt] *n (old car)* vieille bagnole *f*; *(old plane)* vieux coucou *m*

cream [kriːm] **1** *vt* (a) *(defeat)* battre à plates coutures; *Am (beat up)* tabasser (b) **to cream one's jeans** ⚠⚠ *(of man)* décharger dans son froc; *(of woman)* mouiller sa culotte

2 ⚠⚠ *vi* (a) *(become sexually aroused) (of woman)* mouiller (b) *(ejaculate)* décharger

cream crackered [kriːm'krækəd] *adj Br (rhyming slang **knackered**) (exhausted)* crevé, lessivé, naze; *(broken, worn out)* bousillé

crease up [kriːs] *Br* **1** *vt sép* **to crease sb up** *(cause to laugh hysterically)* faire se tordre qn de rire

2 *vi (laugh hysterically)* se tordre de rire

cred [kred] *n Br (abrév **credibility**)* **to have (street) cred** être branché *ou* dans le coup; **he wants to get some (street) cred** il veut faire branché *ou* dans le coup

creep [kriːp] *n* (a) *(unpleasant man)* type *m* répugnant; *Br (obsequious person)* lèche-bottes *mf* (b) **to give sb the creeps** *(scare)* donner la chair de poule à qn; *(repulse)* débecter qn

creepy ['kriːpɪ] *adj* **it's creepy** *(scary)* ça me donne la chair de poule; *(repulsive)* ça me débecte

creepy-crawly ['kriːpɪ'krɔːlɪ] *n* bébête *f*

cretin ['kretɪn] *n (idiot)* crétin(e) *m,f*

crikey ['kraɪkɪ] *exclam* bigre!

crim [krɪm] *n Br & Austr (criminal)* criminel(elle) *m,f*

Crimbo ['krɪmbəʊ] *n Br (Christmas)* Noël ᵈ *m*

crimper ['krɪmpə(r)] *n Br* merlan *m (coiffeur)*

croak [krəʊk] *vi (die)* calancher, passer l'arme à gauche

croc [krɒk] *n (abrév **crocodile**)* crocodile ᵈ *m*

The symbol ᵈ indicates that a translation is neutral in register.

crock [krɒk] n Am **to be a crock** or a **crock of shit** ❗ (nonsense) être des foutaises ou des conneries; **don't believe that crock he told you!** ne crois pas ce qu'il t'a dit, c'est des foutaises!

crone [krəʊn] n **old crone** vieille toupie f

crook [krʊk] adj Austr (ill) mal fichu; (not working) détraqué

cropper ['krɒpə(r)] n **to come a cropper** (fall) prendre une gamelle; (fail) se planter

crown jewels ❗ ['kraʊn 'dʒʊəlz] npl Hum (man's genitals) bijoux mpl de famille

crucial ['kruːʃəl] adj Br (excellent) super, génial; **the DJ at the club last night was well crucial** le DJ de la boîte, hier soir, était vraiment super

crucify ['kruːsɪfaɪ] vt (defeat, criticize) démolir

crud [krʌd] n (a) (dirt) crasse f (b) (nonsense) conneries fpl; **he was talking some crud about the dangers of drugs** il était en train de raconter des conneries sur les dangers de la drogue (c) (person) ordure f, saloperie f

cruddy ['krʌdɪ] adj (a) (dirty) cradingue, dégueulasse (b) (worthless) merdique

cruise [kruːz] 1 vt (person) draguer; (place) aller draguer dans
2 vi (a) (look for sexual partner) draguer (b) Am (leave) mettre les bouts, se casser, s'arracher; **ready to cruise?** on y va? (c) Hum **you're cruising for a bruising!** toi, tu cherches les emmerdes!

crumb [krʌm] n Péj (person) minable mf

crumbly ['krʌmblɪ] n Br (old person) croulant(e) m,f

crummy ['krʌmɪ] adj minable

crumpet ['krʌmpɪt] n Br (women) nanas fpl, gonzesses fpl; **a nice bit of crumpet** une belle nana; **the thinking man's/woman's crumpet** une belle nana /un beau mec intelligent(e)

crust [krʌst] n Br **to earn a** or **one's crust** gagner sa croûte

crustie, crusty ['krʌstɪ] n Br jeune hippie mf crado

Le type "crusty" est apparu au début des années 90 avec l'émergence du mouvement alternatif des "New Age travellers" (communautés néo-hippies parcourant la Grande-Bretagne dans des caravanes et des autobus aménagés, dont les membres sont de tous les combats pour la défense de l'environnement). Le "crusty" est généralement sans emploi et sans domicile fixes, d'une hygiène pas toujours irréprochable, et il se déplace souvent avec un chien tenu au bout d'une ficelle.

cry out [kraɪ] vi **for crying out loud!** c'est pas possible!

cuckoo ['kʊkuː] adj (mad) cinglé, toqué

cuff [kʌf] 1 n (a) (blow) beigne f, torgnole f
2 vt flanquer une beigne à; **to cuff sb round the ear** donner une claque sur l'oreille à qn

cuffs [kʌfs] npl (abrév **handcuffs**) menottes ⁔ fpl, bracelets mpl

cum ‼ [kʌm] n foutre m, jute m

cunt ‼ [kʌnt] n (a) (woman's genitals) chatte f, con m (b) (man) enculé m; (woman) sale pute f; **he's a stupid cunt!** c'est qu'un enculé!; **the poor cunt's smashed his leg to pieces** le pauvre vieux, il s'est bousillé la jambe (c) (thing) **that exam was an absolute cunt!** cet examen était une vraie saloperie!

Il s'agit du terme le plus grossier de la langue anglaise, loin devant "fuck". Même les gens qui ont l'habitude de jurer évitent généralement de l'utiliser, y compris entre amis, car son utilisation ne manquerait pas de choquer. Il est préférable de le bannir complètement de son vocabulaire.

cunted ‼ ['kʌntɪd] adj Br (drunk) complètement bourré ou pété; (on drugs) complètement défoncé

cupcake ['kʌpkeɪk] n (a) (eccentric person) allumé(e) m,f (b) Am Injurieux (homosexual) pédale f, tantouze f

curse [kɜːs] *n* **to have the curse** avoir ses ragnagnas

cushti ['kʊʃtɪ] *adj Br* super, génial

cut [kʌt] *vt* **to cut the cloth** *or* **the cheese** *(break wind)* péter, lâcher une caisse

cut out 1 *vt sép* **cut it out!** ça suffit!
2 *vi Am (leave)* mettre les bouts, calter

D

daffy ['dæfɪ] *adj* loufoque, loufedingue

daftie ['dɑːftɪ] *n Br* cruche *f*, andouille *f*

dag [dæg] *n Austr* (**a**) *(unfashionable)* ringard(e) *m,f* (**b**) *(untidy)* type *m* négligé; *(untidy woman)* bonne femme *f* négligée

daggy ['dægɪ] *adj Austr* (**a**) *(unfashionable)* ringard (**b**) *(untidy)* négligé □

Dago ['deɪgəʊ] *Injurieux* **1** *n* métèque *mf* *(personne d'origine espagnole, italienne, portugaise ou latino-américaine)*
  2 *adj* métèque

daisy ['deɪzɪ] *n* **to be pushing up the daisies** manger les pissenlits par la racine

daks [dæks] *n Austr (trousers)* futal *m*, falzar *m*

damage ['dæmɪdʒ] *n* **what's the damage?** *(how much does it cost?)* ça fait combien?

dame [deɪm] *n Am* gonzesse *f*

dammit ['dæmɪt] **1** *n Br* **as near as dammit** dans ces eaux-là
  2 *exclam* merde!

damn [dæm] **1** *n* (**a**) **I don't give a damn** j'en ai rien à cirer, je m'en balance (**b**) *Br* **damn all** *(nothing)* que dalle; **damn all money/thanks** pas un sou/un merci; **they had damn all to do with it** ils n'y étaient pour rien
  2 *adj* sacré, foutu; **he's a damn nuisance!** c'est un sacré emmerdeur!; **it's one damn thing after another!** ça n'arrête pas!
  3 *adv* vachement; **a damn good idea** une super bonne idée; **you're damn right** t'as parfaitement raison; **he's so damn slow** il est hyper lent; **she knows damn well what I'm talking about** elle sait parfaitement de quoi je parle □
  4 *exclam* **damn (it)!** merde!
  5 *vt* **damn you!** va te faire voir!; **he lied to me, damn him!** il m'a menti, le salaud!; **damn the expense/the consequences!** tant pis pour les frais/les conséquences!; **well, I'll be damned!** eh ben ça alors!; **I'm** *or* **I'll be damned if I'm going to apologize** plutôt crever que de m'excuser ► *voir aussi* **sight**

damnation [dæm'neɪʃən] *exclam* zut!

damned [dæmd] *adj & adv* = **damn**

damnedest ['dæmdəst] **1** *n* **to do one's damnedest (to do sth)** faire tout son possible (pour faire qch)
  2 *adj Am* **it was the damnedest thing!** c'était carrément incroyable!

dandy ['dændɪ] *adj* super; **everything's just (fine and) dandy!** tout baigne!

darky ['dɑːkɪ] *n Injurieux* bronzé(e) *m,f*

darn [dɑːn] **1** *adj* sacré, foutu; **the darn car won't start** cette saloperie de voiture ne veut pas démarrer; **you're a darn fool** t'es un vrai con
  2 *adv* vachement; **we were darn lucky** on a eu la sacrée veine; **you know darn well what I mean!** tu comprends parfaitement ce que je veux dire! □; **it's too darn hot** il fait vraiment trop chaud □
  3 *exclam* **darn (it)!** zut!
  4 *vt* **he's late, darn him!** il est en retard, il fait vraiment chier!; **well, I'll be darned!** eh ben ça alors! ► *voir aussi* **sight**

darned [dɑːnd] *adj & adv* = **darn**

dash [dæʃ] *exclam* **dash (it)!** zut!, mince!

daylights ['deɪlaɪts] *npl* **to beat the living daylights out of sb** flanquer une dérouillée *ou* une raclée à qn; **you scared the living daylights out of me!** tu m'as foutu une de ces trouilles!

dead [ded] **1** *adj* (**a**) *(not alive)* **to be dead from the neck up** ne rien avoir dans le

---

citron; **to be dead to the world** en écraser; **I wouldn't be seen dead there/ in that dress** je préférerais mourir que d'y aller/que de porter cette robe

(b) *(absolute)* **to be a dead ringer for sb** être le portrait tout craché de qn; **he's a dead loss** c'est un bon à rien; **it was a dead loss** ça n'a servi à rien [□]

2 *adv Br (very)* vachement; **it's dead easy/good** c'est vachement facile/bon; **you were dead lucky** tu as eu une sacrée veine; **I'm dead bored** je m'ennuie à mort ▸ *voir aussi* **knock, meat, president**

deadbeat ['dedbiːt] *n Am (lazy person)* glandeur(euse) *m,f; (tramp)* clodo *mf; (parasite)* pique-assiette *mf*

deadly ['dedlɪ] *adj Ir* super, génial, d'enfer

death [deθ] *n* **(a) to look like death warmed up** avoir l'air d'un(e) déterré(e); **to feel like death warmed up** se sentir patraque **(b)** *Am & Austr* **death seat** *(in a vehicle)* place *f* du mort ▸ *voir aussi* **sick**

deck [dek] **1** *n* **(a) to hit the deck** *(get out of bed)* sortir de son pieu, se dépagnoter; *(fall)* se foutre la gueule par terre; *(lie down)* se jeter à terre [□] **(b)** *Hum* **he's not playing with a full deck** c'est pas une lumière, il a pas inventé l'eau chaude

2 *vt* **to deck sb** foutre qn par terre

deep-six ['diːp'sɪks] *vt Am* **(a)** *(throw away)* balancer, foutre en l'air **(b)** *(rule out)* mettre au placard

deep-throat [!] ['diːp'θrəʊt] *vt* faire une pipe à

Il s'agit du titre d'un film pornographique très célèbre, tourné dans les années 70.

def [def] *adj* super, génial

deffo ['defəʊ] *adv Br (abrév* **definitely)** absolument [□]; **are you coming tonight? – deffo!** tu viens ce soir? – je veux!

dekko ['dekəʊ] *n Br* **to have** *or* **take a dekko at sb/sth** mater qn/qch

Delhi belly ['delɪbelɪ] *n Br* **to have Delhi Belly** avoir la courante; **I got severe Delhi belly after that curry the other**

night j'ai eu une sacrée courante après avoir mangé le curry l'autre soir

demo ['deməʊ] *n* **(a)** *(in street)* manif *f* **(b)** *(music sample)* démo *m* **(c)** *(explanation)* démonstration [□] *f*

dense [dens] *adj (stupid)* débile

devil ['devəl] *n* **(a)** *(person)* **the lucky devil!** le veinard!; *Br* **poor devil!** le pauvre!; *Br* **go on, be a devil!** allez, laisse-toi tenter! **(b)** *(for emphasis)* **what/ who/why the devil…?** que/qui/pourquoi diable…?; **how the devil should I know?** comment veux-tu que je sache?; **we had a devil of a job getting here on time** on a eu un mal de chien à arriver à l'heure

dexy ['deksɪ] *n (abrév* **dexamphetamine)** amphé *f,* amphet *f*

diabolical [daɪə'bɒlɪkəl] *adj Br (very bad)* nul

diamond ['daɪəmənd] *adj Br (excellent)* super, génial; **he's a diamond geezer** c'est un type super

dibble ['dɪbəl] *n Br (police)* flics *mpl,* poulets *mpl;* **there were loads of dibble around** il y avait des flics partout

Ce terme vient du dessin animé américain "Top Cat", dont l'un des personnages, un agent de police, se nomme Dibble.

dick [dɪk] *n* **(a)** [!] *(penis)* bite *f,* queue *f* **(b)** [!] *(man)* trou *m* du cul, trouduc *m* **(c)** *Am (detective)* privé *m* ▸ *voir aussi* **clever clogs, features**

dick about, dick around 1 *vt sép* **to dick sb about** *or* **around** faire tourner qn en bourrique

2 *vi* glander, glandouiller; **oh, stop dicking around!** arrête donc de glandouiller!

dickface [!] ['dɪkfeɪs] *n* trou *m* du cul, trouduc *m;* **hey, dickface!** hé, trouduc!

dickhead [!] ['dɪkhed] *n* trou *m* du cul, trouduc *m*

dickless [!] ['dɪkləs] *adj (worthless)* minable, nul; *(lacking courage)* dégonflé, pétochard *m*

dicky-bird ['dɪkɪbɜːd] n Br (rhyming slang **word**) mot [□] m; **not a dicky-bird!** motus et bouche cousue!

diddle ['dɪdəl] vt Am (have sex with) baiser, se taper, s'envoyer; **he's been diddling his secretary for years** ça fait des années qu'il s'envoie sa secrétaire

diddly ['dɪdəlɪ] n Am **that's not worth diddly** ça ne vaut pas un clou

diddlyshit ⚠ ['dɪdəlɪ'ʃɪt] n Am **I don't give a diddlyshit** je m'en balance, je m'en fous complètement

diddlysquat ['dɪdəlɪskwɒt] n Am que dalle; **that's not worth diddlysquat** ça ne vaut pas un clou; **I don't know diddlysquat about computers** l'informatique, j'y connais rien

diesel (dyke) ['diːzəl(daɪk)] n Injurieux gouine f (à l'allure masculine)

dig [dɪg] 1 vt (a) (like) aimer [□], apprécier [□]; **I really dig that kind of music** ça me branche vraiment, ce genre de musique (b) (look at) mater; **dig that guy over there** mate un peu le mec, là-bas (c) (understand) piger

2 vi (understand) piger; **you dig?** tu piges?

dig in vi (start eating) attaquer (un repas)

dike [daɪk] Am = **dyke**

dildo ⚠ ['dɪldəʊ] n Péj (person) trou m du cul, trouduc m

dill [dɪl] n Austr andouille f, courge f

dimwit ['dɪmwɪt] n andouille f, courge f

ding-dong ['dɪŋdɒŋ] n Br (a) (argument) engueulade f (b) (fight) bagarre f

dinkum ['dɪŋkəm] Austr 1 n Australien (enne) m,f de naissance [□]

2 adj (person) franc (franche) [□], sincère [□]; (thing) authentique [□]; **fair dinkum** régulier, vrai de vrai; **dinkum?** sans blague?; **a dinkum Aussie** un vrai Australien [□]/une vraie Australienne [□]; **dinkum oil** la vérité [□]

3 adv franchement [□], vraiment [□]

dip [dɪp] n Am (idiot) andouille f, courge f, cruche f ► voir aussi **wick**

dippy ['dɪpɪ] adj loufoque, loufedingue

dipshit ⚠ ['dɪpʃɪt] n Am taré(e) m,f, crétin(e) m,f

dipso ['dɪpsəʊ] n (abrév **dipsomaniac**) alcolo mf, poivrot(e) m,f

dipstick ['dɪpstɪk] n (idiot) andouille f, cruche f

dirt [dɜːt] n (a) **to dish the dirt (about)** tout raconter (sur); **come on, dish the dirt!** allez, dis-moi tout! (b) Am **to do sb dirt** faire une crasse à qn

dirtbag ['dɜːtbæg] n Am nul (nulle) m,f, nullard(e) m,f

dirtbox ⚠⚠ ['dɜːtbɒks] n Br trou m du cul, boîte f à pâté

dirty ['dɜːtɪ] 1 n Br **to do the dirty on sb** faire une crasse à qn

2 adj **the dirty deed** (sex) = l'acte sexuel; **have you two done the dirty deed yet?** est-ce que vous avez déjà fait crac-crac tous les deux?; **dirty old man** vieux cochon m; **dirty weekend** weekend m coquin; Br Hum **dirty stop-out** débauché(e) m,f qui découche

dis [dɪs] = **diss**

disaster area [dɪˈzɑːstəreəriə] n **to be a walking disaster area** être une catastrophe ambulante

disco biscuit ['dɪskəʊ'bɪskɪt] n Br cachet m d'ecstasy, bonbec m

dishwater ['dɪʃwɔːtə(r)] n **this coffee's like dishwater!** c'est vraiment de l'eau de vaisselle, ce café!

dishy ['dɪʃɪ] adj mignon

diss [dɪs] vt Am débiner

ditch [dɪtʃ] vt (boyfriend, girlfriend) plaquer, larguer; (thing) balancer, foutre en l'air; (plan, idea) laisser tomber

ditz [dɪts] n Am courge f, andouille f, cruche f

ditzy ['dɪtsɪ] adj Am étourdi [□]

div [dɪv] n Br andouille f, cruche f

dive [daɪv] n (place) bouge [□] m

divvy ['dɪvɪ] n Br (idiot) andouille f, courge f, cruche f

DL [diːˈel] n Noir Am = **downlow**

do [duː] 1 vt (a) (take) **to do drugs** se droguer [□]; **let's do lunch** il faudrait qu'on déjeune ensemble un de ces jours

(b) *Br (prosecute)* poursuivre □; **to get done for speeding** se faire pincer pour excès de vitesse

(c) *Br (rob)* **to do a jeweller's/bank** braquer une bijouterie/une banque

(d) *(cheat)* arnaquer; **to do sb out of sth** arnaquer qn de qch; **I've been done!** j'ai été refait!

(e) *(visit)* **to do Paris/the sights** faire Paris/les monuments

(f) *Br (beat up)* tabasser; **I'll do you!** je vais te casser la gueule!

(g) *(kill)* zigouiller, buter

(h) *(have sex with) (of man)* baiser, tringler, troncher; *(of woman)* baiser avec, s'envoyer

2 *n (party)* fête *f*, boum *f*

do in *vt sép Br* **(a)** *(exhaust)* vanner, pomper, crever; **to feel done in** être crevé *ou* naze *ou* sur les rotules **(b)** *(kill)* **to do sb in** buter *ou* zigouiller qn ▶ *voir aussi* **head**

do over *vt sép Br* **(a)** *(beat up)* **to do sb over** tabasser qn **(b)** *(rob)* **to do sb over** dépouiller qn; **to do sth over** dévaliser qch □

do with *vt insép (tolerate)* **I can't be doing with people like that** je peux pas blairer les gens comme ça; **he couldn't be doing with living in London** il pouvait pas supporter de vivre à Londres

dob in [dɒb] *vt sép Austr* moucharder

doddle ['dɒdəl] *n Br* **it's a doddle** c'est hyper fastoche

dodgy ['dɒdʒɪ] *adj Br* **(a)** *(unsafe, untrustworthy)* louche; **he's OK, but all his friends are well dodgy** lui, ça va, mais ses amis craignent vraiment; **the house is nice, but it's in a really dodgy area** la maison est bien mais elle est dans un quartier vraiment craignos; **investing money in a scheme like that is just too dodgy** c'est vraiment trop risqué d'investir dans ce genre de truc; **they were involved in a couple of dodgy business deals** ils ont été impliqués dans des transactions plutôt louches

(b) *(not working properly, unstable)*

merdique; **don't sit on that chair, it's a bit dodgy** ne t'assieds pas sur cette chaise, elle est un peu branlante □; **the ceiling looks a bit dodgy** le plafond n'a pas l'air en très bon état □; **my stomach's been a bit dodgy for the last couple of days** ça fait deux jours que j'ai l'estomac un peu dérangé □; **we can't go camping while the weather's so dodgy** on ne peut pas aller camper alors que le temps risque de se gâter à tout moment □

(c) *(unfashionable, ridiculous)* ringard; **look at him in that dodgy shirt!** regarde-le avec sa chemise de ringard!

dog [dɒg] *n* **(a)** *(ugly woman)* cageot *m*, boudin *m*

(b) **dog's breakfast** *or* **dinner** *(mess)* merdier *m*; **to make a dog's breakfast** *or* **dinner of sth** complètement foirer qch; *Br* **to be dressed up like a dog's dinner** être attifé de façon ridicule

(c) *Br* **to be the dog's bollocks** [!] *(excellent)* être génial

(d) *Br* **to be like a dog with two dicks** [!] avoir l'air très content de soi □; **he's been like a dog with two dicks since he got Jennifer Aniston's autograph** il se sent plus depuis que Jennifer Aniston lui a donné son autographe

(e) *Br (rhyming slang* **dog and bone** = **phone)** bigophone *m*; **get on the dog (and bone) and order a takeaway** prends le bigophone et fais livrer un repas

(f) *Hum* **I'm going to see a man about a dog** *(going to the toilet)* je vais aux toilettes □; *(going somewhere unspecified)* j'ai un truc à faire

(g) *Br* **to give sb dog's abuse** traiter qn de tous les noms

(h) *Am (useless thing)* merde *f*

(i) *Am (foot)* arpion *m*, pinglot *m*; **my dogs are barking!** ce que j'ai mal aux arpions! ▶ *voir aussi* **hair, sausage**

dog-end ['dɒgend] *n Br* mégot □ *m*, clope *m*

doggone ['dɒgɒn] *Am* **1** *adj* sacré, foutu; **I've lost the doggone car keys** j'ai perdu ces saletés de clés de bagnole

2 *adv* vachement; **it's so doggone hot!** il fait une chaleur à crever!

3 *exclam* **doggone (it)!** zut!

doggy-fashion [ˈdɒɡɪfæʃən] *adv (have sex)* en levrette

doll [dɒl] *n* **(a)** *(attractive woman)* canon *m* **(b)** *(term of address)* poupée *f* **(c)** *Am (kind person)* trésor *m*, chou *m*

doll up *vt sép* **to doll oneself up, to get dolled up** se faire belle □

dong [!] [dɒŋ] *n* bite *f*, queue *f*

doobie [ˈduːbɪ] *n* joint *m*, pétard *m*

doodah [ˈduːdɑː], *Am* **doodad** [ˈduːdæd] *n* truc *m*, machin *m*

doo-doo [ˈduːduː] *n* **(a)** *(excrement)* crotte *f*, caca *m*; **the dog's done a doo-doo on the doormat** le chien a fait sa crotte sur le paillasson **(b)** *(trouble)* pétrin *m*; **we're in deep doo-doo!** on est vraiment dans le pétrin!

doofus [ˈduːfəs] *n Am* andouille *f*, cruche *f*, courge *f*

doolally [duːˈlælɪ] *adj Br* zinzin, timbré

Il s'agit à l'origine d'un terme d'argot militaire. Deolali était une ville de garnison britannique située près de Bombay, par où transitaient de nombreux militaires britanniques qui rentraient au pays. Le temps de transit était généralement assez long, et les soldats trompaient leur ennui en fréquentant les bars et les prostituées. Nombre d'entre eux se retrouvaient en prison ou victimes de maladies vénériennes. Le nom Deolali a fini par désigner le comportement étrange de ces soldats désœuvrés.

doorstep [ˈdɔːstep] *n Br (slice of bread)* grosse tranche *f* de pain □

dope [dəʊp] **1** *n* **(a)** *(cannabis)* shit *m* **(b)** *(person)* crétin(e) *m,f*, abruti(e) *m,f*
2 *adj Am (excellent)* génial, super

dopehead [ˈdəʊphed] *n* **to be a dopehead** fumer beaucoup de cannabis □

doper [ˈdəʊpə(r)] *n Am* **to be a doper** fumer beaucoup de cannabis □

dopey [ˈdəʊpɪ] *adj* empoté, cruche

do-re-mi [dəʊreɪˈmiː] *n Am (money)* fric *m*, blé *m*, oseille *f*, artiche *f*

dork [dɔːk] *n* ringard *m*, bouffon *m*

dorky [ˈdɔːkɪ] *adj* ringard, nul

Dorothy [ˈdɒrəθɪ] *npr* **a friend of Dorothy** un homo; **is he a friend of Dorothy, do you think?** tu crois qu'il est homo?

Cette expression trouve son origine dans le film américain "Le Magicien d'Oz" (1939) dans lequel Judy Garland, actrice fétiche de la communauté homosexuelle, incarnait la jeune Dorothy.

dose [dəʊs] *n* **(a)** *(venereal disease)* chtouille *f*; **to catch a dose** attraper la chtouille **(b)** *Br* **to get through sth like a dose of salts** faire qch en deux coups de cuillère à pot

dosh [dɒʃ] *n Br* blé *m*, oseille *f*

doss [dɒs] *Br* **1** *n* **(a)** *(bed)* plumard *m* **(b)** *(sleep)* **to have a doss** piquer un roupillon **(c)** **it was a doss** *(easy)* c'était fastoche
2 *vi (sleep)* roupiller

doss about, doss around *vi Br* traîner

doss down *vi Br* pieuter

dosser [ˈdɒsə(r)] *n Br* **(a)** *(tramp)* clodo *mf* **(b)** *(hostel)* asile *m* de nuit □

doss-house [ˈdɒshaʊs] *n Br* asile *m* de nuit □

dotty [ˈdɒtɪ] *adj* maboule, loufedingue; **to be dotty about sb/sth** être dingue de qn/qch

douche-bag [ˈduːʃbæɡ] *n Am (person)* ordure *f*

dough [dəʊ] *n (money)* blé *m*, oseille *f*

down [daʊn] *vt (eat, drink)* s'enfiler; **he downed his pint and left** il a descendu sa pinte puis il est parti

down-and-out [ˈdaʊnənˈaʊt] **1** *n* clodo *mf*
2 *adj* à la rue □

downer [ˈdaʊnə(r)] *n* **(a)** *(drug)* barbiturique *m*, downer *m* **(b)** *(depressing experience)* **to be on a downer** avoir le bourdon; **it was a real downer** c'était vraiment déprimant □; **the film's a**

complete downer c'est un film qui file le bourdon

downlow [daʊn'ləʊ] *n* Noir Am **on the downlow** *(confidentially)* confidentiellement □; *(in secret)* secrètement □; **I'm telling you this on the downlow** je te dis ça, mais c'est entre nous; **he's seeing someone else on the downlow** il a une maîtresse □

dozey, dozy ['dəʊzɪ] *adj Br (stupid)* couillon; **you dozey plonker, Rodney!** quel couillon *ou* quelle andouille tu fais, Rodney!

drag [dræg] *n* **(a)** *(bore)* truc *m* chiant, galère *f*; **he's such a drag** c'est vraiment un emmerdeur; **the party was a real drag** la soirée était vraiment chiante; **what a drag!** quelle galère!
(b) *(on cigarette, joint)* bouffée *f*, taffe *f*; **she took** *or* **had a drag on her cigarette** elle tira sur sa cigarette
(c) *Am (influence)* influence □ *f*; **to have drag** avoir le bras long ▸ *voir aussi* **main**

drat [dræt] *exclam* **drat (it)!** zut!, mince!

dratted ['drætɪd] *adj* sacré, foutu; **where's that dratted brother of mine?** mais où est passé mon frangin?

draw [drɔː] *n Br (cannabis)* shit *m*

dream [driːm] **1** *n* **in your dreams!** tu peux toujours rêver!
2 *vi* **dream on!** tu peux toujours rêver!

drip [drɪp] *n (person)* mollusque *m*

drippy ['drɪpɪ] *adj* mollasson

drongo ['drɒŋgəʊ] *n Austr (idiot)* abruti(e) *m,f*

drop [drɒp] **1** *vt* **(a) drop it!** *(I don't want to talk about it)* tu me lâches?; *(I don't want to hear about it)* change de disque!
(b) to drop one *(péter)* larguer *ou* lâcher une caisse
2 *vi* **drop dead!** ta gueule! ▸ *voir aussi* **log**

drop-dead gorgeous [drɒpded'gɔː-dʒəs] *adj* hyper canon

dross [drɒs] *n (worthless things)* **it's (a load of) dross** ça ne vaut pas un clou

druggie, druggy ['drʌgɪ] *n* camé(e) *m,f*

dry up [draɪ] *vi* **dry up!** *(be quiet)* la ferme!

ducats ['dʌkəts] *npl Am* fric *m*, blé *m*, oseille *f*

dude [djuːd, duːd] *n Am* **(a)** *(man)* mec *m* **(b)** *(term of address)* mec *m*, vieux *m*; **hey, dude!** *(as greeting)* salut vieux!; *(to attract attention)* excusez-moi! □

duds [dʌdz] *npl (clothes)* fringues *fpl*, frusques *fpl*, nippes *fpl*

duff [dʌf] **1** *n* **(a)** *Br* **up the duff** *(pregnant)* en cloque **(b)** **to get sb up the duff** mettre qn en cloque **(b)** *Am (buttocks)* cul *m*, derche *m*; **get up off your duff!** bouge ton cul!
2 *adj (bad, useless)* merdique

duff up *vt sép* **to duff sb up** tabasser qn

duffer ['dʌfə(r)] *n (incompetent person)* branleur(euse) *m,f*; **old duffer** vieux schnock *m*

dumb [dʌm] *adj Am (stupid)* bête □, débile

dumbass [!] ['dʌmæs] *Am* **1** *n* taré(e) *m,f*, débile *mf*, abruti(e) *m,f*
2 *adj* débile

dumbbell ['dʌmbel] *n (person)* cloche *f*, cruche *f*

dumbfuck [!!] ['dʌmfʌk] *n* connard (connasse) *m,f*

dumbo ['dʌmbəʊ] *n* andouille *f*, gourde *f*, cruche *f*

dump [dʌmp] **1** *n* **(a)** *Péj (house, room)* taudis □ *m*; *(town)* trou *m*, bled *m*; *(pub)* bouge □ *m* **(b) to** *Br* **have** *or Am* **take a dump** [!] *(defecate)* chier, couler un bronze
2 *vt (boyfriend, girlfriend)* plaquer, larguer

dumpling ['dʌmplɪŋ] *n (fat man)* gros patapouf *m*; *(fat woman)* grosse dondon *f*

dunno [dʌ'nəʊ] *contraction (abrév* **I don't know)** j'sais pas!

dunny ['dʌnɪ] *n Austr (toilet)* chiottes *fpl*

dustbins ['dʌstbɪnz] *npl Br (rhyming slang* **dustbin lids = kids)** gosses *mpl*, mômes *mpl*

Dutch [dʌtʃ] **1** *adj* **Dutch courage =** courage puisé dans la bouteille; **I need**

The symbol □ indicates that a translation is neutral in register.

some Dutch courage before I phone him il faut que je boive quelque chose avant de l'appeler

2 *adv* **to go Dutch** payer chacun sa part □

dweeb [dwiːb] *n Am* crétin(e) *m,f*, abruti(e) *m,f*

dyke [daɪk] *n Injurieux (lesbian)* gouine *f*, gousse *f*

E

E [iː] *n* (**a**) (*abrév* **ecstasy**) ecsta *f* (**b**) *Br* (*abrév* **elbow**) **to give sb the big E** plaquer qn, larguer qn

ear [ɪə(r)] *n* (**a**) **to be up to one's ears in work** avoir un boulot dingue *ou* pas possible; **to be up to one's ears in debt** être couvert de dettes (**b**) **to throw sb out on his ear** vider qn (**c**) **to bend sb's ear** pomper l'air à qn ▶ *voir aussi* **pig, thick**

earbashing ['ɪəbæʃɪŋ] *n Br* **to give sb an earbashing** passer un savon à qn, souffler dans les bronches à qn; **to get an earbashing** se faire passer un savon, se faire souffler dans les bronches

earful ['ɪəfʊl] *n* **to give sb an earful** passer un savon à qn, souffler dans les bronches à qn; **to get an earful** se faire passer un savon, se faire souffler dans les bronches; **get an earful of this!** écoute un peu ça!

early doors ['ɜːlɪ'dɔːz] *adv Br* tôt [□]; **we'll have to get there early doors** il faut qu'on se pointe de bonne heure

earner ['ɜːnə(r)] *n Br* **a nice little earner** une affaire juteuse

earth [ɜːθ] *n* (**a**) *Hum* **did the earth move for you?** (*when having sex*) alors, c'était comment pour toi?; **the earth moved!** c'était divin!

(**b**) *Hum* **earth to Jane, earth to Jane, can you hear me?** allô, Jane, est-ce que tu me reçois?

(**c**) (*for emphasis*) **what/who/why on earth...?** que/qui/pourquoi diable...?; **how on earth should I know?** comment veux-tu que je le sache?; **to look like nothing on earth** ne ressembler à rien; **to feel like nothing on earth** n'être vraiment pas dans son assiette ▶ *voir aussi* **scum**

Dans la catégorie (**b**), il s'agit d'une phrase humoristique dont le style rappelle un dialogue de film de science-fiction. On l'utilise pour attirer l'attention d'un interlocuteur distrait.

---

earwig ['ɪəwɪg] *Br* **1** *vt* écouter de façon indiscrète [□]

2 *vi* écouter aux portes [□]

easy ['iːzɪ] **1** *adj* (**a**) *Br* (*promiscuous*) facile (**b**) **to be on easy street** avoir la belle vie

2 *adv* **to take it** *or* **things easy** ne pas s'en faire; **take it easy!** du calme!, calmos! ▶ *voir aussi* **lay**

eat [iːt] *vt* (**a**) (*worry*) **what's eating you?** qu'est-ce qui te tracasse? (**b**) *Am* **eat it** *or* **me** *or* **shit!** [!] va te faire voir! (**c**) [!!] (*perform cunnilingus on*) brouter le cresson à, sucer (**d**) *Am* **to eat sb's lunch** battre qn à plates coutures

eat out *vt sép* (**a**) [!!] (*perform cunnilingus on*) brouter le cresson à, sucer (**b**) **eat your heart out, Victoria Beckham!** ça va faire des jalouses, n'est-ce pas, Victoria Beckham?

eats [iːts] *npl* bouffe *f*

ecofreak ['iːkəʊfriːk] *n* écolo *mf* radical(e)

ecstasy ['ekstəsɪ] *n* (*drug*) ecstasy *f*

'ed [ed] *adv Br* (*abrév* **ahead**) **go 'ed!** vas-y!; **come 'ed!** allez, viens!

Ce terme s'emploie surtout dans la région de Liverpool.

---

eejit ['iːdʒɪt] *n Ir & Scot* andouille *f*, couillon *m*

eff [ef] *vi Br* **to eff and blind** [!] jurer comme un charretier

eff off [!] *vi* se barrer; **eff off!** va te faire!

effing [!] ['efɪŋ] **1** *n Br* **stop that effing**

The symbol [□] indicates that a translation is neutral in register.

and blinding! arrête de jurer comme un charretier!

2 *adj* fichu, foutu; **the effing telly's on the blink** cette saloperie de télé déconne!

3 *adv* sacrément, vachement; **don't be so effing lazy!** remue-toi, espèce de feignasse!

egg [eg] *n* **a good egg** *(man)* un chic type; *(woman)* une brave femme; **a bad egg** *(man)* un sale type; *(woman)* une sale bonne femme

eggbeater ['egbiːtə(r)] *n Am (helicopter)* hélico *m*

egghead ['eghed] *n Hum ou Péj* intello *mf*

eightball ['eɪtbɔːl] *n Am* **to be behind the eightball** être dans la mouise

Il s'agit à l'origine d'un terme de billard; la boule numéro huit est celle qui doit être jouée en dernier et il est donc très délicat de se retrouver dans une position où l'on risque de toucher cette boule avant la fin de la partie.

eighty-six ['eɪtɪ'sɪks] *Am* **1** *adj* **to be eighty-six on sth** *(in restaurant, bar)* manquer de qch □; **tell the customer we're eighty-six on the chicken** dis au client qu'il n'y a plus de poulet

2 *vt* **(a)** *(eject)* vider **(b)** *(kill)* buter, refroidir

elbow ['elbəʊ] *n* **(a)** *Br* **to give sb the elbow** *(employee)* virer qn; *(boyfriend, girlfriend)* plaquer qn, larguer qn; **to get the elbow** *(of employee)* se faire virer; *(of boyfriend, girlfriend)* se faire plaquer *ou* larguer **(b)** *Hum* **to bend one's elbow** *(drink)* lever le coude ▸ *voir aussi* **arse, ass**

El Cheapo [el'tʃiːpəʊ] *Hum* **1** *n* article *m* bas de gamme □

2 *adj* bas de gamme □; **an El Cheapo restaurant** un resto bon marché; **he**

bought her some El Cheapo engagement ring il lui a acheté une bague de fiançailles en toc

elevator ['elɪveɪtə(r)] *n Hum* **the elevator doesn't go up to the top floor** c'est pas une lumière

eliminate [ɪ'lɪmɪneɪt] *vt (kill)* liquider

enchilada [entʃɪ'lɑːdə] *n* **big enchilada** *(person)* huile *f*; **the whole enchilada** *(everything)* tout le tremblement

end [end] *n* **(a)** *Br* **to get one's end away** tremper son biscuit **(b)** **to go off (at) the deep end** péter les plombs, péter une durite **(c)** *Br* **he doesn't know which end is up** il plane complètement

eppy ['epɪ] *n Br (abrév* **epileptic fit**) **to have an eppy** *(lose one's temper)* péter une durite, péter les plombs

equalizer ['iːkwəlaɪzə(r)] *n Am (handgun)* flingue *m*, feu *m*

Essex ['esɪks] *npr Br Péj* **Essex Girl** minette *f* de l'Essex; **Essex Man** ≃ beauf *m*

Il s'agit de stéréotypes sociaux apparus au cours des années 80. L'"Essex Girl" (originaire de l'Essex, comté situé à l'est de Londres) est censée être une jeune femme d'origine modeste aux mœurs légères, vulgaire, bruyante, et peu intelligente. L'"Essex Man" est lui aussi vulgaire et bruyant; de plus, il est réactionnaire et inculte.

eyeball ['aɪbɔːl] *vt* mater

eyeful ['aɪfʊl] *n* **to get an eyeful (of sb/ sth)** mater (qn/qch); **get an eyeful of that!** mate un peu ça!; **she's quite an eyeful!** elle est vachement bien foutue!

eye-popping ['aɪpɒpɪŋ] *adj Am* sensationnel

Eyetie ['aɪtaɪ] *Injurieux* **1** *n* Rital(e) *m,f*, macaroni *mf*

2 *adj* rital

F

FA [ef'eɪ] *n Br* (*abrév* **Fanny Adams** *or* **fuck all**) **sweet FA** que dalle

fab [fæb] *adj Br* (*abrév* **fabulous**) génial, super

face [feɪs] *n* (**a**) *Br* **to be off one's face** (*drunk*) être pété *ou* bourré; (*on drugs*) être défoncé (**b**) **to have a face like a bag of spanners** *or* **a bulldog chewing a wasp** *or* **the back end of a bus** être laid comme un pou (**c**) **in your face** (*unsubtle*) percutant $^\square$ ▸ *voir aussi* **feed**, **shut**, **waste**

faceache ['feɪseɪk] *n Br* **to be a faceache** (*ugly*) être une mocheté; (*miserable*) toujours faire la gueule

fade [feɪd] *vi Am* (*leave*) s'esbigner, calter

faff [fæf] *Br* **1** *n* **what a faff!** quelle histoire!
2 *vi* **stop faffing and let me do it!** arrête tes conneries et laisse-moi faire!

faff about, **faff around** *vi Br* (**a**) (*waste time*) glander (**b**) (*potter*) s'occuper $^\square$, bricoler

fag [fæg] *n* (**a**) *Br* (*cigarette*) clope *f*; **fag end** mégot $^\square$ *m*, clope *m* (**b**) *Am Injurieux* (*homosexual*) pédale *f*, tapette *f*, tantouze *f*; **fag hag** fille *f* à pédés

> Dans la catégorie (b), ce terme perd son caractère injurieux quand il est utilisé par des homosexuels.

fagged (out) [fægd('aʊt)] *adj Br* lessivé, crevé, naze

faggot ['fægət] *n Am Injurieux* (*homosexual*) pédale *f*, tapette *f*, tantouze *f*

> Quand il est utilisé par des homosexuels, ce terme perd son caractère injurieux.

faggy ['fægɪ] *adj Am Injurieux* qui fait tapette; **that pink shirt makes you look a bit faggy** tu fais un peu tapette avec cette chemise

> Quand il est utilisé par des homosexuels, ce terme perd son caractère injurieux.

fairy ['feərɪ] *n Injurieux* (*homosexual*) tante *f*, pédé *m* ▸ *voir aussi* **away**

fall guy ['fɔːlgaɪ] *n* (*dupe*) pigeon *m*; (*scapegoat*) bouc *m* émissaire $^\square$

fall out [fɔːl] *vi Noir Am* (*fall asleep*) s'endormir $^\square$

family jewels ⚠ ['fæməlɪ'dʒuːəlz] *npl Hum* (*man's genitals*) bijoux *mpl* de famille

fancy ['fænsɪ] **1** *adj* (**a**) *Br* **fancy man** amant $^\square$ *m*; **fancy woman** maîtresse $^\square$ *f* (**b**) *Am* **Fancy Dan** (*dandy*) dandy *m*; (*show-off*) frimeur *m*
2 *vt Br* (**a**) (*be attracted to*) **to fancy sb** en pincer pour qn; **to fancy the pants off sb** en pincer drôlement pour qn; **to fancy the arse off sb** ⚠ trouver qn vachement excitant
(**b**) (*have high opinion of*) **to fancy oneself** se gober
(**c**) (*want*) **do you fancy a drink/going to the cinema?** ça te dirait d'aller boire un coup/d'aller au cinéma?

fancy-dan ['fænsɪ'dæn] *adj Am* frimeur

fanny ['fænɪ] *n* (**a**) ⚠ *Br* (*woman's genitals*) chatte *f*, foufoune *f* (**b**) *Am* (*buttocks*) derrière *m*; **fanny pack** banane *f* (*sac*) ▸ *voir aussi* **magnet**

fanny about ⚠, **fanny around** ⚠ *vi Br* perdre son temps à des bricoles, glander

far-out [fɑːˈraʊt] **1** *adj* (**a**) (*strange*) zarbi; (*avant-garde*) d'avant-garde $^\square$ (**b**) (*excellent*) génial, géant
2 *exclam* super!, génial!

The symbol $^\square$ indicates that a translation is neutral in register.

fart [fɑːt] **1** n pet m, prout m; **a boring old fart** (person) un(e) vieux (vieille) con (conne)

2 vi péter ▸ voir aussi **pissed**

fart about, fart around vi perdre son temps à des bricoles, glander

fartsack ['fɑːtsæk] n Am (bed) pieu m, plumard m; (sleeping bag) sac m à viande

fashion victim ['fæʃənvɪktɪm] n Péj esclave mf de la mode

fast [fɑːst] adj **to pull a fast one on sb** rouler qn

fat [fæt] adj **(a) fat cat** richard(e) m,f; Am **to be in fat city** avoir la belle vie

(b) Ironique (for emphasis) **a fat lot of good that'll do me!** ça me fera une belle jambe!; **you're a fat lot of help!** merci! tu m'aides vachement!; **fat chance!** on peut toujours rêver!

(c) Am **fat farm** clinique f d'amaigrissement □

(d) Noir Am (excellent) super, génial ▸ voir aussi **chew**

fathead ['fæthed] n andouille f, courge f

fatso ['fætsəʊ], **fatty** ['fætɪ] n (man) gros lard m; (woman) grosse dondon f

favour ['feɪvə(r)] n Br **do me a favour!** tu rigoles?; **are you going to buy it? – do me a favour!** tu vas l'acheter? – tu rigoles!

faze [feɪz] vt déconcerter □

features ['fiːtjəs] npl Br **monkey features** Duchnoque; **dick features** [!] Ducon

feck [fek] exclam Ir bordel!, merde!, putain!

Il s'agit d'un euphémisme du terme "fuck".

Fed [fed] n Am **(a) the Feds** (abrév **Federal Government**) = toute agence dépendant du gouvernement fédéral, aux États-Unis **(b) the Fed** (abrév **Federal Reserve Board**) = agence gouvernementale américaine dont le rôle est de réguler le système bancaire **(c)** (abrév **Federal Agent**) agent m du gouvernement fédéral □

federal case ['fedərəl'keɪs] n Am **to make a federal case out of sth** faire toute une histoire de qch

feeb [fiːb] n Am crétin(e) m,f, débile mf

feed [fiːd] **1** n (large meal) gueuleton m

2 vt **to feed one's face** s'en mettre plein la lampe, se goinfrer

feedbag ['fiːdbæg] n Am **to put on the (old) feedbag** bouffer

feel up [fiːl] vt sép **to feel sb up** peloter qn

fella ['felə] n Br (man) mec m, type m; (husband, boyfriend) mec m; **old fella** (penis) zob m

fem [fem] n lesbienne f féminine □

fence [fens] **1** n (person) receleur □ m, fourgueur m

2 vi faire du recel □

fender-bender ['fendəbendə(r)] n Am accrochage □ m

fess up [fes] vi Am (confess) se mettre à table

-fest [fest] suffixe **drinkfest** beuverie f; Br **shagfest** séance f de baise intense

Le suffixe "-fest" dénote l'excès. On l'ajoute à des termes désignant une activité.

fierce [fɪəs] adj (excellent) super, génial, de la balle

fifth wheel ['fɪfθ'wiːl] n Am **to feel like a fifth wheel** tenir la chandelle

figure ['fɪgə(r)] vi Am **go figure!** va comprendre!

filth [fɪlθ] n Br Péj **the filth** (the police) les flics mpl, les poulets mpl

fin [fɪn] n **(a)** Am (five-dollar note) billet m de cinq dollars □ **(b)** Br (five-pound note) billet m de cinq livres □

finagle [fɪ'neɪgəl] vt Am obtenir en magouillant

finger ['fɪŋgə(r)] **1** n **to pull one's finger out** s'enlever les doigts du cul; **to give sb the finger**, Br **to give sb the fingers** faire un doigt d'honneur à qn; **to put the finger on sb** (denounce) balancer qn; (blame) accuser qn □

2 vt **(a)** [!] *(woman)* mettre le doigt dans la chatte de, masturber □ **(b)** *(denounce)* balancer; *(blame)* accuser □

En Grande-Bretagne, on utilise l'expression "to give sb the fingers" au pluriel car ce geste se fait à l'aide de l'index et du majeur.

finger-fuck [!!] ['fɪŋgəfʌk] vt *(woman)* mettre le doigt dans la chatte de

fink [fɪŋk] Am **1** n **(a)** *(informer)* mouchard m **(b)** *(unpleasant person)* blaireau m, enflure f **(c)** *(strikebreaker)* jaune m
2 vi moucharder; **to fink on sb** balancer qn

firewater ['faɪəwɔːtə(r)] n tord-boyaux m

fish [fɪʃ] n **(a)** *(person)* **cold fish** pissefroid mf; **queer fish** drôle d'oiseau m **(b)** **to drink like a fish** boire comme un trou

fist-fuck [!!] ['fɪstfʌk] vt insérer le poing dans l'anus de □, pratiquer le fist-fucking sur

fisticuffs ['fɪstɪkʌfs] n Br bagarre f; **if he finds out, there'll be fisticuffs!** s'il s'en rend compte il va y avoir de la bagarre ou du grabuge

fit [fɪt] **1** n **to have** or **throw a fit** piquer une crise, péter les plombs; Br **to be in fits** se tenir les côtes, hurler de rire; Br **to have sb in fits** faire hurler qn de rire
2 adj Br *(attractive)* bien foutu

fit up vt sép **to fit sb up** monter un coup contre qn; **they fitted him up** il a été victime d'un coup monté

fitba ['fɪtbɔː] n Scot *(football)* foot m

five [faɪv] n **(a)** **to take five** faire un break de cinq minutes **(b)** **gimme five!** tapemoi dans la main! ▸ voir aussi **high-five**

Dans la catégorie (b), il s'agit d'une façon de signifier à quelqu'un que l'on veut lui taper dans la main pour le saluer, le féliciter, ou en signe de victoire.

five-o ['faɪv'əʊ] n **the five-o** *(police)* les flics mpl; **the place was teeming with five-o** ça grouillait de flics

Ce terme trouve son origine dans une série télévisée américaine des années 70 intitulée "Hawaii Five-0" ("Hawaii police d'état" en français).

fiver ['faɪvə(r)] n Br *(sum)* cinq livres □ fpl; *(note)* billet m de cinq livres □

five-spot ['faɪvspɒt] n Am billet m de cinq dollars □

fix [fɪks] **1** n **(a)** *(of drugs)* fix m; **I need my daily fix of chocolate** il me faut ma dose quotidienne de chocolat **(b)** **to be a fix** *(of election, contest)* être truqué
2 vt **(a)** *(rig)* truquer **(b)** *(bribe)* graisser la patte à **(c)** *(get even with)* régler ses comptes avec; **I'll fix him!** il va me le payer!

fixer ['fɪksə(r)] n *(person)* combinard(e) m,f, magouilleur(euse) m,f

fizgig ['fɪzgɪg] n Austr *(informer)* mouchard(e) m,f

flake [fleɪk] n *(person)* allumé(e) m,f

flake out vi s'écrouler de fatigue

flaky ['fleɪkɪ] adj loufoque, loufedingue

flamer ['fleɪmə(r)] n Am enflure f

flaming ['fleɪmɪŋ] Br **1** adj *(for emphasis)* **you flaming idiot!** espèce de crétin!; **he's a flaming pest** c'est un sacré emmerdeur; **flaming hell!** merde alors!
2 adv *(for emphasis)* vachement, super; **it was flaming expensive** c'était vachement cher; **you're flaming well staying here!** tu ne bouges pas d'ici, enfonce-toi bien ça dans la tête!

flap [flæp] **1** n **to be in a flap** être dans tous ses états; **to get in a flap** se mettre dans tous ses états, faire un caca nerveux
2 vi s'exciter, paniquer; **stop flapping!** du calme!, calmos! ▸ voir aussi **jaw**

flash [flæʃ] **1** adj Br *(car, clothes, jewellery)* tape-à-l'œil; *(person)* frimeur; **Flash Harry** frimeur m
2 vt Am *(expose oneself to)* s'exhiber devant □
3 vi *(expose oneself)* s'exhiber □; Br **to flash at sb** s'exhiber devant qn

flash on vt insép **to flash on sth** se remémorer qch □; **I flashed on what had**

The symbol □ indicates that a translation is neutral in register.

happened tout d'un coup j'ai revu tout ce qui s'était passé [□]

flashback ['flæʃbæk] *n* (*hallucination*) flashback *m*, retour *m* d'acide

flasher ['flæʃə(r)] *n* (*man*) exhibitionniste [□] *m*

flatfoot ['flætfʊt] *n Am* (*police officer*) flic *m*, poulet *m*

fleabag ['fliːbæg] *n* (**a**) *Br* (*person*) pouilleux (euse) *m,f*; (*animal*) sac *m* à puces (**b**) *Am* (*hotel*) hôtel *m* borgne

fleapit ['fliːpɪt] *n Br* (*cinema*) = vieux cinéma de quartier mal tenu

fleece [fliːs] *vt* (*overcharge*) écorcher; (*cheat*) arnaquer, plumer

flesh [fleʃ] *n* **to press the flesh** = serrer des mains au cours d'un bain de foule

fling [flɪŋ] **1** *n* (**a**) (*sexual relationship*) aventure [□] *f*, passade [□] *f*; **to have a fling (with sb)** avoir une aventure (avec qn) (**b**) (*period of enjoyment*) bon temps [□] *m*; **to have a final fling** s'éclater une dernière fois

flip [flɪp] **1** *vt* **to flip one's lid** *or Am* **wig** (*get angry*) piquer une crise, péter les plombs; (*go mad*) devenir cinglé, perdre la boule; (*get excited*) devenir dingue

2 *vi* (*get angry*) piquer une crise, péter les plombs; (*go mad*) devenir cinglé, perdre la boule; (*get excited*) devenir dingue ▸ *voir aussi* **bird**

flip out *vi* (*get angry*) piquer une crise, péter les plombs; (*go mad*) devenir cinglé, perdre la boule; (*get excited*) devenir dingue

flipping ['flɪpɪŋ] *Br* **1** *adj* (*for emphasis*) foutu, fichu; **get that flipping dog out of here!** fous-moi cette saleté de clébard dehors!; **flipping heck!** mince alors!

2 *adv* (*for emphasis*) sacrément; **he's so flipping annoying!** ce qu'il peut être embêtant!; **don't flipping well talk to me like that!** t'as intérêt à me parler sur un autre ton!

float about, float around [fləʊt] *vi Br* traîner

floater ['fləʊtə(r)] *n* (**a**) (*dead body*) = cadavre à la surface de l'eau (**b**) (*in toilet*) =

étron qui flotte dans la cuvette des toilettes

flog [flɒg] *vt Br* (**a**) (*sell*) fourguer (**b**) *Hum* **to flog one's log** [**!**] (*masturbate*) se tirer sur l'élastique, se taper sur la colonne

floor [flɔː(r)] **1** *n* **to wipe the floor with sb** (*defeat*) battre qn à plates coutures

2 *vt* (**a**) (*knock down*) foutre par terre (**b**) (*shock*) secouer; (*baffle*) dérouter [□]

floosie, floozie, floozy ['fluːzɪ] *n* pétasse *f*, roulure *f*

flop [flɒp] **1** *n* (**a**) (*failure*) bide *m* (**b**) *Am* (*hotel*) hôtel *m* borgne; (*hostel*) asile *m* de nuit [□]

2 *vi* (**a**) (*fail*) faire un bide (**b**) *Am* (*sleep*) pioncer, roupiller

flophouse ['flɒphaʊs] *n Am* (*hotel*) hôtel *m* borgne; (*hostel*) asile *m* de nuit [□]

fluff [flʌf] *n Br* **a bit of fluff**, *Am* **a fluff** une gonzesse, une nana ▸ *voir aussi* **bum**

fluffer ['flʌfə(r)] *n* = personne dont le rôle est de maintenir l'érection d'un acteur de films pornographiques sur le plateau de tournage

flunk [flʌŋk] *Am* **1** *vt* (*exam*) rater [□], foirer; (*student*) ne pas accorder d'unité de valeur à [□]

2 *vi* (*in exam*) échouer [□], se planter

flunk out *vi Am* se faire virer (*à cause de ses mauvais résultats*)

flush [flʌʃ] *adj* (*rich*) **to be flush** avoir des ronds; **I'm feeling flush so I'll pay** j'ai des ronds, donc c'est moi qui paie

fly [flaɪ] **1** *adj* Noir *Am* (*excellent*) génial, super, géant; (*stylish, attractive*) chouette

2 *vt* **to fly the coop** (*escape*) se faire la belle

3 *vi* **to send sb/sth flying** envoyer qn/qch valser; **to fly off the handle** sortir de ses gonds, piquer une crise ▸ *see also* **kite**

fly-by-night ['flaɪbəmaɪt] **1** *n* (*person*) fumiste *mf*, artiste *m*; (*company*) entreprise *f* pas sérieuse

2 *adj* pas sérieux

fogey ['fəʊgɪ] *n* **old fogey** (*man*) vieux schnock *m*; (*woman*) vieille bique *f*; *Hum*

The symbol [□] indicates that a translation is neutral in register.

young fogey jeune con (conne) *m,f* *(vieux avant l'âge)*

foggy ['fɒgɪ] *adj* **I haven't the foggiest (idea)!** aucune idée!

folding ['fəʊldɪŋ] *n Br* biffetons *mpl*, fafiots *mpl*, talbins *mpl*; **got any folding?** t'as pas des biffetons?

fool about, fool around [fu:l] *vi* (**a**) *(act foolishly)* faire l'idiot; **to fool about with sth** jouer avec qch (**b**) *(waste time)* glander, glandouiller (**c**) *(have affairs)* fricoter (**with** avec) (**d**) *(of couple)* se bécoter

foot [fʊt] *n* **my foot!** mon œil!

footer ['fʊtə(r)], **footie** ['fʊtɪ] *n Br* (*abrév* **football**) foot *m*

footsie ['fʊtsɪ] *n* **to play footsie with sb** faire du pied à qn

footy ['fʊtɪ] *n* (**a**) *Br & Austr (soccer)* foot *m* (**b**) *Austr (rugby union)* rugby *m* à quinze; *(rugby league)* rugby *m* à treize; *(Australian rules football)* football *m* australien

fork out [fɔ:k] **1** *vt sép* allonger

2 *vi* casquer (**for** pour)

foul up [faʊl] **1** *vt sép* **to foul sth up** foirer qch, merder qch

2 *vi* foirer, merder

foul-up ['faʊlʌp] *n* ratage ❑ *m*, foirade *f*

four-eyes ['fɔ:raɪz] *n Péj (term of address)* binoclard(e) *m,f*

fox [fɒks] *n Am (woman)* canon *m*

foxy ['fɒksɪ] *adj (sexually attractive)* sexy

fraidy cat ['freɪdɪkæt] *n Am* poule *f* mouillée

frat [fræt] *n Am* (*abrév* **fraternity**) club *m* d'étudiants ❑; **frat rat** membre *m* d'un club d'étudiants ❑

> Les "fraternities" sont des organisations d'étudiants dont chacune possède ses locaux ("fraternity house") et dont la principale raison d'être est de fournir instantanément à ses membres un cercle d'amis et de connaissances. Les étudiants désireux de faire partie d'une "fraternity" doivent être parrainés par des membres et doivent se soumettre à de nombreuses épreuves souvent aussi stupides qu'humiliantes. Le nom de chaque "fraternity" est composé de trois lettres de l'alphabet grec.

frazzled ['fræzəld] *adj (exhausted)* naze, flagada; *(bothered)* à cran

freak [fri:k] **1** *n* (**a**) *(odd person)* monstre *m* (**b**) *(fan)* **a computer/tennis freak** un fana d'informatique/de tennis

2 *vt (shock, scare)* faire flipper

3 *vi (panic, become scared)* flipper, paniquer; *(become angry)* piquer une crise, péter les plombs ▸ *voir aussi* **Jesus**

freak out 1 *vt sép* **to freak sb out** *(shock, scare)* faire flipper qn

2 *vi* (**a**) *(panic, become scared)* flipper, paniquer; *(become angry)* piquer une crise, péter les plombs (**b**) *(abandon restraint)* s'éclater; **look at him freaking out on the dancefloor!** regarde-le s'éclater sur la piste de danse!

freaking [!] ['fri:kɪŋ] *Am* **1** *adj (for emphasis)* sacré, foutu; **where are those freaking kids?** mais où sont passés ces foutus gamins?; **freaking hell!** putain!

2 *adv (for emphasis)* vachement; **it's freaking cold out there** ça pince vachement dehors; **I don't freaking know!** j'en sais foutre rien!

freak-out ['fri:kaʊt] *n* trip *m*

freaky ['fri:kɪ] *adj (strange)* bizarre ❑, zarbi

freebase ['fri:beɪs] *vi* = chauffer de la cocaïne et en inhaler la fumée

freebie ['fri:bɪ] *n (for customer)* cadeau ❑ *m*; *(perk)* à-côté ❑ *m*; **it was a freebie** je l'ai eu gratos

freeload ['fri:ləʊd] *vi* vivre au crochet des autres

freeloader ['fri:ləʊdə(r)] *n* parasite ❑ *m*

French [frentʃ] **1** *n Hum* **pardon** *or* **excuse my French!** *(after swearing)* passez-moi l'expression!

2 *adj* **French kiss** baiser *m* avec la langue ❑, pelle *f*, patin *m*; **to give sb a French kiss** rouler une pelle *ou* un patin à qn; *Br* **French letter** capote *f* anglaise

L'image stéréotypée que se font les Britanniques et les Américains des Français est celle d'un peuple très porté sur le sexe, aux mœurs exotiques. Ces clichés sont à l'origine de nombreuses expressions argotiques. Il est amusant de noter que les "French letters" des Anglais sont les "capotes anglaises" des Français.

French-kiss [frentʃ'kɪs] **1** *vt* rouler une pelle *ou* un patin à
    2 *vi* se rouler une pelle *ou* un patin

fresh [freʃ] *adj Am* (**a**) *(cheeky)* culotté; **don't get fresh with me, young man!** ne soyez pas insolent, jeune homme! (**b**) *(sexually bold)* déluré ᵁ; **to get fresh with sb** faire des avances à qn ᵁ (**c**) *(excellent)* super, génial

fresher ['freʃə(r)] *n Br* étudiant(e) *m,f* de première année ᵁ

fried [fraɪd] *adj* (**a**) *Am (drunk)* bourré, beurré, pété, poivré; *(on drugs)* raide, parti, défoncé (**b**) *Hum* **fried eggs** *(breasts)* œufs *mpl* sur le plat

frig [!] [frɪg] **1** *exclam* **frig (it)!** merde!
    2 *vt* (**a**) *(have sex with) (of man)* baiser, tringler, troncher; *(of woman)* baiser avec, s'envoyer (**b**) *(masturbate)* branler
    3 *vi (masturbate)* s'astiquer le bouton, se branler

frig about [!], **frig around** [!] *vi (act foolishly)* faire le con, déconner; *(waste time)* glander, glandouiller

frigging [!] ['frɪgɪŋ] **1** *adj (for emphasis)* fichu, foutu; **what a frigging waste of time!** tu parles d'une perte de temps!; **shut your frigging mouth!** ferme-la!, ferme ta gueule!
    2 *adv (for emphasis)* **don't frigging lie to me!** ne me mens pas, bordel!; **I'm frigging freezing!** je me les gèle!

frighteners ['fraɪtnəz] *npl Br* **to put the frighteners on sb** menacer qn ᵁ

Frisco ['frɪskəʊ] *npr Am* = surnom donné à la ville de San Francisco

fritz [frɪts] *n Am* **to be on the fritz** *(of TV, machine)* déconner, débloquer

Frog [frɒg], **Froggy** ['frɒgɪ] *Injurieux* **1** *n* Français(e) ᵁ *m,f,* fransquillon(onne) *m,f*
    2 *adj* français ᵁ; **they've got some Frog footballer playing for them** il y a un joueur français dans leur équipe; **I hate Frog food** j'ai horreur de la cuisine française

C'est la réputation de mangeurs de cuisses de grenouilles des Français qui leur valut ce surnom. Selon le ton et le contexte, ce terme peut être soit injurieux, soit humoristique.

front [frʌnt] **1** *adj Hum* **front bottom** *(vagina)* chatte *f,* minou *m*
    2 *vt Am* (**a**) *(pay in advance)* avancer ᵁ; **the cashier can front you the money** le caissier peut vous faire une avance *ou* vous avancer l'argent (**b**) *(give, lend money to)* **can you front me five bucks?** tu pourrais pas me filer cinq dollars?
    3 *vi Noir Am* (**a**) *(show off)* frimer (**b**) *(tell lies)* baratiner, raconter des craques

frosh [frɒʃ] *n Am* étudiant(e) *m,f* de première année ᵁ

fruit [fruːt] *n Am Injurieux (homosexual)* pédé *m,* tapette *f*

fruitcake ['fruːtkeɪk] *n (person)* dingo *mf,* allumé(e) *m,f* ▶ *voir aussi* **nutty**

fry [fraɪ] *Am* **1** *vt (convict)* faire passer à la chaise électrique ᵁ
    2 *vi (of convict)* passer à la chaise électrique ᵁ; **he oughta fry for that!** il mérite de passer à la chaise électrique!

fuck [!!] [fʌk] **1** *n* (**a**) *(sexual intercourse)* baise *f;* **to have a fuck** baiser, s'envoyer en l'air
    (**b**) *(person)* **to be a good fuck** bien baiser, être un bon coup; **you stupid fuck!** espèce d'enculé!
    (**c**) *(for emphasis)* **who the fuck left the window open?** quel est le con qui a laissé la fenêtre ouverte?; **why the fuck didn't you tell me?** pourquoi est-ce que tu m'as pas prévenu, bordel!; **what the fuck are you doing?** mais qu'est-ce que tu fous, bordel!; **I can't really afford it, but what the fuck!** c'est un peu cher pour moi, mais je m'en fous!; **it costs a**

fuck of a lot of money ça coûte la peau du cul; **it's been a fuck of a long day!** putain, la journée a été longue!; **shut the fuck up!** ferme ta gueule!; Br **get to fuck!** va te faire enculer!; **get the fuck out of here!** fous-moi le camp!, dégage!

(**d**) *(expressing surprise, disbelief)* **for fuck's sake!** merde!, putain!; Br **fuck knows where he is!** j'ai pas la moindre idée d'où il peut être!

(**e**) *(in comparisons)* **as stupid as fuck** con comme la lune; **as boring as fuck** chiant comme la pluie; **he ran like fuck** il a pris ses jambes à son cou

(**f**) **not to give a (flying) fuck (about)** se foutre complètement (de); **who gives a fuck!** tout le monde s'en fout!

(**g**) **can I borrow the car? – like fuck you can** *or* Br **can you fuck!** est-ce que je peux prendre la voiture? – alors ta peux te brosser!; **are you going to apologize? – like fuck I am** *or* Br **am I fuck!** est-ce que tu vas t'excuser? – des clous!

(**h**) **fuck all** que dalle; Br **fuck all money/time** pas un flèche/une minute; **she's done fuck all today** elle a rien foutu de la journée; **she knows fuck all about it** elle y connaît que dalle

2 *exclam* **fuck (it)!** bordel de merde!

3 *vt* (**a**) *(have sex with) (of man)* baiser, tringler, troncher; *(of woman)* baiser avec; **he fucked her brains out** il l'a baisée comme il faut

(**b**) *(for emphasis)* **fuck him!** qu'il aille se faire enculer!; **fuck me!** merde alors!; **fuck you!** va te faire enculer!; Br **go and fuck yourself**, Am **go fuck yourself!** va te faire enculer!

4 *vi* (**a**) *(have sex)* baiser (**b**) **to fuck with sb** jouer au con avec qn; **don't fuck with me!** joue pas au con avec moi!; **to fuck with sb's head** faire tourner quelqu'un en bourrique ▸ *voir aussi* **holy, rabbit**

fuck about ‼, **fuck around** ‼ **1** *vt sép* **to fuck sb about** *(treat badly)* se foutre de la gueule de qn; *(waste time of)* faire perdre son temps à qn ▯

2 *vi* (**a**) *(be promiscuous)* baiser à droite à

gauche (**b**) *(act foolishly)* déconner, faire le con; *(waste time)* glander, glandouiller; **to fuck about with sth** tripoter qch

fuck off ‼ **1** *vt sép* **to fuck sb off** faire chier qn; **to be fucked off (with)** en avoir plein le cul (de)

2 *vi* (**a**) *(leave)* se casser, calter; **fuck off!** *(go away)* casse-toi!; *(expressing contempt, disagreement)* va te faire foutre! (**b**) Am *(waste time, be idle)* glander

fuck over ‼ *vt sép* **to fuck sb over** baiser qn, arnaquer qn

fuck up ‼ **1** *vt sép* (**a**) *(person)* rendre cinglé; *(plan, situation)* faire foirer; **she's totally fucked up** *(psychologically)* elle est complètement à côté de ses pompes; **you've fucked everything up** tu as tout fait foirer *ou* merder (**b**) Am **fucked up** *(drunk)* bourré, beurré, pété, poivré; *(on drugs)* raide, parti, défoncé

2 *vi* merder, foirer

fuckable ‼ ['fʌkəbəl] *adj* baisable

fucked ‼ [fʌkt] *adj* (**a**) *(exhausted)* naze, crevé, lessivé

(**b**) *(broken, not working properly)* foutu; **my leg's fucked** j'ai la jambe qui déconne

(**c**) *(in trouble)* foutu; **if they don't win this game, they're fucked** si ils gagnent pas ce match, ils sont foutus

(**d**) *(for emphasis)* **I'm fucked if I'm going to apologize!** plutôt crever que de m'excuser!; **I'm fucked if I know!** j'en sais foutre rien!

fucker ‼ ['fʌkə(r)] *n* (**a**) *(man)* enculé *m*, enfoiré *m*; *(woman)* connasse *f*; **some fucker's stolen my bike** il y a un enculé qui m'a piqué mon vélo; **you lazy fucker!** espèce de grosse feignasse!; **you stupid fucker!** pauvre con! (**b**) *(thing)* saloperie *f*; **I can't get the fucker to start** j'arrive pas à faire démarrer cette saloperie

fuckfest ‼ ['fʌkfest] *n* séance *f* de baise intense

fuckhead ‼ ['fʌkhed] *n* connard (connasse) *m,f*

fucking ‼ ['fʌkɪŋ] **1** *adj* **fucking hell!** merde alors!, putain!; **where the fucking hell have you been?** où est-ce que t'étais passé, bordel?; **she's here all the**

fucking time! elle est toujours fourrée ici!; **where are my fucking cigarettes?** où sont mes putains de cigarettes?; **he's a fucking bastard!** c'est un véritable enculé!; **you fucking idiot!** espèce de crétin!; *Am* **fucking A!** *(absolutely)* absolument!, tu parles!; *(great)* super!, génial!

2 *adv* **it's fucking freezing!** on se les gèle!; **I'm fucking well going home!** merde! moi je rentre chez moi!; **the film was fucking crap!** c'était de la merde ce film!; **we had a fucking amazing weekend!** on a passé un week-end vraiment génial!; **fucking stop it!** arrête, bordel de merde!; **I don't fucking know!** j'en sais foutre rien!

fuck-me [!!] ['fʌkmiː] *adj* **fuck-me dress** robe *f* affriolante; **fuck-me shoes** chaussures *fpl* de pute

fuck-off [!!] ['fʌkɒf] **1** *n Am (person)* glandeur(euse) *m,f*

2 *adj Br (for emphasis)* mastoc, comac, qui se pose là; **they've got a huge fuck-off house in the country** ils ont une baraque comac à la campagne; **they've got a big fuck-off dog** ils ont un clebs qui se pose là

fuckpad [!!] ['fʌkpæd] *n Br* baisodrome *m*

fuck-up [!!] ['fʌkʌp] *n* **(a)** *(bungle)* ratage *m*, foirade *f*; **to make a fuck-up of sth** foirer qch **(b)** *Am (bungler)* manche *m*; *(misfit)* paumé(e) *m,f*

fuckwad [!!] ['fʌkwɒd] *n Am* connard (connasse) *m,f*

fuckwit [!!] ['fʌkwɪt] *n* connard (connasse) *m,f*

fudge-packer [!!] ['fʌdʒpækə(r)] *n Injurieux* tantouze *f*, pédale *f*, tapette *f*

fugly [!!] ['fʌglɪ] *adj (abrév* **fucking ugly**) hyper moche; **she's really fugly** c'est un vrai boudin *ou* cageot

funky ['fʌŋkɪ] *adj* **(a)** *(fashionable, excellent)* cool **(b)** *Am (smelly)* qui pue, qui schlingue

funny farm ['fʌnɪfɑːm] *n* maison *f* de fous

fur burger [!!] [fɜːˈbɜːgə(r)], **furpie** [!!] [fɜːˈpaɪ] *n (woman's genitals)* tarte *f* aux poils

fuzz [fʌz] *n* **the fuzz** *(the police)* les flics *mpl*, les poulets *mpl*

G

gab [gæb] **1** *n* **to have the gift of the gab** avoir du bagout
2 *vi* jacter, jacasser

gabfest ['gæbfest] *n Am* converse *f*

gaff [gæf] *n* (a) *Br* (home) baraque *f*; **he's staying at my gaff for the weekend** il crèche chez moi ce week-end (b) *Am* **to stand the gaff** encaisser ► *voir aussi* **blow**

gaffer ['gæfə(r)] *n* (boss) patron □ *m*, taulier *m*

gag [gæg] **1** *vt Am Hum* **gag me (with a spoon)!** ça me fout la nausée!
2 *vi Br* **to be gagging for it** [!] avoir envie de se faire tirer

gaga ['gɑːgɑː] *adj* (a) (deranged) toqué, timbré; *Br* (senile) gaga (b) (besotted) **to be gaga about** *or* **over sb** être dingue de qn

gal [gæl] *n Am* nana *f*, gonzesse *f*

gallus ['gæləs] *adj Scot* culotté

game [geɪm] *n Br* (a) **to be on the game** se prostituer □, michetonner (b) **fuck** [!!] *or* **sod** [!] *or* **bugger** [!] **this for a game of soldiers!** bon ça va, j'arrête les frais! ► *voir aussi* **mug, skin**

gander ['gændə(r)] *n* **to have a gander (at sb/sth)** jeter un œil (à qn/qch), mater (qn/qch)

ganga ['gændʒə] *n* herbe *f*

gang-bang ['gæŋbæŋ] **1** *n* = coïts entre une femme et plusieurs hommes à la suite; (rape) viol *m* collectif □
2 *vt* **to gang-bang sb** baiser qn à tour de rôle; (rape) commettre un viol collectif sur qn □

gangsta ['gæŋstə] *n Noir Am* = membre d'un gang de Noirs américains

ganja ['gændʒə] = **ganga**

gannet ['gænət] *n Br* (person) morfal(e) *m,f*

garbage ['gɑːbɪdʒ] **1** *n* (a) (nonsense) âneries *fpl*; **don't talk garbage!** ne dis pas n'importe quoi!; **that's garbage, you never said anything of the sort!** tu racontes n'importe quoi, t'as jamais dit ça!
(b) (worthless things) **their new album is a load of garbage** leur dernier album est vraiment nul; **I've been eating too much garbage lately** je mange trop de cochonneries en ce moment
(c) (useless things) bazar *m*; **chuck out all that garbage of yours** fous-moi tout ton bazar en l'air, balance-moi tout ton bazar

garbo ['gɑːbəʊ] *n Austr* éboueur □ *m*, boueux *m*

gas [gæs] **1** *n* (a) (amusing thing, situation) **what a gas!** quelle rigolade!; **the film was a real gas!** c'était un film vachement marrant!; *Br* **to have a gas** se marrer, s'en payer une tranche (b) (amusing person) **he's a real gas!** c'est un vrai boute-en-train! (c) *Am* **to be out of gas** (exhausted) être crevé *ou* naze
2 *vi* (chat) jacter, jacasser ► *voir aussi* **cook**

gasbag ['gæsbæg] *n* (chatterbox) moulin *m* à paroles; (boaster) fanfaron(onne) *m,f*

gas-guzzler ['gæsgʌzlə(r)] *n* voiture *f* qui bouffe beaucoup d'essence

gash [!!] [gæʃ] *n* (woman's genitals) craquette *f*, fente *f*, cramouille *f*

gasp [gɑːsp] *vi* **to be gasping for a cigarette/a drink** mourir d'envie de fumer une cigarette/de boire un verre

gasper ['gɑːspə(r)] *n Br* clope *f*

gassed [gæst] *adj* (drunk) bourré, pété

The symbol □ indicates that a translation is neutral in register.

gasser ['gæsə(r)] *n Am* **to have a gasser** se marrer, s'en payer une tranche; **what a gasser!** quelle rigolade!; **the film was a real gasser!** c'était un film vachement marrant!

gator ['geɪtə(r)] *n Am* (*abrév* **alligator**) alligator ᵈ *m*

gay [geɪ] *adj* (*stupid*) nul

gay-basher ['geɪbæʃə(r)] *n* = individu qui attaque des homosexuels

gay-bashing ['geɪbæʃɪŋ] *n* = violences contre des homosexuels; **they got arrested for gay-bashing** ils se sont fait arrêter pour avoir attaqué des homosexuels

gay plague ['geɪpleɪg] *n* sida ᵈ *m*

> L'expression signifie littéralement "peste gay". Elle est aujourd'hui politiquement incorrecte, mais désignait le sida dans les années 80, à une époque où l'on pensait que cette maladie n'affectait que les homosexuels.

GBH [dʒiːbiː'eɪtʃ] *n* (*abrév* **grievous bodily harm**) *Br Hum* **to give sb GBH of the earholes** raser qn

GD [dʒiː'diː] *adj Am* (*abrév* **goddamn(ed)**) foutu, sacré; **he's a GD fool** c'est un sacré con

gear [gɪə(r)] *n* (**a**) (*equipment*) matos *m*; (*belongings*) barda *m* (**b**) (*clothes*) fringues *fpl* (**c**) *Br* (*drugs*) dope *f* (**d**) *Am* **to get it in gear** se magner ▶ *see also* **arse, ass**

gee [dʒiː] *exclam Am* **gee (whiz)!** ça alors!

geek [giːk] *n* (**a**) (*strange person*) zarbi(e) *m,f*, allumé(e) *m,f* (**b**) (*misfit*) ringard(e) *m,f*

geeky ['giːkɪ] *adj* ringard, débile

geezer ['giːzə(r)] *n* (**a**) *Br* (*man*) mec *m*, type *m*; (*nice man*) chic type *m*; (*streetwise man*) type *m* débrouillard (**b**) *Am* (*old person*) vioque *mf*

gelt [gelt] *n Am* fric *m*, flouze *m*, pognon *m*

gender-bender ['dʒendəbendə(r)] *n* travesti ᵈ *m*, travelo *m*

Geordie ['dʒɔːdɪ] *n Br* = natif de Newcastle-upon-Tyne ou de ses environs

get [get] **1** *n Br* (*man*) salopard *m*; (*woman*) salope *f*

2 *vt* (**a**) (*annoy*) énerver ᵈ, prendre la tête à; **it really gets me the way he's late for everything** il me gonfle à toujours être en retard

(**b**) (*understand*) comprendre ᵈ, piger; **I get it!** j'ai pigé!

(**c**) **to get it** (*be reprimanded*) se faire passer un savon; (*be beaten up*) prendre une raclée

(**d**) **to get it together** se remuer le cul; (*in one's life*) se prendre en main ᵈ

(**e**) **get you!** (*listen to*) écoute-toi!; (*look at*) regarde-toi!

3 *exclam* (*go away*) casse-toi!, dégage!

get away *exclam* (*expressing disbelief*) tu déconnes! ▶ *voir aussi* **end**

get by *vi* (*manage*) y arriver ᵈ, se démerder

get down 1 *vt sép* **to get sb down** foutre le bourdon à qn

2 *vi* (**a**) (*abandon restraint*) s'éclater; (*dance with abandon*) s'éclater en dansant (**b**) *Am* (*get to work, begin*) s'y mettre, attaquer (**c**) *Am* (*have sex*) s'envoyer en l'air

get off *vi* (**a**) (*reach orgasm*) jouir ᵈ (**b**) **to tell sb where to get off** envoyer balader qn; *Br Hum* **to get off at Edge Hill** or **Gateshead** or **Haymarket** or **Paisley** = pratiquer le coït interrompu

> Cette expression humoristique joue sur la métaphore du voyageur descendant du train à la station qui précède la gare principale. Il est donc possible d'adapter l'expression en fonction de l'endroit où l'on habite. Edge Hill, Gateshead, Haymarket et Paisley sont des gares qui se trouvent respectivement à Liverpool, Newcastle, Édimbourg et Glasgow.

get off on *vt insép* **to get off on sth** prendre son pied avec qch; **to get off on doing sth** prendre son pied à faire qch

get off with *vt insép* **to get off with sb** faire une touche avec qn

get on *vt sép* (**a**) **to get it on (with)** (*have sex*) s'envoyer en l'air (avec); *Am* (*fight*) se friter (avec) (**b**) *Am* **to get it**

on (get started, get busy) s'y mettre

get to vt insép **to get to sb** déprimer qn □, foutre le bourdon à qn; **don't let it get to you** il faut pas que ça te sape le moral

get up [!] vt sép **to get it up** bander; **he couldn't get it up** il a pas réussi à bander ▶ voir aussi **nose**

get up to vt insép se livrer à □; **what have you been getting up to?** qu'est-ce que tu deviens?

get-go ['getgəʊ] n Noir Am **from the get-go** (from the beginning) dès le début □; **he's a crook from the get-go** (completely) c'est un escroc total, c'est un véritable escroc

get-together ['gettəgeðə(r)] n réunion f entre amis □

get-up ['getʌp] n accoutrement m

ghetto blaster ['getəʊblɑːstə(r)] n gros radio-cassette m portable □, ghetto blaster m

gig [gɪg] n (a) (concert) concert □ m, gig m (b) (job) boulot m

gimme ['gɪmɪ] contraction (abrév **give me**) donne-moi □; Am **the gimmes** la cupidité □ ▶ voir aussi **five**

ginger[1] ['dʒɪndʒə(r)] n Br rouquin(e) m,f

ginger[2] ['dʒɪndʒə(r)] n Scot = boisson gazeuse

ginormous [dʒaɪˈnɔːməs, Am dʒɪˈnɔːməs] adj énorme □, mastoc

girlfriend ['gɜːlfrend] n Am (term of address) = terme utilisé par les Américaines pour s'adresser les unes aux autres; **yo, girlfriend!** salut frangine!

À l'origine, ce terme n'était utilisé que par les Noires américaines. Aujourd' hui, son usage s'est généralisé.

girlie ['gɜːlɪ] n fille □ f, nana f; **girlie mag** revue f porno; Br **to have a girlie chat** bavarder entre filles □; **she's out seeing some girlie film with her mates** elle est allée voir un film pour les gonzesses avec ses copines

gism ['dʒɪzəm] = **jism (a)**

git [gɪt] n (man) conard m; (woman) conasse f; **you clumsy git!** espèce de manche!

give [gɪv] vi Am **what gives?** quoi de neuf? ▶ voir aussi **one**

give over Br **1** vt insép **give over shouting!** arrête de gueuler comme ça! **2** vi arrêter □

gizmo ['gɪzməʊ] n truc m, bidule m

glaikit ['gleɪkɪt] adj Scot (stupid, vacant) débile

Glasgow ['glɑːzgəʊ] n **Glasgow kiss** coup m de boule; **Glasgow handshake** marron m, patate f

En Grande-Bretagne, Glasgow a la réputation d'être une ville violente.

glitterati [glɪtəˈrɑːtɪ] npl **the glitterati** le beau monde

glitz [glɪts] n clinquant m, tape-à-l'œil m

glitzy ['glɪtsɪ] adj tape-à-l'œil

globes [gləʊbz] npl (breasts) nichons mpl, nénés mpl; **check out the globes on that!** mate un peu les nichons!

glom [glɒm] vt Am (seize) arracher □

glom onto vt insép Am (a) (seize) arracher □ (b) (catch sight of) apercevoir □

G-man ['dʒiːmæn] n Am agent m du FBI □

gnarly ['nɑːlɪ] adj Am (excellent, awful) mortel

gnat [næt] n Br **gnat's piss** [!] (drink) eau f de vaisselle, pipi m de chat

go [gəʊ] vt (a) (say) dire; **so she goes "you're lying!" and I go "no, I'm not!"** alors elle me fait "tu mens!" et je lui fais "non, je mens pas!" (b) **I could really go a beer/ciggy/pizza** je me taperais bien une bière/une clope/une pizza ▶ voir aussi **way**

go down vi (a) (go to prison) aller en taule; **he went down for ten years** il en a pris pour dix ans (b) Br (be received) **to go down like a ton of bricks** or **a lead balloon** faire un bide total, se casser la gueule (c) Am (fall) **to go down like a ton of bricks** se casser la gueule (d) (happen) se passer □, avoir lieu □; **what's going down?** quoi de neuf?

The symbol □ indicates that a translation is neutral in register.

go down on ⚠ *vt insép* **to go down on sb** *(fellate)* sucer qn, tailler une pipe à qn; *(perform cunnilingus on)* sucer qn, brouter le cresson à qn

go for *vt insép* **go for it!** vas-y!

go off *vi Br* **to go off on one** se mettre en pétard, voir rouge

go over *vi Am (be received)* **to go over like a ton of bricks** *or* **a lead balloon** faire un bide total, se casser la gueule

go under *vi (of company)* se casser la gueule

go with *vt insép* **(a)** *(be romantically involved with)* sortir avec □ **(b) to go with the flow** suivre le mouvement □

goat [gəʊt] *n* **(a)** *Br* **to act the goat** *(act foolishly)* faire l'imbécile, déconner **(b) to get sb's goat** *(annoy)* irriter qn □, prendre la tête à qn **(c)** *Péj* **old goat** *(lecherous man)* vieux *m* cochon; *Am (old man)* vieux schnock *m*; *(old woman)* vieille toupie *f*

gob [gɒb] *Br* **1** *n (mouth)* gueule *f*; **shut your gob!** ferme ta gueule!; **to give sb a gob job** ⚠ tailler *ou* faire une pipe à qn **2** *vi (spit)* mollarder **(at/on** vers/sur)

gobble ⚠ ['gɒbəl] *vt (fellate)* sucer, tailler une pipe à

gobbledygook ['gɒbəldɪguːk] *n* **(a)** *(jargon)* charabia *m* **(b)** *(nonsense)* conneries *fpl*

gobby ['gɒbɪ] *adj Br* **to be gobby** être une grande gueule

gobshite ⚠ ['gɒbʃaɪt] *n Br (man)* trouduc *m*; *(woman)* connasse *f*

gobsmacked ['gɒbsmækt] *adj Br* estomaqué

God [gɒd] *n* **(my) God!** mon Dieu!; **for God's sake!** bon Dieu!; **God knows** va savoir; **what in God's name are you doing?** mais qu'est-ce que tu es en train de faire?; **he thinks he's God's gift (to women)** il s'imagine que toutes les femmes sont folles de lui; **the God squad** les culs bénis

godawful ['gɒdɔːfəl] *adj* dégueulasse, nul

goddammit ⚠ [gɒd'dæmɪt] *exclam* bordel!

goddamn ⚠ ['gɒd'dæm], **god-damned** ⚠ ['gɒd'dæmd] **1** *adj* foutu, fichu; **he's a goddamn** *or* **goddamned fool!** c'est un pauvre con!

2 *adv* vachement; **that was goddamn** *or* **goddamned stupid!** c'est vraiment pas malin!

3 *exclam* **goddamn (it)!** bordel!

goer ['gəʊə(r)] *n Br (woman)* **she's a bit of a goer** elle couche à droite à gauche

gofer ['gəʊfə(r)] *n* larbin *m*

> Le terme "gofer" est une altération des termes "go for" qui signifie "aller chercher", ce qui résume le genre de tâches confiées aux employés subalternes.

goldbrick ['gəʊldbrɪk] *Am* **1** *n (malingerer)* tire-au-flanc *m*
2 *vi (malinger)* tirer au flanc

gold-digger ['gəʊld'dɪgə(r)] *n Péj (woman)* croqueuse *f* de diamants

golden showers ⚠ ['gəʊldən'ʃaʊəz] *npl* uro *f*, = pratique sexuelle qui consiste à uriner sur son ou sa partenaire

golly ['gɒlɪ] *exclam* bon Dieu!

gone [gɒn] *adj* **(a) to be gone on sb** être dingue de qn **(b) to be well gone** *(drunk)* être beurré *ou* bourré *ou* pété

goner ['gɒnə(r)] *n* **to be a goner** être foutu

gong [gɒŋ] *n (medal)* médaille □ *f*, breloque *f*; *(prize)* prix □ *m*, récompense □ *f*

gonna ['gənə] *contraction (abrév* **going to)** **I'm gonna kill him!** je vais le buter!

> Cette contraction n'est utilisée que pour exprimer le futur proche.

gonzo ['gɒnzəʊ] *adj Am* dingue, dément

goober ['guːbə(r)] *n Am* crétin(e) *m,f*, andouille *f*, tache *f*

goods [gʊdz] *npl Am* **to have the goods on sb** avoir la preuve de la culpabilité de qn □

goof [guːf] *Am* **1** *n* **(a)** *(person)* crétin(e) *m,f*, andouille *f*, tache *f* **(b)** *(mistake)* boulette *f*, bourde *f*
2 *vi* **(a)** *(make mistake)* faire une boulette

---

ou une bourde (**b**) *(joke)* rigoler; **to goof with sb** *(tease)* faire enrager qn (**c**) *(stare)* **to goof at sb/sth** regarder qn/qch bêtement [□]

goof about, goof around *vi Am* (**a**) *(act foolishly)* faire le con, déconner (**b**) *(waste time)* glander, glandouiller

goof off *Am* **1** *vt insép* **to goof off school** sécher l'école; **to goof off work** ne pas aller bosser
2 *vi* glander, glandouiller

goof up *Am* **1** *vt sép* **to goof sth up** foirer qch, merder qch
2 *vi* foirer, merder

goofball ['gu:fbɔːl] *n Am* (**a**) *(person)* crétin(e) *m,f*, andouille *f*, tache *f* (**b**) *(barbiturate)* mélange *m* de barbituriques et d'amphétamines [□]

goofy ['gu:fɪ] *adj* (**a**) *(stupid)* débile, abruti (**b**) *Br* **to have goofy teeth** avoir les dents qui courent après le biftek

gook [gu:k] *n Am Injurieux* bridé(e) *m,f*

goolies [!] ['gu:lɪz] *npl Br* couilles *fpl*, valseuses *fpl*

goon [gu:n] *n* (**a**) *(idiot)* andouille *f*, cruche *f*, courge *f* (**b**) *(hired thug)* gorille *m*

goose [gu:s] *vt* **to goose sb** mettre la main au cul à qn

gooseberry ['gʊzbərɪ] *n Br* **to play gooseberry** tenir la chandelle

gorblimey [gɔː'blaɪmɪ] *exclam Br* nom de Dieu!, merde alors!

Gordon Bennett ['gɔːdən'benɪt] *exclam Br* nom d'une pipe!

Il s'agit d'un euphémisme du mot "God" utilisé comme juron. Gordon Bennett était un journaliste américain du 19ème siècle haut en couleurs.

gorilla [gə'rɪlə] *n Péj (man)* grosse brute *f*

gosh [gɒʃ] *exclam* la vache!

goss [gɒs] *n Br (abrév* **gossip***)* cancans *mpl*, potins *mpl*; **what's the goss?** quels sont les derniers potins?

gotcha ['gɒtʃə] *exclam (abrév* **I got you***)* *(I understand)* je comprends, d'accord; *(when catching hold of someone)* pris!;

(when catching someone doing something) je t'y prends!; *(when one has an advantage over someone)* je te tiens!

gotta ['gɒtə] *contraction* (**a**) *(abrév* **got to***)* **I('ve) gotta go** (il) faut que j'y aille; **it's gotta be done** il faut que ce soit fait [□] (**b**) *(abrév* **got a***)* **he's gotta new girlfriend** il a une nouvelle copine

grand [grænd] *n (thousand pounds)* mille livres [□] *fpl*; *(thousand dollars)* mille dollars [□] *mpl*

grapes [greɪps] *npl (haemorrhoids)* hémorroïdes [□] *fpl*, émeraudes *fpl*

grass [grɑːs] **1** *n* (**a**) *(marijuana)* herbe *f* (**b**) *Br (informer)* mouchard *m*, balance *f*
2 *vi Br (inform)* moucharder; **to grass on sb** balancer qn, moucharder qn

grass up *vt sép* **to grass sb up** balancer qn, moucharder qn

gravy ['greɪvɪ] *n Am (easy money)* argent *m* facile [□]; **to get on the gravy train** profiter d'un filon

greased lightning [griːst'laɪtnɪŋ] *n* **like greased lightning** à tout berzingue, à fond la caisse

greaser ['griːsə(r)] *n* (**a**) *(biker)* motard *m* (**b**) *Am Injurieux (Latin American)* métèque *mf (d'origine latino-américaine)*

greasy spoon [griːsɪ'spuːn] *n (café)* boui-boui *m*

greedy-guts ['griːdɪgʌts] *n* morfal(e) *m,f*

green [griːn] *n Am (money)* fric *m*, flouze *m*, blé *m*; **let's see your green** aboule ton fric

greenback ['griːnbæk] *n Am* fafiot *m*

greenhorn ['griːnhɔːn] *n* bleu *m*

green-welly [griːn'welɪ] *adj Br Hum* **the green-welly brigade** la grande bourgeoisie rurale

Le terme "green welly" signifie littéralement "botte de caoutchouc verte". Par métonymie, il désigne les aristocrates et les grands bourgeois vivant à la campagne, que l'on voit souvent chaussés de bottes de caoutchouc vertes et vêtus de vestes de chasse.

The symbol [□] indicates that a translation is neutral in register.

greeny ['gri:nɪ] n Br (**a**) (phlegm) mollard m (**b**) (nasal mucus) morve f

grief [gri:f] n (trouble, inconvenience) embêtements mpl; **to give sb grief** embêter qn; **I'm getting a lot of grief from my parents** mes parents n'arrêtent pas de m'embêter ou de me prendre la tête

grifter ['grɪftə(r)] n Am escroc ▫ m, arnaqueur m

grill [grɪl] vt (interrogate) cuisiner

grip [grɪp] n **to get a grip** se ressaisir ▫; **get a grip!** ressaisis-toi!, assure!

grody ['grəʊdɪ] adj Am dégueulasse; **grody to the max** franchement dégueulasse

grogshop ['grɒgʃɒp] n Austr magasin m de vins et spiritueux ▫

groovy ['gru:vɪ] **1** adj bath, super
2 exclam super!, cool!

gross [grəʊs] adj (disgusting) dégueulasse

gross out vt sép **to gross sb out** répugner qn ▫, dégoûter qn ▫, débecter qn

gross-out ['grəʊsaʊt] n Am = chose ou situation répugnante; **what a gross-out!** c'est vraiment dégueulasse!

grot [grɒt] n Br crasse ▫ f

grotty ['grɒtɪ] adj dégueulasse, dégueu

groupie ['gru:pɪ] n groupie f

growler [!!] ['graʊlə(r)] n Br (woman's genitals) cramouille f, craque f

grub [grʌb] n (food) bouffe f; **grub's up!** à la soupe!

grungy ['grʌndʒɪ] adj Am (dirty) dégueulasse, dégueu

grunt [grʌnt] n Am (soldier) bidasse m

guff [gʌf] **1** n (**a**) (nonsense) âneries fpl; **don't talk guff!** ne dis pas d'âneries!;

the film was a load of guff le film était vraiment débile fpl (**b**) (fart) pet m, prout m
2 vi péter, larguer une caisse, lâcher une perle; **who just guffed?** qui est-ce qui vient de larguer une caisse?

guinea ['gɪnɪ] n Am Injurieux (Italian) Rital(e) m,f, macaroni mf

gunk [gʌŋk] n saloperie f (substance)

gutless ['gʌtlɪs] adj **to be gutless** ne rien avoir dans le bide; **a gutless performance** une prestation sans intérêt ▫

gutrot ['gʌtrɒt] n (**a**) (drink) tord-boyaux m (**b**) (stomach upset) mal m de bide

guts [gʌts] npl (**a**) (insides) **to hate sb's guts** ne pas pouvoir blairer qn; **to work one's guts out** travailler comme un nègre (**b**) (courage) cran m; **to have guts** en avoir dans le bide, avoir du cran; **to have the guts to do sth** avoir le cran de faire qch ► voir aussi **spew, spill**

gutsy ['gʌtsɪ] adj (**a**) (courageous) **to be gutsy** en avoir dans le bide, avoir du cran (**b**) (greedy) morfal

gutted ['gʌtɪd] adj Br (disappointed) dégoûté, hyper déçu

guttered ['gʌtəd] adj Br (drunk) bourré, pété, beurré, poivré

guv [gʌv], **guvnor** ['gʌvnə(r)] n Br (**a**) (boss) **the guv** or **guvnor** le patron, le chef (**b**) (term of address) chef m, patron m

guy [gaɪ] n (**a**) (man) mec m, type m (**b**) (person) **hi, guys!** salut!; **what are you guys doing tonight?** qu'est-ce vous faites ce soir? ► voir aussi **tough**

gyp [dʒɪp] **1** n (**a**) Br (pain) **to give sb gyp** faire déguster qn (**b**) Am (swindler) escroc ▫ m, arnaqueur m
2 vt Am (swindle) arnaquer

H

H [eɪtʃ] *n* (*abrév* **heroin**) blanche *f*, héro *f*

habit ['hæbɪt] *n* (*drug addiction*) accoutumance □ *f*; **to have a drug habit** être toxico; **to have a coke/smack habit** être accro à la coke/à l'héro; **to kick the habit** décrocher

hack [hæk] **1** *n* (**a**) *Péj* (*writer*) pisse-copie *mf* (**b**) *Am* (*taxi*) taxi □ *m*, tacot *m*; (*taxi driver*) chauffeur *m* de taxi □

2 *vt* (*cope with*) **he can't hack the pace** il n'arrive pas à tenir le rythme; **he can't hack it** il s'en sort pas

hack off *vt sép* **to hack sb off** prendre la tête à qn; **to be hacked off (with)** en avoir marre (de)

hackette [hæ'ket] *n Br Péj* pisse-copie *f*

hag [hæg] *n* (*ugly woman*) (**old**) **hag** vieille peau *f* ▸ *voir aussi* **fag**

hair [heə(r)] *n* **to get in sb's hair** taper sur les nerfs à qn; **to let one's hair down** se laisser aller; **keep your hair on!** du calme!, calmos!; *Hum* **this'll put hairs on your chest** tiens, bois/mange ça, c'est bon pour la santé!; **I need a hair of the dog (that bit me)** j'ai besoin d'un verre pour soigner ma gueule de bois

hairpie ‼ [heə'paɪ] *n* (*woman's genitals*) tarte *f* aux poils

half [hɑːf] **1** *n* (**a**) **a party/day/hangover and a half** une sacrée nouba/journée/gueule de bois (**b**) **my other** *or* **better half** ma moitié

2 *adv Br* (*for emphasis*) **you don't half talk rubbish** tu racontes vraiment n'importe quoi; **it's not half bad** c'est pas mal du tout; **he hasn't half changed** il a vachement changé; **not half!** et comment!

half-arsed ‼ [hɑːf'ɑːst], *Am* **half-assed** ‼ [hɑːf'æst] *adj* foireux

half-cut [hɑːf'kʌt] *adj Br* (*drunk*) bourré, pété, fait

half-inch [hɑːf'ɪntʃ] *vt Br* (*rhyming slang* **pinch**) piquer, faucher, chouraver; **he got his wallet half-inched** il s'est fait piquer son portefeuille

halfwit ['hɑːfwɪt] *n* abruti(e) *m,f*, débile *mf*

halfwitted [hɑːf'wɪtɪd] *adj* abruti, débile

ham-fisted [hæm'fɪstɪd] *adj* maladroit □, manche

hammer ['hæmə(r)] **1** *n Am* **to let the hammer down** appuyer sur le champignon, mettre les gaz

2 *vt* (**a**) (*beat up*) tabasser (**b**) (*defeat*) écraser, battre à plates coutures (**c**) (*criticize*) éreinter, démolir

hammered ['hæməd] *adj* (*drunk*) bourré, beurré, pété, fait

hammering ['hæmərɪŋ] *n* (**a**) (*beating*) **to give sb a hammering** tabasser qn; **to get a hammering** se faire tabasser
(**b**) (*defeat*) branlée *f*, pâtée *f*; **to give sb a hammering** battre qn à plates coutures, foutre la pâtée à qn; **to get a hammering** être battu à plates coutures
(**c**) (*criticism*) **to give sb/sth a hammering** éreinter *ou* démolir qn/qch; **to get a hammering** se faire éreinter *ou* démolir

hand-job ‼ ['hændʒɒb] *n* **to give sb a hand-job** branler qn

hand shandy ‼ [hænd'ʃændɪ] *n Br Hum* **to have a hand shandy** se branler, faire cinq contre un; **to give sb a hand shandy** branler qn

handsome ['hændsəm] *exclam Br* super!, génial!

hang [hæŋ] **1** *vt Am* **to hang a left/a right** tourner à gauche/à droite □

---

2 *vi* (**a**) *Am (spend time)* traîner; **he's hanging with his friends** il traîne avec ses copains; **what are you up to? – just hanging** qu'est-ce que tu fais? – oh, rien de spécial

(**b**) **how's it hanging?** *(how are you?)* comment ça va?

(**c**) *Am* **to hang loose** rester cool; **hang loose!** détends-toi!, cool!; **to hang tough** s'accrocher

hang about, hang around *vi* (**a**) *(spend time)* traîner; **who does she hang about** or **around with?** avec qui est-ce qu'elle sort? (**b**) *(wait)* poireauter; **to keep sb hanging about** or **around** faire poireauter qn; **hang about, that's not what I meant!** attends voir, c'est pas ce que je voulais dire!

hang in *vi* **to hang in there** tenir bon, tenir le coup; **hang in there!** tiens bon!

hang on *vt sép* **to hang one on** *(get drunk)* prendre une cuite

hang out *vi* (**a**) *(spend time)* traîner; **he hangs out at the local bar** c'est un habitué du café du coin; **who's that guy she hangs out with?** c'est qui ce mec avec qui elle sort? (**b**) **to let it all hang out** être relax

hang up *vt sép* (**a**) **to be hung up on sb/sth** *(obsessed)* être obsédé par qn/qch □ (**b**) *Am* **to hang it up** *(stop)* laisser tomber

hang-out ['hæŋaʊt] *n* **that bar's my favourite hang-out** c'est le bar où je vais d'habitude □; **it's a real student hang-out** c'est un endroit très fréquenté par les étudiants □

hang-up ['hæŋʌp] *n* complexe □ *m*; **she's got a real hang-up about her weight** elle fait un complexe sur son poids

Hank Marvin [hæŋk'mɑːvɪn] *adj Br (rhyming slang* **starving**) **I'm Hank Marvin** j'ai la dalle, j'ai les crocs

Hank Marvin est un guitariste britannique, membre fondateur des Shadows.

hanky-panky ['hæŋkɪ'pæŋkɪ] *n (sexual activity)* galipettes *fpl*; *(underhand behaviour)* coups *mpl* fourrés

happening ['hæpənɪŋ] *adj* branché, dans le coup

happy ['hæpɪ] *adj Hum* **he's not a happy camper** or *Br* **chappy** or **bunny** il est pas jouasse; **to be happy as a pig in clover** or **shit** ! être heureux comme un poisson dans l'eau □, se la couler douce

happy-clappy ['hæpɪ'klæpɪ] *Br Hum Péj* **1** *adj* = agaçant de par sa joie exubérante *(appliqué aux Chrétiens évangéliques)*; **I hate him and his happy-clappy friends** je le déteste lui et ses copains, ces grenouilles de bénitier avec leur sourire béat

2 *n* chrétien(enne) *m,f* évangélique □

hard-ass ! ['hɑːdæs] *n Am (person)* dur(e) *m,f* à cuire

hard-on ! ['hɑːdɒn] *n* **to have a hard-on** bander; **to get a hard-on** se mettre à bander

hard-up [hɑːd'ʌp] *adj* fauché, raide, sans un

hash [hæʃ] *n* (**a**) *(abrév* **hashish**) hasch *m* (**b**) *(mess)* **to make a hash of sth** saloper qch

hassle ['hæsəl] **1** *n (trouble, inconvenience)* embêtements *mpl*; **to give sb hassle** harceler qn □; **it's too much hassle** c'est trop de tintouin, c'est trop galère; **moving house is such a hassle** c'est vraiment galère de déménager

2 *vt* **to hassle sb** harceler qn □; **to hassle sb into doing sth** harceler qn jusqu'à ce qu'il fasse qch □

hatchet ['hætʃɪt] *n* (**a**) **hatchet job** très mauvaise critique □ *f*; **to do a hatchet job on sb/sth** éreinter *ou* démolir qn/qch (**b**) **hatchet man** *(hired killer)* tueur *m* à gages □; *(in industry, politics)* = personne dont le rôle est de restructurer une entreprise ou une organisation, le plus souvent à l'aide de mesures impopulaires

hatstand ['hætstænd] *adj Br (mad)* toqué, timbré, cinglé

have [hæv] *vt* (**a**) **to have had it** *(be ruined, in trouble)* être foutu; *Am (be* *exhausted)* être crevé *ou* naze *ou* lessivé; **to have had it up to here (with)** en avoir marre (de), avoir eu sa dose (de); **to let sb have it** *(physically)* casser la gueule à qn; *(verbally)* souffler dans les bronches à qn; **I tried to convince her but she wasn't having any of it** j'ai essayé de la convaincre, mais elle n'a pas voulu en entendre parler; **he had it coming** il l'a cherché

(b) *(beat up)* casser la gueule à; **I could have you!** si tu me cherches tu vas te trouver!

(c) *(cheat)* **to be had** se faire avoir

(d) ⚠ *(have sex with) (of man)* baiser, s'envoyer; *(of woman)* baiser avec, s'envoyer

have away *vt sép* **to have it away (with sb)** ⚠ s'envoyer en l'air (avec qn)

have in *vt sép* **to have it in for sb** avoir qn dans le nez

have off *vt sép* **to have it off (with sb)** ⚠ s'envoyer en l'air (avec qn)

have on *vt sép* **to have sb on** faire marcher qn

hay [heɪ] *n* **to hit the hay** *(go to bed)* se pieuter, se bâcher

hayseed ['heɪsiːd] *n Am & Austr* bouseux(euse) *m,f*, péquenaud(e) *m,f*

head [hed] *n* **(a)** **to get one's head together** se mettre en train □; **to laugh one's head off** être mort de rire; **to shout one's head off** gueuler comme un sourd; *Br* **to do sb's head in** prendre la tête à qn; *Br* **go and boil your head!** va te faire cuire un œuf!

(b) *Br* **to be off one's head** *(mad)* être cinglé *ou* toqué; **to be out of one's head** *(mad)* être cinglé *ou* toqué; *(drunk)* être bourré *ou* beurré *ou* pété; *(on drugs)* être défoncé *ou* parti

(c) **to give sb head** ⚠ sucer qn ▶ *voir aussi* **hole, honcho, knock, lose, rush, upside**

-head [hed] *suffixe* **she's a bit of a whiskyhead** elle a un faible pour le whisky; **he's a real jazzhead** c'est un vrai fana de jazz

Le suffixe "-head" dénote l'enthousiasme de quelqu'un pour une activité ou une substance.

headbanger ['hedbæŋə(r)] *n* **(a)** *(heavy metal fan)* hardeux(euse) *m,f* **(b)** *Br (mad person)* cinglé(e) *m,f*, toqué(e) *m,f*

headcase ['hedkeɪs] *n* cinglé(e) *m,f*, toqué(e) *m,f*

header ['hedə(r)] *n Ir* cinglé(e) *m,f*, toqué(e) *m,f*

headfuck ⚠ ['hedfʌk] *n* **(a)** *(man)* mec *m* pas net; *(woman)* nana *f* pas nette **(b)** *(thing, experience)* épreuve □ *f*; **this movie is a bit of a headfuck** c'est un peu le bad trip, ce film

headshrinker ['hedʃrɪŋkə(r)] *n Am* psy *mf*

heap [hiːp] *n (car)* poubelle *f*

heaps [hiːps] *Br* **1** *npl (a lot)* **I've got heaps to do** j'ai un tas de trucs à faire; **heaps of time/money** vachement de temps/d'argent
2 *adv* **I like him heaps** je l'aime vachement

heart-throb ['hɑːtθrɒb] *n* idole *f*

heat [hiːt] *n Am* **the heat** les flics *mpl*

heave [hiːv] **1** *n* **to give sb the heave** *(employee)* virer qn, sacquer qn; *(boyfriend, girlfriend)* plaquer qn, larguer qn; **to get the heave** *(of employee)* se faire virer *ou* sacquer; *(of boyfriend, girlfriend)* se faire plaquer *ou* larguer
2 *vi (retch)* avoir un haut-le-cœur □; *(vomit)* gerber, dégueuler, dégobiller

heave-ho [hiːv'həʊ] *n* **to give sb the (old) heave-ho** *(employee)* virer qn, sacquer qn; *(boyfriend, girlfriend)* plaquer qn, larguer qn; **to get the (old) heave-ho** *(of employee)* se faire virer *ou* sacquer; *(of boyfriend, girlfriend)* se faire plaquer *ou* larguer

heaving ['hiːvɪŋ] *adj Br (extremely busy)* hyper animé

heavy ['hevɪ] **1** *n (man)* balaise *m*, grosse brute *f*
2 *adj* **(a)** *(frightening, troublesome)* craignos; **to get heavy with sb** devenir

agressif avec qn □; **things started to get a bit heavy** ça a commencé à craindre **(b)** *(profound, affecting)* profond □; **to get heavy with sb** prendre la tête à qn

hebe [hiːb] *n Am Injurieux* youpin(e) *m,f*; youtre *mf*

heck [hek] **1** *n* **who the heck said you could borrow my car?** bon sang! qui t'a dit que tu pouvais prendre ma voiture?; **why the heck didn't you tell me?** pourquoi est-ce que tu m'as pas prévenu, nom de nom!; **what the heck are you doing?** mais qu'est-ce que tu fous, nom de nom!; **there were a heck of a lot of people there** il y avait un maximum de monde; **he misses her a heck of a lot** elle lui manque vachement; **I can't afford it, but what the heck!** c'est un peu cher pour moi mais je m'en fous!; **to do sth just for the heck of it** faire qch juste pour le plaisir
2 *exclam* mince alors!

heebie-jeebies [ˈhiːbɪˈdʒiːbɪz] *npl* **to have the heebie-jeebies** avoir la trouille *ou* les chocottes; **to give sb the heebie-jeebies** *(scare)* foutre la trouille à qn; *(repulse)* débecter qn

heel [hiːl] *n (person)* chameau *m*

heifer [ˈhefə(r)] *n* **(a)** *Péj (fat woman)* grosse dondon *f* **(b)** *Am (attractive woman)* canon *m*

Heinz [haɪnz] *n Hum (dog)* bâtard □ *m*

C'est parce que la marque Heinz se vantait jadis d'offrir une gamme de 57 variétés de produits différents que l'on gratifie parfois un chien bâtard de cette appellation. Le sous-entendu est que l'animal est issu d'un nombre comparable de variétés canines.

heist [haɪst] **1** *n Am (robbery)* cambriolage □ *m*; *(hold-up)* braquage *m*, casse *m*
2 *vt (money)* rafler; *(bank)* braquer

hell [hel] **1** *n* **(a)** **the boyfriend/flatmate/neighbours from hell** un petit ami/un colocataire/des voisins de cauchemar; **to give sb hell** engueuler qn; **to knock hell out of sb** tabasser qn; **all hell broke loose** ça a chié; **this weather plays hell with my joints** ce temps est mauvais pour mes articulations □; **there'll be hell to pay** on va avoir des embêtements; **hell for leather** à fond la caisse, à tout berzingue; **like a bat out of hell** comme une furie; **go to hell!** va te faire voir!

(b) *(for emphasis)* **what the hell** *or* **in hell's name are you doing?** mais qu'est-ce que tu fous, nom de Dieu!; **who the hell are you talking about?** mais tu parles de qui, nom de Dieu!; **why the hell did you say that?** pourquoi t'as dit ça, nom de Dieu!; **how the hell should I know?** mais comment veux-tu que je le sache?; **what the hell, you only live once!** et puis merde, on ne vit qu'une fois!; **are you going?** – **like** *or* **the hell I am!, am I hell!** est-ce que tu y vas? – tu rigoles!; **get the hell out of here!** fous-moi le camp!; **I did it just for the hell of it** je l'ai fait rien que pour le plaisir; **to hell with it!** et puis merde!; **I wish to hell I knew** c'est ce que j'aimerais bien savoir; **it was hell on wheels** c'était l'enfer; **hell's bells** *or Br* **teeth!** nom de Dieu!

(c) **he's in a hell of a bad mood** il est d'humeur massacrante; **he had a hell of a job carrying the wardrobe** il en a chié pour porter l'armoire; **to have a hell of a time** *(very good)* s'éclater; *(very bad)* passer un très mauvais moment; **he likes her a hell of a lot** il est dingue d'elle; **it could have been a hell of a lot worse** ça aurait pu être bien pire; **it's a hell of a cold day outside** il fait un froid de canard dehors

(d) *(in comparisons)* **to work/run like hell** travailler/courir comme un dingue; **as jealous as hell** hyper jaloux; **as mad as hell** fou à lier; **I'm as sure as hell not going** il est pas question que j'y aille
2 *exclam* bon Dieu!

hellacious [helˈeɪʃəs] *adj Am* **(a)** *(bad, unpleasant)* infernal **(b)** *(excellent)* super, génial

hellhole [ˈhelhəʊl] *n* trou *m* à rats

hellish [ˈhelɪʃ] *adj (very bad)* infernal; **the weather was hellish** il a fait un temps dégueulasse; **I feel hellish** je me sens vraiment pas dans mon assiette

hellishly [ˈhelɪʃlɪ] *adv* vachement

helluva [ˈheləvə] *contraction* (*abrév* **hell of a**) **they're making a helluva noise** ils font un boucan pas possible; **he's a helluva nice guy** c'est un type formidable; **I miss him a helluva lot** il me manque vachement; **it costs a helluva lot of money** ça coûte vachement cher, ça coûte bonbon; **we had a helluva time getting there** on en a chié pour arriver là-bas

helmet [!] [ˈhelmɪt] *n* (*head of penis*) gland □ *m*

hen [hen] *n Scot* (*term of address*) (*to customer*) ma petite dame; (*to relative, friend*) ma chérie

Henry [ˈhenrɪ] *n Br* = un huitième d'once (*environ 3,5 grammes*)

C'est un terme de l'argot de la drogue. Il s'agit d'une référence à Henri VIII (the Eighth).

herb [hɜːb] *n* (*marijuana*) herbe *f*

her indoors [hɜːrɪnˈdɔːz] *n Br Hum* la patronne, ma bourgeoise; **I wanted to go down the boozer, but her indoors wasn't having any of it** je voulais aller au pub mais la patronne *ou* ma bourgeoise n'a pas voulu en entendre parler

hick [hɪk] *n Am* bouseux(euse) *m,f*, péquenaud(e) *m,f*

hickey [ˈhɪkɪ] *n Am* suçon *m*

hide [haɪd] *n* **to tan sb's hide** tanner le cuir à qn

high [haɪ] *adj* (**a**) (*on drugs*) défoncé, parti, raide; **to get high** se défoncer; **as high as a kite** (*on drugs*) complètement parti, raide; *Br* (*very excited*) surexcité □ (**b**) *Br* **he's for the high jump** (*in trouble*) son compte est bon ▶ *voir aussi* **hog**

high-five [ˈhaɪˈfaɪv] *n* (**a**) (*type of handshake*) = tape amicale donnée dans la paume de quelqu'un, bras levé, pour le saluer, le féliciter, ou en signe de victoire (**b**) *Noir Am* (HIV) **he's got the high-five** il est séropo

hightail [ˈhaɪteɪl] *vt* **to hightail it** décamper, mettre les bouts en vitesse; **he hightailed it home** il est rentré chez lui à fond de train

hike [haɪk] *n Am* **take a hike!** va te faire voir!

himbo [ˈhɪmbəʊ] *n Hum* beau mec *m* pas très futé

Il s'agit d'un jeu de mots sur le terme "bimbo" et le pronom "him". Le mot "bimbo" désigne une belle fille pas très intelligente.

hinky [ˈhɪŋkɪ] *adj* (*suspect*) louche

hip [hɪp] **1** *adj* (*fashionable*) branché, tendance; **that's the hippest bar in town** c'est le bar le plus branché *ou* tendance de la ville

2 *vt Am* **to hip sb to sth** mettre qn au courant de qch □; **let me hip you to the latest** je vais te mettre au parfum

hipped [hɪpt] *adj* **to be hipped on sb/sth** être dingue de qn/qch

hissy fit [ˈhɪsɪfɪt] *n* **to have a hissy fit** faire une crise

history [ˈhɪstərɪ] *n* **he's history!** (*in trouble*) il est fini!; (*no longer in my life*) avec lui, c'est terminé

hit [hɪt] **1** *n* (**a**) (*of hard drugs*) fix *m*; (*of joint*) taffe *f*; (*effect of drugs*) effet □ *m* (*procuré par une drogue*); **you get a good hit off that grass** cette herbe fait rapidement de l'effet (**b**) (*murder*) meurtre *m* sur commande □

2 *vt* (**a**) **to hit the road** (*leave*) mettre les bouts, se barrer, s'arracher

(**b**) **to hit the roof** *or Am* **the ceiling** (*lose one's temper*) piquer une crise, péter les plombs

(**c**) (*go to*) **to hit the shops** aller faire du shopping; *Br* **to hit the town** aller faire la fête en ville; *Br* **to hit the pub** aller au pub

(**d**) (*murder*) buter, zigouiller, refroidir

(**e**) **to hit sb for sth** (*borrow*) emprunter qch à qn □; (*scrounge from*) taper qch à qn

(**f**) *Am* **to hit the bricks** (*be released from prison*) sortir de taule

(**g**) *Am* **that hit the spot** (*was satisfying, refreshing*) ça fait du bien par où que ça passe ▶ *voir aussi* **deck, hay, rack, sack**

hit on *vt insép* **to hit on sb** draguer qn, faire du plat à qn

hit up *vt sép* **to hit it up** se piquer, se shooter

hitch [hɪtʃ] *vt* **to get hitched** (*married*) se maquer, se passer la corde au cou

hitman ['hɪtmæn] *n* tueur *m* à gages □, tueur professionnel □

hiya ['haɪjə] *exclam* salut!

ho [həʊ] *n* Noir Am (*abrév* **whore**) pouffiasse *f*, grognasse *f*

> Il s'agit de la transcription phonétique du mot "whore", tel que le prononcent certains Noirs américains. C'est un terme sexiste très employé par les chanteurs de rap et qui désigne une fille ou une femme.

hoaching ['həʊtʃɪŋ] *adj* Scot archibondé; **the town was hoaching with rugby fans** la ville grouillait de supporters de rugby

hog [hɒg] **1** *n* (**a**) Am (*person*) goinfre *m*, porc *m*
(**b**) Am (*motorbike*) grosse bécane *f*, gros cube *m*
(**c**) Noir Am (*luxury car*) voiture *f* de luxe (généralement une Cadillac ou une Lincoln Continental)
(**d**) Am **to live high on the hog** se la couler douce; **to be in hog heaven** être au septième ciel

hogwash ['hɒgwɒʃ] *n* foutaises *fpl*; **that's a lot of hogwash!** tout ça c'est des foutaises!

hokey ['həʊkɪ] *adj* Am (*nonsensical*) absurde □; (*sentimental*) à la guimauve

hokum ['həʊkəm] *n* Am (*nonsense*) foutaises *fpl*; (*sentimentality*) guimauve *f*

hole [həʊl] *n* (**a**) (*house, room*) taudis □ *m*; (*town*) trou *m*, bled *m*; (*pub*) bouge □ *m*
(**b**) (*difficult situation*) **to be in a hole** être dans la mouise; **to get sb out of a hole** sortir qn de la mouise
(**c**) **hole in the wall** (*restaurant*) petit restaurant □ *m*; (*shop*) petite boutique □

f; (*cash dispenser*) distributeur *m* automatique de billets □, crache-thunes *m*; Am (*apartment*) appartement *m* minuscule □
(**d**) **I need that like I need a hole in the head!** j'ai vraiment pas besoin de ça!
(**e**) ‼ (*vagina*) chagatte *f*, chatte *f*; Br **to get one's hole** baiser

hole up *vi* (*hide*) se planquer

-holic ['hɒlɪk] *suffixe* Hum **chocoholic** accro *mf* au chocolat; **workaholic** bourreau *m* de travail; **shopaholic** maniaque *mf* du shopping; Am **foodaholic** goinfre *mf*

holy ['həʊlɪ] *adj* Am (**a**) **holy cow** or **smoke** or **mackerel!** ça alors!; **holy shit** ! or **fuck!** ‼ putain de merde! (**b**) **holy Joe** cul *m* béni

homeboy ['həʊmbɔɪ] *n* Noir Am (**a**) (*man from one's home town*) compatriote *m* (**b**) (*friend*) pote *m* (**c**) (*fellow gang member*) = membre de la même bande

homegirl ['həʊmgɜːl] *n* Noir Am (**a**) (*woman from one's home town*) compatriote *f* (**b**) (*friend*) copine *f* (**c**) (*fellow gang member*) = membre de la même bande

homegrown ['həʊmgrəʊn] *n* = cannabis cultivé chez soi ou dans son jardin

homer ['həʊmə(r)] *n* Br = séance de travail au noir effectuée chez un particulier par un artisan, généralement le soir ou le week-end

homey ['həʊmɪ] = **homeboy, homegirl**

homo ['həʊməʊ] *n* Injurieux (*abrév* **homosexual**) tapette *f*, pédale *f*

> Attention, il s'agit d'un terme injurieux, qui n'est pas l'équivalent du français "homo".

hon [hʌn] *n* Am (*abrév* **honey**) (*term of address*) chéri(e) *m,f*

honcho ['hɒntʃəʊ] *n* Am chef *m*; **head honcho** grand chef *m*

honey ['hʌnɪ] *n* (**a**) (*term of address*) chéri(e) *m,f* (**b**) (*person, thing*) **he's a honey** (*good-looking*) il est vachement mignon; (*nice*) il est vachement gentil; **a honey of a car/dress** une voiture/robe très chouette

honeypot [!] ['hʌnɪpɒt] *n Am (vagina)* chatte *f*, foufoune *f*

honk [hɒŋk] *vi Br* (**a**) *(smell bad)* schlinguer, fouetter (**b**) *(vomit)* gerber, dégueuler

honker ['hɒŋkə(r)] *n Am* (**a**) *(nose)* blaire *m*, tarin *m*, pif *m* (**b**) *(breast)* nichon *m* (**c**) *(device)* bécane *f*

honkie, honky ['hɒŋkɪ] *n Noir Am Injurieux* sale Blanc (Blanche) *m,f*

hooch [hu:tʃ] *n Am* alcool *m* de contrebande ❏

hood [hʊd] *n* (**a**) *(abrév* **hoodlum***)* *(delinquent)* voyou *m*, loubard *m*; *Am (gangster)* truand *m*, gangster ❏ *m* (**b**) *Noir Am (abrév* **neighborhood***)* quartier ❏ *m*

hoodlum ['hu:dləm] *n (delinquent)* voyou *m*, loubard *m*; *Am (gangster)* truand *m*, gangster ❏ *m*

hooey ['hu:ɪ] *n* foutaises *fpl*

hoof [hu:f] *vt* **to hoof it** aller à pinces

hoo-ha ['hu:hɑ:] *n (fuss)* raffut *m*, barouf *m*

hook [hʊk] **1** *n Br* **to sling one's hook** mettre les bouts, foutre le camp, se casser; **sling your hook!** fous le camp!, casse-toi!

2 *vt Am* **to hook school** faire l'école buissonnière

3 *vi Am (work as prostitute)* faire le trottoir

hooked [hʊkt] *adj* **to be hooked (on)** être accro (à)

hooker ['hʊkə(r)] *n* (**a**) *(prostitute)* pute *f* (**b**) *Am (of drink)* **a hooker of gin/bourbon** un bon coup de gin/de bourbon

hookey, hooky ['hʊkɪ] *n Am & Austr* **to play hookey** faire l'école buissonnière

hoon [hu:n] *n Austr* loubard *m*

hoops [hu:ps] *npl Am (basketball)* basket *m*; **to shoot hoops** jouer au basket

Hooray Henry ['hʊreɪ'henrɪ] *n Br* fils *m* à papa *(exubérant et bruyant)*

> Il s'agit d'un homme issu de la grande bourgeoisie, généralement jeune, qui parle très fort et aime se faire remarquer lorsqu'il s'amuse.

hoosegow ['hu:sgaʊ] *n Am* taule *f*; **in the hoosegow** en taule, en cabane

hoot [hu:t] *n* (**a**) **I don't give a hoot** *or* **two hoots (about)** j'en ai rien à fiche (de) (**b**) *(amusing person, situation)* **to be a hoot** être marrant *ou* crevant; **and then he fell over, what a hoot!** et puis après il est tombé par terre, quelle rigolade!

hooter ['hu:tə(r)] *n* (**a**) *(nose)* pif *m*, blaire *m*, tarin *m* (**b**) *Am (breast)* nichon *m*

hop [hɒp] *vt* **to hop it** mettre les bouts, foutre le camp, se casser; **hop it!** casse-toi!, fous le camp!

hophead ['hɒphed] *n Am* toxico *mf*

hopper ['hɒpə(r)] *n Austr* kangourou ❏ *m*

horn [hɔ:n] *n* (**a**) [!] *Br (erection)* érection ❏ *f*; **to have the horn** avoir la trique *ou* le gourdin; **to give sb the horn** *(arouse)* exciter qn (**b**) *Am (telephone)* bigophone *m*; **to get on the horn to sb** passer un coup de fil *ou* de bigophone à qn

horny ['hɔ:nɪ] *adj* (**a**) *(sexually aroused)* excité (**b**) *Br (sexually attractive)* sexy

horror ['hɒrə(r)] *n* (**a**) *(person, thing)* horreur *f*; **that kid's a little horror** ce gosse est un petit monstre (**b**) *Br* **to have the horrors** faire dans son froc; **to give sb the horrors** donner le frisson à qn

horse [hɔ:s] *n (heroin)* blanche *f*, héro *f* ▸ *voir aussi* **hung**

horseshit [!] ['hɔ:sʃɪt] *n Am (nonsense)* conneries *fpl*

hot [hɒt] *adj* (**a**) *(sexually aroused)* excité; **to be hot to trot** *(of man)* être en rut; *(of woman)* être en chaleur

(**b**) *(sexually attractive)* chaud, sexy

(**c**) *(excellent)* génial, super

(**d**) *(stolen)* volé ❏

(**e**) *Am* **the hot seat** *(electric chair)* la chaise électrique ❏

hot-knife ['hɒtnaɪf] *vi* se droguer au hasch *(en coinçant un morceau de haschich entre deux lames de couteau préalablement chauffées)*

hotrod ['hɒtrɒd] *n* bagnole *f* trafiquée

hots [hɒts] *npl* **to have the hots for sb** craquer pour qn

hotshot ['hɒtʃɒt] **1** n (expert) crack m; Br (important person) huile f; Am Péj (self-important person) personne f suffisante □

2 adj **a hotshot lawyer** un super avocat; **a hotshot pool player** un as du billard

hottie ['hɒtɪ] n Am (attractive woman) canon m; (attractive man) beau mec m

hound [haʊnd] n Br (ugly woman) cageot m, mocheté f

house ape ['haʊs'eɪp] n Am Hum (child) môme mf, chiard m

how's-your-father ['haʊzjə'fɑːðə(r)] n Br Hum (sexual intercourse) **a bit of how's-your-father** une partie de jambes en l'air

hubba-hubba ['hʌbə'hʌbə] exclam Am la super gonzesse!

hubby ['hʌbɪ] n mari □ m, bonhomme m, jules m

huff [hʌf] **1** n **to be in a** or **the huff** faire la tête, bouder □; **to take the huff, to go in a huff** se mettre à bouder □

2 vt Am (glue, solvents) sniffer

huffy ['hʌfɪ] adj **to be huffy** (in a bad mood) faire la tête, bouder □; (by nature) être susceptible □, être chatouilleux

hum [hʌm] **1** n (a) Br (bad smell) puanteur □ f; **there's a bit of a hum in here!** ça coince ou ça fouette ici! (b) Am **hum job**‼ pipe f; **to give sb a hum job** tailler ou faire une pipe à qn

2 vi Br (smell bad) coincer, fouetter

humdinger [hʌm'dɪŋə(r)] n **to be a humdinger** être génial; **a humdinger of a football match** un match de foot magnifique; **she's a humdinger!** elle est hyper canon!

hummer‼ ['hʌmə(r)] n Am (fellatio) pipe f, turlute f; **to give sb a hummer** faire ou tailler une pipe à qn, piper qn

humongous [hju:'mʌŋgəs] adj énorme □, mastoc

hump [hʌmp] **1** n (a) Br **to have the hump** être de mauvais poil; **to get** or **take the hump** se mettre à faire la gueule; **to give sb the hump** mettre qn de mauvais poil (b) Am (person) crétin(e) m,f, andouille f □

2 vt (a) ‼ (have sex with) (of man) baiser, se taper; (of woman) baiser avec, se taper (b) (carry) trimballer

3 ‼ vi (have sex) baiser, s'envoyer en l'air

hung [hʌŋ] adj **to be hung like a horse** or **a whale** or Br **a donkey** or Am **a mule**‼ être monté comme un âne ou un taureau ou un bourricot

hunk [hʌŋk] n (man) beau mec m

hunky ['hʌŋkɪ] adj bien foutu

hunky-dory [hʌŋkɪ'dɔːrɪ] adj au poil; **everything's hunky-dory** tout baigne

hurl [hɜːl] vi (vomit) dégobiller, gerber

hurting ['hɜːtɪŋ] adj Am (a) (in need) **to be hurting for sth** avoir méchamment besoin de qch (b) (in trouble) dans la mouise

hush money ['hʌʃmʌnɪ] n = argent versé à quelqu'un pour acheter son silence

hustle ['hʌsəl] Am **1** n (swindle) arnaque f

2 vt (a) (swindle) arnaquer; **to hustle sb out of sth** soutirer qch à qn; **to hustle some pool** jouer au billard pour de l'argent □ (b) (sell) fourguer (c) (obtain dishonestly) soutirer; (steal) piquer, faucher

3 vi (work as prostitute) faire le tapin

hustler ['hʌslə(r)] n Am (a) (energetic person) battant(e) m,f (b) (swindler) magouilleur(euse) m,f (c) (prostitute) pute f

hype¹ [haɪp] **1** n (a) (abrév **hypodermic**) shooteuse f, pompe f (b) (drug addict) toxico mf, camé(e) m,f

2 adj Noir Am (excellent) super, génial, grand

hype² n (publicity) battage m, matraquage m

hype up vt sép **to hype sth up** faire du battage autour de qch

hyper ['haɪpə(r)] adj (excited) surexcité □

hypo ['haɪpəʊ] n (abrév **hypodermic**) shooteuse f, pompe f

The symbol □ indicates that a translation is neutral in register.

I

ice [aɪs] **1** n (**a**) (diamonds) diams mpl (**b**) (drug) ice f
   2 vt (kill) buter, refroidir, zigouiller

icky ['ɪkɪ] adj (repulsive) dégueulasse; (sticky) poisseux; (sentimental) mièvre □, à la guimauve

idea [aɪ'dɪə] n **what's the big idea?** à quoi tu joues?

idiot box ['ɪdɪətbɒks] n Am (television) téloche f

iffy ['ɪfɪ] adj (**a**) (doubtful, unreliable) our

Insults

Son but principal étant de choquer, l'insulte est sans doute la forme la plus pure et la plus immédiate d'utilisation de la langue familière. On trouvera ci-dessous certains des mécanismes de formation les plus répandus en anglais. La forme d'insulte la plus simple est un substantif utilisé comme exclamation (cf colonne "nom") et parfois précédé de "you". Cette combinaison peut à son tour être renforcée par un adjectif. Le tableau ci-dessous illustre ce procédé à l'aide de quelques mots très communs. Il faut remarquer que, bien que les combinaisons soient en principe multiples, certaines sont plus fixes que d'autres.

	ADJECTIF	NOM
	stupid □	idiot □
	Br bleeding	Br pillock
	goddamn	bitch
(you)	Br bloody !	prat
	Br sodding !	bastard !
	Am dumbass !	Br arsehole, Am asshole !!
	fucking !!	Br wanker !!
	Am motherfucking !!	Am motherfucker !!
		cunt !!

Pour un effet tout aussi percutant, on pourra utiliser un impératif, tel que "get lost", "push off", Br "bugger off" !, "piss off" ou "fuck off" !!!

L'expression "go (and)…" est également très productive lorsqu'elle précède un infinitif, comme dans:

      go (and) boil your head!
      go (and) jump in the lake!
      go (and) play in the traffic!
      go (and) fuck yourself! !!!

Enfin, et notamment lorsque le locuteur veut être sarcastique, l'expression "Why don't you…" revient souvent dans la formation d'insultes; elle peut servir à introduire n'importe laquelle des tournures impératives ci-dessus.

The symbol □ indicates that a translation is neutral in register.

holidays are looking very iffy nos vacances risquent de tomber à l'eau; **the brakes are a bit iffy** les freins déconnent un peu; Br **my stomach's been a bit iffy lately** je me sens un peu barbouillé ces temps-ci

(b) (suspicious) louche, chelou; **it all sounded rather iffy** tout ça m'avait l'air plutôt louche; **her new man sounds really iffy** son nouveau copain a l'air vraiment louche

illin' ['ɪlɪn] adj Noir Am (a) (unpleasant) merdique (b) (mad) cinglé, toqué, timbré

in [ɪn] **1** adj (fashionable) in, branché; **it's the in place** c'est l'endroit le plus branché; **it's the in thing/colour** c'est le truc/la couleur à la mode; **the in crowd** les gens branchés

2 adv (a) **to be in on a secret/a plan** être au courant d'un secret/d'un projet ⁰; **I wasn't in on it** j'étais pas dans la confidence; **I want in** (include me) ça me branche (b) **you're going to be in for it!** tu vas voir ce que tu vas prendre!

inhale [ɪn'heɪl] vt Am **to inhale sth** (eat quickly) engouffrer qch; (drink quickly) descendre qch

innit ['ɪnɪt] adv Br (a) (isn't it) hein?; **it's great, innit?** c'est super, hein? (b) (general question tag) hein?; **that was a kicking night out, innit?** on a passé une super soirée, hein?; **you fancy her, innit?** elle te plaît, hein?

"Innit?" est la contraction de "isn't it?". Dans la région de Londres, cependant, cette forme s'utilise de plus en plus pour toutes les personnes du singulier et du pluriel.

inside 1 adj ['ɪnsaɪd] **it was an inside job**

c'est quelqu'un de l'intérieur qui a fait le coup

2 adv [ɪn'saɪd] (in prison) en taule, à l'ombre, au frais; **to put sb inside** mettre qn en taule ou à l'ombre

into ['ɪntʊ] prép (keen on) **to be into sb** en pincer pour qn; **to be into sth** être branché qch; **to be into doing sth** s'éclater à faire qch; **he's into drugs** il se drogue ⁰; **I'm not into that sort of thing** c'est pas mon truc

Irish ['aɪrɪʃ] adj Br (contradictory, illogical) loufoque

"Irish" signifie littéralement "irlandais". En Grande-Bretagne les Irlandais sont la cible de nombreuses plaisanteries où ils apparaissent généralement comme des gens peu intelligents et manquant de bon sens. Bien que ce terme ne témoigne pas nécessairement d'une attitude xénophobe de la part de celui qui l'utilise, il est préférable de ne pas l'employer.

iron ['aɪən] n Br Injurieux (rhyming slang **iron hoof** = **poof**) pédale f, tantouze f, tapette f ▶ voir aussi **pump**

ish [ɪʃ] adv plus ou moins; **is he good-looking? – ish** est-ce qu'il est beau? – mouais...

Il s'agit du suffixe "-ish", dénotant l'approximation, utilisé en tant qu'adverbe.

it [ɪt] pron **she thinks she's IT** elle se prend pas pour de la merde; **it girl** jeune mondaine ⁰ f

item ['aɪtəm] n **they're an item** (of couple) ils sont maqués

J

J [dʒeɪ] n (abrév **joint**) (cannabis cigarette) joint m

Jack [dʒæk] npr Am Péj (term of address) Duchnoque

jack [dʒæk] n (a) **every man jack (of them)** absolument tout le monde (b) **jack shit** ! que dalle

jack around Am 1 vt sép **to jack sb around** (treat badly) se ficher de qn; (waste time of) faire perdre son temps à qn □
2 vi (waste time) glander, glandouiller

jack in vt sép **to jack sth in** laisser tomber qch, plaquer qch; **to jack it all in** tout plaquer

jack off ! 1 vt sép **to jack sb off** branler qn
2 vi se branler, se palucher

jack up 1 vt sép (a) Br (drugs) s'injecter □, se piquer à (b) (prices, profits) gonfler
2 vi Br se piquer, se shooter

jackaroo [dʒækə'ruː] n Austr = apprenti dans un ranch

jackass ['dʒækæs] n Am andouille f, cruche f, crétin m

jacksie, jacksy ['dʒæksɪ] n Br (buttocks) fesses fpl, popotin m; (anus) troufignon m, trou m de balle

Jack-the-lad [dʒækðə'læd] n Br = jeune homme exubérant et insolent d'origine modeste

jaffa ['dʒæfə] n Br Hum homme m stérile □

Cet usage vient du fait que les oranges de la marque Jaffa n'ont pas de pépins.

Jag [dʒæg] n (abrév **Jaguar**) Jaguar □ f

jailbait ['dʒeɪlbeɪt] n fille f mineure □, poids m mort

jake [dʒeɪk] n Br joint m, pétard m

jakey ['dʒeɪkɪ] n Scot clodo m alcolo

jalopy [dʒə'lɒpɪ] n vieille bagnole f, guimbarde f

jam [dʒæm] 1 n (a) (music) **jam (session)** bœuf m, jam-session f; **to have a jam (session)** faire un bœuf ou une jam-session (b) Br **jam jar** (rhyming slang **car**) bagnole f, caisse f (c) Br **jam rag** ! serviette f périodique □ (d) Br **jam sandwich** voiture f de police □
2 vi faire un bœuf ou une jam-session

Dans la catégorie I (d) le terme "jam sandwich" s'utilise en Grande-Bretagne pour désigner les voitures de police car celles-ci sont souvent ornées d'une bande rouge en leur milieu.

jammy ['dʒæmɪ] adj Br (lucky) veinard; **you jammy bugger!** ! sacré veinard!

Jane Doe ['dʒeɪn'dəʊ] npr Am = l'Américaine moyenne

Aux États-Unis Jane Doe est le nom attribué aux femmes dont on ne connaît pas, ou dont on ne veut pas dévoiler, l'identité.

JAP [dʒæp] n Am Péj (abrév **Jewish American Princess**) = jeune Américaine juive issue de la grande bourgeoisie

Jap [dʒæp] Injurieux (abrév **Japanese**) 1 n Jap mf
2 adj jap

jar [dʒɑː(r)] n Br (drink) pot m, godet m; **let's go out for a couple of jars** allons boire un pot

java ['dʒɑːvə] n Am (coffee) kawa m

jaw [dʒɔː] 1 n Am **to flap one's jaw** gueuler
2 vi tailler une bavette

jazz [dʒæz] n (a) **...and all that jazz**

...et tout le tremblement (**b**) **jazz mag** bouquin *m* de cul

jeepers (creepers) [ˈdʒiːpəz(ˈkriːpəz)] *exclam* bon Dieu!, bon sang!

Jeez [dʒiːz] *exclam* bon Dieu!, bon sang!

jelly [ˈdʒelɪ] *n Br (drug)* gélule *f* de Temazepam □

jerk [dʒɜːk] *n (person)* abruti(e) *mf*, crétin(e) *m,f*

jerk about !, **jerk around** ! *vt sép* **to jerk sb about** *or* **around** faire tourner qn en bourrique

jerk off ! **1** *vt sép* **to jerk sb off** branler qn
2 *vi* se branler, se palucher

jerk-off ! [ˈdʒɜːkɒf] *n Am (person)* connard (connasse) *m,f*

jerky [ˈdʒɜːkɪ] *adj Am (stupid)* débile, abruti

jessie [ˈdʒesɪ] *n Scot (feeble man)* mauviette *f*; **stop pretending you're hurt, you big jessie!** arrête de faire semblant d'avoir mal, espèce de mauviette!

Jesus [ˈdʒiːzəs] **1** *n* **Jesus freak** chrétien(enne) *m,f* hippie
2 *exclam* **Jesus (Christ)!** nom de Dieu!; *Br* **Jesus wept!** bon sang!

jiff [dʒɪf], **jiffy** [ˈdʒɪfɪ] *n* seconde □ *f*, instant □ *m*; **in a jiff** dans une seconde

jiggered [ˈdʒɪgəd] *adj Br (exhausted)* naze, crevé, lessivé

jiggy [ˈdʒɪgɪ] *adj Am* **to get jiggy (with it)** s'envoyer en l'air

jillaroo [dʒɪləˈruː] *n Austr* = apprentie dans un ranch

jimjams [ˈdʒɪmdʒæmz] *npl* (**a**) **to have the jimjams** être sur les nerfs (**b**) *Br (pyjamas)* pyjama □ *m*

Jimmy [ˈdʒɪmɪ] *npr Br (rhyming slang* **Jimmy Riddle = piddle**) **to have a Jimmy** pisser; **to go for a Jimmy** aller pisser

jism [ˈdʒɪzəm] *n* (**a**) !! *(semen)* foutre *m* (**b**) *Am (energy)* ressort □ *m*

jive [dʒaɪv] *Noir Am* **1** *n (nonsense)* foutaises *fpl*; *(insincerity)* craques *fpl*
2 *adj (unpleasant)* à la noix

jive-ass ! [ˈdʒaɪvæs] *adj Noir Am* à la noix

jizz !! [dʒɪz] *n (semen)* foutre *m*

joanna [dʒəʊˈænə] *n Br (rhyming slang* **piano**) piano □ *m*

job [dʒɒb] *n* (**a**) *(thing)* truc *m*; **her new car is one of those sporty jobs** sa nouvelle voiture est un de ces modèles style "sport"; **their latest hi-fi is a lovely job** leur nouvelle chaîne stéréo est super
(**b**) *(crime)* coup *m*; **to do** *or* **pull a job** faire un coup; **he did** *or* **pulled that bank job** c'est lui qui a braqué la banque
(**c**) *Br* **to be on the job** ! *(having sex)* être en train de baiser
(**d**) *Br (excrement)* caca *m*
(**e**) *Am* **to do a job on sth** *(ruin, damage)* bousiller qch ▸ *voir aussi* **boob, hatchet, nose, snow**

Jock [dʒɒk] *npr Injurieux (Scotsman)* Écossais □ *m*

"Jock" est un diminutif un peu désuet de "John" qui est parfois utilisé en Écosse. Bien que ce terme ne témoigne pas nécessairement d'une attitude xénophobe de la part de celui qui l'utilise, il est préférable de ne pas l'employer.

jock [dʒɒk] *n Am* (**a**) *(athlete)* sportif(ive) *m,f (pas très brillant intellectuellement)* (**b**) *(abrév* **disc jockey**) disc-jockey *mf*

Joe [dʒəʊ] *npr* (**a**) *Am (man)* mec *m*, type *m*; **a good Joe** *(man)* un chic type; *(woman)* une brave femme; **he's just an ordinary Joe** c'est un type comme les autres (**b**) *Br* **Joe Public, Joe Bloggs, Joe Soap,** *Am* **Joe Blow, Joe Schmo, Joe Six-Pack** Monsieur Tout-le-Monde ▸ *voir aussi* **holy**

John [dʒɒn] *npr Br (term of address)* chef; **got a light, John?** t'as du feu, chef?

Il s'agit d'un terme qui s'utilise surtout à Londres.

john [dʒɒn] *n Am* (**a**) *(toilet)* chiottes *fpl* (**b**) *(prostitute's client)* micheton *m*

John Doe [ˈdʒɒnˈdəʊ] *npr Am* = l'Américain moyen

Aux États-Unis John Doe est le nom attribué aux individus dont on ne connaît pas, ou dont on ne veut pas révéler, l'identité.

johnny ['dʒɒnɪ] n Br (condom) **(rubber) johnny** capote f

johnson ['dʒɒnsən] n Am quéquette f

joint [dʒɔɪnt] n **(a)** (cannabis cigarette) joint m **(b)** (place) turne f; **we ate at some fancy joint** on a mangé dans un resto super classe **(c)** Am (prison) taule f, placard m; **in the joint** en taule, à l'ombre **(d)** [!] Am (penis) pine f, bite f ▸ voir aussi **case, clip**

jollies ['dʒɒlɪz] npl Am **to get one's jollies (doing sth)** prendre son pied (en faisant qch), s'éclater (en faisant qch)

journo ['dʒɜːnəʊ] n Br (abrév **journalist**) journaleux(euse) m,f

joypop ['dʒɔɪpɒp] vi = prendre de la drogue sans devenir dépendant

Juan Doe ['hwæn'dəʊ] npr Am = l'Hispanique moyen

Il s'agit d'une adaptation humoristique du terme John Doe (voir cette entrée), qui s'applique aux Américains d'origine latino-américaine.

jug [dʒʌg] n **(a)** (prison) taule f, cabane f; **in (the) jug** en taule, à l'ombre **(b) jugs** [!] (breasts) nichons mpl, lolos mpl

juice [dʒuːs] n **(a)** (petrol) essence □ f; (electricity) jus m; Br (gas) gaz □ m **(b)** Noir Am (popularity, recognition) succès □; **to have a lot of juice** faire un tabac ▸ voir aussi **jungle**

juiced [dʒuːst] adj Am (drunk) pété, bourré, beurré

juicer ['dʒuːsə(r)] n Am alcolo mf, poivrot(e) m,f

jump [dʒʌmp] vt **(a)** (attack) **to jump sb** sauter sur le paletot à qn; **to get jumped** se faire agresser □ **(b) to jump sb's bones** sauter sur qn ▸ voir aussi **high, throat**

jumping ['dʒʌmpɪŋ] adj (party, nightclub) hyper animé

jungle ['dʒʌŋgəl] n **(a)** Injurieux **jungle bunny** nègre (négresse) m,f **(b) jungle juice** tord-boyaux m (le plus souvent produit artisanalement)

junk [dʒʌŋk] **1** n **(a)** (worthless things) **his new book is a pile of junk** son nouveau bouquin ne vaut pas un clou; **she eats nothing but junk** elle mange que des saloperies **(b)** (useless things) bazar m; **move all that junk of yours off the bed** enlève ton bazar du lit **(c)** (drug) drogue f dure □ (le plus souvent héroïne)
2 vt **(a)** (throw away) balancer, foutre en l'air **(b)** (criticize) débiner, éreinter

junker ['dʒʌŋkə(r)] n Am (old car) vieille bagnole f

junkie ['dʒʌŋkɪ] n junkie mf; **a chocolate/soap opera junkie** un accro du chocolat/des feuilletons télé

K

Kaffir ['kæfə(r)] *n Br Injurieux* nègre (négresse) *m,f* d'Afrique du Sud

kaput [kə'pʊt] *adj* kaput; **theTV's kaput, we can't watch the match!** la téloche est kaput; impossible de regarder le match!

karsey, karzey, kazi ['kɑːzɪ] *n Br* chiottes *fpl*, gogues *mpl*

kazoo [kə'zuː] *n Am (buttocks)* derrière *m*, arrière-train *m*; **to have problems/debts up the kazoo** *(in excess)* avoir des problèmes/des dettes jusqu'au cou

kecks [keks] *npl Br* fute *m*, falzar *m*

keel over [kiːl] *vi* **(a)** *(faint)* tourner de l'œil **(b)** *(die)* calancher, passer l'arme à gauche

keister ['kiːstə(r)] *n Am (buttocks)* fesses *fpl*, derrière *m*, derche *m*

keks [keks] = **kecks**

Kevin ['kevɪn] *npr Br Péj* jeune beauf *m*

Il s'agit d'un stéréotype social comparable à celui de l'Essex Man (voir cette entrée). Le "Kevin" est jeune, d'origine modeste, peu cultivé, parfois violent, et ne fait pas toujours preuve d'un goût très sûr. Kevin est un prénom très courant dans les milieux populaires et, de ce fait, est considéré comme vulgaire par beaucoup de gens.

kick [kɪk] **1** *n (thrill)* **to get a kick out of sth/doing sth** prendre son pied avec qch/en faisant qch; **to do sth for kicks** faire qch histoire de rigoler
   2 *vt* **to kick the bucket** *(die)* calancher, passer l'arme à gauche
   3 *vi Am (die)* calancher, passer l'arme à gauche ▸ *voir aussi* **ass, shit**

kick about, kick around 1 *vt insép (spend time in)* **to kick about the world/Africa** rouler sa bosse *ou* traîner ses guêtres autour du monde/en Afrique; *Br* **is my purse kicking about the kitchen somewhere?** est-ce que mon porte-monnaie traîne quelque part dans la cuisine?
   2 *vi (hang around)* traîner (**with** avec); *Br* **have you seen my lighter kicking about?** t'as pas vu mon briquet (traîner) quelque part?

kick off *vi* **(a)** *Am (die)* calancher, passer l'arme à gauche **(b)** *Br (get violent)* **it's going to kick off** ça va bastonner

kickback ['kɪkbæk] *n (bribe)* pot-de-vin *m*

kicker ['kɪkə(r)] *n Am* **(a)** *(hidden drawback)* os *m*, hic *m* **(b)** *(worst part of situation)* **the work's tough and the kicker is the pay's lousy** le travail est dur, et en plus de ça, c'est payé avec un lance-pierres

kicking ['kɪkɪŋ] **1** *n Br* **to give sb a kicking** tabasser qn à coups de latte; **to get a kicking** se faire tabasser à coups de latte
   2 *adj* **(a)** *(party, nightclub)* hyper animé **(b)** *(excellent)* super, génial

kicky ['kɪkɪ] *adj Am (excellent)* super, génial, géant

kid [kɪd] *n (child)* gosse *mf*; *(young adult)* jeune □ *mf*, gamin(e) *m,f*; *Br* **our kid** *(brother)* le petit frère; *(sister)* la petite sœur

kiddie, kiddy *n Br (child)* gosse *mf*

kiddy-fiddler [!] *n Br* pédophile □ *mf*

kike [kaɪk] *n Am Injurieux* youpin(e) *m,f*, youtre *m,f*

kill [kɪl] **1** *vt Br* **to kill oneself (laughing)** être mort de rire; *Ironique* **you kill me!** toi alors!
   2 *vi* **I'd kill for a beer** je me damnerais pour une bière

The symbol □ indicates that a translation is neutral in register.

killer ['kɪlə(r)] n (**a**) (difficult thing) **those steps were a killer!** ces marches m'ont lessivé!; **the English exam was a killer** l'examen d'anglais était vraiment coton (**b**) (excellent thing) **their new album's a killer** leur dernier album est vraiment génial ou mortel; **this one's a killer** (joke) elle est bien bonne, celle-là

killing ['kɪlɪŋ] adj Br (**a**) (very amusing) marrant, crevant, mortel (**b**) (exhausting) crevant, tuant

kinda ['kaɪndə] contraction (abrév **kind of**) **this is my kinda party!** c'est le genre de soirée que j'aime!; **that kinda thing** ce genre de truc; **you look kinda tired** t'as l'air un peu fatigué; **I kinda expected this** je m'y attendais un peu; **do you like it? – kinda** tu trouves ça comment? – pas mal

kinky ['kɪŋkɪ] adj (person) (sexually) qui a des goûts spéciaux; (eccentric) loufoque; (clothing, sex) très spécial

kip [kɪp] Br **1** n **to have a kip, to get some kip** piquer un roupillon, pioncer; **to get an hour's kip** piquer un roupillon d'une heure; **I didn't get much kip last night** j'ai pas beaucoup roupillé la nuit dernière
2 vi roupiller, pioncer

kip down vi Br pieuter

kiss [kɪs] vt **to kiss sth goodbye, to kiss goodbye to sth** faire une croix sur qch; **you can kiss your money/promotion goodbye!** tu peux faire une croix sur ou dire adieu à ton argent/ta promotion! ► voir aussi **arse, ass, French**

kiss off vt sép Am (**a**) **to kiss sb off** (dismiss) envoyer balader ou promener qn; (kill) buter ou zigouiller qn (**b**) **to kiss sth off** (give up hope of) faire une croix sur qch; **you can kiss off your promotion!** tu peux faire une croix sur ou dire adieu à ta promotion!

kisser ['kɪsə(r)] n (mouth) bec m, museau m

kiss-off ['kɪsɒf] n Am **to give sb the kiss-off** envoyer balader ou promener qn

kit [kɪt] n Br (clothes) **to get one's kit off** se désaper, se mettre à poil; **get your kit off!** à poil!

kite [kaɪt] n **go fly a kite!** va voir ailleurs si j'y suis! ► voir aussi **high**

kittens ['kɪtənz] npl **to have kittens** (become agitated) faire un caca nerveux

Kiwi ['kiːwiː] n (person) Néo-Zélandais(e) □ m,f, kiwi mf

klutz [klʌts] n Am (stupid person) abruti(e) m,f, tache f; (clumsy person) manche m

knacker ['nækə(r)] Br **1** n **knackers** ! (testicles) couilles fpl, balloches fpl
2 vt (**a**) (exhaust) crever, lessiver (**b**) (break, wear out) bousiller

knackered ['nækəd] adj Br (**a**) (exhausted) crevé, lessivé, naze (**b**) (broken, worn out) bousillé

knackering ['nækərɪŋ] adj Br crevant

knees-up ['niːzʌp] n Br (party) sauterie f

knee-trembler ['niːtremblə(r)] n Br **to have a knee-trembler** baiser debout

knickers ['nɪkəz] Br **1** npl **to get one's knickers in a twist** (become agitated) s'affoler, s'exciter; (become angry) piquer une crise, se mettre en pétard; **to get into sb's knickers** s'envoyer qn
2 exclam n'importe quoi!

knife [naɪf] n **he isn't the sharpest knife in the drawer** il n'a pas inventé l'eau chaude ou le fil à couper le beurre

knob [nɒb] **1** n (**a**) ! (penis) bite f, queue f (**b**) ! Br (man) trou m du cul (**c**) Br **the same to you with knobs on!** toi-même!
2 ! vt Br (have sex with) baiser, tringler, troncher

knock [nɒk] vt (**a**) (criticize) éreinter, débiner; **don't knock it till you've tried it!** n'en dis pas de mal avant d'avoir essayé □
(**b**) Br (have sex with) (of man) baiser, tringler, troncher; (of woman) baiser avec, s'envoyer
(**c**) Br **to knock sth on the head** (put a stop to) faire cesser qch □; **knock it on the head, will you!** c'est pas bientôt fini?

The symbol □ indicates that a translation is neutral in register.

(d) Am **to knock sb for a loop** (amaze) scier qn, en boucher un coin à qn

(e) to knock sb dead (impress) en mettre plein la vue à qn; **the Chemical Brothers knocked them dead last night** hier soir, les Chemical Brothers ont fait un tabac

knock about, knock around 1 vt insép (spend time in) **to knock about the world/Africa** rouler sa bosse ou traîner ses guêtres autour du monde/en Afrique; Br **are my keys knocking about the kitchen somewhere?** est-ce que mes clés traînent quelque part dans la cuisine?

2 vi (hang around) traîner (**with** avec); Br **are my fags knocking about?** est-ce que mes clopes sont dans le coin?

knock back vt sép **(a)** (drink) descendre **(b)** Br (cost) coûter à $^{□}$; **it knocked me back a few hundred pounds** ça m'a coûté quelques centaines de livres; **that must have knocked you back a bit!** ça a dû te coûter un paquet de fric! **(c)** Br (reject) **to knock sb back** rejeter qn $^{□}$; **to knock sth back** (offer, invitation) refuser qch $^{□}$; **she knocked him back** il s'est pris une veste

knock off 1 vt sép **(a)** (stop) **knock it off!** arrête!

(b) (steal) piquer, faucher; **to knock off a bank/jeweller's** (rob) braquer une banque/une bijouterie

(c) (murder) buter, refroidir, zigouiller

(d) (have sex with) (of man) baiser, tringler, troncher; (of woman) baiser avec, s'envoyer

2 vi (stop working) dételer

knock out vt sép **to knock oneself out** (indulge oneself) se faire plaisir; **there's plenty food left, knock yourself out!** il reste plein de nourriture, sers-toi autant que tu veux! $^{□}$

knock over vt sép Am (rob) braquer

knock up vt sép **to knock sb up** (make pregnant) engrosser qn

knockback ['nɒkbæk] n Br (rejection) veste f; **to get a knockback** prendre une veste

knockers ⚠ ['nɒkəz] npl (breasts) nichons mpl, roberts mpl

knocking shop ['nɒkɪŋʃɒp] n Br bordel m, boxon m, claque m

knockout ['nɒkaʊt] **1** n (excellent thing) merveille $^{□}$ f; **she's a knockout** (gorgeous) elle est vachement sexy

2 adj super

knockover ['nɒkəʊvə(r)] n Am (robbery) casse m

knot [nɒt] **1** n **to tie the knot** (get married) se maquer, se passer la corde au cou

2 vt Br **get knotted!** (go away) casse-toi!, va te faire voir ailleurs!; (expressing contempt, disagreement) la ferme!

knucklehead ['nʌkəlhed] n andouille f, nouille f

kook [ku:k] n Am zigoto m, zigomar m

kooky ['ku:kɪ] adj Am loufoque, loufedingue

kosher ['kəʊʃə(r)] adj (legitimate, honest) réglo, régulier

Kraut [kraʊt] Injurieux **1** n Boche mf

2 adj boche

kvetch [kvetʃ] vi Am râler, geindre

The symbol $^{□}$ indicates that a translation is neutral in register.

L

lad [læd] n Br (**a**) (young man) garçon $^{\square}$ m, petit gars m; **he's a bit of a lad** c'est un sacré fêtard; **he's one of the lads** on se marre bien avec lui (**b**) **the lads** (friends) les copains; **he's gone out for a couple of drinks with the lads** il est sorti boire un coup avec les copains ▶ voir aussi **new**

laddish ['lædɪʃ] adj Br = typique d'un style de vie caractérisé par de fréquentes sorties entre copains, généralement copieusement arrosées, un comportement arrogant et macho et un goût prononcé pour le sport et les activités de groupe

ladette [læ'det] n Br jeune femme f délurée $^{\square}$ (qui se revendique l'égale des hommes pour ce qui est des sorties, de la vulgarité, etc)

la-di-da [lɑːdɪ'dɑː] **1** adj (person, attitude) prétentieux $^{\square}$, snobinard; (voice) affecté $^{\square}$

2 adv d'une façon prétentieuse $^{\square}$

lager lout ['lɑːgəlaʊt] n Br = jeune voyou buveur de bière

lagered (up) ['lɑːgəd('ʌp)] adj Br bourré à la bière; **he gets lagered up with his mates every Friday night** il se bourre la gueule à la bière avec ses potes tous les vendredi soir

lah-di-dah [lɑːdɪ'dɑː] = **la-di-da**

laid-back [leɪd'bæk] adj décontracté $^{\square}$, relax

lairy ['leərɪ] adj Br **to be lairy** être culotté

La-la land ['lɑːlɑːlænd] n (**a**) Am Péj = surnom donné à la ville de Los Angeles (**b**) **to be in La-la land** être dans le coaltar

laldy ['lældɪ] adv Scot **to give it laldy** s'en donner; **check him out giving it laldy on the dancefloor!** regarde comme il s'en donne sur la piste de danse!; **they were giving it laldy next door again** (arguing) ils étaient encore en train de s'engueuler à côté, et ils faisaient pas semblant

lame [leɪm] Am **1** n (stupid person) andouille f, cruche f, courge f

2 adj (stupid) cloche, nouille

lamebrain ['leɪmbreɪn] n Am andouille f, cruche f, courge f

lamp [læmp] vt Scot (hit) (once) filer un gnon à; (more than once) dérouiller, filer une raclée à

land [lænd] vt (**a**) Br **to get landed with sb/sth** se retrouver avec qn/qch sur les bras; **I got landed with doing the dishes** c'est moi qui me suis tapé ou colliné la vaisselle (**b**) (hit) **to land sb a punch** coller une châtaigne ou un ramponneau à qn; **he landed me one on the chin** il m'a envoyé un marron dans le menton

lardarse ⚠ ['lɑːdɑːs], Am **lardass** ⚠ ['lɑːdæs] n (man) gros m plein de soupe; (woman) grosse vache f

lardy ['lɑːdɪ] adj gros $^{\square}$; **get off your lardy arse and give me a hand!** lève ton gros cul et viens me donner un coup de main!

large [lɑːdʒ] **1** adj **it was a large one last night** on a passé une soirée bien arrosée hier

2 adv (**a**) Br (to a large extent) **Arsenal got thrashed large** Arsenal s'est fait ratatiner ou s'est fait battre à plates coutures; **we got pissed large last night** ⚠ on s'est pris une cuite maison hier soir (**b**) Noir Am **to live large** mener la belle vie

3 vt **to large it** s'éclater (généralement en consommant de grandes quantités d'alcool)

lark [lɑːk] n Br (**a**) (joke) rigolade f; **to do**

---

sth for a lark faire qch histoire de rigoler **(b)** *(activity)* **I'm fed up with this dieting lark** j'en ai marre de ce régime que je suis en train de faire; **I can't be doing with that fancy dress lark** je n'aime pas du tout cette histoire de bal masqué

lark about, lark around *vi Br* faire l'idiot

larrikin ['lærɪkɪn] *n Austr* vaurien *m*

lash [læ∫] *n Br* **to be on the lash** se péter, se bourrer la gueule, prendre une cuite; **to go on the lash** aller se bourrer la gueule, aller prendre une cuite

lashed [læ∫t] *adj Br (drunk)* bourré, pété, fait

later ['leɪtə(r)], *Br* **laters** ['leɪtəz] *exclam* salut!, à la prochaine!

laugh [lɑːf] **1** *n* **to have a laugh** se marrer; **to do sth for a laugh** faire qch histoire de rigoler; **he's always good for a laugh** c'est un marrant; **you're having a laugh, aren't you?** tu déconnes?
     2 *vi* **(a)** **don't make me laugh!** ne me fais pas rigoler!, laisse-moi rire! **(b)** *Br* **if we win this match, we'll be laughing** si on gagne ce match, on n'a plus de souci à se faire; **if your offer's accepted, you'll be laughing** s'ils acceptent ta proposition, ce sera super pour toi

laughing gear ['lɑːfɪŋɡɪə(r)] *n Br* bouche [□] *f*, clapet *m*, bec *m*; **get your laughing gear round this!** *(food, cigar)* fourre-toi ça dans le bec!

lav [læv] *n Br (abrév* **lavatory***)* vécés *mpl*

law [lɔː] *n* **the law** les flics *mpl*; **I'll get the law on you!** j'appelle les flics!

lay [leɪ] **1** *n* **to be a good lay** être un bon coup; **to be an easy lay** avoir la cuisse légère
     2 *vt* **(a)** *(have sex with)* **to lay sb** s'envoyer qn; **to get laid** s'envoyer en l'air **(b)** *Am* **to lay one** *(fart)* péter, larguer une caisse

lay off *vt insép* **(a)** *(stop annoying, nagging)* **to lay off sb** ficher la paix à qn; **just lay off me!** fiche-moi la paix!, fais-moi des vacances! **(b)** *(abstain from)* **to lay off the chocolate** ne plus manger de

chocolat [□]; **to lay off the cigarettes** s'arrêter de fumer [□]; **you'd better lay off the booze for a while** tu devrais t'arrêter de boire pendant quelque temps [□]

lazybones ['leɪzɪbəʊnz] *n* flemmard(e) *m,f*

lead [led] *n* **to fill** *or* **pump sb full of lead** plomber qn; *Am Hum* **to get lead poisoning** *(get shot dead)* se faire buter

leak [liːk] *n* **to take** *or* **have a leak** *(urinate)* pisser un coup

leatherboy ['leðəbɔɪ] *n* cuir *m*, pédé *m* cuir

leatherneck ['leðənek] *n Am* marine [□] *m (américain)*, ≃ marsouin *m*

leave out [liːv] *vt sép Br* **leave it out!** arrête!

leccy ['lekɪ] *n Br (electricity)* électricité [□] *f*, jus *m*; **the leccy got cut off** ils nous ont coupé le jus; **we need to pay the leccy bill** il faut payer la facture d'électricité

lech [let∫] **1** *n* obsédé *m*
     2 *vi* regarder/agir avec concupiscence [□]; **to lech after sb** baver devant qn *(de concupiscence)*

leery ['lɪərɪ] *adj* **to be leery of sb/sth** se méfier de qn/qch [□]

left field [left'fiːld] *n* **to be way out in left field** être complètement loufoque; **it came out of left field** *(comment, question)* c'est tombé comme un cheveu sur la soupe

left-footer [left'fʊtə(r)] *n Br Péj* catholique [□] *mf*, catho *mf*

leftie, lefty ['leftɪ] *n* gaucho *mf*

leg [leg] **1** *n* **(a)** *Br* **to get one's leg over** s'envoyer en l'air **(b)** **to shake a leg** *(get moving)* se magner, se grouiller; **shake a leg!** magne-toi!, grouille-toi!
     2 *vt* **to leg it** *(run, run away)* cavaler

legit [lə'dʒɪt] *adj (abrév* **legitimate***)* réglo, régulier

legless ['leglɪs] *adj Br (drunk)* pété, bourré, beurré

lemon ['lemən] *n* **(a)** *Br (person)* abruti(e) *m,f*; **I felt a total lemon** je me suis senti tout con (**b**) *Am (useless thing)* **it's a lem-on** c'est de la camelote

length [leŋθ] *n Br* **to slip sb a length** ⚠ glisser un bout à qn, tringler qn

lesbo ['lezbəʊ] *n Injurieux (abrév* **lesbian***)* gouine *f*

Ce terme perd son caractère injurieux lorsqu'il est utilisé par des lesbiennes.

let off [let] *vi Br (fart)* larguer, lâcher

lettuce ['letɪs] *n Am (money)* blé *m*, oseille *f*, artiche *m*

level ['levəl] *n* **on the level** réglo, régulier

lez [lez], **lezza** ['lezə], **lezzy** ['lezɪ] *n Injurieux (abrév* **lesbian***)* gouine *f*

Ce terme perd son caractère injurieux lorsqu'il est utilisé par des lesbiennes.

lick [lɪk] *vt (defeat)* battre à plates coutures, mettre la pâtée à, ratatiner; **to get licked** être battu à plates coutures; **to give it big licks** se donner à fond ▸ *voir aussi* **arse**

lick out ⚠⚠ *vt sép* **to lick sb out** brouter le cresson à qn

life [laɪf] *n* **get a life!** t'as rien de mieux à faire de ton temps?; *Br* **my life!** c'est pas vrai!

lifer ['laɪfə(r)] *n* prisonnier *m* condamné à perpète

lift [lɪft] *vt (***a***) (steal)* piquer, faucher (**b**) *Br (arrest)* agrafer, alpaguer; **he got lifted for stealing cars** il s'est fait agrafer *ou* alpaguer pour vol de voitures

light [laɪt] *n Hum* **the lights are on but there's nobody home** c'est pas une lumière

lighten up ['laɪtən] *vi* se détendre □

lightweight ['laɪtweɪt] *n* = personne qui ne tient pas l'alcool

like [laɪk] *adv (***a***)* **there were like three thousand people there** il devait y avoir environ trois mille personnes □; **I was busy, like, that's why I didn't call you** j'étais occupé, c'est pour ça que je t'ai pas appelé, tu comprends?; **he just came up behind me, like** il s'est approché de moi par derrière □

(**b**) *(in reported speech)* **I was like "no way"** alors je lui ai fait "pas question"; **so he was like "in your dreams, pal!"** alors il a dit "c'est ça, compte là-dessus mon vieux!"

"Like" est très souvent utilisé pour combler les temps morts lorsque l'on parle, ou après une expression peu claire ou inhabituelle.

lils [lɪlz] *npl Br (breasts)* nichons *mpl*, nénés *mpl*

limey ['laɪmɪ] *Am* **1** *n* Angliche *mf*, Rosbif *mf*
2 *adj* angliche

limp-wristed [lɪmp'rɪstɪd] *adj* efféminé □, chochotte

line [laɪn] *n (of powdered drugs)* ligne *f*; **to do a line** se faire une ligne ▸ *voir aussi* **main**

lionel ['laɪənəl] *npl Br (rhyming slang* **lionel blairs** = **flares***)* pantalon *m* pattes d'eph

Lionel Blair est un comédien et fantaisiste britannique.

lip [lɪp] *n (cheek)* toupet *m*; **don't give me any of your lip!** ne sois pas insolent! □

lippy ['lɪpɪ] **1** *n Br (abrév* **lipstick***)* rouge *m* à lèvres □
2 *adj (cheeky)* insolent □

lipstick lesbian ['lɪpstɪk'lezbɪən] *n* lesbienne *f* glamoureuse □

liquidate ['lɪkwɪdeɪt] *vt (kill)* liquider, refroidir

load [ləʊd] *n (***a***)* **a load of** un tas de; **it's a load of rubbish** c'est un tas de conneries; **get a load of this!** *(look)* matemoi ça!; *(listen)* écoute un peu ça!
(**b**) **loads of** des tas de; **loads of money/time** vachement d'argent/de temps
(**c**) *Am* **to have a load on** être complètement bourré *ou* beurré *ou* pété ▸ *voir aussi* **shoot**

loaded ['ləʊdɪd] *adj (***a***) (wealthy)* plein aux as (**b**) *(drunk)* bourré, beurré, pété; *(on drugs)* défoncé, raide

loaf [ləʊf] *n Br* (*rhyming slang* **loaf of bread** = **head**) citron *m*, cigare *m*; **use your loaf!** réfléchis une minute!

loaf about, loaf around *vi Br* traîner

loan shark ['ləʊnʃɑːk] *n* usurier(ère) ᵘ *m,f*

lob [lɒb] *vt* (*throw*) balancer

local ['ləʊkəl] *n Br* (*pub*) pub *m* du coin (*où l'on a ses habitudes*)

loco ['ləʊkəʊ] *adj Am* timbré, toqué, cinglé

locoweed ['ləʊkəʊwiːd] *n* (*marijuana*) herbe *f*

log [lɒg] *n Br* **to drop a log** [!] (*defecate*) couler un bronze

lolly ['lɒlɪ] *n Br* (*money*) oseille *f*, artiche *m*, fric *m*, pognon *m*

loo [luː] *n Br* vécés *mpl*; **loo paper** papier *m* cul, PQ *m*

looker ['lʊkə(r)] *n* **she's a real looker** elle est vraiment canon; **she's not much of a looker** c'est pas une beauté

loon [luːn] *n* cinglé(e) *m,f*, dingue *mf*, toqué(e) *m,f*

loony ['luːnɪ] **1** *n* cinglé(e) *m,f*, dingue *mf*, toqué(e) *m,f*; **loony bin** maison *f* de fous; **he's fit for the loony bin!** il est bon pour le cabanon!
2 *adj* timbré, dingue, cinglé

loony-tune ['luːnɪtjuːn] *n Am* cinglé(e) *m,f*, dingue *mf*, toqué(e) *m,f*

loony-tunes ['luːnɪtjuːnz] *adj Am* cinglé, toqué, timbré

loop [luːp] *n Am* **to be out of the loop** ne pas être dans le coup; **to cut sb out of the loop** mettre qn aux oubliettes ▶ *voir aussi* **knock**

loopy ['luːpɪ] *adj* cinglé, chtarbé, dingue

loose [luːs] *adj* (*promiscuous*) facile; **to be loose** être une fille facile ▶ *voir aussi* **hang, screw**

loot [luːt] *n* (*money*) fric *m*, pèse *m*, flouze *m*; (*goods*) marchandise ᵘ *f*; (*presents*) cadeaux ᵘ *mpl*

lorry ['lɒrɪ] *n Br Hum* **it fell off the back of a lorry** c'est de la marchandise volée ᵘ

lose [luːz] *vt* (a) **to lose one's cool** se démonter; **to lose one's head** piquer une crise, voir rouge, se mettre en pétard; **to**

lose it (*go mad*) perdre la boule; (*lose one's temper*) piquer une crise, péter les plombs; *Br* **to lose the plot** perdre la boule; *Br* **to lose the place** devenir gaga
  (b) **get lost!** (*go away*) casse-toi!, tire-toi!; (*expressing contempt, disagreement*) n'importe quoi! ▶ *voir aussi* **lunch, marbles, rag, shirt**

loser ['luːzə(r)] *n* (*man*) raté *m*, loser *m*; (*woman*) ratée *f*

Louis ['luːɪ] *n Br* = un seizième d'once (*environ 1,8 gramme*)

C'est un terme de l'argot de la drogue. Il s'agit d'une référence à Louis XVI.

louse [laʊs] *n* (*person*) peau *f* de vache

louse up *vt sép* **to louse sth up** foirer qch

lousy ['laʊzɪ] *adj* (a) (*very bad*) merdique; **to feel lousy** (*ill*) se sentir vraiment mal fichu; (*guilty*) se sentir coupable ᵘ, avoir les boules *ou* les glandes; **we had a lousy time** on s'est vraiment fait suer; **he's in a lousy mood** il est d'humeur dégueulasse; **all he gave me was twenty lousy quid** il ne m'a filé que vingt malheureuses livres
  (b) **to be lousy with sth** être bourré de qch; **the streets were lousy with cops** les rues étaient pleines de flics; **to be lousy with money** être bourré de fric, être plein aux as

love [lʌv] *n* (a) *Br* (*term of address*) (*to one's spouse, partner, child*) chéri(e) *m,f*; (*to male stranger*) Monsieur *m*; (*to female stranger*) Madame *f* (b) **love handles** poignées *fpl* d'amour

loved up [lʌvdˈʌp] *adj Br* tout gentil (*sous l'effet de l'ecstasy*)

lovely jubbly ['lʌvlɪdʒʌblɪ] *exclam Br* super!, au poil!

Il s'agit d'une expression popularisée par Del Boy, le personnage principal d'une série télévisée comique britannique intitulée 'Only Fools and Horses' diffusée pendant les années 80 et 90.

lover boy ['lʌvəbɔɪ] *n Ironique* **she's**

gone out with lover boy elle est sortie avec son Jules; **when's lover boy coming round to see you?** quand est-ce qu'il vient te voir ton Jules?

lovey-dovey [lʌvɪ'dʌvɪ] *adj (behaviour)* sentimental ❑; **to be all lovey-dovey** *(of two lovers)* être comme des tourtereaux

luck into [lʌk] *vt insép Am* **to luck into sth** dégoter qch

luck out, luck up *vi Am* décrocher le gros lot

luck up on *vt insép* **to luck up on sth** dégoter qch

lucky ['lʌkɪ] *adj* **to get lucky** emballer

lug¹ [lʌg] *n Am (man)* abruti *m*, crétin *m*

lug², lughole ['lʌghəʊl] *n Br (ear)* esgourde *f*, portugaise *f*

lulu ['lu:lu:] *n Am* **to be a lulu** être génial

lumber ['lʌmbə(r)] **1** *vt Br* **to get lumbered with sb/sth** se taper *ou* se coltiner qn/qch; **I got lumbered with doing the dishes** je me suis coltiné *ou* farci la vaisselle

2 *n Scot* **to get a lumber** faire une conquête; **is that your lumber?** c'est ta conquête?

lummox ['lʌməks] *n Br (clumsy person)* empoté(e) *m,f*; *(stupid person)* cruche *f*, andouille *f*

lunch [lʌntʃ] *n* **to be out to lunch** *(mad)* travailler du chapeau, être cinglé; **to lose** *or Am* **shoot one's lunch** *(vomit)* gerber, dégobiller; **liquid lunch** = alcool qui tient lieu de déjeuner; **the boss has had another of his liquid lunches** le patron a passé sa pause déjeuner au pub à picoler

lunchbox ['lʌntʃbɒks] *n Br (man's genitals)* service *m* trois pièces, bijoux *mpl* de famille

lunkhead ['lʌŋkhed] *n Am* cruche *f*, andouille *f*, courge *f*

lush [lʌʃ] **1** *n* alcolo *mf*, poivrot(e) *m,f*

2 *adj Br (attractive)* canon, super bien foutu; *(excellent)* super, génial, de la balle

lushed [lʌʃt] *adj Am* pété, bourré, beurré

luvved up [lʌvd'ʌp] = **loved up**

luvvie, luvvy ['lʌvɪ] *n Br Péj (man)* acteur ❑ *m*; *(woman)* actrice ❑ *f*

M

Mac [mæk] *npr Am (term of address)* chef *m*

mack [mæk] *n* **(a)** *Am (pimp)* maquereau *m*, mac *m* **(b)** *Noir Am (expert seducer)* tombeur *m*

mack on *vt insép* **to mack on sb** draguer qn

mad [mæd] *adj* **(a) to be mad about sb/sth** être dingue de qn/qch; *Br* **to be mad for it** *(raring to go)* être prêt à s'éclater **(b) to run/work like mad** courir/travailler comme un dingue

madam ['mædəm] *n* **(a)** *(of brothel)* mère *f* maquerelle **(b)** *Br (arrogant girl)* **she's a little madam** c'est une petite pimbêche **(c)** *Br (term of address)* madame *f*; **that's enough of your cheek, madam!** ça suffit comme ça, petite insolente!

made up [meɪd'ʌp] *adj Br* hyper content

> Il s'agit d'un terme utilisé surtout dans la région de Liverpool.

madhouse ['mædhaʊs] *n (psychiatric hospital, busy place)* maison *f* de fous; **it's like a madhouse in here** c'est une vraie maison de fous ici

mag [mæg] *n (abrév* **magazine)** revue [□] *f*, magazine [□] *m* ▶ *voir aussi* **girlie, skin, stroke, wank**

magic ['mædʒɪk] *adj* **(a)** *Br (excellent)* super, génial **(b) magic mushrooms** champignons *mpl* hallucinogènes [□], champignons *mpl*

magnet ['mægnɪt] *n* **his new car's a babe** *or* **chick** *or* **fanny**‼ **magnet** sa nouvelle voiture est super pour emballer les gonzesses

main [meɪn] *adj* **(a)** *Am* **main man** *(friend)* pote *m*; **yo, my main man,**

how ya doin'? salut mon pote, comment ça va?; *Br* **when it comes to scoring goals, Michael Owen's the main man** pour ce qui est de marquer des buts, Michael Owen est champion

(b) main squeeze *(boyfriend)* mec *m*, Jules *m*; *(girlfriend)* nana *f*, gonzesse *f*

(c) main line *(vein)* veine *f* apparente [□] *(choisie pour s'injecter de la drogue)*

(d) *Am* **main drag** rue *f* principale [□]

mainline ['meɪnlaɪn] **1** *vt (drugs)* se faire un shoot de; *(habitually)* se shooter à **2** *vi* se shooter, se piquer

mainliner ['meɪnlaɪnə(r)] *n* junkie *mf*, shooté(e) *m,f*

make [meɪk] **1** *n* **to be on the make** *(financially)* chercher à s'en mettre plein les poches; *(sexually)* draguer

2 *vt Am* **to make sb, to make it with sb** coucher avec qn

3 *vi Am* **to make like sb** *(pass oneself off as)* essayer de passer pour qn [□]; **he's always making like a tough guy** il essaie toujours de jouer les durs; **make like you don't know anything** fais comme si tu savais pas

make out *vi Am (sexually)* se peloter; **to make out with sb** peloter qn

mama, mamma ['mæmə] *n Am* **(a)** *(woman)* bonne femme *f* **(b) big mama** *(large object)* mastodonte *m*

man [mæn] **1** *n* **(a)** *Br (husband, boyfriend)* mec *m*; **she's got a new man** elle a un nouveau mec

(b) *(term of address)* **hey, man!** *(as greeting)* salut vieux!; **how are you doing, man?** comment ça va, vieux?; **come on, man!** allez!

(c) *Noir Am* **the Man** *(white people)* les

The symbol [□] *indicates that a translation is neutral in register.*

Blancs *mpl*; *(the police)* les flics *mpl*; *(drug dealer)* dealer *m*

2 *exclam* la vache!; **man, am I tired!** la vache, je suis crevé! ▸ *voir aussi* **con, dog, hatchet, main, new, old, play**

Manc [mæŋk] *n Br (abrév* **Mancunian**) = natif de la ville de Manchester

maneater ['mɛni:tə(r)] *n (woman)* mangeuse *f* d'hommes

manky ['mæŋkı] *adj Br* cradingue, crado

manor ['mænə(r)] *n Br (of police, criminal)* territoire *m*

map [mæp] *n Am (face)* tronche *f*, trombine *f*

marbles ['mɑ:bəlz] *npl* **to lose one's marbles** perdre la boule; **to have all one's marbles** ne pas être gâteux du tout

mare¹ [meə(r)] *n Br Péj (woman)* grognasse *f*; **you silly mare!** espèce d'andouille!

mare² *n Br (abrév* **nightmare**) cauchemar □ *m*; **it was a total mare!** c'était un vrai cauchemar!; **her new boyfriend's a complete mare** c'est une vraie tache son nouveau copain; **we had a bit of a mare finding somewhere to park** on a eu vachement de mal pour trouver une place où se garer

mark [mɑ:k] *n* pigeon *f*, poire *f*

massive ['mæsɪv] **1** *adj Ir (brilliant)* super, génial

2 *n Br (gang)* bande *f*; **the Brighton massive** la bande de Brighton

mate [meɪt] *n Br* **(a)** *(friend)* pote *m* **(b)** *(term of address)* **thanks, mate** *(to friend)* merci vieux; *(to stranger)* merci chef; **watch where you're going, mate!** hé, regarde devant toi!

matey ['meɪtɪ] *Br* **1** *n (term of address)* **how's it going, matey?** comment ça va vieux?; **just watch it, matey!** fais gaffe!

2 *adj (friendly)* **to be matey with sb** être pote avec qn; **they're very matey all of a sudden** ils sont très potes tout d'un coup

max [mæks] *(abrév* **maximum**) **1** *n Am* **to the max** *(totally)* un max; **did you have a good time? – to the max!** tu t'es bien

amusé? – vachement bien!, un max!

2 *adv (at the most)* maxi; **it'll take three days max** ça prendra trois jours maxi

3 *vt Am* **to max an exam** obtenir le maximum de points à un examen □ ▸ *voir aussi* **grody**

max out *Am* **1** *vt sép* **to max out one's credit card** dépenser le maximum autorisé avec sa carte de crédit □

2 *vi* **to max out on chocolate** se goinfrer de chocolat; **to max out on booze** picoler un max

maxed [mækst] *adj Am (extremely drunk)* bourré comme un coing, pété à mort

maxed out [mækst'aʊt] *adj Am* **(a)** **to be maxed out on one's credit card** avoir dépensé le maximum autorisé avec sa carte de crédit □ **(b)** **to be maxed out on chocolate/sci-fi movies** avoir fait une overdose de chocolat/de films de science-fiction

mean [mi:n] *adj (excellent)* super, génial; **she's a mean chess player** elle joue super bien aux échecs, elle touche (sa bille) aux échecs; **he makes a mean curry** il fait super bien le curry

meat [mi:t] *n* **(a)** **you're dead meat!** t'es mort!

(b) !!! *(penis)* bite *f*, queue *f*

(c) **meat rack** lieu *m* de drague *(en particulier chez les homosexuels)*

(d) **meat wagon** *(ambulance)* ambulance □ *f*; *(police van)* panier *m* à salade; *(hearse)* corbillard □ *m*

(e) *Br Péj* **meat market** *(nightclub)* = boîte réputée pour être un lieu de drague ▸ *voir aussi* **beat**

meatball ['mi:tbɔ:l], **meathead** ['mi:thed] *n Am (person)* crétin(e) *m,f*, truffe *f*, andouille *f*

meatheaded ['mi:thedɪd] *adj Am* débile

medallion man [mɪ'dæljənmæn] *n Br* macho *m* à chaîne en or

Le "medallion man" est généralement un homme entre deux âges traversant une crise d'identité. Il porte une chemise ouverte sur un torse velu et des bijoux clinquants (dont le fameux médaillon). Il fréquente les boîtes de nuit en compagnie de gens nettement moins âgés que lui, et tente de séduire les jeunes femmes.

mega ['megə] **1** adj (excellent) génial, super, géant; (enormous) énorme
2 adv (very) hyper, méga

mega- ['megə] préfixe hyper; **mega-rich** hyper riche; **mega-famous** hyper célèbre; **mega-angry** hyper en colère

megabucks ['megəbʌks] n un fric fou, une fortune

megastar ['megəstɑː(r)] n superstar f

megilla [mə'gɪlə] n Am **the whole megilla** tout le tremblement; **I don't need the whole megilla, just give me the main points** t'as pas besoin de tout me raconter en détail ou par le menu, dis-moi le principal

mellow ['meləʊ] **1** n Noir Am (friend) pote m
2 adj (**a**) Noir Am (attractive) sexy, craquant (**b**) Noir Am (fine, acceptable) cool; **see you at six? – yeah, that's mellow** on se voit à six heures? – ouais, ça marche! (**c**) (relaxed, unexcited) cool, décontract, relaxe; **stay mellow!** calmos!, du calme! (**d**) (on drugs) **to be mellow** être parti, planer

mellow out vi (relax) se calmer

melons ['melənz] npl (breasts) nichons mpl, roberts mpl

mensch [menʃ] n Am (man) chic type m; (woman) brave femme f

mental ['mentəl] adj (mad) dingue, cinglé; **to go mental** (go mad) devenir dingue ou cinglé, perdre la boule; (lose one's temper) péter les plombs, péter une durite, piquer une crise; Br **it was a mental party!** c'était une fête vraiment démente ou dingue!; Br **you should have seen the way they were shouting at each other, it was mental!** t'aurais vu comme ils se criaient dessus, c'était dingue!

Merc [mɜːk] n (abrév **Mercedes**) Mercedes □ f

merchant ['mɜːtʃənt] n **speed merchant** Br (fast driver) chauffard m; Am (athlete) = coureur à pied très rapide; Br **gossip merchant** commère f; Br **rip-off** or **con merchant** arnaqueur(euse) m,f

Ce terme peut s'ajouter à de nombreux noms pour désigner quelqu'un qui s'adonne à une activité.

merry ['meri] adj Br (slightly drunk) éméché

meshuga [mə'ʃuːgə] adj Am dingue, taré, cinglé

mess [mes] vi (**a**) Br **no messing!** sans blagues! (**b**) **to mess with sb** embêter qn; **don't mess with him!** le cherche pas!, te frotte pas à lui!

mess about, mess around vi (**a**) (act foolishly) faire l'imbécile (**b**) (waste time) glander, glandouiller (**c**) (potter) bricoler (**d**) **to mess about with sb** (sexually) coucher avec qn

metalhead ['metəlhed] n fan mf de heavy metal □, hardeux(euse) m,f

Mex [meks] Am Injurieux (abrév **Mexican**) **1** n Mexicain(e) □ m,f
2 adj mexicain □

Mick [mɪk] npr Injurieux (Irishman) Irlandais □ m

"Mick" est le diminutif de "Michael", l'un des prénoms les plus courants en Irlande. Bien que ce terme ne témoigne pas nécessairement d'une attitude xénophobe de la part de celui qui l'utilise, il est préférable de ne pas l'employer.

mick [mɪk], **mickey** ['mɪkɪ] n Br **to take the mick out of sb/sth** se ficher de qn/qch; **are you taking the mick?** tu te fiches de moi?

Mickey (Finn) ['mɪkɪ('fɪn)] n = boisson alcoolisée dans laquelle on a versé un sédatif

Mickey Mouse ['mɪkɪ'maʊs] adj Péj à la gomme, à la noix (de coco); **he's got a degree from some Mickey Mouse university** il est titulaire d'un diplôme d'une espèce d'université à la noix; **he works**

for some Mickey Mouse dotcom company il travaille pour une espèce de start-
up à la gomme

middle finger salute [ˈmɪdəl-
fɪŋgəsəˈluːt] n Br doigt m d'honneur; **to
give sb the middle finger salute** faire
un doigt d'honneur à qn

middy [ˈmɪdɪ] n Austr (beer) ≃ demi m
de bière

mighty [ˈmaɪtɪ] adv Am vachement, hyper

Mike [maɪk] npr **for the love of Mike!**
c'est quelque chose!, c'est pas vrai!

miles [maɪlz] adv Br (very much) vachement; **I feel miles better** je me sens
vachement mieux; **it's miles more interesting** c'est vachement plus intéressant;
you're miles too slow t'es vachement
trop lent, t'es mille fois trop lent

million [ˈmɪljən] adj **to look (like) a
million dollars** en jeter; **to feel (like) a**
million dollars être au septième ciel

mince pies [mɪnsˈpaɪz] npl Br (rhyming
slang **eyes**) mirettes fpl, calots mpl

mind [maɪnd] n **to be out of one's mind**
être cinglé ou dingue ou fêlé; **to be bored
out of one's mind** mourir d'ennui; **to be
out of one's mind with worry** être
malade d'inquiétude ▸ voir aussi **blow,
pissed**

mind-blowing [ˈmaɪndbləʊɪŋ] adj
époustouflant

minder [ˈmaɪndə(r)] n Br (bodyguard)
garde m du corps □, gorille m

ming [mɪŋ] vi Br puer, coincer, fouetter,
schlinguer; **it mings in here!** ça schlingue ici!

minge [‼] [mɪndʒ] n Br chatte f

minger [ˈmɪŋə(r)] n Br (unattractive person) mocheté f

minging [ˈmɪŋɪŋ] n Br (unattractive) moche; (of poor quality) merdique; **that**

Pleins feux sur:

Money

Parmi les termes d'argot qui désignent l'argent, **dough** et **bread** sont certainement
les plus courants, bien que les termes **dosh** et **bucks** s'emploient souvent au
Royaume-Uni pour le premier, et aux États-Unis pour le second. Les termes
américains **cabbage** et **lettuce** trouvent leur origine dans le fait que les billets sont
verts, et craquants lorsqu'ils sont neufs. La même allusion à la couleur des billets est
présente dans **greenback** (un billet vert de n'importe quelle valeur). Le yiddish a
donné le terme américain **gelt**. **Dead presidents** est une autre expression
humoristique pour désigner les billets aux États-Unis, qui fait référence au fait que
tous les billets américains portent l'effigie d'un président du pays.

Il existe différents termes pour parler de sommes d'argent précises, tels que a **pony**
(25 livres), **a monkey** (500 livres), **a grand** (1000 livres ou 1000 dollars), **a score**
(20 livres ou 20 dollars), **a tenner** (10 livres ou 10 dollars) et **a fiver** (5 livres). En
Grande-Bretagne, **tenner** et **fiver** peuvent aussi désigner le billet lui-même. Pour
100 livres, on emploiera le mot **ton**, tandis qu'un billet de 100 dollars se nomme **a
C-note**, du chiffre romain C qui équivaut à cent. **Quid** est le mot le plus utilisé
pour désigner la livre sterling; il est invariable au pluriel (**ten quid, a thousand
quid**, etc.).

Pour dire que quelqu'un est très riche, on emploiera les expressions **to be loaded**,
to be rolling in it ou, en anglais américain, **to be rolling in dough**, tandis qu'on
dira d'une personne pauvre qu'elle est **broke**, **hard up**, ou en anglais britannique
skint, **strapped** ou **boracic** (de l'argot rimé **boracic lint** = **skint**). On dira d'un
avare qu'il est **tight**. On dit aussi que c'est un **tightwad** en anglais américain.

The symbol □ indicates that a translation is neutral in register.

wine is absolutely minging! ce vin est vraiment dégueulasse!; **is she going out with him? he's minging!** elle sort avec lui? il est moche comme un pou!

mingy ['mɪndʒɪ] *adj Br (person)* radin; *(sum, portion, amount)* ridicule □, minable

minted ['mɪntɪd] *adj Br* plein aux as, bourré de fric

missis, missus ['mɪsɪz] *n Br (wife)* bourgeoise *f*; **the missis** la patronne, ma bourgeoise

mitt [mɪt] *n (hand)* pogne *f*, patte *f*; **get your mitts off me!** bas les pattes!

mix up [mɪks] *vt sép Am* **to mix it up** *(fight)* se castagner, se bastonner

mo¹ [məʊ] *n Br (abrév* **moment***)* instant □ *m*, seconde □ *f*; **half a mo!, wait a mo!** une seconde!

mo² [məʊ] *adv Noir Am (very, much)* vachement; **we're going to be playing some mo phat sounds** on va vous passer de la super musique

Mob [mɒb] *n* **the Mob** la mafia □

mobster ['mɒbstə(r)] *n* gangster □ *m (particulièrement de la mafia)*

moby ['məʊbɪ] *n Br (mobile phone)* mobile *m*

Mockney ['mɒknɪ] *Br* **1** *n* = personne issue d'un milieu aisé qui affecte l'accent cockney
   2 *adj* = caractéristique des personnes issues d'un milieu aisé qui affectent l'accent cockney

mofo [❗] ['məʊfəʊ] *n Noir Am (abrév* **motherfucker***)* enfoiré *m*

mog [mɒg], **moggy** ['mɒgɪ] *n Br* greffier *m*

mondo ['mɒndəʊ] *adv Am* vachement

money ['mʌnɪ] **1** *n* (a) **to be in the money** avoir du fric (b) *Noir Am (term of address)* chef *m*; **what's up, money?** ça va, chef?
   2 *adj Am (cool)* cool

moneybags ['mʌnɪbægz] *n (person)* richard(e) *m,f*, rupin(e) *m,f*; **lend us a fiver, moneybags!** passe-moi cinq livres, toi qui es plein aux as!

money-grubber ['mʌnɪgrʌbə(r)] *n* rapace *m*, requin *m*

mong [mɒŋ] *n Br (abrév* **mongol***)* mongol(e) *m,f*, gol *m*

Bien que ce terme soit très injurieux et politiquement incorrect lorsqu'il s'applique à un trisomique, il est relativement anodin lorsqu'il désigne simplement un imbécile.

moniker ['mɒnɪkə(r)] *n* blase *m*

monkey ['mʌŋkɪ] *n* (a) *Br (£500)* cinq cents livres □ *fpl*
   (b) *Br* **I don't give a monkey's** je m'en fiche pas mal, j'en ai rien à battre
   (c) **monkey business** magouilles *fpl*
   (d) *Am* **to have a monkey on one's back** être accro
   (e) **to spank the monkey** se branler, se taper sur la colonne
   (f) **monkey suit** *(formal suit)* costard *m* chic; *Am (uniform)* uniforme □ *m* ▸ *voir aussi* **brass, features**

monkey about, monkey around *vi* faire l'imbécile

Montezuma's Revenge ['mɒntɪ-'zuːməzrə'vendʒ] *n Hum* la turista

monty ['mɒntɪ] *n Br* **the full monty** le grand jeu, la totale

moo [muː] *n Br Péj (woman)* vieille bique *f*, vieille toupie *f*; **you silly moo!** espèce d'andouille!; **shut up, you old moo!** la ferme, espèce de vieille toupie!

mooch [muːtʃ] **1** *vt* taper, taxer; **to mooch sth off sb** taper *ou* taxer qch à qn
   2 *vi* taxer

mooch about, mooch around 1 *vt insép* **to mooch about the house** traîner dans la maison
   2 *vi* glander, glandouiller

moocher ['muːtʃə(r)] *n* tapeur(euse) *m,f*

moody ['muːdɪ] *adj Br (goods)* volé □; *(passport, document)* faux □

moola, moolah ['muːlə] *n Am* flouze *m*, fric *m*, pognon *m*

moon [muːn] *vi (expose one's buttocks)* montrer ses fesses

---

moonshine ['mu:nʃaɪn] n Am (a) (non-sense) foutaises fpl (b) (illegal alcohol) alcool m de contrebande ⁿ

moose [mu:s] n (unattractive person) mocheté f

morning glory ['mɔ:nɪŋ'glɔ:rɪ] n Br érection f au réveil ⁿ

moron ['mɔ:rɒn] n crétin(e) m,f, imbécile mf

moronic [mə'rɒnɪk] adj débile

mother ['mʌðə(r)] n (a) (large person, thing) mastodonte m; **I've got a mother of a hangover** j'ai une vache de gueule de bois; **her boyfriend's a big mother** son copain est un balaise
(b) [!] (abrév **motherfucker**) (person) enfoiré m; (thing) saloperie f; **some mother's stolen my drink** il y a un enfoiré qui m'a pris mon verre; **the mother's broken down again** cette saloperie est encore tombée en panne

motherfucker [!!] ['mʌðəfʌkə(r)] n (a) (person) enculé m; **he's a stupid motherfucker** c'est un pauvre con (b) (thing) saloperie f; **the motherfucker won't start** cette saloperie ne veut pas démarrer; **I've a motherfucker of a hangover** j'ai une gueule de bois d'enfer

motherfucking [!!] ['mʌðəfʌkɪŋ] adj foutu; **where's that motherfucking bastard?** où est passé cet enculé?; **open up or I'll kick the motherfucking door in!** ouvre ou j'enfonce cette putain de porte!

mothering [!] ['mʌðərɪŋ] adj Am foutu; **where's that mothering bitch?** où est passée cette conne?

motor ['məʊtə(r)] Br **1** n (car) bagnole f **2** vi **to be motoring** (going fast) foncer

motormouth ['məʊtəmaʊθ] n moulin m à paroles

mouth [maʊθ] n **to be all mouth** n'avoir que (de) la gueule; Br Hum **he's all mouth and no trousers** il a que (de) la gueule; **to shoot one's mouth off** parler à tort et à travers; **me and my big mouth!** j'ai encore perdu une occasion de me taire! ► voir aussi **shut**

mouth off [maʊð] vi (brag) se vanter ⁿ, crâner; (talk impudently) la ramener; (talk indiscreetly) parler à tort et à travers

mouthful ['maʊθfʊl] n (a) (word) mot m imprononçable ⁿ; (name) nom m à coucher dehors (b) Br **to give sb a mouthful** traiter qn de tous les noms (c) Am **you said a mouthful!** tu l'as dit, bouffi!

move [mu:v] n (a) **to get a move on** se magner; **get a move on!** magne-toi! (b) **to make a move** (leave) y aller ⁿ, bouger; **to make a move on sb** faire des avances à qn ⁿ

muck [mʌk] n Br (worthless things) **his book's a load of muck** son livre ne vaut pas un clou; **he eats nothing but muck** il mange que des saloperies

muck up [mʌk] **1** vt sép Br (make a mess of) saloper **2** vi Austr (lark around) faire des bêtises ⁿ

mucker ['mʌkə(r)] n Br (a) (friend) pote m (b) (term of address) vieux m; **alright, me old mucker!** salut vieux!, salut mon pote!

muff [!!] [mʌf] n (woman's genitals) chatte f, con m, cramouille f

muff-diving [!!] ['mʌfdaɪvɪŋ] n descente f au barbu; **to go muff-diving** faire une descente au barbu

mug [mʌg] n (a) (face) tronche f, trombine f; **mug shot** = photo d'identité prise par la police ou en prison (b) (gullible person) poire f; **it's a mug's game** le jeu n'en vaut pas la chandelle; **the lottery's a mug's game** le loto, c'est un attrape-couillons

muggins ['mʌgɪnz] n Br mézique; **muggins (here) paid the bill as usual** comme d'habitude c'est mézigue qui a payé l'addition

mule [mju:l] n (drug smuggler) mule f ► voir aussi **hung**

munch out [mʌntʃ] vi Am se goinfrer, s'empiffrer

mullah, muller ['mʊlə] vt (a) (defeat heavily) écraser, foutre la pâtée à (b) (hit) foutre un gnon à

mullahed, mullered ['mʊləd] adj Br bourré, beurré, pété, fait

---

The symbol ⁿ indicates that a translation is neutral in register.

munchies ['mʌntʃɪz] *npl* (**a**) *(hunger)* fringale *f*; **to have the munchies** avoir la dalle (**b**) *(food)* amuse-gueule *mpl*

munter ['mʌntə(r)] *n Br (ugly woman)* laideron *f*, mocheté *f*, cageot *m*

muppet ['mʌpɪt] *n Br (person)* andouille *f*

murder ['mɜːdə(r)] **1** *n (difficult task, experience)* **it was murder** c'était l'enfer; **the traffic was murder** il y avait une circulation dingue; **it's murder trying to park in the town centre** c'est l'enfer pour trouver à se garer dans le centre-ville; **standing all day is murder on your feet** ça fait vachement mal aux pieds de rester debout toute la journée
2 *vt* (**a**) *(song, language)* massacrer (**b**) *Br* **I could murder a fag/beer** je me taperais bien une clope/une bière (**c**) *(defeat)* ratatiner, écrabouiller, foutre la pâtée à

mush [mʊʃ] *n Br (term of address)* **oi, mush!** hé, Duchenoque!

muso ['mjuːzəʊ] *Br (abrév* **musician***)* musico *m*

mutha ['mʌðə] *Noir Am* = **mother**

muthafucka ['mʌðəfʌkə] *Noir Am* = **motherfucker**

mutt [mʌt] *n* clébard *m*, clebs *m*

mutton ['mʌtn] *adj Br (rhyming slang* **Mutt 'n' Jeff** = **deaf***)* sourdingue

> Mutt and Jeff étaient les personnages d'un dessin animé américain dans les années 30.

N

nab [næb] *vt* (**a**) *(catch, arrest)* pincer, alpaguer (**b**) *(steal)* piquer, faucher

nads ⚠ [nædz] *npl* (*abrév* **gonads**) *Br (testicles)* couilles *fpl*

naff [næf] *adj Br (clothes, place, person)* ringard; *(comment, behaviour)* débile; **naff all** que dalle; **I've got naff all money** j'ai que dalle comme argent

naff off *vi Br* s'arracher, se casser; **naff off!** *(go away)* casse-toi!; *(expressing contempt, disagreement)* va te faire voir!

naffing ['næfɪŋ] *Br* **1** *adj (for emphasis)* foutu, sacré; **shut your naffing mouth!** ferme-la!, ferme ton clapet!; **naffing hell!** putain!
2 *adv (for emphasis)* vachement; **you're so naffing stupid!** t'es vraiment débile!; **you're naffing well coming with me!** tu viens avec moi, un point c'est tout!

nag [næg] *n Br (horse)* bourrin *m*, canasson *m*; **he won a grand and put it all on a nag** il a gagné mille livres et les a misées sur un canasson

Nam [næm] *npr (abrév* **Vietnam**) le Vietnam

Le terme "Nam" n'est utilisé que dans le contexte de la guerre du Vietnam.

nancy (boy) ['nænsɪ(bɔɪ)] *n (effeminate man)* chochotte *f*; *(homosexual man)* homo *m*

narc [nɑːk] *n Am (abrév* **narcotics agent**) agent *m* de la Brigade des stups

nark [nɑːk] **1** *n* (**a**) *(informer)* mouchard(e) *m,f* (**b**) *Br (grumbler)* râleur(euse) *m,f*
2 *vt Br (annoy)* foutre en rogne *ou* en boule
3 *vi (inform)* **to nark on sb** balancer qn

narked [nɑːkt] *adj Br* en rogne

narky ['nɑːkɪ] *adj Br* ronchon

nasty ['nɑːstɪ] **1** *n* **to do the nasty** *(have sex)* faire crac-crac; **have you done the nasty yet?** est-ce que vous avez fait crac-crac?
2 *adj Am (excellent)* super, génial; **she makes a nasty pizza** elle fait super bien la pizza

natch [nætʃ] *exclam (abrév* **naturally**) bien sûr!

natter ['nætə(r)] *Br* **1** *n* converse *f*; **to have a natter** tailler une bavette
2 *vi* papoter

neat [niːt] *Am* **1** *adj (excellent)* super, génial
2 *exclam* super!, génial!

neck [nek] **1** *n* (**a**) *Br (cheek)* culot *m*; **she's got some neck!** elle a un sacré culot! (**b**) *Br* **to get it in the neck** se faire remonter les bretelles
2 *vi (of couple)* se peloter
3 *vt Br (drink)* descendre; **I necked ten pints last night** j'ai descendu dix pintes hier soir ▸ *voir aussi* **brass, dead, pain**

ned [ned] *n Scot* zonard *m*

Il s'agit d'un terme qui s'utilise à Glasgow et dans les environs.

needful ['niːdfʊl] *n Br (what is necessary)* **to do the needful** faire le nécessaire ᵘ; **have you got the needful?** *(money)* t'as du fric?

needle ['niːdəl] **1** *n* **to get the needle** se foutre en boule *ou* en rogne; **to give sb the needle** foutre qn en boule *ou* en rogne
2 *vt (irritate)* foutre en boule *ou* en rogne
3 *vi (inject drugs)* se shooter, se piquer

nelly ['nelɪ] *n Br* **not on your nelly!** des clous!

nerd [nɜːd] *n* ringard *m*

The symbol ᵘ indicates that a translation is neutral in register.

Le "nerd" est une personne, générale-ment jeune, qui par son désintérêt pour les activités prisées par les gens de son âge, son absence de goût en matière vestimentaire et son incapacité à com-muniquer de façon satisfaisante avec au-trui, se rend impopulaire auprès des autres. Le "nerd" est souvent un pas-sionné d'informatique.

nerdy ['nɜːdɪ] adj ringard

never-never ['nevə'nevə(r)] n Br & Austr **to buy sth on the never-never** acheter qch à crédit [□]

new [njuː] adj Br **new lad** jeune homme m moderne [□]; **new man** homme m moderne [□]

Les concepts de "new lad" et de "new man" sont apparus à la fin des années 80. Le "new lad" est un jeune homme dont les centres d'intérêt ne diffèrent en rien de ceux de n'importe quel autre jeune homme (à savoir les sorties, les rencontres, le sport…) mais dont l'atti-tude témoigne d'une certaine sophisti-cation absente chez le "lad" moyen. Le "new lad" sait boire avec modération et n'est pas sexiste. Le "new man", lui, ne craint pas de laisser s'exprimer sa sensi-bilité. Il est constamment à l'écoute des besoins de sa compagne et participe équitablement à l'éducation des enfants et aux tâches ménagères.

newbie ['njuːbɪ] n Am bleu(e) m,f (per-sonne nouvellement recrutée)

newsie ['njuːzɪ] n Am **(a)** (newspaper vendor) vendeur(euse) m,f de journaux [□] **(b)** (journalist) journaleux(euse) m,f

next [nekst] adv Am **to get next to sb** (ingratiate oneself with) faire de la lèche à qn; (become emotionally involved with) se lier avec qn [□]; (have sex with) coucher avec qn

nibs [nɪbz] n Br **his/her nibs** son altesse, cézigue

nice [naɪs] adj Br **nice one!** bravo! ▸ voir aussi **earner**

nick [nɪk] Br **1** n **(a)** (police station) poste m; (prison) bloc m **(b)** (condition) condi-tion [□] f, état [□] m; **in good/bad nick** en bon/mauvais état

2 vt **(a)** (arrest) agrafer, alpaguer; **he got nicked for stealing a car** il s'est fait arrêter pour vol de voiture [□] **(b)** (steal) pi-quer, faucher

nickel ['nɪkəl] n Am **(a)** (five cents) **it's not worth a plugged nickel** ça vaut pas un clou **(b)** (five dollars) cinq dollars [□] mpl; **to buy a nickel of weed** acheter pour cinq dollars d'herbe

nicker ['nɪkə(r)] n Br (pounds sterling) li-vres fpl sterling [□]

niff [nɪf] Br **1** n puanteur [□] f

2 vi refouler, schlinguer, fouetter

niffy ['nɪfɪ] adj Br qui fouette ou refoule

nifty ['nɪftɪ] adj **(a)** (stylish) chouette, classe; **they've got a nifty house** ils ont une chouette baraque; **that's a nifty sweater** il est chouette, ce pull **(b)** (clever) (solution, idea) astucieux [□]; (person) adroit [□], débrouillard; **a nifty little gad-get** un petit gadget très astucieux; **a nifty piece of work** du bon travail **(c)** (quick) rapide [□]; (agile) agile [□]

nigga ['nɪgə] n Noir Am Injurieux nègre (négresse) m,f

Lorsqu'il est utilisé par des Noirs amé-ricains, le terme "nigga" perd son carac-tère injurieux et acquiert une con-notation positive.

nigger ['nɪgə(r)] n Injurieux nègre (né-gresse) m,f

Lorsqu'il est utilisé par des Noirs amé-ricains, le terme "nigger" perd son ca-ractère injurieux et acquiert une con-notation positive.

nimrod ['nɪmrɒd] n Am (fool) crétin(e) m,f, andouille f

Nip [nɪp] n Injurieux Jap mf

nipper ['nɪpə(r)] n Br môme m, gosse m

nippy ['nɪpɪ] adj **(a)** (weather) **it's nippy** ça pince, il fait frisquet **(b)** Br (car) ma-niable [□]

The symbol [□] indicates that a translation is neutral in register.

nit [nɪt], **nitwit** ['nɪtwɪt] *n Br* andouille *f*, courge *f*

nob [nɒb] *n Br* (*rich person*) rupin(e) *m,f*, richard(e) *m,f*

no-brainer [nəʊ'breɪnə(r)] *n Am* crétin(e) *m,f*

noddle ['nɒdəl] *n Br* (*head*) caboche *f*, cafetière *f*, ciboulot *m*; **use your noddle!** fais marcher ton ciboulot *ou* tes méninges!

noggin ['nɒgɪn] *n* caboche *f*, cafetière *f*, ciboulot *m*

noise [nɔɪz] *n Br* **shut your noise!** la ferme!, boucle-la!

no-mark ['nəʊmɑːk] *n* (*pathetic person*) (*male*) nul *m*, pauvre type *m*; (*female*) nulle *f*

nonce [nɒns] *n Br* (*sex offender*) délinquant *m* sexuel (*s'attaquant particulièrement aux enfants*)

no-no ['nəʊnəʊ] *n* **it's a no-no** ça ne se fait pas □; **asking him for more money is a definite no-no** il est hors de question de lui demander plus d'argent

noodle ['nuːdəl] *n* (*head*) caboche *f*, cafetière *f*, ciboulot *m*

nookie, nooky ['nʊkɪ] *n* partie *f* de jambes en l'air; **to have a bit of nookie** *or* **nooky** faire une partie de jambes en l'air

nope [nəʊp] *adv* non □, nan

Norah ['nɔːrə] *npr Br* **flaming Norah!**, punaise!, purée!; **bloody Norah!** [!] putain!

nork [!] [nɔːk] *n Br & Austr* (*breast*) nichon *m*

north and south ['nɔːθən'saʊθ] *n Br* (*rhyming slang* **mouth**) bouche □ *f*, clapet *m*

nose [nəʊz] *n* **to have a nose job** se faire refaire le nez □; *Br* **to get up sb's nose** taper sur les nerfs à qn; **to keep one's nose clean** se tenir à carreau; **to pay through the nose (for sth)** payer le prix fort (pour qch); **nose candy** (*cocaine*) coco *f*, neige *f*

nose-rag ['nəʊzræg] *n* tire-jus *m*

nosey parker [nəʊzɪ'pɑːkə(r)] *n Br* fouine *f*

nosh [nɒʃ] **1** *n* bouffe *f*
2 *vi* bouffer

nosh-up ['nɒʃʌp] *n Br* gueuleton *m*

not [nɒt] *adv* **it was a great party... not!** c'était pas vraiment génial comme soirée!; **he's really gorgeous...not!** c'est pas exactement un Apollon!

> Cette structure a été rendue célèbre par le film comique américain *Wayne's World*, l'histoire de deux adolescents prolongés. Ce film est à l'origine d'expressions désormais couramment utilisées par de nombreux jeunes, aussi bien en Grande-Bretagne qu'aux États-Unis.

nothing doing ['nʌθɪŋ'duːɪŋ] *exclam* pas question!

nowt [naʊt] *pron Br* (*nothing*) rien □, que dalle

nuddy ['nʌdɪ] *n Br Hum* **in the nuddy** (*naked*) à poil

nudge nudge wink wink ['nʌdʒ-'nʌdʒ'wɪŋk'wɪŋk] *exclam Br* vous voyez ce que je veux dire!

> Cette expression fut popularisée par l'émission de télévision *Monty Python's Flying Circus* au cours des années 70. On l'emploie pour indiquer à son interlocuteur que ce que l'on dit comporte des sous-entendus, souvent de nature grivoise.

nuke [njuːk] *vt* (**a**) (*attack with nuclear weapons*) atomiser □ (**b**) (*cook in microwave*) faire cuire au four à micro-ondes □ (**c**) (*defeat*) ratatiner, battre à plates coutures

number ['nʌmbə(r)] *n* (**a**) (*cannabis cigarette*) joint *m* (**b**) **to do a number one/two** (*urinate/defecate*) faire la petite/grosse commission (**c**) **I've got your number!** j'ai repéré ton manège! (**d**) *Am* **to do a number on sth** (*spoil, ruin*) bousiller qch

numb nuts ['nʌmnʌts] *n Am Hum* (*idiot*) andouille *f*, crétin(e) *m,f*, nouille *f*; **you've gone the wrong way, numb nuts!** tu t'es trompé de route, andouille!

numbskull ['nʌmskʌl] *n* crétin(e) *m,f*, andouille *f*, cruche *f*

numero uno ['nuːmərəʊ'uːnəʊ] *n & adj Am* numéro un; **don't forget who's numero uno round here** n'oublie pas qui commande *ou* qui est le patron ici; **he's the numero uno coke dealer** c'est le principal dealer de coke

numpty ['nʌmptɪ] *n Scot (idiot)* crétin(e) *m,f*, cruche *f*, andouille *f*

nurd [nɜːd] *Am* = **nerd**

nut [nʌt] *n* **(a)** *(head)* caboche *f*, cafetière *f*, ciboulot *m*; **to be off one's nut** *(mad)* être dingue *ou* cinglé; **to go off one's nut** *(go mad)* perdre la boule, devenir cinglé; *(get angry)* péter les plombs, péter une durite, piquer une crise; *Br* **to do one's nut** *(get angry)* péter les plombs, péter une durite, piquer une crise

(b) *(person)* cinglé(e) *m,f*, dingue *mf*; **a football/computer nut** un fana de football/d'informatique

(c) **he can't drive/sing for nuts** il conduit/chante comme un pied

(d) **nuts** ! *(testicles)* boules *fpl*, couilles *fpl* ▸ *voir aussi* **sweet**

nutball ['nʌtbɔːl] *n Am* cinglé(e) *m,f*, dingue *mf*

nutcase ['nʌtkeɪs] *n* cinglé(e) *m,f*, dingue *mf*

nuthouse ['nʌthaʊs] *n* maison *f* de fous

nuts [nʌts] **1** *adj (mad)* dingue, cinglé, timbré; **to go nuts** *(go mad)* devenir cinglé, perdre la boule; *(get angry)* péter les plombs, péter une durite; **to drive sb nuts** rendre qn chèvre; **to be nuts about sb/sth** être dingue de qn/qch

2 *exclam* mince!, zut!; **nuts to that!** plutôt crever!

nutso ['nʌtsəʊ] *Am adj* dingue, cinglé, timbré; **to go nutso** *(go mad)* devenir cinglé, perdre la boule; *(get angry)* péter les plombs, péter une durite; **to drive sb nutso** rendre qn chèvre; **to be nutso about sb/sth** être dingue de qn/qch

nutter ['nʌtə(r)] *n Br* cinglé(e) *m,f*, dingue *m,f*

nutty ['nʌtɪ] *adj (mad)* dingue, cinglé, timbré; *Hum* **as nutty as a fruitcake** complètement ravagé

nympho ['nɪmfəʊ] *n (abrév* **nymphomaniac**) nympho *f*

o

-o [əʊ] *suffixe* **sicko** malade *mf*, tordu(e) *m, f*; **thicko** nouille *f*, andouille *f*; **pinko** gaucho *mf*

> Le suffixe "-o" s'utilise pour construire un nom à partir d'un adjectif. Il s'agit d'un procédé générateur en anglais.

oar [ɔ:(r)] *n Br* **to stick one's oar in** ramener sa fraise

oats [əʊts] *npl* **(a) to sow one's (wild) oats** jeter sa gourme; *Br* **to get one's oats** tirer un coup **(b)** *Am* **to feel one's oats** *(feel full of energy)* être en pleine forme □; *(be self-important)* faire l'important □

ocker ['ɒkə(r)] *Austr* **1** *n (boor)* beauf *m*
2 *adj* beauf

OD [əʊ'di:] *(abrév* **overdose) 1** *n* overdose *f*
2 *vi* faire une overdose **(on** de); **I've OD'd on pizzas/soap operas lately** j'ai tellement mangé de pizza/regardé de feuilletons télé ces derniers temps que j'en suis dégoûté

oddball ['ɒdbɔ:l] **1** *n* allumé(e) *m,f*, farfelu(e) *m,f*
2 *adj* loufoque, farfelu

odds [ɒdz] *npl Br (difference)* **it makes no odds** ça change rien; **it makes no odds what I say** ce que je dis ne sert à rien □; **what's the odds?** qu'est-ce que ça peut faire?

ofay [əʊ'feɪ] *n Am Injurieux* sale Blanc (Blanche) *m,f*

off [ɒf] **1** *adj Br (unacceptable)* **that was a bit off** c'est un peu fort de café
2 *vt Am (kill)* buter, refroidir, zigouiller

offie ['ɒfɪ] *n Br (abrév* **off-licence)** magasin *m* de vins et spiritueux □

off-the-wall ['ɒfðə'wɔ:l] *adj* bizarroïde

oi [ɔɪ] *exclam* hé!

oik [ɔɪk] *n Br* plouc *mf*

oiled [ɔɪld] *adj* **(well) oiled** *(drunk)* bourré, beurré, pété

okay-dokay, okey-dokey ['əʊkɪ-'dəʊkɪ] *exclam* OK, d'accord, dac

old [əʊld] *adj* **old lady** *(wife)* bourgeoise *f*; *(mother)* vieille *f*; *Br* **old dear** *(elderly woman)* grand-mère *f*; *(mother)* vieille *f*; *Br* **old lag** truand *m*; **old fella, old man** *(husband)* Jules *m*; *(father)* vieux *m*; *(penis)* zob *m*; **old woman** *(wife)* bourgeoise *f*; *(mother)* vieille *f*; *(timid, fussy man)* chochotte *f*

oldie ['əʊldɪ] *n (person)* vieux (vieille) *m,f*; **(golden) oldie** *(song)* vieux succès □ *m*; *(film)* classique *m* du cinéma populaire □

on [ɒn] **1** *adj* **(a)** *Br* **it's not on!** *(unacceptable)* ça va pas du tout! **(b) fancy a pint? – you're on!** tu bois une bière? – je veux!; **if you wash the dishes, I'll dry them – you're on!** si tu fais la vaisselle, je l'essuie – ça marche! **(c)** *Br* **to be on** *(menstruating)* avoir ses ragnagnas
2 *adv Br* **to be** *or* **go on about sth** jacter de qch sans arrêt; **what's she (going) on about now?** qu'est-ce qu'elle raconte maintenant?
3 *prép* **what's he on?** il se sent bien?

one [wʌn] *n* **(a) to give sb one** ! *(have sex with)* en glisser une paire à qn
(b) to have had one too many avoir bu un coup de trop
(c) *(blow)* **to belt/thump sb one** en coller une à qn
(d) *Br (person)* **you are a one!** toi alors!; **he's a right one, him!** lui alors, il est impayable!
(e) *Br* **to go into one** *(lose one's temper)* péter les plombs, péter une durite ► *voir aussi* **lay, nice**

The symbol □ indicates that a translation is neutral in register.

one-eyed adj Hum **one-eyed trouser snake** anguille f de caleçon

one-night stand [wʌnnaɪt'stænd] n aventure f sans lendemain ▫

oodles ['uːdəlz] npl **oodles of** un max de, des masses de; **to have oodles of money** avoir un max de fric, être plein aux as; **to have oodles of time** avoir vachement de temps

oomph [ʊmf] n (a) (sex appeal) sex-appeal ▫ m; **she's got plenty of oomph** elle est vachement sexy (b) (vigour) punch m, pêche f; **their new album lacks the oomph of the last one** leur nouvel album n'a pas la pêche du précédent

oreo (cookie) ['ɔːrɪəʊ('kʊkɪ)] n Am Péj (person) = personne de couleur qui adopte les valeurs des Blancs

Un "Oreo® cookie" est un type de biscuit au chocolat fourré à la crème: noir à l'extérieur mais blanc à l'intérieur.

orgasmic [ɔː'gæzmɪk] adj (food, smell, taste) jouissif

Oscar ['ɒskə(r)] n Austr (rhyming slang Oscar Asche = cash) pognon m, fric m

OTT [əʊtiː'tiː] adj Br (abrév **over the top**) **the house is nice, but the decor's a bit OTT** la maison est bien, mais la décoration est un peu lourdingue; **it's a bit OTT to call him a fascist** c'est un peu exagéré de le traiter de fasciste; **he went completely OTT when he heard what**

she'd said il a pété les plombs quand il a appris ce qu'elle avait dit

out [aʊt] **1** adj (a) (not in fashion) démodé ▫ (b) (openly homosexual) ouvertement homosexuel ▫

2 adv (a) **to be out of it** (drunk, on drugs) être raide; **I felt a bit out of it** (excluded) je me sentais un peu de trop

(b) **out of order** (unacceptable) inacceptable ▫; **that was a bit out of order!** c'est un peu fort de café!; **you were out of order to call her a slut** t'aurais pas dû la traiter de salope

(c) **I'm out of here** je me casse; **let's get out of here** allez, on se casse

(d) **out there** loufoque; **listen to him, he's completely out there!** écoute-le, il divague complètement!

3 vt (homosexual) dévoiler l'homosexualité de ▫

outta ['aʊtə] contraction (abrév **out of**) **let's get outta here!** allez, on se casse!; **you must be outta your mind!** mais t'es complètement dingue!; Am **outta sight** (excellent) dingue, dément

owt [aʊt] pron Br (anything) quelque chose ▫; **he never said owt** il n'a jamais rien dit ▫; **is there owt the matter?** il y a quelque chose qui va pas?

Oz [ɒz] npr (abrév **Australia**) Australie ▫ f

Ozzie ['ɒzɪ] **1** adj n australien

2 (abrév **Australian**) Australien(enne) ▫ m,f

P

pack [pæk] **1** *vt* **to pack a gun** être armé ❑, être chargé
2 *vi* (**a**) **to be packing** être armé ❑, être chargé (**b**) **to send sb packing** envoyer qn balader ► *voir aussi* **fanny**

pack in *vt sép* **to pack sb/sth in** plaquer *ou* laisser tomber qn/qch; **pack it in!** ça suffit!

pack up *vi Br* (**a**) *(stop work)* dételer (**b**) *(break down)* tomber en panne ❑; **the telly packed up just as Beckham was about to score** la télé m'a/nous a lâché(s) juste au moment où Beckham allait marquer

packet ['pækɪt] *n Br* (**a**) *(large amount of money)* **to cost a packet** coûter bonbon; **to earn a packet** gagner des mille et des cents (**b**) *(man's genitals)* service *m* trois pièces

pad [pæd] *n (home)* casbah *f*; **you can crash at my pad** tu peux pieuter chez moi

Paddy ['pædɪ] *npr Injurieux (Irishman)* Irlandais ❑ *m*

"Paddy" est le diminutif de "Patrick", l'un des prénoms les plus courants en Irlande. Bien que ce terme ne témoigne pas nécessairement d'une attitude xénophobe de la part de celui qui l'utilise, il est préférable de ne pas l'employer.

paddy ['pædɪ] *n* (**a**) *Br* **to be in a paddy** *(angry)* être en rogne (**b**) *Am* **paddy wagon** *(police van)* panier *m* à salade

pain [peɪn] *n* **to be a pain (in the neck)** être casse-pieds; *Am* **to give sb a pain (in the neck)** taper sur le système à qn; **to be a pain in the** *Br* **arse** *or Am* **ass** [!] être casse-couilles *ou* chiant; **it's a real pain in the** *Br* **arse** *or Am* **ass having to get up so early** [!] ça fait vraiment chier de devoir se lever si tôt

Paki ['pækɪ] *n Br Injurieux* (*abrév* **Pakistani**) *(person)* Pakistanais(e) ❑ *m,f*; **Paki shop, Paki's** = épicerie de quartier tenue par un Pakistanais

Lorsqu'il est question d'une épicerie de quartier tenue par un Pakistanais, le terme "Paki" perd sa connotation raciste. Il est toutefois déconseillé de l'utiliser.

Paki-basher ['pækɪbæʃə(r)] *n Br* = individu qui attaque des gens d'origine pakistanaise

Paki-bashing ['pækɪbæʃɪŋ] *n Br* = violences à l'encontre d'immigrés pakistanais

pal [pæl] *n* (**a**) *(friend)* pote *m* (**b**) *(term of address)* **thanks, pal** *(to friend)* merci, vieux; *(to stranger)* merci, chef; **watch where you're going, pal** hé, regarde où tu vas!

pal around *vi* **to pal around with sb** être pote avec qn; **they palled around for a while at high school** il y a un moment où ils étaient potes au lycée

palaver [pə'lɑːvə(r)] *n Br (fuss)* **what a palaver!** quelle histoire!; **it was a real palaver getting a work permit** ça a été la croix et la bannière pour obtenir un permis de travail; **we had the usual palaver about who was going to pay** ça a été le cirque habituel pour décider qui allait payer

pally ['pælɪ] *adj Br* **to be pally with sb** être pote avec qn; **they're very pally all of a sudden** ils sont très potes tout d'un coup

palooka [pə'luːkə] *n Am* (**a**) *(clumsy man)* manche *m*; *(stupid man)* andouille *f*, crétin *m* (**b**) *(inept fighter)* mauvais boxeur ❑ *m*

palsy-walsy ['pælzɪ'wælzɪ] *adj* **to be**

palsy-walsy with sb être comme cul et chemise avec qn, être à tu et à toi avec qn; **they're very palsy-walsy all of a sudden** ils sont très potes *ou* copain-copain tout d'un coup

pan [pæn] **1** *n Br* **to go down the pan** être foutu en l'air; **that's our holidays down the pan** on peut faire une croix sur nos vacances
2 *vt (criticize)* éreinter

panic button ['pænɪkbʌtən] *n Am* **to hit the panic button** paniquer, flipper

pansy ['pænzɪ] *n (effeminate man)* chochotte *f; (homosexual man)* tante *f*

pants [pænts] **1** *npl* **(a)** **to beat the pants off sb** battre qn à plates coutures; **to scare the pants off sb** foutre une trouille pas possible à qn; **to bore the pants off sb** ennuyer qn à mourir; **he charmed the pants off my parents** il a conquis mes parents □ **(b)** **to be caught with one's pants down** être pris sur le fait en train de faire une bêtise
2 *n Br (nonsense)* foutaises *fpl;* **don't listen to him, he's talking pants** ne l'écoute pas, il raconte n'importe quoi; **that TV programme's a load of pants!** c'est n'importe quoi, cette émission de télé; **that's pants!** n'importe quoi!
3 *adj Br (of poor quality)* nul; **that movie was absolute pants!** ce film était particulièrement nul!
4 *exclam Br* zut! ▸ *voir aussi* **pee**

papers ['peɪpəz] *npl Am* **go peddle your papers!** va voir ailleurs si j'y suis!

paralytic [pærə'lɪtɪk] *adj Br (very drunk)* pété à mort, bourré comme un coing, rond comme une queue de pelle

park [pɑːk] *vt* **to park oneself beside sb/on sth** se poser *ou* poser ses fesses à côté de qn/sur qch; **park your** *Br* **bum** *or Am* **butt over here beside me!** pose-toi ici, à côté de moi! ▸ *voir aussi* **walk**

parky ['pɑːkɪ] *adj Br* frisquet; **it's parky today** il fait frisquet aujourd'hui

party ['pɑːtɪ] **1** *n* **party animal** fêtard(e) *m,f;* **party hat** *(condom)* capote *f*
2 *vi* faire la fête

party-pooper ['pɑːtɪpuːpə(r)] *n* rabat-joie *mf*

pass [pɑːs] *n* **to make a pass at sb** faire du plat à qn

past [pɑːst] *prép Br* **to be past it** *(of person)* avoir passé l'âge; *(of thing)* avoir fait son temps

paste [peɪst] *vt (beat up)* tabasser; *(defeat)* battre à plates coutures; **to get pasted** *(beaten up)* se faire tabasser; *(defeated)* être battu à plates coutures

pasting ['peɪstɪŋ] *n* **to give sb a pasting** *(beat up)* tabasser qn; *(defeat)* battre qn à plates coutures; **to** *Br* **get** *or Am* **take a pasting** *(be beaten up)* se faire tabasser; *(be defeated)* être battu à plates coutures

patch [pætʃ] *n Br (of prostitute, salesperson, police officer)* territoire *m*

patsy ['pætsɪ] *n Am* pigeon *m*

paw [pɔː] **1** *n (hand)* pogne *m*, patte *f; Br* **paws off!**, *Am* **keep your (big) paws off!** bas les pattes!
2 *vt (touch sexually)* peloter

payoff ['peɪɒf] *n (bribe)* pot-de-vin *m*

pdq [piːdiːˈkjuː] *adv (abrév* **pretty damn quick)** illico presto

peach [piːtʃ] *n* **she's a peach** elle est canon; **a peach of a goal/dress** un but/une robe magnifique

peachy (keen) ['piːtʃɪ(kiːn)] *adj Am* super, génial, grand

peanuts ['piːnʌts] *npl (small amount of money)* cacahuètes *fpl*

pearl necklace [!!] [pɜːl'neklɪs] *n* collier *m* de perles

pear-shaped ['peəʃeɪpt] *adj Br* **to go pear-shaped** partir en eau de boudin; **when the neighbours called the police it all began to go pear-shaped** quand les voisins ont appelé la police tout est parti en eau de boudin

pecker ['pekə(r)] *n* **(a)** [!] *Am (penis)* bite *f*, queue *f* **(b)** *Br* **to keep one's pecker up** ne pas se laisser abattre □

peckerwood ['pekəwʊd] *n* **(a)** *Noir Am Péj* Blanc (Blanche) *m,f* **(b)** *Am* plouc *mf*

pee [!] [piː] **1** *n* pipi *m;* **to have a pee** faire pipi; **to go for a pee** aller faire pipi

2 vt **to pee oneself** or Br **one's pants** faire pipi dans sa culotte; **to pee oneself (laughing)** rire à en faire dans sa culotte

3 vi faire pipi; **it's peeing (it) down** (raining) il pleut comme vache qui pisse

pee off [!] vt sép (annoy) **to pee sb off** faire chier qn; **to be peed off** être fumasse ou furibard; **to be peed off at sb/about sth** être en pétard contre qn/à cause de qch; **to be peed off with sb/sth** (have had enough of) en avoir ras le bol de qn/qch

peeler ['pi:lə(r)] n Br (policeman) flic m

peg out [peg] vi (die) passer l'arme à gauche, calancher

pen [pen] n (a) Am (abrév **penitentiary**) taule f; **in the pen** en taule, en cabane (b) Br (abrév **penalty**) péno m

pen-and-ink [penən'ɪŋk] vi Br (rhyming slang **stink**) schlinguer, fouetter

penguin suit ['pengwɪnsu:t] n Br costard m chic

penny ['penɪ] n Br **to spend a penny** (urinate) faire la petite commission

perp [pɜ:p] n Am (abrév **perpetrator**) criminel(elle) [□] m,f

perv [pɜ:v] n (abrév **pervert**) Br & Austr pervers(e) [□] m,f, détraqué(e) m,f; **stop staring at me, you dirty perv!** arrête de me fixer comme ça, espèce de détraqué!

pervy ['pɜ:vɪ] adj Br pervers

pet [pet] n Br (term of address) chéri(e) m,f; **be a pet and let the cat out, would you?** laisse sortir le chat, tu seras gentil

Pete [pi:t] npr **for Pete's sake!** bon sang!

peter ['pi:tə(r)] n Am (penis) quéquette f, zizi m

petrolhead ['petrəlhed] n Br dingue m de bagnoles

pew [pju:] n Br **take** or **have a pew!** (sit down) pose-toi quelque part!

phat [fæt] adj Noir Am super, génial; **we got some phat tunes for you tonight** on va vous passer de la super musique ce soir

phwoah [fwɔ:], **phwoar(gh)** [fwɔ:(r)] exclam wouaouh!; **phwoah! that bird's got some rack on her!** wouaouh! elle a des sacrés nichons, la nana!

pick up [pɪk] vt sép **to pick sb up** (sexual partner) lever qn; (criminal) agrafer qn, coffrer qn

pickled ['pɪkəld] adj (drunk) bourré, pété, beurré

picnic ['pɪknɪk] n **it was no picnic!** c'était pas de la tarte! ▸ voir aussi **sandwich**

picture ['pɪktʃə(r)] n (film) film [□] m; Br **the pictures** (the cinema) le cinoche, le ciné

piddle ['pɪdəl] **1** n pipi m; **to have a piddle** faire pipi; **to go for a piddle** aller faire pipi

2 vi faire pipi

piddling ['pɪdəlɪŋ] adj (details) insignifiant [□]; (amount) minable

piece [pi:s] n (a) **a piece of cake**, Br **a piece of piss** [!] un jeu d'enfant (b) Am (gun) flingue m

pie-eyed [paɪ'aɪd] adj rond, bourré

pig [pɪg] **1** n (a) (greedy person) goinfre mf; **to make a pig of oneself** se goinfrer (b) (ugly person) mocheté f; (unpleasant person) chameau m; **he's a real pig to her** il est vraiment salaud avec elle (c) Br (thing) truc m chiant; **cleaning the oven is a pig of a job** c'est vraiment chiant de nettoyer le four; **the desk was a pig to move** le bureau était vachement chiant à déménager (d) (police officer) flic m, poulet m; **the pigs** les flics mpl, les poulets mpl (e) Br **to make a pig's ear of sth** foirer qch; **he made a pig's ear of laying the carpet** il a posé la moquette comme un vrai sagouin

2 vt Br **to pig oneself (on)** se goinfrer (de)

pig out vi se goinfrer (**on** de)

pigeon ['pɪdʒɪn] n Am (person) pigeon m, poire f ▸ voir aussi **stool**

pig-thick ['pɪg'θɪk] adj Br con comme un balai

The symbol [□] indicates that a translation is neutral in register.

pig-ugly ['pɪg'ʌglɪ] *adj Br* moche comme un pou

pillhead ['pɪlhed] *n* accro *mf* aux tranquillisants ou aux speeds

pillock ['pɪlək] *n Br* andouille *f*, courge *f*

pillow-biter ['pɪləʊbaɪtə(r)] *n Injurieux* pédé *m*, tantouze *f*

pill-popper ['pɪlpɒpə(r)] *n* accro *mf* aux tranquillisants ou aux speeds

pinch [pɪntʃ] *vt (arrest)* pincer, alpaguer

pinhead ['pɪnhed] *n* crétin(e) *m,f*, andouille *f*, courge *f*

pinko ['pɪŋkəʊ] **1** *n* gaucho *mf*
2 *adj* gaucho

pins [pɪnz] *npl (legs)* cannes *fpl*, gambettes *fpl*; **she's got a great pair of pins** elle a des super gambettes

pish [pɪʃ] *Scot* = **piss**

pished [pɪʃt] *Scot* = **pissed**

piss [!] [pɪs] **1** *n* **(a)** *(urine)* pisse *f*; **to** *Br* **have** *or Am* **take a piss** pisser; **to go for a piss** aller pisser; *Br* **piss flaps** [!!] grandes lèvres □ *fpl*, escalopes *fpl*
   (b) *Br* **to take the piss out of sb/sth** se foutre de qn/qch; **are you taking the piss?** tu te fous de moi?
   (c) *Br* **to be on the piss** se péter, se bourrer la gueule, prendre une cuite; **to go on the piss** aller se bourrer la gueule, aller prendre une cuite
   (d) *Br (worthless things)* **the film/book was piss** le film/le bouquin ne valait pas un clou; **their beer is piss** leur bière, c'est du pipi de chat
   2 *vt* **to piss oneself** se pisser dessus; **to piss oneself (laughing)** rire à en pisser dans sa culotte
   3 *vi* **(a)** *(urinate)* pisser; **it's pissing down, it's pissing with rain** il pleut comme vache qui pisse **(b)** **to piss all over sb** *(defeat)* battre qn à plates coutures **(c)** *Am* **to piss and moan** geindre, pleurnicher
   4 *adv* **piss poor** merdique; *Br* **piss easy** fastoche ▶ *voir aussi* **gnat, piece, pot, streak**

piss about [!], **piss around** [!] **1** *vt sp Br* **to piss sb about** *(cause problems for)* se foutre de la gueule de qn; *(waste time of)* faire perdre son temps à qn □
   2 *vi (waste time)* glander, glandouiller

piss away [!] *vt sép* **to piss sth away** *(winnings, inheritance)* gaspiller qch □

piss off [!] **1** *vt sép (annoy)* **to piss sb off** faire chier qn; **to be pissed off** être fumasse; **to be pissed off at sb/about sth** être en pétard contre qn/à cause de qch; **to be pissed off with sb/sth** *(have had enough of)* en avoir ras le bol de qn/qch
   2 *vi (go away)* se casser, se tirer; **piss off!** *(go away)* fous le camp!, tire-toi!, dégage! ; *(expressing contempt, disagreement)* va te faire foutre!

piss-artist [!] ['pɪsɑːtɪst] *n Br* poivrot(e) *m,f*, alcolo *mf*

pissbucket [!] ['pɪsbʌkɪt] *n* **(a)** *(toilet)* chiottes *fpl* **(b)** *(person)* ordure *f*, raclure *f*

pissed [!] [pɪst] *adj* **(a)** *Br (drunk)* pété, bourré; **to get pissed** se péter la gueule; **as pissed as a fart** *or* **a newt, pissed out of one's head** *or* **mind** bourré comme un coing, plein comme une barrique, rond comme une queue de pelle
   (b) *Am (annoyed)* **to be pissed** être fumasse; **to be pissed at sb/about sth** être en pétard contre qn/à cause de qch; **to be pissed with sb/sth** *(have had enough of)* en avoir ras le bol de qn/qch

pissed-up [!] ['pɪst'ʌp] *adj Br (drunk)* bourré, pété, beurré

pisser [!] ['pɪsə(r)] *n* **(a)** *(annoying situation)* **what a pisser!** quelle merde! ; **it was a real pisser that the weather wasn't better** c'était vraiment chiant qu'il fasse pas plus beau
   (b) *Am (remarkable situation)* **what a pisser!** c'est génial *ou* super!
   (c) *Am (annoying person)* emmerdeur(euse) *m,f* ; *(remarkable person)* **to be a pisser** être un mec/une nana génial(e)

pisshead [!] ['pɪshed] *n* **(a)** *Br (drunkard)* poivrot(e) *m,f*, alcolo *mf* **(b)** *Am (unpleasant person)* connard (connasse) *m,f*

pisshole [!] ['pɪshəʊl] *n* **his eyes are like**

pissholes in the snow il a des petits yeux

piss-take ⚠ ['pɪsteɪk] n Br satire □ f; **this is a piss-take, isn't it?** non mais tu te fous de ma gueule ou quoi?

piss-up ⚠ ['pɪsʌp] n Br beuverie f; **to have a piss-up** prendre une cuite, se bourrer la gueule; **to go on a piss-up** aller prendre une cuite ou se bourrer la gueule; **Hum he couldn't organize a piss-up in a brewery** c'est un incompétent de première

pit [pɪt] n **(a)** (untidy place) foutoir m **(b)** Br (bed) plumard m, pieu m **(c) to be the pits** être complètement nul

pixilated ['pɪksɪleɪtəd] adj Br bourré, pété, beurré

pizza ['piːtsə] n Hum **to have a face like a pizza** être une vraie calculette

pizza-face ['piːtsəfeɪs] n Hum calculette f

PJs ['piːdʒeɪz] npl (abrév **pyjamas**) pyjama □ m

plank [plæŋk] n Br nouille f, andouille f; **you plank!** espèce d'andouille!

plant [plɑːnt] n (person) taupe f; (thing) = objet caché dans le but d'incriminer quelqu'un

plastered ['plɑːstəd] adj (drunk) bourré, pété, beurré

plastic ['plæstɪk] n (credit cards) cartes fpl de crédit □; **to put sth on the plastic** payer qch avec une carte de crédit; **do they take plastic?** est-ce qu'ils acceptent ou prennent les cartes de crédit?; **can I pay with plastic?** vous prenez les cartes de crédit?

plates [pleɪts] npl Br (rhyming slang **plates of meat** = **feet**) arpions mpl, panards mpl

play [pleɪ] **1** vt Br **play the white man!** sois sympa!
2 vi **(a) to play hard to get** se faire désirer □ **(b) to play with oneself** (masturbate) se caresser, se toucher **(c) to play for the other side** or **team** (to be gay) en être, être de la jaquette; (to be a lesbian) être gouine; **to play for both sides**

or **teams** marcher à voile et à vapeur ▶ voir aussi **deck, hell**

pleb [pleb] n Br Péj (abrév **plebeian**) prolo mf

plebby ['plebɪ] adj Br Péj (abrév **plebeian**) prolo

plod [plɒd] n Br (police officer) flic m; **the plod** les flics, les poulets, la flicaille

plonk [plɒŋk] **1** n Br (wine) piquette f
2 vt (put, place) flanquer, coller, foutre; **just plonk your stuff on the table** t'as qu'à foutre tes affaires sur la table; **plonk yourself down over there** pose-toi là-bas

plonker ['plɒŋkə(r)] n Br **(a)** (person) andouille f, courge f, truffe f **(b)** (penis) quéquette f, zizi m

plowed [plaʊd] adj Am (drunk) pété, bourré, beurré

plug [plʌg] **1** n **to pull the plug on sth** (stop financing) arrêter de financer qch □
2 vt Am (shoot) flinguer

plug-ugly ['plʌg'ʌglɪ] adj moche comme un pou

plums ⚠ [plʌmz] npl Br (testicles) couilles fpl, valseuses fpl

pocket billiards ['pɒkɪt'bɪljədz], Am **pocket pool** ['pɒkɪt'puːl] n Hum **to play** Br **pocket billiards** or Am **pocket pool** se caresser les boules à travers sa poche de pantalon

poison ['pɔɪzən] n **name your poison!**, Br **what's your poison?** qu'est-ce que tu bois?

poke [pəʊk] **1** n **(a)** ⚠ (sexual intercourse) **to have a poke** tirer un coup **(b)** Hum **it's better than a poke in the eye with a sharp stick** c'est mieux que rien □
2 ⚠ vt (have sex with) tringler, troncher

pokey ['pəʊkɪ] n Am (prison) taule f, cabane f; **in the pokey** en taule, en cabane, à l'ombre

pol [pɒl] n Am (abrév **politician**) politicien □ m

polack ['pəʊlæk] n Injurieux Polack mf

pole [pəʊl] n **(a)** Br **to be up the pole** (mad) être dingue ou cinglé; **to be up**

The symbol □ indicates that a translation is neutral in register.

the pole with worry être fou ou malade d'inquiétude ᵁ; **to drive sb up the pole** rendre qn chèvre (**b**) [!] (penis) queue f, bite f

polluted [pəˈluːtɪd] adj Am (drunk) pété, beurré, bourré, rond

pommie, pommy [ˈpɒmɪ] Austr **1** n angliche m,f
 2 adj angliche

ponce [pɒns] n Br (**a**) (effeminate man) chochotte f (**b**) (pimp) maquereau m

ponce about, ponce around vi Br (**a**) (of effeminate man) faire chochotte (**b**) (waste time) glander, glandouiller

poncy [ˈpɒnsɪ] adj Br qui fait chochotte

pond [pɒnd] n (**a**) **the pond** (the Atlantic) l'Océan m Atlantique ᵁ; **across the pond** outre-Atlantique ᵁ (**b**) **pond life** des moins que rien

pong [pɒŋ] Br **1** n puanteur ᵁ f
 2 vi schlinguer, fouetter

pony [ˈpəʊnɪ] n Br (£25) vingt-cinq livres ᵁ fpl

poo [puː] **1** n (**a**) (excrement) caca m; **to**

do or Br **have a poo** faire caca (**b**) Br (worthless things) **it's a load of poo** ça vaut pas un clou; **he's talking a load of poo** il raconte n'importe quoi
 2 vi faire caca

pooch [puːtʃ] n (dog) clébard m, clebs m
 ▶ voir aussi **screw**

poof [puːf], **poofter** [ˈpuːftə(r)] n Br Injurieux pédé f, pédale f, tantouze f, tapette f

poofy [ˈpuːfɪ] adj Br Injurieux qui fait tapette; **he's got a really poofy voice** il parle vraiment comme un pédé

Pool [puːl] npr (abrév **Liverpool**) **the Pool** = surnom donné à la ville de Liverpool

poon [!!] [puːn], **poontang** [!!] [ˈpuːntæŋ] n Am (**a**) (female genitals) chatte f, chagatte f, cramouille f (**b**) (women) gonzesses fpl, meufs fpl; **he's gone out looking for poontang** il cherche une meuf à se mettre sur le bout

poonani [!] [puːˈnænɪ] n chatte f, foufoune f

Pleins feux sur :

Police

Parmi les termes argotiques les plus anciens pour désigner un policier, citons **bobby** et **peeler**, deux mots formés à partir du nom du fondateur de la police britannique, Robert Peel. Cependant, ces deux mots ne sont maintenant que très rarement employés. Aujourd'hui, les termes non péjoratifs **copper** et **cop** (provenant probablement du verbe "to cop" = attraper, arrêter) sont les plus courants. **Rozzer** est aussi fréquent en Grande-Bretagne, où l'on emploie également depuis les années 70 le mot **plod** qui peut désigner un policier (**a plod**) ou la police en général (**the plod**); ce terme a pour origine le nom du policier de la fameuse série pour enfants d'Enid Blyton *Noddy* (*Oui-Oui* en français). Il existe d'autres façons de désigner la police, comme par exemple **the boys in blue** (allusion à la couleur de l'uniforme), **the Bill** ou **the Old Bill**, **the fuzz** et l'expression métonymique **the law**.

Certains termes sont un peu plus péjoratifs. On appelle souvent un agent de police **a pig**. Quant à **flatfoot**, c'est un terme vieilli en anglais britannique, mais il est toujours utilisé aux États-Unis. En Grande-Bretagne, le mot **filth** peut s'employer collectivement pour parler de la police.

D'autres expressions permettent de désigner certains éléments spécifiques de la police. Pour la brigade volante de Scotland Yard, on dira **the Sweeney** (de l'argot rimé Sweeney Todd = flying squad). Aux États-Unis, un membre de la brigade des stupéfiants est appelé **a narc** (de **narcotics agent**) et un agent du FBI, **a Fed**.

The symbol ᵁ indicates that a translation is neutral in register.

poop [puːp] *Am* **1** *n* caca *m*; **to take a poop** faire caca
2 *vi* faire caca

pooped [puːpt] *adj Am* crevé, nase, lessivé

pop[1] [pɒp] **1** *n* (**a**) *(fizzy drink)* soda □ *m* (**b**) **they cost £20 a pop** *(each)* ils coûtent vingt livres pièce
2 *vt* (**a**) **to pop the question** proposer le mariage □ (**b**) **to pop pills** prendre des pilules □ ▶ *voir aussi* **cherry, clogs**

pop[2] *n Am (father)* papa *m*

pop off *vi (die)* calancher, passer l'arme à gauche

Pope [pəʊp] *n Hum* **is the Pope Catholic?** ça me paraît évident

> Il s'agit d'une expression utilisée lorsque quelqu'un vient de poser une question que l'on juge superflue tant il paraît évident que la réponse ne peut être qu'affirmative.

popper [ˈpɒpə(r)] *n (drug)* popper *m*, nitrate *m* d'amyle □

pops [pɒps] = **pop**[2]

pork[!] [pɔːk] **1** *n Hum* **pork (sword)** *(penis)* queue *f*, bite *f*
2 *vt (have sex with)* tringler, troncher

porker [ˈpɔːkə(r)] *n (man)* gros lard *m*; *(woman)* grosse vache *f*

porky [ˈpɔːkɪ] **1** *n Br* **porky (pie)** *(rhyming slang* **lie***)* mensonge □ *m*, craque *f*
2 *adj (fat)* gros □, mastard

posh [pɒʃ] *n Br (cocaine)* coke *f*

posse [ˈpɒsɪ] *n* (**a**) *(group of friends)* bande *f*; **he's out with the posse** il est sorti avec ses potes *ou* avec sa bande (**b**) *Noir Am (entourage)* clique *f* (**c**) *Noir Am (criminal gang)* gang *m*

postal [ˈpəʊstəl] *adj Am* **to go postal** péter les plombs

> Au début des années 90 il y eut plusieurs assassinats qui eurent pour cadre les services postaux américains.

pot [pɒt] *n* (**a**) *(marijuana)* herbe *f*, beu *f* (**b**) **to go to pot** *(deteriorate)* aller à vau-l'eau (**c**) **he hasn't got a pot to piss in**[!] il est complètement fauché ▶ *voir aussi* **shit**

pothead [ˈpɒthed] *n* **to be a pothead** marcher au haschisch

potted [ˈpɒtɪd] *adj Am (drunk)* pété, fait, bourré, rond

potty [ˈpɒtɪ] *adj Br* dingue, cinglé, timbré; **to be potty about sb/sth** être dingue de qn/qch

pox [pɒks] *n Br* **the pox** *(syphilis)* la vérole □

poxy [ˈpɒksɪ] *adj Br (worthless)* minable; **he only gave me a poxy five pounds for it** il me l'a acheté cinq malheureuses livres

prang [præŋ] *Br* **1** *n* accrochage □ *m*; **to have a prang** avoir un accrochage
2 *vt (vehicle)* bigorner

prat [præt] *n* crétin(e) *m,f*, courge *f*, andouille *f*, cruche *f*

prat about, prat around *vi Br (act foolishly)* faire l'idiot; *(waste time)* glander, glandouiller

prawn [prɔːn] *n Austr* **don't come the raw prawn with me!** n'essaie pas de m'embobiner!

preggers [ˈpregəz] *adj* en cloque

preppy [ˈprepɪ] *Am* **1** *n* ≃ BCBG *mf*
2 *adj* ≃ BCBG

president [ˈprezɪdənt] *n Am* **dead presidents** biftons *mpl*, fafiots *mpl*

> Ce terme fait référence au fait que tous les billets américains portent l'effigie d'un président des États-Unis.

pressie, prezzie [ˈprezɪ] *n Br (abrév* **present***)* cadeau □ *m*

previous [ˈpriːvjəs] *n (previous convictions)* casier *m* judiciaire □; **he's got previous for drink-driving** il a déjà été arrêté pour conduite en état d'ivresse

priceless [ˈpraɪslɪs] *adj (amusing)* impayable, crevant

prick[!!] [prɪk] *n* (**a**) *(penis)* bite *f*, queue *f*, pine *f*; **to feel like a spare prick (at a wedding)** tenir la chandelle (**b**) *(man)*

The symbol □ indicates that a translation is neutral in register.

tête *f* de nœud, connard *m*, blaireau *m*; **stop behaving like such a prick!** arrête donc de faire le con!

pricktease !!! ['prɪktiːz], **prick-teaser** !! ['prɪktiːzə(r)] *n* allumeuse *f*

private parts ['praɪvɪt'pɑːts], **privates** ['praɪvɪts] *npl* parties *fpl* génitales □

pro [prəʊ] *n* (a) (*abrév* **prostitute**) pute *f* (b) (*abrév* **professional**) pro *mf*

prob [prɒb] *n* (*abrév* **problem**) problème □ *m*, blème *m*; *Br* **no probs!** pas de problèmes!

Prod [prɒd], **Proddy** ['prɒdɪ] *n Br* (*abrév* **Protestant**) protestant(e) □ *m,f*

profile ['prəʊfaɪl] *vi Noir Am* (*show off*) frimer, crâner

pronto ['prɒntəʊ] *adv* illico (presto), pronto

psycho ['saɪkəʊ] **1** *n* (*abrév* **psychopath**) psychopathe □ *mf*, cinglé(e) *m,f*
2 *adj* (*abrév* **psychopathic**) cinglé, timbré, dingue; **to go psycho** devenir dingue

pub-crawl ['pʌbkrɔːl] *n Br* tournée *f* des bars □; **to go on a pub-crawl** faire la tournée des bars

pubes [pjuːbz] *npl* (*abrév* **pubic hairs**) poils *mpl* pubiens □

puff [pʌf] *n Br* (a) (*marijuana*) herbe *f*, beu *f*; (*cannabis*) shit *m*, hasch *m* (b) (*life*) vie □ *f*; **I've never seen him in my puff!** je le connais ni d'Ève ni d'Adam!

puke [pjuːk] **1** *n* dégueulis *m*
2 *vi* dégueuler, gerber

pukka ['pʌkə] *adj Br* (a) (*excellent*) génial, super (b) (*genuine*) réglo, régulier □

pull [pʊl] **1** *n* (a) **to be on the pull** chercher à lever une nana/un mec (b) (*influence*) piston *m*; **to have a lot of pull** avoir le bras long
2 *vt* (a) (*sexual partner*) lever, emballer (b) *Br Hum* **to pull one's pudding** ! se tirer sur l'élastique, se taper la colonne
3 *vi* (*find sexual partner*) faire une touche ▶ *voir aussi* **fast, plug**

pull off !!! *vt sép* **to pull sb off** branler qn; **to pull oneself off** se branler

pulling power ['pʊlɪŋpaʊə(r)] *n Br* pouvoir *m* de séduction □; **he thinks his new sports car will do wonders for his pulling power** il croit que sa nouvelle voiture de sport l'aidera à lever les nanas

pump [pʌmp] *vt* **to pump iron** faire de la gonflette ▶ *voir aussi* **lead**

pumped [pʌmpt] *adj Am* (*excited*) surexcité; (*enthusiastic*) emballé

punch out [pʌntʃ] *vt sép Br* **to punch sb's lights out**, *Am* **to punch sb out** amocher qn, arranger le portrait à qn

punk [pʌŋk] *n Am* (*worthless person*) ordure *f*

punter ['pʌntə(r)] *n Br* (a) (*gambler*) parieur(euse) □ *m,f* (b) (*consumer, customer*) client(e) □ *m,f* (c) (*prostitute's client*) micheton *m*

push [pʊʃ] **1** *n* (a) *Br* **to give sb the push** (*employee*) virer qn; (*boyfriend, girlfriend*) plaquer qn; **to get the push** (*of employee*) se faire virer; (*of boyfriend, girlfriend*) se faire plaquer (b) *Austr* (*gang*) bande *f*, clique *f*
2 *vt* (a) (*drugs*) dealer (b) **to be pushing forty/fifty** friser la quarantaine/cinquantaine (c) **it'll be pushing it to finish by five** ça va faire un peu juste pour finir à cinq heures; **that's pushing it a bit** c'est un peu exagéré; **don't push your luck!** fais gaffe à toi! ▶ *voir aussi* **daisy**

push off *vi Br* mettre les bouts, se casser, se tirer; **push off!** tire-toi!, casse-toi!

pusher ['pʊʃə(r)] *n* (*drug dealer*) dealer *m*

pushover ['pʊʃəʊvə(r)] *n* (a) (*person*) poire *f*, pigeon *m* (b) (*thing*) jeu *m* d'enfant; **the German exam was a pushover** l'examen d'allemand était hyper fastoche

puss [pʊs] *n* (a) (*cat*) minou *m*, minet *m* (b) (*face*) binette *f*, frimousse *f*

pussy ['pʊsɪ] *n* (a) (*cat*) minou *m*, minet *m* (b) !! (*woman's genitals*) chatte *f*, chagatte *f*, cramouille *f* (c) !! (*women*) nanas *fpl*, cuisse *f*; (*sex*) baise *f*; **they're out looking for pussy** ils cherchent des meufs; **he hasn't had**

The symbol □ indicates that a translation is neutral in register.

any **pussy for weeks** ça fait des semaines qu'il a pas baisé *ou* qu'il a pas tiré un coup
(d) ⚠ *(weak, cowardly man)* lavette *f*

pussy-whipped ⚠ ['pʊsɪwɪpt] *adj* dominé par sa femme □; **he's totally pussy-whipped** c'est sa femme qui porte la culotte

put [pʊt] *vt Br* **put it there!**, *Am* **put 'er there!** *(shake hands)* serrons-nous la pince!

put about *vt sép Br* **(a) to put a rumour about** répandre une rumeur □; **to put it about that...** répandre la rumeur comme quoi... **(b) to put it** *or* **oneself about** *(be promiscuous)* coucher à droite à gauche

put away *vt sép* **(a) to put sb away** *(in prison)* mettre qn à l'ombre; *(in psychiatric hospital)* interner qn □, enfermer qn chez les fous **(b) to put sth away** *(food, drink)* s'envoyer qch; **he can really put it away!** *(food)* il a un sacré appétit!; *(drink)* qu'est-ce qu'il descend!

put on *vt sép* **(a) to put sb on** *(tease)* faire marcher qn **(b) to put it on** *(pretend)* faire du cinéma *ou* du chiqué

put out *vi Am (of woman)* accepter de coucher (**for** avec); **did she put out?** est-ce qu'elle a bien voulu coucher?; **she'd put out for anybody** elle coucherait avec le premier venu

put over *vt sép* **to put one over on sb** gruger qn

putrid ['pju:trɪd] *adj (worthless)* pourri; **that burger was putrid** ce burger était vraiment dégueulasse

put-up ['pʊtʌp] *adj* **a put-up job** un coup monté

putz [pʌts] *n Am* andouille *f*, truffe *f*

putz around *vi Am* **(a)** *(act foolishly)* faire l'idiot, faire l'imbécile **(b)** *(waste time)* glander, glandouiller

---

The symbol □ indicates that a translation is neutral in register.

q.t. [kjuːˈtiː] *n* **on the q.t.** en douce, en loucedé

quack [kwæk] *n Br Péj (doctor)* toubib *m*

queen [kwiːn] *n* (**a**) *(effeminate homosexual)* folle *f* (**b**) *Injurieux (any homosexual man)* pédé *m*, tantouze *f*, tapette *f*

> Ce terme perd son caractère injurieux lorsqu'il est utilisé par des homosexuels. Par ailleurs, lorsqu'il désigne un individu efféminé (sens (a)), il n'est jamais véritablement injurieux. Il convient toutefois de l'utiliser avec circonspection.

queer [kwɪə(r)] **1** *n Injurieux (homosexual)* pédé *m*, pédale *f*, tantouze *f*
  2 *adj* (**a**) *Injurieux (homosexual)* pédé, homo (**b**) *Br* **to be in queer street** être dans la mouise *ou* dans la panade ► *voir aussi* **act, fish**

> Ce terme perd son caractère injurieux quand il est utilisé par des homosexuels.

queer-basher [ˈkwɪəbæʃə(r)] *n* = individu qui se livre à des violences à l'encontre d'homosexuels

queer-bashing [ˈkwɪəbæʃɪŋ] *n* = violences à l'encontre d'homosexuels; **he's into queer-bashing** il aime bien aller casser du pédé

quickie [ˈkwɪkɪ] **1** *n* **to have a quickie** *(drink)* boire un coup en vitesse; *(sex)* tirer un coup vite fait
  2 *adj* **quickie divorce** divorce *m* express

quid [kwɪd] *n Br (pound sterling)* livre *f* sterling □; **to be quids in** être à l'aise, avoir du fric

quim [!!] [kwɪm] *n* chatte *f*, chagatte *f*, con *m*

R

rabbit ['ræbɪt] **1** n Péj **rabbit food** (salad) verdure f; Br **rabbit hutch** (accommodation) cage f à lapins **(b) to fuck like rabbits**‼ baiser comme des lapins

2 vi Br (rhyming slang **rabbit and pork** = **talk**) jacter, jacasser

rabbit on vi Br bavasser (**about** à propos de); **what's he rabbiting on about?** qu'est-ce qu'il bave?

rack [ræk] n **(a)** Am **to hit the rack** (go to bed) se pieuter, se bâcher **(b)** (breasts) nichons mpl, nénés mpl, roberts mpl; **look at the rack on that!** mate un peu les nichons de la nana!

rack back vt sép **to rack sb back** passer un savon à qn, remonter les bretelles à qn

rack off vi Austr se casser; **just rack off, will you!** casse-toi!

racket ['rækɪt] n **(a)** (noise) boucan m, barouf m; **to make a racket** faire du boucan ou du barouf **(b)** (criminal activity) activité f criminelle□; **protection racket** racket m; **drugs racket** trafic m de drogue

rad [ræd] adj (abrév **radical**) super, génial, géant

radical ['rædɪkəl] adj super, génial, géant

rag [ræg] n **(a)** (newspaper) torchon m

(b) Br **to lose one's** or **the rag** piquer une crise, péter les plombs

(c) to be on the rag‼ avoir ses ragnagnas

(d) to feel like a wet rag or Am **a dish rag** se sentir ramollo

(e) Am **rags** (clothes) fringues fpl ▸ voir aussi **chew**

raghead ['ræghed] n Am Injurieux raton m, bicot m

rake in [reɪk] vt sép **to rake sth in** (money) ramasser qch à la pelle; **he must be raking it in!** il doit s'en mettre plein les poches!

rake-off ['reɪkɒf] n commission f illicite□, ristourne f

ralph [rælf] vi gerber, dégueuler

randy ['rændɪ] adj excité (sexuellement)

rank [ræŋk] adj **(a)** Br (worthless) merdique **(b)** (ugly) moche; **she is rank!** c'est un vrai cageot!

rank on vt insép **to rank on sb** agonir qn d'injures, traiter qn de tous les noms

rap [ræp] n **(a)** (blame) **to take the rap (for sth)** écoper (pour qch); Am **to beat the rap** échapper à la condamnation□, être acquitté□; Am **rap sheet** casier m judiciaire□

(b) Am (speech) **don't give me that rap!** raconte pas n'importe quoi!; **he was laying down some rap about the new model** il était en train de faire un baratin sur le nouveau modèle

2 vt Am (criticize) éreinter, descendre

3 vi Noir Am (talk) causer; **what's he rapping about now?** qu'est-ce qu'il raconte maintenant? ▸ voir aussi **bum**

rare [reə(r)] adj Scot (excellent) super, génial; **we had a rare night out last night** on a passé une super soirée hier

raspberry ['rɑːzbərɪ] n Br **(a)** (rhyming slang **raspberry ripple** = **nipple**) mamelon□ m

(b) (**raspberry ripple** = **cripple**) infirme mf

rat [ræt] n **(a)** (person) salaud m, salopard m, ordure f

(b) I don't give a rat's ass‼ je m'en fous pas mal, je m'en balance

(c) Br **to do sth/go somewhere like a rat up a drainpipe** faire qch/aller quelque part à fond de train; **when he**

The symbol □ indicates that a translation is neutral in register.

heard the police siren, he was off like a rat up a drainpipe quand il a entendu la sirène de la police, il est parti comme une flèche ▶ voir aussi frat

rat on vt insép **to rat on sb** balancer qn, moucharder qn

rat out vt sép **to rat sb out** balancer qn, moucharder qn

rat-arsed [!] ['rætɑːst] adj Br bourré comme un coing, pété à mort, plein comme une barrique

ratbag ['rætbæg] n Br salaud m, salopard m, ordure f

ratfink ['rætfɪŋk] n Am salaud m, salopard m, ordure f

ratted ['rætɪd] adj Br bourré comme un coing, pété à mort, plein comme une barrique; **to get ratted** se péter, se torcher

ratty ['rætɪ] adj râleur, rouspéteur

raunchy ['rɔːntʃɪ] adj sexy

raver ['reɪvə(r)] n Br (**a**) (socially active person) noceur(euse) m,f (**b**) (person who attends raves) raver mf

rave-up ['reɪvʌp] n Br boum f

razz [ræz] **1** vt Am (jeer at) chambrer
  2 n Br **to go on the razz** faire la bringue ou la teuf

razzle ['ræzəl] n Br **to go on the razzle** faire la bringue ou la teuf

readies ['redɪz] npl Br liquide m (argent)

real [rɪəl] **1** adj **is he for real?** il est sérieux?; **get real!** arrête de rêver!, redescends sur terre!
  2 adv Am (very) vachement; **you were**

real lucky t'as eu une sacré veine; **it's real hot** il fait vachement chaud; **we had a real good time** on s'est vachement bien amusés

ream out [riːm] vt sép Am **to ream sb out** (scold) passer un savon à qn, remonter les bretelles à qn

rear end [rɪər'end] n (buttocks) arrière-train m

redneck ['rednek] n Am plouc mf, bouseux(euse) m,f (du Sud des États-Unis); **a redneck politician/cop** un homme politique/flic tout ce qu'il y a de plus réactionnaire

reefer ['riːfə(r)] n (cannabis cigarette) joint m, stick m

ref [ref] n (abrév **referee**) arbitre □ m

rellies ['relɪz] n Br (relatives) famille □ f; **are you seeing your rellies at Christmas?** tu vas voir ta famille à Noël?

rent boy ['rentbɔɪ] n Br jeune prostitué m homosexuel □

rents [rents] npl Am (abrév **parents**) vieux mpl, renps mpl

rep [rep] n (abrév **reputation**) réputation □ f; **my rep will take a hammering if they find out she dumped me** ma réputation va en prendre un coup s'ils apprennent qu'elle m'a larguée

repo ['riːpəʊ] **1** n (abrév **repossession**) **repo man** huissier □ m (chargé par une société de saisir des biens non payés)
  2 vt (abrév **repossess**) saisir □

represent [reprɪ'zent] vi Noir Am se pointer

result [rɪ'zʌlt] n Br **to get a result** (in

Rhyming slang

Il s'agit d'un procédé argotique complexe consistant à remplacer un mot par une expression dont le dernier terme rime avec le mot en question; bien souvent n'est prononcé que le premier terme de l'expression, à savoir celui qui ne rime pas avec le mot remplacé. Exemple: kids = dustbin lids = dustbins; head = loaf of bread = loaf. À l'origine ce type d'argot était pratiqué par les Cockneys (les habitants de l'est de Londres) mais certains termes sont maintenant passés dans le langage courant et sont connus de la plupart des Britanniques (c'est le cas de la grande majorité des termes figurant dans ce dictionnaire).

The symbol □ indicates that a translation is neutral in register.

sport) gagner [□], l'emporter [□]; **he had a result last night, he pulled some gorgeous bird** il a fait fort hier soir, il a levé une super nana; **a 20% pay rise? (what a) result!** 20% d'augmentation? tus as fait fort!

retard ['riːtɑːd] *n* crétin(e) *m,f*, débile *mf* mental(e)

Richard [!] ['rɪtʃəd] *npr Br (rhyming slang* **Richard the Third** = **turd**) étron *m*

ride [raɪd] **1** *n* (**a**) [!!] *(sexual partner)* **to be a good ride** être un bon coup (**b**) *Noir Am (car)* bagnole *f*, caisse *f*, tire *f*
  2 [!!] *vt (have sex with) (of man)* baiser, tringler, troncher, sauter; *(of woman)* baiser avec, s'envoyer

rig [rɪg] *n (large truck)* gros-cul *m*

right [raɪt] **1** *adj* (**a**) **too right!** tu l'as dit, bouffi! (**b**) *Am* **a right guy** un chic type
  2 *adv* (**a**) *Br (for emphasis)* vachement, drôlement; **I was right angry** j'étais vachement en colère; **it's a right cold day** ça pince drôlement aujourd'hui, il fait drôlement frisquet aujourd'hui (**b**) **right on!** bravo! ▸ *voir aussi* **yeah**

righteous ['raɪtʃəs] *adj Noir Am* (**a**) *(genuine)* authentique [□] (**b**) *(excellent)* génial, super, géant

right-on ['raɪt'ɒn] *adj (socially aware)* politiquement correct [□]

Riley ['raɪlɪ] *npr* **to lead the life of Riley** se la couler douce, avoir la belle vie

ringpiece [!!] ['rɪŋpiːs] *n* rondelle *f*, troufignon *m*

rinky-dink ['rɪŋkɪdɪŋk] *adj Am (goods)* merdique; *(business, businessman)* minable

riot ['raɪət] *n* (**a**) *(amusing person, thing)* **he's a complete riot** il est vraiment tordant, il est impayable; **the party was a riot** la soirée était vraiment démente (**b**) **to read sb the riot act** souffler dans les bronches à qn, passer un savon à qn

rip [rɪp] *vi Br* **to let rip** *(behave unrestrainedly)* se déchaîner; *(fart)* larguer une caisse; **to let rip at sb** se mettre en pétard contre qn

rip off *vt sép* **to rip sb off** *(cheat, swindle)* arnaquer qn; **to rip sth off** *(steal)* piquer qch, faucher qch

rip-off ['rɪpɒf] *n* arnaque *f*; **what a rip-off!** quelle arnaque! ▸ *voir aussi* **merchant**

ripped [rɪpt] *adj (drunk)* bourré, beurré, pété; *(on drugs)* raide, défoncé; *Br* **ripped to the tits** [!] *(drunk)* bourré comme un coing, plein comme une barrique, rond comme une queue de pelle; *(on drugs)* complètement raide *ou* défoncé

ripper ['rɪpə(r)] *Austr* **1** *n (excellent person, thing)* **he's a ripper** c'est quelqu'un de super; **it's a ripper** c'est super *ou* génial; **you little ripper!** super!, génial!
  2 *adj (excellent)* super, génial

rise [raɪz] *n* **to take** *or* **get a rise out of sb** faire enrager qn

ritzy ['rɪtsɪ] *adj* tape-à-l'œil, clinquant

river ['rɪvə(r)] *n Am* **to send sb up the river** *(to prison)* mettre qn à l'ombre *ou* en taule *ou* en cabane

roach [rəʊtʃ] *n* (**a**) *(of cannabis cigarette)* mégot [□] *m (d'une cigarette de marijuana)* (**b**) *(abrév* **cockroach**) cafard [□] *m*

roadhog ['rəʊdhɒg] *n (man)* chauffard *m*, écraseur *m*; *(woman)* écraseuse *f*

roasting ['rəʊstɪŋ] *n* **to give sb a roasting** souffler dans les bronches à qn, passer un savon à qn; **to get a roasting** se faire souffler dans les bronches, prendre *ou* se faire passer un savon

rob [rɒb] *n* **to go on the rob** aller faucher des trucs

robbery ['rɒbərɪ] *n* **it's** *Br* **daylight** *or Am* **highway robbery** c'est de l'arnaque

rock [rɒk] **1** *n* (**a**) *(diamond)* diam *m*
  (**b**) *(crack cocaine)* crack *m*; *Br (cocaine)* coco *f*, neige *f*
  (**c**) **rocks** [!] *(testicles)* couilles *fpl*, boules *fpl*; **to get one's rocks off** *(have sex)* baiser, s'envoyer en l'air; *(have orgasm)* jouir, prendre son pied; *(enjoy oneself)* s'éclater, prendre son pied; **to get one's rocks off doing sth** s'éclater *ou* prendre son pied en faisant qch
  (**d**) **on the rocks** *(drink)* aux glaçons [□];

(relationship, marriage, business) en train de battre de l'aile

(**e**) *Am* **to have rocks in one's head** être bête comme ses pieds

2 *vi* **the party was really rocking** il y avait une ambiance d'enfer à la soirée; **his new sound system really rocks!** sa nouvelle chaîne hifi est vraiment super *ou* géniale!; **you should meet his sister, she rocks!** il faudrait que tu rencontres sa sœur, elle est super!; **let's rock!** allez, on y va!

rocker ['rɒkə(r)] *n* **to be off one's rocker** *(mad)* être cinglé, avoir une araignée dans le plafond; **to go off one's rocker** *(go mad)* perdre la boule, devenir dingue *ou* cinglé; *(lose one's temper)* péter les plombs, péter une durite, piquer une crise

rocket ['rɒkɪt] *n Br (telling-off)* engueulade *f*; **to give sb a rocket** remonter les bretelles à qn, passer un savon à qn, engueuler qn; **to get a rocket** se faire remonter les bretelles, prendre *ou* se faire passer un savon, se faire engueuler

rockhouse ['rɒkhaʊs] *n Am* = lieu où l'on achète, vend et consomme du crack

rocky ['rɒkɪ] *n Br (abrév* **Moroccan**) *(cannabis)* marocain *m*

rod ⚠ [rɒd] *n (penis)* pine *f*, bite *f*, tige *f*

roger ⚠ ['rɒdʒə(r)] *vt Br* baiser, sauter, sabrer

roid [rɔɪd] *n Am (abrév* **steroid**) roids stéroïdes □ *mpl*; **roid rage** = état d'agressivité extrême causé par l'absorption de stéroïdes

L'expression "roid rage" est un jeu de mots sur l'expression "road rage", qui désigne l'état d'agressivité irrationnel de certains automobilistes.

roll [rəʊl] **1** *n* **to have a roll in the hay** faire une partie de jambes en l'air

2 *vt* (**a**) **to roll one's own** se rouler ses cigarettes □ (**b**) *Am (rob)* faire les poches à *(une personne ivre ou endormie)*

3 *vi* **to be rolling in it** *(very rich)* être plein aux as

Roller ['rəʊlə(r)] *n Br (abrév* **Rolls Royce**) Rolls Royce *f*

rollick ['rɒlɪk] *vt Br* engueuler, remonter les bretelles à

rollicking ['rɒlɪkɪŋ] *n Br* **to give sb a rollicking** engueuler qn, remonter les bretelles à qn; **to get a rollicking** se faire engueuler, se faire remonter les bretelles

rollie ['rəʊlɪ] *n Br* cigarette *f* roulée à la main □

Rolls [rəʊlz] = **Roller**

roll-up ['rəʊlʌp], **roll-your-own** ['rəʊljɔːr'əʊn], **rolly** ['rəʊlɪ] *n Br* cigarette *f* roulée à la main □

roo [ruː] *n Austr* kangourou □ *m*

roofie ['ruːfɪ] *n (abrév* **Rohypnol**) Rohypnol® *m*

rook [rʊk] *vt Am (cheat)* arnaquer

roomie ['ruːmɪ] *n Am (abrév* **roommate**) colocataire *mf*, coloc *mf*

root ⚠ [ruːt] *Austr* **1** *vt (have sex with)* s'envoyer en l'air avec

2 *vi (have sex)* s'envoyer en l'air

rooted ⚠ ['ruːtɪd] *adj Austr (exhausted)* naze, lessivé

rort [rɔːt] *Austr* **1** *n* (**a**) *(trick, fraud)* arnaque *f* (**b**) *(party)* fiesta *f*, bringue *f*

2 *vi* (**a**) *(protest)* gueuler (**b**) *(commit fraud)* faire une arnaque

Rosie Lee, Rosy Lee [rəʊzɪ'liː] *n Br (rhyming slang* **tea**) thé □ *m*

rot [rɒt] *n Br (nonsense)* foutaises *fpl*; **don't talk rot!** arrête de raconter n'importe quoi!

rotgut ['rɒtgʌt] *n* tord-boyaux *m*, gnôle *f*

rotten ['rɒtən] *adj* (**a**) *(worthless)* nul, pourri, merdique; **he's a rotten cook** il est complètement nul comme cuisinier; **the weather was really rotten** le temps était vraiment pourri; **we had a rotten time** on a passé un moment dégueulasse

(**b**) *(unkind)* vache, dégueulasse; **to be rotten to sb** être vache *ou* dégueulasse avec qn; **that was a rotten thing to say/do** c'est vraiment salaud *ou* vache *ou* dégueulasse d'avoir dit/fait ça

---

The symbol □ indicates that a translation is neutral in register.

(c) to feel rotten *(ill)* se sentir patraque; *(guilty)* se sentir coupable □ ► *voir aussi* **something**

rotter ['rɒtə(r)] *n Br* pourriture *f*, ordure *f*

rough [rʌf] **1** *n* **she likes a bit of rough** *(person)* elle aime s'envoyer un prolo de temps en temps; *(sexual activity)* elle aime qu'on la malmène un peu pendant l'amour

2 *adj* **(a)** *Br (ill)* **to feel/look rough** ne pas être/ne pas avoir l'air dans son assiette; **I feel as rough as a badger's arse**[!] je me sens vraiment pas dans mon assiette

(b) *Br (disgusting)* dégueulasse

(c) rough trade *(male prostitute)* = jeune prostitué homosexuel à tendances violentes; *(working-class male homosexual)* homosexuel *m* prolo

rough up *vt sép* **to rough sb up** tabasser qn

roust [raʊst] *vt Am (harass)* harceler; *(arrest)* agrafer, gauler, alpaguer

royal ['rɔɪəl] *adj (for emphasis)* sombre, de première; **her whining gives me a royal pain** elle me fait vraiment chier avec ses jérémiades; **he's a royal idiot** c'est un sombre crétin *ou* un crétin de première

royally ['rɔɪəlɪ] *adv (for emphasis)* dans les grandes largeurs; **they messed up royally** ils se sont plantés dans les grandes largeurs, ils se sont plantés, et pas qu'un peu

rozzer ['rɒzə(r)] *n Br* flic *m*, poulet *m*

rub out [rʌb] *vt sép Am* **to rub sb out** zigouiller *ou* buter *ou* refroidir qn

rubber ['rʌbə(r)] *n* **(a)** *(condom)* capote *f* (anglaise) **(b) rubber** *Br* **cheque** or *Am* **check** chèque *m* en bois

rubberneck ['rʌbənek] *Péj* **1** *n* **(a)** *(at scene of accident)* curieux(euse) *m,f* (qui s'attarde sur le lieu d'un accident) **(b)** *(tourist)* touriste □ *mf* (qui assiste à des visites guidées)

2 *vi* **(a)** *(at scene of accident)* = faire le curieux sur le lieu d'un accident **(b)** *(of tourist)* faire le touriste □ *(en assistant à des visites guidées)*

rubbish ['rʌbɪʃ] *Br* **1** *n (nonsense)* foutaises *fpl*; **don't talk rubbish!** arrête de raconter n'importe quoi!; **his book's a load of rubbish** son livre ne vaut pas un clou, son livre est vraiment nul

2 *exclam* n'importe quoi!

3 *adj (worthless)* nul, pourri; **that was a rubbish film/meal** le film/repas était nul

4 *vt (criticize)* éreinter

rube [ruːb] *n Am* plouc *mf*, péquenaud(e) *m,f*

rub-out ['rʌbaʊt] *n Am* assassinat □ *m*

ruby ['ruːbɪ] *n Br (rhyming slang* **Ruby Murray = curry)** curry □ *m*; **fancy going out for a ruby tonight?** ça te dit d'aller manger indien ce soir?

ruck [rʌk] *n Br (fight)* baston *m ou f*; **there was a bit of a ruck after the match** il y a eu du grabuge *ou* du baston après le match

ruddy ['rʌdɪ] *Br* **1** *adj (for emphasis)* sacré; **you ruddy idiot!** espèce d'andouille!; **he's a ruddy liar!** c'est un sacré menteur!

2 *adv (for emphasis)* sacrément, vachement, drôlement; **you look ruddy ridiculous** t'as l'air vraiment ridicule

rug [rʌg] *n (hairpiece)* moumoute *f*

rug-rat ['rʌgræt] *n (child)* môme *mf*, chiard *m*

rumble ['rʌmbəl] **1** *n (fight)* baston *m ou f*, castagne *f*

2 *vt Br (see through) (scheme, plot)* découvrir □, flairer; *(person)* démasquer □, voir venir

3 *vi (fight)* se friter, se castagner

rum-dum ['rʌmdʌm] *n Am* **(a)** *(idiot)* abruti(e) *m,f*, crétin(e) *m,f* **(b)** *(drunken tramp)* **he's a rum-dum** c'est un clodo et un poivrot

rump [rʌmp] *n (buttocks)* croupe *f*; **move your rump!** pousse tes fesses!

rumpy-pumpy ['rʌmpɪ'pʌmpɪ] *n Br Hum* zig-zig *m*, crac-crac *m*; **to have a bit of rumpy-pumpy** faire une partie de jambes en l'air, faire zig-zig *ou* crac-crac

runner ['rʌnə(r)] *n Br* **to do a runner** *(run away)* décaniller, se débiner, mettre les bouts; *(leave without paying)* partir sans payer □

running jump ['rʌnɪŋ'dʒʌmp] *n Br* **take a running jump!**, *Am* **take a running jump at the moon!** va voir ailleurs si j'y suis!

runs [rʌnz] *npl (diarrhoea)* **the runs** la courante

rush [rʌʃ] *n (after taking drugs)* flash *m*; **I got a real rush from that coffee** ce café m'a donné un coup de fouet; **to get a head rush** avoir la tête qui tourne ▸ *voir aussi* **bum**

rustbucket ['rʌstbʌkɪt] *n (car)* poubelle *f*, tas *m* de ferraille

S

sack [sæk] **1** n (a) (dismissal) **to get the sack** se faire virer *ou* sacquer; **to give sb the sack** virer qn, sacquer qn (b) (bed) pieu m, plumard m; **to hit the sack** se pieuter, se pagnoter; **to be good/no good in the sack** être/ne pas être une affaire au pieu (c) Am **sad sack** (person) raté(e) m,f

2 vt (dismiss) virer, sacquer

sack out vi Am se pieuter, se bâcher, se pager

sad [sæd] adj Péj (pitiful) pitoyable ᵈ; **he's still living with his parents, how sad can you get?** il habite toujours chez ses parents, il est grave *ou* il craint!; **what a sad bastard!** [!] quel branleur!; **he's got really sad taste in music** il écoute de la musique vraiment craignos ▸ *voir aussi* **sack**

saddo ['sædəʊ] n Br nul (nulle) m,f

safe [seɪf] adj Br (good) chouette, cool; **are we still on for tonight? – yeah, safe** ça marche toujours pour ce soir? – ouais, pas de problème; **her boss is a complete tosser, but mine's safe** son patron est un vrai con, mais le mien est cool

salami [sə'lɑːmɪ] n Hum **to play hide the salami** (have sex) s'envoyer en l'air

sambo ['sæmbəʊ] n (a) Br Injurieux (black man) nègre m, bamboula m; (black woman) négresse f (b) Ir (sandwich) casse-dalle m

sandwich ['sændwɪtʃ] n (a) Br Hum **to be one sandwich short of a picnic** ne pas être net (b) **knuckle sandwich** coup m de poing dans la gueule, bourre-pif m; **to give sb a knuckle sandwich** mettre son poing dans la gueule à qn (c) Br Hum **to give sb a tongue sandwich** rouler une pelle *ou* un patin à qn

sap [sæp] n (person) poire f

sarky ['sɑːkɪ] adj Br (abrév **sarcastic**) sarcastique ᵈ

sarnie ['sɑːnɪ] n Br (abrév **sandwich**) casse-dalle m

Saturday night special ['sætədɪnaɪt'speʃəl] n Am (gun) flingue m, feu m (bon marché et de qualité médiocre, que l'on peut se procurer facilement)

sauce [sɔːs] n (a) Br (cheek) insolence ᵈ f; **that's enough of your sauce!** arrête de faire l'insolent! (b) (alcohol) alcool ᵈ m, bibine f; **to hit the sauce** se mettre à picoler; **to be on the sauce** s'être mis à picoler; **to be off the sauce** être au régime sec

sauced [sɔːst] adj (drunk) beurré, bourré, pété

sausage ['sɒsɪdʒ] n Br (a) **not a sausage** (nothing) que dalle; **you silly sausage!** espèce de nouille! (b) **sausage dog** saucisse f à pattes (c) Hum (penis) chipolata f

savvy ['sævɪ] n jugeote f

sawbuck ['sɔːbʌk] n Am billet m de dix dollars ᵈ

sawed-off [sɔːd'ɒf] adj Am Hum (person) petit ᵈ, minus

scab [skæb] **1** n (strikebreaker) jaune m (non-gréviste)

2 vi Am (work as a strikebreaker) briser une grève ᵈ

scabby ['skæbɪ] adj Br (a) (worthless) merdique; **you can keep your scabby car!** tu peux la garder, ta caisse de merde! (b) (shabby) merdique, craignos; (dirty) cradingue, crado, dégueu

scads [skædz] npl Am **scads (of)** un paquet (de), des tas (de), une tapée (de)

scag [skæg] n (a) (heroin) héro f, blanche f

(b) *Am (ugly woman)* boudin *m*, cageot *m*

scally ['skælɪ] *n* arnaqueur(euse) *m,f*

> Il s'agit d'un terme qui s'emploie dans le Nord de l'Angleterre, et principalement à Liverpool.

scam [skæm] **1** *n* arnaque *f*
  2 *vt* arnaquer

scammer ['skæmə(r)] *n* arnaqueur(euse) *m,f*

scank [skæŋk] = **skank**

scanky ['skæŋkɪ] = **skanky**

scants [skænts] *npl Br (men's)* calcif *m*; *(women's)* petite culotte *f*

scaredy cat ['skeədɪkæt] *n* poule *f* mouillée

scarf [skɑːf] *vt Am (eat)* bouffer, boulotter

scarper ['skɑːpə(r)] *vi Br (go away)* se casser, se barrer, trisser, se tirer

scat [skæt] *vi (go away)* se casser, se barrer, se tirer, trisser; **scat!** casse-toi!, dégage!

scene [siːn] *n* **it's not my scene** c'est pas mon truc

schemie ['skiːmɪ] *n Scot* zonard *m*

> Il s'agit d'un terme dérivé de "housing scheme" (cité) et qui ne s'emploie que dans la région d'Édimbourg.

schiz [skɪts] *Am* = **schizo**

schizo ['skɪtsəʊ] *(abrév* **schizophrenic)** **1** *n* cinglé(e) *m,f*, dingue *mf*
  2 *adj* cinglé, timbré, toqué

schlemiel [ʃləˈmiːl] *n Am* minable *mf*

schlep [ʃlep] **1** *n* **(a)** *(person)* lourdaud(e) *m,f* **(b)** *(journey)* trotte *f*; **it's a bit of a schlep to the supermarket** ça fait une trotte jusqu'au supermarché
  2 *vt (carry)* trimballer
  3 *vi (walk)* crapahuter; **to schlep home** rentrer chez soi à pinces; **I had to schlep to the grocery store** il a fallu que je crapahute jusqu'à l'épicerie

schlep around 1 *vt insép* **to schlep around the town** crapahuter en ville
  2 *vi Am* crapahuter

schlock [ʃlɒk] *Am* **1** *n (worthless things)* saloperies *fpl*, daube *f*
  2 *adj (worthless)* qui ne vaut pas un clou, nul; **schlock jewelry** bijoux *mpl* en toc

schlong [!] [ʃlɒŋ] *n Am* queue *f*, bite *f*, pine *f*

schlub [ʃlʌb] *n Am* crétin(e) *m,f*, andouille *f*

schmaltz [ʃmɔːlts] *n* guimauve *f*

schmaltzy ['ʃmɔːltsɪ] *adj* à la guimauve

schmo [ʃməʊ] *n Am (unlucky person)* guignard(e) *m,f*; *(stupid person)* nul (nulle) *m,f* ► *voir aussi* **Joe**

schmooze [ʃmuːz] *vi Am* bavarder, jaspiner, jacasser

schmuck [ʃmʌk] *n Am* andouille *f*, courge *f*

schnook [ʃnʊk] *n Am* poire *f*, pigeon *m*

schnozz [ʃnɒz], **schnozzle** ['ʃnɒzəl] *n* blaire *m*, tarin *m*

schtuk [ʃtʊk] *n Br* **to be in schtuk** être dans le pétrin, être dans la panade

schtum [ʃtʊm] *adj Br* **to keep schtum** ne pas piper mot

schwing [ʃwɪŋ] *exclam* putain, la supernana!

> Il s'agit d'une onomatopée censée reproduire le son que produirait une érection. Ce terme a été popularisé par le film américain *Wayne's World*.

sci-fi ['saɪfaɪ] *(abrév* **science-fiction)** **1** SF *f*
  2 *adj* de SF

scoff [skɒf] **1** *n Br (food)* bouffe *f*, graille *f*
  2 *vt (eat)* bouffer, boulotter

scooby ['skuːbɪ] *n Br (rhyming slang* **Scooby Doo = clue)** **he hasn't got a scooby** *(is incompetent)* il est vraiment nul; *(doesn't suspect)* il se doute de rien; *(doesn't know)* il en a pas la moindre idée

> Ce terme vient du dessin animé américain *Scooby Doo*.

scoop [skuːp] *n Br (drink)* canon *m*, godet *m*; **we went out for a couple of scoops last night** on est allé boire un coup hier soir

scoot [skuːt] *vi* se sauver, filer; **scoot!** du vent!, file!

scoot away, scoot off *vi* se sauver, filer

scope [skəʊp] *vt Am* (**a**) *(look at)* mater, reluquer; **he's at the beach scoping the babes** il est à la plage en train de mater les nanas (**b**) *(see)* voir□; **did you scope that ring he was wearing?** t'as vu un peu la bague qu'il avait au doigt?

scope out *vt* sép = **scope**

scorcher ['skɔːtʃə(r)] *n* journée *f* de forte chaleur□; **today's been a scorcher** il en a fait un plat aujourd'hui

score [skɔː(r)] **1** *n* (**a**) **to know the score** savoir à quoi s'en tenir□; **what's the score?** qu'est-ce qui se passe? (**b**) *Br (20 pounds)* vingt livres□ *fpl* (**c**) *Am (20 dollars)* vingt dollars□ *mpl*
2 *vt (drugs)* acheter□
3 *vi* (**a**) *(buy drugs)* acheter de la drogue□ (**b**) *(find sexual partner)* faire une touche; **to score with sb** emballer qn

Scouse [skaʊs] *Br* **1** *n (person)* = natif de la ville de Liverpool; *(dialect)* = dialecte de la ville de Liverpool
2 *adj* de Liverpool

Scouser ['skaʊsə(r)] *n Br* = natif de la ville de Liverpool

scram [skræm] *vi* se casser, se barrer, trisser, se tirer; **scram!** du vent!, file!

scran [skræn] *n Br* bouffe *f*, graille *f*

scrap [skræp] **1** *n (fight)* baston *m ou f*; **to get into a scrap** se bagarrer; **to get into a scrap with sb** se friter *ou* se castagner avec qn
2 *vi (fight)* se friter, se castagner

scratch [skrætʃ] *n Am (money)* fric *m*, pognon *m*, flouze *m*, oseille *f*

scream [skriːm] *n* **he's a scream** il est impayable; **it was a scream** c'était tordant, c'était à se tordre de rire; **the book/film's a scream** le livre/le film est tordant

screw [skruː] **1** *n* (**a**) [!] *(sexual intercourse)* baise *f*; **to have a screw** baiser, tirer un coup, s'envoyer en l'air; **to be a good screw** *(of person)* être un bon coup

(**b**) **to have a screw loose** *(be mad)* avoir une case de vide
(**c**) *Br (prison officer)* maton(onne) *m,f*
(**d**) *Br (salary)* salaire□ *m*; **to be on a good screw** avoir un super bon salaire
2 *vt* (**a**) [!] *(have sex with) (of man)* baiser, troncher, tringler, limer; *(of woman)* baiser avec, s'envoyer
(**b**) [!] *(for emphasis)* **screw you!** va te faire foutre!; **screw him!** qu'il aille se faire foutre!; **go and screw yourself!** va te faire foutre!
(**c**) *(cheat)* arnaquer
(**d**) *Am* **to screw the pooch** *(blunder)* faire une gaffe *ou* une boulette
3 [!] *vi (have sex)* baiser, s'envoyer en l'air

screw around 1 *vt* sép **to screw sb around** *(treat badly)* se foutre de la gueule de qn; *(waste time of)* faire perdre son temps à qn□
2 *vi* (**a**) *(act foolishly)* faire l'andouille; *(waste time)* glander, glandouiller (**b**) [!] *(be promiscuous)* coucher à droite à gauche

screw over *vt* sép **to screw sb over** arnaquer qn, refaire qn

screw up 1 *vt* sép *(person)* rendre cinglé; *(plan, situation)* faire foirer, foutre en l'air; **she's totally screwed up** elle est complètement à côté de ses pompes; **you've screwed everything up** tu as tout foutu en l'air
2 *vi* foirer, merder

screwball ['skruːbɔːl] **1** *n* allumé(e) *m,f*, barge *mf*
2 *adj* allumé, barge

screwed [skruːd] *adj (in trouble)* **to be screwed** être foutu

screw-loose ['skruːluːs] *adj Am* loufoque, loufedingue

screw-up ['skruːʌp] *n Am (bungler)* manche *m*; *(misfit)* paumé(e) *m,f*

screwy ['skruːɪ] *adj Am* dingue, cinglé, toqué

scrote [!] [skrəʊt] *n Br (abrév* **scrotum**) *(person)* gland *m*, taré *m*

scrubber ['skrʌbə(r)] *n Br (woman)* roulure *f*, salope *f*

The symbol □ indicates that a translation is neutral in register.

scrummy ['skrʌmɪ] *adj Br* délicieux □, super bon

scum [skʌm] *n* (**a**) *(people)* ordures *fpl*; **he's scum** c'est une ordure; **he's the scum of the earth** c'est le dernier des derniers; **she treats him like scum** elle le traite comme de la merde (**b**) [!] *Am (semen)* foutre *m*

scumbag ['skʌmbæg] *n* (**a**) *(person)* ordure *f*, raclure *f* (**b**) [!] *Am (condom)* capote *f* (anglaise)

scumbucket ['skʌmbʌkɪt] *n Am (person)* ordure *f*, raclure *f*

scuzzy ['skʌzɪ] *adj Am* dégueulasse, cradingue

search [sɜːtʃ] *vt* **search me!** *(I don't know)* j'en ai pas la moindre idée!

sec [sek] *n (abrév* **second)** seconde □ *f*, instant □ *m*; **half a sec!** une seconde!; **wait a sec!** attends une seconde!

seeing-to ['siːɪŋtuː] *n Br* **to give sb a good seeing-to** *(beat up)* tabasser qn; *(have sex with)* faire passer qn à la casserole

see ya ['siːjə] *exclam* salut!, à pluss!

semi ['semɪ] *n (half-erection)* **to have a semi** bander mou

serious ['sɪərɪəs] *adj (for emphasis)* **she makes serious money** elle gagne un fric fou; **we did some serious drinking last night** on a picolé hier soir, et on n'a pas fait semblant; **that is one serious computer** c'est pas de la gnognotte, cet ordinateur

seriously ['sɪərɪəslɪ] *adv (for emphasis)* sérieusement, vachement; **she's getting seriously fat** elle devient énorme; **he was seriously drunk** il était sérieusement éméché; **her boyfriend is seriously gorgeous** son petit ami est super beau

---

Pleins feux sur:

Sex

On ne compte plus les termes argotiques anglais désignant l'organe sexuel masculin. Parmi les plus fréquents, on peut citer **dick**, **cock** et **prick**. Les termes **willy** (anglais britannique) et **peter** (anglais américain) sont un peu moins choquants. Le yiddish a donné le mot **schlong**. On trouve également des expressions plus humoristiques telles que **one-eyed trouser snake**. Pour un homme particulièrement "bien équipé", on utilise les expressions **to be hung like a horse**, **a whale**, **a donkey** ou **a mule**. **Balls** est le mot le plus fréquent pour désigner les testicules, mais il existe d'autres synonymes tels que **nuts**, **bollocks** (anglais britannique) et **nads** (ce terme, employé uniquement en Grande-Bretagne, vient de "gonads").

Pour désigner l'organe sexuel féminin, on emploie **pussy**, **snatch** et, en anglais britannique, **fanny**. Il est bon de savoir que **fanny** signifie "fesses" (buttocks) en anglais américain, une différence qui pourrait entraîner quelques malentendus…

"Faire l'amour" a d'innombrables équivalents argotiques en anglais, dont le verbe **to fuck** (très vulgaire) est le plus courant. On peut citer d'autres synonymes tels que **to shag** (très courant en Grande-Bretagne, il s'emploie depuis peu aux États-Unis pour désigner un type de danse), **to screw**, **to shaft**, **to bone** et **to poke**, tous ces verbes étant plutôt vulgaires. Dans un registre un peu moins vulgaire, on trouve **to bonk** en anglais britannique et **to boink** en américain. Certaines expressions britanniques sont un peu plus humoristiques: **rumpy-pumpy**, **a bit of how's your father** et **a roll in the hay** désignent toutes l'acte sexuel. Plusieurs expressions imagées, dont beaucoup contiennent des allitérations ou des rimes, permettent de désigner la masturbation masculine. Citons par exemple **to bash the bishop**, **to beat one's meat** et **to choke the chicken**.

The symbol □ indicates that a translation is neutral in register.

sesh [seʃ] *n Br* (*abrév* **session**) **to have a drinking sesh** se pinter; **we had a bit of a sesh last night** on s'en est donné hier soir

set back [set] *vt sép* (*cost*) coûter à ◻; **it set me back twenty quid** ça m'a coûté vingt livres; **that must have set you back a bit** ça a dû te coûter bonbon

set up *vt sép* (*trap, trick*) piéger ◻; **they were set up** ils ont été victimes d'un coup monté

set-to ['set'tuː] *n Br* baston *m ou f*

set-up ['setʌp] *n* (*trap, trick*) machination ◻ *f*, coup *m* monté

severe [sɪ'vɪə(r)] *adj Br* (*for emphasis*) sacré, vache (de); **he is a severe pain** c'est un sacré emmerdeur

severely [sɪ'vɪəlɪ] *adv Br* (*for emphasis*) sérieusement, vachement; **we were severely drunk last night** on était sérieusement déchirés hier soir; **you are severely annoying me!** tu me cours sérieusement sur le haricot!

sewermouth ['suːəmaʊθ] *n Am* **to be a sewermouth** jurer comme un charretier

sex [seks] *n* **sex god** apollon *m*; **sex goddess** vénus *f*; **sex kitten** nana *f* sexy, joli petit colis *m*; **that girl is just sex on a stick** cette nana est vraiment super sexy

sexpot ['sekspɒt] *n* (*man*) homme *m* hyper sexy; (*woman*) bombe *f* sexuelle

sex-starved ['seks'stɑːvd] *adj* frustré

shack up [ʃæk] *vi* **to shack up with sb** se mettre à la colle avec qn; **to be shacked up (with sb)** être à la colle (avec qn); **they shacked up together** ils se sont mis à la colle

shades [ʃeɪdz] *npl* (*sunglasses*) lunettes *fpl* noires ◻

shaft[!] [ʃɑːft] **1** *n* (**a**) (*penis*) chibre *m*, queue *f* (**b**) *Am* **to get the shaft** (*get cheated*) se faire baiser *ou* arnaquer
2 *vt* (**a**) *Br* (*have sex with*) baiser, tringler, troncher (**b**) (*cheat*) baiser, arnaquer; **to get shafted** se faire baiser *ou* arnaquer

shafted ['ʃɑːftɪd] *adj Br* beurré, bourré, pété

shag[!] [ʃæg] *Br* **1** *n* (**a**) (*sexual intercourse*)

baise *f*; **to have a shag** baiser, tirer un coup, s'envoyer en l'air; **to be a good shag** (*of person*) être un bon coup (**b**) (*boring task*) plaie *f*; **it's a real shag having to get up so early every morning** c'est vraiment chiant *ou* la plaie de devoir se lever si tôt tous les matins
2 *vt* (*have sex with*) (*of man*) baiser, troncher, tringler, limer; (*of woman*) baiser avec, s'envoyer
3 *vi* (*have sex*) baiser, s'envoyer en l'air

shaggable[!] ['ʃægəbəl] *adj Br* baisable

shagged (out) [!] [ʃægd('aʊt)] *adj Br* (*tired*) naze, lessivé

shake [ʃeɪk] **1** *n* (**a**) **in two shakes (of a lamb's tail)** en moins de deux, en deux temps trois mouvements, en deux coups de cuiller à pot (**b**) **it's no great shakes** ça casse pas des briques, ça casse pas trois pattes à un canard ▸ *voir aussi* **leg, stick**
2 *vt Austr* (*rob*) piquer, tirer

shake down *vt sép Am* (**a**) (*blackmail*) **to shake sb down** faire chanter qn ◻ (**b**) (*search*) **to shake sb down** fouiller qn ◻, palper qn; **to shake sth down** fouiller qch ◻

shakedown ['ʃeɪkdaʊn] *n Am* (**a**) (*blackmail*) chantage ◻ *m* (**b**) (*search*) fouille ◻ *f*

shamus ['ʃeɪməs] *n Am* (*private detective*) privé *m*

shank [ʃæŋk] *Am* **1** *n* (*knife*) surin *m*, lame *f*
2 *vt* (*stab*) planter

Sharon and Tracy ['ʃærənən'treɪsɪ] *npr Br* = type de jeune femme d'origine modeste aux mœurs légères, vulgaire, bruyante, et peu intelligente

"Sharon" et "Tracy" sont des prénoms très courants dans les milieux populaires et, de ce fait, sont considérés comme vulgaires par beaucoup de gens. On utilise cette expression de la façon suivante: "the club was full of Sharon and Tracys", "she's a bit of a Sharon and Tracy (type)".

sharp [ʃɑːp] *adj* (*stylish*) chicos, classe ▸ *voir aussi* **poke**

sharpish ['ʃɑːpɪʃ] *adv Br* illico presto, vite fait; **you'd better do it sharpish** t'as intérêt à le faire illico presto, t'as intérêt à faire fissa

shattered ['ʃætəd] *adj Br (exhausted)* naze, lessivé, crevé, claqué

shebang [ʃə'bæŋ] *n* **the whole shebang** et tout le tremblement, et tout le bataclan

shedload ['ʃedləʊd] *n Br* **a shedload of, shedloads of** une tapée de; **she earns a shedload** *or* **shedloads of dosh** elle se fait un fric fou; **he's sold a shedload of albums over the last few years** il a vendu une tapée d'albums ces dernières années

sheep-shagger [!!] ['ʃiːpʃægə(r)] *n Br Injurieux (Welsh person)* Gallois(e) m,f; *(any rural person)* péquenaud(e) m,f

sheesh [ʃiːʃ] *exclam (in surprise)* tiens!; *(in exasperation)* allez!

sheets *npl Br* livres *fpl* sterling □; **his DVD player cost him 500 sheets** son lecteur de DVD lui a coûté 500 livres

sheila ['ʃiːlə] *n Austr* nana *f*

shekels ['ʃekəlz] *npl (money)* fric *m*, flouze *m*, pognon *m*

shell out [ʃel] **1** *vt sép* raquer
  2 *vi* raquer, casquer (**for** pour)

shellac [ʃə'læk] *vt Am (defeat)* battre à plates coutures, écrabouiller, filer une raclée *ou* une déculottée à; **to get shellacked** être battu à plates coutures, se faire écrabouiller, prendre une raclée *ou* une déculottée

shellacking [ʃə'lækɪŋ] *n Am* **(a)** *(beating)* **to give sb a shellacking** tabasser qn, passer qn à tabac; **to take a shellacking** se faire tabasser, se faire passer à tabac, prendre une raclée
  (b) *(defeat)* raclée *f*, déculottée *f*; **to give sb a shellacking** battre qn à plates coutures, écrabouiller qn, filer une raclée *ou* une déculottée à qn; **to take a shellacking** être battu à plates coutures, se faire écrabouiller, prendre une raclée *ou* une déculottée

shemozzle [ʃə'mɒzəl] *n Am* merdier *m*

sherbet ['ʃɜːbət] *n Br* **(a)** *(alcoholic drink)* verre □ *m*; **fancy going for a couple of sherbets?** ça te dirait de sortir prendre un verre? **(b) sherbet dab** *(rhyming slang =* **cab)** taxi □ *m*, tacot *m*

sherman [!] ['ʃɜːmən] *n Br (rhyming slang* **Sherman tank = wank)** branlette *f*; **to have a sherman** se branler, se faire une branlette, faire cinq contre un

shift [ʃɪft] **1** *vt* **(a)** *(sell)* fourguer **(b)** *(eat, drink)* s'envoyer; **hurry up and shift that pint!** dépêche-toi d'écluser ta pinte! **(c) shift yourself!** *(move)* pousse tes fesses!; *(hurry up)* magne-toi!, remue-toi!
  2 *vi (move quickly)* foncer

shifty ['ʃɪftɪ] *adj (person)* louche; *(look)* fuyant □

shill [ʃɪl] *Am* **1** *n* baron *m*
  2 *vt* **(a)** *(lure into swindle)* arnaquer; **they shilled him into handing over his life savings** ils ont réussi à lui soutirer toutes ses économies **(b)** *(hype)* faire de la pub pour; **they've got a quarterback shilling their new frozen yoghurt** il y a un joueur de football américain qui fait la pub pour leur nouveau yaourt glacé

shindig ['ʃɪndɪg] *n* **(a)** *(party)* fête □ *f*, fiesta *f*; **to have a shindig** faire la fiesta **(b)** *(commotion)* raffut *m*, ramdam *m*; **to kick up a shindig** faire du raffut

shine [ʃaɪn] *n Am Injurieux (black man)* nègre *m*, bamboula *m*; *(black woman)* négresse *f*
  2 *vi* **stick it where the sun don't shine!** [!] tu peux te le mettre où je pense! ▸ *voir aussi* **arse**

shiner ['ʃaɪnə(r)] *n (black eye)* œil *m* au beurre noir, coquard *m*

shirt [ʃɜːt] *n* **keep your shirt on!** t'énerve pas!, du calme!; *Br* **to put one's shirt on sth** miser jusqu'à son dernier centime sur qch □; **to lose one's shirt** tout perdre □; **to take the shirt off sb's back** faire cracher jusqu'à son dernier centime à qn; **stuffed shirt** *(person)* collet *m* monté

shirt-lifter ['ʃɜːtlɪftə(r)] *n Br Injurieux* pédé *m*, tantouze *f*, tapette *f*

The symbol □ indicates that a translation is neutral in register.

shit [!] [ʃɪt] **1** n **(a)** (excrement) merde f; **to Br have** or **Am take a shit** chier, couler un bronze; **to have the shits** avoir la chiasse; **to be in the shit** être dans la merde; **to drop sb in the shit** foutre qn dans la merde; **I don't give a shit** j'en ai rien à battre ou à secouer; **who gives a shit?** qu'est-ce que ça peut foutre?; **to treat sb like shit** traiter qn comme de la merde; **to beat the shit out of sb** défoncer la gueule à qn; **to kick** or **beat seven shades of shit out of sb** faire une tête au carré à qn, démolir la gueule à qn; **to scare the shit out of sb** foutre une trouille pas possible à qn; **to get one's shit together** se ressaisir □; **to be up shit creek (without a paddle)** être dans une merde noire; **when the shit hits the fan** quand ça pètera; **he thinks his shit doesn't stink** il se prend pas pour de la merde; **eat shit (and die)!** va te faire foutre!; **tough shit!** tant pis!; **shit happens** ce sont des choses qui arrivent □

(b) (nonsense) conneries fpl; **he's full of shit** il dit que des conneries, il sait pas ce qu'il dit; **to talk shit** raconter des conneries; **that's shit!** c'est des conneries!; **don't believe that shit** n'écoute pas ces conneries; **no shit?** sans déconner?, sans dec?; **no shit!** sans déconner!, sans dec!

(c) (worthless things) **to be a load of shit**, Am **to be the shits** être de la merde; **the film was a piece of shit** c'était vraiment de la merde, ce film

(d) (useless things) bordel m, foutoir m; **clear all that shit off your desk** vire-moi ce bordel de ton bureau

(e) (disgusting substance) merde f, saloperie f; **I can't eat this shit** je peux pas bouffer cette merde

(f) (person) ordure f, bâton m merdeux; **he's been a real shit to her** il s'est vraiment conduit en salaud avec elle

(g) (unfair treatment) **to give sb shit** faire chier qn; **the press have been giving him a lot of shit lately** la presse l'a traîné dans la merde ces derniers temps; **don't take his shit!** le laisse pas te traiter comme de la merde!; **I don't need this shit!** j'ai pas envie de m'emmerder avec ce genre de conneries!

(h) (anything) **he doesn't do shit** il en rame pas une, il en fout pas une rame; **I can't see shit** j'y vois goutte

(i) **to feel/look like shit** (ill) se sentir/avoir l'air patraque

(j) (cannabis) shit m, chichon m; (heroin) héro f, blanche f

2 adj (worthless) merdique; **to feel shit** (ill) se sentir patraque; (guilty) se sentir coupable □, avoir les boules ou les glandes; **I had a really shit time** j'ai passé un moment dégueulasse; **he's a shit driver** il conduit comme un pied

3 adv **to be shit out of luck** ne pas avoir de bol ou de pot

4 exclam merde!

5 vt **(a)** **to shit oneself** (defecate, be scared) chier dans son froc; (react with anger) piquer une crise; (react with surprise) ne pas en revenir; **to shit a brick** or **bricks** chier dans son froc **(b)** **to shit sb** (lie to) raconter des craques à qn; (deceive) se foutre de la gueule de qn

6 vi **(a)** (defecate) chier; **shit or get off the pot!** alors, tu te décides? □

(b) **to shit on sb** (treat badly) traiter qn comme de la merde; Br **to shit on sb from a great height** (treat badly) traiter qn comme de la merde; (defeat) battre qn à plates coutures, écrabouiller qn, foutre une déculottée à qn; Am **shit on that!** et puis merde!

(c) Am (react with anger) piquer une crise; (react with surprise) ne pas en revenir; **your parents will shit when they see what you've done!** tes parents vont piquer une crise quand ils se rendront compte de ce que t'as fait ▶ voir aussi **bear, crock, eat, holy, jack**

shit-ass [!] ['ʃɪtæs] n Am (person) salaud (salope) m,f

shit-can [!] ['ʃɪtkæn] vt Am (discard) balancer, foutre en l'air; (disregard, abandon) laisser tomber

shite [!] [ʃaɪt] Br **1** n **(a)** (excrement) merde f **(b)** (nonsense) conneries fpl; **he's full of shite** il raconte que des conneries, il sait pas ce qu'il dit; **to talk shite** raconter

---

The symbol □ indicates that a translation is neutral in register.

des conneries, déconner; **that's shite!** c'est des conneries!; **don't believe that shit!** n'écoute pas ces conneries!

2 *adj (bad)* merdique; **to feel shite** (*ill*) se sentir patraque; *(guilty)* se sentir coupable ᵈ, avoir les boules *ou* les glandes; **I had a really shite time** j'ai passé un moment dégueulasse; **he's a shite singer** il chante comme un pied

3 *exclam* merde!

shit-faced ⚠ ['ʃɪtfeɪst] *adj (drunk)* bourré, pété, beurré; *(on drugs)* défoncé, raide

shit-for-brains ⚠ ['ʃɪtfəbreɪnz] *n* tache *f*, gogol *mf*

shithead ⚠ ['ʃɪthed] *n* enfoiré(e) *m,f*

shit-heel ⚠ ['ʃɪthiːl] *n Am (person)* pécore *mf*, bouseux(euse) *m,f*

shithole ⚠ ['ʃɪthəʊl] *n (dirty place)* porcherie *f*, taudis *m*; **this town's a complete shithole** *(boring, ugly)* cette ville est un vrai trou

shit-hot ⚠ [ʃɪt'hɒt] *adj* super, génial

shithouse ⚠ ['ʃɪthaʊs] *n* chiottes *fpl*, gogues *mpl*; **to be built like a brick shithouse** être une armoire à glace

shit-kicker ⚠ ['ʃɪtkɪkə(r)] *n Am (farm-hand)* garçon *m* de ferme ᵈ; *(rustic)* pedzouille *mf*, pécore *mf*

shitless ⚠ ['ʃɪtlɪs] *adj* **to be bored shitless** se faire chier à mort; **to be scared shitless** être mort de trouille

shitload ⚠ ['ʃɪtləʊd] *n* **a (whole) shitload (of)** une chiée (de), une tapée (de)

shit-scared ⚠ [ʃɪt'skeəd] *adj* **to be shit-scared** être mort de trouille

shit-stirrer ⚠ ['ʃɪtstɜːrə(r)] *n* fouteur (euse) *m,f* de merde

shitstorm ⚠ ['ʃɪtstɔːm] *n Am* foin *m*; **the announcement caused a helluva shitstorm** la déclaration a fait un sacré foin

shitter ⚠ ['ʃɪtə(r)] *n (toilet)* chiottes *fpl*, gogues *mpl*; **that's two whole days' work down the shitter!** c'est deux jours entiers de travail de foutus!

shitty ⚠ ['ʃɪtɪ] *adj (worthless)* merdique; *(nasty)* dégueulasse; **that was a shitty**

thing to do/say c'est salaud *ou* dégueulasse d'avoir fait/dit ça; **to feel shitty** (*ill*) se sentir patraque; *(guilty)* se sentir coupable ᵈ, avoir les boules *ou* les glandes

shitweasel ⚠ ['ʃɪtwiːzəl] *n Am* ordure *f*, raclure *f*

shiv [ʃɪv] *Am* **1** *n (knife)* surin *m*, lame *f*

2 *vt (stab)* planter

shock jock ['ʃɒkdʒɒk] *n Am* = animateur *ou* animatrice de radio au ton irrévérencieux et provocateur

shonky ['ʃɒŋkɪ] *adj Austr* **(a)** *(risky)* risqué ᵈ; **don't get involved in his shonky schemes** ne te laisse pas embringuer dans ses histoires à la gomme **(b)** *(untrustworthy)* louche; **there's something a bit shonky about him** je le trouve un peu louche **(c)** *(not working properly)* qui déconne; **the brakes are a bit shonky** les freins déconnent un peu

shoo-in ['ʃuːɪn] *n* **it's a shoo-in** c'est couru d'avance; **they're a shoo-in to win the next election** ils vont gagner les prochaines élections, c'est couru d'avance

shoot [ʃuːt] **1** *exclam Am* zut!, mince!

2 *vt* **(a)** *Am* **to shoot the breeze** *or* **the bull** *(chat)* papoter **(b)** **to shoot one's load** *or* **wad** ⚠⚠ *(ejaculate)* décharger, balancer la purée; *Am* **to shoot one's wad** *or* **the works** *(do all one can)* se donner à fond

3 *vi (speak)* **shoot!** vas-y, je t'écoute! ▸ *voir aussi* **blank, cookie, hoops, lunch, mouth**

shoot through *vi Br (leave)* se tirer, mettre les bouts

shoot up 1 *vt sép (drugs)* se faire un shoot de; *(habitually)* se shooter *ou* se piquer à

2 *vi (inject drugs)* se piquer, se shooter

shoot-'em-up ['ʃuːtəmʌp] *n* = film *ou* jeu vidéo comportant de nombreux échanges de coups de feu

shooter ['ʃuːtə(r)] *n (gun)* flingue *m*, feu *m* ▸ *voir aussi* **square, straight**

shooting-gallery ['ʃuːtɪŋgæləɪ] *n Am (for buying drugs)* = lieu où l'on achète, vend et consomme de la drogue

The symbol ᵈ indicates that a translation is neutral in register.

shooting-iron [ˈʃuːtɪŋaɪən] n Am (gun) flingue m, feu m

shooting-match [ˈʃuːtɪŋmætʃ] n **the whole shooting-match** tout le bataclan, tout le tremblement

shop [ʃɒp] vt Br (inform on) dénoncer □, balancer

short [ʃɔːt] adj **to have sb by the short hairs** or Br **by the short and curlies** avoir qn à sa merci □

shortarse [!] [ˈʃɔːtɑːs] n Br rase-bitume mf, bas-du-cul mf

shorts [ʃɔːts] npl (**a**) **to have the shorts** (have little money) être fauché, être raide (**b**) Am **eat my shorts!** tu me gonfles!

shorty [ˈʃɔːtɪ] n rase-bitume mf, bas-du-cul mf; **hey, shorty!** hé, rase-bitume!

shot [ʃɒt] **1** n (**a**) **to do sth like a shot** (speedily) faire qch à tout berzingue; (with no hesitation) faire qch sans hésiter □ (**b**) **big shot** gros bonnet m, huile f (**c**) Noir Am **the whole shot** tout le tremblement
2 adj (**a**) Br **to get shot of sb/sth** se débarrasser de qn/qch □; **I can't wait to be shot of this house** j'ai hâte de me débarrasser de cette maison (**b**) Am (wasted, ruined) fichu, foutu; **that's another day shot!** encore une journée de foutue (en l'air)! ▸ voir aussi **cook, cook up, mug**

shotgun wedding [ˈʃɒtɡʌnˈwedɪŋ] n mariage m forcé □ (lorsque la future mariée est enceinte)

shout [ʃaʊt] **1** n (**a**) Br & Austr (round of drinks) tournée □ f; **it's my shout** c'est ma tournée; **whose shout is it?** c'est la tournée de qui? (**b**) Br (chance) **to be in with a good shout of sth** avoir de bonnes chances de décrocher qch
2 vt Austr (treat) **to shout sb a meal** payer le restaurant à qn
3 vi Austr (pay for drinks) **I'll shout** c'est ma tournée □, c'est moi qui rince

shove off [ʃʌv] vi décaniller, se barrer, se tirer; **shove off!** dégage!, fous le camp!

show [ʃəʊ] vi (arrive) se pointer

showboat [ˈʃəʊbəʊt] Am **1** n (show-off) crâneur(euse) m,f, frimeur(euse) m,f
2 vi (show off) crâner, frimer

shower [ˈʃaʊə(r)] n Br Péj (people) **what a shower!** quel bande de nuls!; **you lazy shower!** bande de flemmards!

shrapnel [ˈʃræpnəl] n (loose change) mitraille f, ferraille f

shredded [ˈʃredɪd] adj Am (drunk) bourré, pété, beurré, fait

shreddies [ˈʃredɪz] npl (underwear) calbute m, calcif m

shrink [ʃrɪŋk] n (psychiatrist) psy mf

shrooms [ʃruːmz] npl (abrév **mushrooms**) champignons mpl hallucinogènes □, champignons mpl

shtuk [ʃtʊk] = **schtuk**

shtum [ʃtʊm] = **schtum**

shuck [ʃʌk] Noir Am **1** n (trick) arnaque f
2 vt (trick) arnaquer
3 vi **to shuck (and jive)** (act foolishly) faire l'andouille; (speak misleadingly, bluff) baratiner

shucks [ʃʌks] exclam mince!, punaise!

shufty [ˈʃʊftɪ] n Br **to have a shufty at sth** jeter un coup d'œil à qch; **have a quick shufty at this!** regarde un peu ça!

shut [ʃʌt] vt **shut your mouth** or **face, shut it!** ferme ton clapet!, la ferme! ▸ voir aussi **noise, trap**

shut up 1 vt sép **to shut sb up** clouer le bec à qn; **that shut him up!** ça lui a cloué le bec!
2 vi fermer son clapet, la fermer, la boucler; **shut up!** la ferme!, ferme ton clapet!, boucle-la!

shut-eye [ˈʃʌtaɪ] n **to get some shut-eye** piquer un roupillon, roupiller

shyster [ˈʃaɪstə(r)] n Am (businessman, politician) homme m d'affaires/politicien m véreux; (lawyer) avocat m marron

sick [sɪk] adj (**a**) **to be sick (and tired) of sb/sth** en avoir marre ou ras le bol de qn/qch; **to be sick to death** or **sick of the sight of sb/sth** en avoir sa claque de qn/qch (**b**) Br (**as**) **sick as a parrot** (disappointed) déçu □, dégoûté (**c**) (perverse) malsain □ ▸ voir aussi **teeth**

sickbag [ˈsɪkbæg] n Br **pass the sickbag!** ça me fout la nausée!

sickie ['sɪkɪ] *n Br & Austr* **to take a sickie** se faire porter pâle *(lorsqu'on est bien portant)*

sicko ['sɪkəʊ] *n* malade *mf*, tordu(e) *m,f*

sight [saɪt] *n* **(a)** **she can't stand** or *Br* **stick the sight of him** elle ne peut pas le voir en peinture
  (b) *(mess)* **to be** or *Br* **look a sight** être dans un bel état; *Br* **what a sight!** quel tableau!
  (c) *(for emphasis)* **a damn** or **darn sight better/easier** vachement mieux/plus facile; **a damn** or **darn sight more/less** vachement plus/moins ▶ *voir aussi* **outta, sick**

signify ['sɪgnɪfaɪ] *vi Noir Am* = se livrer à des joutes verbales entre amis; **they were signifying back and forth** ils se chambraient, ils s'envoyaient des vannes

> Le "signifying" est une sorte de joute verbale improvisée au cours de laquelle des amis se lancent des remarques sarcastiques et grotesques.

simoleon [sɪ'məʊlɪən] *n Am (dollar)* dollar □ *m*

simp [sɪmp] *n Am (abrév* **simpleton)** andouille *f*, crétin(e) *m,f*

sing [sɪŋ] *vi (confess, inform)* cracher *ou* lâcher le morceau ▶ *voir aussi* **blues**

singer ['sɪŋə(r)] *n Br (informer)* indic *mf*

sis [sɪs] *n (abrév* **sister)** frangine *f*

sissy ['sɪsɪ] *n* femmelette *f*

sister ['sɪstə(r)] *n* **(a)** *Noir Am (fellow black woman)* Noire *f* américaine □; **you don't treat your sisters like that!** c'est pas des façons de traiter d'autres Noires! **(b)** *(fellow feminist)* camarade *f* féministe □

six-pack ['sɪkspæk] *n* **(a)** *Hum (stomach muscles)* abdos *mpl*; **he's got a great six-pack** il a des super abdos **(b)** *Br Hum* **to be one can short of a six-pack** ne pas être net

sixty-nine [sɪkstɪ'naɪn] *n (sexual position)* soixante-neuf *m*

skag [skæg] = **scag**

skank [skæŋk] *n Am* cageot *m*, boudin *m*

skanky ['skæŋkɪ] *adj Am* hyper moche

skate [skeɪt] *n* **to get one's skates on** *(hurry up)* se magner, se grouiller; **get your skates on!** magne-toi!, grouille-toi!

skedaddle [skɪ'dædəl] *vi* décamper, se tailler, décaniller

skeezer ['skiːzə(r)] *n Noir Am* **(a)** *(ugly woman)* cageot *m*, boudin *m* **(b)** *(promiscuous woman)* pouffiasse *f*, traînée *f*

skid [skɪd] *n* **(a)** **to be on the skids** *(of company, marriage)* battre de l'aile; *Am* **to hit the skids** *(of company, sales, prices)* dégringoler
  (b) *Am* **skid row** bas-fonds □ *mpl*; **to be on skid row** être dans la dèche
  (c) *Br* **skid lid** casque □ *m (de moto)*
  (d) **skid marks** ⚠ traces *fpl* de pneus *(traces d'excrément sur le slip)*

skin [skɪn] **1** *n* **(a)** *(abrév* **skinhead)** skinhead *mf*, skin *mf*
  (b) *Br (cigarette paper)* papier *m* à cigarette □
  (c) *Am* **gimme some skin!** tape-moi dans la main!
  (d) **skin flick** film *m* de cul; **skin mag** magazine *m* de cul
  (e) *Am* **skin game** *(swindle)* arnaque *f*
  2 *vt* **(a)** *(swindle)* arnaquer **(b)** *Am* **skin me!** tape-moi dans la main!

> Dans les catégories 1(c) et 2(b), il s'agit d'une façon de signifier à quelqu'un que l'on veut lui taper dans la main pour le saluer, le féliciter, ou en signe de victoire.

skin up *vi Br* rouler un joint

skinflint ['skɪnflɪnt] *n* radin(e) *m,f*

skinful ['skɪnfʊl] *n* **to have had a skinful** tenir une bonne cuite

skinny ['skɪnɪ] *n Am (inside information)* renseignements □ *mpl*; **what's the skinny on the situation?** résume-moi la situation □

skinny-dipping ['skɪnɪdɪpɪŋ] *n* **to go skinny-dipping** se baigner à poil

skin-pop ['skɪnpɒp] **1** *vt (drugs)* se piquer *ou* se shooter à

The symbol □ indicates that a translation is neutral in register.

2 vi (inject drugs) se piquer, se shooter

skint [skɪnt] adj Br fauché, raide

skirt [skɜːt] n (women) nanas fpl, gonzesses fpl; **they've gone out looking for skirt** ils sont allés draguer; Br **a bit of skirt** une nana, une gonzesse

skite [skaɪt] Austr **1** n (boastful person) vantard(e) ᵒ m,f; (boasting) vantardise ᵒ f
2 vi (boast) se vanter ᵒ

skitters ['skɪtəz] npl Scot **the skitters** la courante

skive [skaɪv] Br **1** n (easy job) planque f; **she's taking PE because it's such a skive** elle a choisi éducation physique parce que c'est pépère
2 vi tirer au flanc, tirer au cul

skive off Br **1** vt insép **to skive off school** sécher les cours; **to skive off work** ne pas aller bosser
2 vi tirer au flanc, tirer au cul

skiver ['skaɪvə(r)] n Br tire-au-flanc mf, tire-au-cul mf

skivvies ['skɪvɪz] npl Am calbute m, calcif m

skoosh [skuʃ] n Scot (a) (easy thing) **to be a skoosh** être fastoche (b) (carbonated drink) boisson f gazeuse ᵒ

skull [skʌl] n **to be out of one's skull** (drunk) être plein comme une barrique, être rond comme une queue de pelle ▶ voir aussi **thick**

skunk [skʌŋk] **1** n Péj (person) salaud (salope) m,f
2 vt Am (defeat) écraser, battre à plate coutures, mettre la pâtée à; **to get skunked** se faire battre à plates coutures

slacker ['slækə(r)] n bon (bonne) m,f à rien, raté(e) m,f

Il s'agit d'un stéréotype social apparu aux États-Unis, au début des années 90. Ce terme désigne une personne jeune (entre vingt et trente ans), qui a fait des études, mais que le monde du travail et la notion de carrière rebutent, et qui se contente le plus souvent de travaux subalternes qui ne comportent aucune responsabilité.

slag [slæg] Br **1** n (a) (promiscuous woman) pouffiasse f, traînée f (b) Péj (person) enfoiré(e) m,f; **some slag's stolen my fags** il y a un enfoiré qui m'a piqué mes clopes
2 vt (a) (criticize) débiner, éreinter, descendre en flammes (b) (make fun of) se foutre de

slag off vt sép Br (a) (criticize) débiner, éreinter, descendre en flammes (b) (make fun of) se foutre de

slaggy ['slægɪ] adj Br qui fait pute; **she looks really slaggy in all that make-up** elle fait vraiment pute avec tout son maquillage; **you get some really slaggy girls in that bar** dans ce bar il y a des filles qui ont vraiment le genre pute; **that's a really slaggy dress she's wearing** elle porte une robe qui fait vraiment pute

slam [slæm] vt (a) (criticize) éreinter, descendre en flammes; **to get slammed** se faire éreinter, se faire descendre en flammes (b) [!] Am (have sex with) (of man) baiser, s'envoyer; (of woman) baiser avec, s'envoyer (c) (drink quickly) descendre, écluser; **let's go slam some beers** allons écluser quelques bières

slammer ['slæmə(r)] n taule f, cabane f; **in the slammer** en taule, en cabane, à l'ombre

slanging match ['slæŋɪŋmætʃ] n Br prise f de bec, engueulade f; **to have a slanging match (with sb)** avoir une prise de bec (avec qn), s'engueuler (avec qn)

slant [slɑːnt] n Injurieux (Oriental) bridé(e) m,f

slap [slæp] n Br (make-up) maquillage ᵒ m

slaphead ['slæphed] n Br chauve ᵒ m; **he's a slaphead** il n'a pas un poil sur le caillou, il a une casquette en peau de fesse

slapper ['slæpə(r)] n Br (a) (promiscuous woman) pouffiasse f, traînée f, salope f (b) Péj (any woman) gonzesse f, grognasse f

slash [slæʃ] n Br **to have a slash** pisser; **to go for a slash** aller pisser un coup

slasher film ['slæʃəfɪlm] n = film d'horreur particulièrement sanglant

slate [sleɪt] Br **1** n **to have a slate loose**

The symbol ᵒ indicates that a translation is neutral in register.

avoir une case de vide, avoir une araignée
au plafond

   2 vt (criticize) éreinter, débiner, descendre en flammes

slaughter ['slɔːtə(r)] vt (defeat) écrabouiller, battre à plates coutures, mettre
une raclée ou une déculottée à

slaughtered ['slɔːtəd] adj Br (drunk)
bourré, beurré, pété

slay [sleɪ] vt (amuse) faire mourir de rire;
Ironique **you slay me!** tu es impayable!

sleazebag ['sliːzbæg], **sleazeball** ['sliːz-
bɔːl], **sleazoid** ['sliːzɔɪd] n (**a**) (despicable person) ordure f, raclure f (**b**) (repulsive man) gros dégueulasse m

sleep around [sliːp] vi coucher à droite
à gauche

slice-and-dice movie n = film d'horreur particulièrement sanglant

slick up [slɪk] vi Am (dress smartly) se
mettre sur son trente-et-un, se faire beau

slimebag ['slaɪmbæg], **slimeball**
['slaɪmbɔːl] n (**a**) (despicable person) ordure f, raclure f (**b**) (repulsive man) gros
dégueulasse m

slit [!!] [slɪt] n (vagina) craque f, cramouille f

Sloane (Ranger) [sləʊn('reɪndʒə(r))]
n Br ≃ jeune femme f BCBG

> Une "Sloane Ranger" est une jeune
> femme à la mode, fille de grands bour-
> geois ou d'aristocrates. À l'origine, ce
> terme ne désignait que les jeunes
> femmes dont la famille habitait Sloane
> Square (quartier chic du sud-ouest de
> Londres); aujourd'hui, sa sphère géo-
> graphique s'est étendue au reste de
> Londres et à ses environs. "Sloane Ran-
> ger" est un jeu de mots sur "Lone Ran-
> ger", qui est le nom du héros d'une
> série télévisée américaine des années
> 50 qui avait pour cadre le Far West.

Sloaney ['sləʊnɪ] adj Br ≃ BCBG

slob n (dirty person) souillon mf; (lazy person) flemmard(e) m,f; **he's nothing but
a big fat slob** ce n'est qu'un gros flemmard

slob about, slob around 1 vt insép

traînasser; **he just slobs about the
house all day** il passe ses journées à traînasser dans la maison

   2 vi traînasser

slob out vi flemmarder; **he spends
every night slobbing out in front of
the TV** il passe ses soirées affalé devant
la télé

slog [slɒg] **1** n (task) tâche f duraille, corvée f

   2 vi (work hard) trimer; **to slog away
(at sth)** travailler comme un dingue (à
qch)

slope off vi s'esbigner, se débiner, s'esqui-
ver ▫; **he always slopes off when it's
his round** il se débine toujours quand
c'est à lui de payer une tournée

sloshed [slɒʃt] adj bourré, pété, beurré

slug [slʌg] **1** n (**a**) (of drink) goulée f, lampée f; **to take** or **have a slug of sth**
boire une lampée de qch (**b**) (bullet) pruneau m, bastos f

   2 vt (hit) cogner; **to slug it out** se bastonner, se friter, se castagner

slug down vt sép siffler (boire)

slugfest ['slʌgfest] n Am baston m ou f,
castagne f

slut [slʌt] n (**a**) (promiscuous woman) pouffiasse f, traînée f (**b**) (prostitute) pute f

slutty ['slʌtɪ] adj (promiscuous) cou-
cheuse; (clothes, behaviour, make-up) qui
fait pute

smack [smæk] n (heroin) héro f, blanche f

smacker ['smækə(r)] n (**a**) (kiss) gros bi-
sou m (**b**) (pound sterling) livre f sterling ▫;
(dollar) dollar ▫ m; **fifty smackers** cinquante livres/dollars

smalls [smɔːlz] npl Br sous-vêtements ▫
mpl

smart [smɑːt] **1** n Am **smarts** (intelligence) intelligence ▫ f; **to have smarts**
en avoir dans le ciboulot; **he's pretty
low on smarts** c'est pas une lumière

   2 adj **smart alec** petit(e) malin(igne)
m,f, je-sais-tout mf ▸ voir aussi **cookie**

smartarse [!] ['smɑːtɑːs], Am **smart-
ass** [!] ['smɑːtæs] n petit(e) malin(igne)
m,f

smashed [smæʃt] *adj (drunk)* bourré, pété, beurré; *(on drugs)* raide, défoncé

smasher ['smæʃə(r)] *n Br* **to be a smasher** être génial; **that second goal was a smasher** le deuxième but était de toute beauté; **she's a smasher** *(gorgeous)* elle est hyper canon

smashing ['smæʃɪŋ] *adj Br* super, génial, géant

smeg [smeg] *n* saloperies *fpl*

smeggy ['smegɪ] *adj Br (disgusting)* dégueulasse, cradingue

smeghead ['smeghed] *n Br* tête *f* de nœud

smoke [sməʊk] **1** *n* **(a)** *(cigarette)* clope *f*; *(cannabis cigarette)* joint *m*; *(cannabis)* chichon *m*, shit *m*, teuch *m* **(b)** *Br* **the (Big) Smoke** *(London)* = surnom donné à la ville de Londres ▶ *voir aussi* **holy**
  2 *vt Am (defeat)* écraser, mettre la pâtée à, battre à plates coutures; **the Tennessee Titans were smoked for the third time in a row** ça fait trois fois de suite que les Tennessee Titans se font mettre la pâtée

smooch [smuːtʃ] *vi* se bécoter

smoothie, smoothy ['smuːðɪ] *n* individu *m* mielleux

snaffle ['snæfəl] *vt Br* piquer, faire main basse sur; **who's snaffled my pen?** qui est-ce qui m'a piqué mon stylo?

snag [snæg] *n Austr (sausage)* saucisse *f*

snail mail ['sneɪlmeɪl] *n Hum* = terme humoristique désignant les services postaux par opposition aux messageries électroniques

snakebite ['sneɪkbaɪt] *n Br (drink)* = boisson comprenant une mesure de bière et une mesure de cidre

snap [snæp] *exclam Br* **I'm on holiday next week – snap!** je suis en vacances la semaine prochaine – moi aussi!

"Snap" est un jeu de cartes dans lequel deux joueurs retournent leurs cartes une par une et simultanément, jusqu'au moment où deux cartes de la même valeur sont retournées; le premier à dire "snap" remporte alors les cartes accumulées. On utilise cette expression lorsque l'on remarque deux choses identiques.

snapper ['snæpə(r)] *n Ir* môme *mf*, gosse *mf*

snatch ‼ [snætʃ] *n (woman's genitals)* craque *f*, cramouille *f*, chatte *f*

snazzy ['snæzɪ] *adj* chicos, classe

sneak [sniːk] **1** *n* **(a)** *Br (tell-tale)* cafard(e) *m,f*, cafteur(euse) *m,f* **(b)** *Am* **sneaks** *(abrév* **sneakers**) baskets *fpl*
  2 *vi (tell tales)* cafter, cafarder; **to sneak on sb** cafter qn, cafarder qn

snit [snɪt] *n Am* **to be in a snit** être fumasse *ou* furibard

snitch [snɪtʃ] **1** *n* **(a)** *(tell-tale)* cafard(e) *m,f*, cafteur(euse) *m,f* **(b)** *Br (nose)* blaire *m*, tarin *m*, pif *m*
  2 *vi (tell tales)* cafter, cafarder; **to snitch on sb** cafter qn, cafarder qn

snockered ['snɒkəd] *adj Am (drunk)* bourré, pété, fait, beurré

snog [snɒg] *Br* **1** *n* **to have a snog** se bécoter, se rouler des pelles *ou* des patins
  2 *vt* bécoter, rouler des pelles *ou* des patins à
  3 *vi* se bécoter, se rouler des pelles *ou* des patins

snooker ['snuːkə(r)] *vt* **(a)** *Br (thwart)* mettre dans l'embarras ▫; **if that doesn't work, we're snookered!** si ça marche pas, on est foutu! **(b)** *Am (swindle, trick)* arnaquer; **don't get snookered into anything!** te laisse pas arnaquer!

snoot [snuːt] *n (nose)* blaire *m*, tarin *m*, pif *m*

snort [snɔːt] **1** *n (of drug)* **to have a snort** se faire une ligne
  2 *vt (drug)* sniffer

snot [snɒt] *n (mucus)* morve *f*

snotrag ['snɒtræg] *n* tire-jus *m*, tire-moelle *m*

snotty ['snɒtɪ] *adj* **(a)** *(nose, handkerchief)* morveux, plein de morve **(b)** *(haughty)* bêcheur, prétentiard; *(insolent)* insolent ▫

The symbol ▫ indicates that a translation is neutral in register.

snout [snaʊt] n Br (**a**) (cigarette) clope f; (tobacco) tabac[□] m, foin m (**b**) (informer) indic mf

snow [snəʊ] **1** n (**a**) (cocaine) coco f, neige f; (heroin crystals) cristaux mpl d'héroïne[□] (**b**) Am **snow job** baratin m; **to give sb a snow job** baratiner qn, rouler qn dans la farine
2 vt Am **to snow sb** (charm, persuade) baratiner qn, rouler qn dans la farine; **to snow sb into doing sth** baratiner qn pour qu'il fasse qch ▸ voir aussi **bunny, pisshole**

snuff [snʌf] **1** n **snuff movie** = film pornographique au cours duquel un participant est réellement assassiné
2 vt (**a**) Br **to snuff it** (die) calancher, passer l'arme à gauche (**b**) Am (murder) buter, refroidir, zigouiller

soak [səʊk] **1** n **old soak** vieux (vieille) poivrot(e) m,f
2 vt Am **to soak sb** (charge heavily) écorcher qn; (tax heavily) accabler qn d'impôts[□]

soap-dodger ['səʊpdɒdʒə(r)] n Br Hum (man) mec m cradingue; (woman) bonne femme f cradingue

sob [!], **SOB** [!] [esəʊ'biː] n Am (abrév **son-of-a-bitch**) salaud m, fils m de pute

sock [sɒk] **1** n (**a**) (blow) beigne f, châtaigne f; **she gave him a sock in the face** elle lui a filé une beigne (**b**) **to put a sock in it** la fermer, la mettre en veilleuse, la boucler; **put a sock in it!** la ferme!, ferme ton clapet!, mets-la en veilleuse!
2 vt (**a**) (hit) filer une beigne ou une châtaigne à; **she socked him in the face** elle lui a filé une beigne (**b**) **to sock it to sb** montrer à qn ce que l'on sait faire; **sock it to them!** vas-y, montre-leur ce que tu sais faire!, vas-y, donne le maximum!

sod [!] [sɒd] Br **1** n (**a**) (person) con (conne) m,f; **the poor sod** le pauvre, le pauvre bougre; **you're a lazy sod** t'es vraiment un flemmard
(**b**) (thing) saloperie f; **it's a sod of a job** c'est un boulot vraiment chiant
(**c**) **sod all** que dalle; **sod all money** pas un flèche, pas un rond; **there's sod all to**

eat il y a que dalle à bouffer
2 vt **sod it!** merde!; **sod him!** qu'il aille se faire voir!; **sod the expense, let's just go!** tant pis si ça coûte cher, allons-y!

sod off [!] vi Br foutre le camp, décamper, décaniller; **sod off!** fous le camp!, dégage!

sodding [!] ['sɒdɪŋ] Br **1** adj (for emphasis) sacré, foutu; **get that sodding dog out of here!** fous-moi cette saleté de clébard dehors!; **he's a sodding nuisance!** c'est un sacré emmerdeur!; **sodding hell!** merde alors!
2 adv (for emphasis) vachement; **you can sodding well do it yourself!** démerde-toi tout seul pour le faire!; **don't be so sodding lazy!** ce que tu peux être flemmard!

Sod's law [sɒdz'lɔː] n Br la loi de l'emmerdement maximum

softie, softy ['sɒftɪ] n (gentle person) bonne pâte f; (coward) poule f mouillée

solid ['sɒlɪd] Noir Am **1** adj (excellent) génial, super, géant
2 adv (absolutely) absolument[□]; **I solid gotta do it!** il faut absolument que je le fasse!

some [sʌm] adj (**a**) (for emphasis) **that was some party/meal!** c'était une sacrée fête!/un sacré gueuleton!; **she's some cook!** c'est une sacrée cuisinière! (**b**) Ironique **some friend he is!** tu parles d'un copain!; Br **some hope!** on peut toujours rêver!

something ['sʌmθɪŋ] **1** pron **that meal was something else!** c'était quelque chose, ce repas!; **he really is something else!** il est pas possible!
2 adv Br **something rotten** or **awful** (lots) vachement; **he fancies her something rotten** or **awful** il est dingue d'elle

son-of-a-bitch [!!] [sʌnəvə'bɪtʃ] Am **1** n (**a**) (man) salaud m, fils m de pute; **you old son-of-a-bitch, how ya doin'?** comment ça va, enfoiré? (**b**) (object) saloperie f; **this son-of-a-bitch is too heavy to carry** cette saloperie est trop lourde à porter
2 exclam putain!

The symbol [□] indicates that a translation is neutral in register.

son-of-a-bitching[‼] [sʌnəvə'bɪtʃɪŋ] *adj Am (for emphasis)* foutu, putain de; **where'd that son-of-a-bitching letter go?** où est passée cette putain de lettre?

son-of-a-gun [sʌnəvə'gʌn] *Am* **1** *n* salaud *m*; **hi, you old son-of-a-gun!** salut, vieux bandit!
2 *exclam* putain!

sook [sʊk] *n Austr (weak person)* mauviette *f*

soph [sɒf] *n Am (abrév* **sophomore**) étudiant(e) *m,f* de deuxième année ◻

sorehead ['sɔːhed] *n Am (person)* ronchon(onne) *m,f*, grincheux(euse) *m,f*

sorry-ass[!] ['sɔːrɪ'æs], **sorry-assed**[!]['sɔːrɪæst] *adj Am (inferior, contemptible)* à la con; **that sorry-ass bastard stole my woman!** cet enfoiré m'a piqué ma gonzesse!

sorted ['sɔːtɪd] *Br* **1** *adj* **to be sorted** *(psychologically)* être équilibré ◻, être bien dans ses baskets; *(have everything one needs)* être paré; **she's the most sorted person I know** c'est la personne la plus équilibrée que je connaisse ◻; **if I get that pay rise, I'll be sorted** si j'obtiens cette augmentation j'aurai plus à m'en faire; **to be sorted for sth** disposer de qch ◻; **are you sorted for E's/whizz?** t'as ce qu'il te faut comme ecsta/speed?
2 *exclam* super!, génial!

soul [səʊl] *n Noir Am* **soul brother** Noir *m* américain ◻; **soul sister** Noire *f* américaine ◻

> Il s'agit d'expressions utilisées par les Noirs américains pour se désigner eux-mêmes et s'adresser les uns aux autres. Ces expressions sont souvent abrégées en "brother" et "sister".

sound [saʊnd] *Br* **1** *adj* super, génial, géant
2 *exclam* super!, génial!, cool!

sounds [saʊndz] *npl (music)* zizique *f*, zicmu *f*

soup [suːp] *n* **to be in the soup** être dans le pétrin *ou* dans la panade

soup-strainer ['suːpstreɪnə(r)] *n Am*

Hum (large moustache) grosses bacchantes *fpl*

sourpuss ['saʊəpʊs] *n (ill-tempered person)* grincheux(euse) *m,f*

souse [saʊs] *n Am (person)* alcolo *mf*, poivrot(e) *m,f*

soused [saʊst] *adj Am (drunk)* bourré, pété, fait, beurré

sozzled ['sɒzəld] *adj Br* bourré, beurré, pété, fait

SP [es'piː] *n Br (abrév* **starting price**) **to give sb the SP (on)** mettre qn au parfum (à propos de *ou* concernant)

> Il s'agit au départ d'une expression de turfistes. Le "starting price" est la cote d'un cheval juste avant le départ.

space [speɪs] *n (a) Hum* **space cadet**, *Am* **space case** allumé(e) *m,f*; **he's a bit of a space cadet** *or Am* **space case** il est toujours en train de planer *(b) Br* **space cakes** gâteaux *mpl* au cannabis ◻, space cakes *mpl*

spaced out [speɪst'aʊt], **spacey** ['speɪsɪ] *adj* **to be** *or* **feel spaced out** *or* **spacey** *(dazed)* être dans le coaltar; *(after taking drugs)* être raide, planer

spade [speɪd] *n Injurieux (black man)* nègre *m*, bamboula *m*; *(black woman)* négresse *f*

spag bol ['spæg'bɒl] *n Br (abrév* **spaghetti bolognese**) spaghettis *mpl* (à la) bolognaise

spare [speə(r)] *adj (a) (mad) Br* **to go spare** péter les plombs, péter une durite; **to drive sb spare** rendre qn chèvre, faire tourner qn en bourrique *(b) Hum Br* **spare tyre**, *Am* **spare tire** *(roll of fat)* poignée *f* d'amour, pneu *m* de secours ▶ *voir aussi* **prick**

sparkler ['spɑːklə(r)] *n (diamond)* diam *m*

sparks [spɑːks] *n Br (electrician)* électricien(enne) ◻ *m,f*

spastic ['spæstɪk] *n Injurieux* gol *mf*, gogol *mf*

> Ce terme signifie littéralement "handicapé moteur". Il s'agit d'une injure

extrêmement politiquement incorrecte qu'il est préférable de bannir complètement de son vocabulaire.

spaz [spæz] n Injurieux gol mf, gogol mf

Il s'agit d'une abréviation du mot "spastic" utilisé comme injure. Bien que cette injure ne soit pas aussi choquante que le mot dont elle est dérivée, il est préférable de l'utiliser avec beaucoup de circonspection.

spaz out vi faire le con

spazzy ['spæzɪ] = spaz

speccy ['spekɪ] Br **1** n binoclard(e) m,f
2 adj binoclard

special K [speʃəl'keɪ] n (ketamine) spécial K f, vitamine K f

specs [speks] npl (abrév **spectacles**) carreaux mpl, hublots mpl

speed [spi:d] **1** n (a) (amphetamines) amphets fpl, speed m (b) **to be up to speed on sth** être au courant de qch □
2 vi **to be speeding** (have taken amphetamines) être sous amphets, speeder
  ▸ voir aussi **merchant**

speedball ['spi:dbɔ:l] n speedball m (mélange d'héroïne et de cocaïne)

speedfreak ['spi:dfri:k] n **to be a speedfreak** marcher aux amphets

spew [spju:] Br **1** vt dégueuler, gerber; **to spew one's guts up** rendre tripes et boyaux
2 vi dégueuler, gerber

spewing ['spju:ɪŋ] adj Br (angry) fumasse, furax, en pétard

spic, spick [spɪk] n Am Injurieux métèque mf (d'origine latino-américaine)

spieler ['spi:lə(r)] n Austr escroc □ m, arnaqueur m; (card-sharp) tricheur(euse) m,f aux cartes □

spike [spaɪk] n (hypodermic needle) shooteuse f, pompe f

spill [spɪl] **1** vt **to spill the beans, to spill one's guts** vendre la mèche; (under interrogation) cracher ou lâcher le morceau
2 vi vendre la mèche; (under interrogation)

cracher ou lâcher le morceau; **come on, spill!** allez, accouche!

spin [spɪn] n Br **on the spin** (in a row) de suite □; **they've won seven games on the spin** ils ont gagné sept matchs de suite

spins [spɪnz] npl **to have the spins** avoir le tournis (généralement après avoir trop bu)

spit [spɪt] n (a) Br **to be the (very) spit of sb** être le portrait craché de qn
  (b) Br **it's a bit of a spit and sawdust pub** c'est un pub sans prétentions □
  (c) Hum **to swap spit** se rouler des pelles ou des patins
  (d) Am **it doesn't count for spit** ça vaut pas un clou

spit out vt sép **spit it out!** accouche!

splatter movie ['splætəmu:vɪ] n = film violent et sanglant

spliced [splaɪst] adj **to get spliced** (marry) se marier □, se maquer

spliff [splɪf] n spliff m, joint m

split [splɪt] **1** vt **to split one's sides (laughing)** se tenir les côtes (de rire)
2 vi (a) Am (leave) se casser, se barrer, s'arracher; **come on, let's split** allez, on se casse (b) Br (inform) **to split on sb** cafarder qn

spondulicks [spɒn'du:lɪks] npl fric m, pognon m, flouze m

sponge [spʌndʒ] **1** vt **to sponge sth (off sb)** taper qch (à qn)
2 vi jouer au parasite; **to sponge off sb** vivre aux crochets de qn

sponger ['spʌndʒə(r)] n pique-assiette mf

spook [spu:k] **1** n Am (a) (spy) barbouze f (b) Injurieux (black man) nègre m, bamboula m; (black woman) négresse f
2 vt (startle) faire sursauter, foutre la trouille à; (frighten, disturb) donner la chair de poule à

sport [spɔ:t] n Austr (fellow) mon pote, mon vieux

spot-on ['spɒtɒn] Br **1** adj (accurate) **his guess was spot-on** il a mis en plein dans le mille; **his remark was spot-on** sa

remarque était vachement bien vue
2 *exclam (excellent)* super!, génial!

spout [spaʊt] *n Br* **to be up the spout**
(pregnant) être en cloque; *(ruined)* être
foutu; **that's our holidays up the**
spout on peut faire une croix sur nos vacances

spread [spred] *vt Br* **to spread it** *or* **one-**
self about a bit *(be promiscuous)* avoir la
cuisse légère, coucher à droite à gauche

spring [sprɪŋ] **1** *n* **she's no spring chick-**
en *(no longer young)* elle a pas mal d'heures de vol, elle est plus de la première
jeunesse
2 *vt (prisoner)* faire évader □

sprog [sprɒg] *n Br (child)* môme *mf*, gosse
mf

spud [spʌd] *n (potato)* patate *f*

spunk [spʌŋk] *n* **(a)** ⚠ *(semen)* foutre *m*
(b) *Austr (attractive woman)* canon *m*; *(at-*
tractive man) beau mec *m*

spunky ['spʌŋkɪ] *adj Austr (attractive)*
canon

squaddie ['skwɒdɪ] *n Br* bidasse *m*

square [skweə(r)] **1** *n* **(a)** *(unfashionable*
person) ringard(e) *m,f* **(b)** *Am* **square**
shooter *(candid person)* personne *f* franche □
2 *adj (unfashionable)* ringard

square up *vi Am (of criminal)* raccrocher,
se ranger des voitures; *(of drug addict)* décrocher

squawk [skwɔːk] *Am* **1** *n (complaint)*
plainte □ *f*; **what's your squawk?** c'est
quoi ton problème?
2 *vi (complain)* râler

squeal [skwiːl] *vi (inform)* moucharder;
to squeal on sb balancer *ou* moucharder
qn

squealer ['skwiːlə(r)] *n (informer)* indic
mf

squeeze [skwiːz] *n* **(a)** **(main) squeeze**
(boyfriend) mec *m*, Jules *m*; *(girlfriend)*
nana *f*, gonzesse *f* **(b)** **to put the**
squeeze on sb faire pression sur qn □

squiffy ['skwɪfɪ] *adj Br* éméché

squillion ['skwɪljən] *n Br Hum* **squillions**

(of) une foultitude (de), une ribambelle
(de)

squirrelly ['skwɪrəlɪ] *adj Am (eccentric)*
loufedingue

squirt [skwɜːt] *n (person)* avorton *m*,
demi-portion *f*

squits [skwɪts] *npl Br* **the squits** la courante

stache [stæʃ] *n Am (abrév* **mustache)**
bacchantes *fpl*, moustagache *f*

stacked [stækt] *Am* = **well-stacked**

staggered ['stægəd] *adj (amazed)* estomaqué

stallion ['stæljən] *n* **(a)** *(man)* étalon *m*
(b) *Noir Am (woman)* canon *m*, bombe *f*

stand up [stænd] *vt sép* **to stand sb up**
poser un lapin à qn

star [stɑː(r)] *n* **she isn't the brightest**
star in the sky elle n'a pas inventé l'eau
chaude *ou* le fil à couper le beurre

starfucker ⚠ ['stɑːfʌkə(r)] *n* groupie *f*
(qui multiplie les aventures avec des stars)

starkers ['stɑːkəz] *adj Br* à poil

stash [stæʃ] **1** *n* **(a)** *(hidden supply)* provi-
sion □ *f*; *(hiding place)* planque *f* **(b)** *(sup-*
ply of drugs) réserve *f* de drogue □; **the**
police found his stash under the
floorboards la police a trouvé sa réserve
de drogue cachée sous le plancher
2 *vt (hide)* planquer

static ['stætɪk] *n Am* **(a)** *(insolence)* insolence □ *f*; **I'm not taking that static**
from you! arrête de faire l'insolent! **(b)**
(hassle, interference) embêtements *mpl*;
you can expect plenty of static from
mom tu vas avoir Maman sur le dos

steal [stiːl] *n* **to be a steal** *(very cheap)*
être donné

steam in [stiːm] *vi Br (join in)* s'en mêler;
when they started to threaten his
girlfriend that was when he steamed
in quand ils ont commencé à menacer sa
copine il a décidé de s'en mêler

steam up [stiːm] *vt sép Am* **to steam sb**
up *(infuriate)* mettre qn en pétard *ou* en
boule; **to be steamed up** être en pétard
ou en boule

The symbol □ indicates that a translation is neutral in register.

steamboats ['sti:mbəʊts] *adj Br (drunk)* rond comme une queue de pelle, plein comme une barrique, pété à mort

steaming ['sti:mɪŋ] *adj* **(a)** *Br (drunk)* rond comme une queue de pelle, plein comme une barrique, pété à mort **(b)** *Am (angry)* en pétard, en boule

steamy ['sti:mɪ] *adj (erotic)* chaud, sexy

stems [stemz] *npl Am (legs)* quilles *fpl*, gambettes *fpl*, cannes *fpl*

stew [stju:] **1** *n Am (abrév* **stewardess)** hôtesse *f* de l'air □

2 *vi Br* **to be stewing** *(of person)* crever de chaleur; **it's stewing in here** il fait une chaleur à crever ici ▸ *voir aussi* **bum**

stewed [stju:d] *adj* **stewed (to the gills)** rond comme une queue de pelle, plein comme une barrique, pété à mort

stick [stɪk] **1** *n* **(a)** *Br* **up the stick** *(pregnant)* en cloque **(b)** **the sticks** *(place)* la cambrousse; **to live in the sticks** habiter en pleine cambrousse

(c) *Br* **to give sb stick (for sth)** *(tease)* faire enrager qn, chambrer qn (à cause de qch); **they're giving him stick for buying platform shoes** ils le font enrager parce qu'il a acheté des platform shoes **(d)** *Am (cannabis cigarette)* stick *m* **(e)** *Br Hum* **he's won more awards than you can shake a stick at** on lui a décerné une flopée de prix; **there was more talent than you can shake a stick at** ça grouillait de beaux mecs/de belles nanas

2 *vt* **(a)** *(place, put)* flanquer, coller **(b)** *Br (tolerate) (person)* encadrer, blairer, piffer, encaisser; *(thing)* encaisser; **I can't stick him** je peux pas le blairer; **how have you stuck it for so long?** comment t'as fait pour supporter ça aussi longtemps?

(c) **you can stick your job!** ton boulot, tu peux te le mettre où je pense!; **he can stick his money!** son fric, il peut se le mettre *ou* coller où je pense!; **stick it!** va te faire voir! ▸ *voir aussi* **arse, ass, oar, poke, shine, sight**

stickybeak ['stɪkɪbi:k] *Austr* **1** *n* foui-neur(euse) *m,f*, fouinard(e) *m,f*

2 *vi* fouiner

sticky fingers ['stɪkɪ'fɪŋgəz] *npl* **to have sticky fingers** *(steal things)* avoir tendance à piquer tout ce qui traîne

stiff [stɪf] **1** *n* **(a)** *(corpse)* macchabée *m* **(b)** *Br (failure)* bide *m* **(c)** *Am (tramp)* clodo *mf* **(d)** *Am (stupid person)* nul (nulle) *m,f*

2 *adj Am (drunk)* bourré, rond, fait, beurré

stiffy ⚠ ['stɪfɪ] *n Br* **to have a stiffy** bander, avoir la trique *ou* le gourdin; **to get a stiffy** se mettre à bander

sting [stɪŋ] **1** *n* **(a)** *(swindle)* arnaque *f* **(b)** *Am (police operation)* coup *m* monté *(dans le cadre d'une opération de police)*

2 *vt (swindle)* arnaquer, refaire; **to get stung** se faire arnaquer, se faire refaire; **they stung him for a hundred quid** ils l'ont arnaqué *ou* refait de cent livres

stink [stɪŋk] **1** *n (fuss)* foin *m*, pataquès *m*; **to raise** *or* **make** *or* **Br kick up a stink (about sth)** faire toute une histoire (de qch)

2 *vi (be bad)* être nul, craindre; **don't bother going to the concert, it stinks!** ne vas pas au concert, c'est nul!; **what do you think of my plan? – it stinks!** qu'est-ce que tu penses de mon projet? – il est nul! ▸ *voir aussi* **shit**

stinker ['stɪŋkə(r)] *n* **(a)** *(person)* ordure *f* **(b)** *(difficult thing)* **to be a stinker** être vachement dur, être coton; **the German exam was a real stinker** l'examen d'allemand était vraiment coton

(c) *(worthless thing)* **to be a stinker** être nul, être merdique; **his new film's a total stinker** son nouveau film est complètement nul

(d) **to have a stinker of a cold** avoir un sacré rhume *ou* un rhume carabiné

stinking ['stɪŋkɪŋ] **1** *adj* **(a)** *(worthless)* merdique, nul **(b)** **to have a stinking cold** avoir un sacré rhume *ou* un rhume carabiné

2 *adv* **to be stinking rich** être plein aux as, être bourré de fric

stinko ['stɪŋkəʊ] *adj Am (drunk)* pété, bourré, fait

The symbol □ indicates that a translation is neutral in register.

stir [stɜː(r)] **1** *n* (*prison*) taule *f*, placard *m*, cabane *f*; **in stir** en taule, en cabane, à l'ombre; **stir crazy** cinglé (*à force d'être en prison*)

2 *vt Br* **to stir it** semer la zizanie

stitch [stɪtʃ] *n* (**a**) *Am* (*amusing person, thing*) **to be a stitch** être tordant *ou* crevant (**b**) **to be in stitches** (*laugh*) se tenir les côtes (de rire), être plié de rire; **to have sb in stitches** faire rire qn aux larmes

stitch up *vt sép* **to stitch sb up** (*frame*) piéger qn □, monter un coup contre qn; **he was stitched up** il a été victime d'un coup monté

stoater ['stəʊtə(r)] *n Scot* (**a**) (*excellent thing*) **what a stoater of a goal!** quel but d'enfer!; **we had a stoater of an idea** on a eu une idée géniale (**b**) (*beautiful person*) canon *m*; **his new girlfriend's a wee stoater!** sa nouvelle copine est canon!

stocious ['stəʊʃəs] *adj Scot* (*drunk*) bourré, beurré

stogie ['stəʊɡɪ] *n Am* (*cigar*) cigare □ *m*

stoked [stəʊkt] *adj Am* (*excited, enthusiastic*) emballé

stomach ['stʌmək] *vt* (*tolerate*) (*person*) blairer, piffer, encaisser; (*thing*) encaisser; **I like him but I can't stomach his brother** lui, je l'aime bien, mais je peux pas blairer son frère; **I can't stomach the way he looks at me** il a une façon de me regarder qui me débecte ▶ *voir aussi* **throat**

stomp [stɒmp] *vt Am* (*defeat*) flanquer une peignée *ou* une déculottée *ou* une tannée à

stone [stəʊn], **stone-cold** ['stəʊn-'kəʊld] *adj Noir Am* (*absolute, real*) véritable □, total; **she is a stone babe!** c'est une supernana!; **this is turning into a stone drag!** ça devient vraiment galère!

stoned [stəʊnd] *adj* (*on drugs*) raide, défoncé; **to get stoned** se défoncer

stoner ['stəʊnə(r)] *n* adepte *mf* de la fumette

stonker ['stɒŋkə(r)] *n Br* (**a**) (*impressive thing*) **what a stonker of a goal!** quel but d'enfer!; **their latest album's a complete stonker!** leur dernier album est absolument génial! (**b**) (*large thing*) mastodonte *m*; **that new skyscraper is a stonker!** ce nouveau gratte-ciel est un vrai mastodonte (**c**) **!** (*erect penis*) trique *f*, gaule *f*

stonking ['stɒŋkɪŋ] *adj Br* super, génial, d'enfer; **he scored a stonking goal** il a marqué un but d'enfer

stony (broke) ['stəʊnɪ('brəʊk)] *adj* fauché (comme les blés), raide, à sec

stooge [stuːdʒ] *n* (**a**) (*dupe*) pigeon *m*, poire *f* (**b**) (*idiot*) andouille *f*, crétin(e) *m,f*

stool [stuːl], **stoolie** ['stuːlɪ], **stool pigeon** ['stuːlpɪdʒɪn] *n* indic *mf*

storm [stɔːm] *n* **to go down a storm** (*be very successful*) faire un tabac, faire un malheur; **their new Channel Four show is going down a storm with the critics** leur nouvelle émission sur Channel Four fait un vrai malheur auprès de la critique

straight [streɪt] **1** *n* (**a**) (*heterosexual*) hétéro *mf* (**b**) *Am* (*conventional person*) personne *f* conventionnelle *ou* sérieuse □; **don't be such a straight!** sois pas si sérieux!

2 *adj* (**a**) (*heterosexual*) hétéro (**b**) (*not on drugs*) **to be straight** ne pas avoir pris de drogue □ (**c**) (*conventional*) conventionnel □, sérieux □; **her dad's really straight, don't swear in front of him** son père n'est pas du genre rigolo, ne dis pas de gros mots devant lui (**d**) *Am* **a straight arrow** (*man*) un brave type; (*woman*) une brave femme; **a straight shooter** (*person*) une personne franche □ (**e**) *Am* (*true*) vrai □ (**f**) *Am* **to get straight** = prendre une dose d'héroïne (ou d'une drogue comparable) de façon à éviter l'effet de manque

3 *adv* (**a**) **to go straight** (*of criminal*) se ranger des voitures (**b**) *Br* **straight up?** sans déconner?, sans dec?; **straight up!** sans déconner!, je t'assure!, sans dec!

straight-edge [streɪt'edʒ] *adj Am* sérieux [□], rangé [□]

strapped [stræpt] *adj* (**a**) **to be strapped (for cash)** être fauché, ne pas avoir un rond (**b**) *Am (armed)* armé [□], chargé

streak [striːk] *n Br* **he's a long streak of piss** [!] *(tall and thin)* c'est une grande perche; *(insipid in character)* c'est une lavette

street [striːt] *n* (**a**) **to be on the street** *or* **streets** *(of homeless person)* être à la rue; *(of prostitute)* faire le trottoir *ou* le tapin; **to walk the streets** *(of prostitute)* faire le trottoir *ou* le tapin
(**b**) *Br* **this job should be right up your street** ce boulot devrait être dans tes cordes; **there'll be loads of drink and drugs, it should be right up your street** il y aura beaucoup d'alcool et de drogue, c'est tout à fait ton truc ▶ *voir aussi* **cred, easy, queer**

streetwalker ['striːtwɔːkə(r)] *n* prostituée [□] *f*; **to be a streetwalker** faire le trottoir

streetwise ['striːtwaɪz] *adj* qui sait se débrouiller tout seul, déluré

strength [streŋθ] *n* **give me strength!** pitié!

stretch [stretʃ] *n (term of imprisonment)* peine *f* de prison [□]; **to do a stretch** faire de la taule; **he was given a five-year stretch** il a écopé de cinq ans

strewth [struːθ] *exclam Br & Austr (abrév* **God's truth)** mince alors!

strides [straɪdz] *npl Br & Austr (trousers)* bénard *m*, bène *m*, futal *m*, fute *m*

stringbean [strɪŋ'biːn] *n Am (person)* grande perche *f*, asperge *f*

stroke [strəʊk] *vt* (**a**) *Am (flatter)* passer de la pommade à (**b**) **a stroke mag** un bouquin de cul

strop [strɒp] *n Br* **to be in a strop** être mal luné, être de mauvais poil; **we were treated to another of his famous strops** il nous a fait la gueule comme il sait si bien le faire

stroppy ['strɒpɪ] *adj Br* mal luné, de mauvais poil; **there's no need to get stroppy** tu n'as pas besoin d'être désagréable comme ça!

stubby ['stʌbɪ] *n Br & Austr (bottle of beer)* canette *f*

stuck [stʌk] *adj Br* **to get stuck into sb** *(physically, verbally)* rentrer dans le lard à qn; **to get stuck into sth** *(book, work, meal)* attaquer qch; **get stuck in!** attaque!

stud [stʌd] *n (man)* étalon *m*; *Am* **stud muffin** super beau mec *m*

stuff [stʌf] **1** *n* (**a**) *Br* **she's a lovely bit of stuff** elle est vraiment bien balancée, elle est canon; **he was there with his bit of stuff** il était là avec sa gonzesse
(**b**) **go on, do your stuff!** allez, à toi de jouer!; **to know one's stuff** s'y connaître, connaître son affaire; **that's the stuff!** parfait!
(**c**) *(drugs)* came *f*
2 *vt* (**a**) **to stuff oneself** *or* **one's face** se goinfrer, s'empiffrer, s'en mettre plein le lampe, s'en mettre jusque-là
(**b**) **get stuffed!, stuff you!** va te faire cuire un œuf!; **stuff this, I'm going home!** rien à foutre de ce truc, moi je rentre chez moi!; **I've had enough, he can stuff his job!** j'en ai marre, son boulot il peut se le mettre où je pense!
(**c**) *(defeat)* écrabouiller, foutre une déculottée à, battre à plates coutures
(**d**) [!!] *(have sex with)* baiser, troncher, tringler

stuffed [stʌft] *adj Br & Austr (in trouble)* cuit, fichu; **if that cheque doesn't arrive soon, we're stuffed** si ce chèque n'arrive pas bientôt, on est cuits

stumblebum ['stʌmbəlbʌm] *n Am* (**a**) *(drunken vagrant)* clodo *mf* alcolo (**b**) *(clumsy, incompetent person)* manche *m*

stumm [ʃtʊm] = **schtum**

stump up [stʌmp] *Br* **1** *vt sép* cracher, casquer
2 *vi* casquer, raquer (**for** pour); **come on, stump up!** allez, raque!

stunner ['stʌnə(r)] *n Br (woman)* canon *m*, bombe *f*

stupe [stju:p] n Am andouille f, truffe f, crétin(e) m,f

style [staɪl] vi Noir Am (show off) frimer, flamber; (do well) bien se démerder

sub [sʌb] Br 1 n (abrév **subsistence allowance**) (small loan) prêt ᵘ m; **to give sb a sub** dépanner qn; **to get a sub** se faire dépanner
2 vt (lend) **to sub sb sth** dépanner qn de qch; **can you sub me a fiver?** tu peux me dépanner de cinq livres?

suck [sʌk] 1 vt Am **to suck face** se rouler des pelles ou des patins ou des galoches
2 vi (be bad) craindre, être nul ou merdique; **this bar/film sucks** ce bar/film est vraiment nul; **this sucks, let's do something else** c'est nul, si on faisait autre chose?; **I've got to work all weekend – that sucks!** il faut que je travaille tout le week-end – ça craint!

suck off [!!] vt sép **to suck sb off** sucer qn, tailler une pipe à qn, faire un pompier à qn

suck up vi **to suck up to sb** faire de la lèche à qn, cirer les pompes à qn

sucker ['sʌkə(r)] 1 n (a) (gullible person) poire f, pigeon m; **he's a sucker for blondes/chocolate ice-cream** il adore les blondes/la glace au chocolat (b) Am (despicable man) blaireau m (c) Am (object) truc m, machin m, bitoniau m; **what's this sucker for?** à quoi ça sert, ce truc?
2 vt (trick, swindle) arnaquer

sugar ['ʃʊgə(r)] 1 n (a) (term of address) chéri(e) m,f (b) **sugar daddy** = homme âgé qui entretient une jeune maîtresse
2 exclam miel!, punaise!

suit [su:t] n Péj (person) costard-cravate m, employé(e) m,f de bureau ᵘ (en costume ou tailleur) ▸ voir aussi **monkey, penguin**

sunshine ['sʌnʃaɪn] n Br (term of address) chéri(e) m,f; **watch it, sunshine!** fais gaffe, mon coco!

supergrass ['su:pəgrɑ:s] n Br indic mf de choc

Pleins feux sur:

Stupidity and madness

Il existe en anglais un très grand nombre d'expressions argotiques pour exprimer la bêtise ou la folie. Les expressions employées pour exprimer la bêtise d'une personne sont très souvent originales, comme en témoignent les images suivantes: **the lights are on but there's nobody home** et **the elevator doesn't go up to the top floor**. Certaines expressions humoristiques génèrent de nombreuses variantes, et l'on voit régulièrement apparaître de nouvelles trouvailles, souvent éphémères. Parmi les plus courantes, citons **to be one sandwich short of a picnic, one brick short of a load** et **one clown short of a circus**. De même, on peut dire d'une personne **he/she is not the sharpest knife in the drawer** ou bien **not the sharpest tool in the shed** ou encore **not the brightest star in the sky**.

Certains suffixes permettent de former toute une série de mots: par exemple **-head** donne **airhead, bonehead, butthead, dickhead** (plus vulgaire), **fathead, knucklehead** et **pinhead**, pour n'en citer que quelques-uns.

Pour désigner la folie, on emploie très souvent le terme **nut**, ainsi que ses dérivés. Un fou peut alors être **a nut, a nutter, a nutcase** ou **a nutso**. On dira d'une personne qu'elle est **nutty** ou **off one's nut**, qu'elle devient **nuts** (**to go nuts**) ou qu'elle va finir dans une **nuthouse** (**to end up in the nuthouse**).

Il existe d'autres façons de décrire un fou, telles que **to be off one's head, chump, rocker** ou **trolley**. De la même façon, on emploiera les expressions **to go up the wall** ou **the pole, to go round the bend** ou **the twist, to go out of one's tree** ou **mind** pour parler de quelqu'un qui est en train de perdre la raison.

---

sure [ʃɔː(r)] **1** adj **sure thing!** et comment!
2 exclam (**a**) Am (you're welcome) de
rien! ᵁ, il n'y a pas de quoi! ᵁ (**b**) **(for)
sure!** (of course) bien sûr!

surfie ['sɜːfɪ] n Austr surfeur(euse) m,f

suss [sʌs] vt Br (work out) découvrir ᵁ;
(realize) se rendre compte de ᵁ; **I soon
sussed what he was up to** j'ai vite
compris son petit manège; **I haven't
sussed where the good pubs are yet**
j'ai pas encore repéré les bons pubs

suss out vt sép **to suss sth out** (work
out) découvrir ᵁ; (realize) se rendre
compte de ᵁ; **I couldn't suss out how
the modem worked** j'ai pas pigé
comment le modem fonctionnait; **I can't
quite suss her out** c'est quelqu'un que
j'ai du mal à cerner; **I haven't sussed
out his motives yet** j'ai toujours pas pigé
ses motivations; **we have to suss out
the best places to go at night** il faut
qu'on repère les endroits où sortir le soir

sussed [sʌst] adj (**a**) (astute) rusé, malin
(**b**) **I haven't got her sussed yet** je l'ai
pas encore vraiment cernée; **I haven't
got this computer sussed yet** j'ai pas
encore pigé comment fonctionne cet ordinateur; **he's got it sussed, he does no
work and gets paid a fortune** il a
trouvé le bon filon, il ne travaille pas et il
gagne une fortune

swacked [swækt] adj Am (drunk) bourré,
fait, beurré

swally ['swælɪ] n Scot (drinking session)
beuverie f; **fancy a swally?** ça te dirait
de te pinter?

swamp donkey ['swɒmpdɒŋkɪ] n mocheté f

swanky ['swæŋkɪ] adj (**a**) (chic, posh)
classe, chicos (**b**) (boastful) frimeur

sweat [swet] **1** n **no sweat!** pas de problèmes!
2 vt **don't sweat it!** calmos!, relax!

sweeney ['swiːnɪ] n Br (rhyming slang
Sweeney Todd = flying squad) = la
brigade volante de Scotland Yard

Sweeney Todd est un personnage fictif
apparu au XVIIIème siècle; il s'agit d'un
barbier londonien qui assassinait ses cli-
ents pour en faire de la viande hachée.

sweet [swiːt] **1** adj (excellent) génial, super
2 exclam Br **sweet (as a nut)!** cool!,
génial! ▸ voir aussi **FA**

sweetie(-pie) ['swiːtɪ(paɪ)] n (term of
address) mon (ma) chéri(e) m,f

swift [swɪft] adj Am (clever) malin; **that
was a real swift move** c'était bien joué;
she's not real swift c'est pas une lumière, elle est pas très maligne

swifty ['swɪftɪ] n Austr **to pull a swifty
on sb** rouler qn

swine [swaɪn] n Br (person) salaud m;
he's a lazy swine! c'est une grosse feignasse!; **oh, you lucky swine!** sacré
veinard, va!; **he's a jealous swine, just
ignore him** ce n'est qu'un jaloux, ne fais
pas attention à lui

swing [swɪŋ] vi (**a**) (be hanged) être pendu; **he should swing for that!** il mérite-
rait douze balles dans la peau! (**b**)
(exchange sexual partners) faire de
l'échangisme ᵁ (**c**) **to swing both ways**
(be bisexual) marcher à voile et à vapeur
(**d**) **to swing for sb** (hit out at) essayer
d'en coller une à qn

swinger ['swɪŋə(r)] n (**a**) (sociable person) fêtard(e) m,f (**b**) (who exchanges sexual partners) échangiste ᵁ mf

swipe [swaɪp] vt (steal) piquer, chouraver,
barboter; **who's swiped my pen?** qui m'a
piqué ou chouravé ou barboté mon stylo?

swish [swɪʃ] **1** n Am Injurieux (effeminate
homosexual) folle f
2 adj Br (chic) classe, chicos

swishy ['swɪʃɪ] adj Am Injurieux (effeminate) chochotte

switch-hitter ['swɪtʃhɪtə(r)] n Injurieux
(homosexual) pédé m, tante f, tapette f

swizz [swɪz] n Br arnaque f

swot [swɒt] Br **1** n Péj bûcheur(euse) m,f
2 vi bûcher

swot up on vt insép Br bûcher

syrup ['sɪrəp] n Br (rhyming slang **syrup
of figs = wig**) moumoute f

The symbol ᵁ indicates that a translation is neutral in register.

T

ta [tɑː] *exclam Br* merci! □

tab [tæb] *n* (**a**) *(of LSD)* buvard *m* (**b**) *Br (cigarette)* clope *f*, tige *f*, sèche *f*

table ['teɪbəl] *n* **to drink sb under the table** = tenir encore debout quand tout le monde a roulé sous la table

tackle ['tækəl] *n Br Hum* **(wedding) tackle** *(man's genitals)* service *m* trois pièces, bijoux *mpl* de famille

tad [tæd] *n* **a tad** un tantinet; **it's a tad expensive** c'est un peu chérot; **it's a tad long** c'est un peu longuet; **it's a tad worrying** c'est un tantinet inquiétant; **I think you're exaggerating a tad** je crois que t'exagères un tantinet; **you were being a tad naive if you believed him** si tu l'as cru, t'as été un tantinet naïf

tadger ['tædʒə(r)] *n Br (penis)* chipolata *f*

Taffy ['tæfɪ] *n Br Péj (Welshman)* Gallois □ *m*

"Taffy" est censé être la transcription phonétique du prénom "David" tel que le prononcent les Gallois, et désigne une personne originaire du pays de Galles. Bien que ce terme ne témoigne pas nécessairement d'une attitude xénophobe de la part de celui qui l'utilise, il est préférable de ne pas l'employer.

tail [teɪl] **1** *n* (**a**) *(buttocks)* derrière *m*; **to work one's tail off** bosser comme un malade (**b**) *(person following a criminal)* filocheur *m*; **to put a tail on sb** faire filer le train à qn, faire filocher qn (**c**) [!] *Am (woman)* **she's a great piece of tail** c'est une nana super bandante; **he's looking for some tail** il cherche une femme à se mettre sur le bout

2 *vt (follow)* filocher, filer le train à ► *voir aussi* **shake**

tailgate ['teɪlgeɪt] *vt Am* **to tailgate sb** coller au cul à qn

take [teɪk] *n* **to be on the take** toucher des pots-de-vin, palper

take off *vi (leave hurriedly)* se barrer, se tirer

take out *vt sép* **to take sb out** *(kill)* buter qn, zigouiller qn, refroidir qn

tale [teɪl] *n* **to tell tales** *(inform)* cafter; **she's been telling tales to the teacher again** elle est encore allée cafter à la maîtresse

talent ['tælənt] *n Br (attractive men)* beaux mecs *mpl*; *(attractive women)* belles nanas *fpl*; **he's out chatting up the local talent** il est en train de draguer les minettes du coin; **it's an OK bar, but there's not much talent** c'est pas mal comme bar, mais question mecs/nanas, ça casse pas des briques

talk [tɔːk] *vi* **talk about lucky!** tu parles d'un coup de bol!; **talk about a waste of time!** tu parles d'une perte de temps; **now you're talking!** à la bonne heure!, voilà, c'est beaucoup mieux!; **you can talk!, look who's talking!** tu peux parler!

tank [tæŋk] **1** *n* **to be built like a tank** être une armoire à glace

2 *vt Br* **to tank it** foncer

3 *vi Am (lose deliberately)* faire exprès de perdre □

tanked [tæŋkt] *adj Am (drunk)* bourré, beurré, pété; **to get tanked** prendre une cuite

tanked up [tæŋkt'ʌp] *adj Br (drunk)* bourré, beurré, pété; **to get tanked up** prendre une cuite

tap [tæp] *vt Br* **to tap sb for sth** taper qch à qn; **he tapped me for a loan but**

The symbol □ indicates that a translation is neutral in register.

I refused il a voulu me taper du fric, mais j'ai refusé

tapped out ['tæpt'ɑʊt] *adj Am* crevé, lessivé, nase

ta·ra [tə'rɑː] *exclam Br* salut!, ciao!

tart [tɑːt] *n Br* (**a**) *(prostitute)* pute *f* (**b**) *Péj (promiscuous woman)* salope *f*, traînée *f*, Marie-couche-toi-là *f*, pétasse *f*; *Hum* **a tart with a cart** *(air hostess)* hôtesse *f* de l'air □

tart up *vt sép* **to tart oneself up** se pomponner; **to tart sth up** décorer qch □ *(le plus souvent avec mauvais goût)*

tarty ['tɑːtɪ] *adj Br* qui fait pute; **she looks really tarty with her hair bleached like that** elle fait vraiment pute avec ses cheveux décolorés comme ça

tash [tæʃ] *n Br (abrév* **moustache**) moustache □ *f*, bacchantes *fpl*

tasty ['teɪstɪ] *adj (attractive)* bien foutu, bien balancé

tater ['teɪtə(r)] *n Br* patate *f (tubercule)*

tax [tæks] *vt Br (steal)* taxer, piquer, chouraver

tea leaf ['tiːliːf] *n Br (rhyming slang* **thief**) voleur(euse) □ *m,f*

technicolour, *Am* **technicolor** ['teknɪkʌlə(r)] *adj Hum* **to have a** *Br* **technicolour** *or Am* **technicolor yawn** *(vomit)* gerber, dégobiller

teenybopper ['tiːnɪbɒpə(r)] *n* petite minette *f (qui suit la mode)*

teeth [tiːθ] *npl Br* **to be fed up** *or* **sick to the back teeth of sb/sth** en avoir plus que marre de qn/qch ▶ *voir aussi* **hell**

tell-tale ['telteɪl] *n Br* cafteur(euse) *m,f*

tenner ['tenə(r)] *n Br (ten-pound note)* billet *m* de dix livres □; *Am (ten-dollar note)* billet *m* de dix dollars □; *Br (sum)* dix livres □ *fpl*

ten-spot ['tenspɒt] *n Am* billet *m* de dix dollars □

there [ðeə(r)] *adv* **been there, done that (got the T-shirt)** non merci, j'ai déjà donné

thick [θɪk] *adj* (**a**) *(stupid)* bête □, débile; *Br* **to be as thick as two short planks** être bête comme ses pieds *ou* bête à manger du foin; **to be thick as pigshit** [!] être con comme un balai; **will you get that into your thick skull!** tu vas te mettre ça dans la tête, oui ou non?

(**b**) *Br (unreasonable)* **that's a bit thick!** c'est un peu fort!; **it's a bit thick expecting us to take them to the airport!** ils exagèrent de compter sur nous pour les conduire à l'aéroport!

(**c**) *Br* **to give sb a thick ear** flanquer une taloche à qn

thickie ['θɪkɪ], **thicko** ['θɪkəʊ] *n Br* nouille *f*, andouille *f*

thing [θɪŋ] *n* (**a**) **to have a thing about sb/sth** *(like)* avoir un faible pour qn/qch; *(dislike)* avoir horreur de qn/qch; **he's got a real thing about tidiness/punctuality** il est très à cheval sur la propreté/la ponctualité (**b**) *(penis)* chose *f* ▶ *voir aussi* **sure**

thingumabob ['θɪŋəmɪbɒb], **thingumajig** ['θɪŋəmɪdʒɪg], **thingummy** ['θɪŋəmɪ], **thingy** ['θɪŋɪ] *n (person)* Bidule *mf*, Machin(e) *m,f*; *(thing)* truc *m*, machin *m*

third degree ['θɜːdɪ'griː] *n* **to give sb the third degree** cuisiner qn

thrash [θræʃ] **1** *n Br (party)* fiesta *f*
2 *vt* (**a**) *(beat up)* tabasser, casser la gueule à (**b**) *(defeat)* foutre la pâtée *ou* une raclée *ou* une déculottée à, écrabouiller, battre à plates coutures (**c**) *Br (car)* conduire comme un dingue

thrashing ['θræʃɪŋ] *n* (**a**) *(beating)* **to give sb a thrashing** tabasser qn, casser la gueule à qn, foutre une raclée à qn; **to get a thrashing** prendre une raclée, se faire tabasser
(**b**) *(defeat)* déculottée *f*, dégelée *f*, raclée *f*; **to give sb a thrashing** foutre la pâtée *ou* une raclée *ou* une déculottée à qn, écrabouiller qn, battre qn à plates coutures; **to get a thrashing** prendre une raclée *ou* une déculottée, se faire battre à plates coutures

threads [θredz] *npl (clothes)* fringues *fpl*

throat [θrəʊt] *n* (**a**) *Hum* **my stomach**

thinks my throat's cut je crève la dalle (**b**) **to be at each other's throats** (*arguing*) se disputer, se chamailler; **to jump down sb's throat** (*shout at*) rentrer dans qn, gueuler sur qn

throw up [θrəʊ] *vi* (*vomit*) dégobiller

thrupenny bits [!] [θrʌpənɪˈbɪts] *npl Br* (*rhyming slang = **tits***) nichons *mpl*, nénés *mpl*, roberts *mpl*

thunderthighs [ˈθʌndəθaɪz] *n Hum* (*cuisses*) jambonneaux *mpl*; (*woman*) = femme aux grosses cuisses; **she's a real thunderthighs** elle a de sacrés jambonneaux

tick [tɪk] *n Br* (**a**) (*moment*) seconde ᵈ *f*, instant ᵈ *m*; **hang on a tick** *or* **two ticks** attends une seconde; **I'll just be a tick** *or* **two ticks** j'en ai pour une seconde *ou* deux secondes (**b**) (*credit*) **to buy sth on tick** acheter qch à crédit ᵈ

tick off *vt sép* (**a**) *Br* (*scold*) passer un savon à (**b**) *Am* (*annoy*) prendre la tête à; **to be ticked off (with)** en avoir marre (de)

ticker [ˈtɪkə(r)] *n* (*heart*) palpitant *m*

ticket [ˈtɪkɪt] *n* **that's (just) the ticket!** c'est exactement ce qu'il me/te/ *etc* faut!

tiddly [ˈtɪdlɪ] *adj Br* (**a**) (*drunk*) éméché (**b**) (*small*) minus

tie on [taɪ] *vt sép Am* **to tie one on** (*get drunk*) prendre une cuite, se cuiter

tight [taɪt] *adj* (**a**) (*miserly*) pingre, radin (**b**) (*drunk*) pompette

tight-arsed [!] [ˈtaɪtɑːst], *Am* **tight-assed** [!] [ˈtaɪtæst] *adj* (*uptight*) coincé

tight-fisted [taɪtˈfɪstɪd] *adj* pingre, radin

tightwad [ˈtaɪtwɒd] *n* radin(e) *m,f*

time [taɪm] *n* (**a**) **to do time** (*in prison*) faire de la taule (**b**) *Am* **to make time with sb** (*chat up*) draguer qn; (*have sex with*) s'envoyer en l'air avec qn

tinkle [ˈtɪŋkəl] **1** *n* (**a**) *Br* (*phone call*) **to give sb a tinkle** passer un coup de fil à qn (**b**) (*act of urinating*) *Br* **to have** *or* **do a tinkle** faire pipi; **to go for a tinkle** aller faire pipi

2 *vi* (*urinate*) faire pipi

tinnie [ˈtɪnɪ] *n Austr* boite *f* de bière ᵈ

tip [tɪp] *n Br* (*untidy place*) taudis *m* ▸ *voir aussi* **arse**

tipsy [ˈtɪpsɪ] *adj* éméché

tit [!] [tɪt] *n* (**a**) (*breast*) nichon *m*, robert *m*; *Br* **to get on sb's tits** courir sur le haricot à qn, taper sur les nerfs à qn; **to be off one's tits** (*drunk*) être complètement bourré *ou* pété; (*drugged*) complètement défoncé (**b**) *Br* (*person*) con (conne) *m,f*; **I felt a right tit** je me suis senti tout con ▸ *voir aussi* **arse, ripped**

titty [!], **tittie** [ˈtɪtɪ] *n* (**a**) (*breast*) nichon *m*, robert *m*; **titty bar** bar *m* topless ᵈ (**b**) **tough titty!** dur! dur!

toast [təʊst] *n* **to be toast** (*in trouble*) être foutu; (*exhausted*) être naze *ou* crevé *ou* lessivé *ou* claqué; **if Mum finds out, you're toast** si Maman s'en rend compte, t'es mort *ou* foutu!; **I can't drink any more or I'll be toast tomorrow** il faut que j'arrête de boire, sinon demain je serai dans le coaltar

tod [tɒd] *n Br* (*rhyming slang **Tod Sloan** = **own***) **on one's tod** tout seul ᵈ

> Tod Sloan était un célèbre jockey américain du début du XXème siècle.

todger [ˈtɒdʒə(r)] *n Br* (*penis*) chipolata *f*

to-die-for [təˈdaɪfɔː(r)] *adj* craquant

toff [tɒf] *n Br* rupin(e) *m,f*

toffee [ˈtɒfɪ] *n Br* **he can't sing/act for toffee!** il chante/joue comme un pied!

toffee-nosed [ˈtɒfɪnəʊzd] *adj Br* bêcheur, snob

together [təˈɡeðə(r)] *adj* (*well-adjusted*) équilibré ᵈ, bien dans ses baskets

togs [tɒɡz] *npl Br* fringues *fpl*, sapes *fpl*

toilet [ˈtɔɪlɪt] *n* (**a**) **to go down the toilet** (*of plan, career, work*) être foutu en l'air; **that's our holidays down the toilet!** on peut faire une croix sur nos vacances! (**b**) *Br* (*horrible place*) trou ᵈ *m*; **this town is an absolute toilet** c'est vraiment le trou du cul du monde, cette ville

toke [təʊk] **1** *n* (*of joint*) taffe *f*; **to take a toke** prendre une taffe

2 *vi* **to toke on a joint** prendre une taffe d'un joint

tom [tɒm] *n Br* (**a**) *(prostitute)* pute *f* (**b**) *(rhyming slang* **tomfoolery** = **jewellery**) quincaillerie *f* (**c**) ⚠ *(rhyming slang* **tomtit** = **shit**) **to have/go for a tom** couler/aller couler un bronze, faire/aller faire la grosse commission

tomcat around ['tɒmkæt] *vi Am* courir les filles

Tom, Dick and Harry ['tɒm-'dɪkən'hærɪ] *npr* **every** *or Br* **any Tom, Dick and Harry** le premier venu, n'importe qui

tomfoolery [tɒm'fuːlərɪ] *n Br (rhyming slang* = **jewellery**) quincaillerie *f*

tomtit ⚠ [tɒm'tɪt] *n Br (rhyming slang* **shit**) **to have/go for a tomtit** couler/aller couler un bronze, faire/aller faire la grosse commission

ton [tʌn] *n Br* cent ⃞ *m*; *(£100)* cent livres ⃞ *fpl*

tonsil hockey ['tɒnsɪl'hɒkɪ] *n Hum* **to play tonsil hockey** se rouler des pelles *ou* des patins

tool ⚠ [tuːl] *n* (**a**) *(penis)* engin *m* (**b**) *(man)* con *m*, connard *m* (**c**) **he isn't the sharpest tool in the shed** il n'a pas inventé l'eau chaude *ou* le fil à couper le beurre

tool up *Br vt sép* **to tool oneself up, to get tooled up** s'armer ⃞, se charger, s'enfourailler

toot [tuːt] **1** *n* (**a**) *(of cocaine)* prise *f* de cocaïne ⃞ (**b**) *Am (drinking spree)* cuite *f*; **to go out on a toot** sortir prendre une cuite
2 *vt (cocaine)* sniffer
3 *vi (sniff cocaine)* sniffer de la coke

toots [tuːts] *n (term of address)* chéri(e) *m,f*

top [tɒp] **1** *n* (**a**) **to pay top dollar (for sth)** payer le prix fort (pour qch)
(**b**) *Br* **to pay/earn top whack** payer/gagner un max; **we can offer you £50 top whack** on vous propose 50 livres mais pas plus *ou* et c'est notre dernier prix
(**c**) *Hum* **top banana** huile *f*, gros bonnet *m*
2 *adj Br (excellent)* top, génial, super; **that was an absolutely top steak!** ce

steak était vraiment super bon!; **top plan!** super idée!; **his last movie was top** son dernier film était vraiment top
3 *vt Br (kill)* buter, zigouiller, refroidir; **to top oneself** se suicider ⃞, se foutre en l'air ▸ *voir aussi* **blow, totty, up**

tops [tɒps] *adv (at the most)* maxi; **it'll cost a fiver tops** ça coûtera cinq livres maxi *ou* à tout casser

torqued [tɔːkt] *adj Am* (**a**) *(angry)* furibard, furax, fumasse (**b**) *(drunk)* bourré, fait, beurré

tosh [tɒʃ] *Br* **1** *n* foutaises *fpl*; **that's a load of tosh!** c'est des foutaises!
2 *exclam* n'importe quoi!

toss [tɒs] *n Br* **I don't give a toss!** je m'en fiche pas mal!; **who gives a toss?** qu'est-ce que ça peut foutre? ▸ *see also* **cookie**

toss off ⚠ *Br* **1** *vt sép* **to toss sb off** branler qn; **to toss oneself off** se branler, se palucher, se pogner
2 *vi* se branler, se palucher, se pogner

tosser ['tɒsə(r)], **tosspot** ['tɒspɒt] *n Br* tache *f*, branque *m*

total ['təʊtəl] *vt Am (vehicle)* fusiller, bousiller

totally ['təʊtəlɪ] *adv Am (very much)* vachement; **I don't smoke but my parents totally smoke** moi je fume pas, mais mes parents ils fument vachement *ou* ils fument comme des malades

totty ['tɒtɪ] *n Br (attractive women)* belles nanas *fpl*, belles gonzesses *fpl*; **he's at the beach checking out the totty** il est en train de mater les nanas sur la plage; **check out the top totty!** vise un peu les canons!

touch [tʌtʃ] **1** *n* **to be a soft touch** être un pigeon *ou* une poire
2 *vt* **to touch sb for sth** taper qch à qn

touch up *vt sép* **to touch sb up** peloter qn; **to touch oneself up** se toucher

touched [tʌtʃt] *adj (mad)* timbré, toqué, cinglé

tough [tʌf] **1** *adj* **a tough guy** un dur
2 *exclam* tant pis! ▸ *voir aussi* **cookie, hang, shit, titty**

The symbol ⃞ indicates that a translation is neutral in register.

towelhead ['taʊəlhɛd] n *Injurieux* raton m, bicot m

toyboy ['tɔɪbɔɪ] n = jeune amant d'une femme plus âgée

tracks [træks] npl (a) **to make tracks** (*leave*) mettre les bouts, se casser (b) (*on arm*) traces fpl de piquouses

tradesman's entrance [!] ['treɪdzmənz'entrəns] n Br Hum (*anus*) entrée f de service

traffic ['træfɪk] n **go play in the traffic!** va voir ailleurs si j'y suis!

trainspotter ['treɪnspɒtə(r)] n Br Péj ringard(e) m,f

À l'origine, le terme "trainspotter" désigne un passionné des chemins de fer dont le passe-temps consiste à noter les numéros des locomotives qu'il aperçoit. Au sens large, ce terme désigne une personne généralement solitaire et ennuyeuse, qui ne sait pas s'habiller (il porte le plus souvent un anorak). Un "trainspotter" ne s'intéresse pas à l'actualité musicale ou sportive, et ne fréquente aucun endroit branché.

tramlines ['træmlaɪnz] npl Br (*on arm*) traces fpl de piquouses

tramp [træmp] n Péj (*promiscuous woman*) Marie-couche-toi-là f, pétasse f, traînée f

trank [træŋk], **trankie** ['træŋkɪ] n (*abrév* **tranquillizer**) tranquillisant □ m

trannie, tranny ['trænɪ] n Br (*abrév* **transvestite**) travelo m

trap [træp] n (*mouth*) clapet m; **shut your trap!** ferme ton clapet, ferme-la!; **to keep one's trap shut** la fermer, la boucler

trash [træʃ] **1** n (a) (*nonsense*) foutaises fpl; **his new film's a load of trash** son dernier film ne vaut pas un clou (b) (*people*) ordures fpl; **he's just trash** c'est un moins que rien; **white trash** petits Blancs mpl pauvres (c) *Noir Am* **to talk trash** (*converse, gossip*) tailler une bavette **2** vt (a) (*vandalize*) foutre en l'air, bousiller (b) (*criticize*) éreinter, démolir

trashed [træʃt] adj (*drunk*) rond, fait, bourré; (*on drugs*) défoncé, raide

tree [triː] n **to be out of one's tree** (*mad*) être cinglé ou givré; (*drunk*) être rond ou rétamé ou bourré; (*on drugs*) être défoncé ou raide

trendy ['trendɪ] **1** n branché(e) m,f **2** adj branché

trick [trɪk] n (a) **how's tricks?** comment ça va? (b) **to do the trick** faire l'affaire (c) (*prostitute's client*) micheton m; **to turn a trick** faire une passe; **she's been turning tricks for years** ça fait des années qu'elle fait la pute

trim [trɪm] n (*women*) nanas fpl, gonzesses fpl; **that's his new bit of trim** c'est sa nouvelle nana ou gonzesse

trip [trɪp] **1** n (a) (*after taking drugs*) trip m; **to have a good/bad trip** avoir un bon / mauvais trip (b) (*quantity of LSD*) dose f de LSD □, trip m (c) (*experience*) **to be on a guilt trip** culpabiliser; **to be on a power trip** être en plein trip mégalo; **to be on an ego trip** se faire mousser **2** vi (*after taking drugs*) triper

trip out vi (*after taking drugs*) triper

tripe [traɪp] n (*nonsense*) foutaises fpl, conneries fpl; **don't talk tripe!** dis pas n'importe quoi!, raconte pas de conneries!; **what a load of tripe!** n'importe quoi!; **the film is absolute tripe!** il vaut pas un clou, ce film!

trippy ['trɪpɪ] adj psychédélique □

trog [trɒg] n Br (*ugly person*) mocheté f; **he's going out with a real trog** il sort avec un vrai cageot ou un vrai laideron

troll [trɒl] n Br (*ugly person*) mocheté f; **his last bird was well fit but this one's a complete troll** sa dernière nana était canon, mais celle-ci c'est carrément un cageot ou un laideron

trolley ['trɒlɪ] n (a) **to be off one's trolley** avoir un grain, être cinglé (b) Br Péj **trolley dolly** (*air hostess*) hôtesse f de l'air □ (c) Br **trolleys** (*underpants*) calbute m, calcif m

trollied ['trɒlɪd] adj Br bourré, pété, beurré

The symbol □ indicates that a translation is neutral in register.

trots [trɒts] *npl* **the trots** *(diarrhoea)* la courante

trouble ['trʌbəl] *n* **(a)** man/woman **trouble** peines *fpl* de cœur **(b)** *Br* **trouble and strife** *(rhyming slang* **wife***)* femme □ *f*, bourgeoise *f*

trounce [traʊns] *vt* battre à plates coutures, écrabouiller, mettre la pâtée à; **to get trounced** être battu à plates coutures, prendre une déculottée

trousered ['traʊzəd] *adj Br (very drunk)* rond comme une queue de pelle, plein comme une barrique, fin plein

trout [traʊt] *n Péj (woman)* **(old) trout** vieille bique *f*

trump [trʌmp] *Br* **1** *vi* péter, lâcher *ou* larguer une caisse
2 *n* pet *m*, prout *m*

trustafarian [trʌstə'feərɪən] *n Br =* jeune anglais blanc de milieu relativement aisé qui cultive une image rasta

> Il s'agit d'un mélange des termes "rastafarian" et "trust fund".

try on [traɪ] *vt sép Br* **to try it on with sb** *(attempt to deceive)* essayer d'embobiner qn; *(attempt to seduce)* faire des avances à qn □; *(test someone's tolerance)* essayer de faire le coup à qn

tub [tʌb] *n* **a tub of lard** *(man)* un gros lard, un gros plein de soupe; *(woman)* une grosse dondon, une grosse vache

tube [tjuːb] *n* **(a)** **to go down the tubes** *(of plans)* tomber à l'eau; **that's £500 down the tubes** ça fait 500 livres de foutues en l'air
(b) **the tube** *(television)* la téloche
(c) **to have one's tubes tied** *(be sterilized)* se faire ligaturer les trompes □
(d) *Scot (idiot)* andouille *f*, courge *f*, cruche *f* ▸ *voir aussi* **boob**

tubular ['tjuːbjʊlə(r)] *adj Am (excellent)* génial, super, géant

tucker ['tʌkə(r)] *n Br & Austr (food)* bouffe *f*

tug ⚠ [tʌg] *n Br* **to have a tug** *(masturbate)* se tirer sur l'élastique, se polir le chinois

turd ⚠ [tɜːd] *n* **(a)** *(excrement)* merde *f* **(b)** *(person)* ordure *f*

turd-burglar ⚠ ['tɜːdbɜːglə(r)] *n Br Injurieux* pédale *f*, tantouze *f*, lope *f*

turf [tɜːf] *n* **(a)** *(territory)* territoire *m* **(b)** *Am (field of expertise, authority)* domaine □ *m*, truc *m*, rayon *m*; **that's not my turf** c'est pas mon rayon

turf out *vt sép* **to turf sb out** vider qn, foutre qn dehors

turkey ['tɜːkɪ] *n Am* **(a)** *(unsuccessful film, book)* bide *m* **(b)** *(person)* crétin(e) *m,f*, andouille *f*, courge *f* **(c)** **to talk turkey** passer aux choses sérieuses □ ▸ *voir aussi* **cold turkey**

turn off [tɜːn] *vt sép* **to turn sb off** *(repulse)* débecter qn

turn on 1 *vt sép (excite)* **to turn sb on** exciter qn; **to be turned on** être excité; **whatever turns you on!** du moment que tu y trouves ton compte!
2 *vi (take drugs)* se camer

turn over *vt sép Br (rob, burgle)* **to turn sth over** *(house)* cambrioler qch □; *(bank, shop)* cambrioler qch □, braquer qch

turn-off ['tɜːnɒf] *n (sexually)* **it's a turn-off** ça coupe l'envie

turn-on ['tɜːnɒn] *n (sexually)* **it's a real turn-on for him** il trouve ça super excitant

TV [tiː'viː] *n (abrév* **transvestite***)* travelo *m*

twat [twæt] **1** *n* **(a)** ⚠ *(woman's genitals)* chatte *f*, chagatte *f* **(b)** ⚠ *(person)* tache *f*, taré(e) *m,f* **(c)** *Br (tap, knock)* claque □ *f*; **give him a twat on the head!** donne-lui une claque sur la tête!
2 *vt Br (hit)* donner une claque à □; **he twatted her on the head** il lui a donné une claque sur la tête

twatted ['twætɪd] *adj Br (drunk)* rond comme une queue de pelle *ou* comme un boudin, plein comme une barrique

tweaked [twiːkt] *adj Am (drunk)* bourré, fait, beurré; *(on drugs)* raide, défoncé

twenty-four seven ['twentɪfɔː'sevən] *adv (constantly)* sans arrêt □

The symbol □ indicates that a translation is neutral in register.

Cette expression (à laquelle on ajoute parfois "365") signifie littéralement 24 heures par jour, 7 jours par semaine (et 365 jours par an).

twerp [twɜːp] n courge f, nouille f

twink [twɪŋk], **twinkie, twinky** ['twɪŋkɪ] n Am (homosexual) = jeune minet homosexuel, le plus souvent blond et pas très futé

Le Twinkie® est une sorte de biscuit fourré à la crème, vendu aux États-Unis.

twist [twɪst] n Br **to be round the twist** être dingue, avoir un grain; **to go round the twist** devenir dingue ou cinglé, perdre la boule; **to drive sb round the twist** rendre qn chèvre ▸ voir aussi **knickers**

twister ['twɪstə(r)] n (a) Br (crook) arnaqueur(euse) m,f (b) Am (tornado) tornade □ f

twit [twɪt] n Br courge f, nouille f

twitcher ['twɪtʃə(r)] n Br dingue mf d'ornithologie □

two and eight [tuːən'eɪt] n Br (rhyming

slang = state) **to be in a two and eight** être dans tous ses états; **he was in a right two and eight when his missis left him** il était dans tous ses états quand sa nana l'a quitté

two-bit ['tuːbɪt] adj à la noix (de coco), à la gomme; **he plays for some two-bit team** il joue pour une espèce d'équipe à la noix; **she's nothing but a two-bit secretary** ce n'est qu'une petite secrétaire à la gomme

twock [twɒk] vt Br (car) faucher, tirer, chouraver

Il s'agit d'un terme formé à partir des initiales de la phrase "Take Without the Owner's Consent".

twonk [twɒŋk] n (fool) andouille f, cruche f, cloche f

two-time [tuːˈtaɪm] vt **to two-time sb** tromper qn □, faire porter des cornes à qn

two-timer [tuːˈtaɪmə(r)] n personne f infidèle □

tyke [taɪk] n (a) Br (coarse person) lourdaud(e) m,f (b) (child) morveux(euse) m,f, môme mf

U

uh-huh [ˈʌhʌ, ʌˈhʌ] *exclam* ouais!

umpteen [ˈʌmptiːn] *adj* des tas de; **I've told you umpteen times** je te l'ai déjà dit trente-six fois

umpteenth [ˈʌmptiːnθ] *adj* énième; **for the umpteenth time** pour la énième fois

uncool [ʌnˈkuːl] *adj* (a) (*unfashionable, unsophisticated*) ringard; **it's a really uncool place** c'est nul comme endroit; **what an uncool thing to do!** c'est vraiment nul de faire un truc pareil!

  (b) (*not allowed, not accepted*) mal vu □; **I think it's a bit uncool to smoke in here** je pense pas que ce soit permis de fumer ici □

  (c) (*upset*) **she was a bit uncool about me moving in with them** elle tenait pas trop à ce que je m'installe chez eux

undies [ˈʌndɪz] *npl* (*abrév* **underwear**) sous-vêtements *mpl* féminins □

unhip [ʌnˈhɪp] *adj* ringard

uni [ˈjuːnɪ] *n* (a) *Br* (*abrév* **university**) fac *f*; **he's doing law at uni** il fait une fac de droit (b) *Am* (*abrév* **uniform**) uniforme □ *m*

unreal [ʌnˈrɪəl] *adj* (a) (*unbelievable*) pas possible, pas croyable, dingue (b) (*excellent*) dément, super, génial

up [ʌp] **1** *n* (*drug*) amphet *f*, amphé *f*

  2 *adj* (a) **what's up?** (*what's happening*) qu'est-ce qui se passe?; (*what's wrong*) qu'est-ce qui va pas?; *Am* (*as greeting*) salut!; **what's up with him?** qu'est-ce qui lui arrive?; **there's something up with the TV** la télé débloque

  (b) *Br* **we're going clubbing tonight, are you up for it?** on va en boîte ce soir, ça te branche?; **was she up for it?** (*willing*

to have sex) alors, elle a bien voulu coucher?

  3 *adv Br* **he doesn't have very much up top** c'est pas une lumière, il a pas inventé l'eau chaude *ou* le fil à couper le beurre; **she's got plenty up top** elle en a dans le ciboulot

  4 *prép* **up yours!** [!!] va te faire foutre!

upchuck [ˈʌptʃʌk] *vi Hum* dégobiller

uphill gardener [!] [ˈʌphɪlˈgɑːdnə(r)] *n Br Péj Hum* pédale *f*, tantouse *f*

upper [ˈʌpə(r)] *n* (a) (*drug*) amphet *f*, amphé *f*; **he's on uppers** il est sous amphets *ou* amphés (b) *Br* **to be on one's uppers** être dans la dèche

upside [ˈʌpsaɪd] *prép Noir Am* **to go upside sb's head** filer un coup sur le ciboulot *ou* la cafetière à qn

upstairs [ʌpˈsteəz] *adv* (a) **he hasn't got much upstairs** c'est pas une lumière, il a pas inventé l'eau chaude *ou* le fil à couper le beurre (b) **to kick sb upstairs** (*promote*) se débarrasser de qn en lui donnant de l'avancement □

uptight [ʌpˈtaɪt] *adj Noir Am* (*excellent*) super, génial, géant

us [ʌs] *pron Br* (*me*) **give us a kiss** embrasse-moi □; **give us a look** fais voir □; **he bought us a drink** il m'a payé un verre □

use [juːz] *vi* (*take drugs*) se camer

user [ˈjuːzə(r)] *n* drogué(e) □ *m,f*; **heroin user** héroïnomane □ *mf*; **cocaine user** cocaïnomane □ *mf*

usual [ˈjuːʒʊəl] *n* (*drink, food*) **the usual, sir?** comme d'habitude, monsieur?; **I'll just have my usual** je prends comme d'habitude

---

The symbol □ indicates that a translation is neutral in register.

V

V [viː] *n Br* **to give sb the Vs** faire un doigt d'honneur à qn

> Ce geste se fait à l'aide de l'index et du majeur.

vag¹ [!!] [vædʒ] *n* (*abrév* **vagina**) chatte *f*, cramouille *f*

vag² [væg] *n Am* (*abrév* **vagrant**) clodo *mf*

vamoose [vəˈmuːs] *vi* se tirer, se casser; **vamoose!** tire-toi!, casse-toi!

vamp [væmp] *vi Noir Am* (*leave*) se casser, se tirer, s'arracher

veep [viːp] *n Am* (*abrév* **vice-president**) vice-président □ *m*

veg [vedʒ] *npl Br* (*abrév* **vegetables**) légumes □ *mpl*, verdure *f*

veg out *vi* traîner, glandouiller; **I spent the whole weekend vegging out, watching videos** j'ai passé tout le week-end à glandouiller en regardant des vidéos

veggie [ˈvedʒɪ] (*abrév* **vegetarian**) **1** *n* végétarien(enne) □ *m,f*
2 *adj* végétarien □

velvet [ˈvelvɪt] *n Am* (*profit*) bénef *m*; (*easy money*) argent *m* facile □

Vera [ˈvɪərə] *n Br* (*rhyming slang* **Vera Lynn = gin**) gin □ *m*; **go out and get a bottle of Vera** va acheter une bouteille de gin

> Vera Lynn est une chanteuse britannique qui connut son heure de gloire pendant la deuxième guerre mondiale lorsqu'elle alla chanter pour les soldats britanniques.

verbal [ˈvɜːbəl] **1** *n Br* (*insults*) insultes □ *fpl*; **to give sb some verbal** traiter qn de tous les noms
2 *adj Hum* **to have verbal** *Br* **diarrhoea** *or Am* **diarrhea** être atteint de diarrhée verbale

Vette [vet] *n Am* (*abrév* **Corvette®**) Corvette® *f*

vibes [vaɪbz] *npl* (*abrév* **vibrations**) **to get good/bad vibes about sb/sth** bien/mal sentir qn/qch; **he gives me good/bad vibes** il y a quelque chose chez lui que j'aime/que j'aime pas; **this place gives me strange vibes** cet

---

Valley speak

"Valley speak" ou "Valspeak" est le jargon utilisé par les riches adolescentes de la Vallée de San Fernando, près de Los Angeles. C'est Frank Zappa et sa fille Moon Unit qui ont popularisé ce jargon au début des années 80, notamment avec la sortie du disque *Valley Girl* en 1982. Bien que l'engouement pour le "Valley speak" ait été de courte durée, quelques expressions ont survécu et figurent dans ce dictionnaire. Le "Valley speak" a beaucoup emprunté à l'argot des surfeurs. Le sarcasme et l'exagération en sont les caractéristiques principales, ainsi qu'une bonne dose d'ironie qui transparaît dans des expressions telles que "for sure" et "as if". Bien qu'encore adolescente, la "valley girl" jette sur le monde un regard désabusé. Elle constitua le thème de livres, de chansons et de films, le plus célèbre étant *Clueless*, sorti en 1995.

The symbol □ indicates that a translation is neutral in register.

endroit me donne de drôles de sensations

vid [vɪd] *n* (*abrév* **video**) vidéo □ *f*, vidéo-cassette □ *f*

-ville [vɪl] *suffixe* **boresville** hyper chiant; **sleazeville** hyper corrompu

> Le suffixe "-ville" sert à former des noms et des adjectifs. Il indique que le terme qui le précède caractérise ce dont on parle.

vines [vaɪnz] *npl Noir Am* (*clothes*) fringues *fpl*, sapes *fpl*

vino ['viːnəʊ] *n* pinard *m*, picrate *m*

virus ['vaɪrəs] *n* **the virus** le dass, le sida □

vom [vɒm] (*abrév* **vomit**) **1** *n* dégueulis *m* **2** *vi* dégueuler, gerber

---

Pleins feux sur :

Violence

Les origines du vocabulaire de la violence sont variées, avec des expressions appartenant autant au parler de la pègre d'autrefois, que l'on entend encore dans certains films et séries télévisées populaires, qu'à l'argot des quartiers noirs américains où le rap est devenu l'un des principaux moyens de communication. Il existe de nombreux termes pour désigner une arme de poing, notamment **shooter**, **piece** et **equalizer**. L'expression américaine **Saturday night special** désigne un petit pistolet bon marché. Pour parler d'une personne armée, on emploiera les expressions **to be packing** ou **to be tooled up**. On appelle un couteau **a blade**, **a chib** ou **a shiv** (les deux derniers mots étant issus du mot gitan "chiv" qui signifie "lame").

De nombreux verbes sont synonymes de "tuer" : **to blow away**, **to bump off**, **to do in**, **to ice**, **to liquidate**, **to waste** et **to whack**. Pour désigner une bagarre, on emploie les mots **scrap**, **ruck** (anglais britannique) ou **rumble**. Il existe un certain nombre de verbes qui signifient "battre", dont les plus courants sont **to hammer**, **to paste** et **to thrash**. On utilise également la forme substantivée de ces verbes. On peut dire, par exemple, **to give someone a thrashing**, ou **to give someone a hammering**, etc. En anglais britannique, le suffixe **-bashing** permet de former des mots désignant la violence à l'encontre de certaines communautés, comme **Paki-bashing** (violences contre les Pakistanais) ou **queer-bashing** (violences contre les homosexuels).

W

wack [wæk] *adj* Noir Am (**a**) *(worthless)* nul (**b**) *(mad)* cinglé, toqué, timbré (**c**) *(stupid)* débile

wack-job ['wækdʒɒb] *n* Am cinglé(e) *m,f*, dingue *mf*

wacko ['wækəʊ] **1** *n* cinglé(e) *m,f*, dingue *mf*
2 *adj* cinglé, dingue, timbré, toqué

wacky ['wækɪ] *adj* loufoque; *Hum* **wacky baccy** *(marijuana)* herbe *f*

wag [wæg] *vt Br* **to wag it** faire l'école buissonnière

wagman ['wægmæn] *n Br (truancy officer)* = personne employée par la municipalité pour ramener les enfants qui font l'école buissonnière dans leur établissement scolaire

wagon ['wægən] *n* (**a**) **to be on the wagon** être au régime sec; **to be off** *or* **have fallen off the wagon** s'être remis à picoler (**b**) *Ir (unpleasant woman)* chameau *m*; *(ugly woman)* cageot *m*, mocheté *f* ▶ *voir aussi* **meat**, **paddy**

walk [wɔːk] **1** *n* **take a walk!** va voir ailleurs si j'y suis!, dégage!; **it was a walk in the park** *(very easy)* c'était un jeu d'enfant
2 *vt* **to walk it** gagner les doigts dans le nez ▶ *voir aussi* **street**

wall [wɔːl] *n* (**a**) **off the wall** *(eccentric)* loufoque, zarbi (**b**) **to be up the wall** *(mad)* être cinglé *ou* givré, avoir un grain; **to drive sb up the wall** rendre qn chèvre ▶ *voir aussi* **hole**

wallop ['wɒləp] **1** *n* **to give sb a wallop** foutre une beigne *ou* un gnon à qn; **to give sth a wallop** foutre un coup dans qch
2 *vt* (**a**) *(hit) (person)* foutre une beigne *ou* un gnon à; *(object)* foutre un coup dans

(**b**) *(defeat)* foutre la pâtée *ou* une raclée *ou* une déculottée à, écrabouiller, battre à plates coutures

wally ['wɒlɪ] *n Br* andouille *f*, nouille *f*

wank [!!] [wæŋk] *Br* **1** *n* branlette *f*; **to have a wank** se branler, se pogner, se palucher; **wank mag** magazine *m* de cul
2 *vi* se branler, se pogner, se palucher
3 *adj* débile, con

wank off [!!] *Br* **1** *vt sép* **to wank sb off** branler qn; **to wank oneself off** se branler, se pogner, se palucher
2 *vi* se branler, se pogner, se palucher

wanker [!!] ['wæŋkə(r)] *n Br (idiot)* connard *m*

wankered [!!] ['wæŋkəd] *adj Br (drunk)* rond comme une queue de pelle *ou* comme un boudin, plein comme une barrique, fin plein

wanky [!!] ['wæŋkɪ] *adj Br (stupid)* débile, con; **he's OK but all his friends are a bit wanky** lui, ça va, mais tous ses copains son assez cons; **he looks really wanky when he dances** il a vraiment l'air con quand il danse; **what are you wearing that wanky T-shirt for?** pourquoi est-ce que tu portes ce tee-shirt à la con?

wannabe ['wɒnəbiː] *n* (**a**) *(who wants money, success)* arriviste □ *mf* (**b**) *(who wants to be like someone famous)* = personne qui cherche à être comme son idole; **the place was full of Kylie wannabes** c'était plein de filles habillées en Kylie

warpaint ['wɔːpeɪnt] *n Hum (make-up)* maquillage □ *m*; **to put the warpaint on** se maquiller □

washed-up [wɒʃt'ʌp] *adj* **to be (all) washed-up** *(of person)* être fini; *(of plan)* être tombé à l'eau

The symbol □ indicates that a translation is neutral in register.

washout ['wɒʃaʊt] n (failure) fiasco m, bide m

waste [weɪst] vt (attack) casser la gueule à, démonter le portrait à; (kill) buter, refroidir, zigouiller; Br **to waste sb's face** casser ou défoncer la gueule à qn, faire une tête au carré à qn

wasted ['weɪstɪd] adj (drunk) pété, bourré, fait; (on drugs) défoncé, raide

waster ['weɪstə(r)] n Br glandeur(euse) m,f, glandouilleur(euse) m,f

watering hole ['wɔːtərɪŋhəʊl] n Hum (bar) troquet m, rade m

water sports [!!] ['wɔːtəspɔːts] npl uro f, = pratique sexuelle qui consiste à uriner sur son ou sa partenaire

way [weɪ] 1 n (a) **no way!** pas question!; **no way am I going!** il est pas question que j'y aille!; **no way, José!** pas question! (b) **to go all the way** or **the whole way with sb** coucher avec qn; **they went all the way** or **the whole way** ils ont couché ensemble (c) Am **way to go!** super! 2 exclam Am si! (en réponse à "no way!") 3 adv (very) vachement; **he's way crazy** il est vachement atteint ▸ voir aussi **swing**

L'usage figurant dans la catégorie 2 a été popularisé par le film comique américain Wayne's World.

way-out [weɪ'aʊt] adj (eccentric) loufoque

wazoo [wə'zuː] n Am (buttocks) fesses [q] fpl, miches fpl

wazz [wæz] Br 1 n **to have a wazz** faire la petite commission; **to go for a wazz** aller faire la petite commission 2 vi faire la petite commission

wazzed [wæzd] adj Br bourré, pété, cuit, fait

wazzock ['wæzək] n Br andouille f, cloche f, cruche f

wedge [wedʒ] n Br (money) fric m, flouze m, pognon m, oseille f

wedgie ['wedʒɪ] n **to have a wedgie** avoir le slip coincé entre les fesses; **to**

give sb a wedgie remonter brusquement le slip de quelqu'un pour le lui coincer entre les fesses

wee [wiː] Br 1 n pipi m; **to have a wee** faire pipi 2 vi faire pipi

weed [wiːd] n (a) Br (person) femmelette f, mauviette f, lavette f (b) (marijuana) herbe f (c) Am (cigarette) clope f, sèche f, tige f; (cannabis cigarette) joint m (d) **the weed** (tobacco) tabac [q] m; **I've given up the weed** j'ai arrêté de fumer [q]

weedgie ['wiːdʒɪ] = **weegie**

weedy ['wiːdɪ] adj Br (physically) racho; (in character) faible [q], mou

weegie ['wiːdʒɪ] Br Péj 1 n habitant(e) m,f de Glasgow 2 adj de Glasgow

weenie ['wiːnɪ] n Am (a) (frankfurter) saucisse f de Francfort [q] (b) (idiot) andouille f, truffe f, courge f (c) (student) bûcheur(euse) m,f (d) Hum (penis) chipolata f; **to play hide the weenie** (have sex) s'envoyer en l'air

"Weenie" est le diminutif de "wiener" (qui signifie "viennois" en allemand), qui est le nom donné aux saucisses de Francfort aux États-Unis.

weigh into [weɪ] vt insép Br rentrer dans le lard à

weird out [wɪəd] vt sép Am **to weird sb out** faire flipper qn

weirded out ['wɪədɪdaʊt] adj Am (strange) loufoque, zarbi; (mad) cinglé, dingue, timbré

weirdo ['wɪədəʊ] n (man) hurluberlu [q] m; drôle de zèbre m; (woman) hurluberlu [q] m

well [wel] adv Br (very) vachement; **he looks well dodgy** il a l'air vachement louche; **the club was well cool** la boîte était vachement cool

well-hung [!] ['wel'hʌŋ] adj (man) bien monté

wellied ['welɪd] adj Br bourré comme un coing, rond comme une queue de pelle ou comme un boudin

well-stacked ['wel'stækt] adj (woman)

qui a de gros nichons; **she's well-stacked** il y a du monde au balcon

welly ['welɪ] *n Br* **to give it some welly** mettre le paquet

wet [wet] **1** *n Br (feeble person)* mauviette *f*, lavette *f*

　2 *adj* **(a)** *Br (feeble)* faible □, mou **(b) wet blanket** rabat-joie *mf* **(c)** *Am* **to be all wet** *(mistaken)* se gourer ▶ *voir aussi* **rag**

wetback ['wetbæk] *n Am Injurieux* = travailleur clandestin mexicain

> "Wetback" signifie littéralement "dos mouillé". Cette appellation vient du fait que de nombreux Mexicains traversent le Rio Grande à la nage pour aller travailler clandestinement aux États-Unis.

whack [wæk] **1** *n (attempt)* essai □ *m*, tentative □ *f*; **to give sth a whack, to take a whack at sth** essayer qch

　2 *vt (kill)* buter, zigouiller, refroidir ▶ *voir aussi* **top**

whack off [!] *vi* se branler, se pogner, se palucher, faire cinq contre un

whacked [wækt] *adj* crevé, naze, lessivé, claqué

whacky ['wækɪ] = **wacky**

whang [!] [wæŋ] *n Am (penis)* bite *f*, zob *m*, queue *f*

what [wɒt] *pron* **what's up?** comment ça va?

whatever ['wɒtevə(r)] *exclam* laisse tomber!

what-for ['wɒt'fɔ:(r)] *n* **to give sb what-for** *(physically)* foutre une raclée à qn; *(verbally)* passer un savon à qn, remonter les bretelles à qn; **to get what-for** *(physically)* prendre une raclée; *(verbally)* se faire passer un savon, se faire remonter les bretelles

what's-her-face ['wɒtsɜ:feɪs], **what's-her-name** ['wɒtsɜ:neɪm] *n* Machine *f*

what's-his-face ['wɒtsɪzfeɪs], **what's-his-name** ['wɒtsɪzneɪm] *n* Machin *m*

whatsit ['wɒtsɪt], **whatsitsname** ['wɒtsɪtsneɪm] *n* machin *m*, truc *m*, bidule *m*

wheel [wi:l] **1** *n* **(a) (big) wheel** *(person)* huile *f*, gros bonnet *m* **(b) (set of) wheels** *(car)* bagnole *f*, caisse *f*, tire *f*

　2 *vi* **to wheel and deal** magouiller ▶ *voir aussi* **fifth wheel, hell**

wheeler-dealer ['wi:lə'di:lə(r)] *n* magouilleur(euse) *m,f*

whiffy ['wɪfɪ] *adj Br* qui schlingue, qui coince, qui fouette; **it's a bit whiffy in here, don't you think?** ça schlingue ici, tu trouves pas?

whipped [wɪpt] *adj Am* = **pussy-whipped**

whistle ['wɪsəl] *n Br (rhyming slang* **whistle and flute** = **suit)** costard *m* ▶ *voir aussi* **blow**

white [waɪt] *adj* **(a) white stuff** *(morphine)* morphine □ *f*, lili-pioncette *f*; *(heroin)* blanche *f*, héro *f*; *(cocaine)* coco *f*, neige *f*, coke *f* **(b) white lightning** tord-boyaux *m (distillé illégalement)*

whitebread ['waɪtbred] *adj Am Péj (dull, conventional)* conventionnel et ennuyeux □

whitey ['waɪtɪ] *n* **(a) to have a whitey** = devenir tout pâle et être sur le point de dégueuler après avoir fumé trop de hasch **(b)** *Noir Am* **Whitey** Blanc (Blanche) *m,f*

whizz [wɪz] **1** *n* **(a)** *(expert)* as *m*; **a computer whizz** un as de l'informatique; **he's a whizz at chess** c'est un crack aux échecs; **whizz kid** jeune prodige *m* **(b)** *Br (amphetamines)* amphés *fpl*, amphets *fpl* **(c)** *Am* **to take a whizz** *(urinate)* faire pipi

　2 *vi Am (urinate)* faire pipi

whizzbang ['wɪzbæŋ] *adj Am (excellent)* super, génial, géant

whoop [wu:p] *n Am Ironique* **big whoop!** la belle affaire! □

whopper ['wɒpə(r)] *n* **(a)** *(impressive thing)* mastodonte *m*; **that's a whopper of a bruise you've got** tu as un sacré bleu; **that salmon he caught was a whopper** c'est un sacré morceau de saumon qu'il a pêché **(b)** *(lie)* craque *f*, bobard *m*

whopping ['wɒpɪŋ] **1** *adj* énorme, géant; **it costs a whopping £3,000** ça coûte la coquette somme de trois mille livres; **he scored a whopping forty goals last season** il a carrément marqué quarante buts la saison dernière

2 *adv* **a whopping great lie** un bobard énorme; **that was a whopping huge mistake!** c'était une sacrée bourde!

whore [hɔː(r)] *n* (**a**) *(prostitute)* pute *f* (**b**) *(promiscuous woman)* salope *f*, pétasse *f*, traînée *f*

whorehouse ['hɔːhaʊs] *n* bordel *m*, claque *m*

wick [wɪk] *n* (**a**) *Br* **to get on sb's wick** taper sur les nerfs à qn, courir sur le haricot à qn (**b**) **to dip one's wick**[!] tremper son biscuit

wicked ['wɪkɪd] **1** *adj* (**a**) *(excellent)* super, génial, géant (**b**) *Hum* **to have one's wicked way with sb** faire une partie de jambes en l'air avec qn; **so, has he had his wicked way with you yet?** alors, est-ce que tu t'es donnée à lui?

2 *exclam* super!, génial!

3 *adv* vachement; **I was wicked drunk last night** j'étais fin plein hier soir

widdle ['wɪdəl] *Br* **1** *n* **to have a widdle** *(urinate)* faire pipi

2 *vi* faire pipi

wide [waɪd] *adj Br (cocky)* culotté, gonflé; **wide boy** magouilleur *m*

widget ['wɪdʒɪt] *n* (**a**) *(thing, object)* bidule *m*, machin *m* (**b**) *(gadget)* gadget[▢] *m*

wig out [wɪg] *vi Am (get angry)* piquer une crise, péter les plombs; *(go mad)* devenir cinglé, perdre la boule; *(get excited)* devenir dingue

wigged (out) [wɪgd('aʊt)] *adj Am (crazy)* cinglé, tapé, timbré

wigger ['wɪgə(r)] *n Am Péj* = Blanc qui cherche à copier le mode de vie des Noirs

"Wigger" est la contraction de "white" et de "nigger".

wiggy ['wɪgɪ] *adj Am (mad)* cinglé, tapé, timbré; *(eccentric)* loufoque, allumé

wild [waɪld] *adj* (**a**) *(angry)* en pétard, fumasse, furibard, furax; **to go wild** se mettre en pétard

(**b**) *(enthusiastic)* **to be wild about sb/sth** être dingue de qn/qch; **I wasn't exactly wild about it** ça ne m'a pas vraiment emballé

(**c**) *(excellent)* super, génial, géant; **that was a wild film!** ce film était génial!

(**d**) **to do the wild thing** *(have sex)* s'envoyer en l'air

willies ['wɪlɪz] *npl Br* **to give sb the willies** donner la chair de poule à qn

willy ['wɪlɪ] *n* quéquette *f*, zizi *m*

wimp [wɪmp] *n* mauviette *f*, femmelette *f*, lavette *f*

wimp out *vi* se dégonfler; **he wimped out of the fight** il s'est dégonflé au dernier moment et a refusé de se battre; **he wimped out of telling her the truth** finalement il a eu la trouille de lui dire la vérité

wimpy ['wɪmpɪ] *adj (physically)* malingre[▢], racho; *(mentally)* poule mouillée *(inv)*; **he's so wimpy!** quelle mauviette!

wind up [waɪnd] *vt sép Br* **to wind sb up** *(tease)* faire enrager qn, taquiner qn; *(fool)* mettre qn en boîte; *(irritate)* foutre qn en rogne

windbag ['wɪndbæg] *n* moulin *m* à paroles

window ['wɪndəʊ] *n* (**a**) **to go out (of) the window** *(of plans)* tomber à l'eau; **that's my chances of promotion out the window** je peux faire une croix sur mon avancement (**b**) *Péj* **window licker**[!] débile *mf* mental(e)

wind-up ['waɪndʌp] *n Br* mise *f* en boîte; **this has to be a wind-up!** dis-moi que c'est une plaisanterie!

wingding ['wɪŋdɪŋ] *n Am (celebration)* bringue *f*, bombe *f*, fiesta *f*

winkle ['wɪŋkəl] *n Br (penis)* quéquette *f*, zizi *m*

wino ['waɪnəʊ] *n* poivrot(e) *m,f*, alcolo *mf*

wipe out [waɪp] *vt sép* **to wipe sb out** *(exhaust)* lessiver qn; *(kill)* buter *ou* refroidir *ou* zigouiller qn

wiped (out) [waɪpt('aʊt)] *adj (exhausted)* crevé, naze, lessivé, claqué

wired ['waɪəd] *adj (highly strung)* sur les

The symbol [▢] indicates that a translation is neutral in register.

nerfs, à cran; *(after taking drugs)* défoncé *(après avoir pris de la cocaïne ou des amphétamines)*

wise up [waɪz] *vi* **to wise up to sb** voir qn sous son vrai jour ◻; **to wise up to sth** se rendre compte de qch ◻; **wise up!** réveille-toi!, ouvre les yeux!

wiseass [!] ['waɪzæs] *n Am* je-sais-tout *mf*

wiseguy ['waɪzgaɪ] *n Am* **(a)** *(know-all)* je-sais-tout *mf* **(b)** *(criminal)* truand *m*

witch [wɪtʃ] *n (nasty woman)* garce *f*, chameau *m*

with it ['wɪðɪt] *adj* **(a)** *(fashionable)* dans le coup, dans le vent **(b)** *(awake)* bien réveillé ◻; **to get with it** se réveiller ◻

witter ['wɪtə(r)] *vi Br* **to witter (on)** jacasser, bavasser, parler pour ne rien dire; **he's always wittering on about the army** il n'en finit pas de parler de l'armée

wizz [wɪz] = **whizz**

wobbler ['wɒblə(r)], **wobbly** ['wɒblɪ] *n Br* **to throw a wobbler** piquer une crise, péter les plombs, péter une durite

wog [wɒg] *n Injurieux (black man)* nègre *m*, bamboula *m*; *(black woman)* négresse *f*

wolf [wʊlf] *n (womanizer)* coureur *m*

wombat ['wɒmbæt] *n Am (man)* hurluberlu ◻ *m*, drôle de zèbre *m*; *(woman)* hurluberlu ◻ *m*

wonga ['wɒŋgə] *n Br* fric *m*, flouze *m*, pognon *m*

wonk [wɒŋk] *n Am* **(a)** *(student)* bûcheur (euse) *m,f* **(b)** *(intellectual, expert)* intello *mf (qui ne s'intéresse qu'à sa discipline)*

wood [wʊd] *n* **(a)** *Am* **to put the wood to sb** *(beat up)* tabasser qn; *(defeat)* écrabouiller qn, battre qn à plates coutures, mettre une raclée *ou* une déculottée à qn **(b)** [!!] **to get/have wood** *(erection)* bander; **to put the wood to sb** *(have sex with)* tringler *ou* troncher qn

wooden overcoat ['wʊdən'əʊvəkəʊt] *n Hum (coffin)* costume *m* de sapin

woodie [!!] ['wʊdɪ] *n Am (erection)* érection ◻ *f*, bandaison *f*; **to have a woodie**

avoir la trique *ou* le gourdin, bander

woof [wʊf] *vi Noir Am (boast, bluff)* frimer, flamber

woofter ['wʊftə(r)] *n Br Injurieux* tante *f*, tapette *f*

wop [wɒp] *Injurieux* **1** *n* Rital(e) *m,f* **2** *adj* rital

word [wɜːd] *exclam Noir Am* **word (up)!** *(I agree)* parfaitement!; *(it's true)* sans dec!

workie ['wɜːkɪ] *n Br* ouvrier ◻ *m*

working girl ['wɜːkɪŋgɜːl] *n Am (prostitute)* prostituée ◻ *f*, putain *f*

work over [wɜːk] *vt sép* **to work sb over** *(beat up)* tabasser qn, filer une raclée à qn, dérouiller qn

works [wɜːks] *npl* **(a)** **the works** *(everything)* la totale, tout le toutim **(b)** *(drug paraphernalia)* matos *m* de drogué ▶ *voir aussi* **shoot**

worm [wɜːm] *n (person)* larve *f*

worry ['wʌrɪ] *n Austr* **no worries!** pas de problème!

wotcha ['wɒtʃə], **wotcher** ['wɒtʃə(r)] *exclam Br* bonjour! ◻, salut!

wow [waʊ] **1** *exclam* oh là là!, la vache! **2** *vt* en mettre plein la vue à, époustoufler; **he wowed me with a bunch of red roses and a marriage proposal** il m'en a mis plein la vue avec un bouquet de roses rouges puis il m'a demandée en mariage

wowser ['waʊzə(r)] *n Austr* **(a)** *(killjoy)* rabat-joie *mf inv*; *(prude)* puritain(e) ◻ *m,f*

wrap [ræp] *n (for powdered drugs)* sachet *m* de drogue ◻

wrap up [ræp] *vi Br (be quiet)* la fermer, la boucler; **wrap up!** la ferme!, boucle-la!, écrase!

wrecked [rekt] *adj (drunk)* bourré, pété, beurré, fait; *(on drugs)* défoncé, raide; *(exhausted)* crevé, naze, lessivé, claqué

wrinkly ['rɪŋklɪ] *n Br (old person)* croulant(e) *m,f*

wuss [wʊs] *n* mauviette *f*, lavette *f*

wussy ['wʊsɪ] **1** *n* mauviette *f*, lavette *f* **2** *adj* mou, mollasson

---

The symbol ◻ indicates that a translation is neutral in register.

X,Y

X [eks] *n (abrév* **ecstasy***)* X *f*, ecsta *f*

X-rated ['eks'reɪtɪd] *adj (lewd, erotic)* osé, salé; *(violent)* violent □, saignant

"X-rated" signifie littéralement "classé X". Cette appellation n'est plus utilisée par les commissions de censure américaine et britannique mais l'expression perdure.

yabber ['jæbə(r)] *Austr* **1** *vi* jacasser
2 *n* jacassements *mpl*

yack [jæk] = **yak**

yada ['jædə] *n Am* **yada yada (yada)** et patati et patata

yah [jɑː] *n Br Péj* **(OK) yah** ≃ bourge *mf*

"Yah" est la transcription phonétique du mot "yes" tel qu'il est prononcé par certains éléments de la grande bourgeoisie et de l'aristocratie anglaises. Par extension, le mot "yah" désigne une personne d'un milieu très aisé, arrogante et imbue d'elle-même, qui adopte une attitude méprisante avec ceux qu'elle considère comme ses inférieurs.

yak [jæk] **1** *n (conversation)* converse *f*; **to have a yak** papoter
2 *vi* **(a)** *(chat)* papoter **(b)** *Am (vomit)* gerber, dégueuler

Yank [jæŋk] **1** *n* Amerloque *mf*, Ricain(e) *m,f*
2 *adj* ricain

Lorsqu'il est utilisé par les Américains eux-mêmes, ce terme n'a aucune connotation péjorative. Lorsqu'il est utilisé par une personne d'une autre nationalité, il peut être soit injurieux, soit humoristique, selon le ton et le contexte.

yank [jæŋk] **1** [!] *n* branlette *f*; **to have a**

yank se tirer sur l'élastique, se taper sur la colonne
2 *vt* **to yank sb's chain** faire marcher qn; **hey, I'm only yanking your chain!** je te fais marcher!
3 [!] *vi* se tirer sur l'élastique, se taper sur la colonne

Yankee ['jæŋkɪ] **1** *n* **(a)** *Br Injurieux (American)* Amerloque *mf*, Ricain(e) *m,f* **(b)** *Am (person from Northern USA)* = natif du Nord des États-Unis
2 *adj* **(a)** *Br Injurieux (American)* ricain **(b)** *Am (from Northern USA)* du Nord des États-Unis □

Dans la catégorie I (a), ce terme peut être soit injurieux, soit humoristique, selon le ton et le contexte.

yap [jæp] **1** *n* **(a)** *(mouth)* clapet *m*, gueule *f*; **shut your yap!** ferme ton clapet!, la ferme!, écrase! **(b)** *Am (idiot)* andouille *f*, truffe *f*; *(country bumpkin)* pécore *mf*, péquenaud(e) *m,f*
2 *vi* jacasser, bavasser

yawn [jɔːn] *n (boring person, event)* **to be a yawn** être rasoir ► *voir aussi* **technicolour**

yay [jeɪ] *n Am (cocaine)* coco *f*, neige *f*

yeah [jeə] *exclam* ouais!; *Ironique* **yeah, right!, yeah sure!** oui, c'est ça!

yellow ['jeləʊ] *adj (cowardly)* trouillard; **to have a yellow streak** être un peu trouillard sur les bords

yellow-belly ['jeləʊbelɪ] *n (coward)* poule *f* mouillée

yep [jep] *exclam* ouais!

Yid [jɪd] *n Injurieux* youpin(e) *m,f*, youde *mf*

ying-yang [!] ['jɪŋjæŋ] *n Am* **(a)** *(anus)* troufignon *m*, fion *m*, rondelle *f* **(b)** *(penis)* bite *f*, biroute *f*, pine *f*

The symbol □ indicates that a translation is neutral in register.

yo [jəʊ] *exclam Noir Am* salut!

yob [jɒb], **yobbo** ['jɒbəʊ] *n Br* loubard *m*

yonks [jɒŋks] *npl Br* une éternité; **I haven't seen him for yonks** ça fait un bail *ou* une paye que je l'ai pas vu

yup [jʌp] *exclam* = **yep**

yuppie, yuppy ['jʌpɪ] *n* (*abrév* **young upwardly-mobile professional**) yuppie *mf*; **yuppie flu** syndrome *m* de fatigue chronique □

za [tsɑ:] n Am Hum (abrév **pizza**) pizza □ f

zap [zæp] **1** vt (kill) buter, refroidir, zigouiller

   2 vi (change TV channels) zapper

zapper ['zæpə(r)] n (TV remote control) télécommande □ f, zappette f

zebra ['zi:brə] n Am (American football referee) arbitre □ m

> C'est à cause de leur chemise à bandes noires et blanches que l'on donne ce surnom aux arbitres.

zeds [zedz], Am **zees** [zi:z] npl **to catch some** Br **zeds** or Am **zees** piquer un roupillon ▸ voir aussi **cop**

> C'est la bande dessinée qui est à l'origine de cette expression: "zzzz" est l'onomatopée la plus fréquemment utilisée pour évoquer le sommeil.

zero ['zi:rəʊ] **1** n (person) nul (nulle) m,f

   2 adj aucun □; **he's got zero charm** il a aucun charme; **they've got zero chance of winning** ils ont pas la moindre chance de gagner

zilch [zɪltʃ] n (nothing) que dalle

zillion ['zɪljən] n Hum **a zillion** or **zillions (of)** des millions et des millions (de)

zing [zɪŋ] vt Am (tease) vanner, chambrer

zinger ['zɪŋə(r)] n Am (pointed remark) vanne f

zip [zɪp] **1** n Am (nothing) que dalle; (zero) zéro m; **the score was four-zip** le score était de quatre à zéro

   2 vt **to zip it** (be quiet) la fermer, la boucler; **zip it!** la ferme!, ferme ton clapet!, écrase!

zit [zɪt] n (pimple) bouton □ m

zone [zəʊn] n Am **to be in a zone** (dazed) être dans le coaltar; (after taking drugs) être raide, planer

zoned (out) [zəʊnd('aʊt)] adj Am **to be zoned out** (dazed) être dans le coaltar; (after taking drugs) être raide, planer

zonked (out) [zɒŋkt('aʊt)] adj (exhausted) crevé, naze, lessivé, claqué; (drunk) bourré, rond, pété, fait; (on drugs) défoncé, raide

zoom [zu:m] vt Am (**a**) (fool, deceive) se foutre de, duper □ (**b**) (flirt with) faire du rentre-dedans à

zooted ['zu:tɪd] adj Am (drunk) bourré, pété, fait (**b**) (on drugs) raide, défoncé

zowie ['zaʊɪ] exclam Am oh là là!, la vache!

Français-Anglais
French-English

A

abattis [abati] *nmpl* **t'as intérêt à numéroter tes abattis** start saying your prayers!

abeilles [abɛj] *nfpl* **avoir les abeilles** to be hacked off *or* cheesed off

abîmer [abime] *vt* **abîmer qn** to beat sb up, to give sb a hammering *or* a pasting; **se faire abîmer** to get beaten up, to *Br* get *or* *Am* take a hammering *or* a pasting ▶ *see also* **portrait**

abonné, -e [abɔne] *adj* **être abonné à qch** to be prone to sth □; **décidément, je suis abonné!** this is happening to me all the time!

abouler [abule] **1** *vt* (*apporter*) to bring □; (*passer*) to pass □; **allez, aboule le fric!** come on, cough up!
2 s'abouler *vpr* to turn up, to show up, to roll up; **alors, tu t'aboules?** you coming, then? ▶ *see also* **viande**

accoucher [akuʃe] *vi* **accouche!** spit it out!, out with it!

accro [akro] **1** *adj* **être accro à qch** (*drogué*) to be hooked on sth; (*fanatique*) to be really into sth, to be mad about sth
2 *nmf* **(a)** (*drogué*) addict □, junkie; **être accro à qch** to be hooked on sth **(b)** (*fanatique*) addict □, nut, fanatic □; **un accro du jazz** a jazzhead; **un accro du yoga** a yoga nut

accrocher [akrɔʃe] **1** *vi* (*bien fonctionner*) **ça n'a pas accroché entre eux** they didn't hit it off; **j'arrive pas à lire ce roman, j'accroche vraiment pas** I just can't get into this novel
2 s'accrocher *vpr* **(a)** (*persévérer*) to stick at it, to hang in there; **accroche-toi Jeannot!** the best of luck *or* *Br* British! **(b)** **tu peux te l'accrocher!** you can forget it!; **s'il continue comme ça, sa médaille, il peut se l'accrocher** if he carries on like that he can kiss goodbye to his chances of winning a medal

achaler [aʃale] *vt Can* **achaler qn** to bug sb, to get up sb's nose

acide [asid] *nm* (*LSD*) acid

activer [aktive] *vi* to get a move on, to move it, to get one's skates on, *Am* to get it in gear; **allez, active!** come on, get a move on!

ado [ado] *nmf* (*abbr* **adolescent, -e**) teenager □

à donf [adɔ̃f] *adv* (*verlan* **à fond**) (*vite*) *Br* like the clappers, *Am* like sixty; (*très fort*) at full blast; (*beaucoup*) really, like crazy; **je la kiffe à donf, cette nana** I don't half fancy her

affaire [afɛr] *nf* **(a)** **être/ne pas être une affaire (au pieu)** to be good/no good in the sack ▶ *see also* **faire, juteux (b) lâche l'affaire!** (*laisse-moi tranquille*) give me peace!; (*laisse tomber*) just drop it!; **lâche pas l'affaire!** hang on in there!

afficher [afiʃe] **s'afficher** *vpr* to make an idiot of oneself; **il a fait tomber ses lunettes dans le bol de punch; je te dis pas comment il s'est affiché!** his glasses fell off into the punch bowl, what an idiot he made of himself!

affirmatif [afirmatif] *exclam* you bet!, sure thing!

after [aftœr] *nm or nf* (*soirée*) after party; **on a décidé d'aller faire l'after chez Alex** we finished the night off at Alex's place; **je fais une after après la soirée en boîte, d'accord?** everybody back to mine after the clubs shut, yeah?

agace-pissette [!!] [agaspisɛt] *nf Can* pricktease(r)

agité, -e [aʒite] *nm,f Hum* **agité du bocal**

Le symbole □ indique que la traduction n'est pas argotique.

Br nutter, headcase, *Am* wacko, screwball

agrafer [agʁafe] *vt* **(a)** *(retenir)* to corner; **la secrétaire m'a agrafé au début de la réception, et elle m'a tenu la jambe toute la soirée!** the secretary cornered me right at the start of the party and bent my ear all night! **(b)** *(arrêter) Br* to nick, *Am* to bust; **il s'est fait agrafer par les flics en sortant de la banque** he got *Br* nicked or *Am* busted by the cops just as he came out of the bank

aidé, -e [ɛde] *adj* **il est pas aidé** *(bête)* he's not too bright; *(laid)* he's no oil painting

aile [ɛl] *nf* **avoir un coup dans l'aile** to have had one too many; **battre de l'aile** to be in a bad way, to be struggling

-aille [ɑj] *suffix* **boustifaille** food □, chow, grub; **duraille** tough; **la flicaille** the cops, the pigs, *Br* the filth; **marmaille** kids, brats

This suffix is found at the end of many French slang nouns and adjectives and indicates that the word is rather pejorative.

air [ɛʁ] *nm* **de l'air!** get lost!, get out of here!; **ficher** *ou* **foutre**❗ **qch en l'air** *(mettre sens dessus dessous)* to turn sth upside down; *(jeter aux ordures)* to chuck sth (out), to bin sth, *Am* to trash sth; **se foutre en l'air**❗ *(se suicider)* to kill oneself □, *Br* to top oneself; *(avoir un accident de la route)* to have a crash □; **avoir l'air con et la vue basse**❗ to look like a real jerk ▸ see also **envoyer, jambe, pomper**

airbags [ɛʁbag] *nmpl* tits, jugs, knockers, *Am* hooters

aise [ɛz] *nf* **à l'aise** *(facilement)* easily □, no problem, *Br* no probs; **ça coûte 500 balles à l'aise** it's easily worth 500 francs, it's worth 500 francs no problem or *Br* no probs; **et lui il se tournait les pouces, à l'aise, Blaise!** and there HE was, twiddling his thumbs without a care in the world!

alcolo, alcoolo [alkɔlo] *nmf* *(abbr* **alcoolique)** alky, lush, boozer, *Am* juicer

aligner [aliɲe] **1** *vt* **(a)** **les aligner** to pay up, to cough up **(b)** **il s'est fait aligner par un flic en moto** a motorcycle cop slapped a fine on him

2 s'aligner *vpr* to go without; **tu peux**

Focus on:

L'alcool et l'ivresse

In the land of wine and pastis there is no shortage of slang terms to refer to drinking and drunkenness. Tradition dictates that the aperitif, or more familiarly **l'apéro**, is a sacred ritual for many, but there are numerous other occasions, both at home and in bars, to **s'enfiler un verre** or **siffler une bouteille**.

Bourré is the most common slang term for "drunk"; other very commonly used terms include **pété, torché, bituré** and **beurré**. Less crudely, one may describe someone as **rond, paf** or **cuit**. The ensuing hangover is known as a **gueule de bois**.

Colloquial words for an alcoholic include **alcolo, poivrot** and, less commonly, **soûlard, pochetron** and **soiffard**. Drink itself is called variously **la bibine** (a somewhat old-fashioned term now), **la picole** (from the verb **picoler**) and **la tise** (a more recent term which belongs to "l'argot des cités"). Unsurprisingly, wine is the drink best represented in the slang lexicon: **pinard** (from the word **pineau**), **picrate** and **jaja** are all commonly found. A red wine of poor quality may be referred to as **gros rouge** or **gros (rouge) qui tache**. Pastis – the drink favoured by many in the South of France – is known as **pastaga**, while **la gnôle** may refer to alcohol in general or eau-de-vie in particular.

Le symbole □ indique que la traduction n'est pas argotique.

t'aligner pour que je te prête du fric, maintenant! you can get lost if you think I'm going to lend you any money now!

aller [ale] *vi* (a) **tu peux y aller, c'est ce qui se fait de mieux!** you can take it from me, it's the best of stuff! (b) **où tu vas?** are you mad?, have you got a screw loose?, *Br* are you off your head?

aller-retour [alerətur], **aller et retour** [aleertur] *nm* slap on the face □ *(first with the palm and then with the back of the hand)*

allô [alo] *exclam (à quelqu'un qui n'écoute pas)* **allô?** hello?

allocs [alɔk] *nfpl (abbr* **allocations)** *Br* child benefit □, *Am* dependents' allowances □

allonger [alɔ̃ʒe] **1** *vt* (a) *(donner)* **allonger une baffe à qn** to give sb a slap □, to slap sb □; **allonger un coup de poing à qn** to punch sb □ (b) **les allonger, allonger le fric** to pay up, to cough up **2 s'allonger** *vpr (faire des aveux)* to spill the beans

allouf [aluf] *nf* match □ *(for lighting fire, cigarette)*

allumé, -e [alyme] *nm,f* crackpot, crank

allumer [alyme] *vt* (a) *(battre)* to beat up, *Br* to do over; **se faire allumer** to get beaten up or *Br* done over (b) *(tuer)* to kill □, to waste, *Br* to do in (c) *(exciter)* to turn on, to make horny *(deliberately)*

allumeuse [alymøz] *nf* pricktease(r)

allure [alyr] *nf Hum* **à toute allure!** see you later!

This expression, which literally means "at full speed", is a pun on the phrase "à tout à l'heure".

alpaguer [alpage] *vt* to collar, to nab; **se faire alpaguer** to get collared or nabbed

amazone [amazon] *nf* = prostitute who works from a car

amener [amne] **s'amener** *vpr (venir)* to come □; *(arriver)* to turn up, to show up, to roll up ▸ *see also* **viande**

Amerloque [amɛrlɔk] *nmf* Yank, Yankee

ami [ami] *nm* **t'as pas d'amis!** everybody hates you! □, *Br* what a Billy-no-mates!

amocher [amɔʃe] *vt (personne, objet)* to smash up

amortisseurs [amɔrtisœr] *nmpl* tits, jugs, knockers, *Am* hooters

amourette [!!] [amurɛt] *nf* **amourettes** balls, nuts, *Br* bollocks

amphés [ɑ̃fe], **amphets** [ɑ̃fɛt] *nfpl (abbr* **amphétamines)** speed, *Br* whizz

amphi [ɑ̃fi] *nm (abbr* **amphithéâtre)** lecture room or hall □

anar [anar] *nmf (abbr* **anarchiste)** anarchist □

andouille [ɑ̃duj] *nf* dope, *Br* divvy, *Am* dork

Anglais [ɑ̃glɛ] *nmpl* **les Anglais ont débarqué** I've/she's got my/her period □, I'm/she's on the rag

angliche [ɑ̃gliʃ] **1** *adj* British □, Brit **2** *nm (langue)* English □ **3** *nmf* **Angliche** *(personne)* Brit

anglo [ɑ̃glo] *nmf Can Pej* English-speaking Quebecker □

angoisse [ɑ̃gwas] *nf* **c'est l'angoisse!, bonjour l'angoisse!** what a pain or drag or bummer!

angoisser [ɑ̃gwase] *vi* to be all uptight or worked up

anguille [ɑ̃gij] *nf Hum* **anguille de caleçon** one-eyed trouser snake

antisèche [ɑ̃tisɛʃ] *nf Br* crib sheet, *Am* trot

apéro [apero] *nm (abbr* **apéritif)** aperitif □

à pluss [aplys] *exclam* see you later!, ciao!, *Br* laters!

appart' [apart] *nm (abbr* **appartement)** pad, *Br* flat □, *Am* apartment □

appuyer [apɥije] **s'appuyer** *vpr* **s'appuyer qn** to get stuck or *Br* lumbered or landed with sb; **s'appuyer le ménage/la vaisselle** to get stuck or *Br* lumbered or landed with the housework/the dishes ▸ *see also* **champignon**

aprème [aprɛm] *nm or nf (abbr* **après-midi)** **cet** *ou* **cette aprème** this afternoon □

Le symbole □ indique que la traduction n'est pas argotique.

Arbi [arbi] *nm Offensive* = racist term used to refer to a North African Arab

archi- [arʃi] *prefix* extremely □, seriously, *Br* dead, well, *Am* real; **les magasins sont archibondés le samedi après-midi** the shops are *Br* chock-a-block *or Am* jammed on Saturday afternoons; **c'est faux, archifaux!** it's so □ *or Br* dead wrong!; **c'est un air archiconnu** it's a *Br* dead *or Am* real well-known tune

-ard [ar] *suffix* **connard**[!] stupid bastard, prick, *Br* arsehole, *Am* asshole; **faiblard** weakish, on the weak side; **flemmard** lazy so-and-so; **salopard**[!] bastard

> This suffix is found at the end of many French slang nouns and adjectives and indicates that the word is rather pejorative.

ardoise [ardwaz] *nf (pour inscrire des dettes)* slate, tab; **laisser une ardoise** to

disappear without paying one's debts □

aristo [aristo] *nmf (abbr **aristocrate**)* aristo, *Br* toff, nob

arme [arm] *nf* **passer l'arme à gauche** to croak, to kick the bucket, *Br* to snuff it, *Am* to check out

armoire [armwar] *nf* **c'est une armoire à glace** he's built like a tank

arnaque [arnak] *nf* **c'est (de) l'arnaque!** what a rip-off!, it's *Br* daylight *or Am* highway robbery!

arnaquer [arnake] *vt* **arnaquer qn** to rip sb off; **se faire arnaquer** to get ripped off

arnaqueur, -euse [arnakœr, -øz] *nm,f Br* rip-off merchant, *Am* hustler

arpion [arpjɔ̃] *nm* foot □, *Br* plate, *Am* dog

arquer [arke] *vi* to walk □

arracher [araʃe] **1** *vt* **(a)** **ça t'arracherait la gueule de dire merci/de t'excuser?** it wouldn't kill you to say thanks/to

---

Focus on:

L'argent

Fric is the most common of the numerous slang words for "money". Other frequently encountered terms include **pognon**, **flouse** (from the Arabic "el-flouss" = money), **blé** and **pèze**. Two now slightly old-fashioned terms are **grisbi** (as mentioned in the title of the classic film noir "Touchez pas au grisbi") and **oseille**, while conversely the words **caillasse**, **maille** and **genhar** (the verlan term for **argent**) belong to "l'argot des banlieues" (see panel).

Some words are used specifically to refer to small change, such as **mitraille** and **ferraille**. The words **bifton** and **fafiot** are used for banknotes. Someone who is completely penniless may be said to **ne pas avoir un radis, un rond** or **un rotin** whilst a rich person will be described as **plein aux as** or **bourré de fric**.

The most common slang word to refer to francs, before the arrival of the euro rendered this currency obsolete, was **balles**. Terms relating to specific amounts of francs have also been common, for example **une patate**, **une brique** and **un bâton**, all used to refer to 10,000 francs, and **un sac** (10 francs). **Thune** was originally used to mean the sum of 5 francs, but now refers to money in general. Note too its verlan form **neutu**.

It remains to be seen if the euro will have its own slang terms; perhaps "roeu" will soon be heard in the "cités".

Someone with no money is **fauché, à sec** or **dans la dèche**, whilst a rich person is **plein aux as** or is said to **rouler sur l'or**. **Casquer, raquer** and **cracher** mean "to pay a high price", whilst **radin** and **rat** refer to a miser.

Le symbole □ indique que la traduction n'est pas argotique.

apologize! (**b**) **ça arrache (la gueule)** it blows the top of your head off

  2 s'arracher *vpr* to hit the road, to make tracks; **il faut que je m'arrache** I must be off, I've got to make tracks

arranger [arɑ̃ʒe] *vt* **arranger qn** *(battre)* to beat sb up, to clobber sb, *Br* to kick sb's head in

arroser [aroze] **1** *vt* (**a**) *(fêter)* **arroser qch** to celebrate sth with a few drinks □; **il faut arroser ça** that calls for a celebration *or* a drink (**b**) *(mitrailler)* to spray with bullets

  2 s'arroser *vpr* **ça s'arrose** that calls for a celebration *or* a drink

arsouille [arsuj] *nm* hood, hooligan, *Br* yob

Arthur [artyr] *npr* **se faire appeler Arthur** to get one's head bitten off, to get bawled out *or* *Am* chewed out

artiche [artiʃ] *nm* dough, bread, *Br* dosh, *Am* bucks

as [ɑs] *nm* (**a**) *(expert)* whizz; **un as du volant** an ace driver

  (**b**) **passer à l'as** to go out of the window, to go down the tubes *or* *Br* pan

  (**c**) **être fichu** *ou* **foutu** *ou* **fagoté comme l'as de pique** *Br* to be dressed like a scarecrow *or* a tramp, *Am* to look like a bum

  (**d**) **être plein aux as** to be loaded, *Br* to be rolling in it, *Am* to be rolling in dough

asperge [aspɛrʒ] *nf (personne)* beanpole

aspi [aspi] *nm (abbr* **aspirant**) = soldier with the rank of lieutenant engaged in military service

assaisonner [asɛzɔne] *vt* (**a**) *(réprimander)* **assaisonner qn** to give sb a roasting, to bawl sb out, *Am* to chew sb out; **se faire assaisonner** to get a roasting, to get bawled out, *Am* to get chewed out (**b**) *(malmener)* to rough up

asseoir [aswar] **s'asseoir** *vpr* **s'asseoir sur qch** *(ne pas en tenir compte)* not to give a damn *or* a hoot about sth

assis, -e [asi, -iz] *adj* **en rester assis** to be stunned *or* *Br* gobsmacked; **quand il m'a dit qu'il était pédé, j'en suis resté assis** when he told me he was queer, I was completely stunned *or* *Br* gobsmacked

assoce [asɔs] *nf (abbr* **association**) association □

assurer [asyre] *vi* (**a**) *(être compétent)* **il assure vachement en anglais** he's brilliant at English; **elle assure à la batterie** she's a brilliant drummer (**b**) *(garder son sang-froid)* to stay in control, to keep one's head; **vas-y, assure!** go for it!

astap [astap] *adj inv (abbr* **à se taper le cul par terre**) hysterical, side-splitting; **c'était astap** it was a scream *or* a hoot

Athénien [atenjɛ̃] *nm* **c'est là que les Athéniens s'atteignirent** it was at that point that things started to go wrong □ *or* *Br* pear-shaped

atout [atu] *nm (coup)* clout, thump; **prendre un atout** to get clouted *or* thumped

attaque [atak] **d'attaque** *adj* **être d'attaque** to be on top form; **se sentir d'attaque pour faire qch** to feel up to doing sth

attaquer [atake] **1** *vt (entamer)* to tackle, *Br* to get stuck into

  2 *vi (commencer à manger) Br* to get stuck in, *Am* to chow down

atteint, -e [atɛ̃, -ɛ̃t] *adj* **être atteint** *(ne pas être sain d'esprit)* to be touched, to have a screw *or* *Br* slate loose

attrape-couillon [atrapkujɔ̃] *nm* scam, swindle, con, *Am* hustle

auberge [obɛrʒ] *nf* **on n'est pas sortis de l'auberge** we're not out of the woods yet

auge [oʒ] *nf (assiette)* plate □

autre [otr] *pron* **qu'est-ce qu'il a, l'autre?** what's up with him *or* *Br* your man there?; **oh l'autre eh! Il sait pas faire du vélo!** he can't even ride a bike!; **à d'autres!** come off it!, gimme a break!, yeah right!, *Br* do me a favour!

avaler [avale] *vt* (**a**) **avaler son bulletin de naissance** to croak, to kick the bucket, *Am* to cash in one's chips (**b**) **avaler la fumée !!!** *(au cours d'une fellation)* to swallow

avoine [avwan], **avoinée** [avwane] *nf*

Le symbole □ indique que la traduction n'est pas argotique.

thrashing, hammering; **prendre une avoine** to *Br* get *or Am* take a thrashing *or* a hammering; **filer une avoine à qn** to give sb a thrashing *or* a hammering

avoir [avwar] *vt* (**a**) **se faire avoir** to be had *or* conned *or* done (**b**) **en avoir** to have guts *or* balls

azimut [azimyt] **tous azimuts** *adv* all over the place *or Br* shop

azimuté, -e [azimyte] *adj* crackers, *Br* barking, *Am* wacko

B

baba [baba] **1** *adj (stupéfait)* flabbergasted, *Br* gobsmacked; **j'en suis resté baba** I was flabbergasted *or Br* gobsmacked

2 *nmf (hippie)* **baba (cool)** hippy

3 *nm* **l'avoir dans le baba** to be had *or* conned

> "Baba" in sense 2 is a term used to refer to a second-generation hippy who has adopted the image and lifestyle of the original hippy generation of the 60s and 70s.

baboune [babun] *nf Can* **faire la baboune** to be in a huff

babtou [babtu] *nmf Cités (verlan* **toubab)** Frenchman, *f* Frenchwoman □

baby [bebi] *nm* = half-measure of whisky

bac [bak] *nm (abbr* **baccalauréat)** = secondary school examinations qualifying for entry to university, *Br* ≃ A-levels □, *Am* ≃ high school diploma □

bacchantes [bakɑ̃t] *nfpl* moustache □, tash

bâcher [baʃe] **se bâcher** *vpr* to hit the sack *or* the hay *or Am* the rack

bachot [baʃo] *nm* = secondary school examinations qualifying for entry to university, *Br* ≃ A-levels □, *Am* ≃ high school diploma □; **attends d'avoir passé ton bachot, après tu verras** wait till you've got your exams, then you can see; **boîte à bachot** crammer

bachotage [baʃɔtaʒ] *nm* cramming, *Br* swotting

bachoter [baʃɔte] *vi* to cram, *Br* to swot

bachoteur, -euse [baʃɔtœr, -øz] *nm,f* = student cramming for an exam

bacon [bekɔn] *nm Can* **avoir du bacon** to be loaded

badloqué, -e [badlɔke] *adj Can Joual* **être badloqué** to have rotten luck

bâdrage [bɑdraʒ] *nm Can* pain (in the neck)

bâdrant, -e [bɑdrɑ̃, -ɑ̃t] *adj Can* **être bâdrant** to be a pain (in the neck)

bâdrer [bɑdre] *vt Can* **bâdrer qn** to bug sb, *Br* to do sb's head in, *Am* to give sb a pain (in the neck)

baffe [baf] *nf* clout, cuff

baffer [bafe] *vt* to clout, to cuff; **si il continue à m'emmerder, je vais le baffer celui-là!** if he keeps bugging me like that, I'm going to clout him!

bafouille [bafuj] *nf* letter □

bâfrer [bɑfre] *vi* to stuff oneself *or* one's face, to pig out

bâfreur, -euse [bɑfrœr, -øz] *nm,f* pig, *Br* greedy-guts, gannet, *Am* hog

bagne [baɲ] *nm* **c'est le bagne ici** it's like a sweatshop here

bagnole [baɲɔl] *nf* car □, wheels, *Br* motor

bagou [bagu] *nm* gift of the gab; **avoir du bagou** to have the gift of the gab

bagouse [baguz] *nf* **(a)** ring □ *(for finger)* **(b) être de la bagouse** ‼ to be *Br* a poof *or* a shirt-lifter *or Am* a fag

baguenauder [bagnode] **1** *vi* to saunter *or* wander around □

2 se baguenauder *vpr* to saunter *or* wander around □

bahut [bay] *nm* **(a)** *(camion)* lorry □, truck □ **(b)** *(taxi)* taxi □, cab **(c)** *(lycée)* high school □

baigner [beɲe] *vi* **(a) tout baigne (dans l'huile)** everything's hunky-dory *or Am* A-OK **(b) avoir les dents du fond qui baignent** to have stuffed oneself *or* one's face, to have pigged out

Le symbole □ indique que la traduction n'est pas argotique.

baigneur [!] [bɛɲœr] *nm* (**a**) *(sexe de la femme)* pussy, snatch, *Br* fanny (**b**) *(postérieur)* *Br* arse, *Am* ass, fanny

bail [baj] *nm* **ça fait un bail** it's been ages *or Br* yonks

baille [baj] *nf* water□; **tomber à la baille** to fall in□

bain [bɛ̃] *nm* **être/se mettre dans le bain** to be in/get into the swing of things; **je me suis écouté un petit disque à fond avant d'aller en boîte, histoire de me mettre dans le bain** I put a record on full blast before I went out clubbing, just to get me in the mood

baisable [!!] [bɛzabl] *adj* fuckable, *Br* shaggable

baise [!!] [bɛz] *nf (amour physique)* fucking, screwing, *Br* shagging

baisebeige [bɛzbɛʒ] *(abbr* **BCBG**) **1** *adj inv Br* ≃ Sloany, *Am* ≃ preppy
2 *nmf Br* ≃ Sloane (Ranger), *Am* ≃ preppy

> This term is a humorous rephrasing of the term "BCBG" (see entry), itself the abbreviation of "bon chic bon genre".

baise-en-ville [bɛzɑ̃vil] *nm inv* overnight bag□

baise-la-piastre [bɛzlapjas] *nmf Can* skinflint, tightwad

> The word "piastre" is a colloquial term for a dollar in Canadian French.

baiser [!!] [beze] **1** *vt* (**a**) *(faire l'amour avec)* to fuck, to screw, to lay, *Br* to shag (**b**) *(duper)* to shaft, to screw; **se faire baiser** to get shafted *or* screwed (**c**) *(surprendre)* to nab; **se faire baiser** to get nabbed
2 *vi* to fuck, to screw, *Br* to shag; **il baise bien** he's a great fuck *or* lay *or* screw *or Br* shag ▶ *see also* **couille**, **lapin**

baiseur, -euse [!!] [bɛzœr, -øz] *nm,f* **c'est une sacrée baiseuse** she's a great fuck *or* lay *or* screw *or Br* shag

baisodrome [!!] [bɛzɔdrom] *nm* fuckpad

bakchich [bakʃiʃ] *nm Br* backhander, bung, *Am* payoff

balader [balade] *vi* **envoyer balader qn** to tell sb where to go, *Br* to send sb packing; **envoyer balader qch** *(lancer)* to send sth flying; *(abandonner)* to quit sth, *Br* to chuck *or* pack sth in

baladeuse [baladøz] *adj* **avoir les mains baladeuses** to have wandering hands

balai [balɛ] *nm* (**a**) *(an)* year□; **il a cinquante balais** he's fifty□ (**b**) **ce qu'il peut être coincé, ce mec! on dirait qu'il a un balai dans le cul** he can be so uptight, that guy, it's like he's got a poker up his *Br* arse *or Am* ass

> In category (a), this word is used only when referring to people's ages.

balaise [balɛz] **1** *adj* (**a**) *(fort)* *(physiquement)* hefty, burly□; *(intellectuellement)* brainy; **être balaise en qch** to be brilliant at sth (**b**) *(difficile)* tough, tricky
2 *nm* big guy

balance [balɑ̃s] *nf (dénonciateur)* squealer, *Br* grass, *Am* rat

balancé, -e [balɑ̃se] *adj* **être bien balancé** to have a great bod

balancer [balɑ̃se] **1** *vt* (**a**) *(dénoncer)* to squeal on, *Br* to grass on, *Am* to rat on (**b**) *(lancer)* to chuck (**c**) *(mettre aux ordures)* to chuck (out), to bin, *Am* to trash
2 *vi* *(médire)* to dish the dirt, *Br* to bitch
3 **s'en balancer** [!] *vpr* not to give a shit *or Br* a toss *or Am* a rat's ass ▶ *see also* **purée**, **sauce**

balcon [balkɔ̃] *nm* **il y a du monde au balcon** she's well-stacked, she's a big girl, *Br* you don't get many of those to the pound

baliser [balize] *vi* to be scared stiff *or* witless

balle [bal] *nf* (**a**) *(franc)* franc□; **t'as pas cent balles?** got any change? (**b**) **c'est de la balle!** *Br* it's completely top!, *Am* it's totally awesome! ▶ *see also* **peau**, **trou**

balloches [!] [balɔʃ] *nfpl* balls, nuts, *Br* bollocks

ballon [balɔ̃] *nm* (**a**) *(Alcootest®)* **faire**

souffler qn dans le ballon to get sb to blow into the bag **(b) à fond les ballons** *(très vite)* Br like the clappers, Am like sixty; *(très fort)* at full blast

ballot [balo] *nm (idiot)* Br divvy, wally, Am goof, geek

balloune [balun] *nf Can Joual* **prendre une balloune, partir une balloune** to get wrecked *or* wasted; **être en balloune** *(enceinte)* to be in the (pudding) club

> This word comes from the Gallicization of the English word "balloon".

baloche [balɔʃ] *nm* local dance ▫

baltringue [baltrɛ̃g] *nmf Cités* wimp, chicken, Br big girl's blouse

bambou [bãbu] *nm* **avoir le coup de bambou** *(avoir un accès de folie)* to crack up, to go nuts, Br to go off one's head; *(être épuisé)* to be wiped *or* Br shattered *or* Am pooped; **attraper un coup de bambou** *(avoir une insolation)* to get sunstroke ▫; **c'est le coup de bambou** *(c'est très cher)* it costs an arm and a leg *or* Br a bomb *or* a packet

bamboula [bãbula] **1** *nf (fête)* wild party; **faire la bamboula** to party, Br to go on the razzle
2 *nm Offensive (homme de race noire)* nigger, Br wog, Am coon

banane [banan] *nf* **(a)** *(coiffure)* quiff **(b)** *(insulte)* **banane!** you moron *or* Br plonker *or* Am geek! **(c) avoir la banane** ‼ to have a hard-on *or* Br a stiffy

bandaison ‼ [bãdɛzõ] *nf* hard-on, boner, Br stiffy

bandant, -e ‼ [bãdã, -ãt] *adj* **(a)** *(désirable sexuellement)* **elle est bandante** she's really horny, she really turns me on **(b)** *(enthousiasmant)* thrilling ▫

bander ‼ [bãde] *vi* to have a hard-on; **bander mou** to have a semi; **il bande pour elle** he's got the hots for her, she really turns him on, Br he thinks she's really horny; **faire bander qn** *(exciter sexuellement)* to turn sb on, to make sb horny, Br to give sb the horn; **ce genre de musique, ça me fait pas vraiment bander** I can't really get into this sort of music

bandouiller ‼ [bãduje] *vi* to have a semi

bang [bãg] *nm (pipe à eau)* bong

banquer [bãke] *vi* to cough up, to hand over the cash

baquer [bake] **se baquer** *vpr* to go for a dip

baraka [baraka] *nf* **avoir la baraka** to be lucky ▫ *or* Br jammy

baraque [barak] *nf (maison)* place, pad; **casser la baraque** *(remporter un vif succès)* to bring the house down; **casser la baraque à qn** *(faire échouer ses projets)* to mess things up for sb

baraqué, -e [barake] *adj* hefty, burly ▫

baratin [baratɛ̃] *nm (d'un vendeur)* sales talk *or* pitch; *(pour séduire)* sweet talk, Br patter; **c'est du baratin** it's a load of bull *or* tripe *or* Br waffle

baratiner [baratine] *vt* **baratiner qn**

---

l'Argot des banlieues

Around twenty years ago a new form of slang, quite unlike traditional "argot", began to emerge in the impoverished suburban areas of large cities, especially Paris. This new slang reflects the cultural and ethnic diversity of these neighbourhoods, with expressions originating from Arabic (eg "chouf"), African languages (eg "toubab" and its verlan form "babtou") and Romany (eg "bouillaver", "raclo"), whilst the popularity of rap music has led to an influx of English expressions (eg "dope", "shit", "splif").

Verlan (see panel) is omnipresent and words are often abbreviated. It is a form of slang essentially created and used by young people as a linguistic expression of their social, economic and geographical marginalization.

Le symbole ▫ indique que la traduction n'est pas argotique.

(essayer de convaincre) to shoot sb a line, to try to talk sb round; *(pour séduire)* Br to chat sb up, Am to hit on sb; **baratiner qn pour qu'il fasse qch** to try to talk sb into doing sth □

baratineur, -euse [baratinœr, -øz] *nm,f* smooth talker

barbant, -e [barbã, -ãt] *adj* deadly dull; **c'est barbant, mais il faut le faire** it's a drag, but it's got to be done

barbaque [barbak] *nf* meat □

barbe [barb] *nf* **c'est la barbe** it's a drag; **la barbe!** give it a rest!

barber [barbe] **1** *vt* **barber qn** to bore sb stiff *or* to tears
    2 se barber *vpr* to be bored stiff *or* to tears

barbeux, -euse [barbø, -øz] Can **1** *adj* **être barbeux** to be a pain (in the neck)
    2 *nm,f* pain (in the neck)

barboter [barbɔte] *vt (voler)* to pinch, Br to nick; **barboter qch à qn** to pinch *or* Br nick sth from sb; **se faire barboter qch** to get sth pinched *or* Br nicked

barbouze [barbuz] *nf* (**a**) *(barbe)* beard □ (**b**) *(espion)* spy □, plant

barbu [!] [barby] *nm (poils pubiens de la femme)* bush

barda [barda] *nm* stuff, gear

bardeau, -x [bardo] *nm* Can **manquer un bardeau** to be not right in the head, Br to have a slate loose

> The literal meaning of "bardeau" is "shingle", so this expression is almost a word-for-word equivalent of "to have a slate loose".

barder [barde] *v imp* **ça va barder!** there's going to be trouble!

barge [barʒ] *nf* , **barjo, barjot** [barʒo] **1** *adj* nuts, bananas, Br off one's head, Am wacko
    2 *nmf* headcase, nutcase, Br nutter, Am wacko

baron [barɔ̃] *nm (compère)* plant

barouf [baruf], **baroufle** [barufl] *nm* racket, din

barre [bar] *nf* (**a**) **avoir un coup de barre** to be bushed *or* wiped *or* Br shattered *or* Am beat (**b**) **c'est le coup de barre** it costs an arm and a leg *or* a bundle *or* Br a packet ▶ *see also* **couille**

barré, -e [bare] *adj* **être bien barré** to be looking good; **être mal barré** to be heading for trouble

barreau, -x [baro] *nm* (**a**) **barreau de chaise** *(cigare)* fat cigar □, Am stogie (**b**) **être/se retrouver derrière les barreaux** to be/end up behind bars

barrer [bare] **se barrer** *vpr (partir)* to hit the road, to get going, to make tracks; *(se sauver)* to beat it, Br to clear off, Am to book it; **barre-toi!** get out of here!, beat it!, Am take a hike!

barrette [baret] *nf (de haschich)* = thin strip

basket [basket] *nf* (**a**) **être bien dans ses baskets** to be very together *or* Br sorted (in one's head) (**b**) **lâche-moi les baskets!** get off my back!, don't hassle me!

bassiner [basine] *vt* **bassiner qn** to bug sb, Br to do sb's head in, to get up sb's nose, Am to give sb a pain

bassinet [basinɛ] *nm* **cracher au bassinet** to cough up, to hand over the cash

basta [basta] *exclam* that'll do!

Bastoche [bastɔʃ] *nf* **la Bastoche** = the Bastille area of Paris

baston [bastɔ̃] *nm or nf* scuffle, Br punch-up, Am fist fight

bastonner [bastɔne] **1** *v imp* **ça a bastonné** there was a scuffle *or* Br a punch-up *or* Am a fist fight
    2 se bastonner *vpr* to have a scuffle *or* Br a punch-up *or* Am a fist fight

bastos [bastos] *nf* bullet □, slug

bastringue [bastrɛ̃g] *nm* (**a**) *(vacarme)* racket, din (**b**) *(désordre)* shambles (**c**) **et tout le bastringue** blah blah blah

bataclan [bataklã] *nm* **et tout le bataclan** blah blah blah

bataillon [batajɔ̃] *nm* **inconnu au bataillon** never heard of him, who's he when he's at home?

Le symbole □ indique que la traduction n'est pas argotique.

bâtard ‼ [bɑtar] nm bastard

bateau [bato] adj inv (banal) hackneyed ▢, trite ▢

bâton [bɑtɔ̃] nm (dix mille francs) ten thousand francs ▢

battant [batɑ̃] nm (cœur) ticker

battre [batr] **1** vt **j'en ai rien à battre** ! I don't give a shit or Br a toss or Am a rat's ass

   2 se battre vpr **je m'en bats l'œil** I don't give a damn or a hoot or Br a stuff; **je m'en bats les couilles** ‼ I don't give a (flying) fuck ▸ see also **aile**

bavard [bavar] nm (avocat) lawyer ▢, brief

bavarde [bavard] nf (langue) tongue ▢; **tenir sa bavarde** to hold one's tongue, to keep one's mouth shut

bavasser [bavase] vi to yak, Br to natter

bavasseux, -euse [bavasø, -øz] nmf Can Pej (bavard) chatterbox; (indiscret) gossip(monger)

baver [bave] **1** vt **(a)** (dire) **qu'est-ce que tu baves?** what are you rambling or jabbering or Br wittering on about?

   (b) en baver to have a hard or tough time of it; **en faire baver à qn** to give sb a hard time

   (c) Can (contrarier) to mess around; **se faire baver** to be messed around

   2 vi (bavarder) to chat, to yak, Br to natter; **baver sur qn** to dish the dirt about sb, to badmouth sb, Br to bitch about sb

bavette [bavɛt] nf **tailler une bavette (avec qn)** to have a chat or Br a natter (with sb)

baveux, -euse [bavø, -øz] **1** nm,f Can (enfant effronté) brat

   2 nm **(a)** (savon) soap ▢ **(b)** (journal) paper ▢ **(c)** (baiser) sloppy kiss

bazarder [bazarde] vt **(a)** (jeter) to chuck (out), to bin, Am to trash **(b)** (dénoncer) to squeal on, Br to grass on, Am to rat on

bazou [bazu] nm Can (voiture) rustbucket, heap

BCBG [besebeʒe] (abbr **bon chic bon genre**) **1** adj inv Br ≃ Sloany, Am ≃ preppy

   2 nmf Br ≃ Sloane (Ranger), Am ≃ preppy

This term refers to someone whose classic, elegant style of dress suggests a wealthy, conservative social background.

BD [bede] nf (abbr **bande dessinée**) comic strip ▢, cartoon ▢

beauf [bof] (abbr **beau-frère**) **1** adj (caractéristique du Français moyen) = stereotypically narrow-minded and middle-class

   2 nm **(a)** (beau-frère) brother-in-law ▢ **(b)** (Français moyen) = stereotypical narrow-minded, middle-class man

The term "beauf" — short for "beau-frère" — comes from a character in a comic strip created in the 1960s by the French cartoonist Cabu. A "beauf" is the average middle-class Frenchman with a racist, reactionary and jingoistic outlook on life.

beaujolpif [boʒɔlpif] nm Beaujolais ▢

bébé [bebe] nm Can Joual (jolie fille) **un beau bébé** a babe, Am a hottie

bébert [beber] nm Cités = stereotypical reactionary Frenchman

This word has a dual etymology: "bébert" comes firstly from the abbreviation "BBR", which stands for "bleu, blanc, rouge", the colours of the French flag and a symbol of French nationalistic pride. In addition, the name Bébert (a nickname for "Albert") sounds very typically French.

bec [bɛk] nm **(a)** (bouche) mouth ▢, Br gob, cakehole; **clouer le bec à qn** to shut sb up; **puer du bec** to have rotten breath or dogbreath **(b)** Belg, Can & Suisse (baiser) peck, kiss ▢; **donner un bec à qn** to give sb a kiss or peck; Can **bec pincé** snob ▸ see also **claquer**

bécane [bekan] nf **(a)** (bicyclette, moto) bike **(b)** (machine) machine ▢, Am honker

because [bikoz] prep because of ▢

bècebège [bɛsbɛʒ] = **BCBG**

Le symbole ▢ indique que la traduction n'est pas argotique.

bêcheur, -euse [beʃœr, -øz] **1** adj stuck-up, snooty

2 nm,f stuck-up or snooty person

bécosses [bekɔs] nfpl Can Joual Br bog, Am john, can

bécot [beko] nm kiss ▫

bécoter [bekɔte] **1** vt Br to snog, Am to neck

2 se bécoter vpr Br to snog, Am to neck, to suck face

becter [bɛkte] vt & vi to eat ▫

bédave [bedav], **bédaver** [bedave] vi Cités to smoke ▫

bédé [bede] = **BD**

bédo [bedo] nm Cités joint, doobie, spliff, number

before [bifɔr] nm or nf (soirée) = party attended before spending the night clubbing; **où est-ce qu'on va faire le before ce soir?** where are we going to go to start things off this evening?

béger [beʒer] vi (verlan gerber) to puke, to throw up, to barf, to chunder

bégueule [begœl] adj fussy ▫

beigne [bɛɲ] nf clout, cuff; **flanquer une beigne à qn** to clout or cuff sb

belette [bəlɛt] nf chick, Br bird

belle [bɛl] nf **(a) se faire la belle** (faire

Focus on:

La bêtise et la folie

The word **con** is one of the most commonly used insults in French. Despite having the same etymology, it is notably less offensive or taboo than the English word "cunt" and is generally used to refer to a stupid person, its nuances ranging from the slightly forgetful to the completely stupid. This word may also be used to refer to an object, an attitude or even a situation, in, for example, **c'est con que…** used to mean "it's a pity that…". The word often appears in similes; the construction **con comme…** is very common and one may be, variously, **con comme un balai**, **ses pieds**, **pas deux**, **un manche** or **une bite**, the first expression being very similar to the English "daft as a brush". The term **couillon** (from the word **couille**, a common slang term for "testicle") is found more frequently in the South of France, and may have quite affectionate overtones.

Other picturesque expressions to denote stupidity include **il n'a pas inventé la poudre** or **le fil à couper le beurre**, **c'est pas une lumière**, **il en tient une couche** and **il lui manque une case**.

Familiar expressions which are slightly less vulgar than **con** include **crétin**, **andouille**, **cruche**, **cloche**, **nouille** and **banane**, all of which may be used somewhat affectionately. In the "cités", the adjective **grave** is often used to describe someone as stupid, for example, **il est grave, lui…**

Further down the route to madness, many colourful adjectives are used to describe the state of someone who is not so much stupid as deranged, such as **cinglé**, **timbré**, **givré**, **fêlé**, **chtarbé** or **siphonné**.

Electricity-related metaphors are currently popular with the expression **péter les plombs** (literally "to blow the fuses") and, similarly, **disjoncter** ("to short-circuit"). Metaphors connected to transport or driving also exist in terms such as **dérailler** ("to go off the rails", an expression also used figuratively in English, although with a different meaning) and **perdre les pédales**. Also of note is the term **fada**, a word originating in the Provençal dialect, which is still used exclusively in the South of France.

Le symbole ▫ indique que la traduction n'est pas argotique.

une fugue) to run away □, *Br* to do a bunk; (*s'évader*) to break out □

   (b) *Belg* **avoir belle à faire qch** to have no trouble doing sth; **en avoir une belle avec qn** to go through some hard times with sb; **en faire une (bien) belle** to do something really silly *ou* stupid; **ne jamais en faire une belle** to be always putting one's foot in it; **ne pas en faire une belle** to be a total disaster

belle-doche [bɛldɔʃ] *nf* mother-in-law □

bénard [benar], **bène** [bɛn] *nm Br* trousers □, keks, *Am* pants □

bénef [benɛf] *nm* (*abbr* **bénéfice**) profit □; **c'est tout bénef** it's all profit

béni-oui-oui [beniwiwi] *nm inv* yes-man

berceau [bɛrso] *nm* **les prendre au berceau** to be a cradle-snatcher

Bérézina [berezina] *npr* **c'est la Bérézina** it's a disaster □

This expression refers to the Berezina river in Belarus which Napoleon's "Grande Armée" crossed during its hectic retreat from Russia in 1812. Many soldiers lost their lives during the disorganized crossing.

berge [bɛrʒ] *nf* (*an*) year □; **elle a cinquante berges** she's fifty □

This term is used only when referring to people's ages.

berlingot [!] [bɛrlɛ̃go] *nm* **(a)** (*clitoris*) clit **(b)** (*virginité*) **avoir son berlingot** to be a virgin □; **perdre son berlingot** to lose one's virginity □ *or* cherry

berlue [bɛrly] *nf* **avoir la berlue** to be seeing things

berzingue [bɛrzɛ̃g] **à tout berzingue** *adv* at top speed, *Br* like the clappers, *Am* like sixty

bésef [bezɛf] *adv* **pas bésef** not a lot □, not much □; **dix euros par jour pour faire vivre une famille; ça fait pas bésef...** ten euros a day to keep a family, it's not loads

besogner [!] [bəzɔɲe] *vt* to hump, to screw, *Br* to shaft

bête [bɛt] *nf* **(a)** (*expert*) **être une bête (en)** to be brilliant (at) **(b)** **comme une bête** like crazy **(c)** **faire la bête à deux dos** to make the beast with two backs

béton¹ [betɔ̃] *vi* (*verlan* **tomber**) **laisse béton!** forget it!, drop it!

béton² [betɔ̃] *adj* (*argument*) cast-iron; **dis que ton train a déraillé, ça c'est une excuse béton!** say that your train was derailed, that's a cast-iron excuse!

bétonner [betɔne] *vt* (*préparer avec soin*) to work hard on □; **il a bétonné son discours/son dossier** he's worked really hard on his speech/his application

beu [bø] *nf* grass, weed, herb

beur [bœr], **beurette** [bœrɛt] *nm,f* (*verlan* **arabe**) = person born and living in France of North African immigrant parents

beurré, -e [bœre] *adj* (*ivre*) wasted, plastered, loaded, *Br* pissed, legless; **beurré comme un petit Lu** *Br* (as) pissed as a newt, *Am* stewed to the gills

bézef [bezɛf] = **bésef**

bi [bi] *adj inv* (*abbr* **bisexuel, -elle**) bi

biberonner [bibrɔne] *vi* to be a boozer *or* an alky *or* a lush; **qu'est-ce qu'il biberonne!** he can really put it away, he's a terrible boozer *or* alky *or* lush!

bibi [bibi] **1** *nm* (*chapeau*) (woman's) hat □ **2** *pron* (*moi*) yours truly; **et qui c'est qu'a payé l'addition? c'est bibi!** and who paid the bill? yours truly *or Br* muggins here!

biche [bibiʃ] *nf* sweetheart, honey, sugar

bibine [bibin] *nf* (*alcool*) gutrot, rotgut, *Am* alky; (*bière*) dishwater

bibite [bibit] *nf Can* animal □; **il fait froid en bibite** it's freezing, *Br* it's baltic; **être en bibite (contre qn)** to be teed off *or* hacked off (with sb)

bibli [bibli] *nf* (*abbr* **bibliothèque**) library □

biche [biʃ] *nf* **ma biche** darling, sweetheart

Le symbole □ indique que la traduction n'est pas argotique.

bicher [biʃe] vi (a) (bien se passer) **ça biche?** how's it going?, how are things? (b) (être satisfait) to be pleased as Punch or tickled pink; **ça me fait bicher** that makes me happy □; **ça le fait vraiment bicher d'être passé à la télé** he's as pleased as Punch or Br chuffed to bits that he was on TV

biclo [biklo], **biclou** [biklu] nm bike

bicoque [bikɔk] nf (maison) place, pad

bicot [biko] nm Offensive = racist term used to refer to a North African Arab

bicrave [bikrav], **bicraver** [bikrave] vt Cités to sell □, Br to flog; (drogue) to deal

bidasse [bidas] nm Br squaddie, Am grunt

bide [bid] nm (a) (ventre) belly, gut; **être gras du bide** to have a huge gut; **il n'a rien dans le bide** (il n'a pas de courage) he's got no guts or balls (b) (échec) flop, washout, Am bomb; **faire un bide** to be a flop or a washout, Am to bomb

bidoche [bidɔʃ] nf meat □; **j'ai renoncé à bouffer de la bidoche, c'est trop dangereux** I've stopped eating meat, it's too dangerous; **l'été est arrivé; les touristes déballent leur bidoche sur les plages** summer's here, the tourists are baring their flesh on the beaches

bidochon [bidɔʃɔ̃] nmf = stereotypical working-class, reactionary person

This word is an allusion to *Les Bidochon*, a comic strip by the cartoonist Binet, about an ordinary French couple who embody the stereotypical behaviour and values of the working class.

bidon [bidɔ̃] **1** adj inv phoney
  2 nm (a) (ventre) belly, gut (b) **c'est du bidon** it's a load of baloney or garbage or Br rubbish; **c'est pas du bidon** it's gospel, it's the honest truth; **c'est pas du bidon, il a vraiment mal** he's not putting it on, he's in real pain
  3 nmpl Belg **bidons** (habits) togs, gear, threads; (affaires) things □, stuff

bidonnant, -e [bidɔnɑ̃, -ɑ̃t] adj side-splitting, hysterical; **c'était bidonnant!**

it was a scream or a hoot!

bidonner [bidɔne] **1** vt to fix; **il est célèbre pour avoir bidonné une interview de Castro** he's famous for his hoax interview with Castro
  2 se bidonner vpr to kill oneself (laughing), to crack up, to laugh one's head off

bidouillage [biduja3] nm **c'est du bidouillage** it's just been thrown together; **j'appelle pas ça réparer la télé: c'est du bidouillage ce que tu nous as fait là** that's not repairing the TV, that's just patching it up

bidouiller [biduje] vt (bricoler) to tinker with; (trafiquer) to fiddle

bidous [bidu] nmpl Can dough; **avoir des bidous** to be loaded, Br to be rolling in it

bidule [bidyl] **1** nm (chose) thingy, whatsit
  2 npr **Bidule** (personne) thingy, what's-his-name, f what's-her-name

biffe [bif] nf **la biffe** the infantry □

biffeton [biftɔ̃] = **bifton**

biffin [bifɛ̃] nm (a) (soldat) infantryman □ (b) (personne ridicule) buffoon, clown

bifteck [biftɛk] nm **défendre son bifteck** to look after number one; **j'fais pas grève par plaisir mais pour défendre mon bifteck, mon gars!** I'm not on strike for the fun of it, pal, it's to protect my livelihood!; **gagner son bifteck** to earn one's crust or one's bread and butter

bifton [biftɔ̃] nm (billet de banque) note □, Am greenback; (de transport, de spectacle) ticket □

bigler [bigle] **1** vt (observer) to eyeball, to check out, Br to clock
  2 vi (loucher) to have a squint □

bigleux, -euse [biglø, -øz] adj (a) (qui louche) cross-eyed (b) (qui voit mal) short-sighted □

bigophone [bigɔfɔn] nm Br blower, Am horn

bigophoner [bigɔfɔne] vi to make a phone call □; **bigophoner à qn** to give sb a buzz or Br a bell

bigorner [bigɔrne] **1** vt to smash up, Br

Le symbole □ indique que la traduction n'est pas argotique.

to prang; **bigorner sa bagnole contre un arbre** to smash one's car into a tree

2 se bigorner *vpr* to have a scrap *or Br* a punch-up *or Am* a fist fight

bijoux [biʒu] *nmpl Hum* **les bijoux de famille** *(sexe de l'homme)* the crown jewels

bilan [bilã] *nm* **déposer le bilan** *(mourir)* to croak, to kick the bucket, *Br* to snuff it, *Am* to check out; *(déféquer)* to *Br* have *or Am* take a crap *or* a dump

bilingue [bilɛ̃g] **1** *adj Can (bisexuel)* bi
2 *nmf Can (bisexuel)* bi

billard [bijar] *nm* **passer sur le billard** to go under the knife

bille [bij] *nf* **(a)** *(visage)* face ᵁ, mug; **une bille de clown** a funny face ᵁ **(b) reprendre** *ou* **retirer ses billes** to pull out ᵁ *(from a deal)* **(c) toucher sa bille (en** *ou* **à)** to know a thing or two (about)

bimbo [bimbo] *nf* bimbo

bine [bin] *nf Can* **(a)** *(visage)* mug, face ᵁ **(b)** *Joual* **être dans les bines** to be out to lunch; **faire qch en criant bine** to do sth in a flash

> The Joual sense of the word comes from the English word "bean".

binerie [binri] *nf Can Joual Pej* greasy spoon

> This sense comes from the English word "bean".

binette [binɛt] *nf (visage)* face ᵁ, mug

bingo [biŋgo] *nm Can (révolte)* prison riot ᵁ

biniou [binju] *nm (téléphone) Br* blower, *Am* horn; **filer un coup de biniou** to make a phone call ᵁ; **filer un coup de biniou à qn** to give sb a buzz *or Br* a bell

binoclard, -e [binɔklar, -ard] *nm,f* foureyes, *Br* speccy

binz [bins] *nm* **(a)** *(chose compliquée)* **quel binz pour trouver sa maison!** it was a real performance *or* hassle *or Br* carry-on finding his house! **(b)** *(désordre)* shambles

bio [bjo] *nf (abbr* **biographie)** biog; **une bio d'Elvis** an Elvis biog

bique [bik] **1** *nm Offensive* = racist term used to refer to a North African Arab
2 *nf* **une vieille bique** an old bag

biroute [!] [birut] *nf* dick, knob, *Am* schlong

biscoteaux [biskɔto] *nmpl* biceps ᵁ

biscuit [biskɥi] *nm* **(a) tremper son biscuit** [!!] to dip one's wick **(b)** *(amende infligée à un automobiliste)* fine ᵁ

bisoune [bizun] *nf Can* **(a)** *(petite fille)* sweetheart; **ma bisoune** sweetheart, sweetie **(b)** *(pénis) Br* willy, *Am* weener

bistouquette [bistukɛt] *nf Br* willy, *Am* peter

bite [!!] [bit] *nf* dick, cock, prick, knob; **rentrer la bite sous le bras** to go home without getting laid *or Br* without getting one's oats

biter [!] [bite] *vt* **j'y bite rien** I don't understand a *Br* bloody *or Am* goddamn thing

bitoniau [bitɔnjo] *nm* thingy, whatsit, *Br* doodah, *Am* doodad

bitos [bitos] *nm* hat ᵁ

bitu [bity] *adj Belg (ivre)* plastered, drunk ᵁ

biture [bityr] *nf* **il tenait une de ces bitures!** he was completely plastered *or* wasted *or Br* legless *or* pissed!; **prendre une biture** to get plastered *or* wasted *or Br* legless *or* pissed

biturer [bityre] **se biturer** *vpr* to get plastered *or* wasted *or Br* legless *or* pissed

bizut [bizy] *nm* = first-year student in a "grande école"

bizutage [bizytaʒ] *nm Br* ragging, *Am* hazing *(in "grandes écoles")*

bizuter [bizyte] *vt Br* to rag, *Am* to haze *(in "grandes écoles")*

blabla [blabla] *nm inv* baloney, *Br* waffle

blablater [blablate] *vi* to waffle on, *Br* to witter on

black [blak] **1** *nmf (personne de race noire)* Black

2 *nm* **travailler au black** *(clandestinement)* = to work without declaring one's earnings; *(en plus de son travail habituel)* to moonlight

blague [blag] *nf* **(a) sans blague!** *(je t'assure)* no kidding!, it's true!; **sans blague?** *(est-ce vrai?)* no kidding?, yeah?; **j'ai fait la connaissance de ta sœur, elle est vachement plus bandante que toi, dis donc! blague!** I've met your sister, she's way hornier than you! joke! or just kidding! **(b) blagues à tabac** saggy boobs

blair, blaire [blɛr] *nm Br* conk, hooter, *Am* schnozzle, honker

blaireau, -x [blɛro] *nm (individu)* jerk, *Br* prat

blairer [blɛre] *vt* **je peux pas le blairer** I can't stand or stomach or *Br* stick him

blanche [blɑ̃ʃ] *nf (héroïne)* smack, scag, skag

Blanche-Neige [blɑ̃ʃnɛʒ] *nm inv Offensive* nigger, *Br* wog, *Am* coon

blase, blaze [blɑz] *nm* name ▫, handle, moniker

blé [ble] *nm (argent)* dough, *Br* dosh, *Am* bucks

blèche [blɛʃ] *adj* hideous, *Br* pig-ugly

bled [blɛd] *nm (localité)* place ▫; *Pej* hole, dump, dive

blème [blɛm] *nm Cités (abbr* **problème)** problem, *Br* prob

bleu [blø] *nm* **(a)** *(novice)* rookie, *Am* cherry
  (b) un petit bleu a telegram ▫
  (c) *(policier)* cop, *Br* plod, *Am* flatfoot
  (d) *Suisse (permis de conduire) Br* driving licence ▫, *Am* driver's license ▫
  (e) *Can* **avoir les bleus** *(être triste)* to have the blues; **prendre les bleus** *(devenir triste)* to get the blues; *(se mettre en colère)* to go crazy; **être dans les bleus** *(être ivre)* to be wasted

bleubite [bløbit] *nm* rookie, *Am* cherry

bleue [blø] *nf* **la grande bleue** the sea ▫; *(la Méditerranée)* the Med

bleusaille [bløzaj] *nf* **la bleusaille** the new recruits ▫, the rookies

blinde [blɛ̃d] **à toute blinde** *adv* at full speed, like lightning, *Br* like the clappers

blindé, -e [blɛ̃de] *adj* **(a)** *(ivre)* blitzed, plastered, wasted, loaded **(b) être blindé (de monde)** to be swarming or *Br* heaving (with people)

blinder [blɛ̃de] **1** *vi* to bomb along
  2 se blinder *vpr (s'enivrer)* to get blitzed or plastered or wasted or loaded

bloblote [blɔblɔt] *nf* **avoir la bloblote** to have the shakes

bloc [blɔk] *nm* **(a)** *(prison)* slammer, clink, *Br* nick, *Am* pen **(b)** *Can (tête)* head ▫, nut **(c)** *Belg (temps exécrable)* awful weather ▫; **quel bloc aujourd'hui!** the weather's so lousy today!

bloke [blɔk] *nm Can Joual Pej* English-speaking Canadian ▫

blondasse [blɔ̃das] *nf* brassy blonde

blonde [blɔ̃d] *nf Can* girlfriend ▫, *Br* bird

bloquer [blɔke] **1** *vt* **(a)** *Belg (examen)* to cram for, *Br* to swot for, *Am* to grind away for; *(matière)* to cram, *Br* to swot up, *Am* to grind away at **(b)** *Can* to fail ▫, to flunk
  2 *vi* **bloquer sur qn** to have the hots for sb, *Br* to fancy sb

blouser [bluze] *vt* **blouser qn** to put one over on sb, to take sb for a ride; **se faire blouser** to get taken for a ride

bluffer [blœfe] *vt (impressionner)* to blow away; **ils m'ont vraiment bluffé lors de leur passage à Paris** they really blew me away when they played Paris

bobard [bɔbar] *nm* fib, *Br* porky, whopper; **raconter des bobards** to tell fibs or *Br* porkies or whoppers

bobet [bɔbɛ] *Suisse* **1** *adj* dim, thick, *Am* dumb
  2 *nm Br* prat, *Am* jackass

bobinard ⚠ [bɔbinar] *nm* whorehouse, *Br* knocking shop

bobine [bɔbin] *nf (visage)* face ▫, mug

bobo [bobo] *nmf (abbr* **bourgeois(e) bohème)** bobo

bobonne [bɔbɔn] *nf* **(a)** *(épouse)* the old lady, *Br* the missus, her indoors **(b)** *Belg* grandma

Le symbole ▫ *indique que la traduction n'est pas argotique.*

boche [bɔʃ] *Offensive* **1** *adj* Kraut
2 *nmf* **Boche** *(personne)* Kraut

Depending on the context and the tone of voice used, this term may be either offensive or affectionately humorous. It is nonetheless inadvisable to use it unless one is quite sure of the reaction it will receive.

bœuf [bœf] **1** *adj* **faire un effet bœuf** to cause a stir, to make a splash
2 *nm* **(a)** **faire un bœuf** to have a jam session, to jam **(b)** **on n'est pas des bœufs** you can't treat us like slaves

bof [bɔf] *exclam* **c'était bien? – bof** was it good? – not particularly

Normally accompanied by an expression of utter indifference, this term is used in numerous situations to express a disdainful lack of enthusiasm.

bogarter [bɔgarte] *vi* to bogart a joint

bois [bwa] *nm* **ça envoie le bois** it's the business

boîte [bwat] *nf* **(a)** *(société)* firm □, company □ **(b)** **boîte (de nuit)** club, nightclub □; **sortir en boîte** to go clubbing **(c)** **boîte à ouvrage** [!!] box, twat, *Br* fanny; **boîte à pâté** [!!] *Br* dirtbox, arsehole, *Am* asshole ▸ *see also* **bachot**

boit-sans-soif [bwasɑ̃swaf] *nmf inv* alky, lush, boozer, *Am* juicer

bol [bɔl] *nm (chance)* luck □; **un coup de bol** a stroke of luck □; **manque de bol, il était déjà parti** as bad luck would have it, he'd already left □ ▸ *see also* **ras**

bombarder [bɔ̃barde] **1** *vt* **on l'a bombardé ministre** he's been made a minister out of the blue
2 *vi (fumer beaucoup)* to smoke like a chimney

bombe [bɔ̃b] *nf* **(a)** *(fête)* **faire la bombe** to party
  (b) *(jolie fille)* babe, knockout, *Br* cracker, *Am* hottie
  (c) **à toute bombe** at top speed, *Br* like the clappers, *Am* like sixty; **aller à toute bombe** to bomb along, to belt along

  (d) **c'est de la bombe!** *Br* it's fab!, *Am* it's awesome!

bomber [bɔ̃be] *vi* to bomb along, to belt along

bomme [bɔm] *nm Can Joual* tramp, *Am* bum

bommer [bɔme] *vi Can Joual* to bum around

bon app' [bɔnap] *exclam (abbr bon appétit)* enjoy your meal!, *Am* enjoy!

bonbec [bɔ̃bɛk] *nm (cachet d'ecstasy)* E, *Br* disco biscuit

bonbon [bɔ̃bɔ̃] **1** *adv* **coûter bonbon** to cost an arm and a leg *or* a bundle *or Br* a bomb
  2 [!] *nm* **(a)** *(clitoris)* clit **(b)** **bonbons** *(testicules)* balls, *Br* bollocks; **casser les bonbons à qn** to piss sb off, *Br* to get on sb's tits, *Am* to break sb's balls

bonhomme [bɔnɔm] *nm (mari)* old man; **elle a préféré venir sans son bonhomme** she preferred to come without her old man ▸ *see also* **nom**

bonjour [bɔ̃ʒur] *exclam* **bonjour l'ambiance/l'odeur!** what an atmosphere/a smell!; **bonjour les dégâts!** what a mess!

bonnard [bɔnar] *adj* **c'est bonnard!** cool!

bonne [bɔn] **1** *adj Cités (belle)* gorgeous, stunning, *Br* fit; **elle est bonne, la sœur de Frédo** Frédo's sister is a real babe *or Br* cracker
  2 *nf* **avoir qn à la bonne** to like sb □ ▸ *see also* **pâte, poire**

bonnet [bɔnɛ] *nm* **(a)** **un gros bonnet (de)** a big shot *or* big cheese (in) **(b)** **te casse pas le bonnet** don't worry about it □, don't let it bother you □

bonniche [bɔniʃ] *nf* servant □, *Br* skivvy

bord [bɔr] *nm* **sur les bords** a bit □, a tad; **il est un peu menteur sur les bords** he's a bit of a liar

bordel [!!] [bɔrdɛl] **1** *nm* **(a)** *(maison close)* brothel □, whorehouse, *Br* knocking shop **(b)** *(désordre)* shambles, mess; **foutre le bordel (dans)** *(mettre en désordre)* to make a fucking mess (of); **il fout le**

bordel en classe he creates fucking havoc in the classroom
2 *exclam* fuck!; **bordel de merde!** fucking hell!; **mais qu'est-ce qu'il fout, bordel!** what the fuck is he doing?

bordélique [bɔrdelik] *adj* **être bordélique** *(endroit, situation)* to be a mess *or* a shambles; *(personne)* to be messy

borgne [bɔrɲ] *nm Hum* **étrangler le borgne** *(se masturber)* to bang *or Br* bash the bishop

borne [bɔrn] *nf (kilomètre)* kilometre □; **la pompe à essence la plus proche est à quinze bornes** the nearest *Br* petrol station *or Am* gas station is fifteen kilometres away

bosse [bɔs] *nf* **rouler sa bosse** to knock about; **il a roulé sa bosse un peu partout** he's been around a bit

bosser[1] [bɔse] *vi* to work □; **bosser comme un nègre** to slog one's guts out

bosser[2] [bɔse] *vt Can Joual* to boss around; **arrête de me bosser!** stop bossing me around!

bosseur, -euse [bɔsœr, -øz] **1** *adj* hard-working □
2 *nm,f* hard worker □

botcher [bɔtʃe] *vt Can Joual* to botch

botte [bɔt] *nf* **en avoir plein les bottes** to be *Br* knackered *or Am* pooped; **lécher les bottes à qn** to lick sb's boots; **chier dans les bottes à qn** ‼ to piss sb off, *Br* to get on sb's tits, *Am* to break sb's balls; **il lui a proposé la botte** ! he asked her straight out to sleep with him; *Belg* **être bien dans ses bottes** to have a fair bit (of money) tucked away; *Belg* **être** *or* **se sentir droit dans ses bottes** to have an easy conscience □; *Belg* **avoir une pièce dans ses bottes** to have had one too many

botter [bɔte] *vt* **(a)** *(plaire à)* **ça me botte** I like it □, I dig it; **ça te botterait d'y aller?** do you want to go? □, *Br* do you fancy going?
(b) *(donner des coups de pied à)* **botter le cul à qn** ! to give sb *Br* a boot up the arse *or Am* a kick in the ass; **botter les fesses** *ou* **le train à qn** to give sb a kick

in the pants; **à chaque fois qu'on lui pose une question à propos du scandale, le ministre s'empresse de botter en touche** every time the minister gets asked a question about the scandal, he dodges the issue

bottine [bɔtin] *nf Can* **avoir les deux pieds dans la même bottine** *(être maladroit)* to be all (fingers and) thumbs; *(trébucher souvent)* to have two left feet; *(être gaffeur)* to be always putting one's foot in it

boucan [bukɑ̃] *nm* racket, din

boucane [bukan] *nf Can* smoke □

bouché, -e [buʃe] *adj* **être bouché (à l'émeri)** *Br* to be thick (as two short planks), *Am* to have rocks in one's head

boucher [buʃe] *vt* **en boucher un coin à qn** to leave sb flabbergasted *or Br* gobsmacked

boucler [bukle] *vt* **(a)** *(fermer)* to shut □, to close □; **boucler la lourde** to shut *or* close the door □ **(b)** *(emprisonner)* to lock up □, to put away □ **(c) la boucler** *(se taire)* to shut up, to button it, *Br* to belt up; **tu vas la boucler?** shut up *or* button it *or Br* belt up, will you?

boudin [budɛ̃] *nm* **(a)** *(femme laide)* dog, *Br* boot, *Am* beast **(b) faire du boudin** to be in a *or* the huff ▸ see also **eau, rond**

bouffarde [bufard] *nf* pipe □

bouffe [buf] *nf* **(a)** *(aliments)* food □, eats, chow, grub **(b)** *(repas)* meal □; **faire la bouffe** to do the cooking □; **se faire une bouffe** to have a meal together □

bouffer [bufe] **1** *vt (manger)* to eat □; **bouffer de l'essence** to be a gas-guzzler; **bouffer du kilomètre** to clock up a lot of miles; **bouffer du curé/du coco** to be a priest-/commie-hater
2 *vi* to eat □
3 se bouffer *vpr* **se bouffer le nez** to have a shouting match, *Br* to have a go at each other ▸ see also **chancre, vache**

bouffi [bufi] *nm* **tu l'as dit, bouffi!** you said it!, *Am* you said a mouthful!

bouffon [bufɔ̃] *nm (personne ridicule)* buffoon, clown

Le symbole □ indique que la traduction n'est pas argotique.

bougeotte [buʒɔt] *nf* **avoir la bougeotte** to be fidgety; *(beaucoup voyager)* to gad around

bouger [buʒe] *vi (sortir)* to make a move, to move on; **on bouge?** shall we make a move?

bougnoul, bougnoule [buɲul] *nm Offensive* = racist term used to refer to a North African Arab

boui-boui [bwibwi] *nm* greasy spoon

bouillave [bujav], **bouillaver** [bujave] *vt Cités* to screw, to hump, *Br* to shag

bouille [buj] *nf (visage)* face □, mug; **avoir une bonne bouille** to look nice □

bouillie [buji] *nf* **de la bouillie pour les chats** *(texte)* a load of garbage *or Br* rubbish

bouillon [bujɔ̃] *nm (eau)* water □; **tomber dans le bouillon** to fall in □; **boire le bouillon** *(avaler de l'eau)* to get a mouthful of water □; *(faire faillite)* to go bust

boule [bul] *nf* **(a)** *(tête)* **perdre la boule** to crack up, to lose one's marbles, to go round the bend, *Br* to lose the plot; **donner un coup de boule à qn** to headbutt sb; **prendre un coup de boule** to get headbutted; **avoir la boule à zéro** to have a skinhead *(haircut)*
(b) *(angoisse)* **avoir les boules** to be upset □; **ça me fout les boules** it makes me upset; **les boules!** how awful!
(c) **se mettre en boule** to hit the roof *or Am* ceiling, to blow one's top *or Am* stack, to fly off the handle
(d) boules ⚠ *(testicules)* balls, nuts

bouler [bule] *vi* **envoyer bouler qn** to tell sb where to go, *Br* to send sb packing

boulette [bulɛt] *nf (erreur) Br* boob, *Am* boo-boo; **faire une boulette** to make a *Br* boob *or Am* boo-boo

Boul' Mich' [bulmiʃ] *npr* **le Boul' Mich'** = the Boulevard Saint-Michel in Paris

boulonner [bulɔne] *vi* to work □

boulot [bulo] *nm* work □; *(tâche, emploi)* job □; **se mettre au boulot** to get to work □, to get down to it

boulotter [bulɔte] *vi* to eat □

boum [bum] **1** *nf* party □ *(for young people)*
2 *nm* **être en plein boum** to be up to one's neck, to be rushed off one's feet

boumer [bume] *vi* **ça boume?** how are things?, how's it going?

bounty [bunti] *nm* = black person who has adopted the lifestyle and values of a white person, *Br* Bounty bar, *Am* oreo (cookie)

> This term, in a similar way to its English equivalents, comes from the fact that a Bounty® chocolate bar is dark on the outside and white on the inside.

bouquin [bukɛ̃] *nm* book □; **bouquin de cul** skin mag

bouquiner [bukine] *vi* to read □

bourdon [burdɔ̃] *nm* **avoir le bourdon** *(être déprimé)* to feel down, to be on a downer

bourge [burʒ] *Pej (abbr* **bourgeois, -e) 1** *adj* middle-class □
2 *nmf* middle-class person □

bourgeoise [burʒwaz] *nf (épouse)* old lady, *Br* missis

bourlinguer [burlɛ̃ge] *vi* to knock about

bourrage [buraʒ] *nm* **bourrage de crâne** *ou* **de mou** brainwashing □, eyewash

bourre [bur] **1** *nm* cop
2 *nf* **être à la bourre** to be running late □; **coup de bourre** busy time □; **entre midi et deux heures c'est le coup de bourre** it's crazy between twelve and two

bourré, -e [bure] *adj* wasted, plastered, *Br* legless, pissed ▸ *see also* **coing**

bourre-pif [burpif] *nm inv* punch on the nose □

bourrer [bure] **1** ⚠⚠ *vt (posséder sexuellement)* to hump, *Br* to poke, to shaft
2 *vi (aller très vite)* to belt along, to bomb along
3 se bourrer *vpr* **se bourrer la gueule** ⚠ to get shit-faced *or Br* ratarsed *or* pissed ▸ *see also* **mou**

bourrichon [buriʃɔ̃] *nm* **monter le**

bourrichon à qn to put ideas in sb's head; **se monter le bourrichon** to get carried away

bourrin [burɛ̃] **1** adj (qui manque de raffinement) oafish ▫; **il est un peu bourrin avec ses blagues de cul, mon cousin** he's a bit of a Neanderthal, my cousin, what with his dirty jokes

2 nm (a) (cheval) horse ▫ (b) (policier) cop, pig (c) (femme laide) dog, Br boot, Am beast

bourrique [burik] nf (a) (personne têtue) pig-headed person (b) **être soûl comme une bourrique** Br to be (as) pissed as a newt or a fart, Am to be stewed to the gills (c) **faire tourner qn en bourrique** to drive sb round the bend

bouseux, -euse [buzø, -øz] nm,f Pej yokel, peasant, Am hick, hayseed

bousiller [buzije] vt to wreck, to bust, Br to knacker

boussole [busɔl] nf **perdre la boussole** to crack up, to lose one's marbles, to go round the bend or Br the twist

boustifaille [bustifaj] nf food ▫, chow, grub

bout [bu] nm (a) **‼** (sexe de l'homme) dick, prick, cock; **se mettre une femme sur le bout** to get laid, Br to get one's end away; **s'astiquer le bout** to jerk off, Br to toss oneself off, to wank off (b) **tenir le bon bout** to be on the right track; Can **dans mon bout** in my neck of the woods; Can **au bout** great, Br fab ▶ see also **mettre**

boutanche [butɑ̃ʃ] nf bottle ▫ (usually of wine or spirits)

bouteille [butɛj] nf (âge) **avoir de la bouteille** to have been around a long time; **prendre de la bouteille** to be getting on a bit

boutique [butik] nf (a) **parler boutique** to talk shop (b) (sexe de l'homme) dick, Br tadger, Am schlong

bouton **!** [butɔ̃] nm (clitoris) clit

boxon **‼** [bɔksɔ̃] nm (a) (maison close) brothel ▫, whorehouse, Br knocking shop · (b) (désordre) mess, shambles; **foutre le boxon (dans)** (mettre en désordre) to make a fucking mess (of); **il fout le boxon en classe** he creates fucking havoc in the classroom

bracelets [braslɛ] nmpl (menottes) cuffs, bracelets

braire [brɛr] vi **ça me fait braire** it hacks me off, Br it gets up my nose or does my head in, Am it gives me a pain

branché, -e [brɑ̃ʃe] adj (bar, discothèque, personne) hip, trendy; **être branché cinéma/jazz** to be into movies/jazz

brancher [brɑ̃ʃe] **1** vt (a) (plaire à) **ça me branche** I'm really into it; **ça me brancherait de venir avec vous** I'd be into coming with you

(b) (pour séduire) Br to chat up, Am to hit on

(c) (mettre en contact) **brancher qn avec qn** to introduce sb to sb ▫

(d) (faire parler) **brancher qn sur un sujet** to get sb started or to start sb off on a subject

2 se brancher vpr to decide ▫, to make up one's mind ▫

branchitude [brɑ̃ʃityd] nf hipness, trendiness; **cette boîte est l'un des hauts lieux de la branchitude parisienne** this club is one of the trendiest or hippest in Paris

branlée **!** [brɑ̃le] nf (défaite, correction) thrashing, pasting; **prendre une branlée** to get thrashed, to Br get or Am take a pasting

branler [brɑ̃le] **1** **‼** vt to jerk off, Br to toss off, to wank off; **j'en ai rien à branler** I don't give a (flying) fuck or a shit; **mais qu'est-ce qu'il branle?** what the fuck is he doing?, what the fuck is he up to?

2 vi Can to hum and haw

3 **‼** **se branler** vpr to jerk off, Br to toss oneself off, to wank, to have a wank; **s'en branler** not to give a (flying) fuck or a shit

branlette **‼** [brɑ̃lɛt] nf hand-job, Br wank; **se faire une branlette** to jerk off, Br to toss oneself off, to wank, to have a wank; **faire une branlette à qn** to give sb a hand-job, to jerk sb off, Br to toss sb off, to wank sb off

Le symbole ▫ indique que la traduction n'est pas argotique.

branleur, -euse [!] [brɑ̃lœr, -øz] *nm,f*
loser, *Br* waster, *Am* slacker

branleux, -euse [brɑ̃lø, -øz] *Can* **1** *adj*
(qui hésite) dithering □; *(lâche)* chicken
  2 *nm,f (qui hésite)* ditherer □; *(lâche)*
chicken

branque [brɑ̃k] **1** *adj (fou)* bonkers, nuts,
Br off one's head, barking *(mad)*
  2 *nmf (imbécile)* dope, jerk, *Br* prat, *Am*
feeb; *(fou) Br* nutter, headcase, *Am*
wacko, screwball

braque [brak] *adj* crazy, off one's rocker,
Br mental

braquemart [!] [brakmar] *nm* dick,
prick, *Br* knob

braquer [brake] *vt* **(a)** *(voler)* **braquer
une banque/une bijouterie** to hold up
a bank/a jeweller's; **braquer qch à qn** to
pinch *or Br* nick sth from sb **(b)** *(rendre
hostile)* **braquer qn** *Br* to get sb's back
up, *Am* to tick sb off

braqueur, -euse [brakœr, -øz] *nm,f*
armed robber □

bras [brɑ] *nm* **un gros bras** a big guy;
jouer les gros bras to act the tough
guy ▶ see also **bite, pine, yeux**

brêle [brɛl] *nf* **(a)** *(cyclomoteur)* (motor)
scooter □, moped □ **(b)** *(personne)* cretin,
jerk, *Br* tosspot, *Am* fathead

Brésilienne [breziljɛn] *nf (prostitué)* =
Brazilian transsexual or transvestite male
prostitute

bretelles [brətɛl] *nfpl* **remonter les
bretelles à qn** to bawl sb out, *Br* to give
sb an earful, *Am* to chew sb out; **se faire
remonter les bretelles** to get bawled
out, *Br* to get an earful, *Am* to get chewed
out ▶ see also **piano**

bretter [brete] *Can* **1** *vt (chercher)* to look
for □, to be after; **qu'est-ce que tu
brettes ici?** what are you poking around
here for?
  2 *vi* to dawdle

bretteux, -euse [brøtø, -øz] *Can* **1** *adj*
(lent) dawdling; *(fainéant)* lazy □
  2 *nm,f (personne lente) Br* slowcoach,
Am slowpoke; *(fainéant) Br* waster, *Am*
slacker

bricheton [briʃtɔ̃] *nm* bread □

bricole [brikɔl] *nf (chose insignifiante)*
little thing □; **il va lui arriver des bricoles** he's heading for trouble

bricoler [brikɔle] *vi* **(a)** *(faire des petits
boulots)* to do odd jobs, to do this and that
(b) *(se livrer à de menus travaux)* to mess
around, to potter around

bridé, -e [bride] *nm,f Offensive* slant, *Am*
gook

briffer [brife] *vt & vi (manger)* to eat □;
bon, moi j'irais bien briffer right, I'm
up for some grub

brignolet [briɲɔlɛ] *nm* bread □

bringue [brɛ̃g] *nf* **(a)** *(fête)* **faire la
bringue** to party, *Br* to go on the razzle
(b) **une grande bringue** a beanpole

brioche [brijɔʃ] *nf* **avoir de la brioche**
to have a paunch *or* a pot-belly; **prendre
de la brioche** to be getting a paunch *or* a
pot-belly

brique [brik] *nf (dix mille francs)* ten thousand francs □ ▶ see also **casser**

briser [brize] *vt* **il/ça me les brise** he/it
really bugs me *or* hacks me off *or Br* gets
up my nose *or* does my head in

Bronx [brɔ̃ks] *npr* **mettre le Bronx
dans qch** to turn sth upside down, to
make a mess of sth

bronze [brɔ̃z] *nm* **couler un bronze** [!!]
to *Br* have *or Am* take a dump *or* a crap,
Br to drop a log

bronzé, -e [brɔ̃ze] *nm,f Offensive* nigger,
Br darky, *Am* coon

brosse [brɔs] *nf* **prendre une brosse** to
get wrecked *or* smashed *or Br* slaughtered
or pissed; **être en brosse** to be smashed
or pissed

brosser [brɔse] **1** *vt Belg* **brosser un
cours** *Br* to skive off, *Am* to cut a class
  2 **se brosser** *vpr* to do without; **tu
peux te brosser pour que je te prête
ma caisse, maintenant!** if you think I'm
going to lend you my car now, you can forget it!

brosseur, -euse [brɔsœr, -øz] *nm,f*
Belg = pupil who skips school, truant □

Le symbole □ indique que la traduction n'est pas argotique.

broue [bʁu] nf Can lather □; **faire** ou **péter de la broue** to show off; **péteur de broue** show-off

brouille-ménage [bʁujmenaʒ] nm inv red wine □, Br plonk

brouter [bʁute] vt **les brouter à qn** ! to piss sb off, Br to get on sb's tits, Am to break sb's balls; **brouter la tige à qn** !! to go down on sb, to suck sb off, to give sb head; **brouter le cresson à qn** !! to go down on sb, Br to lick sb out

brouteuse !! [bʁutøz] nf dyke

brûlé, -e [bʁyle] adj **être brûlé** (être compromis) to be finished

brut [bʁyt] adj **brut de décoffrage** rough and ready; **il est gentil, son père, mais il est un peu brut de décoffrage: n'espère pas parler philosophie avec lui** his dad's nice but he's a bit rough and ready, don't hope for any philosophical conversations with him

"Brut de décoffrage" literally refers to a type of untreated concrete.

bûche [byʃ] nf **ramasser une bûche** (tomber) to go flying, to measure one's length

bûcher [byʃe] **1** vt Br to swot up on, Am to bone up on
2 vi Br to swot, Am to bone up

bûcheur, -euse [byʃœʁ, -øz] **1** adj hardworking □
2 nm,f hard worker □

buffet [byfɛ] nm (ventre) belly; **il s'est pris une bastos dans le buffet** he took a bullet right in the belly

bulle [byl] nf **(a)** (à un devoir) zero □, Am goose egg; **prendre une bulle** to get a zero □ or Am a goose egg **(b) coincer la bulle** to get some shut-eye or some Br zeds or Am zees ▶ see also **chier**

buller [byle] vi to laze about

burettes ! [byʁɛt] nfpl (testicules) balls, nuts, Br bollocks; **se vider les burettes** !! to shoot one's load; **casser les burettes à qn** to piss sb off, Br to get on sb's tits, Am to break sb's balls

burlingue [byʁlɛ̃g] nm office □

burnes !! [byʁn] nfpl balls, nuts, Br bollocks; **se vider les burnes** to shoot one's load; **casser les burnes à qn** to piss sb off, Br to get on sb's tits, Am to break sb's balls

buser [byze] vt Belg (recaler) **il a été busé** he failed □, Am he flunked

buter [byte] vt to kill □, Br to do in, Am to eighty-six; **se faire buter** to get killed □, Br to get done in, Am to get eighty-sixed

buvable [byvabl] adj **pas buvable** (très antipathique) unbearable □; **c'est un mec pas buvable** he's a complete pain (in the neck)

buvard [byvaʁ] nm (dose de LSD) tab, trip

Byzance [bizɑ̃s] npr **c'est Byzance** it's the last word in luxury; **c'est pas Byzance** it's not exactly luxurious

C

cabane [kaban] *nf (prison)* slammer, clink, *Br* nick, *Am* joint; **en cabane** in the slammer *or* clink *or Br* nick *or Am* joint

cabanon [kabanɔ̃] *nm* **il est bon pour le cabanon** he should be put away

câblé, -e [kɑble] *adj (à la page)* hip, trendy

cabochard, -e [kabɔʃar, -ard] *adj* pig-headed

caboche [kabɔʃ] *nf* head □, nut

cabot [kabo] *nm (chien)* mutt

caca [kaka] *nm* poo, poop; **il nous fait un caca nerveux, l'autre!** he's having kittens!, he's having a fit! ▶ *see also* **nez**

cacaille [kakɑj] *nf Belg* piece of junk

cacheton [kaʃtɔ̃] *nm (cachet d'artiste)* fee □; **courir le cacheton** = to try to get little jobs here and there

cachetonner [kaʃtɔne] *vi (artiste)* = to try to get little jobs here and there

cacou [kaku] *nm* **faire le cacou** to act smart, to show off

cadavre [kadavr] *nm (bouteille vide)* empty, *Br* dead man

cadeau, -x [kado] *nm* **ce mec, c'est pas un cadeau!** that guy's a total pain (in the neck)!

cador [kadɔr] *nm* (**a**) *(chien)* mutt (**b**) *(personne influente)* big shot, big cheese, bigwig, *Am* heavy hitter; *(d'une bande)* leader □

cafard [kafar] *nm* (**a**) *(tristesse)* **avoir le cafard** *ou* **un coup de cafard** to feel down *or* low; **ça m'a foutu le cafard** it got me down (**b**) *(délateur)* sneak, tell-tale, *Am* snitch

cafarder [kafarde] **1** *vt* **cafarder qn** to sneak on sb, to tell tales on sb, *Am* to snitch on sb

2 *vi* (**a**) *(être triste)* to feel down *or* low (**b**) *(rapporter)* sneak, to tell tales, to snitch

cafardeur, -euse [kafardœr, -øz] *nm,f* sneak, tell-tale, snitch

cafardeux, -euse [kafardø, -øz] *adj (personne)* down, low

cafèt' [kafɛt] *nf (abbr cafétéria)* cafeteria □

cafeter [kafte] = **cafter**

cafeteur, -euse [kaftœr, -øz] = **cafteur**

cafetière [kaftjɛr] *nf (tête)* head □, nut

cafouiller [kafuje] *vi* (**a**) *(mal fonctionner)* to be a shambles *or* a muddle; *(machine)* to play up, to be on the blink *or Am* on the fritz (**b**) *(s'embrouiller)* to get in a muddle, to tie oneself in knots

cafouillis [kafuji] *nm* shambles, muddle

cafter [kafte] *vi* to sneak, to tell tales, to snitch

cafteur, -euse [kaftœr, -øz] *nm,f* sneak, tell-tale, snitch

cage [kaʒ] *nf* (**a**) **cage à lapins** *(logement)* rabbit hutch; **il habite dans les cages à lapin, à côté de la zone industrielle** he lives in those rabbit hutches beside the industrial estate (**b**) *(buts)* goal □ *(posts, nets)*

cageot [kaʒo] *nm (femme laide)* dog, *Br* boot, *Am* beast, skank

cagnard [kaɲar] *nm (soleil)* blazing sunshine □; **quel cagnard!** what a scorcher!, *Br* it's roasting!

cagoule [kagul] *nf (préservatif)* condom, rubber, *Br* Durex®

caïd [kaid] *nm (gros bonnet)* big shot, big cheese, bigwig; *(d'une bande)* leader □; **jouer les caïds** to act tough, *Br* to act the hard man

caillassage [kajasaʒ] *nm* throwing *Br*

---

stones or Am rocks (**de** at) ▫; **il a été très souvent question du caillassage des bus dans les banlieues chaudes** the fact that, in the rougher areas, buses often got pelted with Br stones or Am rocks was much talked about

caillasse [kajas] nf (a) Cités (argent) dough, bread, Br dosh, Am bucks, gelt (b) (pierre) Br stone ▫, Am rock ▫

caillasser [kajase] vt to chuck stones at

caille¹ [kaj] nf **ma caille** honey, sweetheart

caille² [kaj] nf Cités (abbr **caillera**) scum

cailler [kaje] **1** v imp **ça caille** it's freezing or Br baltic, Br it's brass monkeys
2 se cailler vpr to be freezing; **se les cailler** ▫! to be freezing one's Br arse or Am ass off

caillera [kajra] nf Cités (verlan **racaille**) scum

caillou, -x [kaju] nm (a) (tête) head ▫, nut; **il a plus un poil sur le caillou** he's as bald as a coot; **elle en a dans le caillou** she's a smart cookie (b) (pierre précieuse) rock, sparkler

cainf [kɛ̃f], **cainfri** [kɛ̃fri] nmf (verlan **Africain**) African ▫

cainri [kɛ̃ri] **1** adj (verlan **ricain**) Yank, Br Yankee
2 nm Yank, Br Yankee

caisse [kɛs] nf (a) (voiture) car ▫, wheels, Br motor (b) **passer à la caisse** (être payé) to collect (c) (pet) **lâcher** ou **larguer une caisse** ▫! to fart, Br to let off, Am to lay one

cake [kɛk] nm (imbécile) dope, jerk, moron, Br plonker, Am goober

calancher [kalɑ̃ʃe] vi to croak, Br to snuff it, Am to check out

calbar [kalbar], **calbute** [kalbyt] nm Br scants, Am shorts, skivvies

calcaire [kalkɛr] nm **avoir** ou **faire un coup de calcaire** to have a fit, to go off (at) the deep end

calcif [kalsif] = **calbar**

calculer [kalkyle] vt (regarder) to check out, to eye (up)

calculette [kalkylɛt] nf pizza face; **elle sort avec un mec, une vraie calculette!** she's going out with this real pizza face guy

The literal sense of the word is "calculator". People with acne are so called because in French the word "bouton" means both "button" (of a calculator, for example) and "pimple".

calebar [kalbar], **calecif** [kalsif] = **calbar**

calendos [kalɑ̃dos] nm Camembert ▫

caleter [kalte] = **calter**

calibre [kalibr] nm (pistolet) shooter, Am piece, equalizer

câlice [kalis] Can Joual **1** nm bastard; **mon câlice!** you bastard!; **en câlice** Br dead, Am real; **il fait froid en câlice** it's freezing or Br baltic; **être en câlice (contre qn)** to be fuming mad (with sb)
2 exclam shit!

câlicer [kalise] vt Can Joual (a) (laisser) to drop; **il a tout câlicé là et il est parti** he dropped everything and left (b) (mettre) to stick; **je vais te câlicer mon poing dans la face** I'm going to sock you one, I'm going to Br bloody well smack you one

calmos [kalmos] exclam chill (out)!, take it easy!

calots [kalo] nmpl (yeux) eyes ▫

calotte [kalɔt] nf **la calotte** (le clergé) the clergy ▫

calter [kalte] vi to beat it, Br to clear off, Am to split

calva [kalva] nm (abbr **calvados**) Calvados ▫

calvaire [kalvɛr] **1** nm Can Joual (juron) bastard; **mon calvaire!** you bastard!
2 exlam shit!

cama [kama] nm Belg (abbr **camarade**) pal, Br mate, Am buddy

Camarde [kamard] nf **la Camarde** death ▫

cambrouse [kɑ̃bruz], **cambrousse** [kɑ̃brus] nf **la cambrousse** the sticks,

Le symbole ▫ indique que la traduction n'est pas argotique.

Am the boondocks; **en pleine cambrousse** in the sticks, in the middle of nowhere, *Br* in the back of beyond

cambuse [kãbyz] *nf* dump, hole, hovel

came [kam] *nf* drugs □, stuff, *Br* gear

camé, -e [kame] **1** *adj* **être camé** to be on something; **il était complètement camé** he was totally loaded *or* wrecked *or* wasted

2 *nm,f* druggie, junkie, *Am* dope fiend

camelote [kamlɔt] *nf* **(a)** *(marchandise)* stuff, *Br* gear **(b)** *(objets de mauvaise qualité)* trash, junk, garbage, *Br* rubbish

camer [kame] **se camer** *vpr* to do drugs; **se camer à l'héroïne/à la cocaïne** to be on heroin/cocaine; **il s'est jamais camé à l'héroïne** he's never done heroin

camp [kã] *nm* **ficher le camp** to clear off, to beat it, *Am* to split; **foutre le camp** ! to go to hell, *Br* to piss off, to bugger off; **fiche(-moi) le camp!** get lost!, beat it!, *Br* sling your hook!, *Am* take a walk!; **fous(-moi) le camp!** ! go to hell!, get the hell out of here!, *Br* piss off!, bugger off!

canard [kanar] *nm* **(a)** *(journal)* rag **(b)** **il fait un froid de canard** it's freezing, *Br* it's baltic ▸ *see also* **casser**

canarder [kanarde] *vt* to snipe at □, to take pot shots at

canasson [kanasɔ̃] *nm* horse □, nag

cané, -e [kane] *adj (épuisé) Br* knackered, shattered, *Am* beat

caner[1] [kane] *vi (renoncer)* to throw in the towel, to chuck it in

caner[2]**, canner** [kane] *vi* **(a)** *(mourir)* to croak, *Br* to snuff it, *Am* to cash in (one's chips) **(b)** *(s'enfuir)* to beat it, *Br* to leg it, *Am* to bug out

cannes [kan] *nfpl (jambes)* legs □, pins; **il est tellement crevé qu'il tient plus sur ses cannes** he's so done in he can hardly stand

canon [kanɔ̃] **1** *adj inv* gorgeous, stunning, *Br* fit

2 *nm (belle femme)* babe, knockout, *Br* smasher, *Am* hottie

canter [kãte] **se canter** *vpr Can* to crash, to hit the sack *or Am* the rack

cantoche [kãtɔʃ] *nf* canteen □

caoua [kawa] = **kawa**

cap [kap] *adj (abbr* **capable) t'es pas cap de…!** I bet you can't…!

capo [kapo] *nm (abbr* **caporal)** *Br* ≃ lance corporal □, *Am* ≃ private first class □

capote [kapɔt] *nf* **capote (anglaise)** condom □, French letter, *Br* Durex®, rubber

capoté, -e [kapɔte] **1** *adj Can* wasted, out of it

2 *nm,f* wacko

capoter [kapɔte] *vi Can (perdre la tête)* to flip, to lose it

capter [kapte] *vt (comprendre)* to get; **répète, j'ai pas capté** say that again, I didn't get it

carabiné, -e [karabine] *adj (café, cocktail)* powerful □; *(rhume)* stinking; *(fièvre)* raging □; **tenir une cuite carabinée** to be off one's face *or* totally plastered *or Br* completely legless

carabistouille [karabistuj] *nf Belg* **(a)** *(mensonge)* **raconter des carabistouilles** to talk nonsense **(b)** *(escroquerie)* con

carafe [karaf] **en carafe** *adv* **rester en carafe** to be left stranded □ *or* high and dry; **je comptais sur lui mais il m'a laissé en carafe** I was counting on him but he left me high and dry; **tomber en carafe** *(en panne)* to break down □

carafon [karafɔ̃] *nm (tête)* head □, nut; **il a vraiment rien dans le carafon** he's got nothing between his ears, *Br* he's as thick as two short planks, *Am* he's got rocks in his head

carapater [karapate] **se carapater** *vpr* to scram, to make oneself scarce

carat [kara] *nm* **dernier carat** *(dernière limite)* at the very most □, max, tops

carburer [karbyre] *vi* **il carbure au whisky/au café** whisky/coffee keeps him going

carne [karn] *nf* bad-quality meat □;

vieille **carne** old bag, old witch

caroline [karɔlin] *nf* (a) *(homosexuel passif)* bitch (b) *(travesti)* TV, *Br* tranny

carotter [karɔte] *vt* **carotter qch à qn** *(dérober)* to pinch or *Br* nick sth from sb; *(escroquer)* to swindle or *Br* do sb out of sth

carpette [karpɛt] *nf (lâche)* doormat; **jamais il tiendra tête à sa bonne femme, c'est une vraie carpette!** he'll never stand up to his wife, he's such a doormat

carreaux [karo] *nmpl (lunettes)* specs

carrer [kare] *vt* **tu peux te le carrer dans le cul** *ou* **dans l'oignon!** !!! you can shove or stick it up your *Br* arse or *Am* ass!

carte [kart] *nf Belg* **taper la carte** to play cards ▢

carton [kartɔ̃] *nm* (a) **faire un carton** *(tirer sur quelqu'un)* to take pot shots at somebody; *(avoir du succès)* to be a hit (b) **(se) prendre un carton** *(essuyer une défaite)* to get thrashed or *Br* trounced; *(avoir une mauvaise note)* to get a bad mark ▢ (c) **taper le carton** *(jouer aux cartes)* to have a game of cards ▢

cartonner [kartɔne] *vi* (a) *(avoir une bonne note)* to pass with flying colours (b) *(musique)* to be mind-blowing

casbah [kazba] *nf (maison)* place, pad, *Br* gaff

case [kaz] *nf* **il lui manque une case** he's got a screw loose, he's off his rocker, he's not all there; **retour à la case départ!** back to square one!

cash [kaʃ] *adv* **payer cash** to pay cash ▢; **y aller cash** *(sans détour)* to get straight to the point, not to mince one's words; **alors je le lui ai dit comme ça, cash** so I just told him straight out

casquer [kaske] *vt & vi* (a) *(payer)* to fork out, to cough up (b) **être casqué !** *(porter un préservatif)* to be wearing a *Br* Durex® or *Am* rubber; **faut pas baiser sans être casqué, c'est trop risqué** best not to ride bareback, it's too risky

casquette [kaskɛt] *nf* (a) **avoir la**

casquette de plomb *ou* **en zinc** to have a hangover ▢, to be hungover ▢ (b) *Cités (contrôleur dans les transports en commun)* ticket inspector ▢ ▸ see also **ras**

casse [kas] **1** *nm* break-in ▢, *Am* heist; **faire un casse chez un bijoutier** to *Br* do over or *Am* boost a jeweller's

2 *nf* trouble; **va y avoir de la casse** there's going to be trouble

cassé, -e [kase] *adj (drogué)* stoned, wrecked, flying; *(ivre)* smashed, plastered, *Br* legless

casse-bonbons ! [kasbɔ̃bɔ̃] **1** *adj inv* **être casse-bonbons** to be a pain (in the neck)

2 *nmf inv* pain (in the neck)

casse-couilles !! [kaskuj] **1** *adj inv* **être casse-couilles** to be a pain in the *Br* arse or *Am* ass

2 *nmf inv* pain in the *Br* arse or *Am* ass

casse-cul !! [kasky] **1** *adj inv* **être casse-cul** to be a pain in the *Br* arse or *Am* ass

2 *nmf inv* pain in the *Br* arse or *Am* ass

casse-dalle [kasdal] *nm inv* sandwich ▢, *Br* butty, sarny

casse-graine [kasgrɛn] *nm inv* snack ▢

casse-gueule [kasgœl] *adj inv (sport, acrobaties)* death-defying ▢; *(entreprise)* risky ▢, *Br* dodgy

casse-pieds [kaspje] **1** *adj inv* **être casse-pieds** to be a pain (in the neck)

2 *nmf inv* pain (in the neck)

casse-pipe [kaspip] *nm inv* **envoyer qn/aller au casse-pipe** *(à la guerre)* to send sb/go to the front ▢

casser [kase] **1** *vt* (a) **casser la figure** *ou* **la gueule !** **à qn** to smash sb's face in, to waste sb's face; **casser la gueule à une bouteille** to down a bottle in one (b) *(critiquer)* to tear or rip to bits (c) *(agresser)* **casser du pédé !** to go queer-bashing or gay-bashing; **casser du flic !** to beat up some cops (d) **les casser à qn !** *(l'importuner) Br* to get on sb's tits, *Am* to break sb's balls (e) **ça casse pas des briques, ça casse pas trois pattes à un canard, ça casse**

Le symbole ▢ indique que la traduction n'est pas argotique.

rien it's nothing to write home about
(f) **à tout casser** (au maximum) max,
tops; **ça doit coûter cent euros à tout
casser** it must cost a hundred euros max
or tops; **faire une fiesta à tout casser**
to have a hell of a party
2 se casser vpr (a) (partir) to clear off,
Am to split; **bon, faut que je me casse**
I'd better be off, I've got to make tracks;
casse-toi! get lost!, get the hell out of
here!
(b) **se casser la figure** ou **la gueule** [!]
(tomber) to fall flat on one's face;
(échouer) to be a flop
(c) (s'inquiéter) **te casse pas!** take it
easy!, chill (out)!
(d) **se casser (à faire qch)** to go out of
one's way (to do sth); **se casser le cul (à
faire qch)** [!] to bust a gut or Am one's ass
(doing sth) ▸ see also **baraque, bonbon, bonnet, burettes, burnes,
couille, croûte, graine, margoulette,
morceau, nénette, pipe, rondelle,
sucre, tronc**

casserole [kasrɔl] nf Hum **passer à la
casserole** (subir un rapport sexuel) Br to
get a good seeing-to, Am to get a balling;
(être assassiné) to get bumped off

castagne [kastaɲ] nf (coup) clout, wallop; **va y avoir de la castagne** there's
going to be a Br punch-up or Am fist fight,
Br it's going to kick off

castagner [kastaɲe] **1** vt to clout, to wallop
2 se castagner vpr to have a Br punch-
up or Am fist fight

cata [kata] nf (abbr **catastrophe**) **c'est la
cata** it's a disaster

catho [kato] adj & nmf (abbr **catholique**)
Catholic □; **il vient d'une famille hyper
catho** he comes from a really churchy
family

causant, -e [kozã, -ãt] adj **il n'est pas
très causant** he's not very chatty, he
doesn't have much to say for himself

causer [koze] vi to chat

cavale [kaval] nf **être en cavale** to be on
the run; **la police n'a toujours pas retrouvé les trois gangsters en cavale**

the police still haven't found the three
gangsters who are on the run

cavaler [kavale] **1** vt **tu commences à
me cavaler!** you're starting to Br get on
my wick or up my nose or Am tick me off!
2 vi (a) (courir, se dépêcher) to run
around, to charge around (b) (recher-
cher les aventures) to chase after wo-
men/men

cavaleur, -euse [kavalœr, -øz] **1** adj
(homme) womanizing; (femme) man-
eating
2 nm,f (homme) womanizer, skirt-
chaser; (femme) man-eater

cave [kav] nm (imbécile) sucker, Br mug,
Am patsy

céfran [sefrã] Cités (verlan **français**) **1** adj
French □
2 nmf (homme) Frenchman, f Frenchwoman □

ceinture [sɛ̃tyr] nf **faire ceinture** (être
privé de nourriture, être forcé à l'absti-
nence) to go without; **ce soir, mon
vieux, ceinture!** you'll have to go without tonight!

cendar [sãdar] nm ashtray □

cerise [səriz] nf Can Joual **faire perdre la
cerise à qn** [!!] to pop sb's cherry

ceusses [søs] pron Hum **les ceusses
qui…** them what…

cézigue [sezig] pron his lordship, Br his nibs

chagatte [!!] [ʃagat] nf pussy, snatch, Br
fanny

chambard [ʃabar] nm (a) (remue-
ménage) upheaval □ (b) (vacarme) racket,
din; **faire du chambard** to make a racket
or a din

chambardement [ʃabardəmã] nm
upheaval □

chambarder [ʃabarde] vt **tout chambarder** (mettre en désordre, bouleverser)
to turn everything upside-down

chambrer [ʃabre] vt (taquiner)
chambrer qn to make fun of sb □, Br to
wind sb up, to take the mickey out of sb,
Am to goof with sb

chameau, -x [ʃamo] **1** adj **être chameau** (homme) to be a Br swine or Am
stinker; (femme) to be a witch or Br a cow

2 nm (homme) Br swine, Am stinker; (femme) witch, Br cow

champ' [ʃɑ̃p] nm (abbr **champagne**) bubbly, Br champers

champignon [ʃɑ̃piɲɔ̃] nm **appuyer sur le champignon** (accélérer) Br to put one's foot down, Am to step on the gas, to let the hammer down

champion, -onne [ʃɑ̃pjɔ̃, -ɔn] adj great, Br fab, Am aces

Champs [ʃɑ̃] npr **les Champs** the Champs-Elysées □

chancre [ʃɑ̃kr] nm **bouffer comme un chancre** to stuff oneself or one's face, to pig out, Br to make a pig of oneself

chandelle [ʃɑ̃dɛl] nf (a) (morve) drip of snot (b) **tenir la chandelle** (être de trop) Br to play gooseberry, Am to be the fifth wheel ▶ see also **trente-six**

chanson [ʃɑ̃sɔ̃] nf **c'est toujours la même chanson** it's always the same old story; **ça va, je connais la chanson!** I've heard it all before!

chapeau [ʃapo] **1** nm **travailler du chapeau** to have a screw loose, to be off one's rocker, to be not all there
2 exclam good for you/him/etc!

char [ʃar] nm (a) **arrête ton char (Ben Hur)!** come off it!, yeah right! (b) Can (voiture) car □, wheels, Br motor; **ça vaut pas les chars** it's not up to much

charas [ʃaras] nm cannabis resin □, black

charbon [ʃarbɔ̃] nm **aller au charbon** (à son travail) to go to work □

charcler [ʃarkle] vt to kill □, to waste, Br to do in, Am to eighty-six; **ça va charcler!** there's going to be trouble!

charclo [ʃarklo] nmf (verlan **clochard**) tramp, Br dosser, Am hobo, bum

charcuter [ʃarkyte] vt (sujet: chirurgien) to butcher, to hack up

chargé, -e [ʃarʒe] adj (ivre, drogué) loaded, wrecked, wasted

charger [ʃarʒe] **se charger** vpr (s'enivrer) to get wrecked or wasted or Br legless or pissed; (se droguer) to get stoned or wrecked or shit-faced

charlot [ʃarlo] nm (personne qui manque de sérieux) clown

charogne [!] [ʃarɔɲ] nf (homme méprisable) bastard; (femme méprisable) bitch

charre [ʃar] = **char**

charrette [ʃarɛt] **1** adj inv (en retard) **être charrette** to be working against the clock
2 nf (a) (voiture) car □, wheels, Br motor (b) Suisse **cette charrette de Paul!** that Br blasted or Am darn Paul!
3 exclam Suisse blast!, Am shoot!

charrier [ʃarje] **1** vt (se moquer de) **charrier qn** to make fun of sb □, Br to take the mickey out of sb, to wind sb up, Am to goof with sb; **il s'est fait charrier** he got made fun of □, Br he got the mickey taken out of him
2 vi **charrier (dans les bégonias)** (exagérer) to go too far; **faut pas charrier!** come off it!, gimme a break!

châsses [ʃɑs] nmpl (yeux) eyes □

châssis [ʃasi] nm (silhouette) chassis, bod; **mate un peu le châssis!** check out the chassis or bod on that!

chat [ʃa] nm **il n'y avait pas un chat** there wasn't a soul ▶ see also **pipi**

châtaigne [ʃatɛɲ] nf (a) (coup) clout, thump; **mettre une châtaigne à qn** to clout or thump sb (b) (bagarre) **il va y avoir de la châtaigne** there's going to be a Br punch-up or Am fist fight, Br it's going to kick off (c) (décharge électrique) **(se) prendre une châtaigne** to get a shock

châtaigner [ʃatɛɲe] **1** vt to clout, to thump; **se faire châtaigner** to get clouted or thumped
2 **se châtaigner** vpr to trade punches

Château [ʃato] nm **le Château** the Élysée Palace □ (official residence of the French President)

Château-Lapompe [ʃatolapɔ̃p] nm Hum **du Château-Lapompe** water □

This humorous expression, imitating a typical name for French wine, is used to mean water when served or ordered instead of wine with a meal.

chatte‼ [ʃat] *nf (sexe de la femme)* pussy, snatch, *Br* fanny; **avoir de la chatte** to be fucking lucky *or Br* jammy

chaud, -e [ʃo, ʃod] **1** *adj* (**a**) *(sexuellement)* hot; **être (un) chaud lapin** to be permanently horny; **être chaud de la pince**❗ to be a horny bastard (**b**) *(difficile)* tricky (**c**) *Can (ivre)* wasted, *Br* pissed **2** *nm* **on a eu chaud (aux fesses)!** we had a narrow escape! ▶ *see also* **eau**

chaude-pisse❗ [ʃodpis] *nf* **la chaude-pisse** the clap

chauffer [ʃofe] *v imp* **ça va chauffer** there's going to be trouble

chausson, -onne [ʃosõ, -ɔn] *adj Can* dimwit, *Am* bozo

chaussure [ʃosyr] *nf* **avoir mis ses chaussures à bascule** *(être ivre)* to be staggering all over the place

chauve [ʃov] *nm Hum* **le chauve à col roulé** one-eyed trouser snake

chébran [ʃebrã] *adj (verlan* **branché**) hip, trendy

chef [ʃɛf] *nm* (**a**) *(terme d'adresse)* pal, *Br* mate, *Am* buddy (**b**) **se débrouiller comme un chef** to do really well □

chefaillon [ʃefajõ] *nm* little Hitler

chela [ʃəla] *vt (verlan* **lâche**) **chela oim!** leave me alone!, get off my back *or* case!

chelou [ʃəlu] *adj (verlan* **louche**) shady, seedy, *Br* dodgy

chèque [ʃɛk] *nm* **chèque en bois** rubber *Br* cheque *or Am* check

chercher [ʃɛrʃe] *vt (provoquer)* to pick a fight with; **tu me cherches, là?** do you want a fight?; **si tu me cherches, tu vas me trouver!** if you're looking for trouble, you've come to the right place, if you're looking for a fight, you'll get one! ▶ *see also* **crosses, midi, pou**

chérot [ʃero] *adj inv* pricey

chetron [ʃətrõ] *nf (verlan* **tronche**) face □, mug

cheval, -aux [ʃəval, -o] *nm* **c'est pas le mauvais cheval** he's a nice enough guy

cheveu, -x [ʃəvø] *nm* **se faire des cheveux (blancs)** to worry oneself sick, to give oneself grey hairs; **venir** *ou* **arriver comme un cheveu sur la soupe** to come at the wrong time; **sa question est tombée comme un cheveu sur la soupe** his question couldn't have come at a worse time

cheville [ʃəvij] *nf* **avoir les chevilles qui enflent** to get big-headed, to get too big for one's *Br* boots *or Am* britches

chèvre [ʃɛvr] *nf* **rendre qn chèvre** to drive sb nuts *or* crazy *or* round the bend; **devenir chèvre** to go nuts *or* crazy *or* round the bend

chevrer [ʃəvre] *vi Suisse* **faire chevrer qn** to drive sb up the wall *or* round the bend

chez [ʃe] *prep* **côté humour, ce film, c'est vraiment lourd de chez lourd** the humour in this film is SO unsubtle; **son nouveau petit copain, c'est le style blaireau de chez blaireau** her new boyfriend is a complete and total jerk; **il est nul ton lecteur de CD, le son est carrément pourri de chez pourri!** your CD player's useless, the sound's as crap as you can get

This very generative expression imitates the wording used in French perfume advertisements, which give the name of the perfume followed by the name of the perfume house, for example "Coco, de chez Chanel".

chiadé, -e [ʃjade] *adj* elaborate □

chiader [ʃjade] *vt* to take care over □; **ce coup-ci j'ai vraiment chiadé ma dissert, j'ai pas envie de me choper une bulle** this time I took loads of care over my essay, I don't want to get a zero *Br* mark *or Am* grade for it

chialer [ʃjale] *vi* (**a**) *(pleurer)* to blubber, to snivel (**b**) *(se plaindre)* to whinge

chiâler [ʃjɑle] *vi Can* to whinge

chiant, -e❗ [ʃjã, -ãt] *adj* (**a**) *(monotone)* *Br* bloody *or Am* goddamn boring; **chiant comme la pluie** as boring as hell, *Br* piss-boring (**b**) *(agaçant)* **être chiant** *Br* to be a bloody nuisance, to be a pain in the *Br* arse *or Am* ass

chiard[!] [ʃjar] *nm* brat

chiasse[!!] [ʃjas] *nf* (a) *(diarrhée)* **la chiasse** the runs, the shits, the trots; **foutre la chiasse à qn** *(lui faire peur)* to scare sb shitless (b) *(ennui)* **quelle chiasse!** what a fucking pain (in the *Br* arse *or Am* ass)!

chiatique[!!] [ʃjatik] *adj* **être chiatique** to be a pain in the *Br* arse *or Am* ass

chibre[!] [ʃibr] *nm* dick, *Br* tadger, *Am* schlong

chicha [ʃiʃa] *nm Cités (verlan* **haschich**) hash, dope, *Br* blow

chichon [ʃiʃɔ̃] *nm Cités* hash, dope, *Br* blow

chicos [ʃikos] *adj* classy, smart

chié, -e[!] [ʃje] *adj* (a) *(formidable)* shit-hot, *Am* awesome (b) *(qui exagère)* **il est chié, lui!** he's got a *Br* bloody *or Am* god-damn nerve!

chiée[!] [ʃje] *nf* **(toute) une chiée de** a (whole) shitload of

chie-en-culotte [!] [ʃiãkylɔt] *nm inv Can* coward □, wimp, wuss

chien, chienne [ʃjɛ̃, ʃjɛn] **1** *adj (méchant)* **être chien avec qn** to be rotten to sb

2 *nm,f* **avoir un mal de chien à faire qch** to have a hell of a job doing sth; **c'est pas fait pour les chiens** it's there for a reason; **les paillassons c'est pas fait pour les chiens!** the doormat's not there as an ornament!; **chienne de vie!** what a life!; *Can* **avoir la chienne** *(avoir peur)* to be scared stiff; *(être paresseux)* to be lazy □ ▸ *see also* **nom**

chienlit [ʃjãli] *nf (désordre)* shambles, muddle; **c'est la chienlit** what a complete shambles *or* muddle

This expression was popularized by French president Charles De Gaulle in 1968, when he commented on the rioting and unrest which marked a turning point in France's social history.

chier[!!] [ʃje] **1** *vt* **tu vas pas nous chier une pendule!** don't make such a fuss *or Br* a bloody song and dance about it!

2 *vi* (a) *(déféquer)* to shit, to *Br* have *or Am* take a shit *or* a crap *or* a dump

(b) **chier dans la colle** to go too far, *Br* to take the piss; **chier dans son froc** *(avoir peur)* to shit oneself, to be shit-scared; **à chier** *(très mauvais)* fucking awful; **y a pas à chier** there are no two fucking ways about it; **en chier (pour faire qch)** to have a hell of a time (doing sth); **ça va chier (des bulles)!** the shit's going to hit the fan!, all hell's going to break loose!; **va chier!** fuck off!; **faire chier qn** *(mettre en colère)* *Br* to piss sb off, to get on sb's tits, *Am* to break sb's balls; *(ennuyer)* to bore sb shitless; **se faire chier** *(s'ennuyer)* to be bored shitless; **se faire chier à faire qch** *(se donner du mal)* to bust a gut *or Am* one's ass doing sth; **envoyer chier qn** to tell sb where to get off, *Br* to tell sb to piss off ▸ *see also* **botte, nul, rat, tortiller**

chierie[!] [ʃiri] *nf* **quelle chierie!** *Br* what a bloody pain!, what a pain in the *Br* arse *or Am* ass!

chieur, -euse[!] [ʃjœr, -øz] *nm,f* pain in the *Br* arse *or Am* ass

chignon [ʃiɲɔ̃] *nm Can (tête)* head □, nut

chinetoc, chinetoque [ʃintɔk] *nmf Offensive* Chink, Chinky

chinois [ʃinwa] *nm* **se polir le chinois**[!] to beat one's meat, to bang *or Br* bash the bishop

chiotte[!] [ʃjɔt] *nf* (a) *(voiture)* car □, wheels, *Br* motor; *(moto)* bike, *Am* hog; *(cyclomoteur)* moped □, *Am* scooter □ (b) *(ennui)* **quelle chiotte!** what a pain in the *Br* arse *or Am* ass! (c) **chiottes** *(W-C) Br* bog, *Am* john; **il a un goût de chiottes** he's got shit taste; **aux chiottes, l'arbitre!** *Br* ≃ the referee's a wanker!, *Am* ≃ kill the umpire!

chiper [ʃipe] *vt* **chiper qch à qn** to pinch *or Br* nick sth from sb

chipolata[!] [ʃipolata] *nf (pénis)* sausage, *Br* pork sword, *Am* salami

chique [ʃik] *nf* **avoir la chique** *(mal aux dents)* to have a swollen cheek □ *(because* *of toothache);* **ça m'a coupé la chique** *(surpris)* I was speechless *or Br* gobsmacked; **mou comme une chique** spineless, *Br* wet; **tirer sa chique !!** to get laid, *Br* to have a shag ▶ *see also* **jus**

chiqué [ʃike] *nm* **c'est du chiqué** it's all put on *or* pretend; **il s'est pas vraiment fait mal, c'est du chiqué!** he hasn't really hurt himself, he's just pretending!

chlass, chlasse, chlâsse [ʃlɑs] = **schlass²**

chleu, chleuh [ʃlø] *nm Offensive* Kraut

> Depending on the context and the tone of voice used, this term may be either offensive or affectionately humorous. It is nonetheless inadvisable to use it unless one is quite sure of the reaction it will receive.

chlinguer [ʃlɛ̃ge] *vi* to stink, *Br* to pong, to hum

chnoc, chnoque [ʃnɔk] = **schnock**

chnouf, chnouffe [ʃnuf] *nf (héroïne)* junk, horse; *(cocaïne)* snow, charlie, coke

chochotte [ʃɔʃɔt] *nf (personne maniérée)* wimp, wuss; **fais pas ta chochotte** stop mincing *or Br* poncing about!

chocolat [ʃɔkɔla] *adj inv* **on est chocolat!** *(on a été dupés)* we've been done!; *(dans une situation sans issue)* we're up shit creek ▶ *see also* **turbine**

chocottes [ʃɔkɔt] *nfpl* **avoir les chocottes** to be scared witless *or* stiff, to have the wind up; **foutre les chocottes à qn** to scare sb witless *or* stiff, to put the wind up sb

choir [ʃwar] *vi* **laisser choir qn** to let sb down □; **tout laisser choir** to pack it all in, *Br* to jack it all in, *Am* to chuck everything

chôm'du, chômedu [ʃomdy] *nm (chômage)* **être au chôm'du** to be out of work □; **pointer au chôm'du** to be *Br* on the dole *or Am* on welfare □

choper [ʃɔpe] *vt* **(a)** *(saisir)* to grab □ **(b)** *(surprendre)* to catch □, to nab; **se faire choper** to get caught □ *or* nabbed **(c)** *(maladie, coup de soleil)* to catch □; **je**

crois que j'ai encore chopé une saloperie I think I've caught something nasty again

chopine [ʃɔpin] *nf* **boire une chopine** to have a drink □

chose [ʃoz] *nf* **être porté sur la chose** to have a one-track mind, *Br* to have sex on the brain

chou, choute [ʃu, ʃut] **1** *adj inv (mignon)* cute

2 *nm,f* **(a)** **rentrer dans le chou à qn** to give sb an earful *or Br* a mouthful **(b)** **mon (petit) chou, ma (petite) choute** darling, sweetie **(c)** **c'est bête comme chou** it's as easy as pie

chouette [ʃwɛt] **1** *adj* great, fantastic, fabulous; *Ironic* **ah t'as l'air chouette, avec cet anneau dans le nez!** you look something else with your nose pierced!

2 *nm* **refiler du chouette !!** to take it up the *Br* arse *or Am* ass

3 *nf* **une vieille chouette** *(femme)* an old bag *or* witch

4 *exclam* **chouette (alors)!** great!, fantastic!, fabulous!

chouf [ʃuf] *exclam Cités* look!

chougner [ʃuɲe] *vi (pleurnicher)* to whine

chouïa [ʃuja] *nm* **un chouïa (de)** a smidgen (of), a touch (of)

chouille [ʃuj] *nf* party □, bash

chouiller [ʃuje] *vi* to party

choune !! [ʃun] *nf (sexe de la femme)* pussy, snatch, *Br* fanny; **avoir de la choune** to be fucking lucky *or Br* jammy

chouraver [ʃurave], **chourer** [ʃure] *vt* to pinch, *Br* to nick; **chouraver** *ou* **chourer qch à qn** to pinch *or Br* nick sth from sb

chrono [krɔno] *adv* **faire du 140 km/h chrono** to be clocked at 140 km/h

chtar [ʃtar] *nm* **(a)** *(cachot)* slammer, clink, *Br* nick, *Am* pen **(b)** *(coup)* clout, wallop **(c)** *(policier)* cop

chtarbé, -e [ʃtarbe] *adj* crazy, nuts, off one's rocker

chtouille ! [ʃtuj] *nf* **la chtouille** the clap

Le symbole □ *indique que la traduction n'est pas argotique.*

chum [tʃɔm] *nm Can* pal, *Br* mate, *Am* buddy

cibiche [sibiʃ] *nf* gasper, cig

ciboire [!] [sibwar] *exclam Can* shit!

ciboulot [sibulo] *nm* **en avoir dans le ciboulot** to have brains, to have a lot between one's ears; **se creuser le ciboulot** to rack *or Am* cudgel one's brains; **travailler du ciboulot** to to be off one's rocker *or Br* trolley, *Br* to have lost the plot

cigare [sigar] *nm* (**a**) *(tête)* head ⃞, nut (**b**) **avoir le cigare au bord des lèvres** [!!] to be dying for a shit (**c**) **cigare à moustaches** [!!] *(sexe de l'homme)* one-eyed trouser snake

cinglé, -e [sɛ̃gle] **1** *adj* crazy, off one's rocker *or Br* head
2 *nm,f* nutcase, *Br* nutter, headcase, *Am* screwball, flamer

cinoche [sinɔʃ] *nm* **aller au cinoche** to go to the *Br* pictures *or Am* movies ⃞; **faire du cinoche** to cause a scene, to make a fuss

cinoque [sinɔk] *adj* crazy, loopy, off one's rocker

cinq [sɛ̃k] *adj inv* **en cinq sec** in no time at all, in two shakes; *Hum* **faire cinq contre un** [!] *(se masturber)* to beat one's meat, *Br* to have a hand shandy

cintré, -e [sɛ̃tre] *adj* cracked, *Br* barmy, *Am* screwy, wacko

cirage [siraʒ] *nm* **être dans le cirage** *(soûl)* to be out of it *or Br* off one's face; *(étourdi)* to be feeling out of it or woozy

cirer [sire] *vt* (**a**) **cirer les pompes à qn** to lick sb's boots (**b**) **j'en ai rien à cirer** [!] I don't give a shit *or Br* a toss *or Am* a rat's ass

citron [sitrɔ̃] *nm* (**a**) *(tête)* head ⃞, nut; **se presser** *ou* **se creuser le citron** to rack *or Am* cudgel one's brains (**b**) *Can Joual (voiture)* useless car ⃞, *Am* lemon

citrouille [sitruj] *nf (tête)* head ⃞, nut

clacos [klakos] *nm* Camembert ⃞

clair [klɛr] *exclam* I get the message!, I hear you!

clamser [klamse] *vi* to croak, to kick the bucket, *Br* to snuff it, *Am* to check out

clando [klɑ̃do], **clandos** [klɑ̃dos] *nm* illegal immigrant ⃞

claouis [!] [klawi] *nmpl* balls, nuts, *Br* bollocks

clapet [klapɛ] *nm* **ferme ton clapet!** shut your trap!, put a lid on it!, *Br* belt up!

claque [klak] **1** *nf* **se prendre une claque** *(subir une défaite cuisante)* to get thrashed; **en avoir sa claque (de)** to have had it up to here (with), to have had a bellyful (of)
2 *nm (maison close)* whorehouse, *Br* knocking shop ▸ *see also* **clique**, **tête**

claqué, -e [klake] *adj (épuisé)* bushed, *Br* knackered, shattered, *Am* beat

claque-merde [!!] [klakmɛrd] *nm (bouche)* trap, *Br* gob; **tu vas le fermer ton claque-merde, dis? j'essaye d'écouter la radio, bordel!** will you shut the fuck up? I'm trying to listen to the radio, for fuck's sake!

claquer [klake] **1** *vt (dépenser)* to blow
2 *vi* (**a**) *(mourir)* to croak, to kick the bucket, *Br* to snuff it, *Am* to cash in (one's) chips (**b**) **claquer du bec** to be starving or ravenous ⃞

classe [klɑs] **1** *adj inv (élégant)* classy; *(formidable)* class
2 *adv* **s'habiller classe** to be a classy dresser
3 *nf* **la classe!** classy!

classieux, -euse [klɑsjø, -øz] *adj* classy

clean [klin] **1** *adj inv* clean-cut ⃞
2 *adv* **s'habiller clean** to dress in a clean-cut way ⃞

clébard [klebar], **clebs** [klɛps] *nm* mutt

clicheton [kliʃtɔ̃] *nm (cliché)* cliché ⃞; **l'histoire est d'une banalité affligeante; tous les clichetons sont au rendez-vous** the story is as banal as can be and completely cliché-ridden

clim [klim] *nf (abbr* **climatisation**) air con

clique [klik] *nf* (**a**) *(bande)* gang, crowd (**b**) **prendre ses cliques et ses claques** to pack one's bags and go

clit [!!] [klit], **clito** [!!] [klito] *nm* clit

Le symbole ⃞ *indique que la traduction n'est pas argotique.*

cloche [klɔʃ] **1** adj daft, thick, Am dumb
2 nf **(a)** (imbécile) jerk, Br prat, pillock, Am geek **(b)** **être de la cloche** to be a tramp or Am hobo **(c)** **se taper la cloche** to feed one's face, Br to have a slap-up meal ▸ see also **sonner**

clocher [klɔʃe] vi **il y a quelque chose qui cloche** there's something wrong somewhere; **qu'est-ce qui cloche?** what's up?

clodo [klɔdo] nmf tramp, Am hobo

clope [klɔp] nf smoke, Br fag, ciggy

cloper [klɔpe] vi to smoke ▢

clopinettes [klɔpinɛt] nfpl **des clopinettes** (presque rien) peanuts; **des clopinettes!** no way!, no chance!

cloque [klɔk] nf **être en cloque** Br to be up the duff or spout, to be in the club, Am to be knocked up

clou [klu] nm **(a)** **ça ne vaut pas un clou** it's not worth a Br penny or Am red cent; Can **cogner des clous** to keep nodding off **(b)** **des clous!** no way!, no chance! **(c)** (bicyclette) bike

coaltar [kɔltar] nm **être dans le coaltar** (étourdi) to be in a daze, to be feeling out of it or spaced out; **j'ai pas dormi de la nuit, je suis complètement dans le coaltar...** I didn't sleep a wink all night, I'm like a complete zombie

cocard [kɔkar] nm black eye ▢, shiner

cochonceté [kɔʃɔ̃ste] nf **(a)** (action obscène) repulsive act ▢; **allez faire vos cochoncetés ailleurs!** go and do that sort of thing somewhere else! **(b)** (remarque obscène) obscenity ▢; **dire des cochoncetés** to talk dirty

cochonner [kɔʃɔne] vt (salir) to dirty ▢, to make a mess of ▢

coco [koko] **1** nm **(a)** (personne) **un drôle de** ou **un sacré coco** a weirdo, an oddball; **toi mon coco, je t'ai à l'œil!** just watch it, pal or Br mate or Am buddy! **(b)** (estomac) **bien se remplir le coco** to stuff oneself or one's face, to feed one's face
2 nmf (abbr **communiste**) commie
3 nf (cocaïne) coke, snow ▸ see also **noix**

cocoter [kɔkɔte] vi to stink, Br to pong, to hum

cocotte [kɔkɔt] nf **ma cocotte** darling, honey

cocotter [kɔkɔte] = **cocoter**

cocu, -e [kɔky] **1** adj **je suis cocu** my wife's cheating on me; **un mari cocu** a man whose wife is cheating on him; **faire qn cocu** to cheat on sb
2 nm deceived husband ▢; **avoir une chance** ou **veine de cocu** to have the luck of the devil

cocufier [kɔkyfje] vt to cheat on

coffrer [kɔfre] vt to put inside or away or behind bars; **se faire coffrer** to get put inside or away or behind bars

cogne [kɔɲ] nm cop, Br bobby, Am flat-foot

cogner [kɔɲe] **1** vt to knock about, to beat (up)
2 vi **(a)** (puer) to stink (to high heaven), Br to pong, to hum **(b)** **ça cogne** (le soleil chauffe) it's scorching or Br roasting
3 se cogner vpr **(a)** **se cogner qn/qch** (corvée) to get stuck or Br lumbered or landed with sb/sth **(b)** **se cogner qn** ‼ (posséder) to screw sb, Br to have it off with sb, Am to ball sb

coincer [kwɛ̃se] **1** vt (attraper) to nab, to collar; **se faire coincer** to get nabbed or collared
2 vi (puer) to stink, Br to pong, to hum ▸ see also **bulle**

coinços [kwɛ̃sos] adj uptight

coing [kwɛ̃] nm **bourré comme un coing** trashed, wasted, plastered, Br off one's face, legless

coke [kɔk] nf (cocaïne) coke

coké [koke] adj (drogué à la cocaïne) coked-up

colbac [kɔlbak] nm **attraper qn par le colbac** to grab sb by the scruff of the neck

colis [kɔli] nm (fille) chick, Br bird; **un joli petit colis** a knockout, a babe, Br a cracker, a bit of all right

colle [kɔl] nf **être à la colle** to be shacked up together ▸ see also **chier, pot**

collé, -e [kɔle] *adj Can* **en avoir de collé** to be loaded

coller [kɔle] **1** *vt* **(a)** *(placer)* to stick, to dump; **il a collé tous les cartons dans un coin** he stuck *or* dumped all the cardboard boxes in a corner

(b) *(administrer)* **coller qch à qn** *(claque, baiser, rhume)* to give sb sth $^\square$; *(amende)* to slap sth on sb; **il m'a collé une de ces beignes!** he gave me a real wallop!; **il m'a collé les gosses pour le week-end** he dumped the kids on me for the weekend; **son bonhomme lui a encore collé un marmot** her old man's knocked her up again

(c) *(retenir à l'école)* *(élève)* to keep in

(d) *(suivre)* **coller qn** to stick to sb like glue, to follow sb around

2 *vi* **(a)** **ça colle!** OK!, cool!; **ça ne colle pas très bien entre eux** they don't really see eye to eye **(b)** **il arrête pas de me coller au cul**❗ he keeps following me around like a lost dog; *(en voiture) Br* he keeps driving up my arse, *Am* he keeps tailgating me

3 s'y coller *vpr* **c'est encore moi qui m'y colle!** I'm stuck *or Br* lumbered with it again!; **c'est toi qui t'y colles** it's your turn ▶ see also **pain**

collimateur [kɔlimatœr] *nm* **avoir qn dans le collimateur** to keep one's eye on sb, to keep tabs on sb

colo [kɔlo] *nf (abbr* **colonie de vacances)** *Br* (children's) holiday camp $^\square$, *Am* summer camp $^\square$

colon [kɔlɔ̃] *nm* **(a)** *(abbr* **colonel)** colonel $^\square$ **(b)** **ben mon colon!** goodness me!, *Br* blimey!, *Am* gee (whiz)! **(c)** *Can (rustre)* yokel, peasant, *Am* hick

colonne [kɔlɔn] *nf* **se taper (sur) la colonne, s'astiquer la colonne**❗❗ to jerk off, to beat off, to beat one's meat

coltiner [kɔltine] **se coltiner** *vpr* **se coltiner qn/qch** to get stuck *or Br* lumbered *or* landed with sb/sth

comac [kɔmak] *adj* ginormous, humongous, massive

comme aç [kɔmas] *adv Cités (verlan* **comme ça)** like that $^\square$; **oh l'autre! t'es**

con ou quoi, faut pas faire comme aç! are you completely stupid or what, you don't do it like that!

comme d'hab [kɔmdab] *adv (abbr* **comme d'habitude)** as per (usual)

commission [kɔmisjɔ̃] *nf* **faire la petite/grosse commission** to do a number one/number two

compagnie [kɔ̃paɲi] *nf* **salut, la compagnie!** hi, guys *or* folks!; **ces mecs, c'est racaille et compagnie** these guys are a bunch of scumbags

compète [kɔ̃pɛt] *nf (abbr* **compétition)** competition $^\square$ *(in sport)*; **faire de la compète** to enter competitions

compil' [kɔ̃pil] *nf (abbr* **compilation)** compilation $^\square$

comprenette [kɔ̃prənɛt] *nf* **avoir la comprenette un peu dure, être lent à la comprenette** to be a bit slow on the uptake

comprenure [kɔ̃prənyr] *nf Belg & Can* **être dur de comprenure** to be slow (on the uptake)

compte [kɔ̃t] *nm* **avoir son compte** *(être condamné)* to have had it, to be done for; *(être ivre)* to have had enough (to drink) $^\square$; **ça va, j'ai eu mon compte** *(j'en ai assez)* that's enough, I've had it; **régler son compte à qn** *(punir sévèrement)* to give sb what for, to give sb what's coming to him/her; *(tuer)* to bump sb off, *Br* to do sb in, *Am* to eighty-six sb; **son compte est bon** he's had it, *Br* he's for it

con, conne [kɔ̃, kɔn] **1** ❗ *adj* **(a)** *(stupide) Br* bloody *or Am* goddamn stupid; **être con comme la lune** *ou* **comme un balai** *Br* to be thick (as two short planks), to be as daft as a brush, *Am* to have rocks in one's head; **t'es con, tu devrais venir avec nous, on va bien se marrer!** don't be stupid, come with us, it'll be a laugh!

(b) *(regrettable)* **c'est con, je ne vais pas pouvoir me libérer** it's a bummer, but I'm not going to be able to get away

(c) **à la con** *(médiocre)* crappy, lousy, *Br* poxy

2 ❗ *nm,f* **(a)** *(imbécile) Br* arsehole, twat,

Le symbole $^\square$ indique que la traduction n'est pas argotique.

Am asshole; **faire le con** (faire le clown) Br to arse around, to piss about, Am to screw around; **faire le con, jouer au con** (faire semblant de ne pas comprendre) to act dumb; **fais pas le con, ça va s'arranger** don't do anything stupid, it'll sort itself out; **fais pas le con, viens avec nous, on va bien se marrer!** don't be stupid, come with us, it'll be a laugh!; **se retrouver comme un con** to be left feeling a complete Br arsehole or Am asshole; **si les cons volaient, tu serais chef d'escadrille** if being an Br arsehole or Am asshole was an Olympic event, you'd be a gold medallist

(**b**) (homme déplaisant) bastard; (femme déplaisante) bitch

3 ‼ nm (sexe de la femme) cunt ▶ see also **air, gueule, piège, tête**

conard, -asse [kɔnar, -as] = **connard**

conclure [kɔ̃klyr] vi (en matière amoureuse) to get a result

concombre [kɔ̃kɔ̃br] nm Can Br pillock, Am bonehead

condé [kɔ̃de] nm (policier) cop

conduite [kɔ̃dɥit] nf **s'acheter une conduite** to turn over a new leaf, to mend one's ways; (criminel) to go straight

confiote [kɔ̃fjɔt] nf (confiture) jam □

congélo [kɔ̃ʒelo] nm (abbr **congélateur**) freezer □

connard, -asse ‼ [kɔnar, -as] nm,f (**a**) (homme stupide) stupid bastard, prick, Br arsehole, Am asshole; (femme stupide) stupid bitch, Br arsehole, Am asshole (**b**) (homme déplaisant) bastard; (femme déplaisante) bitch

connement ‼ [kɔnmɑ̃] adv stupidly □; **il s'est fait connement piquer sa caisse** the stupid idiot got his car pinched; **et connement j'ai accepté** and like the idiot that I am, I said yes

connerie ‼ [kɔnri] nf (**a**) (acte stupide) **faire une connerie** to do a Br bloody or Am goddamn stupid thing; **j'ai peur qu'il fasse une connerie** (un acte inconsidéré) I'm scared he's going to do something Br bloody or Am goddamn stupid (**b**)

(remarque stupide) **dire** ou **raconter des conneries** to talk crap or bullshit (**c**) (caractère stupide) stupidity □; **il est d'une connerie!** he's so Br bloody or Am goddamn stupid!

conso [kɔ̃so] nf (abbr **consommation**) drink □ (in bar, club)

constipé, -e [kɔ̃stipe] adj (gêné) uptight; (sourire) strained □; **ce qu'il peut m'agacer avec son air constipé, ce mec-là!** he really annoys me, the way he's so uptight!

contrat [kɔ̃tra] nm (d'un tueur) contract

contredanse [kɔ̃trədɑ̃s] nf (document) ticket; (amende) fine □

contrefiche [kɔ̃trəfiʃ], **contreficher** [kɔ̃trəfiʃe] **se contrefiche** ou **contreficher de** vpr not to give a damn or a hoot or Br a stuff about

contrefoutre [kɔ̃trəfutr] **se contrefoutre de** vpr not to give a damn or a hoot or Br a stuff about

converse [kɔ̃vɛrs] nf (abbr **conversation**) conversation □, chat □; **faire la converse à qn** to chat to sb

cool [kul] **1** adj inv (**a**) (détendu) laid-back, cool; **cool, mon vieux!** chill (out)!, take it easy! (**b**) (bien, beau) cool

2 exclam cool!

coolitude [kulityd] nf coolness, hipness

coolos [kulos] adj inv (**a**) (détendu) laid-back, cool (**b**) (bien) cool

coopé [kɔpe] nf (abbr **coopération**) (aide aux PVD) aid to developing countries □; (service militaire) = voluntary work overseas carried out as an alternative to national service

copion [kɔpjɔ̃] nm Belg (antisèche) Br crib, Am cheat sheet

coq-l'œil [kɔklœj] **1** adj inv cross-eyed □

2 nmf inv cross-eyed person □

coquard [kɔkar] = **cocard**

corbeau, -x [kɔrbo] nm (personne) Goth

corde [kɔrd] nf (**a**) **se passer la corde au cou** to get spliced or hitched (**b**) **être dans les cordes de qn** to be (right) up

---

Le symbole □ *indique que la traduction n'est pas argotique.*

sb's street (**c**) **il pleut** *ou* **tombe des cordes** it's raining cats and dogs, *Br* it's bucketing down, it's chucking it down (**d**) **faire des cordes** *(être très constipé)* to be all bunged up (**e**) *Can* **coucher sur la corde à linge** to have a wild night of it

corneille [!] [kɔrnɛj] *nf Can (religieuse)* nun □, penguin

cornes [kɔrn] *nfpl* **faire porter des cornes à qn** *(tromper)* to cheat on sb

cornet [kɔrnɛ] *nm (estomac)* **qu'est-ce qu'on s'est mis dans le cornet!** we totally stuffed ourselves *or* our faces!, we really pigged out

corniaud [kɔrnjo] *nm* moron, *Br* twit, *Am* fathead

cornichon [kɔrniʃɔ̃] *nm (niais) Br* plonker, pillock, *Am* lamebrain, meathead

corrida [kɔrida] *nf (agitation)* hassle, *Br* carry-on; **quelle corrida hier soir, pour rentrer chez moi!** what a hassle *or Br* carry-on I had getting home last night!

cossard, -e [kɔsar, -ard] **1** *adj* lazy □
2 *nm,f* lazybones

cossin [kɔsɛ̃] *nm Can* thingy, whatsit

costard [kɔstar] *nm* suit □ *(clothing)* ▸ see also **tailler**

costard-cravate [kɔstarkravat] *nm (personne)* suit

costaud, -e [kɔsto, -od] **1** *adj* (**a**) *(personne)* big □, hefty; *(objet)* sturdy □ (**b**) *(café, alcool)* strong □
2 *nm* big guy

costume-cravate [kɔstymkravat] *nm (personne)* suit; **tous ces sales hippies qui se sont transformés en costume-cravates** all these bloody hippies who sold out and became suits

cote [kɔt] *nf* **avoir la cote (avec qn)** to be popular (with sb) □; **j'ai plus la cote avec le patron depuis notre engueulade de l'autre jour** I haven't been in the boss's good books since that row we had the other day

côte [kot] *nf* (**a**) **avoir les côtes en long** to be bone idle (**b**) **se tenir les côtes** to be in stitches, to kill oneself (laughing), to split one's sides

coton [kɔtɔ̃] **1** *adj inv* tough, tricky
2 *nm* **filer un mauvais coton** to be in a bad way

couche [kuʃ] *nf* (**a**) **en tenir une couche** to have nothing between one's ears, *Br* to be as thick as two short planks, *Am* to have rocks in one's head (**b**) **en remettre une couche** to lay it on thick

coucheries [kuʃri] *nfpl* sleeping around, casual sex □

couchette [kuʃɛt] *nf Can* **être fort sur la couchette** to sleep around

coucou [kuku] *nm (avion)* **un vieux coucou** an old crate

couenne [kwan] *nf* skin □ ▸ see also **sucer**

couillave [kujav], **couillaver** [kujave] *vt Cités* to screw, to shaft *(swindle)*

couille [!!] [kuj] *nf* (**a**) *(testicule)* ball, nut, *Br* bollock; **avoir des couilles (au cul)** to have (a lot of) guts; **baiser à couilles rabattues** to fuck like rabbits; **casser les couilles à qn** *Br* to get on sb's tits, *Am* to break sb's balls; **se faire des couilles en or** to make a bundle *or Br* a packet; **partir en couille** to go down the tubes *or Br* pan; **c'est de la couille (en barre)** it's a load of balls *or Br* bollocks; **mes couilles!** my *Br* arse *or Am* ass!; **couille molle** wimp, *Br* big girl's blouse

(**b**) *(erreur) Br* cock-up, balls-up, *Am* ball-up

(**c**) *(ennui)* problem □; **il m'arrive une couille** I'm in deep shit ▸ see also **battre**, **potage**

couillon, -onne [!] [kujɔ̃, -ɔn] **1** *adj Br* bloody *or Am* goddamn stupid
2 *nm,f Br* arsehole, twat, tosser, *Am* asshole, dumbass; **faire le couillon** *Br* to arse about, to piss about, *Am* to screw around

couillonnade [!] [kujɔnad] *nf* (**a**) *(discours stupide)* **dire des couillonnades** to talk crap *or* bull *or Br* bollocks (**b**) *(acte stupide)* **faire des couillonnades** *Br* to cock *or* balls things up, *Am* to ball things up

couillonner [!] [kujɔne] *vt* to screw, to rip off; **se faire couillonner** to get screwed *or* ripped off

---

Le symbole □ indique que la traduction n'est pas argotique.

coulant, -e [kulɑ̃, -ɑ̃t] **1** adj (arrangeant) easy-going

2 nm (fromage) = very ripe cheese, particularly Camembert

coule [kul] nf **être à la coule** to know the tricks of the trade, to know the ropes, to know what's what

couler [kule] **1** vt (a) (discréditer) **couler qn** to bring sb down, to ruin sb (b) **se la couler douce** to take things easy

2 vi (entreprise) to go under ▸ see also **bronze**

couleur [kulœr] nf **annoncer la couleur** (déclarer ses intentions) to lay one's cards on the table; (au restaurant, au café) = to say what one is having; **allez, annonce la couleur!** what's it to be, then? ▸ see also **voir**

coup [ku] nm (a) (boisson) drink □; **boire un coup** to have a drink □; **un coup de rouge** a glass of red wine □

(b) (acte criminel) job, operation; **il m'a fait le coup de la panne** he tried to pull the old "the car won't start" routine on me; **coup fourré** dirty trick

(c) **un bon coup** [!] (partenaire sexuel) a good lay or screw or Br shag

(d) **avoir le coup (pour faire qch)** to have the knack (of doing sth); **être dans le coup** (être au courant) to know what's going on; (être dans la confidence) to be in on it; **mettre qn dans le coup** to fill sb in, to put sb in the picture; **en mettre un coup** to pull out all the stops; **coup dur** setback □; **en deux coups les gros** in a jiffy, in next to no time ▸ see also **tirer**

coupe-choux [kupʃu] nm inv (rasoir) cut-throat razor □

couper [kupe] **1** vt **ça te la coupe, hein?** you weren't expecting that one, were you!, that shut you up, didn't it?

2 vi **couper à qch** (éviter) to get out of sth ▸ see also **chique, sifflet**

courailler [kuraje] vi Can to chase after women

courailleur [kurajœr] nm Can womanizer, skirt-chaser

courante [kurɑ̃t] nf **la courante** the runs, the trots

courber [kurbe] vt Suisse **courber l'école** to skip school, Br to bunk off, Am to play hookey

coureur, -euse [kurœr, -øz] **1** adj (homme) womanizing; (femme) man-eating

2 nm,f (homme volage) womanizer, skirt-chaser; (femme volage) man-eater

courge [kurʒ] nf Br pillock, plonker, Am meathead, bonehead

courir [kurir] **1** vt **tu commences à me courir!** you're starting to bug me or Br do my head in or Am give me a pain!

2 vi **tu peux toujours courir!** not a chance!, no way!; **tu peux toujours courir pour que je te prête ma caisse!** no way am I lending you my car!; **laisse courir!** forget it!, drop it! ▸ see also **galipote, haricot**

court-jus [kurʒy] nm short-circuit □

cousu [kuzy] adj **c'est du cousu main** (facile) it's in the bag, Br it's a dead cert; (très bien fait) it's a work of art ▸ see also **motus**

couv' [kuv] nf (abbr **couverture**) (de magazine) cover □

couvert [kuvɛr] nm **remettre le couvert** (faire quelque chose à nouveau) to do it again □; (refaire l'amour) to have sex again □; **donne-moi deux minutes pour reprendre mon souffle et puis on remet le couvert, c'est promis** just give me a couple of minutes to get my breath back and I'll be up for round two, promise

couvrante [kuvrɑ̃t] nf blanket □, cover □

crac-crac [krakrak] nm **faire crac-crac** to have a bit of nooky or Br rumpy-pumpy

cracher [kraʃe] **1** vt (argent) to fork out, to cough up

2 vi (a) (payer) to fork out, to cough up (b) **cracher dans la soupe** to bite the hand that feeds; **il crache pas dessus** he never turns up his nose at it, he never says no to it ▸ see also **bassinet, gueule, morceau**

crache-thunes [kraʃtyn] nm inv (distributeur de billets) hole in the wall

Le symbole □ indique que la traduction n'est pas argotique.

crachoir [kraʃwar] *nm* **tenir le crachoir** to go *or* ramble on and on; **tenir le crachoir à qn** to listen to sb go *or* ramble on and on

crack [krak] *nm* (a) *(drogue)* crack (b) *(personne douée)* whizz

crackeur [krakœr] *nm* crackhead

cracra [krakra], **crade** [krad], **cradingue** [kradɛ̃g], **crado** [krado] *adj* filthy □

craignos [krɛɲos] *adj* (a) *(louche)* shady, *Br* dodgy (b) *(laid)* hideous (c) *(mauvais)* crap, lousy, the pits

craindre [krɛ̃dr] *vi* (a) *(être louche)* to be shady *or Br* dodgy (b) *(être laid)* to be hideous (c) *(être mauvais)* to be crap, to be the pits, to suck, *Am* to bite (d) **ça craint!** it's crap!, it sucks!

cramé, -e [krame] *adj (ivre)* blitzed, wasted, *Br* off one's face, *Am* stewed (to the gills)

cramer [krame] **1** *vt* (a) *(brûler)* to burn □ (b) *(repérer)* to spot □, to clock, *Br* to rumble
2 *vi (brûler)* to burn □

cramouille ‼ [kramuj] *nf* pussy, snatch, twat, *Br* fanny

crampe [krɑ̃p] *nf* **tirer sa crampe** ! *(s'enfuir)* to beat it, *Br* to piss off, to bugger off, *Am* to book it; *(coïter)* to screw, *Br* to have a bonk, to have it off, *Am* to bang

crampon [krɑ̃pɔ̃] *nm (personne importune)* leech; **quel crampon, cette nana, impossible de s'en défaire!** what a leech that girl is, you can't get rid of her!

cran [krɑ̃] *nm* (a) *(couteau)* **cran (d'arrêt)** *Br* flick knife □, *Am* switchblade □ (b) **être à cran** to be about to crack up, to have reached boiling point

crâner [krane] *vi* to swagger, to show off

crâneur, -euse [krɑnœr, -øz] **1** *adj* swaggering; **être crâneur** to be a show-off *or* a poser
2 *nm,f* show-off, poser

crapahuter [krapayte] *vi (marcher)* to schlep *or* traipse about

crapoter [krapɔte] *vi* = to smoke without inhaling

crapoteux, -euse [krapɔtø, -øz] *adj* filthy □

craquant, -e [krakɑ̃, -ɑ̃t] **1** *adj (personne)* gorgeous, stunning, *Br* fit
2 *nm Cités (billet de banque) Br* note □, *Am* bill □

craque [krak] *nf* (a) *(mensonge)* lie □, fib, *Br* porky (pie) (b) ‼ *(sexe de la femme)* crack, gash (c) *Can* **avoir une craque** to be off one's rocker

craquer [krake] *vi* (a) *(nerveusement)* to crack up (b) *(succomber)* to crack, to give in □; **finalement j'ai craqué** in the end I couldn't resist it □; **craquer pour qn/qch** to fall for sb/sth; **il me fait vraiment craquer** I've got the hots for him, *Br* I really fancy him (c) **faire craquer un cours** *(ne pas y assister)* to *Br* bunk off *or Am* skip a class

craquette ‼ [krakɛt] *nf* pussy, twat, gash, *Br* minge

craqueur [krakœr] = **crackeur**

crasher [kraʃe] **se crasher** *vpr (avion, automobiliste, motard)* to crash □

craspec [kraspɛk] *adj* filthy □

crasse [kras] *nf* **faire une crasse à qn** to play a dirty trick on sb, *Br* to do the dirty on sb, *Am* to do sb dirt

cravacher [kravaʃe] *vi* to work like mad

cravate [kravat] *nf* **c'est de la cravate** it's a load of baloney *or* bull ▶ *see also* **jeter**

crécher [kreʃe] *vi (habiter)* to live □; **il crèche dans une piaule près de la gare** he's got a place near the station

crémerie [kremri] *nf* **changer de crémerie** to go somewhere else □, to move on □

crétin, -e [kretɛ̃, -in] **1** *adj* cretinous
2 *nm,f* cretin

creuser [krøze] **se creuser** *vpr (réfléchir)* to rack *or Am* cudgel one's brains ▶ *see also* **ciboulot, citron**

crevant, -e [krəvɑ̃, -ɑ̃t] *adj* (a) *(épuisant)* exhausting □, *Br* killing, knackering (b) *(hilarant)* hysterical, side-splitting

crevard, -e [krəvar, -ard] *nm,f (glouton)* pig, *Br* gannet, *Am* hog

Le symbole □ indique que la traduction n'est pas argotique.

crève [krɛv] nf **la crève** a stinking cold

crevé, -e [krəve] adj **(a)** (épuisé) Br knackered, shattered, Am beat **(b)** (mort) dead □

crevée [krəve] nf Suisse gaffe □, Br boob, Am boo-boo

crever [krəve] **1** vt **(a)** (épuiser) to wear out □, Br to knacker
(b) (tuer) to kill □, to waste, Br to do in
(c) crever la dalle to be starving or ravenous
(d) ça crève les yeux (c'est évident) it sticks out a mile; (c'est visible) it's staring you in the face; **c'est lui qui a fait le coup, ça crève les yeux** it's him who did it, it's plain for all to see
2 vi (mourir) to kick the bucket, to croak, Br to snuff it, Am to check out; Suisse (voiture) to stall □; **crever de faim/de chaleur** (avoir faim/chaud) to be starving/boiling; **à crever de rire** hysterical; **c'était à crever de rire** it was hysterical or a scream; **je peux crever la gueule ouverte, t'en as rien à faire!** I could die tomorrow for all you care!; **qu'il crève!** he can go to hell!
3 se crever vpr **(a)** (s'épuiser) to wear oneself out, Br to get knackered **(b)** (se donner du mal) **se crever (à faire qch)** to go out of one's way (to do sth); **se crever le cul (à faire qch)**[!] to bust a gut or Am one's ass (doing sth)

Crim', Crime [krim] nf (abbr **Brigade Criminelle**) **la Crim'** the crime squad □

criminelle [kriminɛl] adj f **elle est criminelle** she's hot, she's a babe

crincrin [krɛ̃krɛ̃] nm racket, din (especially loud music)

crise [kriz] nf **la crise (de rire)!** what a scream or hoot!

criser [krize] vi to lose it, to go ape, Br to go off one's head; **il va criser quand il se rendra compte que tu lui as bousillé son ordinateur** he's going to freak out or lose it when he realizes you've wrecked his computer

crisse [kris] Can Joual **1** nmf bastard; **mon petit crisse** (à un enfant) you little bugger!; **être en crisse** to be hopping mad
2 exclam for Christ's sake!, shit!

This word comes from the word "Christ" as pronounced by a speaker of Joual.

croco [krɔko] nm (abbr **crocodile**) crocodile (skin) □; **un sac en croco** a crocodile handbag □

crocs [kro] nmpl **(a)** (dents) teeth □, Br gnashers, Am choppers **(b) avoir les crocs** (avoir faim) to be hungry □

croire [krwar] **1** vt **j'te crois!** (je suis d'accord) absolutely!, Br too right!; Ironic yeah right!, Br I believe you (thousands wouldn't!)
2 se croire vpr **s'y croire** to think a lot of oneself, Br to fancy oneself

croquenots [krɔkno] nmpl shoes □, clodhoppers

croqueuse [krɔkøz] nf **croqueuse de diamants** gold-digger

croquignolet, -ette [krɔkiɲɔle, -ɛt] adj Ironic flaky, off-the-wall

crosser [!!] [krɔse] **se crosser** vpr Can to jerk off

crosses [krɔs] nfpl **chercher des crosses à qn** to try to pick a fight with sb

crouille [kruj] nm Offensive = racist term used to refer to a North African Arab

croulant, -e [krulɑ̃, -ɑ̃t] nm,f old codger, Br wrinkly, Am geezer

croupion [krupjɔ̃] nm behind, rear (end), rump; **elle marche en ondulant du croupion** she wiggles her Br bum or Am buns when she walks

croûte [krut] nf **(a)** (tableau) bad painting □, daub **(b) casser la** ou **une croûte** to have a snack □ or a bite to eat **(c) gagner sa croûte** to earn a or one's crust

croûter [krute] vi (manger) to eat □, to chow

croûton [krutɔ̃] nm **vieux croûton** old fossil, Br crumbly, Am geezer

cruche [kryʃ] **1** adj dense
2 nf (imbécile) Br plonker, pillock, Am goof, geek

cube [kyb] *nm* **un gros/petit cube** a big/small bike

cucul [kyky] *adj inv* **cucul (la praline)** *(personne, air)* cutesy, *Br* twee; *(film, livre)* corny

cueillir [kœjir] *vt (arrêter)* to pick up, *Br* to lift

cuiller, cuillère [kɥijɛr] *nf* **elle n'y va pas avec le dos de la cuiller** she doesn't go in for half measures, she doesn't do things by halves; **être à ramasser à la petite cuiller** to be completely *Br* shattered *or Am* beat; **en deux *ou* trois coups de cuiller à pot** in next to no time, in two shakes (of a lamb's tail)

cuir [kɥir] *nm* **(a)** *(peau)* skin □; **tanner le cuir à qn** to tan sb's hide **(b)** *(blouson)* leather jacket □ **(c)** *(homosexuel)* leather-boy

cuisiner [kɥizine] *vt (interroger)* to grill

cuisse [kɥis] *nf* **avoir la cuisse légère** to sleep around, to be an easy lay; **il y a de la cuisse!** there's plenty of babes *or Br* talent *or* totty!

cuistot [kɥisto] *nm* cook □

cuit, -e [kɥi, -it] *adj* **(a) être cuit** *(être pris)* to have had it, to be done for; *(être ivre)* to be wasted *or* plastered *or* smashed; **c'est cuit** I've/we've/*etc* had it **(b) c'est du tout cuit** it's in the bag, *Br* it's a dead cert, *Am* it's a lock **(c) les carottes sont cuites** the game's up

cuite [kɥit] *nf* **il tient une sacrée cuite** he's totally wrecked *or* wasted *or Br* leg-less *or* pissed; **prendre une cuite** to get wrecked *or* wasted *or Br* legless *or* pissed; **tu te souviens de ta première cuite?** do you remember the first time you got wrecked *or* wasted *or Br* legless *or* pissed?

cuiter [kɥite] *se cuiter vpr* to get wrecked *or* wasted *or Br* legless *or* pissed

cul [ky] *nm* **(a)** ⚠ *(postérieur)* Br arse, *Am* ass; **en avoir plein le cul (de)** *(en avoir assez)* to be pissed off *or Am* pissed (with); **en avoir plein le cul** *(être fatigué)* to be *Br* shagged *or Am* beat; **l'avoir dans le cul** ⚠⚠ to have been shafted *or*

screwed; **tu peux te le mettre au cul!** ⚠⚠ shove it up your *Br* arse *or Am* ass!; **lécher le cul à qn** ⚠⚠ *Br* to lick *or* kiss sb's arse, *Am* to kiss sb's ass; **trouer le cul à qn** ⚠⚠ to flabbergast sb, to knock sb sideways; **avoir qn au cul** to have sb on one's tail; **en rester sur le cul** to be flabbergasted *or Br* gobsmacked; **avoir le cul bordé de nouilles** to be a lucky bastard; **et mon cul, c'est du poulet?** *Br* you're taking the piss, aren't you!, *Am* gimme a break!; **parle à mon cul, ma tête est malade** ⚠⚠ *(personne ne m'écoute)* I might as well talk to the fucking wall; *(laisse-moi tranquille)* fuck off!; **mon cul!** ⚠⚠ no fucking way!, my *Br* arse *or Am* ass!; **être comme cul et chemise** to be as thick as thieves; **avoir le cul entre deux chaises** to be in an awkward position; **il y a des coups de pied au cul qui se perdent** a kick in the *Br* arse *or Am* ass is too good for some people; *Can* **n'avoir rien que le cul et les dents** to be at rock bottom

(b) ⚠ *(sexe)* screwing, *Br* shagging; **un film de cul** a porn movie, *Am* a skin flick; **un magazine de cul** a porn *or* skin *or* girlie mag; **il s'intéresse qu'au cul** all he thinks about is sex □, *Br* he's got sex on the brain

(c) *(chance)* **avoir du cul** ⚠ to be a lucky bastard

(d) *Pej* **cul béni** ⚠ Bible-basher, Bible-thumper, *Am* holy Joe

(e) *(camion)* **un gros cul** *Br* a juggernaut, *Am* a semi, an eighteen-wheeler

(f) faire cul sec to down one's drink in one; **cul sec!** down in one! ▶ *see also* **carrer, casser, coller, couille, crever, doigt, feu, geler, magner, peau, péter, ras, taper, tête, tirer, tortiller, trou**

culbute [kylbyt] *nf* **faire la culbute** *(faire faillite)* to go bust *or* under

culbuter ⚠ [kylbyte] *vt (posséder sexuellement)* to screw, to shaft, *Br* to shag

culot [kylo] *nm* cheek, nerve; **avoir du culot** to have a lot of nerve, *Br* to have a brass neck; **y aller au culot** to brazen *or* bluff it out

culotte [kylɔt] *nf* **poser culotte** to *Br*
have *or Am* take a dump *or* a crap ▸ see
also **pisser**

culotté, -e [kylɔte] *adj* **être culotté**
to have a lot of nerve, *Br* to have a brass
neck

cul-terreux [kytɛrø] *nm Pej* yokel,
peasant, *Am* hick, hayseed

cureton [kyrtɔ̃] *nm Pej* priest □

curie [kyri] *nm (billet de cinq cents francs)*
five-hundred franc note □

A "curie" is so called because a picture of
Pierre and Marie Curie used to feature
on the banknote.

cuti [kyti] *nf* **virer sa cuti** to change one's
whole lifestyle □; *(changer d'opinion)* to
switch allegiances □; *(devenir homosexuel)*
to become gay □

cuver [kyve] **1** *vt* **cuver son vin/sa bière**
to sleep it off
    2 *vi* to sleep it off

D

dab, dabe [dab] *nm* old man *(father)*

dac [dak] **1** *adv* **je suis/je ne suis pas dac** I agree/don't agree □
2 *exclam* OK!

d'acodac [dakodak] **1** *adv* **je suis/je ne suis pas d'acodac** I agree/don't agree □
2 *exclam* OK!

dalle [dal] *nf* **avoir la dalle** to be hungry □; **avoir la dalle en pente** to be fond of the bottle, to like a drink; **se rincer la dalle** to have a drink □ ▸ *see also* **crever, que dalle**

damer [dame] *vt* **damer le pion à qn** to go one better than sb, to outdo sb □; **se faire damer le pion** to be outdone □

dard [!!] [dar] *nm* dick, prick, cock, *Am* joint ▸ *see also* **pomper**

dare-dare [dardar] *adv* at the double, double quick; **t'as intérêt à rappliquer dare-dare: le patron veut te voir et il est pas content...** you'd better get here right away, the boss wants to see you and he's not a happy camper...

daron [darɔ̃] *nm* old man *(father)*

daronne [darɔn] *nf* old lady, *Br* old dear

dass [das] *nm* Cités *(verlan* **sida***)* the virus

daube [dob] *nf* **(a)** *(chose de mauvaise qualité)* **de la daube** (a load of) garbage *or Br* rubbish; **son dernier film, c'est une vraie daube** his last film is a right load of crap **(b)** *Suisse (personne stupide)* dimwit, *Br* pillock, *Am* jackass

dauber [dobe] *vi* to stink, *Br* to pong, to hum

dauffer [!!] [dofe] *vt* **dauffer qn** to bugger sb, to fuck sb up the *Br* arse *or Am* ass

dawa(h) [dawa] *nm* Cités havoc; **ils arrêtent pas de foutre le dawa en classe** they're always creating havoc in class

deal [dil] *nm* (drug) deal; **il a fait de la taule pour deal d'héro** he did time for dealing smack

dealer[1] [dilœr] *nm* (drug) dealer

dealer[2] [dile] *vt & vi* to deal *(drugs)*

deb [dɛb] *adj (abbr* **débile***)* daft, *Am* dumb

déballer [debale] *vt (avouer)* to pour out, to spill, to come clean about; **il a tout déballé aux flics** he spilled everything to the cops

débander [!!] [debɑ̃de] *vi* to lose one's hard-on

débarquer [debarke] *vi* **tu débarques?** where have you been?, what planet have you been on? ▸ *see also* **Anglais**

débarrasser [debarase] *vt* **débarrasser le plancher** to hit the road, to be off, to make tracks, *Am* to book it; **tu vas me faire le plaisir de me débarrasser le plancher!** would you kindly get lost!

dèbe [dɛb] *adj (abbr* **débile***)* daft, *Am* dumb

débecter [debɛkte] *vt* **débecter qn** to make sb sick

débile [debil] **1** *adj* daft, lame, *Am* dumb
2 *nmf* dope, *Br* divvy, *Am* dork

débilos [debilos] **1** *adj* daft, lame, *Am* dumb
2 *nmf* dope, *Br* divvy, *Am* dork

débine [debin] *nf* **être dans la débine** to be totally broke *or Br* skint *or* strapped

débiner [debine] **1** *vt Br* to bitch about, to slag off, to badmouth
2 se débiner *vpr* to take off, to make oneself scarce, *Br* to scarper, *Am* to bug out

Le symbole □ indique que la traduction n'est pas argotique.

débiter [debite] *vt* (*dire*) to come out with, to trot out

débloquer [deblɔke] *vi* (**a**) (*ne plus avoir toute sa tête*) to be off one's rocker, to be not all there, *Br* to be away with the fairies (**b**) (*dire n'importe quoi*) to talk crap or bull (**c**) (*ne pas fonctionner correctement*) to be on the blink, *Am* to be on the fritz

débouler [debule] *vi* to show up, to turn up; **ils ont déboulé chez moi sans prévenir** they showed up at my place without any warning; **les flics ont déboulé dans le café** the cops burst into the bar

débourrer !! [debure] *vi* to *Br* have or *Am* take a dump or a crap

déboussolé, -e [debusɔle] *adj* lost □, disorientated □; **il est complètement déboussolé depuis que sa femme l'a larguée** he's been all at sea since his wife left him

débrancher [debrɑ̃ʃe] *vt Hum* **débranchez-le!** shut him up, will you!

débris [debri] *nm* **un vieux débris** an old codger, an old fogey, *Am* a geezer

dec [dek] (*abbr* **déconner**) **sans dec** *adv* **sans dec!** (*je t'assure*) no kidding!, *Br* straight up!; **sans dec?** (*est-ce vrai?*) no kidding?, yeah?, *Br* straight up?

décalcifier [dekalsifje] **se décalcifier** *vpr Hum* to take one's *Br* trousers or *Am* pants off □, *Br* to get one's keks off

> This verb derives its humour from the pun on the word "calcif" – slang for "caleçon" – and the literal translation of the verb "to become decalcified".

décalqué, -e [dekalke] *adj* crazy, off one's rocker

décamper [dekɑ̃pe] *vi* to clear off, to make oneself scarce, to take off

décaniller [dekanije] *vi* to clear off, to make oneself scarce, to take off

décarcasser [dekarkase] **se décarcasser** *vpr* to sweat blood, to bust a gut (**pour** over); **se décarcasser pour faire qch** to sweat blood or bust a gut to do sth

décarrer [dekɑre] *vi* (**a**) (*partir*) to make tracks, to hit the road (**b**) (*s'enfuir*) to beat it, to clear off, *Am* to book it

décharger !! [deʃarʒe] *vi* (*éjaculer*) to shoot one's load

dèche [dɛʃ] *nf* poverty □; **être dans la dèche** to be broke or *Br* skint or strapped; **en ce moment c'est la dèche chez nous** we're broke or *Br* skint or strapped at the moment

déchiqueté, -e [deʃikte] *adj Cités* (*ivre*) plastered, trashed, *Br* off one's face, *Am* stiff; (*drogué*) wrecked, ripped, loaded

déchiré, -e [deʃire] *adj* (*ivre*) wasted, trashed, *Br* pissed, *Am* fried; (*drogué*) stoned

déchiros [deʃiros] *nm* weirdo, *Am* wacko

décoiffant, -e [dekwafɑ̃, -ɑ̃t] *adj* mind-blowing

décoiffer [dekwafe] *vi* **ça décoiffe** it's mind-blowing, it takes your breath away

décoller [dekɔle] *vi* (**a**) (*partir*) to be off, to get going, to make a move; **il ne décolle plus de chez nous** we can't get rid of him, he's never away from our place (**b**) (*maigrir*) to lose weight □

déconnade [dekɔnad] *nf* **quelle déconnade!** what a hoot!, what a laugh!

déconner [dekɔne] *vi* (**a**) (*dire n'importe quoi*) to talk crap or bull or *Br* bollocks; **sans déconner!** (*je t'assure*) no kidding!, *Br* straight up!; **sans déconner?** (*est-ce vrai?*) no kidding?, yeah?, *Br* straight up? (**b**) (*faire le clown*) to fool around (**c**) (*ne pas fonctionner correctement*) to play up, to be on the blink, *Am* to be on the fritz (**d**) (*ne plus avoir toute sa tête*) to be off one's rocker, to be not all there, *Br* to be away with the fairies (**e**) (*ne pas être raisonnable*) **allez, déconne pas, viens avec nous!** come on, don't be like that, come with us! □

déconneur, -euse [dekɔnœr, -øz] **1** *adj* **être déconneur** to be a clown or a troublemaker **2** *nm,f* clown, troublemaker

décor [dekɔr] *nm* **la voiture est allée dans le décor** (*hors de la route*) the car left the road □; **envoyer qn dans le**

Le symbole □ indique que la traduction n'est pas argotique.

décor (le faire tomber) to send sb flying

décrocher [dekrɔʃe] **1** vt (obtenir) to land; **son frangin a décroché un super boulot** his brother's landed this great job **2** vi (drogué) to kick the habit

décuiter [dekɥite] vi to sober up □; **ça fait trois jours qu'il décuite pas** he's been wasted or Br bladdered for three days

déculottée [dekylɔte] nf hammering, trouncing; **prendre une déculottée** to get hammered or trounced

défait, -e [defɛ,-ɛt] adj (ivre) wasted, Br slaughtered, Am tanked; (drogué) wrecked, ripped, loaded

défendre [defɑ̃dr] **se défendre** vpr (avoir un niveau honorable) to get by, to hold one's own; **c'est pas un champion mais il se défend** he's not brilliant but he gets by ▶ see also **bifteck**

défonce [defɔ̃s] nf (a) **la défonce** (le fait de se droguer) getting stoned; **à part la défonce, rien ne l'intéresse** the only thing he's interested in is getting stoned (b) **le concert des Foo Fighters, c'était vraiment la défonce intégrale** (extraordinaire) the Foo Fighters concert was totally mind-blowing or totally rocked

défoncé, -e [defɔ̃se] adj (a) (drogué) stoned, wrecked, shit-faced (b) Can (affamé) starving □; **manger comme un défoncé** to eat like a horse

défoncer [defɔ̃se] **1** vt **défoncer la gueule à qn** to smash sb's face in, Br to punch sb's lights out, Am to punch sb out **2 se défoncer** vpr (a) (se droguer) to get stoned or wrecked or shit-faced (b) (faire des efforts) to sweat blood, to work flat out ▶ see also **rondelle**

défriser [defrize] vt **et alors, ça te défrise?** have you got a problem with that?

défroquer [defrɔke] **se défroquer** vpr to take one's Br trousers or Am pants off □, Br to get one's keks off

dég [deg] adj inv (abbr **dégueulasse**) disgusting □, gross

dégager [degaʒe] vi (a) (sentir mauvais) to stink, Br to pong, to hum (b) (produire un effet puissant) (musique) to be mindblowing, to kick ass; (plat, épice) to blow the top of one's head off, to pack a punch (c) (partir) to clear off, to get moving; **allez, dégage!** get out of here!, get lost!, beat it!, Am take a hike!

dégaine [degɛn] nf strange appearance □; **il a vraiment une dégaine pas possible!** he looks like nothing on earth or like something from another planet!

dégelée [deʒle] nf thrashing, hiding; **foutre une dégelée à qn** to give sb a thrashing or a hiding; **prendre une dégelée** to get a thrashing or a hiding

déglingue [deglɛ̃g] nf decay □; **il est en pleine déglingue** he's completely fallen apart

déglingué, -e [deglɛ̃ge] adj (a) (cassé) falling apart, bust, Br knackered (b) (ivre) wrecked, Br off one's face, Am fried

dégobiller [degɔbije] vi to puke, to chunder, to barf

dégoiser [degwaze] **1** vt to come out with, to trot out; **qu'est-ce qu'il peut dégoiser comme conneries!** he can really come out with the biggest load of crap! **2** vi **dégoiser sur qn** Br to bitch about sb, to slag sb off, to badmouth sb

dégommer [degɔme] vt (a) (tuer) to blow away, to gun down (b) (tirer sur) to shoot at □ (c) (évincer) to kick out, to boot out

dégonflard, -e [degɔ̃flar, -ard], **dégonflé, -e** [degɔ̃fle] nm,f chicken (person)

dégonfler [degɔ̃fle] **se dégonfler** vpr to chicken out, Br to bottle out, to lose one's bottle

dégoter, dégotter [degɔte] vt to unearth, to stumble upon; **où est-ce que tu as dégoté ce bouquin?** where did you get hold of this book?; **il faudrait que je réussisse à dégoter une bonne bagnole d'occasion** I had to get my hands on a good second-hand car

dégoûté, -e [degute] adj (découragé) bummed (out), Br gutted; **putain, je suis**

trop dégoûté! what a bummer!, *Br* I'm gutted *or* as sick as a parrot!

dégringoler [degrɛ̃gɔle] *vi* (**a**) *(personne)* to tumble □ (**b**) *(entreprise)* to collapse □; *(prix, cours)* to slump □ (**c**) *(pleuvoir)* **ça dégringole** it's raining cats and dogs, *Br* it's bucketing down, it's chucking it down

dégrouiller [degruje] **se dégrouiller** *vpr* to get a move on, to shake a leg, *Am* to get it in gear

dégueu [degø] *adj inv (abbr* **dégueulasse**) *(sale)* disgusting □, gross; *(mauvais)* crappy, lousy, *Br* poxy; **pas dégueu** *(bon)* pretty good

dégueulasse [degœlas] **1** *adj* (**a**) *(sale)* disgusting □, gross; *(mauvais)* crappy, lousy, *Br* poxy; **pas dégueulasse** *(bon)* pretty good (**b**) *(moralement)* rotten
     2 *nm,f* (**a**) *(sale)* filthy *Br* pig *or Am* hog (**b**) *(moralement) Br* swine, *Am* stinker

dégueulasser [degœlase] *vt* to dirty, to mess up

dégueuler ⚠ [degœle] *vi* to throw up, to puke, to barf, to hurl ▸ *see also* **tripes**

dégueulis ⚠ [degœli] *nm* puke, vom, barf

déguster [degyste] *vi (souffrir)* to have a hellish time of it, to have a hell of a time

déj [deʒ] *nm (abbr* **déjeuner**) **petit déj** breakfast □

déjanté, -e [deʒɑ̃te] *Cités* **1** *adj* wacko, *Br* mental, *Am* gonzo
     2 *nm,f* headcase, *Br* headbanger

déjanter [deʒɑ̃te] *vi* to flip one's lid, to lose it, *Br* to lose the plot

delacroix [dəlakrwa] *nm* one-hundred franc note

> A "delacroix" used to be so called because a picture of the painter Eugène Delacroix used to feature on the banknote.

délire [delir] *nm (moment amusant)* **le délire!** it was wicked *or Br* mental *or Am* awesome!; **on s'est tapés un super délire!** we had a wicked *or Br* mental *or Am* awesome time!, *Am* we had a blast!

délirer [delire] *vi (s'amuser)* to have a wicked *or Br* mental *or Am* awesome time, *Am* to have a blast

déloquer [delɔke] **1** *vt* to undress □
     2 se déloquer *vpr* to get undressed □

démago [demago] **1** *adj (abbr* **démagogique**) crowd-pleasing □
     2 *nmf (abbr* **démagogue**) crowd-pleaser □

déménager [demenaʒe] *vi* (**a**) *(être fou)* to be off one's rocker *or* trolley, to have lost it, *Br* to have lost the plot (**b**) *(produire un effet puissant) (musique)* to be mind-blowing, to kick ass; *(plat, épice)* to blow the top of one's head off, to pack a punch

dément, -e [demɑ̃, -ɑ̃t] *adj (excellent)* brilliant, wicked, *Br* fab, *Am* awesome

démerdard, -e [demɛrdar, -ard] **1** *adj* resourceful □; **il est vachement démerdard** he can wangle *or Am* finagle anything
     2 *nm,f* **être un démerdard** to know a trick or two

démerde [demɛrd] *nf* **dans ce pays, tout marche à la démerde** you have to use your wits to get anything done in this country

démerder [demɛrde] **se démerder** *vpr* (**a**) *(se débrouiller)* to manage □, to get by □; **t'en fais pas, je me démerderai tout seul** don't worry, I'll manage on my own; **tu ne voulais pas que je t'aide, maintenant démerde-toi!** you didn't want me to help you, so you can manage on your own now!; **je sais pas comment il se démerde, il casse tout ce qu'il touche** I don't know how he does it, he breaks everything he lays his hands on
     (**b**) *(dans une discipline)* to manage □, to get by □
     (**c**) *(se dépêcher)* to get a move on, *Am* to get it in gear

demi-portion [dəmipɔrsjɔ̃] *nf* weed, squirt

démolir [demɔlir] *vt (battre)* to thrash, to waste

dent [dɑ̃] *nf* **avoir la dent** to be ravenous or starving; **avoir la dent dure** to be scathing □; **avoir les dents longues** *ou* **avoir les dents qui rayent le parquet** to be extremely ambitious □

dentelle [dɑ̃tɛl] *nf* **ne pas faire** *ou* **donner dans la dentelle** to be really unsubtle □ *or* in your face

dep [dɛp] *nm* Offensive (verlan **pédé**) queer, *Br* poof, *Am* fag

dépaqueter [depakte] **se dépaqueter** *vpr Can Joual* to sober up □

dépatouiller [depatuje] **se dépatouiller** *vpr* to manage □, to get by □; **se dépatouiller de qch** to get (oneself) out of sth

déplumé, -e [deplyme] *adj* bald □

déplumer [deplyme] **se déplumer** *vpr* to go bald □

dépogner [depɔɲe] **se dépogner** *vpr Can* to chill (out)

dépoiler [depwale] **se dépoiler** *vpr* to strip off

dépoter [depɔte] *vi (aller très vite)* to go like a bomb

dépouiller [depuje] *vt* **(a)** *(voler)* **dépouiller qn** to rob sb, *Br* to do sb over; **se faire dépouiller** to get robbed, *Br* to get done over **(b)** *(scandaliser)* **ça me dépouille!** it's an outrage *or* a scandal!

dépuceler [depysle] *vt* **dépuceler qn** to deflower sb □, to pop sb's cherry; **dépuceler une bouteille** to crack open a bottle

dérailler [deraje] *vi (tenir des propos insensés)* to talk drivel, to ramble

derche [!] [dɛrʃ] *nm* butt, *Br* bum, *Am* fanny; **se magner le derche** to move one's butt *or Br* bum; **un faux derche** a two-faced *Br* swine *or Am* stinker

dérouillée [deruje] *nf (correction, défaite)* thrashing, hammering; **flanquer une dérouillée à qn** to thrash *or* hammer sb; **prendre une dérouillée** to get thrashed *or* hammered

dérouiller [deruje] **1** *vt (battre)* **dérouiller qn** to thrash sb, to hammer sb
2 *vi (se faire battre)* to get thrashed *or*

hammered; *(souffrir)* to go through hell, to have a hellish time of it

derrière [dɛrjɛr] *nm* behind, backside; **c'était à se taper le derrière par terre** it was hysterical, it was a scream *or* a hoot

désaper [desape] **se désaper** *vpr* to get undressed □; **allez, désape-toi et viens me faire un gros câlin!** come on, get your clothes off *or Br* get your kit off and come and give me a cuddle!

descendre [desɑ̃dr] *vt* **(a)** *(tuer)* to blow away, to blast **(b)** *(boire)* to put away, to knock back, *Am* to inhale; **qu'est-ce qu'il descend!** he can really put it away *or* knock it back! **(c)** *(critiquer)* **descendre qn en flammes** to give sb a roasting, to crucify sb

descente [desɑ̃t] *nf* **il a une bonne** *ou* **sacrée descente** he can really put it away *or* knock it back

dessin [desɛ̃] *nm* **tu veux que je te fasse un dessin?** do you want me to draw you a map?, do I have to spell it out for you?

dessouder [desude] *vt* to kill □, to waste, *Br* to do in

destroy [dɛstrɔj] *adj (musique)* = loud, fast and aggressive; *(personne)* self-destructive □; *(jean)* ripped □; *(voiture)* beat up, wrecked, *Br* knackered

dételer [detle] *vi (arrêter de travailler)* to knock off; **sans dételer** non-stop

détente [detɑ̃t] *nf* **être long** *ou* **dur à la détente** to be a bit slow on the uptake

déterré, -e [detere] *nm,f* **avoir une mine de déterré** to look like death warmed up

deuche [dœʃ], **deudeuche** [dœdœʃ] *nf* Citroën 2CV □

deuil [dœj] *nm Hum* **il a les ongles en deuil** you could grow potatoes under his nails

deux [dø] *pron* **en moins de deux** in less than no time, in two shakes; **cette bagnole de mes deux** [!] that *Br* bloody *or Am* goddamn car; **les ordinateurs et moi, ça fait deux** I don't know the first thing about computers; **lui et moi, ça**

fait deux he and I are two different people; **il est radin comme pas deux** he's as stingy as they come; **il est menteur comme pas deux** he's an out-and-out liar

deux-pattes [døpat] *nf* Citroën 2CV ⬜

deuz, deuze [døz] (*abbr* **deuxième**) **1** *adj* second ⬜; **je suis deuze!** I'm second! **2** *nmf* second ⬜

deuzio [døzjo] *adv* secondly ⬜

devanture [dvɑ̃tyr] *nf* (a) **se faire refaire la devanture** (*un lifting*) to have a face-lift ⬜; (*se faire battre*) to get one's face wasted *or* one's features rearranged (b) *Can* (*seins*) jugs, rack

déveine [deven] *nf* rotten luck; **être dans la déveine** to have a run of bad luck ⬜

dévierger [!] [devjerʒe] *vt Can* **dévierger qn** to deflower sb ⬜, to take sb's cherry

dézinguer [dezɛ̃ge] *vt* (a) (*détruire*) to wreck (b) (*critiquer*) to pull to pieces, to slam (c) (*tuer*) to bump off

diam [djam] *nm* (*abbr* **diamant**) sparkler, rock

dico [diko] *nm* (*abbr* **dictionnaire**) dictionary ⬜

dingo [dɛ̃go] **1** *adj* crazy, bonkers, *Br* barking (mad), *Am* bonzo **2** *nmf* maniac, nutcase

dingue [dɛ̃g] **1** *adj* (a) (*fou*) crazy, crackers, off one's rocker *or Br* head (b) (*frappant*) unreal, incredible ⬜, crazy; **c'est dingue ce qu'il fait chaud!** it's unreal *or* incredible how hot it is!; **en ce moment j'ai un boulot dingue!** the amount of work I have at the moment is unreal *or* crazy! **2** *nmf* headcase, nutcase, *Br* nutter; **il va finir chez les dingues** he's going to end up in the nuthouse *or* the loony bin

dinguer [dɛ̃ge] *vi* **envoyer dinguer qch** (*jeter brutalement*) to send sth flying; **envoyer dinguer qn** (*le faire tomber*) to send sb flying; (*l'éconduire*) to tell sb where to go, *Br* to send sb packing

dire [dir] *vt* **je te dis pas!** I can't describe it!, you wouldn't believe it!; **il s'est foutu**

dans une colère, je te dis pas! he went absolutely ballistic, you wouldn't have believed it!

direct [direkt], **directo(s)** [direkto(s)] *adv* (*abbr* **directement**) right away, *Br* straight; **si tu continues à faire le con comme ça, tu vas te retrouver en taule direct** if you keep *Br* arsing about *or Am* jerking around like that, you'll be going straight to the slammer

dirlo [dirlo] *nm Br* headmaster ⬜, head, *Am* principal ⬜

discrétos [diskretos] *adv* on the quiet, on the q.t.

discutailler [diskytaje] *vi* to quibble

disjoncter [disʒɔ̃kte] *vi* (*devenir fou*) to crack up, to go round the bend, to lose it, *Br* to lose the plot

disque [disk] *nm* **change de disque!** (*change de sujet*) change the record!

dissert, disserte [disert] *nf* (*abbr* **dissertation**) essay ⬜

djig [dʒig] *nf Cités* chick, *Br* bird

djos [!] [dʒo] *nmpl Can* tits, jugs

doc [dɔk] *nf* (*abbr* **documentation**) info

doigt [dwa] *nm* (a) **faire qch les doigts dans le nez** to do sth standing on one's head *or* with one's eyes closed (b) **s'enlever les doigts du cul** [!!] to pull one's finger out (c) **faire un doigt d'honneur à qn** to give sb the finger, *Am* to flip sb the bird (d) **se mettre** *ou* **se fourrer le doigt dans l'œil (jusqu'au coude)** to be barking up the wrong tree (e) **avoir les doigts de pied en éventail** (*paresser*) to laze around; (*avoir un orgasme*) to come, to get off

domper [dɔ̃pe] *vt Can Joual* (*laisser tomber*) to dump

dondon [dɔ̃dɔ̃] *nf* **grosse dondon** fat lump, fatty

donner [dɔne] **1** *vt* (a) (*dénoncer*) to squeal on, *Br* to grass on, to shop, *Am* to rat on (b) **j'ai déjà donné** been there, done that (,got the T-shirt) **2** *vi* **ça donne** it's something else!, it's wicked *or Br* mental!

Le symbole ⬜ indique que la traduction n'est pas argotique.

3 se donner vpr (a) **s'en donner** to have the time of one's life (b) **se la donner** to show off, to pose

donneur [dɔnœr] nm Br grass, Am fink

donneuse [dɔnøz] nf Br grass, Am fink

"Donneuse" is not used as the feminine form of "donneur" – both terms always refer to a man. The use of the feminine form in this way makes the term sound even more pejorative. See also the entry **salope**.

donzelle [dɔ̃zɛl] nf little madam

dope [dɔp] nf dope, stuff, Br gear

dort-en-chiant [dɔrɑ̃ʃjɑ̃] nm Br slowcoach, Am slowpoke

dos [do] nm **l'avoir dans le dos** to get done or conned; **en avoir plein le dos** (être épuisé) to be Br knackered or shattered or Am beat or pooped; (être excédé) to be hacked off or cheesed off; **avoir qn sur le dos** to have sb on one's back; **je l'ai tout le temps sur le dos** she's always on or never off my back; **il a bon dos, le métro!** blame it on the Br underground or Am subway, why don't you!; **faire un enfant dans le dos à qn** to stab sb in the back ▶ see also **bête, cuiller**

dose [doz] nf (a) **en avoir sa dose** to have had one's fill, to have had it up to here (b) **en tenir une dose** to have nothing between one's ears, Br to be as thick as two short planks, Am to have rocks in one's head

doser [doze] vi **ça dose!** wicked!, Br fab, Am awesome!

douce [dus] **en douce** adv **faire qch en douce** to do sth on the quiet or on the q.t. ▶ see also **couler**

douiller [duje] **1** vt (payer) to fork out for **2** vi (être cher) to cost a bundle or an arm and a leg or Br a bomb

douilles [duj] nmpl (cheveux) hair ᵠ, mop; **se faire couper les douilles** to get one's hair cut ᵠ

douleur [dulœr] nf **si je le chope, il va**

comprendre sa douleur if I catch him, he'll get what's coming to him or his worst nightmares will come true

douloureuse [dulurøz] nf (addition) Br bill ᵠ, Am check ᵠ

drague [drag] nf Br chatting up, Am hitting on; **ce mec-là, c'est un pro de la drague** he's a bit of a pro at Br chatting up or Am hitting on women, that guy; **c'est un lieu de drague idéal** it's an ideal place for Br chatting people up or Am hitting on people

draguer [drage] **1** vt to come on to, Br to chat up, Am to hit on
2 vi to be Br on the pull or Am on the make; **il est parti draguer en boîte** he went out Br on the pull or Am cruising to a club

dragueur, -euse [dragœr, -øz] **1** adj **il est très dragueur** he's always Br chatting up or Am hitting on women; **il n'a jamais été très dragueur** he's never been one for Br chatting up or Am hitting on women
2 nm,f **c'est un dragueur** he's always Br chatting up or Am hitting on women

drauper [drɔper] nm (verlan **perdreau**) (policier) cop

drepou [drəpu] nf (verlan **poudre**) (héroïne) smack, scag, skag; (cocaïne) coke, snow, charlie

Duchnoque [dyʃnɔk] nm his nibs; (terme d'adresse) Br pal, matey, Am bud, buddy

Ducon [!] [dykɔ̃], **Ducon-la-joie** [!] [dykɔ̃laʒwa] nm shit-for-brains, Br dick features

dur, -e [dyr] **1** nm (train) train ᵠ
2 nm,f **un dur à cuire, une dure à cuire** a hard nut
3 exclam **dur dur!** bummer!, what a drag! ▶ see also **coup, détente, feuille**

duraille [dyrɑj] adj tough

durite [dyrit] nf **péter une durite** (se mettre en colère) to go ape or ballistic, to hit the Br roof or Am ceiling

E

eau, -x [o] *nf* **(a)** **finir** *ou* **partir en eau de boudin** *(mal se terminer)* to end in tears; *(échouer)* to go down the tubes **(b)** **il n'a pas inventé l'eau chaude** *ou* **tiède** he's not exactly bright, he's no Einstein, *Br* he'll never set the Thames on fire **(c)** **dans ces eaux-là** thereabouts □, more or less □ **(d)** **il y a de l'eau dans le gaz** there's trouble brewing ▶ *see also* **pomme**

échauffer [eʃofe] *vt* **échauffer les oreilles à qn** to bug sb, *Br* to do sb's head in, to get up sb's nose, *Am* to give sb a pain (in the neck)

éclate [eklat] *nf* **c'est l'éclate** it's a laugh *or* a hoot; **c'est pas l'éclate** it's not exactly a barrel of laughs

éclater [eklate] **1** *vt* **éclater qn, éclater la gueule à qn** to smash sb's face in, to waste sb's face
   2 s'éclater *vpr* to have a fantastic time, *Am* to have a blast

écluser [eklyze] *vt* to knock back, to down, to sink

écolo [ekolo] *adj & nmf* *(abbr* **écologiste)** green

éconocroques [ekɔnɔkrɔk] *nfpl* savings □

écoper [ekɔpe] *vi* **écoper d'une amende/de cinq ans de prison** to get *or* cop a fine/five years in prison

écorcher [ekɔrʃe] *vt* *(faire trop payer)* to fleece, *Am* to soak

écrase-merde [ekrazmɛrd] *nmpl* shoes □, clodhoppers

écraser [ekraze] **1** *vt* **en écraser** to sleep like a log
   2 *vi* **écrase!** shut up!, *Br* belt up!
   3 s'écraser *vpr* to shut up, *Br* to belt up

écroulé, -e [ekrule] *adj* **être écroulé**

(de rire) to be doubled up (with laughter), to be killing oneself (laughing), to be in stitches

ecsta [ɛksta] *nf* *(abbr* **ecstasy)** E

écumoire [ekymwar] *nf* **transformer qn en écumoire** to pump sb full of lead

effeuilleuse [efœjøz] *nf* stripper

emballer [ãbale] **1** *vt* **(a)** *(enthousiasmer)* **ça ne m'a pas emballé** I wasn't wild about it *or* *Br* mad keen on it, it didn't do much for me; **ça l'a vraiment emballé** he was really taken with it **(b)** *(séduire) Br* to pull, to get off with, *Am* to pick up
   2 s'emballer *vpr* to get carried away

emberlificoter [ãbɛrlifikɔte] **1** *vt* to hoodwink; **se laisser emberlificoter** to let oneself be hoodwinked
   2 s'emberlificoter *vpr* to tie oneself in knots; **s'emberlificoter dans ses explications** to get tangled up *or* tied up in one's explanations

embobiner [ãbɔbine] *vt* **embobiner qn** to take sb in, to con sb; **ne te laisse pas embobiner par ce filou** don't let that rogue take you in

embouché, -e [ãbuʃe] *adj* **être mal embouché** *(être de mauvaise humeur)* to be in a foul mood; *(être grossier)* to be foul-mouthed □

embrayer [ãbreje] *vi* to spit it out, to get to the point; **embrayer sur qch** to launch into the subject of sth

embringuer [ãbrɛ̃ge] **1** *vt* **embringuer qn dans qch** to get sb mixed up in sth; **il s'est laissé embringuer dans une histoire de trafic de voitures volées** he got himself mixed up in some scam involving stolen cars
   2 s'embringuer *vpr* **s'embringuer dans qch** to get mixed up in sth; **il s'est**

Le symbole □ indique que la traduction n'est pas argotique.

embringué dans une sale affaire he got himself mixed up in some nasty or Br dodgy affair

embrouille [ãbruj] nf **(a)** (situation confuse) muddle; **il s'est foutu dans une embrouille** he got himself in a complete muddle **(b)** (problème) **tenez-vous tranquilles, je veux pas d'embrouilles!** keep quiet, I don't want any trouble or hassle!; **je vois venir les embrouilles** I can see trouble ahead

embrouiller [ãbruje] vt (duper) to confuse ◻; **n'essaye pas de m'embrouiller, je sais très bien que tu me dois encore du fric** don't try to pull the wool over my eyes, I'm well aware that you still owe me some cash; **ni vu ni connu je t'embrouille** no one is/was/etc any the wiser

éméché, -e [emeʃe] adj tipsy, merry

emmanché [ãmãʃe] nm jerk, Br pillock, Am dork

emmerdant, -e [!] [ãmɛrdã, -ãt] adj **être emmerdant** to be a pain in the Br arse or Am ass, to be damn or Br bloody annoying

emmerde [!] [ãmɛrd] nm or nf trouble ◻, hassle; **avoir des emmerdes** to have a hell of a lot of problems; **en ce moment, j'ai que des emmerdes** at the moment, it's just one damn or Br bloody thing or hassle after another; **j'ai encore eu un emmerde avec la bagnole** I've had more damn or Br bloody trouble with the car

emmerdé, -e [!] [ãmɛrde] adj **avoir l'air/être emmerdé** to look/be in a bit of a mess

emmerdement [!] [ãmɛrd(ə)mã] nm = **emmerde**

emmerder [!] [ãmɛrde] **1** vt **(a)** (contrarier) **emmerder qn** to bug sb to death, to get up sb's nose, Br to piss sb off; **ça m'emmerde de devoir aller à cette réunion** it's a damn or Br bloody nuisance having to go to this meeting
(b) (ennuyer) **emmerder qn** to bore sb stiff or rigid
(c) (mépriser) **le directeur, je l'emmerde!**

the manager can go to hell or Br bugger or sod off!

2 s'emmerder vpr **(a)** (s'ennuyer) to be bored stiff or rigid; **s'emmerder à cent sous de l'heure** to be bored shitless **(b)** (se donner du mal) **s'emmerder à faire qch** to go to the bother or trouble of doing sth **(c)** **tu t'emmerdes pas!** (tu ne te refuses rien) you're not doing too badly for yourself!; (tu as du culot) you've got a Br bloody or Am goddamn nerve! ▶ see also **rat**

emmerdeur, -euse [!] [ãmɛrdœr, -øz] nm,f pain in the Br arse or Am ass, damn or Br bloody nuisance

empaffé [!!] [ãpafe] nm dickhead, prick, Br wanker

empapaouté [!] [ãpapaute] nm arsehole, Am asshole

empapaouter [!] [ãpapaute] vt to bugger, to take up the Br arse or Am ass; **va te faire empapaouter!** go to hell!, Br bugger off!, sod off!

emperlousé, -e [ãpɛrluze] adj dripping with pearls; **l'opéra était plein de vieilles emperlousées** the opera was full of old dears dripping with pearls

empiffrer [ãpifre] **s'empiffrer** vpr to stuff oneself or one's face, to pig out

empiler [!] [ãpile] vt to screw, to fleece; **se faire empiler** to get screwed or fleeced

emplafonner [ãplafɔne] vt to crash or smash into ◻; **il s'est fait emplafonner par un abruti en camionnette** some idiot in a van smashed into him

emplâtre [ãplɑtr] nm Br waster, Am klutz

empoté, -e [ãpɔte] nm,f clumsy or Br cack-handed idiot, Am klutz

en [ã] pron **en être** (être homosexuel) to be one of THEM

encadrer [ãkadre] vt **(a)** (rentrer dans) to smash or crash into ◻; **si tu continues à rouler comme un dingue tu vas finir par encadrer un lampadaire** if you keep driving like a maniac you're going to end up smashing into or wrapping

---

Le symbole ◻ indique que la traduction n'est pas argotique.

yourself round a lamppost **(b) je peux pas l'encadrer** I can't stand (the sight of) him, Br I can't stick him

encaisser [ãkese] **1** vt (tolérer) to stand, Br to stick; **je peux pas l'encaisser** I can't stand (the sight of) him, Br I can't stick him

2 vi (supporter les coups) **il sait encaisser** he can take a lot of punishment; **qu'est-ce qu'il a encaissé!** what a hammering or pasting he took!

encaldosser [!!] [ãkaldɔse] vt to bugger, to fuck up the Br arse or Am ass

enculage [!!] [ãkylaʒ] nm **(a)** (sodomisation) buggery **(b) de l'enculage de mouches** hair-splitting ☐, nit-picking

enculé [!!] [ãkyle] nm prick, Br arsehole, wanker, Am asshole; **c'est cet enculé de Michel qui m'a piqué ma mob** that prick Michel pinched my moped ▶ see also **mère**

enculer [!!] [ãkyle] vt **(a)** (sodomiser) to bugger, to fuck up the Br arse or Am ass; **va te faire enculer!** fuck off!, go and fuck yourself! **(b)** (duper) to screw, to shaft **(c) enculer les mouches** to split hairs ☐, to nit-pick

enculeur, -euse [!!] [ãkylœr, -øz] nm,f **enculeur de mouches** hair-splitter ☐, nit-picker

enfant [ãfã] nm Can **enfant de chienne** [!] son-of-a-bitch; **cet enfant de chienne m'a fait perdre mon boulot** I lost my job because of that son-of-a-bitch; **être en enfant de chienne** to be fuming, Br to be spewing

enfarinée [ãfarine] adj **arriver la gueule enfarinée** to turn up like an idiot or quite unsuspecting

enfer [ãfer] nm **(a) c'est l'enfer** it's hell (on earth) **(b) d'enfer** (excellent) great, wicked, Br fab, Am awesome ▶ see also **look**

enfiler [ãfile] **1** [!!] vt to fuck, to screw, Br to shag

2 s'enfiler vpr **(a)** (nourriture) to scoff; (boisson) to guzzle, to down, to sink **(b)** [!!] (coïter) to fuck, to screw, Br to shag

enfirouâper [ãfirwape] vt Can **(a)** (tromper) to con, to rip off; **se faire enfirouâper** (se faire rouler) to get conned, to get ripped off; (se faire mettre enceinte) to get knocked up **(b)** (nourriture) to gulp down, to wolf down

enflé [!] [ãfle] nm prick, Br arsehole, tosser, Am asshole

enflure [!] [ãflyr] nf prick, Br arsehole, tosser, Am asshole

enfoiré, -e [!!] [ãfware] nm,f (homme) bastard, fucker; (femme) bitch

engin [!] [ãʒɛ̃] nm (pénis) prick, tool

engrosser [!] [ãgrose] vt **engrosser qn** to knock sb up, Br to get sb up the duff; **elle s'est fait engrosser par un mec rencontré en boîte** some guy she met in a club knocked her up

engueulade [ãgœlad] nf bawling out, roasting, earful; **se prendre une engueulade** to get bawled out, to get a roasting or an earful

engueuler [ãgœle] **1** vt **engueuler qn** to bawl sb out, to give sb hell or a roasting; **se faire engueuler** to get bawled out, to get a roasting

2 s'engueuler vpr to be at each other's throats, Br to have a slanging match; **ses parents n'arrêtent pas de s'engueuler** his parents are always at each other's throats ▶ see also **poisson**

enguirlander [ãgirlãde] vt **enguirlander qn** to read sb the riot act; **se faire enguirlander** to get read the riot act

enquiquinant, -e [ãkikinã, -ãt] adj **(a)** (ennuyeux) deadly dull **(b)** (contrariant) **être enquiquinant** to be a pain

enquiquiner [ãkikine] vt **(a)** (ennuyer) to bore stiff or rigid **(b)** (contrarier) **enquiquiner qn** to bug sb, Br to get up sb's nose, Am to give sb a pain

enquiquineur, -euse [ãkikinœr, -øz] nm,f pain (in the neck), pest, nuisance

enrhumer [ãryme] vt to overtake at top speed; **t'aurais vu comme je l'ai enrhumé, ce blaireau, avec sa caisse pourrie!** you should have seen the speed I overtook that jerk in his old banger

---

Le symbole ☐ indique que la traduction n'est pas argotique.

entourloupe [ɑ̃turlup] *nf* dirty trick

entourlouper [ɑ̃turlupe] *vt* **entourlouper qn** to play a dirty trick on sb, *Br* to do the dirty on sb, *Am* to do sb dirt

entourloupette [ɑ̃turlupɛt] = **entourloupe**

entraver [ɑ̃trave] *vt* to understand □, to get; **j'entrave que dalle** I don't understand a damn *or Br* bloody thing

entuber [!] [ɑ̃tybe] *vt (flouer)* to screw; **se faire entuber** to get screwed

envapé, -e [ɑ̃vape] *adj* out of it, ripped, *Br* off one's face

enviandé [!!] [ɑ̃vjɑ̃de] *nm* prick, *Br* arsehole, wanker, *Am* asshole; **c'est cet enviandé d'Alex qui m'a piqué ma mob** that prick Alex pinched my moped

enviander [!!] [ɑ̃vjɑ̃de] *vt* to fuck up the *Br* arse *or Am* ass

envoyer [ɑ̃vwaje] **s'envoyer** *vpr* (a) *(absorber) (nourriture)* to scoff; *(boisson)* to guzzle, to down, to sink; *(livre)* to devour (b) [!] *(avoir des relations sexuelles avec)* *Br* to bonk, to have it off with, *Am* to ball; **s'envoyer en l'air (avec qn)** *Br* to bonk (sb), to have it off (with sb), *Am* to ball (sb) ▸ see also **balader, bouler, chier, décor, dinguer, paître, péter, pisser, promener, rose, vaidinguer, valser, vanne**

épais [epɛ] *adv* **il y en a pas épais** there isn't much/aren't many; **en avoir épais (sur le cœur)** to be feeling down

épate [epat] *nf* **c'est de l'épate** it's just showing off, it's all an act; **faire de l'épate** to show off

épingler [epɛ̃gle] *vt (arrêter)* to nab, *Br* to lift, *Am* to nail; **se faire épingler** to get nabbed *or Br* lifted *or Am* nailed

éponge [epɔ̃ʒ] *nf* (a) *(ivrogne)* lush, alky, boozer, *Am* juicer (b) **éponges** lungs □; **avoir les éponges mitées** = to have a disease of the lungs such as tuberculosis or silicosis

éreinter [erɛ̃te] *vt (critiquer sévèrement)* to pull to pieces, to pan, *Br* to slag off, to slate; **la critique a éreinté son dernier film** the critic pulled his last film to pieces

esbigner [ɛsbiɲe] **s'esbigner** *vpr* to clear off, to take off, *Am* to book it; **il s'est esbigné discrètement** he sloped off

esbroufe, esbrouffe [ɛsbruf] *nf* showing off; **faire de l'esbroufe** to show off; **décrocher un boulot à l'esbroufe** to bluff one's way into a job; **il a eu l'oral à l'esbroufe** he bluffed his way through the oral

esgourde [ɛsgurd] *nf* ear □, *Br* lug, lughole

esgourder [ɛsgurde] *vt (entendre)* to hear □; *(écouter)* to listen □

espèce [ɛspɛs] *nf* **espèce de con!** [!] you *Br* arsehole *or Am* asshole!; **espèce de menteur!** you filthy liar!; **c'est une espèce d'empoté!** he's a *Br* cack-handed idiot *or Am* klutz!; **il s'est marié avec une espèce de pouffiasse** [!] he married some old tart *or Br* slapper

espingouin [ɛspɛ̃gwɛ̃] *Offensive* **1** *adj* Dago

2 *nm* **Espingouin** Dago *(from Spain)*

> Depending on the context and the tone of voice used, this term may be either offensive or affectionately humorous. It is nonetheless inadvisable to use it unless one is quite sure of the reaction it will receive.

esquinter [ɛskɛ̃te] *vt* (a) *(endommager)* to wreck, to bust, *Br* to knacker (b) *(blesser)* to smash up; **se faire esquinter** to get smashed up

estomaquer [ɛstɔmake] *vt* to stagger, to flabbergast; **il a été estomaqué** he was staggered *or* flabbergasted *or Br* gobsmacked

estourbir [ɛsturbir] *vt* (a) *(assommer)* to knock out (b) *(tuer)* to kill □, *Br* to do in

étendre [etɑ̃dr] *vt* (a) *(faire tomber)* to floor, to deck (b) *(tuer)* to kill □, *Br* to do in (c) **se faire étendre (à un examen)** *(échouer)* to fail □ *or Am* flunk (an exam)

Étienne [etjɛn] *npr* **à la tienne, Étienne!** cheers!

étonner [etɔne] *vt Ironic* **tu m'étonnes!**

Le symbole □ indique que la traduction n'est pas argotique.

you're telling ME!, you DO surprise me!; **il s'est barré au moment de régler l'addition? alors là, tu m'étonnes!** he took off as soon as it was time to pay the bill? what a surprise!

étriper [etripe] **s'étriper** *vpr* to knock lumps out of each other, to make mincemeat of each other

étron [etrɔ̃] *nm* turd

exam [ɛgzam] *nm* (*abbr* **examen**) exam

exciter [ɛksite] **s'exciter** *vpr* (*s'énerver*) to get worked up *or* excited; **t'excite pas, je vais te le rendre ton fric!** calm down *or* don't get worked up, I'll give you your money back!

exhibo [ɛgzibo] *nmf* (*abbr* **exhibitionniste**) exhibitionist □

exo [ɛgzo] *nm* (*abbr* **exercice**) exercise □

expliquer [ɛksplike] *vt* **je t'explique pas** I can't describe it, you wouldn't believe it; **on s'est pris un de ces savons, je t'explique pas…** you wouldn't have believed the telling-off we got

exploser [ɛksploze] **1** *vt* (**a**) (*battre*) **exploser qn** to kick sb's head in, to smash sb's face in (**b**) **être explosé (de rire)** to be killing oneself (laughing), to be cracking up, to be in stitches

    2 *vi* **ils ont explosé sur la scène rock il y a vingt ans** they burst onto the rock scene twenty years ago

expo [ɛkspo] *nf* (*abbr* **exposition**) exhibition □

exta [ɛksta] *nf* (*abbr* **ecstasy**) E

extra [ɛkstra] *adj inv* great, terrific, *Br* fab, *Am* awesome

F

fac [fak] *nf* (*abbr* **faculté**) *Br* uni, *Am* school □

façade [fasad] *nf* **se ravaler la façade** to put one's face on, to put on one's warpaint; **se faire ravaler la façade** to have a face-lift □

face [fas] *nf* **face de rat** ratbag, *Am* ratfink; *Can* **avoir une face de bœuf** (*avoir l'air fâché*) to look pissed off *or Am* pissed; (*avoir l'air abruti*) to look spaced-out *or* out of it; **maudite face de bœuf!** you moron!

Note that the word "bœuf" in the expression "face de bœuf" is pronounced [bø] even though it is in the singular and so would normally be pronounced [bœf].

facho [faʃo] *adj & nmf* fascist □

facile [fasil] *adv* easily □, no problem, *Br* no probs

fada [fada] **1** *adj* crazy, crackers, off one's rocker, *Am* wacko
2 *nmf* nutcase, nutter, *Am* wacko

fadé, -e [fade] *adj* **être fadé** to take the *Br* biscuit *or Am* cake; **habituellement, ses films cassent pas des briques, mais le dernier est particulièrement fadé** his films usually aren't much to write home about, but his last one really takes the *Br* biscuit *or Am* cake

fader [fade] **se fader** *vpr* **se fader qn/qch** to get landed with sb/sth

faf¹ [faf] *adj & nmf* (*fasciste*) fascist □

faf², faffe, fafiot [faf], [fafjo] *nm* (**a**) (*billet de banque*) *Br* banknote □, *Am* greenback (**b**) **fafs, faffes, fafiots** (*papiers d'identité*) ID

fagoté, -e [fagɔte] *adj* **être mal/bizarrement fagoté** to be badly-/strangely-dressed ► *see also* **as**

faire [fɛr] **1** *vt* (**a**) **on ne me la fait pas, à moi!** you can't fool me!, there's no flies on me!
(**b**) **faire son affaire à qn** to bump sb off, *Br* to do sb in
(**c**) **ça le fait** it's well cool *or* awesome; **ça le fait pas** it's just not done; **ça le fait pas de se pointer avec une heure de retard le premier jour** it's so crap to show up an hour late on your first day
2 **se faire** *vpr* (**a**) **se faire qn** ! (*avoir des rapports sexuels avec*) to screw *or Br* shag sb; (*battre*) to beat the shit out of sb
(**b**) (*supporter*) **celui-là, il faut se le faire!** he's a total pain (in the neck)!
(**c**) **va te faire!** get out of here!, *Br* sling your hook!, eff off!, *Am* bug off!
(**d**) **on se fait un film/un resto chinois?** do you fancy going to see a film/going for a Chinese?

fait, -e [fɛ, fɛt] *adj* (*ivre*) blitzed, wasted, gassed

falloir [falwar] *v imp* **il l'a remis à sa place, comme il faut** he put him well and truly in his place; **ils leur ont mis la pâtée, comme il faut** they absolutely pasted *or* thrashed them

falzar [falzar] *nm Br* trousers □, strides, keks, *Am* pants □

famille [famij] *nf* **on s'est pris une engueulade des familles** we got a *Br* right *or Am* real roasting; **un petit gueuleton des familles** a nice little meal ► *see also* **bijou**

fana [fana] (*abbr* **fanatique**) **1** *adj* **être fana de football** to be into football, to be a football fan *or* nut
2 *nmf* fan; **un fana de football** a football fan *or* nut

farcir [farsir] **se farcir** *vpr* (**a**) (*consommer*) to scoff, to guzzle; **il s'est farci**

toute la pizza à lui tout seul he scoffed the whole pizza himself

(**b**) *(supporter)* to have to put up with; **celui-là, il faut se le farcir!** he's a total pain!

(**c**) *(faire)* **se farcir qch** to get stuck or *Br* lumbered or landed with sth; **c'est encore moi qui me suis farci toute la vaisselle** I got stuck with doing all the dishes again

(**d**) !! *(posséder sexuellement)* to screw, *Br* to have it off with, *Am* to ball

fard [far] *nm* **piquer un fard** to go red

farine [farin] *nf (héroïne)* smack, scag, skag, H; *(cocaïne)* charlie, snow

fashion [faʃœn] *adj* trendy

fastoche [fastɔʃ] *adj Br* dead or *Am* real easy; **c'était hyper fastoche** it was *Br* dead easy, it was a walk in the park or *Br* a doddle

fauche [foʃ] *nf* thieving □, pinching, *Br* nicking; **à chaque fois, il y a de la fauche** things get pinched or *Br* nicked every time

fauché, -e [foʃe] *adj* broke, *Br* skint, strapped (for cash)

faucher [foʃe] *vt (voler)* to pinch, *Br* to nick

Faucheuse [foʃøz] *nf* **la Faucheuse** *(la mort)* the Grim Reaper

fauteuil [fotœj] *nm* **arriver dans un fauteuil** to win hands down, *Br* to walk it

faux [fo] *adv* **avoir tout faux** *(se tromper)* to have got it all wrong ► *see also* **derche, jeton**

faux-cul [foky], **faux-derche** [fodɛrʃ] *nm* two-faced *Br* swine or *Am* stinker

fax [faks] *nm (femme à la petite poitrine)* ironing board

> This humorous expression probably originates in the image of a flat-chested woman being able to pass through a fax machine.

fayot [fajo] *nm* (**a**) *(personne)* crawler, *Br* creep (**b**) *(haricot)* bean □

fayoter [fajɔte] *vi* to crawl, *Br* to creep; **c'est dingue ce qu'il peut fayoter en classe!** he can be such a crawler or *Br* creep at school!

féca [feka] *nm (verlan* **café**) coffee □, *Am* java

fèche [fɛʃ] *exclam* what a drag!

> This term is a shortened form of the expression "fait chier!" and was popularized by the comic strip character Agrippine, a rebellious teenager created by the cartoonist Claire Brétécher.

Focus on:

Les femmes

Many slang terms are used to refer to women, several of which are, perhaps unsurprisingly, used only by men. There are, however, some less sexist terms which people of both genders may use, such as **nana** (a shortening of Anne, and popularized by the Zola novel) and **nénette**, although since the 1990s both of these have been overtaken in popularity by **meuf** (the "verlan" term for **femme**). A beautiful woman may be called **une belle pépée** or – much more commonly nowadays – **une bombe**, whilst one less blessed with good looks may be **une mocheté, un cageot** or **un thon**. An overweight woman may rather unkindly be called **un boudin**, whilst one who is young and fashionable will be known as **une minette**.

Men will use **gonzesse** (a very colloquial word) when talking among themselves. Terms used to actually insult a woman include **garce** (somewhat dated now), **grognasse** or **pouffiasse**. This last term, together with its shortened form **pouffe**, may also refer to a vulgar woman of low morals.

Le symbole □ indique que la traduction n'est pas argotique.

feeling [filiŋ] *nm* **faire qch au feeling** to do sth by intuition □; **on n'a pas vraiment planifié nos vacances; on va faire ça au feeling** we haven't really planned our holiday, we'll just play it by ear

feignasse [fɛɲas] *nf* lazy so-and-so; **son bonhomme est une vraie feignasse** her old man is a right lazy so-and-so

feignasser [fɛɲase] *vi* to lounge *or* laze around

feinter [fɛ̃te] *vt (duper)* to take in, to con

fêlé, -e [fele] *adj (fou)* crackers, nuts, *Br* barking, *Am* wacko

femmelette [famlɛt] *nf* wimp, drip, sissy, *Br* big girl's blouse

fendant, -e [fɑ̃dɑ̃, -ɑ̃t] *adj* hysterical, side-splitting

fendante [fɑ̃dɑ̃t] *nf* **quelle fendante!**, **la fendante!** what a scream *or* a hoot!

fendard, -e [fɑ̃dar, -ard] **1** *adj (amusant)* hysterical, side-splitting; **c'est fendard** it's hysterical *or* side-splitting
2 *nm (pantalon) Br* trousers □, keks, *Am* pants □

fendre [fɑ̃dr] **se fendre** *vpr* **(a)** *(rire)* **se fendre (la gueule** *ou* **la poire** *ou* **la pêche** *ou* **la pipe)** to kill oneself (laughing), to crack up, to split one's sides
(b) **se fendre de qch** to come up with sth; **je me suis fendu de deux cents balles** I coughed up two hundred francs; **il s'est pas fendu** he wasn't exactly generous, it didn't cost him much; **il s'est même pas fendu d'un sourire** he didn't even crack a smile
(c) *Can* **se fendre le cul en quatre** [!] *(travailler beaucoup)* to work one's *Br* arse *or Am* ass off; *(se donner beaucoup de mal)* to bust a gut, *Am* to bust one's ass

fente [!!] [fɑ̃t] *nf (sexe de la femme)* crack, gash

fer [fɛr] *nm* **se retrouver les quatre fers en l'air** to fall flat on one's back

fermer [fɛrme] *vt* **ferme ta gueule!**, **la ferme!**, **ferme-la!** shut your face *or* mouth!, shut it!, *Br* belt up! ▸ *see also* **clapet**

ferraille [fɛraj] *nf (petite monnaie)* small change □, *Br* coppers

fesse [fɛs] *nf* **(a)** *(sexe)* sex □, *Br* bonking; **il s'intéresse qu'à la fesse** he's got a one-track mind, *Br* he's got sex on the brain; **film de fesse** porn movie, *Am* skin flick; **magazine de fesse** porn *or* skin *or* girlie mag; *Can* **jouer aux fesses** [!!] to screw, *Br* to shag **(b)** **s'occuper de ses fesses** to mind one's own business ▸ *see also* **chaud, feu, peau**

fêtard, -e [fɛtar, -ard] *nm,f* party animal

fête [fɛt] *nf* **faire sa fête à qn** to give sb a hammering, *Br* to do sb over; **ça va être ma/ta/** *etc* **fête** I'm/you're/*etc* in for it

feu, -x [fø] *nm* **(a)** *(pistolet)* shooter, *Am* piece
(b) **avoir le feu au cul** [!] *ou* **aux fesses** *(être pressé)* to be in a hell of a rush; *(aimer les plaisirs charnels)* to be horny as hell *or Br* gagging for it
(c) *Cités* **mettre le feu** to knock them dead; **je suis allé voir Eminem en concert, il a vraiment mis le feu à la salle** I went to see Eminem in concert, he really got the crowd going
(d) *Can* **prendre le feu** to blow a gasket *or* a fuse; **prendre le feu au cul** [!!] to go apeshit ▸ *see also* **péter, plancher[1]**

feuille [fœj] *nf* **(a)** **être dur de la feuille** to be hard of hearing □ **(b)** *(billet de banque)* note □, *Am* greenback

feuj [føʒ] *(verlan juif)* **1** *adj* Jewish □
2 *nmf* Jew □

fiasse [fjas] *nf* **(a)** *(prostituée)* whore, hooker **(b)** *(femme aux mœurs légères)* slut, tart, tramp, *Br* scrubber **(c)** *(femme désagréable)* bitch, *Br* cow

ficelé, -e [fisle] *adj* **(a)** *(habillé)* **être mal ficelé** *Br* to be dressed like a scarecrow *or* a tramp, *Am* to look like a bum **(b)** *(structuré) (histoire, scénario)* **bien/bizarrement ficelé** well-/strangely-structured □

fiche [fiʃ], **ficher** [fiʃe] **1** *vt (faire)* to do □; **mais qu'est-ce qu'il fiche?** what on earth is he doing?
2 se fiche, se ficher *vpr* **se fiche** *ou* **se ficher de qn/qch** not to give a damn about sb/sth; **je m'en fiche pas mal!** I

don't give a damn, I couldn't care less!; **tu te fiches de moi?** are you making a fool of me?

fichu, -e [fiʃy] *adj* (**a**) *(hors d'usage)* **être fichu** to have had it, to be done for, *Br* to be knackered

(**b**) *(condamné à une mort certaine)* **être fichu** to be done for, to have had it

(**c**) *(dépréciatif) Br* blasted, *Am* darn(ed); **il a un fichu caractère** he's so *Br* blasted *or Am* darn(ed) difficult

(**d**) *(fait)* **être bien/mal fichu** to have/ not to have a great bod; **elle est bien fichue, votre cuisine** your kitchen's really well designed □; **un roman bien fichu** a well-structured novel □

(**e**) **mal fichu** *(malade)* under the weather, off-colour

(**f**) *(capable)* **être fichu de faire qch** to be quite capable of doing sth □; **il est pas fichu de le faire** he can't do it □ ▶ see also **as**

fier-pet [fjɛrpɛ] *Can* **1** *adj* pompous □, conceited □

2 *nm* pompous ass

fiesta [fjɛsta] *nf* wild party □; **faire la fiesta** to party

fieu [fjø] *nm Belg* sonny

fifi [fifi] *nm Can* (**a**) *(petit garçon efféminé)* sissy (**b**) *Offensive (homosexuel)* pansy, *Br* poof

fifille [fifij] *nf* girl □, chick

fifine [fifin] *nf Can Offensive (lesbienne)* dyke

fifty-fifty [fiftififti] *adv* fifty-fifty

filer [file] **1** *vt (donner)* to give □; **file-moi une clope** give me a *Br* fag *or Am* cig; **filer une baffe à qn** to smack *or* clout sb

2 *vi (partir)* to get going *or* moving; **il faut que je file** I must be off, I have to get going; **allez, file, tu vas être en retard!** go on, off you go, you're going to be late!

film [film] *nm* **se faire un film** to be living in a dream world

filoche [filɔʃ] *nf* shadowing, tailing

filocher [filɔʃe] **1** *vt (suivre)* to shadow, to tail

2 *vi (se dépêcher)* to get a move on, to move it, to get one's skates on, *Am* to get it in gear

fiole [fjɔl] *nf* (**a**) *(visage)* face □, mug (**b**) *(tête)* head □, nut

fion [!][fjɔ̃] *nm* (**a**) *(postérieur) Br* arse, *Am* ass; **se casser le fion (pour faire qch)** to bust a gut *or Am* one's ass (doing sth) (**b**) *(anus) Br* arsehole, *Am* asshole; **l'avoir dans le fion** *(se faire avoir)* to get shafted (**c**) *(chance)* luck □; **avoir du fion** to be lucky □; **ne pas avoir de fion** to be unlucky □

fiotte [!!][fjɔt] *nf Offensive* queer, *Br* poof, *Am* fag

fissa [fisa] *adv* **faire fissa** to get a move on, to get one's skates on, *Am* to get it in gear

fix, fixe [fiks] *nm* fix *(of drug)*

fixette [fiksɛt] *nf* **faire une fixette sur qn/qch** to be obsessed with sb/sth □, *Br* to have sb/sth on the brain

flag [flag] **en flag** *adv (abbr* **en flagrant délit)* **être pris en flag** to get caught red-handed *or* with one's pants down

flagada [flagada] *adj inv* washed-out; **je me sens tout flagada depuis quelques jours** I've been feeling all washed-out for several days

flamber [flɑ̃be] **1** *vt (dépenser)* to blow; **il flambe un fric fou** he spends money like water

2 *vi* (**a**) *(jouer avec passion)* to be a heavy gambler □ (**b**) *(se donner des airs)* to show off

flambeur, -euse [flɑ̃bœr, -øz] *nm,f* (**a**) *(joueur)* heavy gambler □ (**b**) *(personne qui se donne des airs)* show-off

flan [flɑ̃] *nm* (**a**) **en rester comme deux ronds de flan** to be flabbergasted *or Br* gobsmacked (**b**) **c'est du flan** it's a load of nonsense *or Br* rubbish

flancher [flɑ̃ʃe] *vi (abandonner)* to chuck it in, to throw in the towel; **son cœur a flanché** his heart gave out; **j'ai la mémoire qui flanche** my memory's going

flanc-mou [flɑ̃mu] *nm Can Br* skiver, *Am* goldbrick

Le symbole □ indique que la traduction n'est pas argotique.

flanquer [flãke] **1** vt **flanquer une claque/un coup à qn** to smack/punch sb; **flanquer qch par terre** (en le faisant exprès) to chuck or fling sth on the floor; (accidentellement) to knock sth onto the floor ᵁ; **flanquer qn à la porte** to kick sb out; **flanquer la trouille à qn** to put the wind up sb, to scare sb stiff or witless
 2 se flanquer vpr **se flanquer (la gueule) par terre** to fall flat on one's face

flapi, -e [flapi] adj dead beat, bushed, Br knackered

flash [flaʃ] nm rush (after taking drugs)

flasher [flaʃe] vi (a) (après absorption de drogue) to get a rush (b) **flasher sur qn** to fall for sb; **flasher sur qch** to fall in love with sth

flèche [flɛʃ] nm **j'ai pas un flèche** I'm totally broke or Br skint or strapped

flémingite [flemɛ̃ʒit] nf Hum laziness ᵁ, lazyitis; **être atteint de flémingite aiguë** to suffer from acute laziness or lazyitis

flemmard, -e [flemar, -ard] **1** adj lazy ᵁ
 2 nm,f lazy so-and-so

flemmarder [flemarde] vi to laze or lounge about

flemme [flɛm] nf laziness ᵁ; **j'ai la flemme** I can't be bothered doing anything, I don't feel like doing anything; **j'ai la flemme de le faire maintenant** I can't be bothered doing it just now; **je me traîne une de ces flemmes depuis quelque temps** I haven't felt like doing anything for a while now

flic [flik] nm cop, Br plod, Am flatfoot

flicage [flikaʒ] nm police surveillance ᵁ; **ils craignent le flicage du courrier électronique par la direction** they are afraid that the management are checking their e-mails ᵁ

flicaille [flikaj] nf **la flicaille** the cops, the pigs, Br the filth

flingue [flɛ̃g] nm shooter, Am piece

flinguer [flɛ̃ge] **1** vt (a) (tuer) to blow away (b) (casser) to wreck, to bust, Br to knacker
 2 se flinguer vpr to blow one's brains out

flip [flip] nm (a) (déprime) **être en plein flip** to be on a real downer; **c'est le flip!** what a downer! (b) (après l'absorption de drogue) depression ᵁ, downer (as the after-effect of taking cocaine or amphetamines)

flippant, -e [flipã, -ãt] adj (déprimant) depressing ᵁ; **être flippant** to be a downer

flipper [flipe] vi (a) (être angoissé) to feel down, to be on a downer; **faire flipper qn** to get sb down (b) (avoir peur) to be scared ᵁ (c) (après absorption de drogue) to feel down (as the after-effect of taking cocaine or amphetamines) ▶ see also **mère**

fliqué, -e [flike] adj crawling or heaving with cops

fliquer [flike] vt Pej (a) (population, employés) to keep under surveillance ᵁ; **il flique complètement sa femme** he watches his wife like a hawk (b) (quartier) to police ᵁ

flo [flo] nmf Can (adolescent) teenager ᵁ, Am teen

flopée, floppée [flɔpe] nf **une flopée (de)** a whole bunch (of), loads (of), tons (of)

flotte [flɔt] nf (eau) water ᵁ; **prendre la flotte** to get soaked (in the rain); **tomber à la flotte** to fall in ᵁ; **t'as pas autre chose que de la flotte à nous proposer?** have you got nothing better than water to offer us?

flotter [flɔte] vi (pleuvoir) to rain ᵁ

flouse, flouze [fluz] nm cash, dough, Br dosh, Am bucks

flûte [flyt] nf (a) (mensonges) lies ᵁ, Br porkies (b) **jouer de la flûte** ‼, **tailler une flûte** ‼ to give sb a blow job, to suck sb off, to give sb head

flûter [flyte] vi (dire des mensonges) to tell lies ᵁ or Br porkies

flûteur, -euse [flytœr, -øz] nm,f liar ᵁ

flyé, -e [flaje] Can Joual **1** adj spaced-out, spacey
 2 nm,f (paumé) space cadet; (drogué) junkie

Le symbole ᵁ indique que la traduction n'est pas argotique.

flyer [flajœr] nm (prospectus de club) flier □, flyer □

foies [fwa] nmpl **avoir les foies** to be scared stiff or to death or out of one's wits

foin [fwɛ̃] nm (a) **faire du foin** (du tapage) to make a racket; (du scandale) to make waves, to cause a stink (b) Can **avoir du foin** (être riche) to be loaded; **il a du foin à vendre** (sa braguette est ouverte) he's flying low, his flies are undone □

foire [fwar] nf (a) (désordre) chaos □, Br bedlam; **c'est la foire, là-dedans!** it's a madhouse or Br it's bedlam in there! (b) **faire la foire** to have a wild time; **il ne pense qu'à faire la foire** all he thinks about is having a good time

foirer [fware] **1** vt (rater) to make a Br cock-up or balls-up or Am ball-up of; **j'ai complètement foiré l'interro d'anglais** I made a complete Br cock-up or balls-up or Am ball-up of the English exam **2** vi (a) (échouer) to be a Br cock-up or balls-up or Am ball-up; **le coup a complètement foiré** the job was a complete Br cock-up or balls-up or Am ball-up (b) ‼ (déféquer) to shit, to crap; **il a foiré dans son froc tellement il a eu la trouille** he was so scared he shat himself

foireux, -euse [fwarø, -øz] adj hopeless, useless; **j'en ai marre de lui et de ses plans foireux** I've had it up to here with him and his useless schemes

foldingue [fɔldɛ̃g] adj crazy, loopy, Br mental, Am wacko

folichon, -onne [fɔliʃɔ̃, -ɔn] adj **pas folichon** not much fun; **ça n'a rien de folichon** it's no fun

folkeux, -euse [fɔlkø, -øz] nm,f (amateur de musique folklorique) folkie

folklo [fɔlklo] adj inv (abbr **folklorique**) bizarre, weird and wonderful; (personne) eccentric □, loopy, off-the-wall, Am kooky

folle [fɔl] nf (homosexuel) queen; **c'est vraiment une folle perdue ce mec-là, on croirait qu'il sort tout droit de "La Cage aux Folles"** that guy really is a screaming queen, he's like something out of "La Cage aux Folles"

foncedé, -e [fɔ̃sde] adj Cités (verlan **défoncé**) stoned, wrecked

fondu, -e [fɔ̃dy] adj (fou) round the bend, out to lunch, off one's rocker or trolley

fonsdé, -e [fɔ̃sde] adj Cités (verlan **défoncé**) stoned, wrecked

foot [fut] nm (abbr **football**) soccer □, Br football □, footie

footeux [futø] nm (amateur de football) Br footie fan, Am soccer fan □

foqué ‼ [fɔke] Can Joual **1** adj fucked-up **2** nm,f fuck-up

> This word comes from the English word "fuck".

foquer ‼ [fɔke] vt Can Joual (voiture) to fuck; (personne, famille) to fuck up

> This word comes from the English word "fuck".

fort [fɔr] **1** adj **c'est fort** that's quite something; **c'est un peu fort (de café)** that's a bit much or rich **2** adv (a) **y aller un peu fort** to go a bit over the top or Br OTT; **tu y es allé un peu fort avec le poivre** you overdid it a bit with the pepper (b) **faire fort** to do really well □, to excel oneself □ ▶ see also **gueule**

fortiche [fɔrtiʃ] adj clever □, smart □; **il est fortiche aux échecs, mon cousin** my cousin's brilliant at chess

fortifs [fɔrtif] nfpl = the old defence works around Paris, once a favourite area for criminals

fossile [fosil] nm (individu rétrograde) fossil

fouetter [fwɛte] vi (sentir mauvais) to stink, Br to pong

foufoune ! [fufun] nf (a) (sexe de la femme) pussy, Br fanny, snatch (b) Can **foufounes** (fesses) buns, butt

fouille [fuj] nf (poche) pocket □

fouille-merde ! [fujmɛrd] nmf inv busybody, Br nosey parker

fouiller [fuje] **se fouiller** ! vpr **tu peux toujours te fouiller!** you haven't a hope in hell!

fouiner [fwine] *vi* to nose *or* ferret about (**dans** in)

fouler [fule] *se fouler* *vpr* **se fouler (la rate)** to strain *or* overexert oneself □; **t'aurais pu te fouler un peu plus!** you could have made a bit more of an effort!; **tu t'es vraiment pas foulé (la rate)!** you didn't exactly strain *or* overexert yourself!

foultitude [fultityd] *nf* **une foultitude (de)** masses (of), loads (of), tons (of)

foune [!] [fun] *nf* pussy, *Br* fanny, snatch; **avoir de la foune** *(avoir de la chance) (habituellement)* to have the luck of the devil; *(ponctuellement)* to have a stroke of luck □

four [fur] *nm (échec)* flop, *Br* washout, *Am* bomb, turkey; **faire un four** to be a flop *or Br* a washout, *Am* to bomb

fourbi [furbi] *nm* **(a)** *(désordre)* shambles, mess **(b)** *(affaires)* stuff, *Br* gear

fourguer [furge] *vt* **(a)** *(vendre)* to flog; *(placer)* to unload, to palm off; **fourguer qch à qn** *(vendre)* to flog sth to sb; *(placer)* to unload sth on sb, to palm sth off on sb **(b)** *(dénoncer)* to squeal on, *Br* to grass on, to shop, *Am* to rat on

fourmi [furmi] *nf (petit revendeur de drogue)* (small-time) dealer

fourrer [fure] *vt* **(a)** *(mettre)* to stick, to shove **(b)** [!!] *(posséder sexuellement)* to shaft, to poke, to ride; *Can Joual* **fourrer le chien** *(perdre son temps)* to fuck around ▶ *see also* **doigt**

foutage [futaʒ] *nm* **c'est du foutage de gueule** you/they/*etc* gotta be kidding!, *Br* that's just taking the piss!

foutaise [futɛz] *nf* **de la foutaise, des foutaises** crap, bull; **raconter des foutaises** to talk crap *or* bull

fouteur, -euse [futœr, -øz] *nm,f* **fouteur de merde** [!] shit-stirrer, *Am* buttinski

foutoir [futwar] *nm* shambles; **quel foutoir dans sa chambre!** her room's a complete pigsty *or* tip!

foutraque [futrak] *adj* nuts, *Br* crackers

foutre [futr] **1** *vt* **(a)** [!] *(faire)* to do □; **ne**

rien foutre, ne pas en foutre une to do damn all *or Br* bugger *or* sod all; **j'en ai rien à foutre!** I don't give a shit!; **qu'est-ce qu'il fout?** what the hell is he doing?; **qu'est-ce que tu veux que ça me foute?** what the hell do I care?, what the hell does it matter to me?; **qu'est-ce que j'ai bien pu foutre de mes clés?** what the hell can I have done with my keys?

(b) [!] *(mettre)* to stick, to dump, *Br* to bung; **il sait pas où il a foutu les clés** he doesn't know what the hell he's done with the keys; **il peut pas bouffer sans en foutre partout** he can't eat without getting his food everywhere; **foutre qch par terre** *(en le faisant exprès)* to stick *or* dump *or Br* bung sth on the floor; *(accidentellement)* to knock sth onto the floor □; **foutre qn à la porte** to chuck *or* kick sb out; **foutre son poing dans la gueule à qn** to give sb a punch in the face; **foutre la paix à qn** to get off sb's back; **ça la fout mal** it doesn't look too good; **foutre qn dedans** to mislead sb □; **j't'en foutrais, moi, de l'esprit d'équipe!** team spirit, I'll give you *Br* bloody *or Am* goddamn team spirit!; **qui est-ce qui m'a foutu un empoté pareil?** how the hell did I end up with such a total *Br* arsehole *or Am* asshole?

(c) va te faire foutre [!!] fuck off!; **qu'il aille se faire foutre!** [!!] he can fuck right off!

2 *vi* **foutre sur la gueule à qn** [!] to waste sb's face, to smash sb's face in

3 *se foutre* [!] *vpr* **(a)** *(se mettre)* **se foutre à faire qch** to start doing sth □; **il s'est foutu de l'encre partout** he covered himself in ink □; **s'en foutre plein les poches** to rake it in; **se foutre par terre, se foutre la gueule par terre** [!!] to fall flat on one's face; **se foutre dedans** to screw up

(b) se foutre de qch not to give a shit about sth; **se foutre de qn** *(être indifférent)* not to give a damn *or* a shit *or Br* a toss about sb; *(se moquer)* to make a fool of sb, *Br* to take the piss out of sb; **une montre en or! elle s'est pas foutue**

de toi! a gold watch! she didn't make a fool of you or Br take the piss out of you!

4 !!! nm spunk, come, cum ▶ see also **air, camp, gueule**

foutrement ! [futrəmɑ̃] adv damn(ed), Br bloody

foutu, -e ! [futy] adj **(a)** (hors d'usage) **être foutu** to have had it, to be done, Br to be knackered or buggered

(b) (condamné à une mort certaine) **être foutu** to have had it, to be done for

(c) (sans espoir) **c'est foutu, jamais on n'y arrivera** we're Br buggered or Am screwed, we'll never manage it

(d) (dépréciatif) damn(ed), godawful, Br bloody; **elle a un foutu caractère** she's so damn(ed) or Br bloody difficult

(e) (fait) **être bien/mal foutu** to have/not to have a great bod; **elle est bien foutue, votre cuisine** your kitchen's really well designed □; **un roman bien foutu** a well-structured novel □

(f) mal foutu (souffrant) under the weather, Br off-colour, Am off-color

(g) (capable) **être foutu de faire qch** to be quite capable of doing sth □; **ne pas être foutu de faire qch** to be incapable of doing sth □ ▶ see also **as**

fracasse [frakas], **fracassé, -e** [frakase] adj Cités smashed, wrecked, wasted

fraîche [frɛʃ] nf (argent) cash, dough, Br dosh, Am bucks

frais¹ [frɛ] nm **mettre qn au frais** to put sb inside or away or behind bars

frais² [frɛ] nmpl **(a) aux frais de la princesse** (aux frais de l'État) at the taxpayer's expense □; (aux frais d'une société) at the company's expense □ **(b) arrêter les frais** to throw in the towel

frais-chié, -e ! [frɛʃje] nm,f Can (homme) cocky bastard; (femme) cocky bitch

fraise [frɛz] nf **ramener sa fraise** (arriver) to turn up, to show (up), to show one's face; (intervenir inopportunément) to stick one's nose or oar in; **mais je t'ai rien demandé! pourquoi il faut toujours que tu ramènes ta fraise?** I didn't

ask you, why do you always have to stick your oar in?; **ramène ta fraise!** get over here! ▶ see also **sucrer**

franchouillard, -e [frɑ̃ʃujar, -ard] **1** adj typically French □

2 nm,f typical Frenchman, f Frenchwoman □

> This word, whilst not overly pejorative, describes the average French person complete with the stereotypical characteristics of narrow-mindedness and jingoism.

franco [frɑ̃ko] adv **vas-y franco!** (pour encourager quelqu'un) go for it!; **vas-y franco si tu veux que ça rentre** you'll have to hit/push/etc it hard for it to go in; **il y est allé franco avec le piment** he didn't hold back with the chilli; **elle lui a dit ce qu'elle pensait de lui et elle y est allé franco** she told him what she thought of him and she didn't mince her words

frangibus [frɑ̃ʒibys] nm brother □, bro

frangin [frɑ̃ʒɛ̃] nm brother □, bro

frangine [frɑ̃ʒin] nf **(a)** (sœur) sister □, sis **(b)** (femme, fille) chick, Br bird

frappadingue [frapadɛ̃g] adj crazy, bonkers, Br mental

frappe [frap] nf **une (petite) frappe** a (little) hoodlum or Am hood

frappé, -e [frape] adj (fou) crazy, loopy, touched

frapper [frape] se **frapper** vpr **ne pas se frapper** not to get worked up; **te frappe pas** take it easy!, chill out!

frérot [frero] nm brother □, bro

fric [frik] nm cash, dough, Br dosh, Am bucks

frichti [friʃti] nm cooked meal □; **ça sent bon le frichti** there's a nice smell of cooking □

> This word comes from an Alsatian word similar to the German word "Frühstück", which means "breakfast".

fricot [friko] nm food □, eats, chow, grub

Le symbole □ indique que la traduction n'est pas argotique.

fricoter [frikɔte] **1** *vt* **qu'est-ce qu'il fricote?** what's he up to?

2 *vi* **fricoter avec qn** *(avoir des relations sexuelles)* to have a thing going with sb; *(avoir des relations)* to have shady *or Br* dodgy dealings with sb; **il paraît que ce politicien fricote avec la Mafia** apparently this politician has some shady *or Br* dodgy dealings with the Mafia

Fridolin [fridɔlɛ̃] *nm Offensive* Kraut

This term is somewhat dated now and is normally used in the context of Franco-German conflicts, such as the two World Wars. Depending on the context and the tone of voice used, it may be either offensive or affectionately humorous.

frigo [frigo] *nm (abbr* **Frigidaire®***)* fridge

frime [frim] *nf* **(a)** *(fanfaronnade)* **les lunettes noires, c'est pour la frime** dark glasses are just for posing in; **bon, t'arrête ta frime?** will you stop showing off!; **tu l'aurais vu avec son nouveau cuir, la frime!** you should have seen him in his new leather jacket, what a poser! **(b)** *(comportement trompeur)* **c'est de la frime** it's all an act, it's all put on

frimer [frime] *vi* to show off

frimeur, -euse [frimœr, -øz] *nm,f* show-off

fringale [frɛ̃gal] *nf* hunger □; **avoir la fringale** to have the munchies

fringue [frɛ̃g] *nf* piece of clothing □; **j'ai plus une fringue à me mettre** I haven't a thing to wear; **des fringues** clothes □, threads, *Br* gear

fringuer [frɛ̃ge] **se fringuer** *vpr* to get dressed □; **être bien/mal fringué** to be well-/badly-dressed □; **elle aime bien se fringuer pour sortir** she likes to get all dressed up to go out; **il sait pas se fringuer** he's got no dress sense; **elle se fringue très seventies** she wears really seventies clothes, she dresses really seventies

fripé, -e [fripe] *adj Can* bushed, *Br* knackered, shattered

friqué, -e [frike] *adj* loaded, *Br* rolling in it, *Am* rolling in dough

Frisé [frize] *nm Offensive (Allemand)* Kraut

This term is somewhat dated now and is normally used in the context of Franco-German conflicts, such as the two World Wars. Depending on the context and the tone of voice used, it may be either offensive or affectionately humorous.

frisquet, -ette [friskɛ, -ɛt] *adj* chilly □, *Br* nippy, parky; **il fait frisquet ce matin** it's a bit chilly *or Br* nippy this morning

frite [frit] *nf* **(a)** *(énergie)* **avoir la frite** to be on top form, to have bags of energy **(b)** *(coup)* flick; **faire une frite à qn** to flick sb on the bottom **(c)** *(visage)* face □, mug; **se fendre la frite** to crack up, to howl (with laughter)

friter [frite] **1** *vt (battre)* **friter qn** to beat sb up, to kick sb's head in

2 se friter *vpr* to have a *Br* punch-up *or Am* fist fight; **il y avait deux mecs en train de se friter dans la rue** there were two guys having a *Br* punch-up *or Am* fist fight in the street

fritz [frits] *nm Offensive* Kraut

This term is somewhat dated now and is normally used in the context of Franco-German conflicts, such as the two World Wars. Depending on the context and the tone of voice used, it may be either offensive or affectionately humorous.

froc [frɔk] *nm (pantalon) Br* trousers □, keks, *Am* pants □; **faire dans son froc** *(déféquer, avoir peur)* to shit *or* crap oneself; **baisser son froc** to demean oneself □; **il a encore baissé son froc devant le patron** he behaved like a total wimp with the boss again ▶ *see also* **chier, pisser**

from [frɔm] *nmf (abbr* **fromage blanc***)* *(Français de souche)* = French person of native stock as opposed to immigrants or their descendants

fromage [frɔmaʒ] *nm* (a) **il n'y a pas de quoi en faire tout un fromage** there's no need to make such a big deal *or* a song and dance about it, *Am* there's no need to make a federal case out of it (b) **fromage blanc** *(Français de souche)* = French person of native stock as opposed to immigrants or their descendants

fromgi [frɔmʒi], **frometon** [frɔmtɔ̃] *nm* cheese ⁰

frotte-manche [frɔtmɑ̃ʃ] *nmf Belg* bootlicker

frotter [frɔte] *vt Belg* **frotter la manche à qn** to butter sb up

frotteur [frɔtœr] *nm* = pervert who enjoys rubbing himself against women in crowded places

froussard, -e [frusar, -ard] *adj & nm,f* chicken *(person)*

frousse [frus] *nf* **avoir la frousse** to be scared ⁰; **foutre la frousse à qn** to scare the living daylights out of sb

frusques [frysk] *nfpl* clothes ⁰, threads, *Br* gear

fumant, -e [fymɑ̃, -ɑ̃t] *adj* **un coup fumant** a masterstroke ⁰

fumantes [fymɑ̃t] *nfpl (chaussettes)* socks ⁰

fumasse [fymas] *adj* fuming, livid

fumer [fyme] *vt* (a) *(battre)* to clobber, to thump (b) *(tuer)* to kill ⁰, *Br* to do in

fumette [fymɛt] *nf* getting stoned; **c'est un habitué de la fumette** he gets stoned regularly; **il y a que la fumette qui l'intéresse** all he's interested in is getting stoned

fumier ⚠ [fymje] *nm* bastard, shit; **espèce de fumier!** you bastard!

fumiste [fymist] **1** *adj (attitude, personne)* lazy ⁰; **il est un peu fumiste** he's a bit of a shirker
2 *nmf* shirker, *Br* layabout; **c'est un fumiste** he doesn't exactly kill himself working

fumisterie [fymistəri] *nf* sham, farce; **une vaste fumisterie** an absolute farce

fun [fœn] **1** *adj inv* fun ⁰
2 *nm* fun ⁰; **faire qch pour le fun** to do sth just for fun *or* for the fun of it

furax [fyraks], **furibard, -e** [fyribar, -ard] *adj* seething, livid

fusée [fyze] *nf* **lâcher une fusée** *(vomir)* to throw up, to puke, to chunder; *(faire un pet)* to fart, *Br* to let off

fusiller [fysije] *vt (briser)* to wreck, to bust, *Br* to knacker; **baisse le volume, autrement tu vas fusiller tes enceintes** turn it down or you're going to wreck *or Br* knacker your speakers

futal [fytal], **fute** [fyt] *nm Br* trousers ⁰, keks, *Am* pants ⁰

fute-fute [fytfyt] *adj* **elle n'est pas fute-fute** she's not exactly bright, *Am* she's no rocket scientist

G

G [ʒe] nm Belg (abbr **GSM**) (téléphone portable) mobile

gadin [gadɛ̃] nm **prendre** ou **se ramasser un gadin** to fall flat on one's face

gadji [gadʒi] nf Cités chick, Br bird

gadjo [gadʒo] nm Cités guy, Br bloke

gaffe [gaf] nf (a) (bévue) gaffe, blunder, Br boob, Am boo-boo; **faire une gaffe** to put one's foot in it, to boob, Am to make a boo-boo, to goof
(b) **fais gaffe, tu risques de glisser!** watch out, you might slip!; **faire gaffe à qch** (y prendre garde) to be careful of sth, to watch out for sth; **fais gaffe à toi!** (prends soin de toi) take care of yourself!; (menace) be careful!, watch it!; **fais gaffe à ce que tu dis!** be careful or watch what you say!

gaffer [gafe] vi to put one's foot in it, Br to boob, Am to make a boo-boo, to goof

gaffeur, -euse [gafœr, -øz] **1** adj **être gaffeur** to be always putting one's foot in it
2 nm,f **c'est un gaffeur** he's always putting his foot in it

gaga [gaga] adj gaga, Br away with the fairies

gagedé [gaʒde] exclam Cités (verlan **dégage**) get out of here!, get lost!

galère [galɛr] **1** adj **c'est galère** what a pain or hassle; **lui et ses plans galères!** him and his lousy ideas!
2 nf (situation pénible) pain, hassle; **c'est la galère!, quelle galère!** what a pain or hassle!; **se foutre dans une galère** to get oneself into a mess

galérer [galere] vi to have a hard time (of it); **tu vas galérer pour trouver à te garer dans le quartier** you're going to have a hard time or a lot of hassle finding

a parking space in the area; **il a beaucoup galéré dans sa jeunesse** he had a really hard time of it when he was young

galette [galɛt] nf (a) (argent) cash, dough, Br dosh, Am bucks (b) (disque) record □

galipote [galipɔt] nf Can **courir la galipote** to chase anything in a skirt

galoche [galɔʃ] nf French kiss; **rouler une galoche à qn** to French-kiss sb, Br to snog sb

galure [galyr], **galurin** [galyrɛ̃] nm hat □

gamberger [gɑ̃berʒe] vi (a) (réfléchir) to think hard □ (b) (ruminer) to brood □

gambette [gɑ̃bɛt] nf leg □, pin ▶ see also **tricoter**

gamelle [gamɛl] nf (a) (baiser) French kiss; **rouler une gamelle à qn** to French-kiss sb, Br to snog sb (b) **prendre une gamelle** to fall flat on one's face

ganache [ganaʃ] nf Br divvy, wally, Am dork

gâpette [gɑpɛt] nf (flat) cap □

garage [garaʒ] nm Hum **garage à bites** ‼ nympho; **c'est un vrai garage à bites** ‼ she's seen more ceilings than Michelangelo

garce [gars] nf bitch, Br cow

garde-à-vous [gardavu] nm Hum **être au garde-à-vous** (avoir une érection) to have a hard-on or boner

garetteci [garetsi] nf Cités (verlan **cigarette**) Br fag, Am cig

garrocher [garɔʃe] Can **1** vt to chuck, to fling
2 se garrocher vpr to get a move on, to move it, Am to get it in gear

gaspard [gaspar] nm rat □

Le symbole □ indique que la traduction n'est pas argotique.

gastos [gastos] *nm (bistrot)* bar[□], *Br* boozer

gâteau [gɑto] *nm* **c'est pas du gâteau** *(c'est pénible)* it's no picnic, it's no walk in the park; *(ça demande un effort intellectuel)* it's no walkover, it's not as easy as it looks, *Am* it's no cakewalk

gâterie [gɑtri] *nf* Hum **faire une gâterie à qn** ! *(fellation)* to go down on sb, to suck sb off; *(cunnilingus)* to go down on sb, to lick sb out; **se faire faire une petite gâterie** to get some oral

gatter [gate] *vt* Suisse *(cours)* to skip, to cut; **gatter l'école** *Br* to bunk off, to wag it, *Am* to play hooky

gauche [goʃ] *nf* **mettre de l'argent à gauche** to stash some money away; **jusqu'à la gauche** totally[□], completely[□]; **il s'est fait entuber jusqu'à la gauche** he got totally *or* completely screwed ▶ see *also* **arme**

gaucho [goʃo] *nmf* leftie, lefty

gaule [gol] *nf* **avoir la gaule** !! to have a hard-on

gaulé, -e [gole] *adj* **être bien/mal gaulé** to have/not to have a great bod

gauler [gole] *vt (attraper)* to nab, *Br* to nick; **se faire gauler** to get nabbed *or Br* nicked

gaulois, -e [golwa, -az] *nm,f* Cités = French person of native stock, as opposed to immigrants or their descendants

gaver [gave] *vt (importuner)* **gaver qn** to bug sb, *Br* to do sb's head in, to get up sb's nose, *Am* to give sb a pain (in the neck); **putain, qu'est-ce qu'il peut me gaver avec ses questions!** fucking hell, he *Br* does my head in *or Am* gives me a real pain with all his questions!

gay [gɛ] *adj & nm* gay[□]

gaz [gaz] *nm* **être dans le gaz** to be out of it

gazer [gaze] *v imp* **ça gaze?** how's it going?, how's things?; **ça gaze** everything's fine

GDB [ʒedebe] *nf (abbr* **gueule de bois)** hangover[□]

géant, -e [ʒeɑ̃, -ɑ̃t] *adj (excellent)* wicked, cool, *Br* fab, *Am* awesome

gégène [ʒeʒɛn] **1** *adj* brilliant, great, terrific

2 *nf* **la gégène** = torture by electric shock

gelé, -e [ʒəle] *adj* Can *(drogué)* wasted, wrecked

geler [ʒ(ə)le] **se geler** *vpr* to freeze to death; **se geler le cul** ! , **se les geler** ! to freeze one's *Br* arse *or Am* ass off

gencives [ʒɑ̃siv] *nfpl* **qu'est-ce qu'il s'est pris dans les gencives!** he really got it in the neck!; **elle lui a envoyé dans les gencives que...** she told him straight to his face that...

genhar [ʒɑ̃ar] *nm (verlan* **argent)** cash, dough, *Br* dosh, *Am* bucks

génial, -e [ʒenjal] *adj (excellent)* great, brilliant, fantastic

genre [ʒɑ̃r] *nm* **(a)** *(environ)* **ça fait genre 200 euros** it's something like *or* somewhere around 200 euros **(b)** *(type)* **son copain c'est un mec genre hippie** her boyfriend's the hippy type

géo [ʒeo] *nf (abbr* **géographie)** geography[□]

gerbe [ʒɛrb] *nf (vomissement)* puke, vom, barf; **foutre la gerbe à qn** to make sb want to puke *or* barf; **avoir la gerbe** to want to puke *or* barf; **ça me fout la gerbe de voir un tel étalage de luxe alors qu'il y a des gens qu'arrivent à peine à se nourrir** it makes me sick to see such a show of wealth when there are people who can barely afford to eat

gerber [ʒɛrbe] *vi* to puke, to throw up, to barf, to chunder; **gerber sur qch** *(en dire du mal)* to slate, *Br* to slag off; **la critique a carrément gerbé sur le film** the critic tore the film to shreds

gicler [ʒikle] *vi* to be off, to push off, *Am* to split

giga [ʒiga] *adj inv* wicked, mega, *Br* fab, *Am* awesome

gigue [ʒig] *nf* **une grande gigue** a beanpole

girond, -e [ʒirɔ̃, -ɔ̃d] *adj* gorgeous, stunning, *Br* fit

---

givré, -e [ʒivʀe] adj (fou) crackers, crazy, Br bananas

glamour [glamuʀ] adj inv glam

gland [!] [glɑ̃] nm (imbécile) dick, prick

glander [glɑ̃de] **1** vt **qu'est-ce que tu glandes?** what the hell are you doing?; **j'en ai rien à glander** I don't give a damn or Br a toss

2 vi to hang around, to bum around

glandes [glɑ̃d] nfpl **avoir les glandes** (être énervé) to be hacked off or cheesed off; (être triste) to be upset ᵁ; **foutre les glandes à qn** (énerver) to hack or cheese sb off; (attrister) to upset sb ᵁ

glandeur, -euse [glɑ̃dœʀ, -øz] nm,f layabout, Am goldbrick

glandouiller [glɑ̃duje] = **glander**

glandouilleur, -euse [glɑ̃dujœʀ, -øz] = **glandeur**

glandu [glɑ̃dy] nm halfwit, dope, Br plonker, Am flamer

glaouis [glawi] = **claouis**

glauque [glok] adj (personne, endroit) shady, Br dodgy; (ambiance) creepy

glaviot [!] [glavjo] nm spit ᵁ, Br gob

glavioter [!] [glavjɔte] vi to spit ᵁ, Br to gob; **il est constamment en train de glavioter, c'est dégueulasse!** he's always spitting or Br gobbing everywhere, it's gross!

gnangnan [nɑ̃nɑ̃] adj inv (personne, air) drippy; (film, livre) corny; **ce qu'elle peut m'agacer celle-là avec son air gnangnan!** she's so drippy it really gets on my nerves!

gnaque, gniac [njak] nf fighting spirit ᵁ, drive; **avoir la gniac, être plein de gniac** to have plenty of drive

gnognotte [nɔɲɔt] nf **de la gnognotte** junk, trash, Br rubbish; **c'est pas de la gnognotte** it's quite something

gnole, gnôle [nol] nf firewater, Am alky

gnon [nɔ̃] nm thump, clout; **donner** ou **mettre un gnon à qn** to thump or clout sb

gnouf [nuf] nm glasshouse (prison)

go [go] vi **on y go?** shall we go?, shall we be off?

gober [gɔbe] **1** vt **(a)** (croire) to swallow; **il gobe tout ce qu'on lui raconte** he swallows everything you tell him **(b)** (supporter) **j'ai jamais pu la gober, celle-là!** I've never been able to stand her! **(c) mais reste donc pas là à gober les mouches!** don't just stand there gawping!, don't just stand there like a Br lemon! or Am lump!

2 vi (prendre un cachet d'ecstasy) to drop an E

3 se gober vpr to fancy oneself

godasse [gɔdas] nf shoe ᵁ

gode [!] [gɔd] nm (abbr **godemiché**) dildo

godet [gɔdɛ] nm **prendre un godet** to have a drink ᵁ

godiche [gɔdiʃ] **1** adj (maladroit) ham-fisted; (niais) daft, Am dumb

2 nf **c'est une godiche** she's a ham-fisted or Br cack-handed idiot or Am klutz

godillot [gɔdijo] nm **(a)** (chaussure) shoe ᵁ, clodhopper **(b)** (personne) yes-man

gogo [gogo] nm sucker, Br mug, Am patsy

gogol [gɔgɔl] = **gol**

goguenots [gɔgno], **gogues** [gɔg] nmpl Br bog, Am john

goinfre [gwɛ̃fʀ] nmf pig, Br greedy-guts, gannet, Am hog

goinfrer [gwɛ̃fʀe] **se goinfrer** vpr to stuff oneself or one's face, to pig out

gol [gɔl] nmf (abbr **mongolien, -enne**) spaz, Br mong

> This term is used as a mild reproach to someone silly but because of its origins is extremely politically incorrect.

goldo [gɔldo] nf = Gauloise® cigarette

gomme [gɔm] nf **mettre la gomme** (en voiture) to step on it, Br to put one's foot down, Am to step on the gas; **à la gomme** useless, pathetic

gommé [gɔme] nm (cocktail) = cocktail consisting of beer and lemon-flavoured syrup

gommer [gɔme] **se gommer** vpr Cités

to clear off, *Am* to split; **allez, gomme-toi!** get out of here!, get lost!, beat it!, *Am* take a hike!

gondoler [gɔ̃dɔle] **se gondoler** *vpr* (*rire*) to fall about laughing, to crack up; **qu'est-ce que vous avez à vous gondoler?** what's so hilarious?

gonflant, -e [gɔ̃flɑ̃, -ɑ̃t] *adj* maddening; **être gonflant** to be a pain (in the neck)

gonflé, -e [gɔ̃fle] *adj* **être gonflé** to have a cheek *or* a nerve; **je le trouve gonflé de me demander de lui prêter ma caisse** I think he's got a cheek *or* a nerve asking me to lend him my car

gonfler [gɔ̃fle] *vt* (*ennuyer*) **gonfler qn** to bug sb, *Br* to get up sb's nose, to get on sb's wick, *Am* to tick sb off; **bon, t'arrêtes de me gonfler avec tes questions?** look, will you stop bugging me with your questions?

gonflette [gɔ̃flɛt] *nf* pumping iron; **faire de la gonflette** to pump iron; **il a de gros muscles, mais c'est de la gonflette** he's got big muscles, but that's coz he pumps iron

gonze [gɔ̃z] *nm* guy, *Br* bloke

gonzesse [gɔ̃zɛs] *nf* chick, *Br* bird

gorgeon [gɔrʒɔ̃] *nm* drink □

gosse [gɔs] **1** *nmf* kid; **beau/belle gosse** good-looking guy/girl
2 *nm* **gosses** [!] *Can* (*testicules*) balls, nuts, *Br* bollocks

gosser [gɔse] *vt Can* to whittle □

gouape [gwap] *nf* hoodlum, *Am* hood

goudou [!] [gudu] *nf Offensive* dyke, *Br* lezbo

gougnafier [guɲafje] *nm* (*individu grossier*) yokel, peasant, *Am* hick; (*bon à rien*) good-for-nothing, *Br* waster, *Am* slacker; (*mauvais ouvrier*) careless workman □, *Br* cowboy

gouine [!!] [gwin] *nf Offensive* dyke

goulot [gulo] *nm* mouth □, *Br* gob; **repousser** *ou* **refouler du goulot** to have rotten breath *or* dogbreath

goupiller [gupije] **1** *vt* (*arranger*) to cook up, to set up

2 se goupiller *vpr* (*se passer*) to turn out, to work out; **finalement, tout s'est bien goupillé** everything turned out fine in the end

gourbi [gurbi] *nm* dump, hovel

gourdin [!!] [gurdɛ̃] *nm* (*pénis*) dick, prick, *Br* knob; **avoir le gourdin** to have a hard-on

gourer [gure] **se gourer** *vpr* (**a**) (*se tromper*) *Br* to boob, *Am* to goof (up); **je me suis gouré de train** I got the wrong train; **se gourer de jour** to get the day wrong; **je me suis gouré dans les horaires** I got the times mixed up (**b**) (*se douter*) **je m'en gourais!** I thought as much!

gourmandise [!] [gurmɑ̃diz] *nf Hum* (*fellation*) blow-job; **faire une gourmandise à qn** to give sb a blow-job, to go down on sb

gousse [!!] [gus] *nf Offensive* (*lesbienne*) dyke

goutte [gut] *nf* **boire la goutte** to have a drop of brandy

grabuge [grabyʒ] *nm* trouble, *Br* aggro; **tirons-nous d'ici, je sens qu'il va y avoir du grabuge** let's get out of here, I sense trouble brewing

graff [graf] *nm* graffiti □

graffeur, -euse [grafœr, -øz] *nm,f* graffiti artist □

graillaver [grajave] *vi Cités* to eat □, to chow

graillé [!] [graje] *adj Can* well-hung

grailler [!] [graje] *vt & vi* to eat □

graillon [grajɔ̃] *nm* **sentir le graillon** to smell of burnt fat □; **avoir un goût de graillon** to taste of burnt fat □

graillonner [grajɔne] *vi* to clear one's throat noisily □

grain [grɛ̃] *nm* **avoir un grain** to be not all there, to be not right in the head, to have a screw loose

graine [grɛn] *nf* (**a**) **casser la graine** to have a bite to eat; **de la graine de voyou** a future hooligan □; **graine de con** [!] *Br* bloody *or* *Am* goddamn fool; **c'est de la mauvaise graine** he's a bad egg;

prends-en de la graine! take note!, take a leaf out of his/her book! **(b)** [!] *Can (pénis)* dick, cock

grand-duc [grɑ̃dyk] *nm* **la tournée des grands-ducs** a big night out on the town; **faire la tournée des grands-ducs** to go for a big night out on the town

grand-mère [grɑ̃mɛr] *nf* **et ta grand-mère, elle fait du vélo?** mind your own business!

graph [graf] = **graff**

grapheur, -euse [grafœr, -øz] = **graffeur**

grappe [grap] *nf* **lâcher la grappe à qn** to get off sb's back *or* case

grappin [grapɛ̃] *nm* **mettre le grappin dessus à qn** *(arrêter)* to collar *or Br* lift *or* nick sb; *(accaparer)* to get one's hands on sb, to corner sb; **mettre le grappin sur qch** to get one's hands on sth

gras [gra] **1** *nm* **discuter le bout de gras** to chew the fat *or* the rag
2 *adv* **il y a pas gras de monde dans les rues aujourd'hui** there's not many people out today

gratin [gratɛ̃] *nm (élite)* **le gratin** high society □, *Br* the upper crust; **le gratin du monde du spectacle** the showbiz elite

gratiné, -e [gratine] *adj* over the top, *Br* OTT

gratos [gratos] *adv* free (of charge) □, for nothing □; **on a réussi à entrer gratos** we managed to get in for nothing

gratte [grat] *nf* guitar □, *Br* axe, *Am* ax

gratter [grate] **1** *vt (devancer)* to overtake □; **personne n'arrive à le gratter au démarrage** nobody can beat him off the mark when the lights turn green
2 *vi (travailler)* to work □
3 se gratter *vpr* **tu peux toujours te gratter!** nothing doing!, no way!

gratteux [gratø] *nm (guitariste)* guitarist □

grave [grav] **1** *adj (dérangé)* **il est grave** he's not all there, he's off his rocker *or Br* head
2 *adv* seriously, in a bad way; **il me prend la tête grave** he seriously bugs

me; **grave de chez grave** seriously, in a big way, big time

Grecs [grɛk] *nmpl* **va te faire voir chez les Grecs!** [!] go to hell!, *Br* sod off!, *Am* eat it!

greffier [grɛfje] *nm (chat)* puss, moggy

grelot [grəlo] *nm* **(a)** *(téléphone)* **un coup de grelot** a phone call □; **filer un coup de grelot à qn** to give sb a buzz *or Br* a bell **(b) grelots** [!] *(testicules)* balls, nuts, *Br* bollocks

greluche [grəlyʃ] *nf* chick, *Br* bird

greum [grœm] *adj* Cités *(verlan* **maigre)** thin □

grillé, -e [grije] *adj* **il est grillé** he's had it

griller [grije] **1** *vt* **(a)** **griller qn** *(devancer)* to leave sb standing, to leave sb for dead; **jamais tu réussiras à me griller au démarrage!** you'll never beat me off the mark when the lights turn green!
(b) *(compromettre)* to land sb in it; **vous avez grillé notre indic avec vos indiscrétions** you've landed our *Br* grass *or Am* rat right in it with your blabbing
(c) **en griller une** to have a smoke *or Br* a fag
2 se griller *vpr (se démasquer)* **il s'est grillé en disant cela** he gave himself away by saying that; **se griller auprès de qn** to blot one's copybook with sb

grimpant [grɛ̃pɑ̃] *nm Br* trousers □, keks, *Am* pants □

grimper [!] [grɛ̃pe] *vt (posséder sexuellement)* to ride, to shaft, *Br* to shag

grimpion, -onne [grɛ̃pjɔ̃, -ɔn] *nm,f* Suisse careerist □; **il n'y a que des grimpions dans mon service** my department's full of people who want to climb the career ladder at all costs

gringue [grɛ̃g] *nm* **faire du gringue à qn** to come on to sb, *Br* to chat sb up, *Am* to hit on sb

grisbi [grisbi] *nm* cash, dough, *Br* dosh, *Am* bucks

griveton [grivtɔ̃] *nm* private (soldier) □, *Br* squaddie, *Am* grunt

groggy [grɔgi] *adj inv (épuisé, sous l'effet de l'alcool)* out of it; *(étourdi)* dazed

Le symbole □ indique que la traduction n'est pas argotique.

grognasse [grɔɲas] *nf Pej (fille)* tart, *Br* slapper; *(copine)* girlfriend □, (main) squeeze, *Br* slapper

grolle [grɔl] *nf* shoe □

gros, grosse [gro, gros] *nm,f* **un gros/ une grosse plein(e) de soupe** a tub of lard

gros-cul [groky] *nm (camion) Br* large lorry □, *Am* large truck □

grouiller [gruje] **se grouiller** *vpr* to get a move on, *Br* to shake a leg, *Am* to get it in gear; **allez, grouille-toi** *ou* **grouille!** come on, get a move on!

grue [gry] *nf* **(a)** *(fille facile) Br* tart, slapper, *Am* hooker **(b) faire le pied de grue** to hang about *or* around

guèche [gɛʃ] *nmf* Portuguese □

> This term comes from shortening the word "portuguèche", a pronunciation of "portugais" that mimics the "sh" sound characteristic of the Portuguese language. Depending on the context and the tone of voice used, this term may be either offensive or affectionately humorous. It is nonetheless inadvisable to use it unless one is quite sure of the reaction it will receive.

guenon [gənɔ̃] *nf (femme laide)* dog, *Br* boot, *Am* beast

guêtres [gɛtr] *nfpl* **traîner ses guêtres quelque part** to wander about *or* around □; **j'en ai plein les guêtres** *(après une marche)* I'm *Br* knackered *or* *Am* bushed; *(j'en ai assez)* I've had it up to here

gueulante [gœlɑ̃t] *nf* **pousser une gueulante** to kick up a stink, to hit the *Br* roof *or* *Am* ceiling

gueulard, -e [gœlar, -ard] *nm,f* **(a)** *(personne qui parle fort)* **quel gueulard!** he's got a voice like a foghorn! **(b)** *(protestataire)* grouch, whinger

gueule [!] [gœl] *nf* **(a)** *(bouche)* mouth □, *Br* gob; **emporter** *ou* **arracher la gueule** to take the roof off one's mouth off; **puer de la gueule** to have rotten breath *or* dogbreath; **une grande gueule** a loudmouth; **être fort en gueule** to be a loudmouth, to have too much to say for oneself; **ta gueule!** shut your mouth *or* face!, shut it!; **pousser un coup de gueule** to kick up a stink, to hit the roof

(b) *(visage)* face □, mug; **avoir une sale gueule** *(personne) (avoir l'air antipathique)* to look shady *or* *Br* dodgy; *(avoir l'air malade)* to look under the weather *or* off-colour; *(plat, aliment)* to look horrible; **il s'est fait arrêter pour délit de sale gueule** he got arrested just because they didn't like the look of him; **prendre un coup dans la gueule** *ou* **sur le coin de la gueule** to get hit in the face □; **il s'est pris le ballon en pleine gueule** the ball hit him right in the face □; **en mettre plein la gueule à qn** *(critiquer)* to give sb a mouthful; *(frapper)* to smash sb's face in; **en prendre plein la gueule (pour pas un rond)** *(se faire critiquer)* to get a real mouthful; *(se faire frapper)* to get one's face smashed in; **ça va me retomber sur la gueule** it's all going to come back on me, I'm going to get the blame for it all □; **se foutre sur la gueule** to go for each other; **foutre sur la gueule à qn** to sock sb in the face; **faire** *ou* **tirer la gueule** to be in a *or* the huff; **faire une gueule d'enterrement** to have a face like a wet weekend; **il en fait une gueule, qu'est-ce qu'il a?** he looks really down, what's wrong with him?; **faire la gueule à qn** to be in the huff with sb; **cracher à la gueule de qn** to spit in sb's face; **gueule de bois** hangover □; **avoir la gueule de bois** to have a hangover □, to be hungover □; **avoir de la gueule** *(avoir du style)* to have something; **cette bagnole a de la gueule** that's some car, that car's quite something, *Br* that's a car and a half; **gueule de con** *Br* arsehole, *Am* asshole; **gueule de raie** fishface

(c) *(individu)* **ma/ta/**etc **gueule** me/ you/etc □; **se fiche** *ou* **se foutre de la gueule de qn** to make a fool of sb, *Br* to take the piss out of sb; **du coq au vin! elle s'est pas foutue de notre gueule!**

coq au vin! she didn't make a fool of us *or Br* take the piss out of us!; **se foutre de la gueule du monde** *Br* to treat people like idiots, *Br* to take the piss; **c'est pour ma gueule** it's for me ▸ see also **arracher, bourrer, casser, crever, défoncer, éclater, enfarinée, fendre, fermer, flanquer, foutre, ouvrir, péter, soûler**

gueuler [gœle] *vi* (**a**) *(crier)* to yell (one's head off) (**b**) *(protester)* to kick up a fuss *or* stink

gueuleton [gœltɔ̃] *nm* blowout, feast, feed; **je vous ai préparé un petit gueuleton dont vous me direz des nouvelles** I've made a bit of a feast for you, I think you'll like it

gugus [gygys] = **gus**

guibolle [gibɔl] *nf* leg ᵁ, pin; **j'en ai plein les guibolles** my legs are killing me; **elle a des guibolles de rêve** she's got a lovely pair of pins on her

guidoune [gidun] *nf Can* slut, *Br* tart, slapper

guignard, -e [giɲar, -ard] *nm,f* unlucky person ᵁ, *Am* schmo

guigne [giɲ] *nf* rotten luck ᵁ; **avoir la guigne** to have a run of bad luck ᵁ

guignol [giɲɔl] *nm (personne ridicule)* clown, joker; **faire le guignol** to play the fool, to clown around; **mais qui est-ce qui m'a fichu un guignol pareil?** how on earth did I get landed with such a clown?

guimbarde [gɛ̃bard] *nf (voiture)* heap, rustbucket, *Br* banger

guincher [gɛ̃ʃe] *vi* to dance ᵁ, to bop

guindaille [gɛ̃daj] *nf Belg* student party ᵁ; **il adore faire la guindaille** he loves to party

guindailler [gɛ̃daje] *vi Belg* to attend a student party ᵁ

guindailleur, -euse [gɛ̃dajœr, -øz] *nm,f Belg* = student who likes to party; **c'est un sacré guindailleur** he's a total party animal

gus, gusse [gys] *nm* guy, *Br* bloke

H

H [aʃ] *nm (haschisch)* hash, *Br* blow

habiller [abije] *vt* **habiller qn** to bad-mouth sb, *Br* to slag sb off

haine [ɛn] *nf* **avoir la haine** to be full of rage □

> This expression was brought to a wider audience by the 1995 film *La Haine* by Mathieu Kassovitz. Describing the lives of three teenagers of different backgrounds living in a deprived Paris suburb, it used a lot of slang vocabulary, and in particular "verlan" (see panel). See also the panel **l'argot des banlieues** (p. 9, French-English side).

hallu [aly] *nf (abbr* **hallucination***)* hallucination □; **je dois avoir des hallus!** I must be seeing things!

halluciner [alysine] *vi* **c'est pas vrai, j'hallucine!** I must be seeing things!

hardeux, -euse [ardø, -øz] *nm,f* **(a)** *(homme)* rocker; *(femme)* rock chick **(b)** *(acteur, actrice de films pornographiques)* porn actor/actress

hardos [ardos] *nm (musicien de hard-rock)* hard rocker; *(amateur de hard-rock)* hard rocker, metalhead

haricot [ariko] *nm* **courir sur le haricot à qn** *Br* to get on sb's wick *or* up sb's nose, *Am* to tick sb off; **c'est la fin des haricots** I've/we've/*etc* had it now; **des haricots!** not a chance!; **travailler pour des haricots** to work for peanuts

harponner [arpɔne] *vt (retenir)* to corner, to waylay

hasch [aʃ] *nm (abbr* **haschisch***)* hash

haute [ot] *nf* **la haute** high society □, *Br* the upper crust

hebdo [ɛbdo] *nm (abbr* **hebdomadaire***)* weekly (magazine) □

herbe [ɛrb] *nf (marijuana)* grass, weed

héro [ero] *nf (abbr* **héroïne***)* smack, scag, skag

hétéro [etero] *adj & nmf (abbr* **hétérosexuel, -elle***)* straight, hetero

heure [œr] *nf* **à pas d'heures** at an ungodly hour; **elle est rentrée à pas d'heures** she didn't get home until some ungodly hour

hic [ik] *nm* **il y a un hic** there's a snag

histoire [istwar] *nf* **(a)** **qu'est-ce que c'est que cette histoire?** what the hell is going on? **(b)** **faire qch histoire de rigoler** to do sth just for a laugh; **je l'ai fait histoire de me changer les idées** I did it just to take my mind off things

homme [ɔm] *nm Can* **un homme aux hommes** *(un homosexuel)* a gay man □

homo [omo] *(abbr* **homosexuel, -elle***)* **1** *adj* gay □
2 *nmf* gay □

> In French, the word "homo" has no pejorative or homophobic connotations and is therefore not used in the same way as the English word "homo".

honte [ɔ̃t] *nf* **avoir la honte, se taper la honte** to be embarrassed □ *or* mortified; **(c'est) la honte!** the shame of it!

horreur [ɔrœr] *nf* **c'est l'horreur** it's the pits, it sucks, *Am* it bites; **il y avait une de ces circulations en ville, c'était l'horreur** there was so much traffic in town, it was hideous!

hostie [!] [ɔsti] *exclam Can* fucking hell!, for fuck's sake!

hosto [ɔsto] *nm (abbr* **hôpital***)* hospital □

hotte [ɔt] *nf* **en avoir plein la hotte** to be bushed *or Br* knackered *or Am* beat

---

Le symbole □ indique que la traduction n'est pas argotique.

HP [aʃpe] *nm* (*abbr* **hôpital psychiatrique**) psychiatric hospital ▫; **elle tourne pas rond, ça m'étonnerait pas qu'elle finisse en HP** she's not all there, it wouldn't surprise me if she ended up in the loony bin

HS [aʃɛs] *adj* (*abbr* **hors service**) (**a**) (*objet*) bust, *Br* knackered (**b**) (*personne*) bushed, *Br* knackered, shattered, *Am* beat

hublots [yblo] *nmpl* specs

huile [ɥil] *nf* (*personnage important*) big shot, big cheese, big enchilada ▸ *see also* **pomme**

hyper [ipɛr] *adv* mega, *Br* dead, *Am* real, mondo; **on s'est hyper bien amusés** we had a blast, we had a great *or* wicked *or* *Am* awesome time

hypra [ipra] *adv* mega, *Br* dead, *Am* real, mondo

I

iech ⚠, **ièche** ⚠ [jɛʃ] *vi* (verlan **chier**)
faire iech qn *Br* to piss sb off, to get on
sb's tits, *Am* to break sb's balls; **se faire
iech** to be bored shitless

illico [iliko] *adv* pronto

imbibé, -e [ɛ̃bibe] *adj (ivre)* tanked up,
Br sozzled, legless

imbitable [ɛ̃bitabl] *adj* incomprehen-
sible □; **il est imbitable son article** I
can't make head nor tail of his article

imbuvable [ɛ̃byvabl] *adj (insupportable)*
unbearable □; **je le trouve imbuvable,**

Insultes

Abuse is perhaps the purest form of slang, and is certainly the most direct, as it is
always meant to be rude. Some of the more typical patterns found in French insults
are given below:

The simplest insult of all is a noun used as an exclamation (see the noun column
below). This can itself be reinforced by a slang adjective (see column below). The
table below shows this pattern with some of the most common words. Although
some "mixing and matching" is possible, note that some combinations work better
than others.

ADJECTIVE	NOUN	TAG
pauvre	andouille	de merde
sale	idiot(e)	
espèce de (sale)	con (conne) ⚠	
	connard (connasse) ⚠	
	salaud (salope) ⚠	
	enfoiré(e) ⚠⚠	
	pouffiasse ⚠⚠	
	enculé ⚠⚠	

Speakers of "banlieue"-type slang (see entry **l'argot des banlieues** on p. 9 of the
French-English side) often use tags such as "de ta race" or "de ta mère" (eg: "espèce
d'enculé de ta mère ou de ta race!").
Many more colourful insults using a verbal construction begin with "va", eg

va voir ailleurs si j'y suis!
va te faire cuire un œuf!
va te faire voir (chez les Grecs)! ⚠
va te faire mettre! ⚠⚠
va te faire foutre! ⚠⚠
va te faire enculer! ⚠⚠

All of the above imperatives with the structure "va te faire" can be modified into "tu
peux aller te faire... !"

Le symbole □ indique que la traduction n'est pas argotique.

ce mec I can't stand (the sight of) that guy, I can't stomach *or Br* stick that guy

impasse [ɛ̃pas] *nf (sujet non étudié)* **faire une impasse** = to miss out part of a subject when revising

impayable [ɛ̃pɛjabl] *adj (amusant)* priceless

impec [ɛ̃pɛk] **1** *adj (abbr* **impeccable)** *(très propre)* spotless; *(parfait)* perfect □ **2** *adv (abbr* **impeccablement)** perfectly □; **tout s'est passé impec** everything went off like a dream; **ils nous ont reçus impec** they made us incredibly welcome; **c'est du travail de pro, il a fait ça impec** it's a really professional job, his work was faultless

in [in] *adj inv* in, trendy, hip

incendier [ɛ̃sɑ̃dje] *vt* **incendier qn** *(le réprimander)* to give sb hell, to haul sb over the coals; **il s'est fait incendier par ses parents** he caught hell from his parents

incruste [ɛ̃kryst] *nf* **si on l'invite, il va encore taper l'incruste** if we invite him, we'll never get rid of him; **il a tapé l'incruste à ma boum** he gatecrashed my party

incruster [ɛ̃kryste] **s'incruster** *vpr* **j'espère qu'il va pas s'incruster** I hope he doesn't overstay his welcome □, I hope we can manage to get rid of him; **il s'est incrusté à ma boum** he gatecrashed my party

indé [ɛ̃de] *adj (abbr* **indépendant)** indie; **le rock indé** indie (rock)

indic [ɛ̃dik] *nm (abbr* **indicateur)** squealer, *Br* grass, *Am* rat

infichu, -e [ɛ̃fiʃy] *adj* **être infichu de faire qch** to be incapable of doing sth □

info [ɛ̃fo] *nf (abbr* **information)** (a) **une info** a piece of info (b) **les infos** *(les nouvelles)* the news □

infoutu, -e [ɛ̃futy] *adj* **être infoutu de faire qch** to be incapable of doing sth □

inquiéter [ɛ̃kjete] **s'inquiéter** *vpr* **t'inquiète!** don't worry! □, take it easy!

instit [ɛ̃stit] *nmf (abbr* **instituteur, -trice)** (primary school) teacher □

intello [ɛ̃telo] *(abbr* **intellectuel, -elle) 1** *adj* intellectual □, highbrow □ **2** *nmf* egghead

interpeller [ɛ̃tɛrpəle] *vt* **ça m'interpelle (quelque part)** I can relate to that

interro [ɛ̃tero] *nf (abbr* **interrogation)** test □ *(at school)*

intox [ɛ̃tɔks] *nf (abbr* **intoxication)** **de l'intox** brainwashing □

inventer [ɛ̃vɑ̃te] *vt* **il n'a pas inventé l'eau chaude** *ou* **le fil à couper le beurre** *ou* **la poudre** he's not exactly bright, he's no Einstein, *Br* he'll never set the Thames on fire

invite [ɛ̃vit] *nf (abbr* **invitation)** invite

iroquoise [irɔkwaz] *nf (coupe de cheveux)* mohican

J

jacasser [ʒakase] *vi* to chatter, to yap, *Br* to witter (on), to natter

Jacques [ʒak] *npr* **faire le Jacques** to play the fool, to clown around

jacter [ʒakte] *vi* to chatter, to yap, *Br* to witter (on), to natter

jaffe [ʒaf] *nf (nourriture) Br* scran, food □, grub; *(repas)* meal □

jaffer [ʒafe] *vi* to eat □

jaja [ʒaʒa] *nm* wine □, vino

jambe [ʒɑ̃b] *nf* (**a**) **tenir la jambe à qn** to drone on and on at sb (**b**) **faire une partie de jambes en l'air**[!] *Br* to have a bonk, *Am* to get down (**c**) **ça me fait une belle jambe!** a fat lot of good that does me! (**d**) **en avoir plein les jambes** to be *Br* knackered *or* shattered *or Am* beat *or* pooped

jambonneaux [ʒɑ̃bɔno] *nmpl (cuisses)* thunderthighs; **elle a une sacrée paire de jambonneaux** she's got a real pair of thunderthighs on her!

jap [ʒap] *Offensive* **1** *adj (abbr* **japonais, -e)** Jap
   2 *nmf* Jap *(abbr* **Japonais, -e)** Jap, Nip

jaquette [ʒakɛt] *nf Offensive* **la jaquette flottante**[!] *(les homosexuels) Br* poofs, *Am* fags; **être** *ou* **refiler de la jaquette (flottante)**[!] to be a *Br* poof *or Am* fag

jaspiner [ʒaspine] *vi* to chat, to yak, *Br* to natter

jaune [ʒon] *nm* (**a**) *(apéritif anisé)* pastis □ (**b**) *(ouvrier non gréviste)* strikebreaker □, scab, *Br* blackleg

java [ʒava] *nf (fête)* party □, bash, do; **faire la java** to party

jean-foutre[!] [ʒɑ̃futr] *nm inv* loser, nohoper, *Br* waster

jeannette [ʒanɛt] *nf Belg Offensive (homosexuel)* queer, poof, *Am* fag

je-m'en-foutisme [ʒmɑ̃futism] *nm* couldn't-care-less attitude

jeté, -e [ʒte] *adj (fou)* crazy, off one's rocker, *Br* barking (mad), *Am* loony-tunes

jeter [ʒ(ə)te] **1** *vt* (**a**) *(abandonner) (personne)* to chuck, to dump; **il s'est fait jeter par sa gonzesse** his chick *or Br* bird dumped him
   (**b**) *(chasser)* to throw *or* chuck out, *Am* to eighty-six; **se faire jeter** to get thrown *or* chucked out, *Am* to get eighty-sixed
   (**c**) **jeter du jus, en jeter** to be quite *or* really something, to be something else
   (**d**) **n'en jetez plus (la cour est pleine)!** give it a rest!, pack it in!
   2 se jeter *vpr* **s'en jeter un (derrière la cravate)** to have a drink

jeton [ʒtɔ̃] *nm* (**a**) **être un faux jeton** to be two-faced (**b**) **avoir les jetons** to be

---

Javanais

More a source of amusement for French schoolchildren than a true form of slang, "javanais" is formed by inserting the syllable "-av-", "-va-" or "-ag-" immediately after each consonant or group of consonants. "Chatte", for example, becomes "chagatte" and "pute" becomes "pavute". It is probably so called because the word "javanais" contains the syllable "av" and suggests an exotic, secret language.

Le symbole □ indique que la traduction n'est pas argotique.

scared ❑, to be spooked, *Br* to have the wind up; **foutre les jetons à qn** to give sb a fright ❑, to spook sb, *Br* to put the wind up sb

jeune [ʒœn] *adj (insuffisant)* **ça fait un peu jeune** it's cutting it a bit fine, it's pushing it a bit; **trois bouteilles de vin pour vingt personnes, ça fait un peu jeune** three bottles of wine for twenty people, that's cutting it a bit fine *or* that's pushing it a bit

jeunot [ʒœno] *nm* lad, youngster ❑

job [dʒɔb] *nm* job ❑

jobard, -e [ʒɔbar, -ard] **1** *adj* gullible ❑
2 *nm,f* sucker, *Br* mug, *Am* schnook

jobine [ʒɔbin], **jobinette** [ʒɔbinɛt] *nf Can* casual job ❑; **faire des jobines** to do odd jobs

joint [ʒwɛ̃] *nm* joint, spliff

jojo [ʒoʒo] **1** *adj inv (beau, correct)* **pas jojo** not very nice ❑; **il est pas jojo son petit ami** her boyfriend's no oil painting; **c'est pas jojo ce qu'il a fait là** that wasn't a very nice thing for him to do
2 *nm* **un affreux jojo** a little horror *or* monster, a holy terror

jos-connaissant [djokɔnɛsɑ̃] *nm Can Br* know-all, *Am* know-it-all

joual [ʒwal] *nm Can* joual

> Joual is the traditional working-class variant of French used in Quebec. The word "joual" is derived from the vernacular French Canadian pronunciation of the word "cheval". Although initially derided by purists as a bastardized and highly anglicized form of French, the reputation of "joual" was rehabilitated in the sixties when it was championed by Quebec intellectuals as a symbol of Quebécois identity. Many words bear a close resemblance to their English equivalents, such as "badloqué" (from "bad luck"), "bomme" (from "bum") and "crisse" (from "Christ").

jouasse [ʒwas] *adj* pleased ❑, *Br* chuffed; **qu'est-ce que t'as, t'es pas jouasse?** got a problem?; **il avait pas l'air jouasse** he didn't look too pleased *or Br* chuffed

jouer [ʒwe] **1** *vt* **où t'as vu jouer ça?** are you mad?, have you got a screw loose?, are you off your rocker?
2 se jouer *vpr* **se la jouer** to show off, to pose ▸ *see also* **caïd, touche-pipi, tripes**

joufflu [ʒufly] *nm Hum (postérieur)* butt, *Br* bum, *Am* fanny

jouir [ʒwir] *vi* (**a**) *(atteindre l'orgasme)* to come (**b**) *Ironic (souffrir)* to go through hell; **j'ai joui quand je me suis foutu un coup de marteau sur les doigts** it hurt like hell *or Br* like a bastard when I whacked my fingers with the hammer; **qu'est-ce qu'il m'a fait jouir ce salaud de dentiste!** that bastard dentist put me through hell!

jouissif, -ive [ʒwisif, -iv] *adj* (**a**) *(qui procure un grand plaisir)* orgasmic (**b**) *Ironic (douloureux) Br* bloody *or Am* goddamn painful; **s'écraser le petit orteil, c'est jouissif!** stubbing your little toe is a real barrel of laughs!

journaleux, -euse [ʒurnalø, -øz] *nm,f Pej* hack

joyeuses [!] [ʒwajøz] *nfpl (testicules)* balls, nuts, *Br* bollocks

JT [ʒite] *nm* (*abbr* **journal télévisé**) TV news ❑

juif, -ive [ʒɥif, -iv] *nm,f* (**a**) *(avare)* tightwad, skinflint (**b**) **le petit juif** the funny bone

> This term as used in category (a), although not overtly racist, is nonetheless very politically incorrect and should be used with extreme caution.

Jules [ʒyl] *npr* boyfriend ❑, man, (main) squeeze; **elle est venue avec son Jules** she came with her man; **elle se cherche un Jules** she's trying to find a man

Julie [ʒyli] *npr* girlfriend ❑, (main) squeeze, *Br* bird

jus [ʒy] *nm* (**a**) *(eau)* **tomber au jus** to fall in ❑ (**b**) *(café)* coffee ❑, *Am* java; **jus de chique** *ou* **de chaussette** dishwater (**c**) *(courant électrique)* juice; **prendre le jus**

to get a shock; **être au jus** to know □ ▸ see also **jeter**

jusque-là [ʒyskəla] *adv* (**a**) **s'en mettre jusque-là** to stuff oneself or one's face, to pig out, *Am* to munch out (**b**) **en avoir jusque-là (de)** to have had it up to here (with); **j'en ai jusque-là de tes imbécilités** I've had it up to here with your stupid behaviour

juter !! [ʒyte] *vi (éjaculer)* to come, to shoot one's load, to spurt

juteux[1] [ʒytø] *nm (adjudant) Br* ≃ warrant officer class II □, *Am* ≃ warrant officer (junior grade) □

juteux[2]**, -euse** [ʒytø, -øz] *adj (fructueux)* lucrative □; **une affaire juteuse** a goldmine, *Br* a nice little earner

kakou [kaku] *n* **faire le kakou** to act smart

kaput [kaput] *adj* kaput; **la téloche est kaput; impossible de regarder le match!** the TV's kaput, we can't watch the match!

kawa [kawa] *nm* coffee □, *Am* java

kebla [kəbla] *nmf Cités (verlan* **black***)* Black

kéblo [keblo] *adj Cités (verlan* **bloqué***)* hung-up, full of hang-ups

kébra [kebra] *vt Cités (verlan* **braquer***)* *(banque, bijouterie)* to hold up; **kébra qch à qn** to pinch *or Br* nick sth from sb

ken ! [ken] *vt (verlan* **niquer***)* **(a)** *(posséder sexuellement)* to screw, to shaft, *Br* to have it off with, *Am* to slam **(b)** *(endommager)* to bust, *Br* to knacker, to bugger **(c)** *(duper)* to rip off, *Am* to rook **(d)** *Cités (attraper)* to nab, to collar; **se faire ken** to get nabbed *or* collared

késako [kezako] = **quès aco**

keuf [kœf] *nm (verlan* **flic***)* cop, *Am* flatfoot

keum [kœm] *nm Cités (verlan* **mec***)* guy, *Br* bloke

keupon [køpɔ̃] *nm (verlan* **punk***)* punk

keusse [køs] *nm Cités (verlan* **sac***)* ten francs □

kif [kif] *nm* kif, kef

kiffer [kife] *Cités* **1** *vt* to get off on, to get a kick out of
2 *vi* to get off; **nous, on fait de la musique pour faire kiffer les gens** we make music so people can get off on it

kif-kif [kifkif] *adv* **c'est kif-kif** it's six of one and half a dozen of the other, it's six and two threes

kiki [kiki] *nm* **(a)** *(cou)* neck □; *(gorge)* throat □; **serrer le kiki à qn** to wring sb's neck □ **(b)** *(type d'homosexuel)* = homosexual man who habitually wears jeans, a bomber jacket and baseball boots, and whose hair is either shaved or worn with a Tintin-style quiff **(c)** **c'est parti mon kiki** here we go!

kil [kil] *nm* **un kil de rouge** a bottle of red wine □

kisdé [kisde] *nm Cités (policier)* cop, pig

klébard [klebar], **klebs** [klɛps] *nm* mutt

klondike [klɔ̃dajk] *nm Can* plum job

kopeck [kɔpɛk] *nm* **pas un kopeck** not a bean *or Am* a cent; **il me reste plus un kopeck** I haven't a bean *or Am* a cent

kro [kro] *nf* Kronenbourg® beer □

kroumir [krumir] *nm* **(vieux) kroumir** old fogey, *Am* geezer

---

Le symbole □ indique que la traduction n'est pas argotique.

L

là [la] *adv* **il est un peu là, il se pose là** *(il est remarquable)* he makes his presence felt □; **elle se pose là comme cuisinière** she's a mean cook, she's some cook; *Ironic* she's a mean cook…not!, she's a mean cook, I don't think!; **comme emmerdeur/menteur, il se pose là!** he's a total pain/liar!

labo [labo] *nm (abbr* **laboratoire)** lab

lâcher [lɑʃe] **1** *vt* **(a)** *(laisser tranquille)* **lâche-moi!** leave me alone!, get off my back *or* case!

(b) *(abandonner) (emploi)* to quit, *Br* to chuck *or* pack in; *(famille, associé)* to walk out on; *(amant)* to chuck, to dump

(c) **les lâcher** *(payer)* to cough up, to fork out; **il les lâche pas facilement** he's a real tightwad, he's really tight-fisted

(d) **en lâcher une** !| to fart, *Br* to let off, *Am* to lay one

2 !| *vi (émettre des gaz intestinaux)* to fart, *Br* to let off, *Am* to lay one ► *see also* **basket, caisse, fusée, grappe, louise, morceau, perle, perlouse, rampe**

lambin, -e [lɑ̃bɛ̃, -in] *nm,f Br* slowcoach, *Am* slowpoke

lambiner [lɑ̃bine] *vi* to dawdle

lambineur, -euse [lɑ̃binœr, -øz], **lambineux, -euse** [lɑ̃binø, -øz] *nm,f Can Br* slowcoach, *Am* slowpoke

lampe [lɑ̃p] *nf* **s'en mettre** *ou* **s'en foutre** !| **plein la lampe** to stuff oneself *or* one's face, to pig out

lance-pierres [lɑ̃spjɛr] *nm inv* **manger avec un lance-pierres** to wolf one's food down; **payer qn avec un lance-pierres** to pay sb peanuts *or Am* chump change

lancequiner !| [lɑ̃skine] *vi* **(a)** *(pleuvoir)* **il lancequine** it's pissing down **(b)** *(uriner)* to pee, to piss, *Br* to have a slash

lapin [lapɛ̃] *nm* **(a)** **poser un lapin à qn** to stand sb up **(b)** **baiser comme des lapins** !!| to fuck like rabbits ► *see also* **cage, chaud, pet¹, tirer**

lard [lar] *nm* **un gros lard** a big fat slob; **rentrer dans le lard à qn** to lay into sb, to set about sb, to go for sb; **faire du lard** to sit around and get fat

lardon [lardɔ̃] *nm (enfant)* kid; **il a préféré venir sans ses lardons** he preferred to come without his kids

lardu [lardy] *nm* cop, *Am* flatfoot

larfeuil, larfeuille [larfœj] *nm Br* wallet □, *Am* billfold □

largeur [larʒœr] *nf* **dans les grandes largeurs** totally □, big time, in a big way; **ils se sont fait entuber dans les grandes largeurs** they got totally ripped off, they got ripped off big time *or* in a big way

---

Largonji

"Largonji" is a type of slang formed by replacing the initial consonant of a word with the letter "l" and moving the original consonant to the end of the word, where it is followed by a vowel to aid pronunciation. "À poil" thus becomes "à loilpé"; "en douce" becomes "en loucedé". The word "largonji" is itself the result of this procedure applied to the word "jargon".

Le symbole □ indique que la traduction n'est pas argotique.

largué, -e [large] adj **être largué** to be lost, not to have a clue

larguer [large] **1** vt (abandonner) (emploi) to quit, Br to chuck or pack in; (famille, associé) to walk out on; (amant) to chuck, to dump; **il s'est fait larguer par sa nana** his chick or Br bird dumped him

2 [!] vi (émettre des gaz intestinaux) to fart, Br to let off, Am to lay one ▶ see also **caisse**

larmichette [larmiʃɛt] nf tiny drop ▭; **tu me remets une larmichette de vin?** will you pour me another smidgeon of wine?

larve [larv] nf (personne faible) wimp, drip

lascar [laskar] nm Cités rogue, Br dodgy geezer

latino [latino] adj & nmf (abbr **latino-américain, -e**) Latino

latte [lat] nf (chaussure) **un coup de latte** a kick ▭, a boot; **il m'a filé un coup de latte** he gave me a kick or a boot, he kicked or booted me; **ils lui ont défoncé la gueule à coups de lattes** they kicked or booted his head in

latter [late] vt to kick ▭, to boot, Br to put the boot into

lavasse [lavas] nf **de la lavasse** (café, bière) dishwater

lavette [lavɛt] nf (personne) wimp, drip; **quand sa femme l'a traité de lavette, il a failli lui répondre quelque chose** when his wife called him a wimp, he almost answered her back

lèche [lɛʃ] nf **faire de la lèche** to be a bootlicker; **faire de la lèche à qn** to lick sb's boots

lèche-bottes [lɛʃbɔt] nmf inv bootlicker

lèche-cul [!!] [lɛʃky] nmf inv brown-nose, Br arse-licker, Am ass-licker

lécheur, -euse [leʃœr, -øz] nm,f bootlicker

lèdge [lɛdʒ] adj (abbr **léger**) (insuffisant) (excuse) weak; **deux bouteilles pour quatre, ça va faire un peu lèdge, non?** two bottles for four people, that's

going to be cutting it a bit fine, do you not think?

légitime [leʒitim] nf **ma légitime** my old lady, Br the missus, Br my indoors

lerche [lɛrʃ] adv **il y en a pas lerche** there isn't much /aren't many

lerga [lɛrga] nf Cités (verlan **galère**) pain, hassle

lessivé, -e [lesive] adj (épuisé) washed out, wiped

lever [ləve] vt (a) (séduire) to pick up, Br to pull, to get off with (b) **lever le pied** (ralentir) to slow down ▭; **lève le pied, il y a un radar par ici** slow down, there's a speed camera round here (c) **lever le coude** (boire) to bend one's elbow

levrette [ləvrɛt] **en levrette** adv doggy-fashion

lézard [lezar] nm (difficulté) **il y a pas de lézards** no problem, no sweat, Br no probs

lézarder [lezarde] vi to soak up the sun, to catch some rays

ligne [liɲ] nf (a) (dose de cocaïne) line; **se faire une ligne** to do a line (b) **sur toute la ligne** from beginning to end ▭

limace [limas] nf (chemise) shirt ▭

limer [!!] [lime] vt (posséder sexuellement) to hump, to screw, Br to shaft

limite [limit] adj inv **je me suis pas mis en colère, mais c'était limite** I didn't lose my temper, but it was a close thing; **question propreté, c'était limite** it certainly wasn't the cleanest place in the world; **ses blagues sont un peu limite** his jokes are a bit close to the bone; **j'hésite à me déchausser, mes chaussettes sont un peu limite** I'm not sure whether I should take my socks off, they're a bit iffy or Br dodgy

linge [lɛ̃ʒ] nm **du beau linge** high society ▭, Br the upper crust; **il y avait que du beau linge à la réception** the upper crust were out in force at the reception

liquette [likɛt] nf shirt ▭; **mouiller sa liquette** to work up a sweat; **il se fatigue pas trop celui-là, pas de danger qu'il mouille sa liquette** he doesn't exactly

---

Le symbole ▭ indique que la traduction n'est pas argotique.

tire himself out, there's not much chance of him breaking sweat

liquider [likide] vt (**a**) (tuer) to bump off, to liquidate, to ice (**b**) (nourriture) to scoff, to guzzle; (boisson) to sink, to down, Am to inhale

litron [litrɔ̃] nm bottle of red wine □

locdu [lɔkdy] = **loquedu**

loche [lɔʃ] nf (sein) tit, boob; **regarde un peu la paire de loches!** check out those tits!

loilpé [lwalpe] **à loilpé** adv stark naked, in the buff, Br starkers

lolo [lolo] nm (**a**) (sein) boob (**b**) (lait) milk □

longe [lɔ̃ʒ] nf (année) year □

> This term is never used when referring to people's ages.

longuet, -ette [lɔ̃gɛ, -ɛt] adj longish, on the long side; **j'ai trouvé le film un peu longuet** I found the film a bit on the long side

look [luk] nm look, image; **avoir un look d'enfer** to look great or wicked or Br fab

looké, -e [luke] adj **être looké punk/ grunge** to have a punky/grungy look or image

lope [lɔp], **lopette** [lɔpɛt] nf (**a**) Offensive (homosexuel) Br poof, poofter, Am fag, faggot (**b**) (lâche) wimp, Br big girl's blouse

loquedu [lɔkdy] nm (**a**) (bon à rien) good-for-nothing, loser, no-hoper, Br waster (**b**) (individu méprisable) scumbag, Br swine, Am stinker

loser [luzœr] nm loser

lot [lo] nm (femme) **un joli (petit) lot** a babe, a knockout, Br a smasher, a bit of all right

loub [lub] nm (abbr **loubard**) hood, hooligan □, Br yob

loubard [lubar] nm hoodlum, hooligan □, Br yob

loucedé [lusde] **en loucedé** adv on the quiet or sly

louche [luʃ] nf (main) hand □, mitt, paw;

serrer la louche à qn to shake hands with sb □

loucher [luʃe] vi **loucher sur qch** to eye sth up, to have one's eye on sth

louf [luf], **loufedingue** [lufdɛ̃g] adj crazy, Br barking (mad), off one's head, Am loony-tunes

loufe [luf] nm (pet) fart

loufer ！, **louffer** ！ [lufe] vi to fart, Br to let off, Am to lay one

loufiat [lufja] nm waiter □ (in a café)

louise [lwiz] nf fart; **lâcher une louise** to fart, Br to let off, Am to lay one

loulou, -oute [lulu, -ut] nm,f (**a**) (personne) hoodlum, hooligan □ (**b**) (appellation affectueuse) **mon loulou, ma louloute** sweetheart, honey, babe

louper [lupe] **1** vt (examen) to fail □, Am to flunk; (train, cible) to miss □

2 vi **j'étais sûr qu'il pleuverait, et ça n'a pas loupé!** I was sure that it would rain, and sure enough it did!

3 se louper vpr (**a**) (échouer dans une tentative de suicide) to bungle one's suicide attempt □; **il s'est coupé les cheveux tout seul et il s'est pas loupé!** he cut his own hair and made some job of it!; **je me suis blessé avec l'ouvre-boîte – dis-donc, tu t'es pas loupé!** I've cut myself on the tin-opener – you certainly have! (**b**) **vous vous êtes loupés de peu** you just missed each other □ ▸ see also **une**

loupiot [lupjo] nm kid

loupiote [lupjɔt] nf lamp □, light □

lourd, -e [lur, lurd] **1** adj (sans subtilité) unsubtle □, in your face, Br OTT

2 adv **il en fiche pas lourd** he doesn't exactly overtax himself, he doesn't kill himself with overwork; **il en reste pas lourd** there's not that much/many left □

lourde [lurd] nf (porte) door □

lourder [lurde] vt **lourder qn** to give sb the boot, to kick sb out; **ils l'ont lourdé quand ils se sont rendu qu'il piquait dans la caisse** they gave him the boot when they found out he had his hand in the till

lourdingue [lurdɛ̃g] adj unsubtle □, in

your face, *Br* OTT; **il est vraiment lour-dingue avec ses blagues de cul** he's so in your face with his dirty jokes

loustic [lustik] *nm* (**a**) *(individu)* guy, *Br* bloke (**b**) *(farceur)* clown, joker; **c'est un sacré loustic** he's quite a character, he's a real case

loute [lut] *nf* chick, *Br* bird

louzeda [luzda] *nf* Cités **avoir la louzeda** to be starving *or* ravenous □

LSD [!] [εlεsde] *nf Hum (femme de petite taille)* shorty, squirt

> This humorous but somewhat vulgar expression comes from a pun on LSD the drug and LSD, the initial letters of "elle (L) suce debout", meaning "she sucks standing up". The image is thus of a woman who is short enough to perform oral sex on a man while in a standing position.

luc [!] [lyk] *nm (verlan* **cul**) *Br* arse, *Am* ass

luette [lɥεt] *nf Can* **se mouiller** *ou* **se rincer la luette** *(prendre un verre)* to wet one's whistle, *Br* to have a couple of scoops; *(se soûler)* to get plastered *or* wasted *or Br* ratted *or* legless

lugée [lyʒe] *nf Suisse (échec)* failure □; **il s'est pris une fameuse lugée** he failed miserably, *Am* he totally flunked

luger [lyʒe] *Suisse* **1** *vi (échouer)* to fail □, *Am* to flunk
2 se luger *vpr (échouer)* to fail □

lune [lyn] *nf (derrière)* butt, *Br* bum, *Am* fanny; **se faire taper dans la lune** [!] to take it up the *Br* arse *or Am* ass, to get buggered ▶ *see also* **con**

luné, -e [lyne] *adj* **être bien/mal luné** to be in a good/bad mood □

M

maboul, -e [mabul] *adj* crazy, bananas, *Br* mental, *Am* wacko

mac [mak] *nm* (*abbr* **maquereau**) pimp, *Am* mack

macache [makaʃ] *exclam* **macache (bono)!** no way (José)!, no chance!, *Br* nothing doing!

macadam [makadam] *nm* **faire le macadam** to walk the streets, to be on the game, *Am* to hook

macaroni [makarɔni] *nm Offensive (Italien)* wop, Eyetie, *Am* guinea

> Depending on the context and the tone of voice used, this term may be either offensive or affectionately humorous. It is nonetheless inadvisable to use it unless one is quite sure of the reaction it will receive.

macchabée [makabe] *nm* stiff *(corpse)*

machin, -e [maʃɛ̃, -in] **1** *nm* (**a**) *(chose)* thing ⁰, thingy (**b**) **espèce de vieux machin!** you old fool!

2 *npr* **Machin, Machine** *(personne)* thingy, what's-his-name, *f* what's-her-name

maganer [magane] *vt Can (personne)* to beat up; *(objet)* to wreck

magner [maɲe] **se magner** *vpr* **se magner (le train** *ou* **le popotin)** to get a move on, to get one's skates on, *Am* to get it in gear; **se magner le cul**[!] to move *or* shift one's *Br* arse *or Am* ass

magnéto [maɲeto] *nm* (*abbr* **magnétophone**) tape recorder ⁰, cassette player ⁰

magot [mago] *nm* stash, hoard, pile; **il se souvient plus où il a planqué le magot** he can't remember where he hid the stash

magouille [maguj] *nf* scheme; **magouilles électorales** vote-rigging; **se**

livrer à des magouilles to scheme, to do some wheeling and dealing

magouiller [maguje] *vi* to scheme, to do some wheeling and dealing

magouilleur, -euse [magujœr, -øz] *nm,f* schemer, wheeler-dealer

mahous, -ousse [maus] = **maous**

maigrichon, -onne [megriʃɔ̃, -ɔn] *adj* skinny

maille [maj] *nf Cités (argent)* cash, *Br* dosh, *Am* bucks

maison [mezɔ̃] *adj inv* **une engueulade/une râclée maison** an almighty ticking-off/thrashing

mal [mal] *nm* **ça me ferait mal!, ça me ferait mal aux seins**[!] it would kill me!; **ça te ferait mal de t'excuser?** it wouldn't hurt you to apologize!

malabar [malabar] *nm* hulk; **il s'est retrouvé nez à nez avec un malabar qui lui barrait le passage** he found himself nose to nose with some big hulk who was blocking his way

malade [malad] **1** *adj (inconscient)* crazy, crackers, *Br* mental, *Am* gonzo

2 *nmf* (**a**) *(inconscient)* maniac, headcase, *Br* nutter, *Am* screwball; **il conduit comme un malade** he drives like a maniac; **bosser comme un malade** to work like crazy *or* like mad; **il a flippé comme un malade** he totally flipped *or* freaked out (**b**) *(fanatique)* nut, freak

malaise [malɛz] *nm* **il y a comme un malaise** there's a bit of a snag *or* a hitch

mal-baisée [!!] [malbeze] *nf* **c'est une mal-baisée** she needs a good fuck

maldonne [maldɔn] *nf* **il y a maldonne** something's gone wrong somewhere

malengueulé, -e [malɑ̃gœle] *Can* **1** *adj* vulgar ⁰, uncouth ⁰; **être malengueulé**

Br to have a mouth like a sewer, *Am* to be a sewermouth

2 *nm,f* **être un malengueulé** *Br* to have a mouth like a sewer, *Am* to be a sewermouth

malle [mal] *nf* **se faire la malle** *(partir)* to beat it, *Br* to clear off, *Am* to book it; *(se détacher)* to fall off □

manche [mɑ̃ʃ] **1** *adj (maladroit)* ham-fisted, *Br* cack-handed

2 *nm (personne maladroite) Br* cack-handed idiot, *Am* klutz, lug; *(personne incapable)* prat, *Br* pillock, *Am* lame; **tu t'y prends comme un manche** you're making a real mess of it; **il conduit comme un vrai manche** he's a lousy or hopeless driver ▸ *see also* **paire**

manche-à-balle [mɑ̃ʃabal] *nm Belg* crawler, bootlicker

mandale [mɑ̃dal] *nf* clout, slap; **filer une mandale à qn** to clout or slap sb

manettes [manɛt] *nfpl* **à fond les manettes** at full speed, *Br* like the clappers, *Am* like sixty

manger [mɑ̃ʒe] **se manger** *vpr* **se manger qch** *(percuter)* to go head-first into sth; **il s'est mangé un sapin en pleine tronche** he went head-first into a fir tree

manif [manif] *nf (abbr* **manifestation)** demo

manip [manip] *nf (abbr* **manipulation)** process □; **tu veux que je te réexplique ou tu as compris la manip?** do you want me to explain it to you again or do you understand how to do it? □

manitou [manitu] *nm* **un grand manitou** a big shot or cheese or enchilada

maous, -ousse [maus] *adj* ginormous, humongous, massive

maqué, -e [make] *adj* **être maqué(e)** *(homme)* to have a woman; *(femme)* to have a man; **ils sont maqués** they're an item

maquer [make] **se maquer** *vpr (se marier)* to get hitched or spliced, to tie the knot; *(s'établir en couple)* to shack up together; **se maquer avec qn** *(se marier*

avec) to get hitched or spliced to sb; *(s'établir en couple avec)* to shack up with sb

maquereau, -x [makro] *nm (proxénète)* pimp, *Am* mack

maquerelle [makrɛl] *nf* **(mère) maquerelle** madam *(in brothel)*

marave¹ [marav] *nf* scuffle, *Br* punch-up, *Am* slugfest

marave², maraver [marave] *vt* **(a)** *(battre)* **marave qn** to waste sb's face, *Am* to punch sb out **(b)** *(tuer)* to kill □, to waste, *Am* to snuff

marcel [marsɛl] *nm Hum (maillot de corps sans manches) Br* vest □, *Am* undershirt □; **il se balade toujours en marcel** he always walks around in his *Br* vest or *Am* undershirt

marcher [marʃe] *vi* **(a)** *(croire naïvement quelque chose)* to fall for it, to swallow it; **faire marcher qn** to pull sb's leg, *Br* to wind sb up; **il a pas marché, il a couru** he fell for it or swallowed it hook, line and sinker **(b)** *(accepter)* **je marche** count me in; **je marche pas** count me out **(c)** *(fonctionner)* **il marche au whisky/aux speeds** he runs on whisky/speed ▸ *see also* **pompe, radar**

margoulette [margulɛt] *nf* **casser la margoulette à qn** to smash sb's face in, to rearrange sb's features; **se casser la margoulette** to fall flat on one's face

margoulin [margulɛ̃] *nm* **(a)** *(escroc)* con man, crook, *Am* grifter **(b)** *(incompétent)* prat, *Br* pillock, *Am* lame

Marie-Chantal [mariʃɑ̃tal] *npr inv Br* ≃ Sloane (Ranger), *Am* ≃ preppy

Marie-couche-toi-là [marikuʃtwala] *nf inv* trollop, slut

marie-jeanne [mariʒan] *nf inv (cannabis)* Mary Jane, pot

mariole, mariolle [marjɔl] *nmf* clown, *Am* klutz; **faire le mariole** to act smart

marlou [marlu] *nm (voyou)* hoodlum, thug, hooligan □; *(proxénète)* pimp, *Am* mack

marmaille [marmaj] *nf* brood, kids; **elle**

est venue avec toute sa marmaille she came with her whole brood

marmot [marmo] *nm* kid

marner [marne] *vi* to slog, to sweat blood; **il nous fait marner** he keeps us hard at it *or* slaving away

maronner [marɔne] *vi* (**a**) *(protester)* to grumble, to grouch, to gripe (**b**) *(attendre)* to hang about *or* around; **il nous fait toujours maronner** he always has us hanging about *or* around waiting

marrant, -e [marɑ̃, -ɑ̃t] **1** *adj (amusant, bizarre)* funny; **c'est marrant, j'aurais pourtant juré qu'il était homo** that's funny, I could have sworn he was gay; **t'es marrant toi, comment veux-tu que j'entre si j'ai pas la clef?** very funny, how am I meant to get in if I don't have the key?; **t'es pas marrant!** you're no fun!

2 *nm,f* **être un marrant** to be fun, to be a laugh *or* a riot; **son père, c'est pas un marrant** his dad's not much fun *or* not much of a laugh

marre [mar] *adv* **en avoir marre (de)** to be fed up (with) *or* hacked off (with) *or* sick and tired (of); **en avoir marre de faire qch** to be fed up with *or* hacked off with *or* sick and tired of doing sth; **j'en ai marre de tes jérémiades** I'm sick and tired of your moaning; **c'est marre!** that's enough!, that'll do!

marrer [mare] **se marrer** *vpr* to have a laugh; **on s'est bien marré hier soir avec les potes** we had a good laugh last night with the guys *or Br* lads; **il nous a bien fait marrer avec ses histoires de régiment** he gave us a good laugh with his army stories; *Ironic* **alors là, je me marre!** that's a laugh!, don't make me laugh!; **tu me fais marrer avec tes histoires de télépathie!** you make me laugh with all your stuff about telepathy!

marron [marɔ̃] **1** *adj* (**a**) *(qui exerce clandestinement)* unqualified □ (**b**) *(dupé)* **être marron** to have been taken in, to have been taken for a ride, *Am* to have been rooked; **faire qn marron** to take sb in, to take sb for a ride, *Am* to rook sb

2 *nm (coup)* belt, wallop; **coller un mar-**

ron à qn to belt *or* wallop sb one

marteau [marto] *adj (fou)* **être marteau** to be not all there, to have a screw *or Br* a slate loose

maso [mazo] *(abbr* **masochiste**) **1** *adj* masochistic □

2 *nmf* masochist □

masse [mas] *nf* (**a**) **être à la masse** to be off one's head, to be *Br* barking (mad) *or Am* wacko (**b**) **il y en a pas des masses** there isn't much/aren't many □

mastard [mastar] *nm* hulk; **c'est un sacré mastard, le copain de ma cousine** my cousin's boyfriend is a huge hulk of a guy

mastoc [mastɔk] *adj inv* (**a**) *(énorme)* ginormous, humongous (**b**) *Belg (fou)* crazy, *Br* barking, *Am* loony-tunes

mat' [mat] *nm (abbr* **matin**) **deux/trois heures du mat'** two/three a.m. *or* in the morning □

mater¹ [mate] *vt* to check out; *(avec concupiscence)* to eye up; **mate-moi ça!** check it out!, *Br* get a load of that!

mater² [mater], **maternelle** [maternel] *nf* old lady, *Br* old dear *(mother)*

mateur, -euse [matœr, -øz] *nm,f* **c'est un sacré mateur** he's always eyeing up women

maton, -onne [matɔ̃, -ɔn] *nm,f* screw *(prison warder)*, *Am* hack, bull

matos [matos] *nm* stuff, gear; **les musiciens se sont fait piquer leur matos pendant leur tournée** the band got all their gear pinched *or Br* nicked while they were on tour

maudit, -e [!] [modi, -it] *Can* **1** *adj (très)* **c'est une maudite belle fille** she's a hell of a good-looking girl; **être en maudit** to be fuming *or Br* spewing; **c'est un beau film en maudit** it's a damn *or Br* bloody good film; **il court vite en maudit** he's a damn *or Br* bloody fast runner

2 *exclam* shit!, *Br* bloody hell!

mauditement [moditmɑ̃] *adv Can* damn, *Br* bloody; **mauditement cher** damn *or Br* bloody expensive

mauvaise [movɛz] *adj* **l'avoir** *ou* **la**

Le symbole □ indique que la traduction n'est pas argotique.

trouver mauvaise to be hacked off or bummed

mauviette [movjɛt] *nf* wimp, *Br* big girl's blouse

max [maks] *nm* (*abbr* **maximum**) **un max de monde/de voitures** stacks or a ton of people/cars; **assurer un max** to do brilliantly; **sur scène ils assurent un max** they really kick ass on stage

maxi [maksi] *adv* (*abbr* **maximum**) **on sera vingt maxi** there'll be twenty of us max or tops; **ça prendra deux heures maxi** it'll take two hours max or tops

mec [mɛk] *nm* (a) (*individu*) guy, *Br* bloke; **salut les mecs!** hi, guys! (b) (*compagnon*) boyfriend ᐤ, man; **elle est venue sans son mec** she came without her man

meca [məka] *nf Cités* (*verlan* **came**) drugs ᐤ, stuff, *Br* gear

méchamment [meʃamã] *adv* (*très, beaucoup*) really ᐤ, terribly, *Am* real

méchant, -e [meʃã, -ãt] *adj* (*remarquable*) amazing, terrific

mecton [mɛktɔ̃] *nm* guy, *Br* bloke

médoc [medɔk] *nm* medicine ᐤ; **il est dépressif et bourré de médocs** he suffers from depression and he's stuffed full of drugs or he's a walking pharmacy

mégalo [megalo] (*abbr* **mégalomane**) **1** *adj* megalomaniac ᐤ, power-mad
2 *nmf* megalomaniac ᐤ, power maniac, control freak

mégoter [megɔte] *vi* to skimp (**sur** on); **arrête de mégoter, achète du vrai Champagne!** don't be stingy, buy real champagne!; **il a pas mégoté sur le piment** he didn't skimp on the chilli

meilleure [mejœr] *nf* **ça c'est la meilleure!** that just tops it all!

mélanger [melãʒe] **se mélanger** *vpr Hum* (*avoir des rapports sexuels*) to exchange bodily fluids

mêler [mele] **se mêler** *vpr* **de quoi je me mêle?** what's that got to do with you/him/etc?

mêle-tout [mɛltu] *nmf inv* busybody, *Br* nosey parker

mélo [melo] **1** *adj* (*abbr* **mélodramatique**) melodramatic ᐤ, over-the-top, *Br* OTT
2 *nm* (*abbr* **mélodrame**) melodrama ᐤ

melon [məlɔ̃] *nm Offensive* (*Maghrébin*) = racist term used to refer to a North African Arab

membré [mãbre] *adj* **être bien/mal membré** to be/not to be well-hung

mémérage [memeraʒ] *nm Can* gossip ᐤ

mémère [memɛr] **1** *nf* (*femme d'un certain âge*) old biddy, *Br* old dear
2 *adj* frumpy, frumpish; **faire mémère** to look like an old woman ▶ *see also* **pousser**

mémérer [memere] *vi Can* to gossip ᐤ

méninges [menɛ̃ʒ] *nfpl* **se remuer les méninges** to rack or *Am* cudgel one's brains

menteuse [mãtøz] *nf* (*langue*) tongue ᐤ

merde ! [mɛrd] **1** *nf* (a) (*excrément*) shit, crap; **être dans la merde** to be in the shit, to be up shit creek (without a paddle); **traîner qn dans la merde** to drag sb's name through the mud; **ne pas se prendre pour de la merde** to think one's shit doesn't stink, *Br* to think the sun shines out of one's arse; **il a de la merde dans les yeux** he never sees a thing, he can't see what's going on right in front of him
(b) (*individu méprisable*) shit
(c) (*chose de mauvaise qualité*) **c'est une merde cet ordinateur** this computer's (a load of) shit; **de la merde** (a load of) shit; **c'est de la merde ce rasoir** this razor's (a load of) shit!; **un boulot/un quartier de merde** a shit or shitty job/area; **tu vas l'éteindre, ta radio de merde, oui?** will you turn that *Br* bloody or *Am* goddamn radio off!
(d) (*désordre*) **semer** ou **foutre la merde** to create havoc; **c'est la merde dans le pays en ce moment** the country's a *Br* bloody or *Am* goddamn mess or shambles at the moment; **c'est la merde pour circuler dans Paris en ce moment** driving in Paris is a *Br* bloody or *Am* goddamn nightmare at the moment

---

Le symbole ᐤ *indique que la traduction n'est pas argotique.*

(e) *(problème)* problem [□]; **et si il nous arrivait une merde?** what if we ended up in the shit?; **il m'est arrivé une merde** something shit's happened
2 *exclam* **(a)** *(pour exprimer l'exaspération)* shit!; **dire merde à qn** to tell sb to piss off *or Br* bugger off; **alors, tu viens, oui ou merde?** are you coming or not, for Christ's sake?; **avoir un œil qui dit merde à l'autre** to have a squint [□]
(b) *(pour souhaiter bonne chance)* break a leg! ▶ see also **bordel, fouteur**

merder ! [mɛrde] **1** *vt (rater)* to screw up, *Br* to cock up, to balls up *Am* to ball up
2 *vi (personne)* to screw up; *(situation)* to be a *Br* cock-up *or* balls-up *or Am* ball-up; **le coup a complètement merdé** the job was a complete *Br* cock-up *or* balls-up *or Am* ball-up

merdeux, -euse ! [mɛrdø, -øz] **1** *adj (coupable)* **se sentir merdeux** to feel shit *or* shitty
2 *nm,f* **(a)** *(personne méprisable)* shit **(b)** *(enfant)* kid

merdier ! [mɛrdje] *nm Br* bloody *or Am* goddamn mess *or* shambles

merdique ! [mɛrdik] *adj* shit, shitty

merdouille ! [mɛrduj] *nf* **(a)** *(situation déplaisante) Br* bloody *or Am* goddamn mess *or* shambles; **être dans la merdouille** to be in the shit **(b)** *(chose sans valeur)* **de la merdouille** (a load of) shit

merdouiller ! [mɛrduje], **merdoyer** ! [mɛrdwaje] *vi* to screw up, *Br* to cock up, to balls up, *Am* to ball up

mère [mɛr] *nf Cités* **ta mère!** ! *Br* piss off!, *Am* take a hike!; **enculé de ta mère!** !! you fucking prick *or Br* arsehole *or* wanker *or Am* asshole!; **niquer sa mère à qn** !! to kick sb's fucking head in, *Am* to punch sb out; **flipper sa mère** to be scared stiff; **ouah! il est beau sa mère ce mec!** wow! that guy is a total babe *or Am* hottie! ▶ see also **maquerelle, niquer**

The word "mère", literally translated as "mother", appears in numerous slang expressions of the "banlieues" (see panel **l'argot des banlieues** on p. 9, French-English side) and functions as an intensifier. This usage almost indisputably has its origins in North African culture.

mérinos [merinos] *nm Hum* **laisser pisser le mérinos** to let things take their course [□]

merlan [mɛrlɑ̃] *nm* **(a)** *(coiffeur)* hairdresser [□] **(b)** **regarder qn avec des yeux de merlan frit** *(sans comprendre)* to gaze blankly at sb [□], to gape at sb [□]; *(amoureusement)* to make sheep's eyes at sb

métèque [metɛk] *nmf Offensive* = racist term used to refer to any dark-skinned foreigner living in France, especially one from the Mediterranean; **sa fille s'est mise en ménage avec un métèque** his daughter's shacked up with some Dago-looking guy

métro [metro] *nm* **(a)** **il a toujours un métro de retard** he's always the last one to know what's going on **(b)** **métro, boulot, dodo** the daily grind, the nine-to-five routine

mettable !! [mɛtabl] *adj* fuckable, *Br* shaggable

mettre [mɛtr] **1** *vt* **(a)** !! *(posséder sexuellement)* to fuck, to screw, *Br* to shag; **va te faire mettre!** up yours!, fuck off!, go and fuck yourself! **(b)** **les mettre, mettre les bouts** to make tracks, to hit the road, *Am* to book it
2 se mettre *vpr* **(a)** **son contrat, il peut se le mettre quelque part!** !! he can shove his contract up his *Br* arse *or Am* ass!
(b) **s'en mettre jusque-là** to stuff oneself *or* one's face, to pig out, *Am* to munch out; **qu'est-ce qu'on s'est mis!** we really stuffed ourselves *or* our faces!, we really pigged *or Am* munched out!
(c) **qu'est-ce qu'ils se sont mis!** *(dans une bagarre)* they really laid into each other!, they were going at it hammer and tongs! ▶ see also **coup, grappin, nez, paquet, veilleuse, voile, vue**

meuf [mœf] *nf (verlan* **femme***)* **(a)** *(fille)*

Le symbole [□] indique que la traduction n'est pas argotique.

chick, Br bird (**b**) (compagne) girlfriend ᵁ, woman, Br bird

meule [møl] nf (**a**) (moto) (motor)bike ᵁ (**b**) **meules** (postérieur) butt, Br bum, Am fanny (**c**) Suisse (personne ou chose fastidieuse) drag

mézigue [mezig] pron yours truly, Br muggins (here)

mic [majk] nm Cités mike

miches [miʃ] nfpl (**a**) (postérieur) butt, Br bum, Am buns, fanny (**b**) (seins) boobs, knockers

micheton [miʃtɔ̃] nm Br punter, Am john

michetonner [miʃtɔne] vi (**a**) (avoir recours à une prostituée) to go to a hooker (**b**) (se prostituer) to turn tricks

mickey [mikɛ] nm nobody ᵁ, nonentity ᵁ

micmac [mikmak] nm muddle, shambles

midi [midi] nm (**a**) **chercher midi à quatorze heures** to look for complications (where there are none) ᵁ; **pas besoin de chercher midi à quatorze heures pour expliquer son départ** no need to look too far to understand why he left (**b**) **marquer midi** ‼ (avoir une érection) to have a boner

millefeuille ‼ [milfœj] nm (sexe de la femme) muff, beaver, snatch

mimi [mimi] **1** adj inv cute ᵁ
2 nm (**a**) (baiser) kiss ᵁ (**b**) (chat) pussy (cat) (**c**) ! (sexe de la femme) pussy, Br fanny

minable [minabl] **1** adj (**a**) (mesquin, pauvre) shabby, grotty (**b**) (incompétent, insuffisant) pathetic, lousy
2 nmf loser, no-hoper, dead loss

mince [mɛ̃s] exclam (pour exprimer l'exaspération) blast!, sugar!, Am shoot!; (pour exprimer la surprise) wow!, Br blimey!, strewth!, Am gee (whiz)!

minch [minʃ] nf Cités (**a**) (femme) chick, Br bird (**b**) ! (sexe de la femme) pussy, beaver, snatch

minet, -ette [minɛ, -ɛt] **1** nm (**a**) (chat) pussy (cat) (**b**) ! (sexe de la femme) pussy, beaver, snatch
2 nm,f (jeune personne à la mode) trendy

3 ! nf (sexe de la femme) pussy, beaver, snatch; **faire minette (à qn)** to go down (on sb), to give (sb) head

minou [minu] nm (**a**) (chat) pussy (cat) (**b**) ! (sexe de la femme) pussy, beaver, snatch

mioche [mjɔʃ] nmf kid

mirettes [miɛt] nfpl eyes ᵁ; **en mettre plein les mirettes à qn** to blow sb away

miro [miro] adj short-sighted ᵁ; **il est complètement miro** he's as blind as a bat; **elles sont devant ton nez, tes clés; t'es miro ou quoi?** your keys are right under your nose, are you blind?

mitan [mitɑ̃] nm **le mitan** the underworld, gangland

mitard [mitar] nm disciplinary cell ᵁ, cooler; **se retrouver au mitard** to end up in solitary

miteux, -euse [mitø, -øz] **1** adj (costume, chambre, hôtel) shabby, grotty; (personne) seedy-looking, shabby; (situation, salaire) pathetic
2 nm,f (indigent) bum, Br dosser

mitraille [mitraj] nf (petite monnaie) small change ᵁ, Br coppers

mob [mɔb] nf (abbr mobylette) moped

moche [mɔʃ] adj (**a**) (laid) ugly ᵁ, hideous (**b**) (moralement répréhensible) rotten, lousy; **c'est moche ce qu'il a fait** that was a rotten or lousy thing he did (**c**) (regrettable) rotten; **c'est moche ce qui lui est arrivé** it was rotten or terrible what happened to him

mocheté [mɔʃte] nf (**a**) (femme laide) dog, hag, horror, Br boot, Am beast; (homme laid) horror (**b**) (chose laide) eyesore

mofflé, -e [mɔfle] nm,f Belg failed (exam) candidate ᵁ

moffler [mɔfle] vi Belg **j'ai été mofflé** I failed my exam ᵁ, Am I flunked my exam

moine ‼ [mwan] nm Can (pénis) prick, dick

moite-moite [mwatmwat] adv fifty-fifty, half-and-half

Le symbole ᵁ indique que la traduction n'est pas argotique.

molard !, **mollard** ! [mɔlar] *nm*
spit □, *Br* gob of spit

molarder !, **mollarder** ! [mɔlarde]
vi to spit □, *Br* to gob

mollasson, -onne [mɔlasɔ̃, -ɔn] **1** *adj*
slow □, sluggish □
2 *nm,f* lazy so-and-so

mollo [mɔlo] **1** *adv* **y aller mollo** to take
it easy; **vas-y mollo avec la sauce** go
easy on *or* take it easy with the sauce
2 *exclam* take it easy!

môme [mom] **1** *nmf (enfant)* kid
2 *nf* **(a)** *(fille)* chick, *Br* bird **(b)** *(compagne)* girlfriend □, *(main)* squeeze, *Br*
bird

monaco [mɔnako] *nm* = cocktail consisting of beer, grenadine and lemonade

monnaie [mɔnɛ] *nf (argent)* cash, *Br*
dosh, *Am* gelt, bucks

monstre [mɔ̃str] *adj* monstrous, ginormous, humongous; **j'ai un boulot
monstre!** I've got loads *or* tons *or* piles
of work to do!; **il a un culot monstre**
he's got a damned nerve *or Br* a bloody
cheek

monté [mɔ̃te] *adj* **être bien monté** to be
well-hung; **être monté comme un âne**
ou **un bourricot** *ou* **un taureau** ! to be
hung like a horse *or Br* a donkey *or Am* a
mule

montesquieu [mɔ̃tɛskjø] *nm (billet de
deux cents francs)* two-hundred franc
note □

The "montesquieu" used to be so called
because a picture of the writer Charles
Montesquieu used to feature on the
banknote.

morbac, morbaque [mɔrbak] *nm* **(a)**
! *(pou du pubis)* crab **(b)** *(enfant)* kid

morceau, -x [mɔrso] *nm* **(a)** *(personne)*
un beau morceau a babe, a knockout, *Br*
a nice bit of stuff, a bit of all right; **un
sacré morceau** a big bruiser **(b)** **casser**
ou **cracher** *ou* **lâcher** *ou* **manger le
morceau** to spill the beans, to let the cat
out of the bag **(c)** **casser le morceau à
qn** to give sb a piece of one's mind **(d)**

emporter *ou* **enlever le morceau** to
get one's own way

mordache [mɔrdaʃ] *nf Suisse* **avoir la
mordache** to have the gift of the gab

mordicus [mɔrdikys] *adv* stubbornly □;
il soutient mordicus que c'est vrai he
absolutely insists that it's true □

mordu, -e [mɔrdy] **1** *adj (amoureux)*
madly in love, completely smitten
2 *nm,f* fan, fanatic □; **un mordu de
football** a football fan *or* fanatic □

morfale [mɔrfal] **1** *adj* greedy □
2 *nmf* pig, *Br* greedy-guts, gannet, *Am*
hog

morfler [mɔrfle] **1** *vt* **(a)** *(recevoir)* to
get □; **il a morflé une claque dans la
tronche** he got a slap in the face **(b)** *(se
voir infliger une peine de)* to get □, to cop
2 *vi* **(a)** *(être abîmé)* to get smashed up;
(être blessé) to get injured □; **les suspen-
sions de la voiture ont drôle-
ment morflé** the car suspension's totally
wrecked *or Br* knackered **(b)** *(être sévèrement puni)* to catch it, *Br* to cop it

moricaud, -e [mɔriko, -od] **1** *adj* dark-
skinned □, swarthy □
2 *nm,f Offensive* **(a)** *(personne de race
noire)* nigger, *Br* wog **(b)** *(personne à la
peau foncée)* dark-skinned *or* swarthy person □

morlingue [mɔrlɛ̃g] *nm (porte-monnaie) Br* purse □, *Am* change purse □;
(portefeuille) Br wallet □, *Am* billfold □;
avoir des oursins dans le morlingue
(être très avare) to be a total skinflint *or*
tightwad, *Br* to have moths in one's wallet

mornifle [mɔrnifl] *nf* **(a)** *(argent)* bread,
Br dosh, *Am* bucks, gelt **(b)** *(gifle)* slap,
cuff

morpion [mɔrpjɔ̃] *nm* **(a)** *(pou du pubis)*
crab **(b)** *(enfant)* kid

mort, -e [mɔr, mɔrt] **1** *adj* **(a)** *(hors
d'usage)* **être mort** to be dead, to have
had it, *Br* to be knackered **(b)** *(fatigué)*
dead **(c)** **être mort de rire** to be killing
oneself (laughing); **être mort de
trouille** to be scared to death
2 à mort *adv* **freiner à mort** to slam on

Le symbole □ indique que la traduction n'est pas argotique.

the brakes; **déconner à mort** ⚠ to talk complete crap or bull or Br bollocks; **bander à mort** ⚠⚠ to have a raging hard-on ▶ see also **rat**

mortel, -elle [mɔrtɛl] **1** adj **(a)** (excellent) wicked, Br fab, Am awesome, gnarly **(b)** (très mauvais) hellish, Am gnarly **(c)** (ennuyeux) deadly boring

2 adv **on s'est éclatés mortel!** we had a wicked or Br fab or Am awesome time!; **on s'est fait chier mortel** ⚠⚠ we were fucking bored to death

3 exclam wicked!, Br fab!, Am awesome!

mortibus [mɔrtibys] adj dead □

morue ⚠ [mɔry] nf **(a)** (prostituée) whore, hooker **(b)** (femme) tart, Br slapper

morveux, -euse [mɔrvø, -øz] **1** adj snotty-nosed

2 nm,f **(a)** (enfant) kid **(b)** (jeune prétentieux) snotty little upstart

motte ⚠⚠ [mɔt] nf (sexe de la femme) snatch, twat, pussy, Br minge; **s'astiquer la motte** to finger oneself, to play with oneself

motus [mɔtys] exclam **motus (et bouche cousue)!** not a word!, mum's the word!

mou [mu] **1** adv (doucement) **y aller mou** to go easy, to take it easy; **vas-y mou avec le piment** go easy on or take it easy with the chilli

2 nm **(a) bourrer le mou à qn** to pull the wool over sb's eyes **(b) c'est du mou** (c'est faux) it's a load of garbage or Br rubbish **(c) rentrer dans le mou à qn** (agresser qn) to go for sb, to lay into sb, to set about sb ▶ see also **bourrage, chique**

mouais [mwɛ] exclam well, yeah; **alors, t'as aimé le film? – mouais, j'ai vu pire...** did you like the movie, then? – well, yeah, I've seen worse

mouchard, -e [muʃar, -ard] nm,f squealer, Br grass, Am rat; (à l'école) snitch, Br sneak, tell-tale, Am tattle-tale

moucharder [muʃarde] **1** vt to squeal on, Br to grass on, to shop, Am to rat on; (à l'école) to snitch on, Br to sneak on, to tell tales on

2 vi to squeal, Br to grass, Am to rat; (à l'école) to snitch, Br to sneak, to tell tales, Am to tattle

mouflet, -ette [muflɛ, -ɛt] nm,f kid

moufter [mufte] vi **ne pas moufter** to keep one's mouth shut, Br to keep schtum

mouille ⚠ [muj] nf (sécrétions vaginales) lube, love juice; (sexe de la femme) pussy, twat, gash, Br minge

mouiller [muje] **1** vt **(a)** (compromettre) to involve □, to drag in **(b)** Can (fêter) **il va falloir mouiller ça!** we'll have to have a drink to celebrate! □, this calls for a celebration! □

2 vi **(a)** ⚠ (avoir peur) to wet oneself **(b)** ⚠⚠ (être excitée sexuellement) to be wet

3 se mouiller vpr **(a)** (se compromettre) to stick one's neck out **(b)** Can **se mouiller la dalle** ou **le gargoton** ou **le canayen** to get wasted or Br ratted ▶ see also **liquette**

mouise [mwiz] nf (misère) poverty □; (ennuis) grief, hassle, Br aggro; **être dans la mouise** (être dans la misère) to be hard up or broke or Br skint; (avoir des ennuis) to be in a hole, Am to be behind the eight-ball

moule ⚠⚠ [mul] nf (sexe de la femme) pussy, snatch, twat, Br fanny, minge; **avoir de la moule** (de la chance) (ponctuellement) to be lucky □; (toujours) to have the luck of the devil

moumoune [mumun] nf Can Offensive fairy, queer, Br poof, Am fag

moumoute [mumut] nf wig □, rug, Br syrup

mourir [murir] vi **plus débile/macho, tu meurs!** they don't come any more stupid/macho than that!

mouron [murɔ̃] nm **se faire du mouron** to worry oneself sick

mousse [mus] nf **(a)** (bière) beer □; **on se boit une mousse?** fancy a Br pint or Am brew? **(b) se faire de la mousse** to worry oneself sick

moutard [mutar] *nm* kid

mouv' [muv] *nm* (*abbr* **mouvement**) **c'est dans le mouv'** it's dead hip, it's totally cool

moyen [mwajɛ̃] *nm* **y'a moyen!** can do!

muflée [myfle] *nf* **prendre une muflée** to get wrecked *or* wasted *or Br* legless *or* pissed; **il tenait une sacrée muflée** he was totally wrecked *or* wasted *or Br* legless *or* pissed

mule [myl] *nf* (*passeur de drogue*) mule

mur [myr] *nm* **tenir le mur** to bum around all day (*because one is unemployed*)

murge [myrʒ] *nf* **prendre une murge** to get wrecked *or* wasted *or Br* legless *or* pissed; **il tenait une sacrée murge** he was totally wrecked *or* wasted *or Br* legless *or* pissed

muscu [mysky] *nf* (*abbr* **musculation**) body-building □; **faire de la muscu** to do body-building

musiciens [myzisjɛ̃] *nmpl* (*haricots*) beans □

musicos [myzikos] *nm* (*musicien*) muso

must [mœst] *nm* must; **c'est un must** it's a must

mytho [mito] *nmf* (*abbr* **mythomane**) (**a**) (*menteur*) compulsive liar □ (**b**) *Cités* (*mensonge*) lie □, whopper, *Br* porky

N

nager [naʒe] *vi (ne rien comprendre)* to be totally lost, not to have a clue

nana [nana] *nf (femme)* chick, *Br* bird; *(petite amie)* girlfriend ⃞, (main) squeeze, *Br* bird

nanar [nanar] *nm* (**a**) *(marchandise sans valeur)* junk, trash, garbage (**b**) *(mauvais film)* lousy film, *Am* turkey

NAP [nap] *(abbr* **Neuilly-Auteuil-Passy)**
1 *adj Br* ≃ Sloany, *Am* ≃ preppy
2 *nmf Br* ≃ Sloane (Ranger), *Am* ≃ preppy

> Neuilly, Auteuil and Passy are areas in the west of Paris, and are among the wealthiest and most middle-class in the city, although strictly speaking Neuilly is not part of Paris, but in the adjoining département Hauts-de-Seine. A "NAP" is typically rich, expensively dressed, and politically to the right.

nase [naz] = **naze**

naseaux [nazo] *nmpl (narines)* nostrils ⃞; **on a pris toute la fumée dans les naseaux** all the smoke went right up our noses

navet [navɛ] *nm (mauvais film)* lousy film, *Am* turkey

naze [naz] *adj* (**a**) *(épuisé)* bushed, *Br* knackered, shattered, *Am* beat (**b**) *(hors d'usage)* kaput, bust, *Br* clapped-out (**c**) *(stupide)* thick, dense, *Am* dumb (**d**) *(de mauvaise qualité)* crap, crappy, lousy, *Am* rinky-dink

nèfles [nɛfl] *nfpl* **des nèfles!** no way!, no chance!

négatif [negatif] *exclam* no! ⃞, nope!

negifran [nəʒifrã] *nf (verlan* **frangine)** chick, *Br* bird

négro [negro] *nm Offensive* nigger

neige [nɛʒ] *nf (cocaïne)* snow

nénés [nene] *nmpl* tits, knockers, jugs, *Am* hooters

nénette [nenɛt] *nf* (**a**) *(femme, fille)* chick, *Br* bird (**b**) *(tête)* **se casser la nénette (à faire qch)** to go to a lot of bother (to do sth); **te casse pas la nénette** don't worry about it, don't let it bother you

nerfs [nɛr] *nmpl* **avoir les nerfs** to be hacked off; **foutre les nerfs à qn** to hack sb off, to get sb's back up ► *see also* **paquet**

net, nette [nɛt] *adj* **pas net** *(louche)* shady, *Br* dodgy; *(ivre, drogué)* off one's face, wasted, wrecked; *(pas complètement sain d'esprit)* not all there, *Br* one sandwich short of a picnic

nettoyer [netwaje] *vt* (**a**) *(dépouiller)* to clean out, to take to the cleaners (**b**) *(tuer)* to bump off, *Am* to rub out, to off

neuf-trois [nœftrwa] *nm (département de la Seine-Saint-Denis)* Seine-Saint-Denis ⃞

> This term comes from the two-digit number of the Seine-Saint-Denis département, which is located on the outskirts of Paris and contains many impoverished housing estates.

neuneu [nønø] *adj* daft, *Am* dumb

neutu [nœty] *nf Cités (verlan* **thune)** cash, dough, *Br* dosh, *Am* bucks

nez [ne] *nm* (**a**) **avoir un coup dans le nez** to have had one too many (**b**) **elle m'a dans le nez** she can't stand *or* stomach me *or Br* stick me, *Br* I get right up her nose (**c**) **mettre à qn le nez dans son caca** *ou* **dans sa merde** ‼ to call sb to order ⃞, to pull sb up ► *see also* **doigt, pendre, tirer**

Le symbole ⃞ indique que la traduction n'est pas argotique.

niac [njak] *nmf Offensive (Asiatique)* slant, *Am* gook

niacoué, -e [njakwe] *nm,f Offensive (Asiatique)* slant, *Am* gook

niaiser [njeze] *Can* **1** *vt* **niaiser qn** *(faire perdre patience à)* to drive sb crazy; *(se moquer de)* to laugh at sb, *Br* to wind sb up, *Am* to razz sb; *(raconter des histoires à)* to pull sb's leg, *Br* to wind sb up, to have sb on
2 *vi (ne rien faire)* to hang around

niaiseux, -euse [njezø, -øz] *Can* **1** *adj* dense, *Am* dumb
2 *nm,f* moron, jerk, *Am* geek

niaque [njak] = **gnaque**

nibard ⚠ [nibar] *nm* tit, knocker, jug

nichon [niʃɔ̃] *nm* boob, tit

nickel [nikɛl] **1** *adj inv* **nickel** *ou* **nickel chrome** *(très propre)* spotless ◻, gleaming ◻
2 *adv* **faire qch nickel** *ou* **nickel chrome** to do sth really well ◻

nickelé [nikle] *adj* **avoir les pieds nickelés** *(être trop paresseux pour marcher)* to be too lazy to walk anywhere ◻; *(avoir de la chance)* to be lucky ◻ *or Br* jammy

niet [njɛt] *exclam* no way!, not a chance!

nimportenawaque [nɛ̃pɔrtnawak] *adv Cités Br* rubbish, *Am* BS; **ce film, je te raconte pas, c'était nimportenawaque!** that film, my God, what a load of *Br* rubbish *or Am* BS

nipper [nipe] **se nipper** *vpr* to get dressed ◻; **il sait pas se nipper** he's got no dress sense

nippes [nip] *nfpl* clothes ◻, gear, *Br* threads

nique [nik] *nf* **faire la nique à qn** to thumb one's nose at sb

niquer ⚠ [nike] **1** *vt* **(a)** *(posséder sexuellement)* to fuck, to screw, *Br* to shag, *Am* to ball; **va te faire niquer!, nique ta mère!** fuck off!, go and fuck yourself!
(b) *(endommager)* to bust, *Br* to knacker, to bugger; **il m'a niqué ma mob** he's bust *or Br* knackered *or* buggered my moped; **il s'est niqué le genou** he's bust *or Br* knackered *or* buggered his knee; **je vais lui niquer sa gueule!** I'm going to waste his fucking face!; *Cités* **niquer sa mère** *ou* **sa race à qn** to waste sb's face, *Br* to punch sb's lights out, *Am* to punch sb out
(c) *(attraper)* to nab, to collar; **il s'est fait niquer par les contrôleurs** he got nabbed *or* collared by the ticket collectors
(d) *(duper)* to shaft, to screw; **c'est un faux, tu t'es fait niquer!** it's a fake, you've been shafted *or* screwed!
2 *vi* to fuck, to screw, *Br* to shag, *Am* to ball

niquet [nikɛ] *nm Belg* snooze, nap; **faire un niquet** to have a snooze or a nap *or Br* a kip

noce [nɔs] *nf* **(a)** **faire la noce** to live it up **(b)** **être à la noce** to have the time of one's life, to have a whale of a time; **on n'était pas à la noce** it was no picnic

nœud ⚠⚠ [nø] *nm (pénis)* cock, dick, prick; **à la mords-moi le nœud** lousy, crappy, *Br* poxy ▶ *see also* **tête**

nœud-pap [nøpap] *nm (abbr nœud papillon)* bow tie ◻

noiche [nwaʃ] *nmf Cités (verlan chinois)* Chinese ◻

noir, -e [nwar] **1** *adj (ivre)* plastered, smashed, wasted
2 *nm* **un petit noir** a black coffee ◻

noircir [nwarsir] **se noircir** *vpr (s'enivrer)* to get plastered *or* smashed *or* wasted

noisettes ⚠ [nwazɛt] *nfpl (testicules)* balls, nuts, *Br* bollocks

noix [nwa] *nf* **à la noix (de coco)** lousy, *Br* poxy

nom [nɔ̃] **1** *nm* **nom à coucher dehors** mouthful; **il a un nom à coucher dehors** his name's a real mouthful; **petit nom** first name ◻
2 *exclam* **nom de nom!, nom d'un petit bonhomme!, nom d'une pipe!** for goodness' sake, *Br* blimey!, *Am* gee (whiz)!; **nom d'un chien!** hell!; **nom de Dieu!** for Christ's sake!, Christ (Almighty)!

nono, -ote [nono, nɔnɔt] *nm,f Can* jerk, *Br* pillock, plonker, *Am* schmuck

noraf [nɔraf], **nordaf** [nɔrdaf] nm Offensive = racist term used to refer to a North African Arab

nouba [nuba] nf party □; **faire la nouba** to party

nougats [nuga] nmpl (pieds) feet □, Br plates, Am dogs

nouille [nuj] nf (a) (personne stupide) dimwit, Br berk, divvy, Am meathead (b) ⚠(pénis) dick, tool, Br knob, Am schlong; **égoutter la nouille** to Br have or Am take a piss, Br to have a slash or a leak

nuigrave [nɥigrav] nf smoke, Br fag

> This term is a contraction of the words "nuit gravement à la santé", the government health warning which appears on every cigarette pack in France.

nul, nulle [nyl] **1** adj crap, garbage, Br rubbish; (personne) useless, hopeless, clueless; **il est nul en anglais** he's crap or useless or hopeless at English; **c'est nul de pas l'avoir invité à ta boum** it was crap not to invite him to your party; **nul à chier**‼ fucking awful
2 nm,f useless idiot, prat

nullache [nylaʃ] adj (abbr **nul à chier**) godawful, Br bloody awful; **son dernier skeud, il est nullache** his last record is godawful or Br bloody awful

nullard, -e [nylar, -ard] **1** adj crap, lousy
2 nm,f useless idiot, prat

nullissime [nylisim] adj totally useless, pathetic

nullité [nylite] nf (personne) useless idiot, prat

nullos [nylos] **1** adj useless
2 nmf useless idiot, prat; **mais qui est-ce qui m'a fichu une bande de nullos pareille?** how did I get stuck with such a bunch or Br shower of useless idiots?

numéro [nymero] nm (a) (personne originale) character, case; **quel numéro!** what a character or case!; **c'est un drôle de numéro!** he's a strange character!, Br he's a right one! (b) **avoir tiré le bon numéro** to have found Mr/Miss Right

nunuche [nynyʃ] adj daft, Am dumb

nympho [nɛ̃fo] nf (abbr **nymphomane**) nympho

O

occase [ɔkaz] *nf* (*abbr* **occasion**) chance □, opportunity □; **c'est le genre d'occase à ne pas laisser passer** you shouldn't let an opportunity like that pass you by; **d'occase** second-hand □; **je n'achète que des voitures d'occase** I only buy second-hand cars

occuper [ɔkype] **s'occuper** *vpr* **t'occupe!** mind your own business!, keep your nose out!, butt out! ▶ *see also* **oignon**

-oche [ɔʃ] *suffix* **baloche** local dance □; **cantoche** canteen □; **cinoche** *Br* pictures, *Am* movies; **fastoche** *Br* dead or *Am* real easy

> This suffix is found at the end of many French slang nouns and adjectives and is used for either pejorative or humorous effect.

œil [œj] *nm* **mon œil!** my eye!, my foot!; **faire de l'œil à qn** to give sb the eye; **œil au beurre noir** black eye □, shiner; **à l'œil** free (of charge) □; **avoir qn à l'œil** to have one's eye on sb, to keep an eye on sb ▶ *see also* **battre, doigt, rincer, taper, tourner, yeux**

œuf [œf] *nm* (**a**) **va te faire cuire un œuf!** take a running jump, go and jump in the lake, *Am* take a hike! (**b**) *Hum* **œufs sur le plat** (*seins*) fried eggs

oigne [‼] [waɲ] *nm Br* arsehole, *Am* asshole; **l'avoir dans l'oigne** to have been shafted or screwed

oignon [ɔɲɔ̃] *nm* (**a**) [‼] (*anus*) *Br* arsehole, *Am* asshole; **l'avoir dans l'oignon** to have been shafted or screwed (**b**) **s'occuper de ses oignons** to mind one's own business; **c'est pas tes oignons!** it's none of your business! (**c**) **aux petits oignons** great, terrific ▶ *see also* **carrer**

oilpé [walpe] = **loilpé**

oinj [wɛ̃ʒ] *nm* (*verlan* **joint**) joint, spliff

oiseau, -x [wazo] *nm* **un drôle d'oiseau** an odd character, a funny old bird; **se donner des noms d'oiseaux** to throw insults at each other

ombre [ɔ̃br] *nf* (**a**) **être à l'ombre** (*en prison*) to be behind bars or inside; **mettre qn à l'ombre** to put sb behind bars or inside (**b**) **marche à l'ombre!** (*conseil*) keep a low profile!; (*menace*) stay out of my sight!

ordure [ɔrdyr] *nf* (*individu méprisable*) scumbag, *Br* rotter, *Am* stinker

orphelines [‼] [ɔrfəlin] *nfpl* (*testicules*) balls, nuts, *Br* bollocks

os [ɔs] *nm* (**a**) (*problème*) snag, hitch; **il y a un os** there's a snag or a hitch; **tomber sur un os** to hit a snag (**b**) **l'avoir dans l'os** [‼] to get screwed or shafted; **jusqu'à l'os** totally □, completely □ ▶ *see also* **sac**

-os [ɔs] *suffix* **chicos** classy, smart; *Offensive* **portos** Dago (*from Portugal*); **nullos** useless idiot; **rapidos** pronto; **ringardos** uncool, unhip, square

> This suffix is found at the end of many French nouns and adjectives and often indicates that the word is rather pejorative.

oseille [ozɛj] *nf* (*argent*) dough, *Br* dosh, *Am* bucks

ostrogoth [ɔstrogo] *nm* boor

où [u] *adv Cités* **d'où tu me parles comme ça, toi?** who do you think you're talking to?

ouais [wɛ] *exclam* yeah!

oublier [ublije] *vt* **oublie-moi!** get off my back or case!

Le symbole □ indique que la traduction n'est pas argotique.

ouf [uf] **1** *adj* (*verlan* **fou**) crazy, *Br* mental, barking, *Am* nutso

2 *nm* (*verlan* **fou**) nutcase, *Br* nutter, *Am* screwball; **c'est un truc de ouf** it's for nutcases

3 *exclam* **il n'a pas eu le temps de dire ouf** he didn't even have time to catch his breath

ouïe [wi] *nf Can* (*oreille*) ear □

-ouille [uj] *suffix* **magouille** scheme; **merdouille** mess; *Pej* **pedzouille** yokel, peasant, *Am* hick

> This suffix is found at the end of many French nouns and adjectives and often indicates that the word is rather pejorative.

-ouse [uz] *suffix* **bagouse** ring □;

partouse orgy; **perlouse** pearl □; **piquouse** shot, *Br* jab; *Offensive* **tantouse** queer, *Br* poof, *Am* fag

> This suffix is found at the end of many French nouns and adjectives and often indicates that the word is rather pejorative.

outil [uti] *nm Hum* (*pénis*) tool ▶ *see also* **remballer**

outillé [utije] *adj Hum* **être bien outillé** to be well-hung

ouvrir [uvrir] *vt* **l'ouvrir, ouvrir sa gueule** [!] (*parler*) to open one's big mouth

-ouze [uz] = **-ouse**

P

pacson [paksɔ̃] nm (**a**) *(paquet)* parcel □, package □ (**b**) **toucher le pacson** *(dans une affaire)* to make a bundle *or* Br a packet; *(au jeu)* to win a bundle *or* Br a packet

paddock [padɔk] nm *(lit)* bed □, Br pit

paf [paf] **1** adj inv smashed, plastered, sozzled

2 [!] nm *(pénis)* dick, knob, Am pecker

pagaïe, pagaille [pagaj] nf (**a**) *(désordre)* mess, shambles (**b**) **il y en a en pagaïe** there's loads *or* tons of it/them

page [paʒ], **pageot** [paʒo] nm *(lit)* bed □, Br pit

pager [paʒe], **pagnoter** [paɲɔte] **se pager, se pagnoter** vpr to hit the sack *or* the hay *or* Am the rack

paillasse [pajas] nf *(ventre)* stomach □, belly, guts; **trouer la paillasse à qn** to knife sb in the guts

paillasson [pajasɔ̃] nm *(personne servile)* doormat; **traiter qn comme un paillasson** to treat sb like a doormat

paille [paj] nf (**a**) **être/finir sur la paille** to be/end up completely broke *or* Br on one's uppers *or* Am without a dime (**b**) *Ironic (petite somme)* **il a perdu vingt mille euros à la roulette – une paille!** he lost twenty thousand euros at the roulette table – chickenfeed! *or* small change! *or* peanuts!

pain [pɛ̃] nm (**a**) *(coup)* belt, smack; **coller un pain à qn** to belt *or* smack sb (**b**) **ça mange pas de pain** it won't do any harm ▶ see also **planche**

paire [pɛr] nf (**a**) **se faire la paire** *(s'enfuir)* to take off, to make oneself scarce, Br to scarper; *(s'évader)* to break out □; *(faire une fugue)* to run away □, Br to do a bunk (**b**) **c'est une autre paire de manches** that's a different kettle of fish, that's a whole different ball game (**c**) **en glisser une paire à qn** [!] to give sb one, Br to slip sb a length

paître [pɛtr] vi **envoyer qn paître** to tell sb where to go, Br to send sb packing

paix [pɛ] nf **fiche-moi** *ou* **fous-moi** [!] **la paix!** get off my back!; **la paix!** shut up!

pâle [pɑl] adj (**a**) **se faire porter pâle** to call in sick □ *(when one is well enough to work)*, Br to take a sickie (**b**) **être pâle des genoux** to be Br knackered *or* shattered *or* Am beat

paletot [palto] nm **tomber sur le paletot à qn** to jump on sb, to go for sb; **mettre la main sur le paletot à qn** to nab *or* Br nick *or* lift sb

pâlichon, -onne [pɑliʃɔ̃, -ɔn] adj a bit pale □, on the pale side □

pallot [!] [palo] nm French kiss; **rouler un pallot à qn** to French-kiss sb, Br to snog sb

palmée [palme] adj Hum **les avoir palmées** to be bone idle *or* a complete lay-about

This expression literally means "to have webbed hands", a condition that would, obviously, make work somewhat difficult.

palper [palpe] vi *(toucher de l'argent)* to get one's money □, to collect; **t'en fais pas pour lui, il a déjà palpé** don't worry about him, he's already got his share

palpitant [palpitɑ̃] nm *(cœur)* ticker

paluche [palyʃ] nf hand □, mitt, paw

palucher [!] [palyʃe] **1** vt to grope, to feel up, to touch up

2 se palucher vpr to play with oneself, to touch oneself up

Le symbole □ indique que la traduction n'est pas argotique.

panade [panad] nf **être dans la panade** to be penniless □ or Br on one's uppers

panais [!!] [panɛ] nm **tremper son panais** to dip one's wick

Paname [panam] npr = nickname given to Paris

panard [panar] nm (a) (pied) foot □, Br plate, Am dog (b) (plaisir intense) **quel panard!** great!, cool!, Br fab!; **prendre son panard** (éprouver un grand plaisir) to get one's kicks; (atteindre l'orgasme) to come, to get off

panier [panje] nm (a) (derrière) **mettre la main au panier à qn** to goose sb (b) **panier à salade** Br Black Maria, Am paddy wagon

pantouflard, -e [pãtuflar, -ard] 1 adj **être pantouflard** to be a real stay-at-home or homebody

2 nm,f stay-at-home, homebody

papa [papa] **à la papa** adv leisurely □; **on va faire ça à la papa** we'll take it easy, we'll do it at our own pace

papelard [paplar] nm (a) (papier) paper □ (b) (article de journal) (newspaper) article □, piece (c) **papelards** (papiers d'identité) ID; **les flics lui ont demandé ses papelards** the cops asked to see his ID

papi [papi] nm (homme âgé) granddad

papier-cul, papier Q [papjeky] nm Br bog roll, Am TP

papillon [papijɔ̃] nm (contravention) (parking) ticket □; **on m'a encore collé un papillon** I've got another parking ticket

papoter [papɔte] vi to chat, to yak, Br to natter

papouilles [papuj] nfpl **faire des papouilles à qn** to stroke sb □, to caress sb □; **c'est un gamin qui aime bien qu'on lui fasse des papouilles** he's a very cuddly child

pâquerette [pakrɛt] nf **voler au ras des pâquerettes** (conversation, plaisanterie) to be a bit on the basic side

paquet [pakɛ] nm (a) **mettre le paquet** to pull out all the stops, to go all out (b) **tout un paquet de** a pile or stack of; **il**

m'a montré sa collection de disques et je peux te dire qu'il y en a pour un **paquet de fric!** he showed me his record collection and I can tell you it must be worth a bundle or Br packet (c) **un paquet de nerfs** a bag of nerves

parachuter [paraʃyte] vt (faire venir de l'extérieur) to parachute in □; **personne ne le connaît, il a été parachuté d'une autre boîte** no one knows him, he's been parachuted in from another company

parano [parano] 1 adj (abbr **paranoïaque**) paranoid □

2 nmf (abbr **paranoïaque**) paranoid person □

3 nf (abbr **paranoïa**) paranoia □; **personne ne veut ta peau, t'es en pleine parano!** nobody's after you, you're just being paranoid!

pardon [pardɔ̃] exclam **qu'est-ce qu'on a bien bouffé, alors là, pardon!** you should have seen how well we ate, it was something else!; **elle a une paire de lolos, pardon!** you should see the pair of boobs she's got on her!; **Sophia Loren, ah pardon! ça c'est une femme!** Sophia Loren, now that's what I call a woman!

pare-chocs [parʃɔk] nmpl Hum (seins) headlights, bumpers, knockers

parfum [parfœ̃] nm **être au parfum** to be in the know; **mettre qn au parfum** to fill sb in, to put sb in the picture

parigot, -e [parigo, -ɔt] 1 adj Parisian □
2 nm,f **Parigot, Parigote** Parisian □

parler [parle] vi **tu parles!** (absolument) you're telling me!, absolutely!, Br too right!; (absolument pas) you must be joking!, are you kidding!; **tu parles d'une cuisinière! elle est pas fichue de faire cuire un œuf...** some cook she is, she can't even boil an egg!

parlote, parlotte [parlɔt] nf chat, chitchat

parole [parɔl] exclam cross my heart!, I swear to God!

parti, -e [parti] adj (ivre) wasted,

plastered, *Br* legless, *Am* polluted, plowed

partie [parti] *nf* **partie fine** orgy; **partie carrée** foursome

partousard, -e [partuzar, -ard] *nm,f* = person who takes part in an orgy

partouse [partuz] *nf* orgy

partouser [partuze] *vi* = to take part in an orgy

partouzard, -e [partuzar, -ard] = **partousard**

partouze [partuz] = **partouse**

partouzer [partuze] = **partouser**

pascal [paskal] *nm* (*billet de cinq cents francs*) five-hundred franc note ᵒ

> The "pascal" used to be so called because a picture of the writer and philosopher Blaise Pascal used to feature on the banknote.

passe [pɑs] *nf* (*d'une prostituée*) trick; **faire une passe** to turn a trick

passe-lacet [pɑslasɛ] *nm* **raide comme un passe-lacet** completely broke *or Br* skint *or* strapped (for cash)

passer [pɑse] *vi* (**a**) **y passer** to croak, *Br* to snuff it, *Am* to kick off, to cash in (**b**) *Hum* **il y a que le train qui lui soit pas passé dessus** she's the town bike, she's seen more ceilings than Michelangelo, they'll bury her in a Y-shaped coffin ▸ *see also* **arme, as, billard, casserole, pommade, savon, sentir, tabac**

passoire [paswar] *nf* (**a**) **transformer qn en passoire** to pump sb full of lead, to riddle sb with bullets (**b**) (*mauvais gardien de but*) **c'est une vraie passoire, ce gardien** this keeper lets everything in (**c**) **ma mémoire est une vraie passoire** I've got a memory like a sieve

pastaga [pastaga] *nm* (*pastis*) pastis ᵒ

patapouf [patapuf] *nm* **gros patapouf** fatso, fatty

pataquès [patakɛs] *nm* mess, shambles; **faire un pataquès** to cause a stink, to set tongues wagging

patate [patat] *nf* (**a**) (*pomme de terre*) potato ᵒ, spud

(**b**) (*coup*) thump, clout

(**c**) (*dans les jeux de balle*) powerful shot ᵒ

(**d**) (*dix mille francs*) ten thousand francs ᵒ

(**e**) **en avoir gros sur la patate** to be down in the mouth

(**f**) (*imbécile*) dork, *Br* divvy, wally, *Am* putz

(**g**) *Can* **lâche pas la patate!** hang in there!

patati [patati] *exclam* **et patati et patata** blah blah blah, and so on and so forth

patatras [patatra] *exclam* crash!

patauger [patoʒe] *vi* **patauger (dans la semoule)** to be totally lost; **je ne comprends rien à ces histoires de logarithmes, je patauge...** I don't understand the first thing about this logarithm nonsense, I'm totally lost

pâte [pɑt] *nf* **être bonne pâte** to be a good sort

pâtée [pɑte] *nf* thrashing, hammering; **foutre la pâtée à qn** (*correction, défaite*) to give sb a thrashing *or* a hammering

patelin [patlɛ̃] *nm* (*village*) village ᵒ; (*petite ville*) small town ᵒ

pater [patɛr], **paternel** [patɛrnɛl] *nm* (*père*) old man

patin [patɛ̃] *nm* (**a**) [!] (*baiser*) French kiss; **rouler un patin à qn** to French-kiss sb, *Br* to snog sb (**b**) **donner** *ou* **filer un coup de patin** (*un coup de frein*) to slam on the brakes

patraque [patrak] *adj* out of sorts, under the weather, *Br* off-colour, *Am* off-color

patron, -onne [patrɔ̃, -ɔn] *nm,f* (*conjoint*) old man; (*conjointe*) old lady; **j'en sais rien, demande à la patronne** I've no idea, ask my old lady

patte [pat] *nf* (**a**) (*jambe*) leg ᵒ, pin; **tirer dans les pattes à qn** to cause trouble for sb; **retomber sur ses pattes** to land on one's feet; **un pantalon pattes d'eph** a pair of flares *or Br* lionels; **en avoir plein les pattes** to be *Br* knackered *or Am* bushed (**b**) (*main*) hand ᵒ, mitt, paw; **tomber dans les pattes de qn** to fall into sb's clutches; **graisser la patte à**

qn to grease sb's palm; **bas les pattes!** paws off!, keep your paws to yourself! ▸ see also **casser**

paturon [patyrɔ̃] *nm* foot □, *Br* plate, *Am* dog

paumé, -e [pome] **1** *adj* **(a)** *(reculé)* godforsaken; **il habite une ferme dans un coin paumé** he lives on a farm in the middle of nowhere **(b)** *(perdu, embrouillé)* lost
2 *nm,f* loser, dropout, *Br* waster, *Am* slacker

paumer [pome] **1** *vt* to lose □
2 se paumer *vpr* to get lost □

pavé [pave] *nm* **(a)** *(livre épais)* doorstop **(b)** *(dent)* tooth □

paveton [pavtɔ̃] *nm* *(pavé)* paving stone □

pavute ! [pavyt] *nf* whore, hooker

paye [pɛj] *nf* **ça fait une paye** it's been ages *or Br* yonks

payer [pɛje] **se payer** *vpr* **il a brûlé un feu rouge et s'est payé un piéton** he went through a red light and hit a pedestrian □; **il s'est payé un arbre en moto** he crashed *or* smashed his motorbike into a tree □; **si il continue à m'énerver, celui-là, je vais me le payer!** if he carries on annoying me, I'm going to swing for him *or* thump him one!; **se payer la tête** *ou* **la tronche** ! **de qn** *Br* to take the mick *or* mickey out of sb, to take the piss out of sb, *Am* to razz sb; **il s'est payé une crève carabinée** he came down with a stinking cold; **se payer du bon temps, s'en payer** to have a wicked *or Br* mental time, *Am* to have a blast ▸ see also **tranche**

peau, -x [po] *nf* **faire la peau à qn** to bump sb off, *Br* to do sb in; **trouer la peau à qn** to fill *or* pump sb full of lead; **avoir qn/qch dans la peau** to be mad *or* crazy about sb/sth; **avoir le rythme dans la peau** to have rhythm in one's blood; **il sait pas quoi faire de sa peau** he doesn't know what to do with himself; **coûter la peau des fesses** *ou* **du cul** ! to cost an arm and a leg; **peau de balle** *ou* **de zébi!** no way!, no chance!, *Br* nothing doing!; **peau d'âne** diploma □;

peau de vache *(homme) Br* swine, *Am* stinker; *(femme)* bitch, *Br* cow

pébroc, pébroque [pebrɔk] *nm* umbrella □, *Br* brolly

pêche [pɛʃ] *nf* **(a)** *(coup)* thump, wallop; **prendre une pêche** to get thumped *or* walloped **(b) avoir la pêche** to be on (top) form, to be full of go **(c) poser une pêche** ! to *Br* have *or Am* take a dump, to drop a log ▸ see also **fendre**

pécho [peʃo] *vt (verlan* **choper)** **(a)** *(saisir)* to grab □ **(b)** *(surprendre)* to catch □, to nab; **se faire pécho** to get caught *or* nabbed **(c)** *(maladie, coup de soleil)* to catch □

pêchu, -e [pɛʃy] *adj* on (top) form, full of go

pécore [pekɔr] *nmf Pej* yokel, peasant, *Am* hick

pécos [pekos] *nm* bomber, cone *(cannabis cigarette)*

pécu [peky] *nm Br* bog roll, *Am* TP

pédale [pedal] *nf* **(a)** *Offensive (homosexuel)* queer, *Br* poof, *Am* fag; **être de la pédale** to be a queer *or Br* poof *or Am* fag **(b) perdre les pédales** to lose one's marbles, *Br* to lose the plot; **s'emmêler les pédales** to get all mixed up, to get hopelessly lost

pédaler [pedale] *vi* **pédaler dans la choucroute** *ou* **dans la semoule** *ou* **dans le yaourt** to get nowhere

pédé !! [pede] *Offensive (abbr* **pédéraste)** **1** *adj* queer, *Br* bent; **pédé comme un phoque** *Br* as bent as a nine-bob note *or* as a three-pound note, *Am* as queer as a three-dollar bill
2 *nm* queer, *Br* poof, *Am* fag

pédégé [pedeʒe] *nm Hum Br* MD □, *Am* CEO □

> This expression comes from the humorous spelling of "P-DG", the abbreviation of "président-directeur général", as it is pronounced.

pédibus [pedibys] *adv* on foot □; **il y est allé pédibus** he went on foot □, he hoofed it

pedzouille [pɛdzuj] *nmf Pej* yokel, peasant, *Am* hick

péfli [pefli] *vi Cités (verlan* **flipper**) to be scared ◻, *Br* to be bricking it

peigne-cul [pɛɲky] *nm (individu méprisable)* jerk, *Br* tosser; *(individu grossier)* pig, boor, *Am* hog

peignée [pɛɲe] *nf* thrashing, hiding, hammering; **flanquer une peignée à qn** to give sb a thrashing *or* hiding *or* hammering; **recevoir une peignée** to get a thrashing *or* hiding *or* hammering

peinard, -e [pɛnaʀ, -aʀd] **1** *adj* **(a)** *(tranquille)* **être peinard** to have it easy, to have an easy time of it; **ils sont peinards dans leur nouvelle baraque** they're nice and comfortable in their new place; **il a trouvé un coin peinard pour pioncer** he found a quiet corner to crash out; **tiens-toi peinard!** keep your nose clean! **(b)** *(peu fatigant)* **un boulot peinard** a cushy job *or* number
   2 *adv (tranquillement)* in peace ◻, peacefully ◻

pékin [pekɛ̃] *nm (individu)* guy, *Br* bloke

pelant, -e [pəlɑ̃, -ɑ̃t] *adj Belg (agaçant)* annoying ◻; *(assommant)* deadly dull; **c'est pelant!** *(agaçant)* it's a real pain (in the neck) *or* a real nuisance!; *(assommant)* it's a real drag!

pelé [pəle] *nm* **il y avait trois pelés et un tondu** there was hardly a soul there

peler [pəle] **1** *vi* to be freezing (cold); **ça pèle** it's freezing (cold) *or Br* brass monkeys
   2 se peler *vpr* **se (les) peler** to be freezing (cold)

pèlerin [pɛlʀɛ̃] *nm (individu)* guy, *Br* bloke

pelle [pɛl] *nf* **(a)** ❗ *(baiser)* French kiss; **rouler une pelle à qn** to French-kiss sb, *Br* to snog sb **(b)** **à la pelle** in spades, by the bucketful; **des nanas comme elle, il y en a à la pelle** there's loads of chicks *or Br* birds like her **(c)** **(se) prendre** *ou* **(se) ramasser une pelle** *(tomber)* to fall flat on one's face; *(subir un échec)* to come unstuck ▸ *see also* **rond**

pelloche [pɛlɔʃ] *nf* film ◻ *(for camera)*

pélo [pelo] *nm (individu)* guy, *Br* bloke

pelote ‼ [plɔt] *nf Can (sexe de la femme)* pussy, *Br* fanny; *(femme)* a bit of *Br* skirt *or Am* tail

peloter [plɔte] **1** *vt* to grope, to feel up, to touch up
   2 se peloter *vpr* to grope each other, to feel *or* touch each other up

pelouse [pluz] *nf (marijuana)* grass, weed, herb

pelure [plyʀ] *nf (manteau)* coat ◻

pendouiller [pɑ̃duje] *vi* to dangle ◻, to hang down ◻

pendre [pɑ̃dʀ] *vi* **ça te pend au nez** you've got it coming to you; **être toujours pendu au téléphone** to be never off the phone, to spend one's life on the phone

péniches [peniʃ] *nfpl (grandes chaussures)* shoes ◻, clodhoppers

péno [peno] *nm (abbr* **penalty**) penalty ◻, *Br* pen *(in football)*

penser [pɑ̃se] *vt* **il peut se le mettre où je pense** he knows where he can stick it; **elle lui a fichu un coup de pied où je pense** she gave him a kick up the you-know-where

people [pipɔl] *nm (célébrité)* celeb

pépé [pepe] *nm (homme âgé)* granddad

pépée [pepe] *nf* chick, *Br* bird

pépère [pepɛʀ] **1** *adj* **(a)** *(tranquille)* relaxing ◻ **(b)** *(peu fatigant)* **un boulot pépère** a cushy job *or* number
   2 *adv* leisurely ◻; **on a fait ça pépère** we took it easy, we did it at our own pace
   3 *nm* **(a)** *(homme âgé)* granddad **(b)** **un gros pépère** a big fatty *or* fatso

pépètes, pépettes [pepɛt] *nfpl* **(a)** *(argent)* cash, dough, *Br* dosh, *Am* bucks **(b)** *Belg* **avoir les pépètes** to be scared stiff *or* witless

pépin [pepɛ̃] *nm* **(a)** *(problème)* hitch, snag; **avoir un pépin** to have a problem ◻ **(b)** *(parapluie)* umbrella ◻, *Br* brolly

péquenaud, -e [pekno, -od] *nm,f Pej* yokel, peasant, *Am* hick

péquenot [pekno] nm Pej yokel, peasant, Am hick

perche [pɛrʃ] nf (a) **grande perche** (personne) beanpole, Am stringbean (b) **tendre la perche à qn** to throw sb a line, to give sb a helping hand

percuter [pɛrkyte] vi (comprendre) to catch on

perdreau, -x [pɛrdro] nm (policier) cop

perfecto® [pɛrfɛkto] nm biker's jacket

périf, périph' [perif] nm (abbr **boulevard périphérique**) **le périf** = the ring road around Paris

perle [!] [pɛrl] nf (a) (pet) fart; **lâcher une perle** to fart, Br to let off, Am to lay one (b) (faute grossière) howler; **il collectionne les perles de ses élèves** he collects the howlers that his pupils come out with (c) **enfiler des perles** to mess around; **bon, faudrait peut-être se mettre au boulot, on n'est pas là pour enfiler des perles** right, it's maybe time to get to work, we're not here to twiddle our thumbs

perlouse, perlouze [pɛrluz] nf (a) (perle) pearl □ (b) [!!] (pet) fart; **lâcher une perlouse** to fart, Br to let off, Am to lay one

perm, perme [pɛrm] nf (abbr **permission**) leave □

Pérou [peru] npr **c'est pas le Pérou** it won't break the bank

perpète [pɛrpɛt] **à perpète** adv (abbr **à perpétuité**) (a) (pour toujours) **être condamné à perpète** to get life (b) (très loin) miles away; **n'y va pas à pied, c'est à perpète** don't walk there, it's miles away

perroquet [pɛrɔkɛ] nm (cocktail) = cocktail consisting of pastis and mint-flavoured syrup

perso [pɛrso] adv (abbr **personnellement**) **être** ou **jouer perso** to hog the ball

personne [pɛrsɔn] pron **quand il s'agit de faire la vaisselle/de payer, il n'y a plus personne** when it's time to do the dishes/to pay, you can't see anyone for dust

pervenche [pɛrvɑ̃ʃ] nf (contractuelle) Br (female) traffic warden □, Am meter maid □

pèse [pɛz] = **pèze**

pet¹ [pɛ] nm (a) (gaz intestinaux) fart; **ça vaut pas un pet de lapin** it's not worth a monkey's fart; **celui-là, il a toujours un pet de travers** there's always something up with him (b) **faire le pet** (faire le guet) to keep watch □ or a lookout □

pet² [pɛt] = **pète**

pétage [petaʒ] nm **pétage de plombs** (fait de se mettre en colère) going ballistic, hitting the roof or Am ceiling, blowing one's top or Am stack; (fait de craquer nerveusement) cracking up; **le patron nous a fait un pétage de plombs maison quand il s'est aperçu de ce qui s'était passé** the boss went totally ballistic or totally hit the roof or Am ceiling when he saw what had happened; **il faut que je prenne des vacances parce que là je suis au bord du pétage de plombs** I need to take a holiday coz I'm on the verge of cracking up

pétant, -e [petɑ̃, -ɑ̃t] adj **à cinq heures pétantes** at five sharp or on the dot

Pétaouchnock [petauʃnɔk] npr = imaginary distant place; **ils l'ont envoyé à Pétaouchnock** they sent him to some place in the back of beyond or to Timbuktu

pétard [petar] nm (a) (cigarette de cannabis) joint, spliff, reefer, number (b) **être en pétard** (en colère) to be fuming or livid; **se mettre en pétard** to go ballistic, to hit the roof or Am ceiling, to blow one's top or Am stack (c) (pistolet) shooter, Am piece = (d) (postérieur) butt, Br bum, Am fanny (e) Can (belle fille) stunner, Br cracker (f) **faire du pétard** (du bruit) to make a racket or a din; (du scandale) to kick up a fuss, to cause a stink

pétasse [petas] nf (a) (femme vulgaire) slut, Br slapper, scrubber (b) (prostituée) whore, hooker

pète [pɛt] nm (trace de coup) dent □, bash □

pété, -e [!] [pete] *adj (ivre)* shit-faced, *Br* rat-arsed, pissed

pète-dans-le-sable [pɛtdɑ̃lsabl] *nmf* runt, squirt, shorty

péter [pete] **1** *vt* **(a)** *(briser)* to break □; *(mettre hors d'usage)* to bust, *Br* to knacker, to bugger; **péter la gueule à qn** to smash sb's face in, to waste sb's face **(b)** **péter le feu** *ou* **des flammes** to be bursting with energy **(c)** **la péter** *(avoir très faim)* to be starving *or* ravenous □ **(d)** **se la péter, péter sa frime** to show off, to pose

2 *vi* **(a)** [!] *(émettre des gaz intestinaux)* to fart; **péter plus haut que son cul** to think one's shit doesn't stink, *Br* to think the sun shines out of one's arse; **péter dans la soie** to live in the lap of luxury; **envoyer qn péter** to tell sb where to go *or* where to get off **(b)** *(casser)* to break □, to bust **(c)** **tu vas la fermer? j'en ai rien à péter de tes histoires!** will you shut up? I don't give a *Br* monkey's *or* Am rat's ass about your nonsense

3 **se péter** *vpr* **(a)** *(se casser)* **se péter le poignet/la cheville** to break one's wrist/ankle □; **la poutre s'est pétée en deux** the beam broke in two □ **(b)** **se péter la gueule** *(tomber)* to fall flat on one's face; **se péter (la gueule)** [!!] *(s'enivrer)* to get shit-faced *or Br* rat-arsed *or* pissed ▸ see also **durite, plomb, sous-ventrière**

pète-sec [pɛtsɛk] **1** *adj inv* abrupt □, snippy

2 *nmf inv* abrupt □ *or* snippy person

péteux, -euse [petø, -øz] *adj* **(a)** *(lâche)* chicken, yellow-bellied **(b)** *(prétentieux)* stuck-up, snooty

2 *nm,f* **(a)** *(lâche)* chicken **(b)** *(prétentieux)* upstart

pétochard, -e [petɔʃar, -ard] *adj & nm,f* chicken *(coward)*

pétoche [petɔʃ] *nf* fear □; **avoir la pétoche** to be scared stiff *or* witless

pétocher [petɔʃe] *vi* to be scared stiff *or* witless

pétoire [petwar] *nf Hum* old rifle □

peton [pətɔ̃] *nm* foot □, *Br* plate, *Am* dog

pétouiller [petuje] *vi Suisse* to hang around

pétrin [petrɛ̃] *nm* **être/se mettre dans le pétrin** to be in/get into a fix *or* a mess

pétrolette [petrɔlɛt] *nf Hum (cyclomoteur)* moped □

peu [pø] *nm* **un peu (mon neveu)!** you bet!, sure thing!, *Br* too right!; **il est un peu bête, ce mec – un peu beaucoup!** the guy's a bit stupid – more than a bit!; **pas qu'un peu** more than a little

peuple [pœpl] *nm* **(a)** *(monde)* **il y avait du peuple** there were tons of people there **(b)** **que demande le peuple?** what more could you ask for?

peupons [pøpɔ̃] *nfpl (verlan* **pompes)** shoes □

pèze [pez] *nm* cash, dough, *Br* dosh, readies, *Am* bucks

philo [filo] *nf (abbr* **philosophie)** philosophy □

phosphorer [fɔsfɔre] *vi* to think hard □; **il faut trouver une solution, alors c'est le moment de phosphorer, les mecs!** we need to find a solution, so let's put our heads together, guys

photo [foto] *nf* **tu veux ma photo?** what are YOU staring at?; **y'a pas photo** there's no two ways about it; **des deux frangines, c'est elle la mieux roulée, y'a pas photo** of the two sisters, that one's got the best body, no two ways about it

> The expression "y a pas photo" comes from the world of horseracing, where a photo-finish decides the result of a race in which it has been impossible to see which horse won.

piaf [pjaf] *nm (oiseau)* bird □; *(moineau)* sparrow □

piailler [pjaje] *vi (criailler)* to squeal □; **on entendait la marmaille en train de piailler dans la cour de récré** you could hear the kids squealing in the playground

piane-piane [pjanpjan] *adv* slowly □; **vas-y piane-piane!** take your time!, there's no rush!

piano [pjano] **1** adv **piano (-piano)** (doucement) slowly □; **vas-y piano-piano!** take your time!, there's no rush!

2 nm **piano du pauvre, piano à bretelles** squeezebox

piasse [pjas] nf Can dollar □, buck

piastre [pjastr] nf Can dollar □, buck

piaule [pjol] nf (bed)room □

picaillons [pikajɔ̃] nmpl dough, bread, Br dosh, Am bucks

pichtegorne [piʃtəgɔrn] nm wine □, vino, Br plonk

picole [pikɔl] nf boozing; **la picole, il n'y a que ça qui l'intéresse** boozing's the only thing he/she's interested in

picoler [pikɔle] **1** vt to knock back **2** vi to booze, to knock it back

picoleur, -euse [pikɔlœr, -øz] nm,f boozer, alky, Br pisshead, Am boozehound

picrate [pikrat] nm wine □, vino, Br plonk

pièce [pjɛs] nf (a) **une belle pièce** (femme) a babe, Br a nice bit of stuff, a bit of all right (b) **on n'est pas aux pièces** we're not on piecework, there's no great hurry

pied [pje] nm **prendre son pied** (atteindre l'orgasme) to come, to get off; (prendre du plaisir) to get one's kicks; **c'est le pied** it's great or fantastic or Br fab or Am awesome; **il a fait ça comme un pied** he made a dog's breakfast or Br a pig's ear of it; **il chante/conduit comme un pied** he can't sing/drive to save his life; **être bête comme ses pieds** Br to be thick (as two short planks), to be as daft as a brush, Am to have rocks in one's head ▶ see also **grue, lever, nickelé**

piège [pjɛʒ] nm **piège à cons** con, scam

piercé, -e [pirse] **1** adj pierced □ (part of body)

2 nm,f = person with body piercings

pierrot [pjɛro] nm (moineau) sparrow □

pieu, -x [pjø] nm (lit) bed □, Br pit; **se mettre au pieu** to hit the sack or the hay or Am the rack ▶ see also **affaire**

pieuter [pjøte] **1** vi to crash, to kip

2 se pieuter vpr to hit the sack or the hay or Am the rack

pif [pif] nm (a) (nez) Br conk, hooter, Am schnozzle; **je l'ai dans le pif** I can't stand the sight of him, Br he gets right up my nose (b) (abbr **pifomètre**) **faire qch au pif** to do sth by guesswork

pifer, piffer [pife] vt **je ne peux pas le piffer** I can't stand or stomach or Br stick him, Br he gets right up my nose

pifomètre, piffomètre [pifɔmɛtr] nm **faire qch au piffomètre** to do sth by guesswork

pige [piʒ] nf year □; **il a au moins soixante-dix piges** he's at least seventy □

pigeon [piʒɔ̃] nm (dupe) sucker, Br mug, Am patsy

pigeonner [piʒɔne] vt **pigeonner qn** to take sb for a ride, to take sb in, Am to rook sb

piger [piʒe] vt to get it, to catch on; **il est pas question que je te prête ma caisse, tu piges?** no way am I lending you my car, got it?

pignoler [piɲɔle] **se pignoler** !͟ vpr to jerk off, to beat off, Br to toss oneself off

pignouf [piɲuf] nm slob, boor

pile [pil] **pile-poil!** adv wicked!, great!

> This expression was popularized in Les Guignols de l'Info, a television programme in the form of a satirical puppet show.

piler [pile] vi to slam on the brakes

pillave [pijav], **pillaver** [pijave] vi to booze, to knock it back

pilule [pilyl] nf **dorer la pilule à qn** to Br sugar or Am sweeten the pill for sb; **se dorer la pilule** to catch some rays; **il a dit ça pour faire passer la pilule** he said it to Br sugar or Am sweeten the pill

pinailler [pinaje] vi to split hairs □, to nit-pick

pinard [pinar] nm wine □, vino, Br plonk

pince [pɛ̃s] nf (a) (main) hand □, mitt, paw; **serrer la pince à qn** to shake hands with sb □ (b) **aller à pinces** to go on foot$^□$, to hoof it ▸ see also **chaud**

pinceaux [pɛ̃so] nmpl (pieds) feet$^□$, Br plates, Am dogs; **s'emmêler les pinceaux** (trébucher) to trip up$^□$, to stumble$^□$; (s'embrouiller) to tie oneself in knots

pincer [pɛ̃se] **1** vt (a) (arrêter) to collar, to nab; **se faire pincer** to get collared or nabbed (b) **en pincer pour qn** to be crazy about sb, to have the hots for sb, Br to fancy sb like mad

2 v imp **ça pince** (il fait froid) it's chilly or Br nippy or parky

pincettes [pɛ̃sɛt] nfpl **ne pas être à prendre avec des pincettes** to be like a bear with a sore head

pine ‼ [pin] nf dick, prick, cock; **rentrer la pine sous le bras** to go home without getting laid or Br without getting one's oats

piner ‼ [pine] vt & vi to fuck, Br to shag

pinglot [pɛ̃glo] nm foot$^□$, Br plate, Am dog

pinté, -e [pɛ̃te] adj smashed, sozzled, trashed

pinter [pɛ̃te] **se pinter** vpr to get smashed or sozzled or trashed

pinteur, -euse [pɛ̃tœr, -øz] nm,f Belg & Suisse boozer, alky

pintocher [pɛ̃tɔʃe] vi Suisse to booze

pion, pionne [pjɔ̃, pjɔn] nm,f (surveillant) supervisor$^□$ (student paid to supervise pupils outside class hours) ▸ see also **damer**

pioncer [pjɔ̃se] vi to sleep$^□$, to crash out; **tu peux rester pioncer chez moi si tu veux** you can crash at mine if you like; **à trois heures de l'après-midi il était toujours en train de pioncer** he was still crashed out at three in the afternoon

pipe [pip] nf (a) ‼ (fellation) blow-job; **tailler** ou **faire une pipe à qn** to give sb a blow-job, to suck sb off, to give sb head (b) **casser sa pipe** to croak, to kick the bucket, Br to snuff it, Am to check out (c) (cigarette) smoke, Br fag, ciggy ▸ see also **fendre, nom, tailleuse**

pipeau [pipo] nm **c'est du pipeau** it's a load of garbage or Br rubbish

pipeauter [pipote] vi to talk crap or bull

pipelette [piplɛt] nf chatterbox, gasbag

pipette [pipɛt] nf Suisse **ça ne vaut pas pipette** it's not worth a bean or Am a red cent

pipi [pipi] nm (a) (urine) pee; **faire pipi** to pee, to have a pee (b) **du pipi de chat** (boisson insipide) dishwater, gnat's piss

pipi-room [pipirum] nm Br loo, Am bathroom$^□$

piqué, -e [pike] adj (a) (fou) crazy, loopy, Br bonkers, barking (mad) (b) **un film pas piqué des vers** ou **des hannetons** a heck of a good film; **un rhume pas piqué des vers** ou **des hannetons** a stinking cold

piquer [pike] **1** vt (a) (voler) to pinch, Br to nick (b) (surprendre) to nab, Br to nick; **se faire piquer** to get nabbed or Br nicked (c) (faire) **piquer une colère** to go ballistic, to hit the roof or Am ceiling, to blow one's top or Am stack; **piquer un cent mètres** to sprint off$^□$; **piquer une tête** (plonger) to dive in$^□$; (se baigner) to have a dip

2 se piquer vpr (se droguer) to shoot up, to hit it up, to jack up ▸ see also **fard, ronflette, roupillon, ruche**

piquette [pikɛt] nf (a) (défaite) thrashing, pasting; **foutre la piquette à qn** to thrash or paste sb (b) (vin de mauvaise qualité) cheap wine$^□$, Br plonk

piquouse, piquouze [pikuz] nf shot, Br jab; **c'est un adepte de la piquouse** he's into shooting up

pisse ‼ [pis] nf piss; **c'est de la pisse d'âne, ta bière!** your beer's like (gnat's) piss!

pisse-copie [piskɔpi] nmf inv hack

pisse-froid [pisfrwa] nmf inv cold fish

pissenlit [pisɑ̃li] nm **manger les pissenlits par la racine** (être mort) to be pushing up the daisies

pisser [pise] **1** vt (a) **pisser du sang** ‼ to piss blood; **pisser des lames de rasoir** ‼ (souffrir au cours de la miction) to piss razor blades (b) **son bras pissait**

le sang blood was pouring or gushing from his arm

2 vi **(a)** [!] *(uriner)* to piss; **c'est comme si je pissais dans un violon** it's a complete waste of time, it's like pissing in the wind; **laisse pisser!** forget it!, drop it!; **c'était à pisser de rire** it was an absolute scream; **pisser dans sa culotte** ou **son froc** to piss oneself or one's pants; **ils en pissaient dans leur culotte** ou **froc** they were pissing themselves (laughing); **envoyer pisser qn** to tell sb to piss off; **ça lui a pris comme une envie de pisser** the urge just came over him; **ça pisse pas loin** it's no great shakes, it's not up to much; **pisser à la raie à qn** [!!] not to give a shit about sb **(b)** *(fuir)* to leak □ ▶ see also **mérinos, sentir**

pissette [pisɛt] *nf Can (pénis)* dick, prick

pisseuse [pisøz] *nf* little girl □

pisseux, -euse [pisø, -øz] *adj (couleur)* washed-out

pissodrome [!] [pisodrom] *nm Belg* public urinal □

pissotière [pisɔtjɛr] *nf* (public) urinal □

pissou [pisu] *nm Can* wimp, wuss

pistoche [pistɔʃ] *nf* swimming pool □

pistolet [pistɔlɛ] *nm* **un drôle de pistolet** a shady or *Br* dodgy character; *Can* **être en pistolet** to be fuming or *Br* spewing

piston [pistɔ̃] *nm (népotisme)* string-pulling; **avoir du piston** to have friends in the right places; **il a eu son job au piston** he got his job by having friends in the right places

pistonner [pistɔne] *vt* **pistonner qn** to pull strings for sb; **il s'est fait pistonner** he got someone to pull strings for him

pitonner [pitɔne] *vi Can (zapper)* to zap, to (channel-)surf; *(sur un clavier, une calculatrice)* to tap □

placard [plakar] *nm (prison)* slammer, clink, *Br* nick, *Am* pen; **mettre qn au placard** *(en prison)* to put sb behind bars or inside or away; *(l'écarter)* to sideline sb □

placardisation [plakardizasjɔ̃] *nf* sidelining □

placardiser [plakardize] *vt* to sideline □

placer [plase] *vt* **ne pas pouvoir en placer une** to be unable to get a word in (edgeways)

placoter [plakɔte] *vi Can* to chew the fat or the rag

placoteur, -euse [plakɔtœr, -øz], **placoteux, -euse** [plakɔtø, -øz] *nm,f Can* gossip □, gossipy person □

plafond [plafɔ̃] *nm* **(a) être bas de plafond** to be a bit slow on the uptake **(b) avoir une araignée au plafond** to have bats in the belfry

plaire [plɛr] *vi Ironic* **il commence à me plaire, celui-là!** he's starting to bug me or *Br* do my head in or get up my nose or *Am* give me a pain (in the neck)!

plan [plɑ̃] *nm* **(a)** *(projet)* plan □; **lui et ses plans foireux!** him and his lousy plans!; **on se fait un plan ciné/resto?** shall we go to the *Br* cinema □ or *Am* movies □/go out for a meal? □; **y'a pas plan** no can do; **je t'aurais bien accompagné, vieux, mais là, vraiment, y'a pas plan!** I'd have gone with you, pal, but no can do **(b) laisser qn en plan** to leave sb in the lurch; **tout laisser en plan** to drop everything

planant, -e [planɑ̃, -ɑ̃t] *adj (drogue)* relaxing □; *(musique)* mellow □

planche [plɑ̃ʃ] *nf* **(a) avoir du pain sur la planche** to have a lot on one's plate **(b) c'est une vraie planche à pain** ou **à repasser** *(elle a de petits seins)* she's as flat as a pancake or as an ironing-board

plancher¹ [plɑ̃ʃe] *nm* **(a) le plancher des vaches** dry land □, terra firma □ **(b) avoir un feu de plancher** = to be wearing trousers which are too short ▶ see also **débarrasser**

plancher² [plɑ̃ʃe] *vi* to be tested □, to have a test □ *(at school)*

planer [plane] *vi* **(a)** *(être sous l'influence d'une drogue)* to be flying, to be high (as a kite), to be spaced out **(b)** *(ne pas avoir le sens des réalités)* to always have one's head in the clouds, to be a space cadet; *(penser à autre chose)* to be miles away, to have one's head in the clouds

Le symbole □ indique que la traduction n'est pas argotique.

plan-plan [plãplã] *adj* routine ⁿ, humdrum ⁿ; **il a une vie tout ce qu'il y a de plus plan-plan** he has the most humdrum life imaginable

planque [plãk] *nf* (**a**) *(cachette)* hiding place ⁿ, hidey-hole (**b**) *(surveillance)* stakeout; **ils étaient en planque autour de la maison** they were staking out the house (**c**) *(emploi tranquille)* cushy job *or* number

planqué, -e [plãke] *nm,f* person with a cushy job *or* number

planquer [plãke] **1** *vt* to hide ⁿ, to stash
2 se planquer *vpr* (**a**) *(se cacher)* to hide ⁿ (**b**) *(se protéger)* to take cover ⁿ

planter [plãte] **1** *vt (tuer à l'arme blanche)* to knife to death ⁿ; *(blesser à l'arme blanche)* to knife ⁿ, *Am* to shank, to shiv
2 *vi (ordinateur)* to go down ⁿ, to crash ⁿ
3 se planter *vpr* (**a**) *(se tromper)* to get it wrong ⁿ, to boob (**b**) *(avoir un accident de la route)* to have a crash ⁿ (**c**) *(échouer)* to fail ⁿ, *Am* to flunk; **il s'est planté à son examen** he failed ⁿ *or Am* flunked his exam

plaque [plak] *nf* (**a**) **être à côté de la plaque** to be wide of the mark, to be off target, to be barking up the wrong tree (**b**) *(dix mille francs)* ten thousand francs ⁿ

plaquer [plake] *vt (emploi)* to quit, *Br* to chuck *or* pack in; *(famille)* to walk out on; *(amant)* to chuck, to dump; **tout plaquer** *Br* to chuck *or* pack it all in, *Am* to chuck everything

plastoc, plastoque [plastɔk] *nm* plastic ⁿ

plat [pla] *nm* (**a**) **faire du plat à qn** *Br* to chat sb up, *Am* to hit on sb (**b**) **faire tout un plat de qch** to make a big song and dance *or* a big fuss about sth (**c**) **il en fait un plat** *(il fait très chaud)* it's a scorcher, *Br* it's roasting ▶ *see also* **œuf**

platiniste [platinist] *nmf* DJ ⁿ

plâtrée [platre] *nf* huge helping; **une plâtrée de nouilles** a huge helping of noodles

plein, -e [plɛ̃, plɛn] *adj (ivre)* **être plein (comme une barrique), être fin plein**
to be plastered, to have had a skinful ▶ *see also* **as, botte, cul, dos, hotte, jambe**

pli [pli] *nm* **ça ne fait pas un pli** there's no doubt about it ⁿ, it's bound to happen ⁿ; **je me doutais qu'il se blesserait, et ça n'a pas fait un pli** I was just waiting for him to hurt himself, and sure enough he did

plié, -e [plije] *adj* **être plié (de rire), être plié en quatre** to be doubled up *or* bent double (with laughter)

plier [plije] *vt (voiture)* to smash up, to wreck

plomb [plɔ̃] *nm* **péter les plombs** *(se mettre en colère)* to go ballistic, to hit the roof *or Am* ceiling, to blow one's top *or Am* stack; *(craquer)* to crack up; **la pression était tellement forte au boulot que j'ai cru que j'allais péter les plombs** the pressure was so bad at work that I thought I was going to crack up ▶ *see also* **casquette**

plombe [plɔ̃b] *nf* hour ⁿ; **il nous a encore fait attendre trois plombes** he kept us waiting for ages again ⁿ

plombé, -e ⚠ [plɔ̃be] *adj (atteint par une MST)* **être plombé** to have a dose

plomber [plɔ̃be] *vt* (**a**) *(tuer à l'aide d'une arme à feu)* to fill sb with lead, to pump sb full of lead (**b**) *(transmettre une MST à)* **plomber qn** ⚠ to give sb a dose (**c**) *(compromettre)* to compromise ⁿ, to jeopardize ⁿ; **les négociations ont été plombées par les récentes grèves** the negotiations have been compromised by the recent strikes

plonge [plɔ̃ʒ] *nf* **faire la plonge** to wash dishes ⁿ *(in a restaurant)*, to be a washer-upper

plonger [plɔ̃ʒe] *vi* (**a**) *(être envoyé en prison)* to be put inside *or* away, *Br* to be sent down (**b**) *(prendre une décision importante)* to take the plunge, to go for it

plouc [pluk] *nmf* yokel, peasant, *Am* hick

pluie [plɥi] *nf* **pluie d'or** ⚠ *(pratique sexuelle)* golden showers

plumard [plymaʁ], **plume¹** [plym] *nm (lit)* bed ⁿ, *Br* pit

---

Le symbole ⁿ *indique que la traduction n'est pas argotique.*

plume² [plym] *nf* (a) ‼️ *(fellation)* blow-job; **tailler une plume à qn** to give sb a blow-job, to suck sb off, to go down on sb (b) *(cheveux)* **perdre ses plumes** to go thin on top (c) **il y a laissé des plumes** he didn't come out of it unscathed ᵘ (d) **voler dans les plumes à qn** to go for sb, to let fly at sb (e) **on a eu chaud aux plumes** we had a narrow escape ▶ see *also* **tailleuse**

plumer [plyme] *vt (escroquer)* to fleece

pochard, -e [pɔʃar, -ard] *nm,f* alky, boozer, *Br* pisshead, *Am* boozehound

poche [pɔʃ] *nf* **c'est dans la poche** it's in the bag; **faire les poches à qn** to go through sb's pockets; **mets ça dans ta poche (et ton mouchoir par-dessus)!** put that in your pipe and smoke it!; **ne pas avoir les yeux dans sa poche** to have eyes in the back of one's head; **s'en mettre** *ou* **s'en foutre** ‼️ **plein les poches** to rake it in

pochetron [pɔʃtrɔ̃] *nm* alky, boozer, *Br* pisshead, *Am* boozehound

pochette-surprise [pɔʃɛtsyrpriz] *nf* **tu l'as eu dans une pochette-surprise, ton permis?** where did you get your licence – in a cornflakes packet *or* in a Christmas cracker?

pogne [pɔɲ] *nf* hand ᵘ, paw, mitt; **se faire une pogne** ‼️ to jerk off, to beat off, *Br* to have a wank

pogner ‼️ [pɔɲe] **1** *vi Can (se caresser mutuellement)* to neck, *Am* to make out; *(avoir des relations sexuelles)* to screw, *Br* to shag
  2 se pogner *vpr* (a) to jerk off, to beat off, *Br* to have a wank (b) *Can* **se pogner le cul** *(se caresser mutuellement)* to neck, *Am* to make out; *(avoir des relations sexuelles)* to screw, *Br* to shag

pognon [pɔɲɔ̃] *nm* cash, *Br* dosh, *Am* bucks

pogo [pogo] *nm* pogo *(dance)*

pogoter [pogɔte] *vi* to pogo

poignée [pwaɲe] *nf* **poignées d'amour** love handles

poil [pwal] *nm* **à poil** in the buff, *Br* starkers; **torse poil** *(homme)* bare-chested ᵘ; *(femme)* topless ᵘ; **être au (petit) poil** to be just the ticket; **tomber au poil** to arrive just at the right moment ᵘ; **au (petit) poil!** great!, terrific!; **il a raté le train à un poil près** he missed the train by a hair's breadth *or* by a whisker; **son analyse est juste, à un poil près** his analysis is correct apart from one or two small details ᵘ; **avoir un poil dans la main** to be bone idle; **être de bon/mauvais poil** to be in a good/bad mood ᵘ; **rentrer dans qch au quart de poil** to fit into sth perfectly ᵘ; **démarrer au quart de poil** to start right away *or* first time ᵘ; **tomber sur le poil à qn** to jump on sb, to go for sb ▶ see *also* **tarte**

poilant, -e [pwalɑ̃, -ɑ̃t] *adj* hysterical, side-splitting

poiler [pwale] **se poiler** *vpr (rire)* to kill oneself (laughing), to laugh one's head off, to split one's sides; *(s'amuser)* to have a ball *or Am* a blast

point [pwɛ̃] *nm* **point barre** end of story; **tu rentres à minuit ou bien tu n'y vas pas; point barre** you'll be home by midnight *or* you're not going at all and that's it, end of story

pointer [pwɛ̃te] **se pointer** *vpr* to turn up, to show up

pointure [pwɛ̃tyr] *nf (personne remarquable en son genre)* **une (grosse) pointure** a big name; **tous les musiciens qui l'accompagnent sont des pointures** all his/her backing musicians are big names in their own right

poire [pwar] *nf* (a) *(visage)* face ᵘ, mug, *Am* map; **il s'est pris le ballon en pleine poire** the ball hit him right in the face (b) *(personne facile à duper)* **une (bonne) poire** a sucker, *Br* a mug, *Am* a patsy ▶ see *also* **fendre**

poireau, -x [pwaro] *nm* (a) ‼️ *(pénis)* dick, cock, prick; **souffler dans le poireau à qn** to give sb a blow-job, to suck sb off, to give sb head (b) **faire le poireau** to hang about *or* around

poireauter [pwarote] *vi* to hang about *or* around; **faire poireauter qn** to keep sb hanging about or around; **ça fait presque une heure que je poireaute!** I've been hanging about or around for nearly an hour!

poiscaille [pwaskaj] nm (poisson) fish ᵁ

poisse [pwas] nf (malchance) bad luck ᵁ; **avoir la poisse** to be unlucky ᵁ; **porter la poisse** to bring bad luck ᵁ

poisson [pwasɔ̃] nm **engueuler qn comme du poisson pourri** to bite sb's head off, to bawl sb out, to jump down sb's throat, to call sb every name under the sun

poivré, -e [pwavre] adj (ivre) wasted, trashed, Br legless, Am lushed

poivrer [pwavre] **se poivrer** vpr to get wasted or trashed or Br legless or Am lushed

poivrot, -ote [pwavro, -ɔt] nm,f alky, boozer, wino, lush

Polac, Polack [pɔlak] nmf Offensive Polack; **être soûl comme un Polack** to be wasted or Br ratted

> Depending on the context and the tone of voice used, this term may be either offensive or affectionately humorous. It is nonetheless inadvisable to use it unless one is quite sure of the reaction it will receive.

polar [pɔlar] nm whodunnit

polichinelle [pɔliʃinɛl] nm **avoir un polichinelle dans le tiroir** to have a bun in the oven, Br to be up the spout or the duff, Am to be knocked up

pommade [pɔmad] nf **passer de la pommade à qn** (flatter) to butter sb up

pomme [pɔm] nf (a) **tomber dans les pommes** to pass out ᵁ, to keel over (b) **aux pommes** (excellent) great, super, terrific (c) **pomme (à l'eau** ou **à l'huile)** (personne naïve) sucker, Br mug, Am patsy (d) **ma pomme** (moi) yours truly; **ta/sa pomme** (toi/lui ou elle) you/him/her ▸ see also **sucer**

pompe [pɔ̃p] nf (a) **avoir un coup de pompe** to suddenly feel bushed or Br knackered or shattered or Am beat

(b) (chaussure) shoe ᵁ; **un coup de pompe** a kick ᵁ; **être** ou **marcher à côté de ses pompes** to be screwed up

(c) **à toute pompe** like lightning, Am like sixty

(d) (aide-mémoire) Br crib, Am trot

(e) **un soldat de deuxième pompe, un deuxième pompe** Br a squaddie, Am a grunt

(f) (seringue) hype, hypo ▸ see also **cirer**

pompé, -e [pɔ̃pe] adj (épuisé) bushed, Br knackered, shattered, Am beat

pomper [pɔ̃pe] **1** vt (a) **pomper qn, pomper l'air à qn** (l'importuner) to get on sb's nerves, to bug sb, Br to get on sb's wick, Am to give sb a pain

(b) (copier) to copy ᵁ, to crib; **il a pompé tout ça dans une encyclopédie** he copied or cribbed it all out of an encyclopedia

(c) (boire) to knock back; **qu'est-ce qu'il pompe!** he can really knock it back!

(d) (épuiser) to wear out, Br to knacker, to do in

(e) **pomper qn**‼, **pomper le dard à qn**‼ (lui faire une fellation) to give sb a blow-job, to suck sb off, to go down on sb

2 vi (copier) to copy ᵁ, to crib; **pomper sur qn/dans qch** to copy or crib from sb/sth

pompette [pɔ̃pɛt] adj tipsy, merry

pompier‼ [pɔ̃pje] nm (fellation) blow-job; **faire un pompier à qn** to give sb a blow-job, to suck sb off, to give sb head, to go down on sb

pompon [pɔ̃pɔ̃] nm **c'est le pompon!** that's the limit!; **avoir** ou **décrocher** ou **tenir le pompon** to take the Br biscuit or Am cake; **j'ai connu des gens de mauvaise foi mais toi, vraiment, tu tiens le pompon!** I've known insincere people before, but you really take the Br biscuit or Am cake!

pondeuse [pɔ̃døz] nf Hum (femme très féconde) **c'est une sacrée pondeuse** she breeds like a rabbit, she's like a battery hen

pondre [pɔ̃dr] vt (a) (mettre au monde) to produce ᵁ, to drop; **sa bonne femme lui a encore pondu un marmot** his old lady's had another kid or Br dropped another sprog **(b)** *(produire)* to produce [□], to come up with; **il pond deux romans par an** he churns out two novels a year

Popaul [!!] [pɔpol] *npr (pénis)* dick, prick, cock; **étrangler Popaul** to beat one's meat, to bang or Br bash the bishop

popof [pɔpɔf] = **popov**

popote [pɔpɔt] **1** *adj inv* overly house-proud [□]

2 *nf* cooking [□]; **faire la popote** to do the cooking [□]

popotin [pɔpɔtɛ̃] *nm* butt, Br bum, Am fanny ▶ *see also* **magner**

popov [pɔpɔf] **1** *adj inv* Russian [□]
2 *nmf inv* **Popov** Russki

poppers [pɔpœrz] *nmpl* poppers

populo [pɔpylo] *nm* **(a)** *(peuple)* **le populo** the plebs, the riff-raff, the rabble **(b)** *(monde)* crowd [□]; **il y avait un de ces populos en ville** the town was jam-packed or Br chock-a-block or heaving

poquer [pɔke] *vt Can Joual (contusionner)* to bruise [□]; *(emboutir)* to dent [□], to bump [□]; *(érafler)* to scratch [□]; *(frapper)* to hit [□]; **se faire poquer la gueule** to get one's face smashed in or wasted

porno [pɔrno] **1** *adj (abbr* **pornographique)** porn, porno
2 *nm (abbr* **pornographie) (a)** *(genre)* porn **(b)** *(film)* porn movie

porte [pɔrt] *nf* Lyon, ce n'est pas la porte à côté it's a fair way to Lyons; **il n'habite pas la porte à côté** he doesn't exactly live round the corner

portenawak [pɔrtnawak] *exclam* garbage!, Br rubbish!

porte-poisse [pɔrtpwas] *nm inv* jinx [□]

portillon [pɔrtijɔ̃] *nm* **(a)** **ça se bouscule au portillon** he/she/etc can't get his/her/etc words out **(b)** **ça se bouscule pas au portillon** *(il y a peu de monde)* people are staying away in droves

portos [pɔrtos] *nmf Offensive* Dago (from Portugal)

Depending on the context and the tone of voice used, this term may be either offensive or affectionately humorous. It is nonetheless inadvisable to use it unless one is quite sure of the reaction it will receive.

portrait [pɔrtrɛ] *nm (visage)* **abîmer le portrait à qn** to waste sb's face, to rearrange sb's features; **se faire tirer le portrait** to have one's photo taken [□]

portugaises [pɔrtygɛz] *nfpl (oreilles)* ears [□]; **avoir les portugaises ensablées** to be as deaf as a post

"Portugaises" are so called after the variety of oyster with the same name whose shape is reminiscent of that of an ear.

positiver [pozitive] *vi* to be positive [□], to look on the bright side [□]; **arrête donc de te morfondre comme ça, essaye de positiver!** stop moping around like that, try to look on the bright side!

This term originated in an advertising campaign for Carrefour (a chain of French supermarkets); the slogan used was "avec Carrefour, je positive!"

posse [pɔsi] *nf (bande)* posse

pot [po] *nm* **(a)** *(chance)* (good) luck [□]; **avoir du pot** to be lucky [□]; **manque de pot, la banque était fermée** as (bad) luck would have it, the bank was closed **(b)** *(boisson)* drink; **prendre un pot** to go for a drink; **je suis invité à un pot ce soir** I've been invited out for drinks tonight **(c)** *(postérieur)* butt, Br bum, Am fanny **(d)** **plein pot** *(à toute vitesse)* Br like the clappers, Am like sixty **(e)** **être sourd comme un pot** to be as deaf as a post **(f)** **être un vrai pot de peinture** *(très maquillée)* to wear make-up an inch thick, to put one's make-up on with a trowel; **quel pot de colle, ce mec, impossible de s'en défaire!** he sticks to you like glue, that guy, you just can't get rid of him!

potable [pɔtabl] *adj (passable)* reasonable [□], just about OK

Le symbole [□] indique que la traduction n'est pas argotique.

potache [pɔtaʃ] *nm* schoolboy [□], schoolkid; **des plaisanteries de potaches** schoolboy jokes *or* humour

potage [pɔtaʒ] *nm* (a) **être dans le potage** *(être évanoui)* to be out cold; *(être dans une situation pénible)* to be in the soup (b) **il y a une couille dans le potage** *(un problème)* there's a bit of a glitch

potasser [pɔtase] **1** *vt Br* to swot up on, *Am* to bone up on; **il a potassé ses leçons d'histoire pendant toute la nuit** he *Br* swotted up on *or Am* boned up on his history all night
2 *vi Br* to swot, *Am* to bone up

pote [pɔt] **1** *adj* **être pote avec qn** to be pally with sb; **ils sont très potes** they're very pally
2 *nm* pal, *Br* mate, *Am* buddy; **salut mon pote!** hi pal *or Br* mate *or Am* buddy!

poteau, -x [pɔto] *nm* pal, *Br* mate, *Am* buddy

potin [pɔtɛ̃] *nm* racket, din

pou, -x [pu] *nm* **chercher des poux dans la tête à qn** to pick a quarrel with sb

poubelle [pubɛl] *nf (voiture)* heap, banger, rustbucket

pouce [pus] *nm Can* **faire du pouce** to thumb *or Br* lift *or Am* ride ▶ see also **tourner**

poudre [pudr] *nf (héroïne)* smack, skag, H; *(cocaïne)* coke, charlie, *Am* nose candy ▶ see also **inventer**

pouffe ⚠️ [puf], **pouffiasse** ⚠️, **poufiasse** ⚠️ [pufjas] *nf* (a) *(prostituée)* whore, hooker (b) *(femme aux mœurs légères)* slut, tart, tramp, *Br* scrubber (c) *(femme désagréable)* bitch, *Br* cow

poulaille [pulaj] *nf* **la poulaille** the cops, *Br* the pigs, the fuzz

poule [pul] *nf* (a) *(prostituée)* whore, hooker (b) *(femme)* tart, *Br* slapper (c) *(terme d'affection)* sweetheart, honey, babe

poulet [pulɛ] *nm (policier, gendarme)* cop, pig

poulette [pulɛt] *nf* (a) *(fille, femme)* chick, *Br* bird (b) *(terme d'affection)* sweetheart, honey, babe

poumons [pumɔ̃] *nmpl Hum (seins)* knockers, jugs, *Am* hooters; **elle a des sacrés poumons** she's got a great pair of lungs on her

poupée [pupe] *nf (femme, fille)* babe, doll; **comment ça va, poupée?** how are you doing, babe?

poupoule [pupul] *nf* **ma poupoule** sweetheart, honey, babe

pourave [purav] *adj* crap, garbage, *Br* rubbish; **une bagnole pourave** a heap, a banger

pourliche [purliʃ] *nm* tip [□] *(money)*

pourri, -e [puri] **1** *adj* (a) *(en mauvais état)* falling apart, *Br* knackered (b) *(mauvais)* rotten; **il a fait un temps pourri** the weather was rotten (c) *(de mauvaise qualité)* crappy, *Br* rubbish, *Am* rinky-dink (d) *(corrompu)* rotten to the core, *Br* bent
2 *nm,f (homme méprisable)* scumbag, *Br* swine, *Am* stinker; *(femme méprisable)* bitch, *Br* cow ▶ see also **poisson**

pourrir [purir] *vt (dire du mal de)* to badmouth, *Br* to slag off

pousse-au-crime [pusokrim] *nm inv* firewater, rotgut

pousser [puse] *vt* (a) **faut pas pousser (mémé** *ou* **mémère dans les orties)** that's pushing it a bit (b) **pousser la chansonnette, en pousser une** to sing a song [□]

PQ [peky] *nm Br* bog roll, *Am* TP

praline [pralin] *nf* (a) *(coup)* belt, wallop (b) *(balle d'arme à feu)* bullet [□], slug (c) ⚠️ *(clitoris)* clit

précieuses ❗ [presjøz] *nfpl Hum (testicules)* crown jewels, *Br* wedding tackle

première [prəmjɛr] **de première** *adj* first-class; **c'est un crétin de première** he's a first-class idiot

prems [prɔms] = **preums**

prendre [prɑ̃dr] *vt* (a) **qu'est-ce qu'il a pris!** he really caught it! (b) **ça prend pas!** give me a break!, yeah right!, *Br* pull the other one!

pression [presjɔ̃] nf **mettre la pression à qn** to pressurize sb □, to put pressure on sb □

preums [prœms] (abbr **premier, -ère**) **1** adj first □
2 nmf first □

primo [primo] adv first of all □, for starters

privé [prive] nm (abbr **détective privé**) private eye, Am dick, shamus

pro [pro] nmf (abbr **professionnel, -elle**) pro

prof [prɔf] nmf (abbr **professeur**) teacher □

professionnelle [prɔfesjɔnɛl] nf (prostituée) pro, streetwalker

profonde [prɔfɔ̃d] nf (poche) pocket □

projo [prɔʒo] nm (abbr **projecteur**) projector □

prolo [prɔlo] (abbr **prolétaire**) **1** adj plebby
2 nmf prole, pleb

promener [prɔmne] **1** vi **envoyer promener qn** (l'éconduire) to send sb packing, to tell sb where to go; **tout envoyer promener** Br to chuck or pack it all in, Am to chuck everything
2 se promener vpr (éprouver de la facilité) **il se promène en anglais** he finds English a pushover

promo [prɔmo] nf (abbr **promotion**) promotion □, promo

pronto [prɔ̃to] adv pronto; **tu vas me débarrasser ton bordel pronto, OK?** get your shit out of here pronto, OK?

proprio [prɔprijo] nmf (abbr **propriétaire**) landlord, f landlady □

prose [prɔz] = **proze**

protal [prɔtal] nm Br headmaster □, head, Am principal □

prout [prut] nm (a) (pet) fart; **faire un prout** to fart, Br to let off, Am to lay one (b) **prout, ma chère!** (pour singer un homosexuel) ooh, ducky!

prout-prout [prutprut] adj snobby, up oneself; **qu'est-ce qu'elle peut être prout-prout, sa gonzesse!** his girlfriend can be so up herself!

provo [provo] nm Br headmaster □, head, Am principal □

provoc [prɔvɔk] nf (abbr **provocation**) provocation □; **il ne pense pas vraiment ce qu'il dit, c'est de la provoc** he doesn't really believe what he's saying, he's just trying to Br wind you up or Am yank your chain

proxo [prɔkso] nm (abbr **proxénète**) pimp, Am mack

proze [!][prɔz], **prozinard** [!][prɔzinar] nm butt, Br bum, Am fanny

prune [pryn] nf (a) (coup de poing) punch □, thump, clout (b) **pour des prunes** (pour rien) for nothing □ (c) (contravention) fine □

pruneau, -x [pryno] nm (balle d'arme à feu) bullet □, slug; **il s'est pris un pruneau dans la jambe** he took a bullet in the leg

pseudo [psødo] nm (abbr **pseudonyme**) alias □

psy [psi] nmf (abbr **psychanalyste**) shrink, Am bug doctor

puant, -e [pɥɑ̃, -ɑ̃t] **1** adj (très vaniteux) cocky, full of oneself; **c'est le genre de mec qui n'arrête pas de se faire mousser, je le trouve puant** he's the kind of guy who's always blowing his own trumpet, he's so full of himself
2 nm (fromage) smelly cheese □

puceau, -x [pyso] nm virgin □

pucelage [pyslaʒ] nm virginity □; **c'est avec lui qu'elle a perdu son pucelage** she lost her cherry to him

pucelle [pysɛl] nf virgin □

pucier [pysje] nm (lit) bed □, Br pit

pue-la-sueur [pylasɥœr] nm inv Pej workman □, Br workie

puissant, -e [pɥisɑ̃, -ɑ̃t] adj (remarquable) wicked, Br fab, Am awesome

punaise [pynɛz] exclam heck!, Br blast!, sugar!, Am shoot!

punkette [pœ̃kɛt] nf punkette

pur, -e [pyr] adj (excellent) wicked, cool, Am awesome

purée [pyre] **1** nf **balancer la purée** [!!]

Le symbole □ indique que la traduction n'est pas argotique.

(éjaculer) to shoot one's load; **balancer la purée** ☐! *(tirer avec une arme à feu)* to open fire ☐

2 *exclam* heck!, *Br* blast!, sugar!, *Am* shoot!

putain ☐! [pytɛ̃] **1** *nf (prostituée)* whore, hooker; *(femme aux mœurs légères)* tart, slut, *Br* slapper, scrubber, slag; **faire la putain** *(chercher à plaire)* to prostitute oneself; **putain de bagnole/de temps!** fucking car/weather!

2 *exclam* fuck!, fucking hell!

putassier, -ère [pytasje, -ɛr] *adj* (**a**) *(vulgaire)* tarty (**b**) *(servile, obséquieux)* ingratiating ☐

pute ☐! [pyt] *nf (prostituée)* whore, hooker; *(femme facile)* tart, slut, *Br* slapper, scrubber, slag; **faire la pute** *(chercher à plaire)* to prostitute oneself; **fils de pute** son-of-a-bitch

Q

quadra [kadra] *nmf (abbr* **quadragénaire**) = person in his/her forties; **être quadra** to be in one's forties □; **c'est un quadra** he's in his forties □

quart [kar] *nm* **quart de brie** *(nez)* beak, *Br* conk, hooter, *Am* schnozzle ► *see also* **poil**

quatre [katr] *adj inv* **un de ces quatre (matins)** one of these days ► *see also* **fer**

quat'zyeux [katzjø] **entre quat'zyeux** *adv* in private □; **il a demandé à me voir entre quat'zyeux** he asked to see me in private

quebri [kəbri] *nf (verlan* **brique**) ten thousand francs □

que dalle [kədal] *pron* zilch, sweet FA, *Br* bugger all, sod all; **j'y comprends que dalle** I don't understand a damn *or Br* bloody thing

quelque chose [kɛlkəʃoz] *pron* **(a)** **il s'est viandé, quelque chose de bien** he got smashed up something awful; **il lui a passé un savon, quelque chose de bien** he gave him an almighty telling-off; **il tenait quelque chose comme cuite!** he was totally plastered!; **il y a quelque chose comme vent dehors** there's a terrible wind outside **(b)** **mais c'est quelque chose!** that's a bit much!

quelque part [kɛlkəpar] *adv* **il lui a mis son pied quelque part** *(au derrière)* he gave him a kick up the you-know-what; **elle lui a foutu un coup de genou quelque part** *(dans les testicules)* she kneed him in the you-know-where *or* where it hurts most

quenotte [kənɔt] *nf* tooth □

quenouille [kənuj] *nf Can* **quenouilles** *(jambes)* long skinny legs □, matchstick legs

que pouic [kəpwik] *pron* zilch, sweet FA, *Br* bugger all, sod all; **j'y comprends que pouic** I don't underdstand a damn *or Br* bloody thing

quéquette [kekɛt] *nf* willy, *Am* peter, johnson

quès aco [kezako] *adv* what's that? □

question [kɛstjɔ̃] *nf* **(a)** **question soleil, on n'a pas été gâtés** we didn't see much in the way of sunshine; **question argent, j'ai pas à me plaindre** moneywise, I can't complain **(b)** **alors, tu te magnes le cul? question!** so, are you going to move your *Br* arse *or Am* ass or what?

que tchi [kətʃi] *pron* zilch, sweet FA, *Br* bugger all, sod all; **il y comprend que tchi** he doesn't understand a damn *or Br* bloody thing

queude [kœd] = **que dalle**

queue [kø] *nf* **(a)** ‼ *(pénis)* dick, prick, cock; **se faire** *ou* **se taper une queue** to jerk off, *Br* to wank, to have a wank **(b)** **il y en avait pas la queue d'un/d'une** there wasn't a single one, there wasn't one to be seen; **ne pas en avoir la queue d'un** to be broke *or Br* skint **(c)** **des queues!** ⚠ no way!, no chance! ► *see also* **rond**

queutard ‼ [køtar] **1** *adj* horny as fuck **2** *nm* horny bastard

queuter ‼ [køte] *vt* to screw, to shaft

quillard [kijar] *nm* = soldier about to be discharged or nearing the end of his national service

quille [kij] *nf* **(a)** *(jambe)* leg □, pin; **jouer des quilles** to beat it, to leg it **(b)** *(petite fille)* little girl □ **(c)** *(fin de service militaire, démobilisation)* discharge □, *Br* demob

quincaillerie [kɛ̃kajri] *nf* **(a)** *(armes à*

Le symbole □ *indique que la traduction n'est pas argotique.*

feux) weapons □ (**b**) *(bijoux)* jewellery □, sparklers, *Br* tom

quinquets [kɛ̃kɛ] *nmpl (yeux)* eyes □,

peepers; **ouvre bien grand tes quinquets** open your eyes wide

quiquette [kikɛt] = **quéquette**

R

rab [rab], **rabiot** [rabjo] *nm* **(a)** *(excédent)* leftovers □, extra □; **il y a du rab de poulet** there's some chicken left over; **qui veut du rab?** who wants seconds?; **t'aurais pas une clope en rab?** can I bum a smoke *or Br* fag?, have you got a spare smoke *or Br* fag?; **vous auriez pas un oreiller en rab?** do you have a spare pillow? □

   (b) faire du rab *(au travail)* to put in a bit of overtime *or* a few extra hours; *(à l'armée)* to serve extra time □

rabioter [rabjote] *vt (obtenir en supplément)* to wangle

   2 *vi* to skimp; **rabioter sur qch** to skimp on sth

râble [rɑbl] *nm* **tomber sur le râble à qn** to lay into sb, to go for sb

raccrocher [rakrɔʃe] **1** *vt* **raccrocher le client** *(prostituée)* to solicit □, *Am* to hustle, to hook

   2 *vi (cesser une activité)* to pack it in, *Am* to hang it up

raccuser [rakyze] *vt Belg* to snitch on

raccusette [rakyzɛt] *nf Belg* snitch

race [ras] *nf Cités* **ta race!** [!] *Br* piss off!, *Am* take a hike!; **enculé de ta race!** [!!] you fucking prick *or Br* arsehole *or* wanker *or Am* asshole!; **défoncer** *ou* **faire** *ou* **éclater sa race à qn** to waste sb's face, *Br* to punch sb's lights out, *Am* to punch sb out; **niquer sa race à qn** [!!] to beat the shit out of sb

> The word "race" appears in numerous slang expressions of the "banlieues" (see panel **l'argot des banlieues**) and functions as an intensifier. See also the entry for **mère**, which has a similar function.

racho [raʃo] *(abbr* **rachitique) 1** *adj (personne, arbre)* weedy, scrawny; *(portion)* mean, stingy

   2 *nmf* scrawny person

raclée [rakle] *nf (correction, défaite)* thrashing, hammering; **flanquer une raclée à qn** to give sb a thrashing *or* a hammering; **prendre une raclée** to *Br* get *or Am* take a thrashing *or* a hammering

racli [rakli] *nf Cités* chick, *Br* bird

raclo [raklo] *nm Cités* guy, *Br* bloke

raclure [!] [raklyr] *nf (homme méprisable)* bastard, *Am* son-of-a-bitch; *(femme méprisable)* bitch

raconter [rakɔ̃te] *vt* **(a) je te raconte pas!** you can't imagine!; **on s'est pris une de ces cuites, je te raconte pas...** you can't imagine how plastered we got **(b) se la raconter** to show off

radar [radar] *nm* **marcher** *ou* **être au radar** *(ne pas être bien réveillé)* to be on automatic pilot

radasse [!!] [radas] *nf* **(a)** *(prostituée)* tart, hooker **(b)** *Pej (femme)* tart, *Br* slapper

rade¹ [rad] *nm (café)* bar □, *Br* boozer

rade² [rad] **en rade** *adv* **(a)** *(en panne)* **être en rade** to have broken down □ *or* conked out; **tomber en rade** to break down □, to conk out **(b)** *(abandonné)* stranded □; **laisser qn en rade** to leave sb stranded □ *or* in the lurch

radin, -e [radɛ̃, -in] **1** *adj* stingy, tight-fisted

   2 *nm,f* skinflint, tightwad

radiner [radine] **1** *vi* to turn up, to show up, to roll up; **alors, tu radines?** are you coming, then?

   2 se radiner *vpr* to turn up, to show up, to roll up; **il se radine toujours quand on l'attend pas, celui-là!** he always turns up when you least expect him to!

radis [radi] *nm (sou)* **j'ai plus un radis** I haven't a bean *or Am* a red cent; **sans un radis** broke, *Br* skint

raffut [rafy] *nm* **(a)** *(bruit)* racket, din; **c'est pas bientôt fini ce raffut?** is this racket *or* din going to go on for much longer? **(b)** *(scandale)* **faire du raffut** to cause a stink, to set tongues wagging

rafiot [rafjo] *nm* old tub *(boat)*

rageant, -e [raʒɑ̃, -ɑ̃t] *adj* maddening ⁿ, infuriating ⁿ; **c'est vraiment rageant, j'ai loupé le train à trente secondes près** it's really maddening, I missed the train by thirty seconds

ragnagnas [!] [raɲaɲa] *nmpl* **avoir ses ragnagnas** to have one's period ⁿ, to be on the rag

raide [rɛd] *adj* **(a)** *(drogué)* stoned, wasted, ripped; *(ivre)* plastered, *Br* off one's face, legless, *Am* shredded, tanked **(b)** *(sans argent)* broke, *Br* skint **(c)** **elle est raide, celle-là!** that's a bit far-fetched *or* hard to swallow! ▸ *see also* **passe-lacet**

raie [rɛ] *nf* **taper dans la raie à qn** [!!!] *(sodomiser)* to fuck sb up the *Br* arse *or Am* ass ▸ *see also* **gueule, pisser**

rail [rɑj] *nm (de cocaïne)* line; **se faire un rail** to do a line

ralléger [raleʒe] *vi (venir)* to come ⁿ; *(revenir)* to come back ⁿ

ramasser [ramase] **1** *vt* **(a)** *(recevoir)* to get; **ramasser une gifle/un coup/un PV** to get a slap/a clout/a parking ticket **(b)** **se faire ramasser** *(se faire emmener par la police)* to get picked up *or Br* lifted *or* nicked; *(subir un échec)* to fail ⁿ, *Br* to come a cropper
    2 *vi (recevoir une correction)* to get it, to catch it
    3 se ramasser *vpr* **(a)** *(tomber)* to fall flat on one's face, to go flying **(b)** *(échouer)* to fail ⁿ, *Br* to come a cropper **(c)** *(recevoir)* **se ramasser une gifle/un coup/un PV** to get a slap/a clout/a parking ticket ▸ *see also* **bûche, cuiller, gadin, pelle**

rambo [rãbo] *nm Cités* = security officer patrolling the Parisian railway network or underground

ramdam [ramdam] *nm* racket, din; **faire du ramdam** to make a racket *or* a din

> This word comes from "ramadan", the Muslim festival during which people fast during the day and tend to be active at night.

rame [ram], **ramée** [rame] *nf* **ne pas en fiche** *ou* **en foutre** [!] **une rame** *ou* **une ramée** to do zilch *or Br* bugger all *or* sod all

ramener [ramne] **1** *vt* **la ramener** *(intervenir de façon intempestive)* to stick one's oar in; *(se vanter)* to show off; **il faut toujours qu'il la ramène quand on lui demande rien** he always has to stick his oar in when nobody's asked him anything
    2 se ramener *vpr* to turn up, to show up, to roll up ▸ *see also* **fraise**

ramer [rame] **1** *vt* **ne pas en ramer une** to do zilch *or Br* bugger all *or* sod all
    2 *vi (éprouver des difficultés)* to have a hard time of it; **ramer pour faire qch** to sweat blood *or* to bust a gut to do sth

ramier [ramje] **1** *adj (fainéant)* lazy ⁿ
    2 *nm (fainéant)* lazybones, lazy so-and-so

ramollo [ramolo] **1** *adj* washed out, wiped; **je me sens tout ramollo aujourd'hui** I feel like a wet rag today
    2 *nmf* wet rag *(person)*

ramoner [!!!] [ramone] *vt (posséder sexuellement)* to screw, to shaft, to hump, *Br* to shag

rampe [rãp] *nf* **lâcher la rampe** *(mourir)* to croak, to kick the bucket, *Br* to snuff it, *Am* to check out

ramponneau, -x [rãpono] *nm* clout, thump

rancard [rãkar] = **rencard**

rancarder [rãkarde] = **rencarder**

rancart [rãkar] *nm* **mettre** *ou* **jeter qn au rancart** to throw sb on the scrap heap; **mettre** *ou* **jeter qch au rancart** *(objet)* to chuck sth out; *(projet)* to scrap sth

---

Le symbole ⁿ indique que la traduction n'est pas argotique.

ranger [rɑ̃ʒe] **se ranger** vpr **se ranger des voitures** to settle down; *(criminel)* to go straight; **être rangé des voitures** to have settled down; *(criminel)* to have gone straight

raousse [raus] exclam (get) out!, *Br* on your bike!, *Am* take a hike!

> This term comes from the German "heraus", meaning "out". It entered the French language during the Second World War, when France was occupied by Germany.

râpe [rɑp] nf (**a**) *(guitare)* guitar □, *Br* axe, *Am* ax (**b**) *Suisse (avare)* skinflint, tightwad

râpé [rɑpe] adj **c'est râpé** we've/you've/ etc had it; **c'est râpé pour nos vacances en Australie!** bang goes our holiday in Australia!, that's our holiday in Australia out the window!

rapiat, -e [rapja, -at] **1** adj stingy, tight-fisted
  2 nm,f skinflint, tightwad

rapido [rapido], **rapidos** [rapidos] adv quickly □; **boire un coup rapidos** to have a quick drink; **on se fait une petite partie rapidos?** shall we have a quick game?

raplapla [raplapla] adj inv washed out, wiped

rappliquer [raplike] vi *(arriver)* to come □; *(revenir)* to get back □; **ma belle-mère rapplique ce week-end** my mother-in-law's coming this week-end □

raquer [rake] **1** vt to cough up, to fork out; **combien t'as raqué pour ton blouson?** how much did your jacket set you back?
  2 vi to pay up, to cough up

ras [rɑ] adv **en avoir ras le bol** ou **ras la casquette** ou **ras le cul**[!] to have had it up to here, to be fed up (to the back teeth) ▸ see also **pâquerette**

rasant, -e [razɑ̃, -ɑ̃t] adj deadly dull; **c'était rasant** it was a real drag

rasdep[!] [rasdɛp] *Offensive (verlan pédéraste)* **1** adj queer, *Br* bent

2 nm queer, *Br* poof, *Am* fag, faggot

rase-bitume [razbitym] nmf inv runt, squirt

raser [raze] **1** vt (**a**) *(ennuyer)* **raser qn** to bore sb stiff or to tears (**b**) **comme la société a eu de bons résultats cette année, on aura peut-être droit à une prime... – oui, c'est ça, et demain on rase gratuit!** since the company has done well this year maybe we'll get a bonus – yeah right, dream on!
  2 se raser vpr *(s'ennuyer)* to be bored stiff or to tears

raseur, -euse [razœr, -øz] nm,f bore; **quel raseur!** what a bore or drag!

rasibus [razibys] adv (**a**) *(court)* short □, very close □; **il s'est fait couper les cheveux rasibus** he's been scalped (**b**) *(très près)* very close □; **la balle est passée rasibus** the bullet whizzed past

rasif [razif] nm razor □; **ils se sont battus à coups de rasif** they were going at each other with open razors

rasoir [razwar] adj deadly dull; **ce qu'il peut être rasoir!** he's such a drag! ▸ see also **pisser**

rassis [rasi] nm **se taper un rassis**[!!] to jerk off, to beat off, *Br* to have a wank

rasta [rasta] nmf *(abbr* **rastafari**) Rasta

rat [ra] **1** adj *(avare)* stingy, tight-fisted
  2 nm (**a**) *(avare)* skinflint, tightwad (**b**) **s'emmerder** ou **se faire chier comme un rat mort**[!] to be bored shitless ▸ see also **face**

rata [rata] nm food □, grub, chow; **ne pas s'endormir sur le rata** not to fall asleep on the job

ratatiner [ratatine] vt *(vaincre)* **ratatiner qn** to thrash sb, *Am* to kick sb's ass

rate [rat] nf (**a**) **se dilater la rate** to be in stitches, to kill oneself (laughing), to split one's sides (**b**) *(femme)* chick, *Br* bird ▸ see also **fouler**

râteau [rato] nm (**a**) *(peigne)* comb □ (**b**) **se prendre un râteau** *(être rejeté)* to get turned down □, *Br* to get a knockback (**c**) *Suisse* stingy, tight-fisted

râtelier [rɑtəlje] nm (**a**) *(dentier)*

dentures □ **(b) manger à tous les râte-liers** to have a finger in every pie

ratiboiser [ratibwaze] *vt* **(a) ratiboiser qn** *(au jeu)* to clean sb out, to take sb to the cleaners; **ratiboiser qch à qn** *(au jeu)* to clean sb out of sth; *(le lui voler)* to pinch *or Br* nick sth from sb **(b) se faire ratiboiser (la colline)** *(se faire couper les cheveux)* to get scalped

ratiche [ratiʃ] *nf* tooth □

raton [ratɔ̃] *nm Offensive* = racist term used to refer to a North African Arab

ravagé, -e [ravaʒe] *adj (fou)* crazy, nuts, bonkers, *Br* barking, *Am* loony-tunes

rave [rɛiv] *nf* rave

raymond [rɛmɔ̃] *adj & nm* square, straight

> This term comes from the first name "Raymond", which is nowadays considered rather unfashionable.

rayon [rɛjɔ̃] *nm* **c'est/c'est pas mon rayon** that's/that's not my department *or Am* turf; **en connaître un rayon** to know a thing or two, to be well clued-up

réac [reak] *adj & nmf (abbr* **réactionnaire)** reactionary □

rebelote [rəbəlɔt] **1** *nf* **faire rebelote** to do it again □; **la dernière fois le service était nul donc je préfère essayer ailleurs, j'ai pas envie de faire rebelote** last time the service was crap so I'd rather try elsewhere, I don't want to go there again; **leur premier album était excellent, et ils ont fait rebelote avec le deuxième** their first album was excellent and they've done it again with their second one **2** *exclam* here we go again!

rebeu [rəbø] *nmf (verlan* **beur)** = person born and living in France of North African immigrant parents

> "Beur" is itself the "verlan" term for "Arabe". "Rebeu", then, is an example of a word which has been "verlanized" twice. See the panel at **verlan**.

récré [rekre] *nf (abbr* **récréation)** *Br* break time □, *Am* recess □

rectifier [rɛktifje] **1** *vt* **(a)** *(casser)* to break □ **(b)** *(tuer)* to bump off, *Br* to do in, *Am* to off **(c)** *(dépouiller)* to rob □, to mug, *Br* to do over
2 se rectifier *vpr (s'enivrer)* to have a skinful, to get wasted

recui [rəkɥi] *nm (verlan* **cuir)** leather jacket □

récup' [rekyp] *nf (abbr* **récupération)** **(a) de la récup'** *(matériaux)* scrap **(b)** *(récupération idéologique)* exploitation □

redescendre [r(ə)desãdr] *vi (après une prise de drogue)* to come down

refaire [r(ə)fɛr] **1** *vt (duper)* to do, to have, to con; **j'ai été refait!** I've been done *or* had *or* conned! **je me suis fait refaire de cinquante euros** I've been done out of fifty euros
2 se refaire *vpr (regagner une somme perdue)* to recoup one's losses □ ▸ see also **devanture**

refiler [r(ə)file] *vt* **(a)** *(donner)* to give □; **il m'a refilé son vieux blouson** he gave me his old jacket **(b)** *(transmettre)* to give □; **le salaud, il m'a refilé son rhume!** ! the bastard's given me his cold! **(c) refiler de la jaquette** ! *ou* **de la dossière** !!, **en refiler** !! to take it up the *Br* arse *or Am* ass ▸ see also **chouette**

refouler !! [r(ə)fule] *vi (sentir mauvais)* to stink □, *Br* to pong, to niff ▸ see also **goulot**

refroidir [r(ə)frwadir] *vt (tuer)* to ice, to bump off, to liquidate

regarder [r(ə)garde] *vt* **non mais tu m'as bien regardé?, tu m'as pas regardé?** what do you take me for?; **non mais tu t'es regardé?** who do you think you are?

réglo [reglo] **1** *adj inv (personne)* straight, on the level; *(opération, transaction)* legit, kosher
2 *adv* by the book, fair and square; **il a intérêt à jouer réglo** he'd better play fair; **on fait ça réglo, hein?** we'll do it by the book, OK?

régulière [regyljɛr] **1 à la régulière** adv fair and square; **ils se sont battus à la régulière** they had a good, clean fight

2 nf **(a)** (épouse) old lady, Br missus **(b)** (maîtresse) mistress □, Br bit on the side

relax [rəlaks] **1** adj laid-back

2 adv **faire qch relax** to take it easy doing sth; **on a fait ça relax** we took it easy

3 exclam **relax, Max!** take it easy!, chill out!

relooker [r(ə)luke] **1** vt to revamp

2 se relooker vpr to change one's image □

reloquer [r(ə)lɔke] **se reloquer** vpr to put one's clothes back on □, Br to get one's kit back on

relou [rəlu] adj (verlan **lourd**) **(a)** (qui manque de subtilité) unsubtle □, in your face, over the top, Br OTT; **ce que tu peux être relou avec tes blagues de cul!** you can be so over the top with your dirty jokes! **(b)** (stupide) thick, dumb, Am lame

reluire [rəlɥir] vi (atteindre l'orgasme) to come

reluquer [r(ə)lyke] vt to eye up, to check out, Am to scope (out); **sa bonne femme n'aime pas qu'il pas reluque les gonzesses** his other half doesn't like him checking out other chicks or Br birds

remballer [rɑ̃bale] vt Hum **remballer ses outils** to put one's Br trousers □ or keks or Am pants □ back on

rembarrer [rɑ̃bare] vt **rembarrer qn** to tell sb where to go or where to get off, Br to knock sb back; **se faire rembarrer** to get told where to go or where to get off, Br to get knocked back

remettre [r(ə)mɛtr] vt **(a)** (reconnaître) to recognize □, to place; **tu me remets?** can you place me? **(b)** **remettre ça** (recommencer) to start again □; (prendre un autre verre) to have another one □ ▸ see also **couvert**

rempiler [rɑ̃pile] vi (se rengager) to sign up again □

remplumer [rɑ̃plyme] **se remplumer** vpr **(a)** (reprendre du poids) to put a bit of weight back on □ **(b)** (améliorer sa situation financière) to improve one's cash flow □, to get back on one's feet

renauder [r(ə)node] vi to whinge, to gripe, to moan and groan

rencard [rɑ̃kar] nm **(a)** (rendez-vous) appointment □; (amoureux) date; **avoir un rencard avec qn** to have an appointment/a date with sb; **filer un rencard à qn** to fix an appointment/a date with sb **(b)** (renseignement) tip-off

rencarder [rɑ̃karde] **1** vt **rencarder qn** (renseigner) to tip sb off; (donner rendez-vous à) to arrange to meet sb

2 se rencarder vpr (se renseigner) to get information □

renifler [r(ə)nifle] vi (sentir mauvais) to stink, Br to pong, to niff

reniflette [rəniflɛt] nf (cocaïne) coke, charlie

renoi [rənwa] Cités (verlan **noir**) **1** adj black □

2 nmf Black

renps [rɑ̃p(s)] nmpl (verlan **parents**) folks, Br old dears, Am rents

rentre-dedans [rɑ̃tdədɑ̃] nm **faire du rentre-dedans à qn** to come on to sb, Br to chat sb up, Am to hit on sb

repasser [r(ə)pase] **1** vt (escroquer) to do, to rip off

2 vi **tu repasseras!** no way!, no chance!, not on your life!; **il peut toujours repasser** he hasn't a hope, he's got another think coming ▸ see also **planche**

repiquer [r(ə)pike] **1** vt (classe) to repeat □

2 vi **(a)** (redoubler une classe) to repeat a Br year or Am grade □ **(b)** **repiquer au truc** (reprendre une activité ou une habitude) to be at it again

replonger [r(ə)plɔ̃ʒe] vi **(a)** (retourner en prison) to go back inside **(b)** (reprendre une habitude) to be at it again

répondant [repɔ̃dɑ̃] nm **avoir du répondant** (avoir des économies) to have plenty of cash stashed away

repousser [r(ə)puse] vi (sentir mauvais)

Le symbole □ indique que la traduction n'est pas argotique.

to stink, *Br* to pong, to niff ▸ *see also* **goulot**

restau, resto [rɛsto] *nm* (*abbr* **restaurant**) restaurant □; **restau-U** university cafeteria *or Br* canteen *or* refectory □

resté, -e [rɛste] *adj Can* (*épuisé*) *Br* knackered, shattered, *Am* beat

resucée [rəsyse] *nf* (**a**) (*quantité supplémentaire*) **une resucée** some more □; **t'en prendras bien une petite resucée?** will you have some more? □ (**b**) (*copie*) rehash

résultat [rezylta] *nm* **résultat des courses,...** the upshot was... □, as a result,... □; **résultat des courses, on s'est retrouvés au poste** the whole thing ended up with us in the police station

rétamé, -e [retame] *adj* (**a**) (*ivre*) wasted, trashed, *Br* legless, *Am* fried (**b**) (*épuisé*) bushed, *Br* knackered, shattered, *Am* out of gas (**c**) (*hors d'usage*) wrecked, bust, *Br* knackered

rétamer [retame] **1** *vt* (**a**) (*rendre ivre*) **rétamer qn** to get sb wasted *or* trashed *or Br* legless *or Am* fried (**b**) (*épuiser*) to wear out, *Br* to knacker (**c**) (*mettre hors d'usage*) to wreck, to bust, *Br* to knacker
2 se rétamer *vpr* (*tomber*) to go flying, to take a tumble; (*échouer*) to fail □, *Am* to flunk; **elle s'est rétamée à l'oral** she failed □ *or Am* flunked the oral

retape [rtap] *nf* (**a**) **faire la retape** (*en parlant de prostituées*) *Br* to be on the game, *Am* to hustle (**b**) **faire de la retape pour qch** to plug sth for all it's worth; **ça fait bizarre de voir ce soit-disant comédien alternatif faire de la retape pour une marque de lessive** it's strange to see a so-called alternative comedian plugging a brand of washing powder for all it's worth

retourne [rturn] *nf* **les avoir à la retourne** to be bone idle

rétro [retro] *nm* (*abbr* **rétroviseur**) rear-view mirror □

reuch [rœʃ] *adj Cités* (*verlan* **cher**) expensive □, pricey

reuf [rœf] *nm Cités* (*verlan* **frère**) brother □, bro

reum [rœm] *nf Cités* (*verlan* **mère**) old lady, *Br* old dear

reunoi [rənwa] = **renoi**

reup [rœp] *nm Cités* (*verlan* **père**) old man

reur [rœr], **reureu** [rœrø] *nm Cités* (*RER*) = express rail network serving Paris and its suburbs

reuss [rœs] *nf Cités* (*verlan* **sœur**) sister □, sis

reviens [rəvjɛ̃] *nm* **je te prête mon dico mais il s'appelle reviens** I'll lend you my dictionary but I'll need it back □

revoyure [rvwajyr] *nf* **à la revoyure!** see you!

revue [rvy] *nf* **être de la revue** to have to go without

This expression has its origins in military slang: the soldiers selected to take part in a military parade had to endure many hours of training for the event during what would have been their free time.

ribambelle [ribɑ̃bɛl] *nf* **une ribambelle de** tons of, loads of

ricain, -e [rikɛ̃, -ɛn] (*abbr* **américain, -e**)
1 *adj* Yank, *Br* Yankee
2 *nm,f* **Ricain, Ricaine** Yank, *Br* Yankee

richard, -e [riʃar, -ard] *nm,f* money-bags, *Br* nob

riche [riʃ] *adj* **baiser à la riche** !! (*pratiquer la sodomie*) to have anal sex □; **il l'a baisée à la riche** he fucked her up the *Br* arse *or Am* ass

ric-rac [rikrak] *adv* **c'était ric-rac** it was touch and go, it was a close thing

rideau [rido] *exclam* enough!, that'll do!

rien [rjɛ̃] *adv* (**a**) (*très*) very □, seriously, *Br* well, *Am* real; **elle est rien moche, sa copine** his girlfriend's a real dog *or Am* beast (**b**) **c'est rien de le dire** you can say that again, you said it ▸ *see also* **casser**

rififi [rififi] *nm* trouble, *Br* aggro; **il va y avoir du rififi** there's going to be trouble *or Br* aggro

riflard [riflar] *nm* umbrella □, *Br* brolly

riflette [riflɛt] nf (guerre) war □

rigolade [rigɔlad] nf (a) (amusement) **quelle rigolade!** what a hoot or a scream!; **prendre qch à la rigolade** (avec humour) to see the funny side of sth, to treat sth as a joke; (avec légèreté) not to take sth too seriously □ (b) **c'est de la rigolade!** (facile) it's a piece of cake!, it's a walkover!; **c'est pas de la rigolade!** it's no picnic!

rigoler [rigɔle] vi to laugh □; **histoire de rigoler, pour rigoler** for a laugh, for fun; **fais ce que je te dis, je ne rigole pas!** do as you're told, I'm not kidding or joking!; **tu rigoles?** are you kidding?, are you joking?; **ils rigolent pas avec la sécurité dans cet aéroport** they don't mess about or take any chances with security at this airport; Ironic **tu me fais rigoler, tiens!** you make me laugh!, don't make me laugh!

rigolo, -ote [rigɔlo, -ɔt] **1** adj funny □
2 nm,f (a) (personne amusante) hoot, scream (b) (personne peu sérieuse) clown, joker

rikiki [rikiki] = **riquiqui**

rincée [rɛ̃se] nf (averse) downpour □

rincer [rɛ̃se] **1** vt **se faire rincer** to get caught in a downpour
2 vi (offrir à boire) to buy the drinks □; **c'est moi qui rince!** I'm buying the drinks!, the drinks are on me!; **c'est le patron qui rince!** the drinks are on the house!
3 se rincer vpr **se rincer l'œil** to get an eyeful ▸ see also **dalle**

ringard, -e [rɛ̃gar, -ard] **1** adj tacky, Br naff
2 nm,f square, nerd, Br anorak

ringardise [rɛ̃gardiz] nf tackiness, Br naffness; **la déco était d'une ringardise, je te dis pas!** the decor was unbelievably tacky or Br naff!

ringardos [rɛ̃gardos] = **ringard**

ripatons [ripatɔ̃] nmpl feet □, Br plates, Am dogs

riper [ripe] vi to beat it, to push off, Am to beat feet, to book it

ripou, -x [ripu] nm (verlan **pourri**) Br bent or Am bad cop

> This expression was popularized by Claude Zidi's 1984 comedy film about corruption in the police force, Les Ripoux.

riquiqui [rikiki] adj inv teeny-weeny

rital, -e [rital] Offensive **1** adj wop, Eyetie
2 nm (langue) Italian □
3 nm,f **Rital, Ritale** wop, Eyetie

> Depending on the context and the tone of voice used, this term may be either offensive or affectionately humorous. It is nonetheless inadvisable to use it unless one is quite sure of the reaction it will receive.

roberts [!] [rɔbɛr] nmpl (seins) tits, knockers, jugs

> This term comes from a once famous make of baby's bottle.

robineux [rɔbinø] nm Can tramp, Am hobo

rodéo [rɔdeo] nm (en voiture volée) joyride

rogne [rɔɲ] nf anger □, rage □; **être/se mettre en rogne** to be/go mad or crazy or ape

rognons [!!] [rɔɲɔ̃] nmpl (testicules) balls, nuts, Br bollocks

roi [rwa] nm **c'est le roi des cons** [!]**/des poivrots** he's a complete prick/alky

roille [rɔj] nf Suisse downpour □; **pleuvoir à la roille** to bucket down, Br to chuck it down

roiller [rwaje] vi Suisse (pleuvoir) to bucket down, Br to chuck it down

romano [rɔmano] nmf Pej (abbr **romanichel, -elle**) gypsy □, gippo

rombière [rɔ̃bjɛr] nf (a) (femme désagréable) **(vieille) rombière** stuck-up old cow (b) (épouse) other half, old lady; (maîtresse) mistress □, Br bit on the side, fancy woman

rond, -e [rɔ̃, rɔ̃d] **1** adj (ivre) wasted,

loaded, *Br* pissed, *Am* fried; **rond comme une queue de pelle** *ou* **comme un boudin** *Br* as pissed as a newt, *Am* stewed to the gills

2 *adv* **ne pas tourner rond** *(machine)* to be on the blink, *Am* to be on the fritz; *(personne)* to be not all there, to have a screw *ou Br* a slate loose

3 *nm* **(a)** *(argent)* **ne pas avoir un rond** *Br* not to have a penny to one's name, *Am* not to have a red cent; **t'as des ronds sur toi?** got any cash on you? **(b)** **prendre** *ou* **filer du rond** [!!] to get fucked in the *Br* arse *or Am* ass ▸ see also **flan, gueule**

rondelle [!!] [rɔ̃dɛl] *nf (anus)* ringpiece, *Br* arsehole, *Am* asshole; **défoncer** *ou* **casser la rondelle à qn** to fuck sb in the *Br* arse *or Am* ass; **se faire taper dans la rondelle** to get fucked in the *Br* arse *or Am* ass

ronflette [rɔ̃flɛt] *nf* **piquer une ronflette** to have a nap *or* a snooze

roploplos [!] [roploplo] *nmpl* tits, knockers, jugs

Rosbif [rɔsbif] *nmf Offensive (Britannique)* Brit

> This term originates in the stereotypical notion among the French that the British consume large quantities of roast beef. Depending on the context and the tone of voice used, this term may be either offensive or affectionately humorous.

rose [roz] *nf* **(a)** **ça sent pas la rose** it stinks a bit, *Br* it's a bit whiffy **(b)** **envoyer qn sur les roses** to send sb packing, to tell sb where to go *or* where to get off

rosette [!] [rozɛt] *nf (anus)* ring, *Br* arsehole, *Am* asshole

roteuse [rɔtøz] *nf (bouteille de champagne)* bottle of bubbly *or Br* champers

rotin [rɔtɛ̃] *nm (sou)* **ne pas avoir un rotin** to be totally broke *or Br* skint

rotoplots [rotoplo] = **roploplos**

rotule [rɔtyl] *nf* **être sur les rotules** to be wiped (out) *or Br* knackered; **mettre**

qn sur les rotules to wipe sb out, *Br* to knacker sb

roubignoles, roubignolles [rubiɲɔl] = **roupettes**

rouflaquettes [ruflakɛt] *nfpl* sideburns □

rouge [ruʒ] *nm (vin rouge)* red wine □; **une bouteille de rouge** a bottle of red; **un coup de rouge** a glass of red wine □; **du gros rouge** cheap red wine □

roulée [rule] *adj* **bien roulée** curvy

rouler [rule] **1** *vt* **(a)** **rouler les mécaniques** to walk with a swagger **(b)** **rouler une pelle** *ou* **une galoche** *ou* **un pallot** *ou* **un patin à qn** [!] to French-kiss sb, *Br* to snog sb

2 *vi (aller bien)* **ça roule** things are fine, everything's OK

3 se rouler *vpr* **(a)** **s'en rouler une** to roll a smoke *or Br* a fag **(b)** **se les rouler** to twiddle one's thumbs ▸ see also **bosse**

roulottier [rulɔtje] *nm (voleur)* = thief who robs parked cars

roulure [!] [rulyr] *nf* **(a)** *(prostituée)* hooker, whore **(b)** *(homme méprisable)* bastard, *Am* son-of-a-bitch; *(femme méprisable)* bitch

roupettes [!] [rupɛt], **roupignolles** [!] [rupiɲɔl] *nfpl* balls, nuts, *Br* bollocks

roupiller [rupije] *vi* to sleep □, *Br* to kip; **il faudrait que tu arrêtes de roupiller en classe** you need to stop sleeping in class

roupillon [rupijɔ̃] *nm* snooze, nap, *Br* kip; **piquer un roupillon** to have a snooze *or* a nap *or Br* a kip

rouquin [rukɛ̃] *nm (vin rouge)* red wine □

rouscailler [ruskaje] *vi* to gripe, to whinge, to moan and groan

rouspétance [ruspetɑ̃s] *nf* **pas de rouspétance!** I don't want to hear any moaning and groaning *or* whingeing *or* grumbling!

rouspéter [ruspete] *vi* to moan and groan, to whinge, to grumble

rouspéteur, -euse [ruspetœr, -øz] *nm,f* moan, whinge, grumbler

rousse [rus] *nf* **la rousse** *(la police)* the cops, the pigs

rouste [rust] *nf* thrashing, hammering; **flanquer une rouste à qn** to give sb a thrashing *or* a hammering

roustons [!] [rustɔ̃] *nmpl* balls, nuts, *Br* bollocks

royaumer [rwajome] **se royaumer** *vpr Suisse* to lounge about

RU [ry] *nm (abbr* **restaurant universitaire)** university cafeteria *or Br* canteen *or* refectory □

ruche [ryʃ] *nf* **se piquer la ruche** to get wasted *or* trashed *or Br* pissed

ruper [rype] *vt Suisse (manger)* to stuff oneself with

rupin, -e [rypɛ̃, -in] **1** *adj (personne)* loaded, *Br* rolling in it, *Am* rolling in dough; *(quartier)* plush, *Br* posh
   2 *nm,f* moneybags

Ruskoff [ryskɔf] *nmf Offensive* Russki

> Depending on the context and the tone of voice used, this term may be either offensive or affectionately humorous. It is nonetheless inadvisable to use it unless one is quite sure of the reaction it will receive.

S

sabrer [sɑbre] vt (**a**) *(couper) (texte)* to slash (**b**) *(noter sévèrement) (personne)* to slate (**c**) *(refuser) (candidat)* to fail □, Am to flunk (**d**) [!] *(posséder sexuellement)* to poke, Br to shaft

sac [sak] nm (**a**) *(dix francs)* ten francs □; **dix/vingt sacs** a hundred/two hundred francs (**b**) **sac d'os** *(personne maigre)* bag of bones

> In sense (a), "sac" used to be used in multiples of ten.

sacquer [sake] vt (**a**) *(congédier)* to fire, to sack (**b**) **je ne peux pas le sacquer** I can't stand or Br stick him

sacrant, -e [sakrɑ̃, -ɑ̃t] adj Can (**a**) *(fâcheux)* annoying □; **cet accident est bien sacrant!** this accident is a real pain! (**b**) **au plus sacrant** *(au plus vite)* as quickly as possible □

sacré, -e [sakre] adj **un sacré con** [!] a total Br arsehole or Am asshole; **un sacré fouteur de merde** [!] a hell of a shit-stirrer; **c'est un sacré numéro** he's quite a character or case!; **cette sacrée bagnole est encore en panne** the damn or Br bloody car's broken down again; **c'est un sacré veinard** he's a lucky or Br jammy devil

sacrément [sakremɑ̃] adv damn, Br bloody; **il s'est sacrément foutu de notre gueule** [!] he made a total damn or Br bloody fool of us; **il est sacrément radin celui-là!** he's so damn or Br bloody tight!; **il fait sacrément froid** it's damn or Br bloody cold

sado [sado] nmf *(abbr* **sadique)** sadist □

sado-maso [sadomazo] *(abbr* **sado-masochiste)** **1** adj SM, S & M
2 nmf sado-masochist □

sagouin, -e [sagwɛ̃, -in] nm,f *(personne malpropre)* filthy slob; **du travail de sagouin** sloppy work

saigner [seɲe] **1** vt *(tuer à l'arme blanche)* to stab to death □
2 vi **ça va saigner** there's going to be trouble

sainte-nitouche [sɛ̃tnituʃ] nf goody-two-shoes; **avec ses airs de sainte-nitouche** looking as though butter wouldn't melt in his/her mouth

> This term is a corruption of "sainte", meaning "saint", and "ne pas y toucher", meaning "not to touch", suggesting someone who avoids any activities of a sexual nature.

saint-frusquin [sɛ̃fryskɛ̃] nm **tout le saint-frusquin** the whole caboodle, Br the full monty, Am the whole megilla

Saint-Glinglin [sɛ̃glɛ̃glɛ̃] nf **attendre jusqu'à la Saint-Glinglin** to wait forever or until doomsday; **c'est maintenant qu'il faut le faire, pas à la Saint-Glinglin** it has to be done now, not whenever

salade [salad] nf (**a**) *(situation embrouillée)* muddle, mess; **quelle salade!** what a muddle or mess! (**b**) **vendre sa salade** to make a pitch □, to try to sell an idea □ (**c**) **raconter des salades** to tell fibs or Br porkies ▸ *see also* **panier**

salamalecs [salamalɛk] nmpl bowing and scraping

salaud [!] [salo] **1** adj **c'est salaud de faire/dire ça** that's a really shitty thing to do/say, that's a bastard of a thing to do/say; **il a été salaud avec elle** he's been a real bastard to her
2 nm bastard, Am son-of-a-bitch

sale [sal] adj **pas sale** pretty good, not

Le symbole □ indique que la traduction n'est pas argotique.

bad; **il est pas sale, ton pinard** this wine of yours is pretty good

salé, -e [sale] *adj* (**a**) *(élevé) (note, addition)* steep (**b**) *(osé)* steamy, X-rated

salement [salmɑ̃] *adv (beaucoup)* badly❑; *(très) Br* dead, *Am* real; **salement blessé** badly injured; **salement déçu** *Br* dead *or Am* real disappointed; **il a salement vieilli** he's really aged

saleté [salte] *nf* (**a**) *(en injure)* **saleté!** *(à un homme)* swine!, bastard!; *(à une femme)* bitch!, *Br* cow!; **c'est une vraie saleté** he's a real louse (**b**) **saleté de bagnole/de temps!** this blasted *or Am* darn car/weather!

saligaud [!] [saligo] *nm (individu malpropre)* filthy pig; *(individu méprisable)* bastard, *Am* son-of-a-bitch

salingue [!] [salɛ̃g] **1** *adj* filthy

2 *nmf* filthy pig

salopard [!] [salɔpar] *nm* bastard, *Am* son-of-a-bitch

salope [!] [salɔp] *nf* (**a**) *(femme méprisable)* bitch, *Br* cow; *(femme aux mœurs légères)* tart, slut, *Br* slapper (**b**) *(homme méprisable)* bastard, *Am* son-of-a-bitch

saloper [salɔpe] *vt* (**a**) *(salir)* to dirty❑, to mess up (**b**) *(mal exécuter)* to make a dog's breakfast *or Br* a pig's ear of

saloperie [salɔpri] **1** *nf* (**a**) *(acte méprisable)* dirty trick; **faire une saloperie à qn** to play a dirty trick on sb, *Br* to do the dirty on sb, *Am* to do sb dirt

(**b**) *(marchandise de mauvaise qualité)* garbage, junk, *Br* rubbish; **saloperie de bagnole/d'ordinateur!** this blasted *or Am* darn car/computer!

(**c**) *(maladie, virus)* something nasty; **il a attrapé une saloperie en vacances** he caught something nasty on *Br* holiday *or Am* vacation; **c'est une vraie saloperie, ce nouveau virus** this new virus is really nasty

(**d**) *(homme méprisable)* bastard, *Am* son-of-a-bitch

2 saloperies *nfpl* (**a**) *(saletés)* crud, *Br* muck (**b**) *(propos orduriers)* filthy language; **dire des saloperies** to use filthy language (**c**) *(aliments malsains)* junk (food), garbage, *Br* rubbish; **il bouffe que des saloperies** he just eats garbage *or* junk *or Br* rubbish

salsifis [salsifi] *nmpl (doigts)* fingers❑

sang [sɑ̃] *nm* **bon sang!** *(de surprise)* for Pete's sake!, *Br* blimey!, *Am* gee (whiz)!; *(de colère)* blast it!, hell! ▸ *see also* **pisser**

sans [sɑ̃] *prep* **sans un** broke, *Br* skint, strapped ▸ *see also* **dec, déconner**

santé [sɑ̃te] **1** *nf* **avoir de la santé** *(avoir de l'audace)* to have a nerve *or Br* a brass neck

2 *exclam* cheers! ▸ *see also* **voleuse**

santiags [sɑ̃tjag] *nfpl* cowboy boots❑

saper [sape] **1** *vt* to dress❑

2 se saper *vpr (s'habiller)* to get dressed❑; *(s'habiller chic)* to get all dressed up❑; **être bien/mal sapé** to be well-/badly-dressed❑; **elle aime bien se saper pour sortir** she likes to get all dressed up to go out; **il sait pas se saper** he's got no dress sense; **elle se sape très seventies** she wears really seventies clothes, she dresses really seventies

sapes [sap] *nfpl* clothes❑, threads, *Br* gear, clobber

sapeur [sapœr] *nm* = young, well-dressed African man

sapin [sapɛ̃] *nm Hum* **ça sent le sapin** he's/she's/*etc* on his/her/*etc* last legs; **une toux qui sent le sapin** a worryingly unhealthy cough❑, a death-rattle of a cough

saquer [sake] = **sacquer**

saton [satɔ̃] *nm* **coup de saton** kick❑, boot; **donner des coups de saton à qn/dans qch** to boot sb/sth, to give sb/sth a kicking

satonner [satɔne] *vt* **satonner qn/qch** to boot sb/sth, to give sb/sth a kicking

saturer [satyre] *vi* to have had enough, to have had as much as one can take

sauce [sos] *nf* (**a**) *(pluie)* rain❑; **prendre la sauce** to get soaked *or* drenched❑ (**b**) **mettre la sauce** to pull out all the stops, to go all out (**c**) **balancer la sauce** [!!] *(éjaculer)* to shoot one's load *or* wad

saucée [sose] *nf* downpour❑; **prendre**

une saucée to get drenched □

saucer [sose] *vt* **se faire saucer** to get soaked or drenched □

sauciflard [sosiflar] *nm* (dried) sausage □

saucisse [sosis] *nf* **grande saucisse** (personne) beanpole; **saucisse à pattes** sausage dog □

saucissonné, -e [sosisɔne] *adj* trussed up; **il était tout saucissonné dans son pardessus** he was trussed up like a turkey in his overcoat □

saucissonner [sosisɔne] **1** *vt* (ligoter) to tie up □

 2 *vi* to grab a quick snack

saumâtre [somatr] *adj* **il l'a trouvée saumâtre** he didn't appreciate it at all □, he wasn't amused or impressed □

saute-au-paf [!] [sotopaf] *nf inv* nympho, Br goer

sauter [sote] **1** *vt* (a) [!!] (posséder sexuellement) to fuck, to screw, Br to shag (b) **la sauter** (avoir faim) to be starving or ravenous

 2 *vi* (a) **se faire sauter la cervelle** ou **le caisson** to blow one's brains out (b) **et que ça saute!** jump to it!, make it snappy! (c) (perdre son emploi) to get fired or Br sacked

sauterelle [sotrɛl] *nf* (fille, femme) chick, Br bird

sauterie [sotri] *nf* party □, do, get-together

sauvage [sovaʒ] *adj* (excellent) wild

savate [savat] *nf* (a) **il chante comme une savate** he can't sing to save his life, Br he can't sing for toffee (b) **traîner la savate** to be completely broke or Br on one's uppers or Am without a dime

savater [savate] *vt* to kick □, to boot

savon [savɔ̃] *nm* **passer un savon à qn** to give sb a roasting, to bawl sb out, to read sb the riot act, Am to chew sb out; **se faire passer** ou **prendre un savon** to get a roasting, to get bawled out or Am chewed out

savonnette [savɔnɛt] *nf* (de cannabis) = 250-gramme block of hashish

SBAB [!!] [zbab] *nf* (abbr **super bonne à baiser**) horny bitch

scato [skato] *adj* (abbr **scatologique**) (blague) disgusting □; **humour scato** toilet humour

schizo [skizo] *adj & nmf* (abbr **schizophrène**) schizo, Am schiz

schlass[1] [ʃlas] *nm* (couteau) knife □, blade, Am shiv

schlass[2], **schlasse** [ʃlas] *adj* (ivre) sozzled, trashed, wasted

schlinguer [ʃlɛ̃ge] = **chlinguer**

schlof [ʃlɔf] *nm* bed □, Br pit; **se mettre au schlof** to hit the sack or the hay or Am the rack

schmilblick [ʃmilblik] *nm* **faire avancer le schmilblick** to make progress □, to get somewhere; **tout ça, ça fait pas avancer le schmilblick** that's not getting us any further forward

> This expression comes from a radio quiz show of the early 1970s, in which the contestants had to identify the mystery object (the "schmilblick") by asking the presenter a series of questions to which he could answer only yes or no. "Faire avancer le schmilblick" thus signified asking a question which gave the contestant additional clues to the object in question. The expression was popularized by the comedian Coluche, who performed a famous sketch based on this show.

schmitt [ʃmit] *nm* cop

schneck [!!] [ʃnɛk] *nm* Cités pussy, snatch

schnock, schnoque [ʃnɔk] *nm* half-wit, dope, Br divvy, Am goober; **un vieux schnock** an old fogey, an old codger

schnouf, schnouffe [ʃnuf] = **chnouf**

schtarbé, -e [ʃtarbe] = **chtarbé**

schwartz [ʃwarts] *nm* (a) (policier) cop, Am flatfoot (b) (Noir) Black

scier [sje] *vt* (a) (surprendre) to amaze □, to stagger, to flabbergast, Am to knock for a loop; **ça m'a scié d'apprendre que...** I was staggered or Br gobsmacked or Am knocked for a loop to find out that… **(b)** *Suisse* **scier du bois** to snore like a pig

scotché, -e [skɔtʃe] *adj* **(a)** *(stupéfait)* **je suis resté scotché** I was staggered *or Br* gobsmacked **(b) être scotché devant la télé** to be glued to the TV

scotcher [skɔtʃe] *vt (stupéfaire)* to flabbergast, to knock sideways; **ça m'a vraiment scotché!** I was staggered *or Br* gobsmacked

scoumoune [skumun] *nf* rotten luck; **avoir la scoumoune** to be jinxed

scratcher [skratʃe] **se scratcher** *vpr* to go off the road; **il s'est scratché**

avec la moto de son frère he went off the road on his brother's motorbike

sec [sɛk] *adv* **(a)** *(beaucoup)* a lot □; **il boit sec** he can really knock it back; **ils ont dérouillé sec pendant la guerre** they went through total hell during the war **(b) l'avoir sec** to be bummed (out) *or Br* gutted **(c) être à sec** to be broke *or Br* skint ▸ *see also* **cinq**

sèche [sɛʃ] *nf (cigarette)* smoke, *Br* fag, *Am* cig

sécher [seʃe] **1** *vt (ne pas assister à) (cours) Br* to bunk off, *Am* to skip

---
Focus on:

Le sexe

There are countless slang terms used to describe the male sex organ, among the most common of which are **bite**, **queue** and **pine**. **Bout** is also encountered in the extremely vulgar expressions **s'astiquer le bout** and **se mettre quelqu'un sur le bout**. The female equivalent is usually referred to as **la chatte**. **Couilles** is the most frequently used term for testicles, but it has several synonyms, including the humorous-sounding **roubignolles** and **valseuses**, a term popularized by the 1974 Bertrand Blier film *Les Valseuses*. A man with an erection is said to **bander (comme un taureau)** or to **avoir la gaule** or **la trique.**

The verb "to have sex" also has many slang equivalents. The most common is **baiser**, which originally meant "to kiss", but is no longer used to mean this; fortunately so, as the potential for misunderstandings would be great. **Baiser** has several related words: **baise**, **baiseur** or **baiseuse** and **baisable**, together with more humorous inventions such as **baisodrome** (a place where much sexual activity takes place) and **baise-en-ville** (used to mean an overnight bag, a much less vulgar term than the others).

The verb **tirer** is also used to refer to sex, on its own or in the expression **tirer un coup**. By extension, a good sexual partner is **un bon coup**. Transitive verbs meaning "to have sex with" include **s'enfiler**, **s'envoyer**, **se faire**, **sauter** and **bourrer** (an especially vulgar expression). **Niquer** and a more recent coinage, **bouillave(r)**, are often used by young people in the Parisian "banlieues". It is interesting to note that unlike similar English verbs, the above terms can only have a man as their subject.

Fellatio has several colourful slang expressions: the most frequently encountered are **tailler une pipe**, **une plume** or **une flûte**. The verbs **enculer** and, less frequently, **empapaouter** or **empaffer**, refer to sodomy.

The use of the passive voice with some verbs referring to sex often gives a figurative sense to the verb. The expression **se faire baiser** thus means "to get swindled", similar to the notion in English of getting screwed or shafted. It is worth noting that **foutre** used to refer to the sex act but has now lost any erotic connotation.

Le symbole □ indique que la traduction n'est pas argotique.

2 *vi (ne pas aller en classe) Br* to bunk off, *Am* to play hookey

sécoin [sekwɛ̃] *(verlan* **coincé**) **1** *adj* uptight

2 *nmf* **c'est une vraie sécoin cette bonne femme** she's so uptight, that woman!

sécot [seko] *adj* (**a**) *(sec)* dry □ (**b**) *(maigre)* skinny, lanky

secoué, -e [skwe] *adj (fou)* off one's nut or rocker, *Br* crackers, *Am* nutso

secouer [s(ə)kwe] *vt* (**a**) **j'en ai rien à secouer** ! I don't give a damn *or Br* a toss (**b**) **secouer les puces à qn** *Br* to tick sb off, *Am* to chew sb out

Sécu [seky] *nf (abbr* **Sécurité sociale**) *Br* ≃ Social Security □, *Am* ≃ welfare □

sensass [sãsas] *adj inv (abbr* **sensationnel**) sensational, terrific, *Br* smashing

sentiment [sãtimã] *nm* **la faire au sentiment à qn** to get round sb

sentir [sãtir] **1** *vt* (**a**) **je ne peux pas la sentir** I can't stand *or Br* stick her; **je le sens pas bien, ce mec-là** there's something about that guy I don't like (**b**) **je l'ai senti passer!** *(à propos d'une douleur, d'une facture, d'une réprimande)* I knew all about it!

2 se sentir *vpr Hum* **ne plus se sentir** *(se comporter de façon étrange)* to have taken leave of one's senses; **ne plus se sentir (pisser)** *(être vaniteux)* to be too big for one's *Br* boots *or Am* britches ▶ see also **rose, sapin**

sérieux [serjø] **1** *adv (sérieusement)* seriously; **ils se sont foutus sur la gueule sérieux** they seriously went for each other; **sérieux?** seriously?

2 *nm (chope de bière)* litre of beer □

séropo [seropo] *(abbr* **séropositif, -ive**) **1** *adj* HIV-positive □

2 *nmf* HIV-positive person □

serre-la-piastre [sɛrlapjastr] *nm Can (avare)* stingy, tight-fisted

serre-patte [sɛrpat] *nm* sergeant □

serrer [sere] *vt (arrêter) Br* to nick, to lift, *Am* to bust ▶ see also **kiki, louche, pince, vis**

service [sɛrvis] *nm Hum* **entrée de service** ! *(anus)* back door, tradesman's entrance

seulabre [sølabr] *adj* alone □, *Br* on one's tod

sévère [sevɛr] *adv (gravement)* severely, seriously; **il déjante sévère en ce moment** he's severely *or* seriously lost it at the moment; **on a morflé sévère** we went through total hell

SF [ɛsɛf] *nf (abbr* **science fiction**) sci-fi, SF

shit [ʃit] *nm* hash, shit, *Br* blow, draw

shoot [ʃut] *nm (de drogue)* fix, shot; **se faire un shoot** to shoot up, to jack up

shooté, -e [ʃute] **1** *adj* (**a**) *(drogué)* **être shooté** to be a druggie *or* a junkie (**b**) *(fou)* crazy, *Br* barking (mad), *Am* wacko

2 *nm,f* (**a**) *(drogué)* druggie, junkie (**b**) *(fou)* headcase, fruitcake, *Br* nutter, *Am* wacko

shooter [ʃute] **se shooter** *vpr* to shoot up, to jack up

shooteuse [ʃutøz] *nf* hype, hypo

sifflard [siflar] *nm* (dried) sausage □

siffler [sifle] **1** *vt (boire)* to sink, to down, to knock back

2 se siffler *vpr* **il s'est sifflé un litre de rouge à lui tout seul** he sank *or* downed *or* knocked back a whole litre of red wine on his own

sifflet [siflɛ] *nm* **couper le sifflet à qn** to leave sb speechless, to shut sb up

sinoque [sinɔk] = **cinoque**

siphonné, -e [sifɔne] *adj (fou)* crazy, bonkers, *Br* barking (mad)

situasse [situɑs] *nf (abbr* **situation**) situation □

six-quatre-deux [siskatdø] **à la six-quatre-deux** *adv* **faire qch à la six-quatre-deux** to do sth any old how

skeud [skœd] *nm Cités (verlan* **disque**) record □

skin [skin] *nm (abbr* **skinhead**) skin, skinhead

slibar [slibar] *nm Br* scants, *Am* shorts, skivvies

smack [smak] *nm* smack, scag, skag

---

smala, smalah [smala] nf family □, tribe, clan

sniffer [snife] vt to sniff, Am to huff; (cocaïne) to snort, to sniff, Am to huff

snobinard, -e [snɔbinar, -ard] **1** adj stuck-up, snobby, lah-di-dah **2** nm,f snob □

snul [snyl] nm Belg cretin, Br dipstick

socialo [sɔsjalo] adj & nmf (abbr **socialiste**) socialist □, leftie, lefty

sœur [sœr] nf (a) (femme) chick, Br bird (b) **et ta sœur!** mind your own business!

soft [sɔft] nm soft porn

soif [swaf] nf (a) **jusqu'à plus soif** to one's heart's content (b) **il fait soif** I'd kill for a drink, Br I could murder a drink

soiffard, -e [swafar, -ard] nm,f alky, lush, boozer, Br pisshead, Am boozehound

soigné, -e [swaɲe] adj (remarquable en son genre) **une engueulade soignée** a hell of a telling-off, a telling-off and a half; **il lui a fichu une raclée, quelque chose de soigné!** he thrashed him to within an inch of his life!; **l'addition était soignée** the Br bill or Am check was exorbitant

soigner [swaɲe] vt **faut te faire soigner!** you need your head examined!

soixante-neuf [swasɑ̃tnœf] nm (position) sixty-nine

sonné, -e [sɔne] adj (a) (fou) crazy, nuts, Br crackers, Am loony-tunes (b) (étourdi) groggy

sonner [sɔne] vt (a) (assommer) to knock out (b) **sonner les cloches à qn** to bawl sb out, to give sb what-for (c) **toi, on t'a pas sonné!** nobody asked you!

sono [sɔno] nf (abbr **sonorisation**) sound system □

sortable [sɔrtabl] adj **il n'est pas sortable** you can't take him anywhere

sortir [sɔrtir] **1** vt (dire) to come out with; **ce qu'il peut sortir comme conneries!** [!] he can come out with some real crap or bullshit! **2** vi **d'où tu sors?** where have you been?, what planet have you been on?;

il me sort par les trous de nez ou **par les yeux** I can't stand the sight of him

souci [susi] nm **il n'y a pas de soucis!** no worries!

souffler [sufle] **1** vt (a) (surprendre) to amaze □, to stagger, to flabbergast, Am to knock for a loop; **ça m'a soufflé d'apprendre ça** I was staggered to hear that (b) (dérober) **souffler qch à qn** to pinch or Br nick sth from sb **2** vi **souffler dans les bronches à qn** to bawl sb out, Br to give sb dog's abuse, Am to rank on sb ▸ see also **ballon, poireau**

souk [suk] nm (désordre) mess; **c'est le souk dans sa piaule!** his/her room's an absolute bombsite or pigsty!; **foutre le souk (dans)** (mettre en désordre) to make a mess (of); **il fout le souk en classe** he creates havoc in the classroom

soulager [sulaʒe] **1** vt **soulager qn de qch** (lui voler quelque chose) to relieve sb of sth **2** **se soulager** vpr (a) (uriner, déféquer) to relieve oneself (b) (se masturber) to give oneself relief

soûlard, -e [sular, -ard] nm,f alky, lush, boozer, Am boozehound

soûler [sule] vpr **se soûler la gueule** [!] Br to get pissed, Am to hang or tie one on

soûlon [sulɔ̃] nm Can & Suisse (ivrogne) alky, lush, boozer, Am boozehound

soûlot, -ote [sulo, -ɔt] nm,f alky, lush, boozer, Am boozehound

soupe [sup] nf (a) **par ici la bonne soupe!** that's the way to make money! (b) **faire la soupe à la grimace** to sulk □, to be in the huff (c) **à la soupe!** grub's up! (d) **être soupe au lait** to fly off the handle easily (e) (musique insipide) supermarket or elevator music ▸ see also **cheveu, cracher**

souper [supe] vi **en avoir soupé de qn/qch** to have had enough of sb/sth, to be fed up (to the back teeth) with sb/sth

sourdingue [surdɛ̃g] adj deaf □

souris [suri] nf (femme) chick, Br bird

sous-fifre [sufifr] nm underling, minion

Le symbole □ indique que la traduction n'est pas argotique.

sous-marin [sumarɛ̃] *nm* (a) *(véhicule de surveillance)* = converted van used for police surveillance (b) *(boisson)* = cocktail consisting of a pint of beer with a shot glass of tequila in the bottom of the beer glass, served with a straw

sous-merde[!] [sumɛrd] *nf* nobody □, non-entity □; **traiter qn comme une sous-merde** to treat sb like shit

sous-off [suzɔf] *nm* (*abbr* **sous-officier**) non-commissioned officer □

sous-ventrière [suvɑ̃trijɛr] *nf* **manger à s'en faire péter la sous-ventrière** to pig out, to stuff oneself *or* one's face, *Am* to munch out

soutif [sutif] *nm* bra □

speed [spid] **1** *adj (nerveux)* hyper **2** *nm (amphétamine)* speed

speedé, -e [spide] *adj* (a) *(nerveux)* hyper (b) *(drogué aux amphétamines)* **être speedé** to be speeding

speeder [spide] *vi* (a) *(être sous l'effet d'amphétamines)* to be speeding (b) *(se dépêcher)* to get a move on, *Am* to get it in gear; **il va falloir speeder si on veut pas arriver à la bourre** we're going to have to get a move on *or Am* get it in gear if we don't want to be late (c) *(être hyperactif)* to be hyper; **mais arrête donc de speeder comme ça, détends-toi!** stop being so hyper, relax!

splif [splif] *nm* spliff, joint, number

sport [spɔr] *nm* (a) **il va y avoir du sport** now we're going to see some fun (b) *Hum* **sport en chambre** *(rapports sexuels)* bedroom sports

squatter [skwate] **1** *vt* (a) *(monopoliser)* to take over, to hog; **il squatte toujours la télécommande quand on regarde un film** he always hogs the remote control when we're watching a film; **arrête de squatter le joint, fais tourner!** stop bogarting that joint, pass it round! (b) *Cités (vivre aux dépens de)* to scrounge off

2 *vi* to squat; **ça fait trois semaines qu'il squatte chez moi** he's been squatting at mine for three weeks now

starsky [starski] *nm* cop, *Am* flatfoot

> This term comes from *Starsky and Hutch*, the popular 1970s American TV series about two policemen.

stick [stik] *nm* (thin) joint *or* spliff *or* number

stonba [stɔ̃ba] *nf* Cités *(verlan* **baston**) scuffle, *Br* punch-up, *Am* slugfest

stone [ston], **stoned** [stond] *adj* stoned

student [stydɛnt] *nm Belg* student □

stups [styp] *nmpl* **la Brigade des stups, les stups** the Drug Squad, *Am* the narcs

suant, -e [sɥɑ̃, -ɑ̃t] *adj (fâcheux)* **être suant** to be a pain (in the neck)

subclaquant, -e [sybklakɑ̃, -ɑ̃t] *adj* **être subclaquant** to be on one's last legs, to have one foot in the grave

sucer [syse] *vt* (a) [!!] **sucer qn** *(pratiquer la fellation sur)* to go down on sb, to give sb head, to suck sb off; *(pratiquer le cunnilinctus sur)* to go down on sb, to give sb head, *Br* to lick sb out
(b) **sucer la pomme** *ou* **la couenne à qn** *Br* to snog sb, *Am* to make out with sb; **se sucer la pomme** *ou* **la couenne** *Br* to snog, *Am* to make out, to suck face
(c) **il suce pas que de la glace** he drinks like a fish
(d) *(essence)* to guzzle; **il faudrait que je me trouve une bagnole qui suce un peu moins d'essence** I need to find a car that guzzles a bit less gas *or* that's a bit less thirsty

sucette [sysɛt] *nf* **partir en sucette** to go down the tubes *or* pan

suceur[!] [sysœr] *nm (flatteur) Br* arse-licker, *Am* ass-licker

suceuse[!!] [sysøz] *nf (femme qui pratique la fellation)* **c'est une sacrée suceuse** she gives a great blow-job, she gives great head

sucre [sykr] *vt* **casser du sucre sur le dos de qn** to bad-mouth sb, *Br* to slag sb off

sucrer [sykre] **1** *vt* (a) *(supprimer) (permis, licence)* to take away □; *(permission, prime)* to cancel □; *(argent de poche)* to stop □ (b) **sucrer les fraises** to have shaky hands

2 se sucrer *vpr (s'octroyer un bénéfice)* to line one's pockets

suer [sɥe] *vi* (a) **faire suer qn** *(l'embêter)* to bug sb, *Br* to get up sb's nose, to get on sb's wick, *Am* to tick sb off (b) **faire suer le burnous** to exploit one's workforce □, to be a real slavedriver

suif [sɥif] *nm* **faire du suif** to kick up a fuss

sulfateuse [sylfatøz] *nf (mitraillette)* submachine gun □

sup [syp] *adj inv (abbr* **supplémentaire)** **heures sup** overtime □

super [syper] **1** *adj inv* super, great, terrific **2** *adv Br* dead, *Am* real; **un bouquin super chiant** a *Br* dead *or Am* real boring book; **on s'est super bien marrés** we had a *Br* fab *or Am* awesome time

This is by far the most common word used to describe the excellence of someone or something. "Super" and its accompanying term are often written as one word, eg "supernana", "super-plan","superchiant".

surgé [syrʒe] *nmf (abbr* **surveillant, -e général(e))** head supervisor □ *(in charge of school discipline)*

surin [syrɛ̃] *nm* knife □, blade, *Am* shiv, shank

suriner [syrine] *vt (blesser avec un couteau)* to knife □, to cut, *Am* to shiv; *(tuer avec un couteau)* to stab to death □

survêt [syrvɛt] *nm (abbr* **survêtement)** tracksuit □, trackies

sympa [sɛ̃pa] *adj (abbr* **sympathique)** nice □; **c'est quelqu'un de très sympa** he's/she's really nice; **j'ai dégoté un petit resto très sympa** I've found a really nice little restaurant

syphilo [sifilo] *nmf (abbr* **syphilitique)** = person suffering from syphilis

système [sistɛm] *nm* (a) **taper sur le système à qn** *Br* to get on sb's wick, to get up sb's nose, to do sb's head in, *Am* to give sb a pain (in the neck), to tick sb off (b) **le système D** resourcefulness □

T

tabac [taba] *nm* (**a**) **faire un tabac** to be a big hit (**b**) **passer qn à tabac** to beat sb up, to give sb a hammering; **passage à tabac** beating up, hammering (**c**) **c'est le même tabac** it's the same difference, it amounts to the same thing ► *see also* **blague**

tabasser [tabase] *vt* **tabasser qn** to beat sb up, to give sb a hammering; **se faire tabasser** to get beaten up, to *Br* get *or Am* take a hammering

tabernacle [tabɛʁnakl] *exclam Can* damn!

table [tabl] *nf* **se mettre** *ou* **passer à table** *(faire des aveux)* to spill the beans; **on a encore mangé à la table qui recule** we had to go without food again ᵘ

tablette [tablɛt] *nf* **tablette de chocolat** *(abdominaux)* six-pack

This expression derives from the fact that a set of well-toned stomach muscles are somewhat reminiscent of the squares of a bar of chocolate.

tablier [tablije] *nm Hum* **tablier de sapeur** *ou* **de forgeron**[!] *(poils pubiens)* bush, pubes, beaver

tache [taʃ] *nf* (**a**) *(personne nulle)* nonentity ᵘ, loser, no-hoper; **quelle tache ce mec-là!** what a total non-entity *or* loser *or* no-hoper that guy is! (**b**) **faire tache** *(jurer)* to stand *or* stick out like a sore thumb

tacot [tako] *nm* (**a**) *(vieille voiture)* heap, banger, rustbucket (**b**) *(taxi)* taxi ᵘ, cab, *Am* hack

taf [taf] *nm (travail)* work ᵘ; *(tâche, emploi)* job ᵘ

taffe [taf] *nf* drag, puff

taffer [tafe] *vi (travailler)* to work ᵘ

tag [tag] *nm* tag *(piece of graffiti)*

tagger¹ [tage] *vt* to cover in graffiti ᵘ

tagger² [tagœʁ] *nm* graffiti artist ᵘ, tagger, *Am* writer

taguer [tage] = **tagger**¹

tagueur, -euse [tagœʁ, -øz] *nm,f* = **tagger**²

tailler [taje] **1** *vt* (**a**) **tailler une pipe** *ou* **une plume** *ou* **une flûte à qn**[!!] to give sb a blow-job, to suck sb off, to give sb head (**b**) **tailler un costard à qn** *Br* to slag sb off, *Am* to badmouth sb (**c**) **tailler la route** *(parcourir beaucoup de chemin)* to eat up the miles; *(partir)* to beat it, *Br* to scarper, *Am* to book it

2 se tailler *vpr (partir)* to beat it, *Br* to scarper, *Am* to book it ► *see also* **bavette**

tailleuse [tajøz] *nf* **c'est une sacrée tailleuse de pipes** *ou* **de plumes**[!!] she gives a great blow-job, she gives great head

talbin [talbɛ̃] *nm Br* banknote ᵘ, *Am* greenback; **qu'est-ce que t'as foutu des talbins?** what have you done with the dough *or Br* dosh *or Am* bucks?

taloche [talɔʃ] *nf* clout, cuff; **flanquer une taloche à qn** to clout *or* cuff sb

talocher [talɔʃe] *vt* to clout, to cuff

tambouille [tãbuj] *nf* food ᵘ, grub, chow; **faire la tambouille** to do the cooking ᵘ

tamponne [tãpɔn] *nf Belg (drinking)* binge; **prendre une tamponne** to get wasted *or Br* trousered

tamponner [tãpɔne] **se tamponner** *vpr* (**a**) **s'en tamponner (le coquillard)** not to give a damn *or Br* a toss *or* a monkey's *or Am* a rap (**b**) *Belg* to get wasted *or Br* trousered

tanche [tãʃ] *nf Br* pillock, plonker, *Am* meathead

Le symbole ᵘ indique que la traduction n'est pas argotique.

tangente [tãʒãt] nf **prendre la tangente** to slip off or away, to make oneself scarce

tango [tãgo] nm (boisson) = cocktail consisting of beer and grenadine

tannant, -e [tanã, -ãt] adj (a) (importun) annoying ▫; (énervant) maddening ▫; **ce que tu peux être tannant avec tes questions!** you're a real pain with all these questions! (b) Can (remuant) rowdy

tanné, -e [tane] adj Can **être tanné** (en avoir assez) to be fed up, to have had it up to here; **je suis tannée à faire le ménage** I'm fed up or I've had it up to here doing housework

tannée [tane] nf (correction, défaite) thrashing, hammering; **filer une tannée à qn** to thrash or hammer sb, to give sb a thrashing or a hammering; **prendre une tannée** to get thrashed or hammered

tanner [tane] vt (importuner) to pester, to badger, to bug ▸ see also **cuir**

tante [tãt], **tantouse, tantouze** [tãtuz] nf Offensive (homosexuel) fairy, queer, Br poof, Am fag

tapant, -e [tapã, -ãt] adj **à cinq heures tapantes** at five o'clock sharp or on the dot

tapé, -e [tape] adj (fou) nuts, Br crackers, Am loony-tunes

tapecul, tape-cul [tapky] nm (véhicule) boneshaker

tapée [tape] nf **(toute) une tapée de** loads of, tons of

taper [tape] vt (a) (emprunter) to bum, to cadge, Br to tap; **taper qch à qn, taper qn de qch** to bum or cadge sth off sb, to hit or Br tap sb for sth; **il m'a tapé dix euros** he bummed or cadged ten euros off me, he hit or Br tapped me for ten euros
(b) (atteindre) **taper le cent/le deux cents** to hit a hundred/two hundred (kilometres an hour)
(c) **elle lui a tapé dans l'œil** (elle lui a plu) he was really taken with her, he took quite a shine to her
(d) (faire) **taper la frime** to show off;

taper la discussion to chew the fat, to shoot the breeze
2 se taper vpr (a) (subir) **on s'est tapé ses parents tout le week-end** we got stuck or Br landed or lumbered with his/her parents all weekend; **se taper le ménage/les courses** to get stuck or Br landed or lumbered with the housework/the shopping; **on s'est tapé de la pluie pendant trois semaines** we had rain every day for three weeks; **on s'est tapé deux heures d'embouteillages** we got stuck in traffic jams for two hours; **se taper la honte** to be totally mortified
(b) (absorber) (nourriture) to guzzle, to scoff; (boisson) to sink, to lower; **je me taperais bien une petite choucroute!** I'd kill for or Br I could murder a plate of sauerkraut!; **il a fallu que je me tape tout Proust pour l'examen** I had to devour the entire works of Proust for the exam
(c) ‼ (posséder sexuellement) **se taper qn** to screw or Br shag sb
(d) ❗ (se désintéresser) **je m'en tape** I don't give a shit or Br a toss or Am a rat's ass
(e) **à se taper le derrière** ou **le cul** ❗ **par terre** hysterical, side-splitting ▸ see also **carton, cloche, colonne, honte, incruste, lune, queue, raie, rassis, système**

tapette [tapɛt] nf Offensive (homosexuel) queer, fairy, Br poof, Am fag

tapeur, -euse [tapœr, -øz] nm,f moocher, sponger, scrounger

tapin [tapɛ̃] nm **faire le tapin** to walk the streets, Br to be on the game, Am to hook

tapiner [tapine] vi to walk the streets, Br to be on the game, Am to hustle; **elle tapine du côté du port** she walks the streets or Am hustles down at the port

tapineur, -euse [tapinœr, -øz] nm,f streetwalker

tapocher [tapɔʃe] vt Can (frapper) to tap ▫; (battre) to beat up

taponner [tapɔne] Can **1** vt (tâter) to touch ▫, to feel ▫; (sexuellement) to feel up, to grope

Le symbole ▫ indique que la traduction n'est pas argotique.

2 *vi (ne rien faire)* to hang around

tarba [tarba] *nm (verlan* **bâtard***)* bastard

taré, -e [tare] **1** *adj* crazy, off one's head or rocker, *Br* barking (mad)

2 *nm,f* nutcase, headcase, *Br* nutter

targettes [tarʒɛt] *nfpl* **(a)** *(pieds)* feet ⁰, *Br* plates, *Am* dogs **(b)** *(chaussures)* shoes ⁰

tarin [tarɛ̃] *nm Br* conk, hooter, *Am* schnozzle

tarpé [tarpe] *nm (verlan* **pétard***)* joint, spliff, reefer, number

tarte [tart] **1** *adj* **(a)** *(ridicule)* ridiculous ⁰, *Br* naff **(b)** *(stupide) Br* dim, thick, *Am* dumb

2 *nf* **(a)** *(coup)* clout, wallop; **flanquer une tarte à qn** to clout *or* wallop sb **(b)** **c'est pas de la tarte** *(c'est difficile)* it's no walkover, it's no picnic **(c)** **tarte aux poils**‼ *(sexe de la femme)* bush, hairpie; **bouffer de la tarte aux poils** to go muff-diving

Tartempion [tartɑ̃pjɔ̃] *npr* thingy, what's-his-name, *f* what's-her-name

tartignol, tartignolle [tartiɲɔl] *adj* ridiculous ⁰, *Br* naff

tartine [tartin] *nf* **(a)** *(pied)* foot ⁰, *Br* plate, *Am* dog **(b)** *(chaussure)* shoe ⁰ **(c)** *(texte long)* **en mettre une tartine** *ou* **des tartines** to write screeds, to waffle on

tartiner [tartine] **1** *vt* **(a)** *(écrire)* to churn out **(b)** *(enduire en grande quantité)* **tartiner qn/qch de qch** to cover sb/sth in sth ⁰

2 se tartiner *vpr* **se tartiner de qch** to cover oneself in sth ⁰

tartir [tartir] *vi* **se faire tartir**! to be bored shitless

tas [tɑ] *nm* **(a)** **tas de ferraille** *(voiture en mauvais état)* rusty old heap **(b)** **un tas** *ou* **des tas de** *(un grand nombre de, une grande quantité de)* a lot of ⁰; **tas de paresseux/menteurs!** you bunch of lazybones/liars!, *Br* you lazy/lying lot! **(c)** **un gros tas** *(gros individu mou)* a big fat lump; *(grosse fille laide)* a fat old boot

tasse [tɑs] *nf* **(a)** **boire la tasse** *(avaler de l'eau)* to get a mouthful of water ⁰ **(b)** **tasses** *(urinoirs)* street urinals ⁰

tassé, -e [tɑse] *adj* **il a la cinquantaine bien tassée** he's fifty if he's a day, he's on the wrong side of fifty

tassepé! [taspe] *nf (verlan* **pétasse***)* **(a)** *(fille)* slut, *Br* slapper, scrubber **(b)** *(prostituée)* whore, hooker

tata [tata] *nf Offensive (homosexuel)* queer, fairy, *Br* poof, *Am* fag

tatane [tatan] *nf* shoe ⁰

tataner [tatane] *vt* **tataner qn/qch** to give sb/sth a kicking

taulard, -e [tolar, -ard] *nm,f* jailbird, con

taule [tol] *nf* **(a)** *(prison)* slammer, clink, *Br* nick, *Am* pen; **faire de la taule** to do time, to do a stretch **(b)** *(lieu de travail)* workplace ⁰ **(c)** *(chambre)* room ⁰

taulier, -ère [tolje, -ɛr] *nm,f* **(a)** *(d'un hôtel)* boss **(b)** *(logeur)* landlord, *f* landlady ⁰

taupe [top] *nf* **avoir la taupe au bord du trou**‼ to be dying for a shit

tauper [tope] *vt Suisse* **tauper qch à qn** *(emprunter)* to bum *or* to cadge sth from sb; *(soustraire)* to do *or* to con sb out of sth

taxer [takse] *vt* **(a)** *(emprunter)* **taxer qch à qn** to scrounge *or* sponge *or* bum sth from sb **(b)** *(voler)* to pinch, *Br* to nick; **je me suis fait taxer mon cuir par une bande de skins** I got my leather jacket pinched *or* *Br* nicked by a bunch of skinheads

TBM [tebeɛm] *adj (abbr* **très bien monté***)* hung like a horse *or* a whale *or* *Br* a donkey *or* *Am* a mule

tchatche [tʃatʃ] *nf* **de la tchatche** the gift of the gab; **tout ça c'est de la tchatche** that's just a lot of talk

tchatcher [tʃatʃe] *vi* to chat

tchatcheur, -euse [tʃatʃœr, -øz] *nm,f* smooth talker

techi [tœʃi] *nm (verlan* **shit***)* shit, hash, *Br* blow, draw

tehon [tœɔ̃] *nf (verlan* **honte***)* **avoir** *ou* **se taper la tehon** to be embarrassed ⁰ *or*

Le symbole ⁰ indique que la traduction n'est pas argotique.

mortified; **(c'est) la tehon!** the shame of it!

tèj [tɛʒ] vt (verlan **jeter**) (chasser) to throw or chuck out, Am to eighty-six; (abandonner) to chuck, to dump; **il s'est fait tèj par sa meuf** his woman chucked or dumped him

téléphoné, -e [telefɔne] adj **c'était téléphoné** you could see it coming (a mile off); **un gag téléphoné** a joke you can see coming (a mile off)

téloche [telɔʃ] nf TV, tube, Br telly

tendance [tɑ̃dɑ̃s] adj trendy

tenir [tənir] vt **tenir une bonne cuite** to be totally wrecked or wasted or Br legless or pissed; **qu'est-ce qu'il tient!** (il est vraiment stupide) what a jerk or Br tosser or Am klutz!; (il est complètement ivre) he's totally wrecked or wasted or Br legless or pissed! ▸ see also **bavarde, bout, chandelle, côte, couche, crachoir, dose, jambe**

tension [tɑ̃sjɔ̃] nf **avoir deux de tension** to be all sluggish

terre [tɛr] nf **ne plus toucher terre** to be run off one's feet; Can **être à terre** (déprimé) to be or feel down

têtard [tɛtar] nm (enfant) kid, brat

tête [tɛt] nf **être une tête** to be brainy, to have brains; **tête de con**‼, **tête de nœud**‼ dickhead; Can Pej **tête carrée** English-speaking Canadian▢; **quelle tête à claques ce mec!** he's got a face you want to slap!; **c'est quinze euros par tête de pipe** it's fifteen euros a head; **prendre la tête à qn** Br to get up sb's nose, to get on sb's wick, Am to tick sb off; **prise de tête** pain (in the neck); **tomber sur la tête** to go off one's rocker, to lose it, Br to lose the plot; **non mais t'es tombé sur la tête ou quoi?** were you dropped on the head or something?; **ça va pas la tête?** are you mad?; **avoir ou attraper la grosse tête** to have a big head, to be big-headed; **faire une (grosse) tête** ou **une tête au carré à qn** to smash sb's face in, Br to punch sb's lights out, Am to punch sb out; **avoir la tête dans le cul**‼ to be out of it ▸ see

also **cul, payer, piquer, pou, yeux**

téter [tete] vi (boire avec excès) to knock it back, to drink like a fish

tétons [tetɔ̃] nmpl (seins) tits, boobs, knockers

teuch¹ [tœʃ] nm (verlan **shit**) shit, hash, Br blow, draw

teuch²‼ [tœʃ] nf Cités (verlan **chatte**) pussy, snatch, Br minge

teuf [tœf] nf (verlan **fête**) (a) (soirée) party▢ (b) (rave) rave▢

teufeur [tœfœr] nm (a) (dans une soirée) party animal (b) (dans une rave) raver▢

teup‼ [tœp] nf Cités (verlan **pute**) (prostituée) whore, hooker; (femme facile) tart, slut, Br slapper, scrubber, slag

texto [tɛksto] adv (abbr **textuellement**) word for word▢

thon [tɔ̃] nm (femme laide) dog, Br boot, Am beast

thune [tyn] nf (a) (argent) cash, Br dosh, Am bucks; **ils ont de la thune dans sa famille** his/her family's loaded or Br rolling in it (b) (pièce) **j'ai plus une thune** I haven't a bean or Am a cent

tiags [tjag] nfpl (abbr **santiags**) cowboy boots▢

ticket [tikɛ] nm **avoir le ticket (avec qn)** to have made a hit (with sb); **profites-en, je crois que t'as le ticket avec elle** get in there, I think you're well in with her

tickson [tiksɔ̃] nm ticket▢

tiéquar [tjekar] nm Cités (verlan **quartier**) neighbourhood▢

tifs [tif] nmpl hair▢; **il faut que j'aille me faire couper les tifs** I have to go and get my hair cut

tige [tiʒ] nf (a) (cigarette) Br fag, Am cig (b) ‼ (pénis) dick, prick, cock ▸ see also **brouter**

tignasse [tiɲas] nf (cheveux) mane, mop

tilt [tilt] nm **ça a fait tilt** the penny dropped, it clicked

timbré, -e [tɛ̃bre] adj (fou) nuts, crazy, Br barking, Am loco

tintin [tɛ̃tɛ̃] nm (a) **tintin!** no way (José)!,

Le symbole ▢ indique que la traduction n'est pas argotique.

no chance!, nothing doing! (**b**) **faire tintin** to go without

tintouin [tɛ̃twɛ̃] nm (**a**) (vacarme) racket, din (**b**) (souci) grief, hassle; **elle me donne bien du tintouin** she's giving me so much trouble or hassle; **tous ces invités, ça fait du tintouin** all these guests is just a lot of hassle

tip-top [tiptɔp] adj tip-top

tiquer [tike] vi to wince □; **il a pas tiqué** he didn't bat an eyelid or turn a hair; **ça l'a fait tiquer** it gave him a shake or a jolt

tire [tir] nf (voiture) car □, Br motor, Am ride

tire-au-cul [!] [tiroky], **tire-au-flanc** [tiroflɑ̃] nm inv Br skiver, Am gold-brick

tirée [tire] nf haul, trek; **ça fait une tirée d'ici à là-bas** it's a bit of a haul or trek from here

tire-jus [!] [tirʒy] nm snot-rag

tire-larigot [tirlarigo] **à tire-larigot** adv **boire à tire-larigot** to drink like a fish; **il y en a à tire-larigot** there's loads or tons of them

tirelire [tirlir] nf (**a**) (visage) face □, mug; **se fendre la tirelire** to split one's sides (laughing), Br to kill oneself laughing (**b**) (tête) head □, nut, Br bonce

tire-moelle [!] [tirmwal] nm inv snot-rag

tirer [tire] 1 vt (**a**) (voler) **tirer qch à qn** to pinch or Br nick sth from sb

(**b**) (prendre pour cible) **ils tiraient les passants comme des lapins** they were picking off passers-by one by one

(**c**) [!!] (posséder sexuellement) to fuck, to screw, to hump, Br to shag

(**d**) [!!] **tirer un coup** to get laid, to have a fuck or a screw or Br a shag; **ça fait des semaines que j'ai pas tiré mon coup** I haven't got laid in weeks

(**e**) (passer) **il est en train de tirer dix piges pour vol à main armée** he's doing a ten-year stretch for armed robbery; **encore deux mois à tirer avant les vacances** another two months to get through before the Br holidays or Am vacation

(**f**) **tirer les vers du nez à qn** to worm or drag it out of sb

2 vi **tirer au flanc** ou **au cul** [!] to shirk, Br to skive

3 **se tirer** vpr (**a**) (partir) to hit the road, to get going, to make tracks; (se sauver) to beat it, Br to clear off, Am to book it (**b**) **se tirer sur l'élastique** [!] to jerk off, to beat off, Br to wank, to have a wank ▸ see also **crampe, gueule, numéro, patte, portrait**

tiroir [tirwar] nm (ventre) stomach □, belly ▸ see also **polichinelle**

tise [tiz] nf Cités boozing

tiser [tize] 1 vt to knock back
2 vi to booze, to knock it back

tis-jos-connaissant [tiʒokɔnɛsɑ̃] nm Can Br know-all, Am know-it-all

titi [titi] nm = Parisian street urchin

tocante [tɔkɑ̃t] nf watch □

tocard, -e [tɔkar, -ard] 1 nm,f (personne insignifiante) non-entity □, dead loss, loser
2 nm (mauvais cheval de course) rank outsider □

tof, toffe [tɔf] adj Belg great, fantastic

toile [twal] nf (**a**) **se faire une toile** to go to the Br pictures or Am movies (**b**) **toiles** (draps) sheets □; **se mettre dans les toiles** to hit the sack or the hay or Am the rack

tomate [tɔmat] nf (cocktail) = cocktail consisting of pastis and grenadine

tombeau [tɔ̃bo] nm **à tombeau ouvert** at breakneck speed

tomber [tɔ̃be] 1 vt (**a**) (séduire) to pick up, Br to pull (**b**) (enlever) to take off □; **il a tombé la veste** he took his jacket off
2 vi (**a**) (être arrêté) to get nabbed or Br lifted or nicked (**b**) (pleuvoir) to rain □; **qu'est-ce qu'il est tombé hier soir!** it was raining cats and dogs or Br bucketing down or chucking it down last night! (**c**) **laisse tomber!** forget it! (**d**) Belg **tomber dans l'œil de qn** to catch sb's eye ▸ see also **carafe, cordes, jus, os, paletot, patte, poil, pomme, râble, rade, tête**

Le symbole □ indique que la traduction n'est pas argotique.

tombeur [tɔ̃bœr] nm (a) (séducteur) womanizer □, Am mack (b) (vainqueur) **c'est
lui le tombeur du champion du
monde** he's the man who defeated the
world champion □

-ton [tɔ̃] suffix **biffeton** (billet de banque)
note □, Am greenback; (de transport, de
spectacle) ticket □; **cureton** priest □; **frometon** cheese □; **mecton** guy, Br bloke

This suffix is found at the end of many
French nouns and is used for either humorous or pejorative effect.

top [tɔp] **1** adj great, Br top, Am awesome
2 adv (très) Br dead, Am real; **putain, sa
gonzesse elle est top bonne!** fuck, his
girlfriend is one horny babe!
3 nm **c'est le top (du top)** it's the best
of stuff, Br it's the business!

topo [tɔpo] nm report □; **faire un topo à
qn sur qch** to give sb the lowdown on
sth, Am to hip sb to sth; **tu vois (un
peu) le topo?** (you) see what I mean?;
c'est toujours le même topo it's always
the same old story

toqué, -e [tɔke] **1** adj crazy, nuts, Br
mental, Am gonzo
2 nm,f headcase, Br nutter, Am wacko

torche [tɔrʃ] nf Can (grosse femme) fat
cow

torche-cul [!] [tɔrʃ(ə)ky] nm (journal)
rag; (texte) trash, Br rubbish

torchée [tɔrʃe] nf (correction) thrashing,
hammering; **filer une torchée à qn** to
thrash or hammer sb

torcher [tɔrʃe] **1** vt (a) (faire en vitesse) to
knock off, to dash off; **j'ai torché ma dissert en une heure** I knocked off my
essay in an hour; **bien torché** well put-
together (b) [!!] (essuyer le derrière de)
torcher (le cul de) qn to wipe sb's Br
arse or Am ass
2 se torcher vpr (a) (se battre) to knock
lumps out of each other, to have a Br
punch-up or Am slugfest (b) [!!] (s'essuyer)
se torcher (le cul) to wipe one's Br arse
or Am ass; **je m'en torche!** I don't give a
shit or Am a rat's ass! (c) [!] (s'enivrer) to
get shit-faced or Br pissed or rat-arsed

torchon [tɔrʃɔ̃] nm (mauvais journal) rag;
(devoir mal présenté) dog's breakfast or
dinner

tordant, -e [tɔrdɑ̃, -ɑ̃t] adj (amusant)
hysterical, side-splitting

tord-boyaux [tɔrbwajo] nm inv gutrot,
rotgut, Am alky

tordre [tɔrdr] **se tordre** vpr **se tordre
(de rire)** to be in stitches, to kill oneself
(laughing), to be doubled up (with laughter)

tordu, -e [tɔrdy] nm,f nutcase, headcase, Br nutter, Am wacko

torgnole [tɔrɲɔl] nf (gifle) clout, wallop;
flanquer une torgnole à qn to clout or
wallop sb

torrieu [tɔrjø] exclam Can oh hell!

tortiller [tɔrtije] vi **y a pas à tortiller, y
a pas à tortiller du cul pour chier
droit** [!!] there's no getting away from it,
there are no two ways about it

tortore [tɔrtɔr] nf cooking □; **elle fait de
la vachement bonne tortore** she
makes really great food or Br scran

tos [tos] nmf Offensive Dago (from Portugal)

Depending on the context and the tone
of voice used, this term may be either
offensive or affectionately humorous. It
is nonetheless inadvisable to use it unless one is quite sure of the reaction it
will receive.

tosser [tɔse] vi to get stoned

total [tɔtal] adv **total, j'ai perdu mon
boulot/il a fallu que je recommence**
the upshot is, I lost my job/I had to start
again

totale [tɔtal] nf **quand il m'a demandée
en mariage, il m'a fait la totale** when
he proposed to me, he really went all
out; **on a eu droit à la totale: verglas,
embouteillages, barrages de routiers**
black ice, traffic jams, lorry drivers' road
blocks, you name it, we had it

This expression originates from "la totale" meaning a hysterectomy. It is used

Le symbole □ indique que la traduction n'est pas argotique.

to abbreviate a long list and may have
either positive or negative connota-
tions.

toto [toto] *nm* louse ᵁ, *Am* cootie

toubab [tubab] *nmf* = French person of
native stock, as opposed to immigrants
or their descendants

toubib [tubib] *nm* doctor ᵁ, doc

touche [tuʃ] *nf* (**a**) *(aspect)* look ᵁ; **il a
une de ces touches avec sa veste à
franges!** he looks like something from
another planet with that fringed jacket of
his! (**b**) *(personne séduite)* conquest ᵁ;
faire une touche to score, *Br* to pull (**c**)
Can **tirer** *ou* **prendre une touche** *(fumer)* to have a smoke

touche-pipi [tuʃpipi] *nm inv* **jouer à
touche-pipi** to play at doctors and nurses

toucher [tuʃe] **1** *vi* (**a**) *(être doué)* to be
brilliant (**en/à** at) (**b**) *(recevoir de l'argent)*
to collect
    2 se toucher *vpr* (**a**) ‼ *(se masturber)*
to play with oneself, *Br* to touch oneself
(up) (**b**) **se toucher (la nuit)** to fool oneself, to kid oneself on ▸ *see also* **bille,
pacson**

touffe ‼ [tuf] *nf (toison pubienne)* bush,
pubes; **une jupe ras la touffe** a micro
mini-skirt ᵁ, *Br* a bum-freezer

touiller [tuje] *vt* to stir ᵁ

toupie [tupi] *nf* **une vieille toupie** an old
crone *or* bag *or Am* goat

tournant [turnã] *nm* **attendre qn au
tournant** to be waiting for a chance to
get even with sb

tourner [turne] **1** *vi* (**a**) *(devenir)* **tourner
homo/hippie** to become gay/a hippy ᵁ
(**b**) **tourner de l'œil** to pass out ᵁ, to keel
over
    2 se tourner *vpr* **se tourner les
pouces, se les tourner** to twiddle one's
thumbs ▸ *see also* **rond**

tournicoter [turnikɔte] *vi* to wander
around aimlessly

toutim, toutime [tutim] *nm* **et tout
le toutim** the works, the whole enchilada, *Br* the full monty

toutou [tutu] *nm* doggy, doggie

touzepar [tuzpar] *nf (verlan* **partouze***)*
orgy

toxico [tɔksiko] *nmf (abbr* **toxicomane***)*
addict ᵁ, junkie, *Am* hophead

tracer [trase] *vi (aller vite)* to belt along,
to bomb along; *(déguerpir)* to beat it, *Br*
to clear off, *Am* to book it

traduc [tradyk] *nf (abbr* **traduction***)*
translation ᵁ

train [trɛ̃] *nm (postérieur)* backside, *Br*
bum, *Am* fanny; **filer le train à qn** to
shadow *or* tail sb ▸ *see also* **botter,
magner, passer**

traînailler [trenaje] *vi* (**a**) *(être lent)* to
dawdle (**b**) *(perdre son temps)* to hang
about, *Br* to faff about

traînard, -e [trenar, -ard] *nm,f Br* slowcoach, *Am* slowpoke

traîne [trɛn] *nf* **être à la traîne** to lag behind

traînée [!] [trene] *nf (femme)* tart, *Br*
slapper, scrubber

traîner [trene] *vi (être posé)* to lie around,
to hang around ▸ *see also* **guêtres,
merde, savate**

traîne-savates [trensavat] *nm inv*
down-and-out, *Br* dosser, *Am* bum

traîneux [trenø] *nm Can* slob, waster

traiter [trete] *vt (insulter) Br* to slag off,
Am to bad-mouth

tralala [tralala] *nm* **et tout le tralala** the
works, the whole enchilada, *Br* the full
monty

tranche [trɑ̃ʃ] *nf* **s'en payer une
tranche** to have a ball *or Am* a blast

tranquillos [trãkilos] *adv (tranquillement)* **vas-y tranquillos, inutile de
faire des excès de vitesse** take your
time, there's no need to break the speed
limit; **ils étaient dans le canapé en
train de siroter mon whisky, tranquillos** they were on the sofa sipping away at
my whisky, without a care in the world

transbahuter [trãsbayte] *vt* to shift, to
hump, to lug; **comment on va faire
pour transbahuter tout ton bordel?**

Le symbole ᵁ indique que la traduction n'est pas argotique.

how are we going to shift all your mess?

transfo [trãsfo] nm (abbr **transforma-teur**) transformer □

transpirer [trãspire] vi Cités **transpirer sa race** to be crapping oneself, Br to be bricking it

trappe [trap] nf Can (bouche) trap, Br gob

trapu, -e [trapy] adj (a) (difficile) tough, tricky (b) (expert) brainy, brilliant (**en/à** at)

travail [travaj] nm **et voilà le travail!** and that's all there is to it!, Br and Bob's your uncle!; **qu'est-ce que c'est que ce travail?** what's going on here?, what's the meaning of this?

travelo [travlo] nm drag queen, TV, Br tranny

traviole [travjɔl] **de traviole** adv **marcher de traviole** to be staggering all over the place; **être de traviole** to be lop-sided or skew-whiff

trèfle [trɛfl] nm (a) (argent) cash, dough, Br dosh, Am bucks (b) (foule) crowd □; **qu'est-ce qu'il y avait comme trèfle en ville!** the town was totally jam-packed or Br heaving or chock-a-block

tremblement [trãbləmã] nm **et tout le tremblement** the works, the whole enchilada, Br the full monty

tremblote [trãblɔt] nf **avoir la tremblote** (de peur) to have the jitters; (de froid, à cause de la fièvre) to have the shivers; (à cause d'une maladie) to have the shakes; (vieillard) to be shaky

trempe [trãp] nf (correction) thrashing, pasting; **prendre une trempe** to Br get or Am take a thrashing or a pasting; **flanquer une trempe à qn** to give sb a thrashing or a pasting

tremper [trãpe] vi **tremper dans qch** to be mixed up in sth ▸ see also **biscuit, panais**

trempette [trãpɛt] nf **faire trempette** to have a dip

trente-six [trãtsis] adj **tous les trente-six du mois** once in a blue moon; **il y en a pas trente-six** there aren't that many of them; **des raisons, je pourrais t'en**

citer trente-six I could give you umpteen reasons; **il y a pas trente-six solutions** there's no getting away from it, there are no two ways about it; **voir trente-six chandelles** to see stars

trente-sixième [trãtsizjɛm] adj **être au trente-sixième dessous** to be in a tight spot

tricard, -e [trikar, -ard] **1** adj = prohibited from entering a certain area
2 nm,f = ex-convict prohibited from entering a certain area

trichlo [triklo] nm (abbr **trichloréthylène**) trichloroethylene □ (used as a drug)

tricoter [trikɔte] vi (marcher vite) **tricoter (des gambettes)** to leg it, to belt along

trifouiller [trifuje] **1** vt (a) (fouiller) to rummage through (b) (toucher à) to fiddle with, to tinker with
2 vi **trifouiller dans qch** to rummage around in sth

Trifouillis-les-Oies [trifujilezwa] npr = fictional name for the archetypal isolated, dull village

trimarder [trimarde] vi to be on the road

trimardeur [trimardœr] nm tramp, Am hobo

trimballer [trɛ̃bale] **1** vt (a) (transporter) to hump, to schlep, to lug around; **il trimballe sa famille partout où il va** he has his family in tow everywhere he goes (b) **qu'est-ce qu'il trimballe!** what a total halfwit or Br tosser or Am klutz!
2 se **trimballer** vpr to schlep around, to trail around

trimer [trime] vi to slog away, to slave away; **faire trimer qn** to keep sb hard at it, to keep sb's nose to the grindstone; **qu'est-ce qu'ils peuvent nous faire trimer dans cette boîte!** they really keep us hard at it in this company!

tringler [!!] [trɛ̃gle] vt to fuck, to screw, Br to shag

trinquer [trɛ̃ke] vi (subir un désagrément) to be the one who suffers □, to pay the price

trip [trip] *nm* (**a**) *(centre d'intérêt)* kick; **il est en plein trip écolo en ce moment** he's on some environmental kick at the moment; **c'est vraiment pas mon trip, ce genre de truc** I'm not really into that kind of thing, it's not my scene, that kind of thing (**b**) *(produit par la drogue)* trip

tripaille [tripaj] *nf* innards, guts

tripant, -e [tripɑ̃, -ɑ̃t] *adj Can* great, terrific

tripatouiller [tripatuje] *vt* (**a**) *(truquer)* *(document)* to tamper with ⁰; *(chiffres, résultats)* *Br* to fiddle, *Am* to doctor; **tripatouiller les comptes** to cook the books (**b**) *(modifier)* *(texte)* to alter ⁰ (**c**) *(tripoter)* *(personne)* to paw, to feel up; *(cheveux)* to play *or* fiddle with; *(bouton)* to pick at

triper [tripe] *vi* to trip *(after taking drugs)*; **ça me fait vraiment triper, ce genre de musique** this type of music just blows me away

tripes [trip] *nfpl* (**a**) **jouer avec ses tripes** to give it one's all (**b**) **rendre** *ou* **vomir** *ou* **dégueuler tripes et boyaux** to be as sick as a dog, *Br* to spew one's guts up

tripette [tripɛt] *nf* **ça ne vaut pas tripette** it's a load of tripe *or* dross, *Am* it's not worth diddly

tripotée [tripɔte] *nf* (**a**) **une tripotée (de)** tons (of), loads (of) (**b**) *(correction, défaite)* thrashing, hammering; **filer une tripotée à qn** to thrash *or* hammer sb, to give sb a thrashing *or* a hammering; **prendre une tripotée** to get thrashed *or* hammered

tripoter [tripɔte] **1** *vt* (**a**) *(toucher)* to fiddle with, to play with (**b**) *(se livrer à des attouchements sur)* to feel up, to grope, *Br* to touch up
   2 se tripoter [!] *vpr* to touch oneself up, to play with oneself

trique [!!] [trik] *nf* *(érection)* hard-on, boner; **avoir la trique** to have a hard-on *or* a boner

triquer [!!] [trike] *vi* to have a hard-on *or* a boner

triso [trizo] *Offensive* *(abbr* **trisomique**) **1** *adj* spazzy, *Br* mong
   2 *nmf* spaz, *Br* mong

trisser [trise] **1** *vi* to hightail it, to scoot, *Am* to split
   2 se trisser *vpr* to hightail it, to scoot, *Am* to split

tristounet, -ette [tristunɛ, -ɛt] *adj* sad ⁰, down ⁰; **il m'a l'air un peu tristounet** he looks a bit down to me

trogne [trɔɲ] *nf* *(visage)* face ⁰, mug, *Am* map

trognon [trɔɲɔ̃] **1** *adj* *(mignon)* cute, sweet
   2 *nm* **jusqu'au trognon** [!] well and truly; **il s'est fait avoir jusqu'au trognon** [!] he's been well and truly had

trom [trom] *nm* *(verlan* **métro**) *Br* underground ⁰, *Am* subway ⁰

trombine [trɔ̃bin] *nf* face ⁰, mug

trombiner [!!] [trɔ̃bine], **tromboner** [!!] [trɔ̃bɔne] *vt* *(posséder sexuellement)* to fuck, to screw, to shaft, *Br* to shag

tromé [trome] = **trom**

tronc [trɔ̃] *nm* **se casser le tronc** to worry ⁰, *Br* to get one's knickers in a twist

tronche [trɔ̃ʃ] *nf* (**a**) *(visage)* face ⁰, mug; **il a une drôle de tronche** he looks really odd, he's really odd-looking; **faire la tronche** to sulk ⁰, to be in a *or* the huff; **t'en fais une tronche, qu'est-ce qui t'arrive?** you look really down, what's up?; **une tronche de cake** *(personne)* a complete jerk (**b**) *(personne intelligente)* brain, brainy person; **ce mec-là, c'est une tronche!** that guy's a real brain *or* so brainy! ▶ *see also* **payer**

troncher [!!] [trɔ̃ʃe] *vt* to fuck, to screw, to hump, *Br* to shag

trône [tron] *nm Hum* **être sur le trône** *(aux toilettes)* to be on the throne

trop [tro] **1** *adj inv* *(incroyable)* too much, unreal
   2 *adv* *(très)* **j'étais trop dégoûté** I was so bummed *or Br* gutted; **il est trop mortel, son plan** his plan's so *or* too brilliant; **j'étais trop mort de rire** I was absolutely killing myself; **ah ouais, je l'ai vu, ce**

film, il est trop bien! oh yeah, I've seen that film, it was totally *Br* fab or top or *Am* awesome!

troquet [tʀɔkɛ] *nm* bar □, *Br* boozer

trotte [tʀɔt] *nf* hike, stretch, schlep; **il y a ou ça fait une trotte d'ici à là-bas** it's quite a hike or stretch or schlep from here

trottoir [tʀɔtwaʀ] *nm* **faire le trottoir** to be on the game, *Am* to hook

trou [tʀu] *nm* (a) *(prison)* slammer, clink, *Br* nick, *Am* pen (b) *(endroit isolé)* hole; **il n'est jamais sorti de son trou** he's never been out of his own backyard (c) **boire comme un trou** to drink like a fish (d) **trou de balle** [!], **trou du cul** [!!] *Br* arsehole, *Am* asshole ▸ *see also* **taupe, yeux**

trouduc [!] [tʀudyk], **trou-du-cul** [!] [tʀudyky] *nm (imbécile) Br* arsehole, *Am* asshole

troufignon [!] [tʀufiɲɔ̃] *nm Br* arsehole, *Am* asshole

troufion [tʀufjɔ̃] *nm* (a) *(simple soldat) Br* squaddie, *Am* grunt (b) [!] *(postérieur) Br* arse, *Am* ass

trouillard, -e [tʀujaʀ, -aʀd] *nm,f* chicken *(person)*

trouille [tʀuj] *nf* fear □; **avoir la trouille** to be scared stiff; **foutre la trouille à qn** to scare the living daylights out of sb, to scare sb stiff

trouillomètre [tʀujɔmɛtʀ] *nm* **avoir le trouillomètre à zéro** to be scared stiff

trouilloter [!] [tʀujɔte] *vi* (a) *(avoir peur)* to be scared shitless, to be shit-scared (b) *(sentir mauvais)* to stink, *Br* to pong

trousser [!] [tʀuse] *vt (posséder sexuellement)* to hump, *Br* to have it away or off with

truander [tʀyɑ̃de] **1** *vt* to swindle, to rip off, to con, *Am* to rook; **se faire truander** to get swindled or ripped off or conned or *Am* rooked
2 *vi (tricher)* to cheat □ **(à** in); *(resquiller)* to sneak in

truanderie [tʀyɑ̃dʀi] *nf* con, scam

truc [tʀyk] *nm* thing □; **c'est pas mon truc** it's not my scene or thing or bag or *Br* cup of tea; **c'est tout à fait son truc**

it's just his/her sort of thing, *Br* it's right up his/her street

trucider [tʀyside] *vt* to bump off, to ice, to waste

Trucmuche [tʀykmyʃ] *npr* thingy, what's-his-name, *f* what's-her-name

truffe [tʀyf] *nf (imbécile) Br* divvy, dipstick, *Am* lamebrain, schmuck

trumeau, -x [tʀymo] *nm (femme laide)* dog, *Br* boot, *Am* beast

truster [tʀœste] *vt (monopoliser)* to monopolize □, to hog

tubard, -e [tybaʀ, -aʀd] **1** *adj* **être tubard** to have TB
2 *nm,f* TB sufferer

tuber [tybe] *vt (téléphoner à)* **tuber qn** to give sb a buzz or *Br* a bell

tuer [tɥe] *vt* **ça me tue!** it kills me!; **ça tue!** it's a killer!

tuile [tɥil] *nf (problème)* hassle; **il m'arrive une tuile** I'm in a bit of a mess

tune [tyn] = **thune**

turbin [tyʀbɛ̃] *nm* work □

turbine [tyʀbin] *nf* **turbine à chocolat** [!!] *Br* arsehole, dirtbox, *Am* asshole

turbiner [tyʀbine] *vi* (a) *(travailler)* to slog or slave away (b) *(se livrer à la prostitution)* to turn tricks, *Br* to be on the game

turbo [tyʀbo] *nm* **mettre le turbo** to get a move on, to get one's skates on, *Am* to get it in gear

turbo-prof [tyʀbopʀɔf] *nmf* = teacher who works in a town in the provinces and commutes there from Paris every day

turf [tyʀf] *nm* (a) *(prostitution)* prostitution □; **faire le turf** to turn tricks, *Br* to be on the game (b) *(travail)* work □; *(lieu de travail)* workplace □

turista [tyʀista] *nf* **la turista** Montezuma's revenge, Delhi belly, Spanish tummy

turlupiner [tyʀlypine] *vt* to bother □, to bug

turlute [!] [tyʀlyt] *nf* blow-job; **faire une turlute à qn** to give sb a blow-job, to go down on sb, to give sb head

turne [tyrn] *nf* room □

tuyau, -x [tɥijo] *nm* (**a**) *(conseil)* tip, hint, pointer; *(aux courses)* tip; *(renseignement)* tip-off; **un tuyau percé** a useless tip / tip-off (**b**) **la famille tuyau de poêle** = family whose members have an incestuous relationship

tuyauter [tɥijɔte] *vt (renseigner)* to tip off

tuyauterie [tɥijɔtri] *nf (organes de la digestion)* innards, guts; *(poumons)* lungs □

type [tip] *nm* guy, *Br* bloke; **un chic type** a nice guy, *Am* a mensch, a good Joe; **un sale type** a bad egg, a nasty piece of work; **un pauvre type** a sad individual

---

Le symbole □ indique que la traduction n'est pas argotique.

U

une [yn] *adj* **et d'une** for a start, for starters; **ne faire ni une ni deux** not to think twice; **il n'en loupe** *ou* **rate pas une** he's forever screwing up

uni [yni], **unif, univ** [ynif] *nf Belg Br* uni, *Am* school □

unité [ynite] *nf (dix mille francs)* ten thousand francs □

urger [yrʒe] *vi* to be urgent □

uro [yro] *nf (urolagnie)* water sports

usiner [yzine] **1** *vi (travailler dur)* to slog *or* slave away, to be hard at it
   2 s'usiner *vpr* to jerk off, *Br* to have a wank

v

vacciné, -e [vaksine] *adj* **être vacciné** to have learnt one's lesson; **être vacciné au vinaigre** to be in a foul mood; **être vacciné à la merde** ⚠ to be in a shit mood

vachard, -e [vaʃar, -ard] *adj* rotten, mean, nasty

vache [vaʃ] **1** *adj* (a) *(méchant)* rotten, mean, nasty; **ce qu'elle peut être vache!** she can be so bitchy *or* such a bitch! (b) *(remarquable)* **il a un vache (de) coquard** he's got a hell of a black eye; **il a eu une vache d'idée** he had a hell of a good idea

2 *nf* (a) *(homme méchant) Br* swine, *Am* stinker; *(femme méchante)* bitch, *Br* cow; **elle lui a fait un coup en vache** she played a dirty trick on him, *Br* she did the dirty on him, *Am* she did him dirt; **elle a dit ça en vache** she just said that to be bitchy *or* a bitch

(b) **manger** *ou* **bouffer de la vache enragée** to have a hard *or* tough time of it

(c) **la vache!** *(de surprise)* God!, *Br* blimey!, *Am* gee (whiz)!; *(d'admiration)* wow!

(d) **mort aux vaches!** *(à bas la police)* kill the pigs! ► *see also* **peau, plancher**

vachement [vaʃmã] *adv* really □, *Br* dead, *Am* real; **on s'est vachement bien marrés** we had a really *or Br* dead *or Am* real good time; **il y a vachement de monde en ville** there are loads *or* tons of people in town

vacherie [vaʃri] *nf* (a) *(méchanceté)* meanness □, nastiness □ (b) *(action méchante)* dirty trick; **faire une vacherie à qn** to play a dirty trick on sb, *Br* to do the dirty on sb, *Am* to do sb dirt (c) *(parole blessante)* nasty remark □; **il m'a dit un tas de vacheries** he said loads of nasty things to me

vachté [vaʃte] *adv* really □, *Br* dead, *Am* real

va-comme-je-te-pousse [vakɔmʒtəpus] **à la va-comme-je-te-pousse** *adv* **faire qch à la va-comme-je-te-pousse** to do sth any old how

vadrouille [vadruj] *nf* wander □; **être en vadrouille** to be wandering *or* roaming around □; **il est rarement à son bureau, il est toujours en vadrouille** he's hardly ever at his desk, he's always wandering around somewhere

vadrouiller [vadruje] *vi* to wander *or* roam around □; **il est constamment en train de vadrouiller dans le bureau** he's always wandering around the office

valda [valda] *nf (balle d'arme à feu)* bullet □, slug

> This term comes from the name of a famous brand of throat pastilles, the shape of which is reminiscent of that of a bullet.

valdinguer [valdɛ̃ge] *vi* to go flying; **envoyer valdinguer qn/qch** to send sb/sth flying

valise [valiz] *nf* (a) **valises** *(poches sous les yeux)* bags (under one's eyes) (b) *Can* sucker, mug

valoche [valɔʃ] *nf* (a) *(valise)* suitcase □, case □ (b) **valoches** *(poches sous les yeux)* bags (under one's eyes)

valse [vals] *nf* (a) *(correction)* hammering, thrashing; **foutre une valse à qn** to give sb a hammering *or* a thrashing (b) *(cocktail)* = cocktail consisting of beer and mint-flavoured syrup

valser [valse] *vi* (a) *(perdre l'équilibre)* **il est allé valser contre la porte** he went flying into the door; **envoyer valser qch**

---

to send sth flying; **envoyer valser qn**
(l'éconduire) to send sb packing, to show
sb the door; *(pousser)* to send sb flying
(b) *(abandonner)* **j'ai envie de tout envoyer valser!** I feel like packing it all in or
Br jacking it all in or Am chucking everything!

valseur [valsœr] *nm (postérieur)* bum,
Am fanny

valseuses ! [valsøz] *nfpl (testicules)*
balls, nuts, Br bollocks

This word became popular after the
success of Bertrand Blier's 1974 film *Les
Valseuses*, which told the story of two
young dropouts, one of whom was
played by Gérard Depardieu.

vanne [van] *nf* **(a)** *(remarque désobli-
geante)* snide remark □, dig, jibe, Am zinger; **envoyer des vannes à qn** to make
digs at sb, Am to zing sb **(b)** *(plaisanterie)*
joke □, crack

vanné, -e [vane] *adj* dead beat, bushed,
Br knackered, Am pooped

vanner [vane] *vt (se moquer de)* to make
digs at, Am to zing

vapes [vap] *nfpl* **être dans les vapes** to
be out of it or in a daze or Am punchy;
tomber dans les vapes to pass out □,
to keel over

variétoche [varjetɔʃ] *nf* middle-of-the-
road music

vaser [vɑze] *v imp* to rain cats and dogs,
Br to bucket down, to chuck it down

vaseux, -euse [vɑzø, -øz], **vasouil-
lard, -e** [vɑzujar, -ard] *adj* **(a)** *(mauvais)* **plaisanterie/excuse vaseuse**
feeble or pathetic joke/excuse; **raisonne-
ment vaseux** woolly or Br dodgy reason-
ing **(b)** *(mal en point)* under the weather,
out of sorts, Br off-colour, Am off-color

vasouiller [vɑzuje] *vi* to flounder

vautrer [votre] **se vautrer** *vpr (tomber)*
to go flying

va-vite [vavit] *nm Can* **avoir le va-vite**
to have the runs, to have the trots

veau, -x [vo] *nm (véhicule poussif)* hair-
drier on wheels

vécés [vese] *nmpl Br* loo, Am john

veille [vɛj] *nf* **c'est pas demain la veille**
that's not going to happen in a hurry;
c'est pas demain la veille qu'ils te

Verlan

"Verlan" is the most frequently used form of slang among young French people,
particularly in the impoverished areas of large cities. It is formed by inverting the
syllables of the word and making any spelling changes necessary to aid
pronunciation. The word "verlan" is itself the inverted form of "l'envers" meaning
"the other way round".

Some verlan terms have passed into spoken French generally and are used or
understood by a great many speakers, eg "laisse béton" (laisse tomber) –
popularized by the singer Renaud – "ripou" (pourri) and "meuf" (femme). It is,
however, an extremely generative form of slang and any word can, in theory, be
"verlanized". Some examples: "pétard" becomes "tarpé", "bizarre" becomes "zarbi",
and "pute" becomes "teupu" which is then shortened to "teup".

Monosyllabic words can also be "verlanized", eg "chaud" becomes "auch"; an "e" is
frequently added to aid pronunciation, eg "flic" becomes "keufli" which is shortened
to "keuf"; "mère" becomes "reumè", which is in turn shortened to "reum". A term may
be "verlanized" twice – the term "rebeu", for example, comes from the verlan for
"Arabe" – "beur" – which is then "re-verlanized" to give "rebeu".

See also the panel at **l'argot des banlieues** on p. 9 of the French-English side.

---

proposeront un boulot they're not going to be offering you a job in a hurry

veilleuse [vɛjøz] *nf* **la mettre en veilleuse** to shut up, to put a sock in it

veinard, -e [vɛnar, -ard] **1** *adj* lucky □, *Br* jammy

2 *nm,f* lucky *or Br* jammy devil

veine [vɛn] *nf (chance)* luck □; **avoir de la veine** to be lucky □ *or Br* jammy ▸ *see also* **cocu**

vélo [velo] *nm* **avoir un petit vélo dans la tête** to be off one's rocker, to be not all there ▸ *see also* **grand-mère**

vénère [venɛr] *Cités* **1** *adj (verlan* **énervé***)* *Br* wound up, *Am* ticked off

2 *vt (verlan* **énerver***)* **vénère qn** to bug sb, *Br* to wind sb up, *Am* to tick sb off

vent [vã] *nm* **(a)** **avoir du vent dans les voiles** to be three sheets to the wind **(b)** **du vent!** clear off!, buzz off!, get lost! **(c)** **se prendre un vent** *(être rejeté)* to get turned down □, *Br* to get a knockback **(d)** **je me suis pris un vent, je lui ai parlé pendant un bon quart d'heure et elle a rien écouté...** it was like talking to a brick wall, I was talking to her for a good quarter of an hour and she didn't listen to a word I was saying...

ventre [vãtr] *nm* **en avoir dans le ventre, avoir quelque chose dans le ventre** to have guts; **ne rien avoir dans le ventre** to be gutless

verni, -e [vɛrni] *adj (qui a de la chance)* lucky □, *Br* jammy

---

Focus on:

La violence

Violence-related slang originates both in the speech of the criminal underworld, popularized by detective novels and films, and in everyday colloquial language, although it is worth noting that the latter has often borrowed from the former.

Slang equivalents of "to kill" include the euphemisms **descendre**, **étendre**, **refroidir**, **dessouder** and **dézinguer**. **Flinguer** is the most common term used to mean "to shoot dead", and **suriner** means "to stab to death" (from "surin" = knife).

Also found are **faire la peau à quelqu'un** and **régler son compte à quelqu'un**.

Several expressions meaning "to hit" or "to beat up" use the same image, with slight variations each time: **casser la gueule**, **péter la gueule**, or, more humorously, **abîmer le portrait** (rather old-fashioned now) and **faire une tête au carré**.

Tabasser, from the expression **passer à tabac**, and **buter** are very common expressions. Less frequently encountered is **maraver** (a Romany term now reclaimed by the young people of the "cités") and the ironic term **arranger** (now dated).

A fight is most commonly called **castagne** (the verb **se castagner** is also commonly used) and **baston**, an obsolete form of the word **bâton** which has resurfaced to become popular in contemporary slang (note, too, the verb **se bastonner**). A more dated term is **rififi**, which is highly evocative of the films noirs of the 1950s and 1960s, such as the 1955 film *Du rififi chez les hommes*.

Colourful terms used to mean "a blow" often come from words suggestive of either the fist or a projectile. The most common examples are **châtaigne**, **marron**, **prune**, **patate**, **pain**, **gnon** (from **oignon**). Other examples include **beigne**, **taloche**, **raclée**, **torgnole** and, more recently, **mandale**.

Someone who is about to be attacked is said to be going to **déguster** or **morfler**.

Le symbole □ indique que la traduction n'est pas argotique.

vérole [verɔl] *nf* (a) *(syphilis)* **la vérole** the pox (b) **quelle vérole!** what a pain!

verrat [!] [vera] **1** *nm Can (homme méprisable)* swine, bastard; **en verrat** *Br* dead, *Am* real; **un beau film en verrat** a damn *or Br* bloody good film

2 *exclam* **(maudit) verrat!** shit!, *Br* bloody hell!

vesse [vɛs] *nf* silent but deadly fart

veste [vɛst] *nf* **(se) prendre une veste** *(échouer)* to come unstuck; *(être rejeté)* to get turned down $^{\square}$, *Br* to get a knockback

véto [veto] *nm (abbr* **vétérinaire)** vet $^{\square}$

veuve [vœv] *nf Hum* **la veuve Poignet** masturbation $^{\square}$; **fréquenter la veuve Poignet** to bang *or Br* bash the bishop, to beat one's meat

viande [vjɑ̃d] *nf (corps humain)* **amène** *ou* **aboule ta viande!** get your butt *or* carcass over here!; **il y a de la viande soûle dans les rues** the streets are full of drunken bodies; **de la viande froide** *(un cadavre)* a stiff; *(des cadavres)* stiffs

viander [vjɑ̃de] **se viander** *vpr* to get smashed up

vibure [vibyr] *nf* **à toute vibure** at full speed, at top speed

vicelard, -e [vislar, -ard] **1** *adj* (a) *(retors)* crafty, sneaky (b) *(lubrique)* kinky, *Br* pervy

2 *nm,f* (a) *(personne retorse)* crafty *or* sneaky person (b) *(personne lubrique)* perv; **un vieux vicelard** a dirty old man

vidé, -e [vide] *adj (épuisé)* wiped, dead beat, *Br* done in, *Am* pooped, out of gas

vider [vide] *vt* (a) *(expulser, licencier)* **vider qn** to throw sb out (on his ear), *Br* to turf sb out, *Am* to eighty-six sb (b) *(épuiser)* to drain, to wipe out ▸ *see also* **burettes, burnes**

videur [vidœr] *nm* bouncer

vieille [vjɛj] *nf (mère)* old lady, *Br* old dear

vieux [vjø] *nm* (a) *(père)* old man; **mes** *ou* **les vieux** *Br* my old dears, *Am* my rents (b) *(terme d'adresse)* pal, *Br* mate, *Am* buddy; **comment ça va, vieux?** how are you doing, pal *or Br* mate *or Am* buddy?

vinaigre [vinɛgr] *nm* (a) **faire vinaigre** to get a move on, to get one's skates on, *Am* to get it in gear (b) **tourner au vinaigre** *(discussion, relation)* to turn sour; *(opération, expédition)* to go wrong $^{\square}$, to screw up, *Br* to cock up ▸ *see also* **vacciné**

vinasse [vinas] *nf* cheap wine $^{\square}$, *Br* plonk

vingt-deux [vɛ̃ddø] *exclam (attention)* watch out!, watch it!

vioc [vjɔk] = **vioque**

violon [vjɔlɔ̃] *nm (prison)* slammer, clink, *Br* nick, *Am* pokey; **il s'est retrouvé au violon** he wound up in the slammer *or* clink *or Br* nick *or Am* pokey ▸ *see also* **pisser**

vioque [vjɔk] **1** *adj* old $^{\square}$

2 *nmf* old fossil, *Br* wrinkly, *Am* geezer; **mes** *ou* **les vioques** *Br* my old dears, *Am* my rents

virer [vire] **1** *vt (congédier)* to chuck out, to kick out

2 *vi (devenir)* **virer homo** to become gay $^{\square}$; **virer voyou** to become *or* turn into a thug $^{\square}$ ▸ *see also* **cuti**

virolo [virɔlo] *nm* bend $^{\square}$ *(in road)*; **il a pris le virolo à fond la caisse** he took the bend at top speed

vis [vis] *nf* **serrer la vis à qn** *(sévir)* to crack down on sb, to tighten the screws on sb; *(être strict)* to be hard on sb

viser [vize] *vt (regarder)* to check out, *Am* to scope; **vise un peu la gonzesse!** check out that girl!

vissé, -e [vise] *adj* **être bien vissé** *(de bonne humeur)* to be in a good mood; **être mal vissé** *(de mauvaise humeur)* to be in a foul mood

vite [vit] *adv* **vite fait** quickly $^{\square}$; **boire un coup vite fait** to have a quick drink; **faire qch vite fait bien fait** to do sth in next to no time; **à vite vite!** see you in a bit!

vitriol [vitrijɔl] *nm (mauvais vin)* cheap wine $^{\square}$, *Br* plonk; *(mauvais alcool)* gutrot

v'là [vla] *prep* **et juste à ce moment-là, v'là t-y pas qu'il se met à pleuvoir!** and just then, would you believe it, it starts raining!

Le symbole $^{\square}$ indique que la traduction n'est pas argotique.

voile [vwal] *nf* (**a**) **être** *ou* **marcher à voile et à vapeur** to be AC/DC, to swing both ways (**b**) **mettre les voiles** to get going, to make tracks ▶ *see also* **vent**

voir [vwar] *vt* (**a**) **va te faire voir (chez les Grecs)!** ⚠ go to hell!, *Br* bugger off!, piss off! (**b**) **en voir (de toutes les couleurs)** to go through hell, to have a hellish time of it; **en faire voir (de toutes les couleurs) à qn** to make sb's life a misery, to put sb through hell (**c**) **j'en ai jamais vu la couleur** I haven't seen hide nor hair of it

vol [vɔl] *nm Hum* **elle a pas mal d'heures de vol** she's no spring chicken

volaille [vɔlaj] *nf* **la volaille** the pigs

volée [vɔle] *nf (correction)* thrashing, hammering; **flanquer une volée à qn** to thrash *or* hammer sb; **recevoir une volée** to get thrashed *or* hammered

voleuse [vɔløz] *nf Hum* **voleuse de santé** nympho, *Br* goer

vouloir [vulwar] *vt* (**a**) **en vouloir** *(être ambitieux)* to want to make it (**b**) **je veux!** absolutely!, you bet!, *Br* too right!

voyage [vwajaʒ] *nm* (**a**) **être en voyage** *(être en prison)* to be inside *or* behind bars (**b**) *Ironic* **si il vient se plaindre à moi, il va pas être déçu du voyage!** if he comes complaining to me, he'll wish he hadn't bothered!

vrille [vrij] *nf* **partir en vrille** to go down the tubes *or* pan

vu [vy] *adj* **vu?, c'est vu?** OK?, all right?, got it? ▶ *see also* **embrouiller**

vue [vy] **1** *nf* **en mettre plein la vue à qn** to knock sb dead, to blow sb away
2 *nfpl Can* **les vues** *(le cinéma) Br* the pictures, *Am* the movies □; **aller aux (petites) vues** to go to the *Br* pictures *or Am* movies ▶ *see also* **air**

vulgos [vylgos] *adj* vulgar □, coarse □

Le symbole [□] indique que la traduction n'est pas argotique.

W, X, Y

wakos [wakos] *nm* (*abbr* **Walkman**®) Walkman® □

witz [vits] *nm Suisse* (*plaisanterie*) joke □

WW [dubləvedublə və] *adj inv* brand new □

In France new cars are given temporary registration plates marked with the letters WW until full registration has taken place.

X [iks, εks] *nf* (*ecstasy*) X, E

yaourt [jaurt] *nm* (*charabia*) = type of gibberish which imitates English sounds without forming actual words, used by people who want to sound as if they are talking or singing in English ► *see also* **pédaler**

yecs [jɛks] *nfpl Cités* (*verlan* **couilles**) balls, nuts, *Br* bollocks

yeux [jø] *nmpl* **avoir les yeux qui se croisent les bras** to be cross-eyed □; **coûter les yeux de la tête** to cost a fortune *or* a bundle *or Br* a packet; **il n'a pas les yeux en face des trous** (*il est mal réveillé*) he hasn't come to yet, his brain isn't in gear yet; (*il n'est pas observateur*) he's as blind as a bat, he never sees what's going on right in front of him; **il a une petite amie/une bagnole, attention les yeux!** you should see his girlfriend/car!, his girlfriend/car is an absolute *Br* cracker *or Am* crackerjack!; **il n'a pas froid aux yeux** he's got plenty of nerve, he's not backward in coming forward; **il/ça me sort par les yeux** I can't stand *or Br* stick him/it; **il a les yeux plus grands que le ventre** (*il est trop gourmand*) his eyes are bigger than his belly *or* his stomach; (*il est trop ambitieux*) he's bitten off more than he can chew ► *see also* **crever, merde, merlan, œil, poche**

yo [jo] *exclam* yeah!

youde [jud] *Offensive* **1** *adj* Jewish □, yid **2** *nmf* yid, kike, *Am* hebe

yougo [jugo] *Offensive* **1** *adj* (*abbr* **yougoslave**) Yugoslav □ **2** *nmf* **Yougo** (*abbr* **Yougoslave**) Yugoslav □

Depending on the context and the tone of voice used, this term may be either offensive or affectionately humorous. It is nonetheless inadvisable to use it unless one is quite sure of the reaction it will receive.

youpin, -e [jupɛ̃, -in] *Offensive* **1** *adj* Jewish □, yid **2** *nm,f* yid, kike, *Am* hebe

youtre [jutr] *Offensive* **1** *adj* Jewish □ **2** *nmf* yid, kike, *Am* hebe

youve [juv], **youvoi** [juvwa] *nm* (*verlan* **voyou**) hood, hooligan □, *Br* yob

yoyoter [jɔjɔte] *vi* (**a**) (*mal fonctionner*) to be on the blink, *Am* to be on the fritz (**b**) (*déraisonner*) to have a screw *or Br* a slate loose, to be off one's trolley

yvette [ivet] *nf Can Pej* housewife □, homemaker □

Le symbole □ indique que la traduction n'est pas argotique.

zapper [zape] *vt* (**a**) *(supprimer)* to scrap, to scratch (**b**) **zapper qn** to drop sb; **j'ai décidé de zapper ce loser, il a pas changé de portable depuis au moins six mois!** I've decided to drop that loser, he's had the same mobile for at least six months now!

2 *vi (changer de chaîne)* to channel-surf, to channel-hop

zappette [zapɛt] *nf* remote control □, zapper

zarbi [zarbi] *adj (verlan* **bizarre**) strange □, weird □, odd □

zarma [zarma] *exclam* wow!, God!, *Br* blimey!, *Am* gee (whiz)!

zen [zɛn] *adj inv* **être/rester zen** to be/stay cool

zeph [zɛf] *nm (abbr* **zéphyr**) wind □

zéro [zero] **1** *adv* **il est bien gentil, mais pour le travail, zéro!** he's nice enough, but when it comes to work he's a dead loss **2** *nm* (**a**) *(individu nul)* non-entity □, nobody □, zero (**b**) **les avoir à zéro** to be scared stiff *or* witless ▸ see also **boule, trouillomètre**

zézette [zezɛt] *nf (sexe de l'homme)* dick, willy, *Am* peter; *(sexe de la femme)* pussy, *Br* fanny

zgueg [!] [zgɛg] *nm* dick, willy, *Am* peter

ziav [ziav] *exclam (verlan* **vas-y**) stop it!, get out of here!

zicmu [zikmy] *nf (verlan* **musique**) music □, sounds, tunes

zieuter [zjøte] *vt* to check out, to eyeball, *Am* to scope

zieverer [zivəre] *vi Belg* to talk drivel *or Br* rubbish

zig [zig] *nm* guy, *Br* bloke

zigomar [zigɔmar], **zigoto** [zigɔto] *nm* crackpot, crank, *Am* kook; **faire le zigoto** to act the fool, to clown around

zigouigoui [zigwigwi] *nm Hum* (**a**) *(pénis)* willy, *Am* peter (**b**) *(sexe de la femme)* pussy, *Br* fanny (**c**) *(objet)* thingy, whatsit

zigouiller [ziguje] *vt* to bump off, to liquidate, to ice

zigoune [zigun] *nf Can* roll-up, rollie, rolly

zigue [zig] = **zig**

zig-zig [zigzig] *nm* **faire zig-zig** to have a bit of nookie *or Br* rumpy-pumpy

zinc [zɛ̃k] *nm* (**a**) *(comptoir de café)* bar □ (**b**) *(avion)* plane □

zinzin [zɛ̃zɛ̃] *adj* loopy, *Br* hatstand, *Am* loony-tunes

zique [zik] *nf* music □, sounds, tunes

ziva [ziva] *exclam (verlan* **vas-y**) stop it!, no way!, get out of here!; **ziva! je l'invite pas à ma boum, ce junkie!** no way! *or* get out of here!, I'm not inviting that junkie to my party!

zizi [zizi] *nm* (**a**) *(pénis)* willy, *Am* peter (**b**) *(sexe de la femme)* pussy, *Br* fanny (**c**) **faire zizi panpan** *Br* to have a bit of rumpy-pumpy, *Am* to get jiggy with it

zizique [zizik] *nf* music □, sounds, tunes

zob [!] [zɔb] *nm* dick, knob

zomblou [zɔ̃blu] *nm (verlan* **blouson**) jacket □

zonard, -e [zonar, -ard] *nm,f (marginal)* dropout

zone [zon] **1** *adj (sans intérêt, de mauvaise qualité)* crap, lousy

2 *nf* (**a**) **la zone** *(banlieue misérable)* slum area □, rough area □; *(endroit pauvre)* dump, hole, dive; *(endroit sale)* tip, pigsty, bombsite (**b**) **c'est la zone!** it sucks!, it's the pits!, *Am* it bites!

zoner [zone] **1** *vi* (**a**) *(traîner)* to hang

Le symbole □ indique que la traduction n'est pas argotique.

around, to bum around (**b**) *(faire)* **qu'est-ce que tu zones?** what are you up to?
  2 se zoner *vpr* to hit the sack *or* the hay *or Am* the rack

zonga [zɔ̃ga] *nm Cités (verlan* **gazon**) *(marijuana)* grass, weed, herb

zonzon [zɔ̃zɔ̃] *nf Cités* slammer, clink, *Br* nick, *Am* pen

zoulette [zulɛt] *nf Cités* chick, *Am* bird

zoulou [zulu] *nm (jeune noir)* = young black man

zozo [zozo] *nm* jerk, *Br* arse

zwanze [zwɑ̃z] *nf Belg* joke ; **faire la zwanze** to go out and have fun , to party ; **mettre de la zwanze** to liven things up , to get things going

zwanzer [zwɑ̃ze] *vi Belg (plaisanter)* to joke ; *(faire la fête)* to go out and have fun , to party

zyeuter [zjøte] = **zieuter**

zyva [ziva] = **ziva**

Le symbole  indique que la traduction n'est pas argotique.

HARRAP

RUDE FRENCH

AN ALTERNATIVE FRENCH PHRASEBOOK

HARRAP PARDON MY SPANISH!
ISBN 0245 60721 8
pp 176
£5.99

HARRAP

PARDON MY SPANISH!

POCKET SPANISH SLANG DICTIONARY

SPANISH-ENGLISH/ENGLISH-SPANISH